THE OXFORD HANDBOOK OF

HEALTH CARE MANAGEMENT

THE OXFORD HANDBOOK OF

HEALTH CARE

MANAGEMENT

Edited by
EWAN FERLIE,
KATHLEEN MONTGOMERY,
and
ANNE REFF PEDERSEN

OXFORD
UNIVERSITY PRESS

OXFORD
UNIVERSITY PRESS

Great Clarendon Street, Oxford, OX2 6DP,
United Kingdom

Oxford University Press is a department of the University of Oxford.
It furthers the University's objective of excellence in research, scholarship,
and education by publishing worldwide. Oxford is a registered trade mark of
Oxford University Press in the UK and in certain other countries

Published in the United States of America by Oxford University Press
198 Madison Avenue, New York, NY 10016, United States of America

British Library Cataloguing in Publication Data

Data available

Library of Congress Control Number: 2016933503

ISBN 978-0-19-870510-9

Printed in Great Britain by
Clays Ltd, St Ives plc

CONTENTS

PART I THEORETICAL AND POLITICAL APPROACHES TO HEALTH CARE MANAGEMENT AND ORGANIZATIONS

PART II   PEOPLE IN HEALTH CARE ORGANIZATIONS: PATIENTS, PROFESSIONALS, AND LEADERS

PART III   ORGANIZATIONAL PROCESSES AND PRACTICES IN HEALTH CARE MANAGEMENT

PART IV ISSUES IN THE HEALTH CARE ORGANIZATIONAL FIELD

List of Figures

LIST OF TABLES

List of Contributors

Rachael Addicott Senior Research Fellow, the King's Fund, and Visiting Fellow at King's College London, United Kingdom

Roland Bal Professor of Health Care Governance and Chair of the Health Care Governance group and Director of Education, Erasmus University, the Netherlands

Simon Bishop Assistant Professor in Organisational Behaviour, University of Nottingham, United Kingdom

Jeffrey Braithwaite Director, Centre for Clinical Governance Research, and Professor of Health Systems Research, Macquarie University, Australia

Haldor Byrkjeflot Professor of Sociology, Department of Sociology and Human Geography, University of Oslo, Norway

Mariline Comeau-Vallee PhD Candidate, HEC Montréal, Canada

Graeme Currie Professor of Public Management, University of Warwick, United Kingdom

Huw Davies Professor of Health Care Policy and Management, University of St Andrews, United Kingdom

Jean-Louis Denis Canadian Research Chair in the Governance and Transformation of Health Care Organizations and Systems, Ecole Nationale d'Administration Publique, Montreal, Canada.

Sir Liam Donaldson Chair in Health Policy at the Department of Surgery and Cancer, Imperial College, London, United Kingdom

Bill Doolin Professor of Technology and Organization, Auckland University of Technology, New Zealand

Evan Doran Associate Research Fellow, Centre for Values, Ethics and the Law in Medicine, the University of Sydney, Australia

Ewan Ferlie Professor of Public Services Management, King's College London, United Kingdom

Louise Fitzgerald Visiting Professor of Organizational Change, Said Business School, Oxford and Emeritus Professor, De Montfort University, Leicester, United Kingdom

Elizabeth Goodrick Associate Professor of Health Administration, Florida Atlantic University, United States

Julia Gracheva Independent researcher, New York, and IKON, Warwick Business School, United Kingdom

C. R. Bob Hinings Professor Emeritus in the Faculty of Business, University of Alberta, Canada

Christopher Jordens Associate Professor in Bioethics, Centre for Values, Ethics and the Law in Medicine, the University of Sydney, Australia

Ian Kerridge Associate Professor in Bioethics and Director, Centre for Values, Ethics and the Law in Medicine, the University of Sydney, Australia

Ian Kirkpatrick Professor of Work and Organisation, University of Leeds, United Kingdom

Martin Kitchener Professor, Dean and Head of Cardiff Business School, Cardiff University, United Kingdom

Peter Kjær ProRector, Roskilde University. From 1997 to 2014 he was assistant Professor, Associate Professor at Head of the Department of Organization at Copenhagen Business School, Denmark

Ann Langley Professor of Management, HEC Montréal, Canada

Charlotta Levay Associate Professor in Business Administration, Department of Business Administration, Lund University, Sweden

Jenny M. Lewis Professor of Public Policy and Australian Research Council Future Fellow, the University of Melbourne, Australia

Wendy Lipworth Senior Research Fellow, Centre for Values, Ethics and the Law in Medicine, the University of Sydney, Australia

Chris Lonsdale Reader in Procurement and Supply Management, University of Birmingham, United Kingdom

Maria Lusiani Resaercher, Università Ca'Foscari, Venice, Italy

Laura E. McClelland Assistant Professor of Health Administration, Virginia Commonwealth University, United States

Russell Mannion Professor of Health Systems, University of Birmingham, United Kingdom

Lynn Markiewicz Managing Director, Aston Organisation Development, Farnborough, United Kingdom

Graham Martin Professor of Health Organisation and Policy, University of Leicester, United Kingdom

Kathleen Montgomery Professor of the Graduate Division and Emerita Professor of Organizations and Management, University of California, Riverside United States

Indraneth Neogy Research Associate, Centre for Innovation in Health Management, University of Leeds, United Kingdom

Ainsley J. Newson Senior Lecturer in Bioethics, Centre for Values, Ethics and the Law in Medicine, the University of Sydney, Australia

Davide Nicolini Professor of Organization Studies, University of Warwick, United Kingdom

Sandra Nutley Professor of Public Policy and Management, School of Management, University of St Andrews, United Kingdom

Lieke Oldenhof PhD candidate, Erasmus University, the Netherlands

Jeroen Postma PhD candidate, Erasmus University, the Netherlands

Alison Powell Senior Research Fellow, School of Management, University of St Andrews, United Kingdom

Cheryl Rathert Associate Professor of Health Administration, Virginia Commonwealth University, United States

Trish Reay Professor of Entrepreneurship and Innovation, University of Alberta, Canada

Anne Reff Pedersen Associate Professor of Organization studies, Department of Organization at Copenhagen Business School, Denmark

Harry Scarbrough Professor in Information Systems and Management, Cass Business School, City University, United Kingdom

Jill Schofield Professor and Head of School, School of Economics, Finance and Management, University of Bristol, United Kingdom

Viviane Sergi Assistant Professor, Department of Management and Technology, University of Quebec, Montreal, Canada

Rod Sheaff Professor in Health Services Research, Plymouth University School of Government, United Kingdom

Stephen M. Shortell Blue Cross of California Distinguished Professor of Health Policy and Management and Director, Center for Healthcare Organizational and Innovation Research, School of Public Health, and Professor of Organization Behavior, Haas School of Business, University of California, Berkeley, United States

Anja Svejgaard Pors Assistant Professor, Metropolitan University College, Copenhagen, Denmark

Richard Thomas PhD candidate, Cardiff University, United Kingdom

Timothy J. Vogus Associate Professor of Management, Vanderbilt Owen Graduate School of Management, United States

Karsten Vrangbæk Professor in the Political Science and Public Health Department and Director of Center for Health Economics and Policy (CHEP), Copenhagen University, Denmark

Justin Waring Professor of Organisational Sociology, University of Nottingham, United Kingdom

Michael A. West Professor of Work and Organizational Psychology, Lancaster University Management School, United Kingdom and Senior Fellow at the King's Fund, London.

EDITORS' INTRODUCTION

The State of Health Care Management Research: A Critical Overview

EWAN FERLIE, KATHLEEN MONTGOMERY,
AND ANNE REFF PEDERSEN

INTRODUCTION: PURPOSE
AND CONTRIBUTION

WHY should anyone wish to edit, contribute a chapter to—or take the time to read—this Handbook? Firstly, the Handbook offers extensive and contemporary academic commentary on a major sector of societal, moral, scientific, policy, and economic importance. The Handbook secondly explores various themes and perspectives in a more discursive manner than is possible in a conventional academic article. It thirdly seeks to operate at a broader level than the national level at which much health management writing too often becomes trapped. Thus, the core purpose of the Handbook is to offer a variety of current scholarly perspectives to explore important policy developments evident in the health care management practice field and to do so on an international basis.

The prime focus is on the meso level of the health care organization, in contrast to the macro level of health policy conventionally found in political science literature or the micro level of service delivery evident in an expanding body of health service research (HSR). The Handbook relates academically to various perspectives drawn from organization studies and related social science disciplines. It seeks to develop a more theoretically informed perspective than apparent in much conventional health management writing.

REFLECTIONS ON THE STATE OF MUCH
HEALTH MANAGEMENT RESEARCH

We begin by critiquing much existing health management research, where two rather different streams of literature can be distinguished: health services research (HSR) and managerial practice research. The first body of literature, HSR, includes a growing field of applied and evaluative work on health service program and practice innovations. HSR has been advancing as a research area over the last two decades, building its own funding streams, academic communities, professional associations, and new journals.

Nevertheless, there are several reasons why HSR has struggled to build an autonomous academic identity and a cumulative knowledge base of its own. It often tends to be near-clinical in orientation, with a focus on the measurement of patient outcomes and other performance indicators. Many HSR research designs call for multi-disciplinary, large-scale service evaluations, akin to other approaches in the biological and clinical sciences, but without attention to using and further developing underlying social science theory.

While the exploration of performance is a legitimate concern and reflects a cost-containment agenda in the policy domain, this angle often dominates, crowding out more exploratory prisms available in the social sciences. Because much of the work is technicist and apolitical, it tends to neglect wider questions of power, politics, and the influence of dominant ideologies and values on health care restructuring. For example, HSR-based organization studies often focus on measuring the impact of a focal intervention or service innovation, often within a quasi-experimental design that mimics the logic of a randomized control trial, rather than assessing and analyzing the influence of the wider organizational contexts in which the innovation sits. However, elements of the contexts may be so toxic (e.g., low levels of trust, no organizational memory, weak organizational learning, or poor change management capacity) that nearly all interventions are doomed to fail. Moreover, the search for external generalizability is typically pursued empirically rather than conceptually.

Further constraining its external generalizability, HSR is commonly heavily embedded in national health care systems and therefore can be somewhat parochial. It is often too close to short-term local bubbles in health policy and reform, and lacks the critical distance of a long-term or comparative perspective (not asking, for example, why previous similar reorganizations have had mixed results).

We recognize the value of much HSR-orientated work, typically characterized by a large-scale data collection strategy and sophisticated statistical methods of analysis. But we suggest that HSR faces the danger of a descent into empiricism and capture by the field of managerial and clinical practice, being too often atheoretical, parochial, and divorced from wider social science currents, particularly those that have developed more recently or come from international rather than national authors (see Greenhalgh, 2012 for a related critique of the intellectual limits of Cochrane Reviews, especially when applied in broader fields than originally intended).

A second strand of generic business literature also has gained influence in health management practice, especially in more market-like health care systems such as the US (e.g., Porter and Teisberg's 2006 text outlining a new model of value-led competition for American health care), but now in other systems too, such as the UK National Health Service (NHS). Such work comes from a very different source than the near-clinical and technicist HSR stream. It is often produced by business school gurus or management consultants involved in corporate change programs. These management texts help to diffuse models, concepts, and large-scale organizational change programs from their origins in private firms into the health care sector internationally. There is also a developing social science-based literature that explores the diffusion and impact of such change programs, which can be taken as topics for scholarly inquiry in their own right.

Many of these popularly written blockbuster texts promote managerial "fads and fashions" (to use an analytic framing set up by Abrahamson, 1991, 1996), which have been diffused widely into health care settings, starting with cultural change programs (e.g., Peters and Waterman, 1982), later followed by business process re-engineering (BPR) (Hammer and Champy, 1993, represent the initial text; then explored in McNulty and Ferlie's 2002 academic study of the diffusion and only partial implementation of BPR into a UK NHS hospital), then knowledge management initiatives (see the foundational text by Davenport and Prusak, 1998; explored in more social science terms in NHS settings by Currie, Waring, and Finn, 2008) and most recently the Lean production approach (see the well cited book from Womack, Jones, and Roos, 1990; explored in the NHS by Radnor, Holweg, and Waring, 2012).

The appeal of these managerial texts is that they promote bold and accessibly written ideas that capture the managerial imagination and stimulate more action in the field than would be likely in the case of academic writing. On the other hand, they typically are not well linked to a broader academic base and do not take the form of traditional peer reviewed science. They are often functionalist and performance orientated, overly aligned with a managerial perspective, and cast clinicians, if considered at all, in the role of change resisters. Finally, while HSR is often methodologically sophisticated, these texts can be methodologically opaque.

Reviving Academic Rigor and Policy Relevance

This Handbook represents an opportunity to develop—or rather revive—a third approach to writing in the health care management domain. We asked our distinguished authors to present a carefully considered overview of their areas of expertise. We did not expect them to present a mass of primary data, but rather to take stock and reflect widely. We envisioned that the chapters would reconnect the analysis of the health management field with wider social science literatures and to revive its theoretical base. We see this mode of writing as one that can fruitfully combine academic rigor and policy relevance, albeit in a long-term, more indirect, and broader manner than in a highly applied mode of policy-driven research.

In reflecting on earlier social science-based scholarship that has enriched health care management research, we note the distinguished body of work, much of it qualitative, which emerged in the 1960s and 1970s. For example, Goffman's (1968) ethnography of an American psychiatric hospital as an organization helped developed the more general concept of a total institution. Freidson's (1970a, 1970b) sociological analysis of American medicine as a dominant profession informed Alford's (1977) political science-based analysis of the multiple forces involved in (resisting) plans for large-scale health service reconfiguration in New York, together with an exploration of their differential power bases. Managers (here termed corporate rationalizers) began to emerge as actors in decision making in the health care field, although at that stage still secondary to domi-nant professional groups. Mintzberg's (1983) archetype of decision making in a profes-sionalized bureaucracy moved an analysis of the effects of professional dominance up to the organizational level, with its suggestion that strategy making could in this situation be largely bottom up, coming from dominant professional segments.

Continuing this social science-based tradition, Scott et al. (2000) explored the rise of new organizational forms in American managed care in the 1980s and 1990s, which challenged professional dominance. Similarly, academic literature within the UK explored the effects of the new public management (NPM) reforms of the 1980s and 1990s on health care and the extent to which managerialization was eroding professional dominance (Harrison et al., 1992; Pettigrew, Ferlie, and McKee, 1992). The relationship between the health care professions and a more activist and reforming state seeking to reshape the health care system remains a key strand in the current academic literature, as does the exploration of the emergence of new organizational forms, often driven by pressures for productivity. However, we will argue that this fine scholarly tradition could be updated and broadened. With this goal in mind, we articulate three propositions that guided our plans for the Handbook:

Proposition 1: Bringing Social Science Back into Health Management Research

We invited contributors to the Handbook to use social science and theoretically based perspectives to inform their analysis of substantive policy developments. This orien-tation is another source of external—but conceptually generated—generalizability, distinct from the search for empirical generalizability often found in large-scale HSR designs. Our contributors demonstrate several ways that theory can be fruitfully and creatively incorporated into examinations of health care management topics: First, clas-sic theories can be reassessed for their relevance in today's health care environment, with the potential for extending and modifying taken-for-granted assumptions inherent in these traditional theories. Second, well-developed organization theory can be examined within a new context. Third, theories from several perspectives can be synthesized into a new framework from which to study emerging and prevailing phenomena. And fourth, non-traditional theories can cast a new light and prompt new questions about long-standing relationships. We next illustrate how chapters in the Handbook use these various approaches.

Several chapters draw on classic streams of literature that were developed originally within the general discipline of organization studies. This represents a base discipline that has been broadening considerably since its early roots in contingency theory introduced in the 1960s that explored organization/environment fit and focused on questions of organizational structure. Early organization theorists embraced the notion of professionalized bureaucracy as a new organizational form to explore strategy making in the context of powerful organizational members, who accepted professional authority structures that were distinct from typical bureaucratic control mechanisms. In their chapter, Shortell and Addicott demonstrate that the classic tenet "form follows function" no longer applies in the development of many new health care organizational forms in health care today.

Since the 1980s, several new perspectives have emerged within the broad discipline of organizational studies (Clegg and Hardy, 1996), encouraging analyses that go beyond a focus on formal structure and take into account newer prisms such as gender, sustainability, and micro practices. This shift is evident in several Handbook chapters that demonstrate an enhanced interest in organizing as a human activity rather than the study of formal organization. Thus, there is an increased interest in processes instead of, or as they interact with, structure, suggesting that day-to-day working life in health care organizations often is not directed by formal policy or regulations, but rather is dependent on micro negotiations reflecting dimensions as learning, culture, communication, and knowledge. Chapters by Nicolini, Scarbrough, and Gracheva; Mannion and Davies; Kjær, Pedersen, and Pors; and Davies, Powell, and Nutley all reflect this approach. In order to study such softer topics, we also see greater use of qualitative methods, including ethnography, organizational case studies, and a discursive analysis of texts.

Perhaps the strongest and most enduring theoretical influence on the health care management research field has been the sociology of the professions literature. Initially associated with concepts of professional power and dominance, this literature expanded to explorations of how a hierarchy of professions engages with one another (e.g., doctors and nurses) and with organizational bureaucracies (e.g., doctors and hospitals), as well as how professional powers and jurisdictional claims for occupational turf are made and maintained, often through labor market shelters like credentialism (Abbott, 1988; Freidson, 1970a, 1970b, 2001; Larson, 1977) and how intraprofessional segmentation takes place (Montgomery, 1990; Montgomery and Oliver, 2007). Over the past two decades, this literature stream broadened to explore a counter current of possible de-professionalization, driven by the marketization and/or managerialization of health care fields evident from the 1980s onwards (e.g., Scott et al., 2000; Ferlie et al., 1996). Sociologists of the professions are now considering how technological changes are fostering shifts within the hierarchy of health care occupations and professions. In her chapter on professional interactions and professional boundaries, Fitzgerald suggests that multiple currents of role shifts and maintenance of boundaries are simultaneously occurring.

Another strong theoretical stream that figures prominently in health care is the new institutionalist perspective, which typically analyzes a whole organizational field and examines different field-level logics of action associated with a variety of institutionalized actors. This theory has been applied in various substantive sectors, and health care settings are especially fruitful for analysis, as they are caught between the different logics of two major entrenched forces: the professions and the state. All too often, the traditionally dominant professions and tightly coupled nature of these actors in the health care field means that the status quo has been readily reproduced, and periods of radical change are rare (although occasionally evident, Scott et al., 2000). For example, Reay and Hinings (2005, 2009) use a new institutionalist perspective to model long-term dynamics in the Albertan health care field, where rising political/managerialist and entrenched professional logics appeared to co-exist over an extended period of time. In her chapter, Lipworth takes an institutionalist perspective into a new context that brings pharmaceutical firms and other commercial interests into an analysis of multiple logics in the health care organizational field.

In addition to these classic social science perspectives, the authors of several chapters synthesize multiple theoretical streams in presenting their topics. Reay, Goodrick, and Hinings provide a compelling synthesis of the classic theories of institutionalism and professionalization. Another example is the chapter by Doran et al. on clinical ethics support, which incorporates themes from bioethics into organizational and professional development frames. Similarly, the chapter by Rathert, Vogus, and McClelland on patient-centered care and the chapter by Oldenhof, Postma, and Bal on replacing care combine theories of professional power and control with new developments that challenge traditional organizational structure and processes.

Finally, we see the value of bringing a critical theory lens to examine power and the prevailing status quo within health care, as articulated in the chapter by Kitchener and Thomas reviewing critical management studies and the chapter by Currie and Martin on political narratives in the health policy domain. As with all instances in social science when introducing emerging theory and modifications to existing theory, our contributors worked hard to tread a fine line between advocacy and discussion of new ways to conceptualize themes in health care. We encouraged authors to make links between general theory and the health care context and to discuss the limitations of their chosen approach.

We observe there is no one master theory that recurs across the chapters. Instead the chapters combine to offer a rich picture of the varied ways that social science perspectives can be borrowed, re-examined, recontextualized, synthesized, and developed in the study of health care management and policy.

Proposition 2: Exploring Health Policy Developments Academically

The chapters often address—and also seek to reconceptualize in more academic and theorized terms—major developments in the health care policy field. As well as being theoretically informed, therefore, the chapters also relate to major domains of health policy and practice. They do so often in an indirect and autonomous way, rather than being captured by a short-term and narrow policy agenda.

Some policy-related themes are well known in the general management literature and have been brought into the health care domain over the years. Many of these themes capture organizational policies and practices for optimal performance. For example, policies of long standing in the human resources field that relate to performance management and measurement are becoming more prominent in health care (explored in the chapter by Lewis); also receiving renewed attention in health care are elements of accountability and transparency (Chapter 17 in this volume by Levay and Chapter 21 by Vrangbæk and Byrkjeflot).

Similarly, the themes of organizational culture, leadership, and teamwork have long occupied scholars in general management, and three chapters demonstrate how insights from the general literature are affecting policy and practice in health care (see chapters in this volume by Mannion and Davies on culture; Sergi et al. on plural leadership; and West and Markiewicz on team working). More recent themes in the general management domain that have relevance for health care include knowledge mobilization (Davies, Powell, and Nutley), situated learning (Nicolini, Scarbrough, and Gracheva), communication discourses (Kjær, Pedersen, and Pors), partnerships (Bishop and Waring), and networks (Sheaff and Schofield).

Other themes have developed within health care itself and have figured prominently in health care policies and practices over the long term, some of which have then diffused from health care into the general management literature. These include themes related to professional-organizational dynamics and to cost-containment, which are policy concerns to many organizations both inside and outside health care. For example, the long-running debate about the classic model of professional dominance in health care and the extent to which it has been eroded by managerialism, is explored in the chapters by Reay, Goodrick, and Hinings and by Fitzgerald. The organizational consequences of a cost-containment and productivity-based policy agenda represent another long-standing theme that arose within health care (addressed by Shortell and Addicott).

Several emerging policy issues of particular consequence in the health care domain are also explored in the Handbook. These represent policies specific to patient care, including patient safety and quality (Braithwaite and Donaldson), patient care delivery models (Rathert, Vogus, and McClelland), clinical ethics support (Doran et al.), e-Health (Doolin), and spatial arrangements for patient care (Oldenhof, Postma, and Bal).

We observe that there has been a long-term proliferation of macro-level health policy initiatives and programs, which then seek to influence health care organizations at the meso level. The field is becoming more crowded and receptive to a variety of approaches and dictates, which seem to co-exist rather than to displace one another. This proliferation perhaps reflects the increased production and diffusion of general management knowledge, models, and texts in advanced and knowledge-based capitalist economies (Thrift, 2005). As noted earlier, such management ideas typically move from their original base in private firms to public and health services settings (Sahlin-Andersson and Engwall, 2002) and across national borders. Idea carriers—management consultants, business gurus, and think tanks—play an important diffusion role, stimulating new health policy initiatives (e.g., ideas around TQM, quality management, and how Lean came originally from Japanese car firms such as Toyota).

It also is important to recognize the question of how enduring a policy-related theme has to be before it becomes mature enough to attract broader academic exploration and review. Several general management related themes now go back several decades (e.g., Peters and Waterman, 1982, was the first culture-related management text to diffuse extensively into health care settings), and some themes that were developed within health care have also benefitted from decades of academic study (e.g., professional dominance models developed by Freidson in the 1970s). Others are more emergent and only now receiving attention in the academic literature. For these newer policy themes, both in the general management literature and in the health care field, several decades may indeed need to elapse before a substantial academic knowledge base accumulates. It is our hope that the chapters in this Handbook will serve as important contributions to advancing the future literature for these policy-related topics.

Proposition 3: Building an International Literature Base

Health systems differ from one country to another, and therefore the field faces the danger of parochial thought. All too often, academic writers face a strong pull to the field, perhaps with too much immersion in national detail, such as exploring the impact of the latest reorganization or a short-term policy bubble that generates transient excitement. The aim of having an international focus taken, in the sense of including case examples from different countries, gives the reader an understanding of the local setting, emphasizing that health care management always is embedded in a local and national context. Yet, some of the phenomena explored in the Handbook, such as the patient-centered care movement or the development of quality standards, are of long-standing interest comparatively and internationally, while at the same time operating within different national economies and health care delivery systems. There is much to be learnt from the more frequent crossing of national frontiers and defamiliarization from policy phenomena in order to avoid being too readily taken for granted or appearing as common sense in a particular country.

While not going down a formally comparativist route (such as that taken by Painter, Martin, and Peters, 2010; and Pollitt and Bouckaert, 2011), we deliberately tried to incorporate an international dimension in our selection of authors and topics to counteract the tendency for much health management research work to remain narrowly in its own health system. We also sought to move beyond the predominance of perspectives from North America and the UK, to attract authors from other health systems and academic cultures. And we encouraged authors to cite appropriate examples from systems other than their own. To write and to read internationally is not therefore linked only to nationality, but to the ability to present relevant problems and broad areas of interest that communicate across national borders.

On reflection, we were only partially successful in this endeavor: The set of chapters includes authors from several North European countries, notably in Scandinavia and the Netherlands, as well as from Australia and New Zealand. However, contributions from Germany, France, Israel, and countries in Southern Europe remain a major gap, despite highly developed health care systems in these countries that could enrich the body of health management literature included in the Handbook. Chapters are also absent from Asia, Africa, and countries in the developing world, where challenges may be of a different sort than confronted in systems represented here. Clearly, more work is needed to broaden the international and comparative element of health management research and writing.

CHAPTER OVERVIEWS

The Handbook contains four parts, which operate at different levels of analysis and display different foci.

Part I: Theoretical and Political Approaches to Health Care Management and Organizations

Part I operates at the macro level of health care and health policy, with an overarching theme of exploring the value of distinct theoretical perspectives that can be brought to bear on key health policy issues.

Part I opens with Chapter 1 by Reay, Goodrick, and Hinings on institionalization and professionalization, recognizing the central role that these two classic theoretical perspectives have had over the long term in analyzing health care issues across organizations and national systems. These authors see the health care field as both highly institutionalized and highly professionalized; they suggest that these two perspectives and literature streams should be brought more closely together. They review recent developments in what is now a rapidly expanding literature, highlighting three streams of work: the first stream reflects on different institutional logics now apparent in the health care field (professionalism, managerialism, and the market), where each logic is associated with a different power base and claim for control. The second stream considers institutional agents of change and resistance within an institutional entrepreneurship prism. Institutional entrepreneurship refers to the activities of social actors who use different resources and institutional positions to create new institutions, transform existing ones, and resist changes imposed by others. The third stream supports calls to bring back a consideration of front-line work—and the meaning of such work. Strong professionalization and institutionalization produce embedded work routines at the local level, which may prove to be resistant to top-down or radical change, evolving instead through an incremental pattern of change that reproduces the professionalized *status quo*. Work practices are thus firmly embedded in wider institutional contexts. This approach provides important insights into challenges when implementing major change initiatives.

Chapter 2 by Shortell and Addicott examines the nature and significance of organizational innovations and their links to function, using examples from the US and UK. They argue that policy pressures and scientific advances are triggering attempts to reorganize the provider side of health care to reduce costs, assure quality and safety, and add value. The chapter examines the link between form (the macro-level organizational innovation) and function (micro-level goal-orientated activity), which is seen as emergent and negotiated rather than pre-determined. Shortell and Addicott suggest that, rather than form following function, the reverse may be taking place, where organizational forms emerge first, followed by functions that are enabled by the newly emerged forms. They suggest that it is helpful theoretically to complement traditionally influential approaches, such as institutionalism and a markets/hierarchy/networks typology, with newer perspectives that are better equipped to handle the relational aspects of complex, network-based modes of organizing. This perspective not only opens the door to a substantial literature on network-based modes of organizing (see Ferlie et al., 2013 for a review), but also to work on complex adaptive systems, which has been applied to health care settings (Plsek and Greenhalgh, 2001; Trenholm and Ferlie, 2013). Shortell and Addicott also suggest that, rather than representing ideal types, health care organizations are hybrid forms, some of which may endure over considerable time periods.

Chapter 3 by Currie and Martin connects to a small but interesting narrative-based stream of literature (Pollitt, 2013) on the rhetorical justification of public policy reforming that appears in public administration scholarship. These authors take as their focal case the rise of important and enduring NPM reform doctrines in UK health care (and more broadly across the public services) from the 1980s onwards, which they see as linked to the Thatcherite political economy. The construction of the NHS quasi market in 1990 reforms serves as an emblematic example of such politically driven change. Previous to these initiatives, the health sector had been protected from top-down reforming, whereas it now became an early target for state-imposed reforms, given the scale, costs, and visibility of the health care sector (Scott et al., 2000). The analysis thus proceeds over several decades, rather than offering a conventional short-term focus. Currie and Martin connect the recomposition of the health care field to long-run changes in the broader political economy, which generates ideologically informed narratives of reforming.

In Chapter 4, Mannion and Davies examine the question of culture in health care organizations, returning to a theme that has assumed prominence over the last thirty years in health policy and practice in many countries. The authors unpick the rise of the culture wave in the health care sector and explore various ways in which the term can be defined. They note that increased interest in culture may reflect disillusion with the effects of recurrent and structurally based reform strategies in health care systems. The interest in culture brings in a body of organizational knowledge from anthropology and sociology, as opposed to economics-based knowledge. It appears to be particularly relevant in such areas as quality and safety, and sometimes is linked to the use of tools and techniques pioneered in Japanese firms (such as TQM and Lean). Possible associations with the building of high performance organizations are also explored, and models for planned cultural change are introduced and discussed. In the midst of explicit attempts to manage cultural change and to create high performance cultures in health systems, Mannion and Davies explore ways to understand such grand change projects and question the extent to which deep organizational culture is readily malleable to such top-down interventions. They argue that the field of culture and cultural change in health care organizations is a complex and contested one where more debate is needed.

The last chapter in Part I, by Kitchener and Thomas, constructs an argument for a critical stream in the health management literature. Critical management studies (CMS) has developed as a growing subfield in general management research, associated with post-modern forms of organizational sociology, and it has begun appearing in the health management domain, especially evident in the UK and Nordic countries. Much of the focus is on anti-NPM, drawing on a prism that considers NPM as over-emphasizing narrow questions of performance. The authors argue that a critical perspective should act to defamiliarize taken-for-granted assumptions and to explore how these assumptions are constructed by political economic formations. Kitchener and Thomas also note that there is a "booming silence" in mainstream health management research on issues related to social movements and social movement organizations. This approach does not eschew value-laden concepts and terms, such as exploitation and surveillance, prompting the long-debated issue of value freedom versus value commitment within social science.

As a group, the chapters in Part I provide an exciting flavor of the rich and creative ways that theories from the social sciences can be brought into the health care domain, paving the way for the remainder of the Handbook to address substantive policy issues.

Part II: People in Health Care Organizations: Patients, Professionals, and Leaders

The five chapters in Part II take the perspective of key actors in health care organizations: patients (and their loved ones); professionals (physicians, nurses, and others engaged in the clinical delivery of care; and leaders (those who assure the smooth

operations of the organization). Although these groups are thought of as distinct entities, they are of course interdependent; and it is their interactions that serve both as
facilitators and barriers to the delivery of high quality health care. The thorough reviews
and innovative conceptual analyses in these five chapters advance our understanding
of emerging challenges and exigencies within the health care sector today. In so doing,
they reveal how approaches to health care delivery are affecting, and being affected by,
shifting roles and goals among the people in health care organizations.

The first chapter, by Rathert, Vogus, and McClelland, examines the rich literature on
the increasingly popular model of health care delivery known as patient-centered care.
They point out that, although the term is widely used, efforts to measure the effectiveness of patient-centered care are thwarted by a lack of conceptual clarity about what
the term actually means. As a result, this approach can be interpreted and implemented
across organizations quite differently. While most studies include the notion that patient
preferences and values are key components of patient-centered care, these authors identify the goal of alleviating patient vulnerabilities as a central theme across studies. They
encourage greater attention, both in delivery of health care and in studies of its impact,
to the therapeutic relationship that supports caring and compassion for patients, as well
as for care providers. In order to accomplish this goal, the authors emphasize the importance of the work environment that facilitates the ability of health care professionals to
enrich the therapeutic relationship.

The second chapter, by a team of scholars at the Centre for Values, Ethics, and the
Law in Medicine at the University of Sydney, introduces the growing presence of clinical
ethics support services (CESS) in health care organizations across the globe. Doran and
colleagues define CESS as an individual or group who can provide a suite of services to
help identify and manage ethical issues that inevitably arise in the design and delivery
of health care today. They argue that an interest in CESS has been generated by technological and societal changes that reveal the ethical complexities of patient care, several of
which have received widespread media attention. Drawing on literature from multiple
perspectives including bioethics, sociology of the professions, and patient advocacy, the
authors provide a careful analysis of concerns that have been raised about the appropriate goals, functions, and models of clinical ethics support services. Many of these
debates include how, where, and with whom the interactions encompassed by CESS can
or should occur, as well as the training expected of CESS professionals. This analysis
demonstrates that, similar to the patient-centered care movement, even the most well-
intentioned initiatives like providing CESS within health care face implementation
challenges when stakeholders' perspectives and priorities diverge.

In the third chapter of Part II, Fitzgerald revisits long-standing debates about the
nature of interactions among health care professionals in the delivery and management of health care. Using the theme of professional autonomy and shifting boundaries, she offers a nuanced analysis of the interactions that key professional groups engage
in, from high-level physicians to uncertified health care assistants. Her examination of
much of the empirical data on this topic reveals that the broad system of professions can
be characterized by paradoxical dynamics: First, Fitzgerald reports that the boundaries

between physicians and nurses have remained relatively unchanged over time, with physicians maintaining their traditional professional dominance, and experiencing only a selected loss of task autonomy that is not accompanied by evidence of jurisdictions being extended to other professions. At the same time, her analysis shows substantial role blurring between nurses and other health care assistants, with many instances of task off-loading by nurses onto other occupations lower in the professional hierarchy. The issue of training and credentials for those at the lower ends of the system of health care professions remains inconsistent across locales, contributing to blurred legal and task boundaries. Fitzgerald also examines another form of role blurring that is occurring at the elite levels of health care delivery: the hybridization of clinical and managerial roles, undertaken by a subset of physicians. She observes that this phenomenon is generating new sub-boundaries both within and between professions and management.

The fourth chapter in Part II provides an in-depth look at the challenges confronting health care delivery from the perspective of leadership. Reflecting some of the same issues raised in the first three chapters, Sergi and colleagues observe that health care organizations are typically characterized by diffuse authority structures and diverse value systems. This reality renders decision-making especially challenging, because the main actors—whether they are patients, professionals, or leaders—do not necessarily share the same priorities and concerns. These authors point to the need for plural forms of leadership, and they draw from an extensive literature to discuss several ways that plural leadership can be organized and practiced in health care organizations. Their analysis includes case studies to illustrate when a particular form of plural leadership would be appropriate. Shared leadership, for example, may be most effective with interprofessional teams dealing with complex clinical cases, where team members bring different clinical expertise; whereas pooled leadership may be most effective when the management of a clinical program requires co-leaders who bring clinical and managerial expertise to the table. (This contrasts with the hybrid professionals discussed by Fitzgerald, where the clinical and managerial functions are merged in one individual.) The authors conclude with a call for further research into the conditions under which the four forms of plural leadership are likely to flourish and whether they can be deliberately implemented or need to emerge organically.

Regardless of the form of plural leadership that may occur, the interdependence of people involved in health care delivery and management inevitably requires a teamwork approach, which is the topic of the last chapter in Part II. West and Markiewicz argue that, while team working is essential, its effectiveness is often assumed, masking a reality that teamwork does not always contribute to higher quality of patient care or higher quality of staff morale. The complex nature of health care delivery and management, as noted in all the chapters in Part II, is seen as both a primary need for, as well as a major challenge to, working in teams. Also echoing concerns raised in other chapters, these authors lament a lack of conceptual clarity about what is a team and how to measure team effectiveness. Their review of the literature highlights some of the key issues, such as objectives and task assignments, roles and interactions, conflict, member diversity, and leadership. While such issues can arise regardless of context, the authors offer a rich analysis of the way these issues are confronted by teams working within health care, along with cautions about the danger to patients and staff when teams fail to perform as intended.

Taken together, the chapters in Part II present a compelling picture of the challenges confronting the people in health care delivery and management as they strive, through various forms of interdependency, to achieve the goals of the system. Although the overarching goal of health care delivery is high quality of care for patients in need, the methods for accomplishing this fundamental goal are fraught with conflicts over values, priorities, and power. These authors do not present us with clear answers, but their cogent reviews and conceptual analyses give us some important guidance about how to think through the debates and issues, and highlight where additional research can be of value.

Part III: Organizational Processes and Practices

When health care management studies move beyond a focus on people in health care, they often explore the practices and processes that enable health care organizations to function. A practice perspective means that health care management can be understood from an everyday angle by looking at how management goals and health policy reforms are translated into practice, and how the clinic or the department life is a part of a community of practice. A process perspective means that organizations are more than structures and forms; organizations also emerge from work processes or organizing processes, which involve interactions, learning, communications, and knowledge. The first three chapters in Part III examine the importance of fundamental organizational processes within health care organizations that cut across specific policy issues, and how these processes can be understood as learning practices, knowledge mobilization processes, and communication practices, while the remaining four chapters focus on practices and processes as they relate to particular policy issues.

The first chapter, by Nicolini, Scarbrough, and Gracheva, explores learning in health care management; they define learning as community of practice and argue that the concepts of learning have been used both to illuminate the challenges of creating a learning culture in health care and to establish initiatives promoting knowledge transfer and sharing. The chapter illustrates how the ideas of community of practice and situated learning have been applied in diverse ways by health care organizations, and how these ways of knowing and learning have been inserted into established institutional order, and the mixed, but sometimes promising, outcomes which have flowed from them.

The second chapter, by Davies, Powell, and Nutley, examines the concept of knowledge mobilization, a broad term they use to cover activities aimed at collating and communicating research-based knowledge within health care organizations. Noting the international trend that emphasizes evidence-based knowledge, the authors illustrate how research-based knowledge interacts with other forms of knowing within organizations and how it can inform health care policy and management. They review the conceptual variations in the meaning of knowledge and knowledge flows within and between organizations. They point out that knowledge flow in health care is often slow, intermittent, and uncertain; and they discuss reasons why this is so, such as complex dynamics at the organizational level that must take into account issues of leadership, culture, and performance assessment. They also note the impact of the wider political context on knowledge mobilization and call for further research into how individuals and groups create and use knowledge to ensure that research-based knowledge informs policy and practice.

The third chapter explores the organizational consequences resulting from an increased interest in health care communication. A discursive communication perspective highlights that one should not only look for the desired outcomes of communication initiatives, but also focus on unintended consequences in terms of changes in management roles, challenges to professional values, and the reshaping of patients' identities. The authors, Kjær, Pedersen, and Pors, describe the expansion of organizational health communication and identify three distinct types of communications: clinical communication, extra-clinical communication, and corporate communication. To discuss the consequences of these types of communication, the authors present examples of the institutionalization of communication ideals, the communicative management of meaning, and the role of communication tools as organizing technologies.

Taken together, the first three chapters in Part III demonstrate that organizational practices of health care management can be described in analytical terms of learning, knowledge, and communication. That is, learning as "communities of practice," knowledge as "mobilization processes," and communication as "discursive practices" all require an understanding of health care practice as places where the organizational actors engage in interpretations, social relations, and knowledge strategies. They have in common a shared understanding of health care management as social processes, which involve complex types of interactions, different types of knowledge strategies, and different layers of communications and interpretations.

The next four chapters in Part III focus on specific policy issues and their translation into organizational practice. Four important issues are examined: patient safety, e-health, performance, and transparency—each of which can be seen as having a global impact on health care organizations, as well as raising challenges to health care management in practice.

Patient safety and quality are fundamental issues in health care delivery and management; yet, as Braithwaite and Donaldson report, avoiding harm and improving quality of care has proved to be a challenging goal around the globe. The authors review the substantial literature that has developed in recent decades, in order to reveal the scope of the problem and to uncover factors contributing to its persistence, at the individual, organizational, and institutional levels. They then explore various approaches, strategies, and tools designed to tackle harm and improve care, discussing in some detail several of the more promising systems-based initiatives, which factor in the challenges of complexity and build on the naturally occurring resilience of health systems. They argue for partnerships between politicians, policy makers, managers, clinicians, patients, researchers, and other groups in order to meet the expectation of creating better safety and quality in health care management.

E-health, defined as the application of information and communication technology to support the organization, management, and delivery of health care, has become an issue of great interest and importance. There is much optimism internationally about the potential for e-health to drive widespread change in health care practice, as well as to improve the quality and efficiency of health care delivery. In this chapter, Doolin explores the multi-level conceptualizations of e-health in practice, starting with the point of care at the bedside, moving to relations between health care providers across time and space, and ultimately to the consumers of health care, in the form of lifetime personal health records. Despite the promise of e-health, its implementation is a complex and emergent process that requires consideration of local health care contexts, including substantial changes in work processes, interactions, and behaviors. Doolin concludes with observations about some unintended consequences of a poorly implemented e-health policy and suggestions for future approaches that allow local flexibility, with agreed-upon standards and guidelines that avoid neither a top-down nor a bottom-up implementation approach.

In the next chapter, Lewis examines the link between performance measurement and performance management, pointing out many of the unintended effects of poorly implemented measurement practices. Although the need for performance management is well accepted in many countries, Lewis explains that its substantial focus in the health care sector derives from reasons that are both financial (e.g., the size of expenditures in health care and associated cost-containment policies) and existential (i.e., the essential life-and-death nature of the quality of health care). She reviews arguments justifying performance measurement, including for accountability and performance improvement purposes; and continues with a discussion of the challenges of measurement itself and its relationship to management, illustrated with case examples of various management approaches to improve performance in health care organizations. She cites the conclusions in one inquiry that point to some of the distortions on performance management and measurement, noting that priority was placed on the achievement of targets and that statistics and reports were preferred to patient experience data. Lewis positions her analysis on what she terms a paradox of "too much and too little," by which she means there is a theme of overload and duplication in terms of complicated statistical measures, in the midst of inadequate attention to the more difficult-to-measure qualitative indicators of patient care. Lewis concludes with some suggestions for moving toward a mixture of central and local measurement, combined with greater local flexibility and dialogue.

The last chapter in Part III continues the theme of performance management, in this case through the lens of accountability to outside constituents and transparency in those efforts. Levay notes that the increased pressures from outside actors are driven by policy reforms intended to make health care more efficient and accountable to general audiences, by applying business- and market-like forms of control. Yet, there are many reasons why these approaches do not readily lend themselves to assessments of performance that lead to improvements in health care and why they are not universally considered to be of value. Levay observes that relevant research comes from two distinct perspectives: a practitioner and policy-oriented lens aimed at providing guidance for transparency initiatives, and a social science lens that focuses on challenges resulting from the complex social relationships in health care. Quoting Donabedian (1980), she proposes that the question of performance and quality should be "What goes on here?" rather than "What is wrong, and how can it be made better?" She concludes that social science perspectives and policy-based perspectives can be mutually reinforcing in order to reap the potential benefits from transparency efforts. She urges a shared framework that would allow more systematic study of strategies that professionals, patients, and organizations engage in when creating and receiving public quality information.

The second set of chapters in Part III explore policy and management technologies that represent major movements within health care, each of which have garnered increased international attention in the last decade. Within these chapters, the authors provide illustrative stories behind these management practices, along with valuable insights that enable greater understanding of the pressures and barriers to successful implementation of the relevant practices. In so doing, the chapters allow critical reflection of strategies for translating these management and policy initiative into organizational practices.

As a whole, the seven chapters in Part III provide analytical perspectives of essential organizational practices and processes, beginning with a focus on learning, knowledge, and communication processes and practices, and concluding with in-depth assessments of the challenges of implementing specific health care initiatives related to safety, e-health, performance, and transparency. A key underlying theme appearing in all chapters is the importance of understanding health care practices as situated, complex social processes, which are not easily controlled. Instead they reveal various mobilizing strategies and behaviors, including inertia and resistance, used by the professionals and managers to cope, learn, understand, and work in the everyday practice of health care organizations.

Part IV: Issues in the Health Care Organizational Field

The final Part of the Handbook focuses on issues that go beyond the health care organization and incorporates institutional actors and publics in the broader organizational field. The use of a field-level lens widens the analytical frame to shed light on the interactions among important members of the organizational field that can have substantial influence on governance and decision making about the policies and practices of health care management. Such field-level actors include members of local communities (as explored by Oldenhof, Postma, and Bal); networks of multiple health care organizations (Sheaff and Schofield); partnerships between public and private organizations in the delivery of care (Bishop and Waring); external actors involved in developing and overseeing accountability regimes (Vrangbæk and Brykjeflot); powerful representatives of the pharmaceutical industry (Lipworth); and managerial consultants (Kirkpatrick, Lonsdale, and Neogy). Taken together, these chapters reveal the varied sets of public and private actors in the health care organizational field, whose different interests and priorities complicate decision making in health care management.

The Oldenhof, Postma, and Bal paper from the Netherlands brings in a distinctive spatial perspective, drawing on concepts from human geography (Massey, 1997), which they argue are underexplored in the health care management field. They seek to make a "space for space" in the analysis of the location, and especially the relocation, of health care services, which constitute an important aspect of the governance of health care. They draw on Pollitt's (2011) work in public administration scholarship, which suggests that space matters in influencing the trajectory of public management reforms in each country: local divergence is more likely than global convergence on one master reform paradigm. The authors develop this general argument by looking at three concrete developments in the health care field: (i) e-health or the notion of placeless care; (ii) the concentration and replacement of hospital care; and (iii) replacing care by re-imagined neighborhoods. For example, they note that large-scale service reconfigurations and centralization are often justified on the grounds of better clinical outcomes, but such efforts may also generate perverse social and equity effects, especially in less technical or scientifically based areas of health care. This chapter reflects echoes of a policy rhetoric about new modes of co-production in health care, linked to decentralization, participation, and partnership with informal and third sector care providers. Interestingly, this theme relates to a strand of political science work (Lowndes and Sullivan, 2008; Newman and Clarke, 2009) on modes of neighborhood governance, along with a consideration of their political and power effects.

The second chapter, by Sheaff and Schofield, explores networks as a growing form of governance in health care (as opposed to alternative market or hierarchy based modes). The literature has so far concentrated more on market-based reforms in health care, rather than on these network-based reforms (see Ferlie et al., 2013), so this chapter is a welcome corrective to an overly market-centric view. Sheaff and Schofield draw examples from the UK NHS in the New Labour period in the early 2000s, when managed network-based forms were seen as a reform reflecting politically preferred values of collaboration, as opposed to NPM-style competition. They also briefly review some international examples, as health care networks are also evident outside the UK Network-based forms of working are one way of pursuing the goal of more integrated care. The question of how a network-based governance mode plays out and how it relates to markets and hierarchy as alternatives is then an important one. Using Donabedian's work (1980), Sheaff and Schofield develop a typology of different variants of networks (especially program and care forms of network) and consider what desired outcomes might be associated with each type. They call for more comparative research in what is still a developing area.

The third chapter, by Bishop and Waring, examines the growing number of public-private partnerships in health care, apparent internationally but taking the example of the English NHS. Not only has there been a straightforward marketization of functions moving into the private sector, but there also is a growing number of hybrid spaces and organizational forms (Skelcher and Smith, 2015), which cross traditional sectoral boundaries and are sometimes associated with NPM reforms. In UK health care, major examples of partnerships include the Private Finance Initiative (PFI) designed to attract private capital to help build new hospitals; Independent Sector Treatment Centres providing elective surgical services for NHS-funded patients; and now increased tendering for community health services by private and third-sector providers, but under contract to NHS commissioners. The remainder of the chapter considers four broad organizational and management challenges brought about by the growth of public-private partnerships in health care: namely, governance and accountability, management culture and identity, managing workforce and employment, and managing learning and innovation.

Vrangbæk and Byrkjeflot's paper on Norwegian and Danish health care settings examines different forms of accountability regimes fostered by continuing reforms. They draw on an expanding stream of political science-orientated work (e.g., Bovens, 2007), which seeks to develop a typology of different accountability regimes in the public services. They suggest that forms of accountability in health care have proliferated, yet somehow co-exist and therefore become sedimented, similar to the multiple-logics perspective explored in other chapters. Their review of the literature suggests traditional professional forms of accountability remain but have become more transparent and explicit, and have further been challenged by rising managerial and market-based modes, especially in high-NPM health systems. In post-NPM systems, lateral and whole-systems forms of accountability become more important. They also note that an emerging rights-based discourse opens up a possibility of more activist forms of judicial review. In the Danish and Norwegian cases, various shifts to traditional accountability regimes are noticeable, which complement professional dominance and traditional democratic notions. Specialist national-level agencies have recently been developing new quality indicators and accreditation standards. The authors echo observations in earlier chapters regarding growing expectations of performance accountability in health care organizations, in addition to the traditional constitutional and democratic role that accountability regimes have played in these Nordic societies. A growth of legislation enshrining patient rights and enhanced patient expectations of their rights is also recognized.

The fifth chapter in Part IV, by Lipworth, examines the pharmaceutical sector as an increasingly important actor in the health care field, using an institutionalist prism and specifically tracing multiple institutional logics associated with different players in the field. Using examples from Australia, the chapter explores the widespread influence of the bio-pharma sector on other players in the field, by creating various new organizational forms, such as the medicines policy think tanks in Australia often funded by commercial firms; or by changing existing forms, such as an expanding number of pharma-funded randomized control trials (RCTs) within hospitals. The economics of the biotechnology sector and its links with venture capitalists as new actors are also of interest. Lipworth observes that there appears to be a nuanced or ambivalent reaction from established players to the growing presence of big pharma, as it brings a new commercial logic into a traditionally professionalized field. She identifies a common response of compartmentalization, as one mechanism for accommodating multiple institutional logics in complex fields, which enables traditional actors in the field to place limits around the rightful role of pharma.

Finally, Kirkpatrick, Lonsdale, and Neogy explore the increasingly prominent question of the role of management consultancy as advisers within health care systems, given the extensive use of such consultants across health systems, especially in the US and the UK. This trend is attracting scholarly examination of the role and impact of management consultancy in general, although there is little analysis of their role specifically in the health care sector. Mainly, this scholarly work has focused on patterns of knowledge production, diffusion, and consumption. Illustrating their argument with an overview of management consulting activities in the UK, which seems particularly receptive to such involvement, the authors observe that such actors have not only played a key role in sponsoring NPM reforms, but they also have become well-embedded partners to reformist governments, who look to consultants because they may be suspicious of provider dominance and in-house advice. The chapter serves as a useful ground-clearing exercise in what is a still emergent field and offers an ambitious research agenda in the conclusion.

FINAL REFLECTIONS

We hope in this Handbook first of all to have contributed to bringing theory back into the academic study of health care management and to help reconnect it with a developing social science base. We see this task as a reanimation of some of the field's founding texts. Many of the chapters clearly illustrate different ways such theories can helpfully illuminate important aspects of current health care policy and practice.

We need, secondly, to continue to develop more international and comparative work so that we get beyond excessive local concerns with the details of our national health care systems. We need to bring in scholars from more health systems than have been represented in the Handbook so far. Comparative analysis is, of course, most demanding to do well. Strong theoretical grounding provides one good basis for the stimulation of cross-national conversations. Building cross-national academic teams that can work on the more empirically related phenomena in different health systems on a comparative basis is another potential way forward.

We hope finally that various chapters—notably in emergent areas such as clinical ethics support services, knowledge management, and management consulting in health care—have not only taken a broad overview of their fields but have used such an overview to propose a forward-looking research agenda in order to stimulate a future cycle of work.

REFERENCES

Abbott, A. (1988). *The system of professions: An essay on the division of expert labor.* Chicago: University of Chicago Press.

Abrahamson, E. (1991). Managerial fads and fashions: The diffusion and rejection of innovations. *Academy of Management Review*, 16(3): 586–612.

Abrahamson, E. (1996). Management fashion. *Academy of Management Review*, 21(1): 254–285.

Alford, R. R. (1977). *Health care politics: Ideological and interest group barriers to reform.* Chicago: University of Chicago Press.

Bovens, M. (2007). Analysing and assessing accountability: A conceptual framework. *European Law Journal*, 13(4): 447–468.

Clegg, S. and Hardy, C. (1996). Introduction: Organizations, organization and organizing. In *Handbook of organization studies*, ed. Clegg, S., Hardy, C., and Nord, W., pp. 1–28. London: Sage.

Currie, G., Waring, J., and Finn, R. (2008). The limits of knowledge management for UK public services modernization: The case of patient safety and service quality. *Public Administration*, 86(2): 363–385.

Davenport, T. H. and Prusak, L. (1998). *Working knowledge: How organizations manage what they know.* Boston, MA: Harvard Business Press.

Donabedian, A. (1980). *The definition of quality and approaches to its assessment.* Ann Arbor, MI: Health Administration Press.

Ferlie, E., Ashburner, L., FitzGerald, L., and Pettigrew, A. (1996). *The new public management in action.* Oxford: Oxford University Press

Ferlie, E., Fitzgerald, L., McGivern, G., Dopson, S., and Bennett, C. (2013). *Making wicked problems governable? The case of managed health care networks.* Oxford: Oxford University Press.

Freidson, E. (1970a). *Professional dominance: The social structure of medical care.* New York: Atherton Press.

Freidson, E. (1970b). *The profession of medicine: A study in the sociology of applied knowledge.* Chicago: University of Chicago Press.

Freidson, E. (2001). *Professionalism: The third logic.* Chicago: University of Chicago Press.

Goffman, E. (1968). *Asylums: Essays on the social situation of mental patients and other inmates.* New York: Aldine Transaction Books.

Greenhalgh, T. (2012). Outside the box: Why are Cochrane reviews so boring? *British Journal of General Practice*, 62(600): 371.

Hammer, M. and Champy, J. (1993). *Reengineering the corporation.* New York: Harper Collins

Harrison, S., Hunter, D., Marnoch, G., and Pollitt, C. (1992). *Just managing: Power and culture in the NHS.* Basingstoke: Palgrave Macmillan.

Larson, M. S. (1977). *The rise of professionalism.* Berkeley: University of California Press.

Lowndes, V. and Sullivan, H. (2008). How low can you go? Rationales and challenges for neighourhood governance. *Public Administration* 86(1): 53–74.

McNulty, T. and Ferlie, E. (2002). *Reengineering health care: The complexities of organizational transformation.* Oxford: Oxford University Press.

Massey, D. (1997). A global sense of place. In *Reading human geography*, ed. Barnes, T. and Gregory, D., pp. 315–323. London: Arnold.

Mintzberg, H. (1983). *Structure in fives.* Englewood Cliffs, NJ: Prentice Hall.

Montgomery, K. (1990). A prospective look at the specialty of medical management. *Work and Occupations*, 17(2): 178–198.

Montgomery, K. and Oliver, A. L. (2007). A fresh look at how professions take shape: Dual-directed networking dynamics and social boundaries. *Organization Studies*, 28(5): 661–687.

Newman, J. and Clarke, J. (2009). *Publics, politics and power: Remaking the public in public services*: London: Sage.

Painter, M. J., Martin, J., and Peters, B. G. (eds) (2010). *Tradition and public administration*. Basingstoke: Palgrave Macmillan.

Peters, T. J. and Waterman, R. H. (1982). *In search of excellence: Lessons from American best-run companies*. New York: Harper & Row.

Pettigrew, A., Ferlie, E., and McKee, L. (1992). *Shaping strategic change*. London: Sage.

Plsek, P. E. and Greenhalgh, T. (2001). Complexity science: The challenge of complexity in health care. *British Medical Journal*, 323(7313): 625.

Pollitt, C. (2011). Time and place in public administration: Two endangered species? *Acta Wasaensia*, 238(4): 33–53.

Pollitt, C. and Bouckaert, G. (2011). *Public management reform: A comparative analysis-new public management, governance, and the neo-Weberian state*. Oxford: Oxford University Press.

Pollitt, C. (2013). The evolving narratives of public management reform: 40 years of reform white papers in the UK. *Public Management Review*, 15(6): 899–922.

Porter, M. E. and Teisberg, E. O. (2006). *Redefining health care: Creating value-based competition on results*. Cambridge, MA: Harvard Business Press.

Radnor, Z. J., Holweg, M., and Waring, J. (2012). Lean in healthcare: The unfilled promise? *Social Science & Medicine*, 74(3): 364–371.

Reay, T. and Hinings, C. R. (2005). The recomposition of an organizational field: Health care in Alberta. *Organization Studies*, 26(3): 351–384.

Reay, T. and Hinings, C. R. (2009). Managing the rivalry of competing institutional logics. *Organization Studies*, 30(6): 629–652.

Sahlin-Andersson, K. and Engwall, L. (2002). The dynamics of management knowledge expansion. In *The expansion of management knowledge*, ed. Sahlin-Andersson, K. and Engwall, L., pp. 277–296. Stanford, CA: Stanford Business Books

Scott, W. R., Ruef, M., Mendel, P., and Caronna, C. (2000). *Institutional change and health-care organizations: From professional dominance to managed care*. Chicago: University of Chicago Press.

Skelcher, C. and Smith, S. R. (2015). Theorizing hybridity: Institutional logics, complex organizations, and actor identities: The case of nonprofits. *Public Administration*, 93(2): 433–448.

Thrift, N. (2005). *Knowing capitalism*. London: Sage

Trenholm, S. and Ferlie, E. (2013). Using complexity theory to analyse the organizational response to resurgent tuberculosis across London. *Social Science & Medicine*, 93: 229–237.

Womack, J. P., Jones, D. T., and Roos, D. (1990). *The machine that changed the world*. New York: Simon and Schuster.

PART I

THEORETICAL AND POLITICAL APPROACHES TO HEALTH CARE MANAGEMENT AND ORGANIZATIONS

CHAPTER 1

....

INSTITUTIONALIZATION
AND PROFESSIONALIZATION

....

TRISH REAY, ELIZABETH GOODRICK,
AND BOB HININGS

HEALTH care systems around the world are both highly institutionalized and highly professionalized (Abbott, 1988; Scott et al., 2000). This means that the many tightly interconnected mechanisms that constitute the health care system tend to consistently reproduce the status quo. As well, the highly professionalized nature of health care results in the traditionally conservative professions holding power to resist externally imposed change and to maintain stability in the system. And yet, we know that significant change can be greatly needed. Quality and cost concerns are substantial motivators and have led to the development of carefully crafted change initiatives—however, observations show that sometimes change occurs and sometimes it does not. As Scott et al. (2000) noted in their examination of health care change in the San Francisco Bay area, empirical studies of health care have provided scholars with "a marvelous opportunity to examine an institutional arena undergoing rapid, even 'profound' change" (2000, xvii). In contrast, McNulty and Ferlie (2002) investigated a large-scale change initiative in the UK health system and found that very little actually changed. In this chapter, we are interested in the nature of health care systems and how the power dynamics associated with such highly institutionalized structures and professionalized delivery systems can lead to either stability or change.

In addressing power, and in particular, the notion of power dynamics, we are stressing the idea that actors (individual and collective) are affected by other actors, the social systems within which they are embedded, and the technologies with which they work (Scott, 2001; Clegg, Courpasson, and Phillips, 2006; Lawrence, Malhotra, and Morris, 2012). Thus, power is about "the dimension of relationships through which the behaviours, attitudes, or opportunities of an actor are affected by another actor, system, or technology" (Lawrence, Malhotra, and Morris, 2012, 105). Power is enacted. The dynamics of power are about those relationships of effect between actors.

Our focus on power dynamics reflects our conviction that they are central to understanding how the status quo is protected and change is enabled. Both the highly institutionalized nature of the system and its reliance on highly professionalized service providers lead to particular power dynamics among field level actors who are able to significantly impact organizational change, or resistance against change. The professions and professional control over broad bodies of knowledge perpetuate established ways of thinking through tightly controlled professional education and regulation of the professional membership. As a result and as clearly illustrated by McNulty and Ferlie (2002), many well-intentioned, large-scale radical change initiatives lead to limited or patchy alterations at best. On the other hand, some innovations such as micro-surgery have become implemented quickly and resulted in significant reorganization of basic work patterns (Ferlie et al., 2005). This suggests that when actors are aligned in particular ways, change is very difficult if not impossible, but in other cases it occurs relatively easily. More work is needed to understand the similarities and differences and how power dynamics play out in different ways.

The health care context has provided fertile ground for scholars of both institutions and professions. While most studies focus on either institutionalization or professionalization, we suggest it is critical to consider both these characteristics of the system to improve our understanding of change and stability, and the role of power dynamics in those processes. To this end, we provide here a short and selective review of the commonly separate literatures on institutionalization and professionalization in health care, and then highlight more current work that attempts to bring these concepts together in ways that reveal the underlying power dynamics and their impact on stability or change. We show how early conceptualizations in the institutional literature focused on context and structure as a way to understand similarity across health care organizations, and later shifted to view context as a source that could enable radical change. We also show that somewhat in parallel, the sociology of the professions literature first focused on the distinctive basis of professionalized occupations such as physicians and their legislatively protected right to provide particular services (Freidson, 1988), then expanded the focus to a system of professions (Abbott, 1988). Later, this literature re-focused on the challenges facing professions, with particular attention to the ways in which conflict among professions and conflict between management and professions has impacted the health system. More recently, and what we argue is essential for the future, we see that a growing number of studies are bringing together knowledge about institutionalization together with professionalization in ways that help to illuminate the inherent power dynamics that can either maintain stability or facilitate institutional change. We group this research into three general approaches—(1) institutional logics, allowing specific attention to the professional logic as an organizing principle, (2) institutional agency, including "professionals as institutional agents" (Scott, 2008) and other examples of institutional work, and (3) a constructivist approach focused on meanings of everyday work. We discuss studies within each of these approaches, showing how power dynamics are portrayed and the impact on organizational change. Finally, and in conclusion, we propose three ways in which future research could improve our understanding of change in health care.

INSTITUTIONALIZATION

Researchers of health care organizations have long been interested in the highly institutionalized nature of the health system. Scholars such as Borum (1995) and Pettigrew, Ferlie, and McKee (1992) in Europe, and Shortell (1988) and Alexander and Amburgey (1987) in the US focused their research attention on organizational change within the institutional environment of health care. These studies formed a foundation of work suggesting that health care organizations responded to changes in their environment, not only in response to technical demands, but also to normative and regulative forces (Alexander and D'Aunno, 1990). This attention to the power of forces within an institutionalized environment was consistent with, but also extended the early (neo) institutional literature focused on similarity across organizations (Meyer and Rowan, 1977). Institutional theory at that time focused on isomorphic pressures as explanations for the observed similarity of organizations and stability of systems, thus situating sources of power within the "self-regulating" system structure. This approach led to the concept of an organizational field: a set of actors consisting of key suppliers, resource and product consumers, regulatory agencies, and other organizations that produce services or products and that participate in a common meaning system (DiMaggio and Powell, 1983; Scott, 2014). Health care scholars provided many excellent examples of organizational change within a highly institutionalized field where coercive, mimetic, and normative isomorphic pressures convene in ways that lead to stability and predictability.

However, fundamental changes in health care organizational forms, authority and control patterns, and the implementation of "business" practices during the 1980s led researchers to question the value of current theory to explain observed changes (Alexander and D'Aunno, 1990; D'Aunno, Succi, and Alexander, 2000). By investigating these changes, scholars revealed new insights into the development and diffusion (or not) of new practices or organizational forms throughout the broader health care system (e.g., Burns, 1982; Fennell and Warnecke, 1988; Kimberly, 1978). They showed that mimetic forces (copying others) and normative forces (networking) were important factors in diffusion. Through further studies regarding the significant differences in uptake of new medical advancements (both technical and organizational innovations), researchers contributed to the development of institutional theory more broadly by showing the relationships between organizational characteristics or position and the relatively quick or slow adoption of innovation (e.g., Burns and Wholey, 1993).

D'Aunno, Sutton, and Price's (1991) study of addiction treatment clinics is an example of a further advancement in understanding how the highly institutionalized environment of health care impacted processes of organizational change. They showed that organizations not only responded to changes in their environment, but they also found ways to accommodate institutional pressures even if the pressures were dissociated from performance improvement (Greenwood and Hinings, 1996). Drawing on the "old" institutionalism (Selznick, 1949) and focusing more specifically on differences among organizational responses to institutional pressures, Greenwood and Hinings (1996) proposed that power dependencies were important enabling dynamics for organizational change. This theoretical advancement was important to an institutional understanding of health care because it not only drew on previous studies of change in health care (e.g., Burns and Wholey, 1993; D'Aunno, Sutton, and Price, 1991), it opened up consideration of new frameworks where power to change (or not) resided at the organizational level as well as within the institutionalized system.

Other scholars have also engaged with an institutional approach to understand change in health care settings. Earlier studies showed the importance of context and legitimation efforts in analyzing the effectiveness of change initiatives (Pettigrew, McKee, and Ferlie, 1988). Building on concepts from the literature on transformational or radical change, scholars showed how health care reform initiatives could be characterized by many twists and turns as change leaders responded to institutional pressures and unexpected resistance (Hinings et al., 2003; McNulty and Ferlie, 2002). These studies tend to show how powerful actors attempt to manage large scale change, and at the same time how other powerful actors try to resist.

In dealing with institutionalization and the power dynamics of both stability and change, a central feature is the highly professionalized nature of health care. In most jurisdictions, there are physicians who are often seen as the key players. But there are many other professions involved in the delivery of health care, such as nurses, physiotherapists, pharmacists, occupational therapists, dieticians, psychologists. It is this profusion of professions and their relative status and power in particular health care systems that is critical to an understanding of stability and change. So, it is to professionalization that we now turn.

PROFESSIONALIZATION

Literature on the sociology of the professions shows a long-standing interest in physicians since they are one of the classic professions characterized by exclusive control over an abstract body of knowledge and autonomous practice (Freidson, 2001). Sociologists' fascination with physicians extended to studying the health care system more broadly, especially with the rise of multiple allied health professions (e.g., nurses, dieticians, psychologists, rehabilitation therapists) that provide services within a system of professions (Abbott, 1988). The earliest writing presented the professions in general as being functional for society by sustaining social order and providing a moral foundation (e.g., Carr-Saunders and Wilson, 1933; Durkheim, 1957; Parsons, 1951). During the mid-1900s, physicians enjoyed the "Golden Age of Medicine" (Freidson, 2001) during which they held considerable control over the content and economic conditions of their work. Researchers studied how medical students were initiated into a system that was almost entirely self-governing (Becker et al., 1961) and attributes of physicians' work often served as comparison for other occupations (Freidson, 1988). Overall, these studies showed the stability of professions in society, and presented the health care system as resilient and strong, largely because of the influence of professionals. There was little, if any, attention to change in health care organizations.

In the 1970s, consistent with a general shift in sociology to focus on power and conflict, the study of professions moved toward explanations of professionalization as a mechanism by which members of an occupation exerted control over their work (Johnson, 1972). This perspective placed power at the center of professional studies, emphasizing the political and social power of the medical profession in health care (Larson, 1977; Starr, 1982). Physicians were viewed as leveraging their resources to gain a monopolistic position in the marketplace (Freidson, 1970). This process was portrayed as a somewhat subversive "professional project" (Larson, 1977), where occupations acquired government support to require credentialing for specialized skills, thus maximizing status and financial rewards for members of the profession.

Both the functionalist and conflict view of professions focus on the professionalization of single occupations. In contrast, Abbott (1988) set out the idea that professions operate as part of an interdependent system. This view is particularly relevant in health care because of the large numbers of professions engaged in the provision of care; systems of professions must be the focus of analysis rather than any profession in isolation, since professionalization takes place in relationship to other professions. The dominance of physicians can be explained in terms of successful jurisdictional claims over a particular task domain which closes specific work to other occupational groups, resulting in "occupational closure" (Witz, 1992). Since shifts in the occupational domain of one profession have an impact on nearby professions or in the creation of new occupations, change in work activities are key to understanding changes in professionalization. Consequently, the construction of boundaries between professions is important for their establishment and reproduction (Fournier, 2000).

Successful and unsuccessful jurisdictional claims derive from relative power and status. The successful claims of physicians and their continued dominance in most health care systems arise from the higher status that they have acquired over a long period of time, resulting in greater power. Introducing change into a health care system not only will encounter the "usual" issues of change (Greenwood and Hinings, 1996), but also the specific professional issues of jurisdictional boundaries (Reay, Golden-Biddle, and GermAnn, 2006). Consequently, power dynamics across different professional groups are a source of change and resiliency in health care organizations.

As Abbott (1988) emphasized, these disciplinary boundaries between professional groups can be fluid. In health care, professional boundaries have been challenged as a result of cost concerns and associated personnel shortages in medicine, nursing, and allied health; tasks that were previously reserved for one professional group have been reassigned to other groups and unskilled workers have taken on tasks previously under professional control (Nancarrow and Borthwick, 2005). Similarly, the introduction of inter-professional health care teams and new technology has reconfigured professional boundaries by changing the distribution of work between different professions (e.g., Barley, 1986; Haland, 2012; Reay et al., 2013). However, most studies focusing on the highly professionalized nature of health care continue to view professions collectively as key field level actors that bring stability to the system by commonly resisting change initiatives.

Combining Institutionalization and Professionalization

In the sections above we have shown how attention to institutionalization and professionalization in health care has occurred somewhat in parallel. However, in reality, these two concepts are tightly intertwined in health care, and we see that researchers are now bringing them together in three different ways that we discuss below.

Competing Logics of Professionalism, Managerialism, and Market

A growing number of studies in health care have adopted a logics perspective as a way to examine the influence of professionalism in light of other guiding principles such as managerialism and the market. Two important studies for health care were published in close proximity that drew on a framework of multiple logics grounded in the writings of Weber (1978). In the sociology of the professions literature, Freidson (2001) set out an argument of consistent and generalized deprofessionalization over the past decades by labeling professionalism as the "third" logic, in comparison to the market and managerial logics. Of particular interest to health care is Freidson's approach to understanding the battle between physicians and managers for control over how services are organized. He set out a systematic framework to analyze professions and the pressures challenging their status and position in society. The second study of particular relevance was by Scott et al. (2000). They explained macro-level changes in the US health care system by showing that older models of service provision were clearly guided by a professional logic—"medical professionalism" based on the unique knowledge and expertise of physicians that was used to determine appropriate patient care. However, this study shows that over time a new guiding logic of managerialism arose to challenge professionalism, suggesting a change process requiring the replacement of one dominant logic with another. Although they approach the issue of professionalism in competition with other organizing principles from different perspectives, both studies employ the construct of "logics" to identify sources of power held by particular actors in the field. That is, physicians hold power associated with professionalism while managers hold sources of power aligned with a corporate or managerial model of organizing and potentially also aligned with market principles. Thus, both these approaches present the introduction of change initiatives as a battlefield where strength and strategy determine the course of events and the ultimate winner.

The conceptualization of a battle between professional and managerial (and possibly market) values is evident in a number of health care studies investigating organizational change, although the term "logic" is not always invoked. For example, researchers have identified regulatory, market, and organizational changes that reduced professional oversight, changed the nature and content of professionals' work, and decreased professional autonomy (Borum, 2004; Doolin, 2002). Regulatory changes have been conceptualized as undermining traditional professional privileges and redefining the regulatory contract for professional groups (Adams, 2015; Coburn, 1999; White, 2000). Light (1993, 1995) attributed diminished professional control to the states' counteractions to the professions' power to shape its own domain. In addition, market principles have been touted as the way to bring much needed discipline into health care under the guise of innovations such as managed competition and accountable care organizations (Light, 2001; Fisher et al., 2012). While bureaucracy was noted to be in conflict with professional modes of organizing as early as the 1960s (e.g., Scott, 1965), changing employment arrangements due to the continually increasing numbers of professional groups within health care has resulted in a much stronger role for management and thus increasing influence of managerialism over professionalism (Everts, 2011). For example, some scholars suggest that physician autonomy has been diminished by the diffusion of clinical guidelines that replace traditional physician decision-making with procedural rules standardizing elements of clinical practice—a shift toward bureaucratic control of medical activity (Adler and Kwon, 2013; Nigam, 2013). In other words, the relative power of different occupational groups has changed with the waxing and waning of competing logics, changing the dynamics of professional relationships.

Other studies of health care have specifically drawn on the theoretical foundation of "institutional logics" to understand processes of change. Institutional logics are the commonly held values and beliefs that guide the behavior of actors within a field (Friedland and Alford, 1991). Kitchener (2002) showed that health care executives were expected to adopt particular managerial innovations in support of a political agenda to repress the logic of professionalism and shift to one of managerialism. Dunn and Jones (2010) showed how medical education, the supplier of medical professionals, was alternatively dominated by the logics of care and science. Reay and Hinings (2005) investigated a government-led change initiative to transform health care from being guided by the professional logic, to one guided by a logic of "business-like healthcare," and found that the power of the medical profession was too much for the health care managers to overcome. The result was an "uneasy truce" characterized by the co-existence of two field level logics, with neither able to gain dominance. In their follow-up study, Reay and Hinings (2009) provided more depth of understanding about how two competing logics can co-exist when key actors associated with different logics hold relatively equal power. Drawing on the concept of collaboration, they found that physicians and health care managers were able to work together in the same field, but be guided by different logics because they engaged in processes that allowed physicians to maintain control over some aspects of health care, while managers held the power to control over-arching, system-level issues. The relatively equal levels of power held by physicians and managers meant that change initiatives could only succeed when goals were viewed as mutually beneficial. These studies that are based on the concept of co-existing competing institutional logics give particular attention to the strength of professionalism (and medical professionalism in particular). They suggest that the power of professionalism must be respected. Change must be negotiated with the professions, even when there are strong competing logics such as the managerial or market logics that governments enact in their attempts to achieve increased efficiency and external measures of effectiveness.

More recently, a growing number of studies in health care settings suggest that the relationship between logics may be cooperative as well as competitive and that multiple logics can be conceptualized as existing in combination or arranged in a constellation (Goodrick and Reay, 2011; Waldorff, Reay, and Goodrick, 2013). Competitive relations among logics imply that strengthening one logic necessarily results in weakening another logic, or that logics can be equally strong, resulting in a truce. Alternatively, cooperative relationships among logics imply that different logics can jointly influence practice and that strengthening one logic may even result in strengthening another logic. For example in their study of pharmacists, Goodrick and Reay (2011) showed that the professional, market, corporate, and state logics all influenced pharmacist practice to some extent. In analyzing changes over time, they showed that both the professional and corporate logics increased in strength as pharmacists shifted from being small business owners to being employees of large drug stores.

Somewhat similarly, McDonald et al. (2013) studied a UK change initiative designed to move health care away from medical professionalism toward a logic of "population based medicine." They found that instead of competition between logics, each of the logics was simultaneously reflected in different dimensions of organizational activity. This concept of complementarity among logics is important for health care management because it moves away from a battlefield mentality, suggesting that change can occur without threatening the professionalism of physicians or other health professionals. From this perspective, successful change relies on the recognition of intertwined power dynamics, and the cooperation of key actors within system is paramount. Power is not viewed as a zero-sum game, but as something that can be increased by all parties.

Institutional Agents of Change or Resistance

In contrast to the focus on logics outlined above, the second way that ideas about institutionalization and professionalization have been brought together to understand health care change is through a focus on the ability of institutional actors (organizations and individuals) to influence the process of change within an institutionalized context. From this perspective, power resides in the actors themselves. Some scholars have adopted the concept of institutional entrepreneurship as a way to "reintroduce agency, interests and power into institutional analyses of organizations" (Garud, Hardy, and Maguire, 2007, 957). The term "institutional entrepreneurship" refers to the activities of social actors with resources and interests in particular institutional arrangements to create new institutions or transform existing ones (Maguire, Hardy, and Lawrence, 2004). This conceptualization has served as an interesting theoretical platform to better understand how some health care actors can accomplish change more successfully than others. For example, Battilana and Casciaro (2012) showed that the network position of change agents affected their ability to initiate and facilitate the adoption of change in health care organizations. In addition, Maguire, Hardy, and Lawrence (2004) showed how the position of key individuals allowed them to bridge across diverse stakeholders in ways that connected otherwise disparate values and facilitated the development of new HIV/AIDS practices. More recently, Lockett et al. (2012) drew on the concept of institutional entrepreneurship in analyzing the success of change agents in cancer care networks. They found that actors in "medium" field positions (neither central nor peripheral) were best situated for successful agency because they were cognitively distant enough to envision desired changes, but central enough to hold power to enact those changes. Collectively, these studies focus on the power of particular positions in the health care system, and suggest that it is the creative and strategic use of positional power that facilitates successful change.

Other scholars have focused specifically on professionals themselves as the most powerful agents of stability or change. That is, the power to make or resist changes to the highly institutionalized arrangements in health care is concentrated in the professions. DiMaggio and Powell (1983) recognized the importance of professionals in their now classic paper in which they delineated professionalization as one of the sources of isomorphic organizational change. They suggested that because professionals hold prominent roles within organizations and fields, they are well placed to influence institutions through their normative power. Building on these concepts, Scott (2008) claimed that the professions are the most important institutional agents in modern society. He argued that the primary social function of the professions involves "creating, testing, conveying, and applying cultural-cognitive, normative, and or regulative frameworks" (2008: 233) that govern social spheres. Therefore, by defining reality, providing prescriptive guidance, and controlling rewards and penalties, professionals hold significant levels of power in facilitating and regulating a broad range of activities (Scott, 2008, 2014). By focusing on an institutionally agentic role for the professions, this approach suggests that power dynamics are controlled by the professions. The action of professions is a key mechanism through which institutions are created and tended, and efforts at change in the health care context must take into account the ability of professionals to advance, transform, and resist change.

Although it is hardly news that professionals such as physicians hold significant power and the ability to facilitate or derail change initiatives (e.g., McNulty and Ferlie, 2002; Pettigrew, Ferlie, and McKee, 1992), we still lack knowledge about how the influence of professionals plays out. Several scholars suggest that institutional entrepreneurs (change agents) are more or less successful depending on their relationship to the dominant professional hierarchy and their embeddedness in the field. For example, Battilana (2011) studied the relationship between professional status of the change agent and the likelihood of social actors initiating change initiatives that diverge from the institutional status quo of medical professionalism where physicians dominate all other professionals. She found that non-physician professionals were more likely than physicians to initiate changes that diverged from the model of medical professionalism. Somewhat similarly but in a different context, Reay, Golden-Biddle, and GermAnn (2006) showed that professionals who were embedded in the established system could use their knowledge of "how things work" to advance change initiatives designed to diverge from the status quo. They found that that nurse practitioners already working in the health care system in experimental projects were able to use their embeddedness as a resource to enact change. Castel and Friedberg's (2010) study of the modernization of French cancer centers also shows the importance of embeddedness as a resource for change. They showed that because physician directors understood the connections between different components of the health system, they were able to engage in "bricolage" (Rao, Monin, and Durand, 2003) and successfully blend together programs and ideas taken from different cancer treatment settings. These studies suggest that successful change agents in health care are savvy political actors who take advantage of their unique power sources (especially their knowledge of the setting) to achieve particular goals.

The concept of institutional work (Lawrence and Suddaby, 2006) is a theoretical development grounded in the concept of institutional entrepreneurship that holds potential to improve our understanding of processes through which actors can enact change or maintain stability in professionalized contexts (Muzio, Brock, and Suddaby, 2013). Institutional work was introduced by Lawrence and Suddaby (2006) as a way of conceptualizing the role of embedded social actors in the processes of institutional creation, maintenance, and change. Institutional work is fundamentally about power dynamics. Rather than emphasizing how institutions govern action, the concept of institutional work focuses on how action affects institutions (Battilana and D'Aunno, 2009; Lawrence, Suddaby, and Leca, 2009). Social actors are viewed as having the awareness, reflexivity, and skill (Fligstein, 2001) to engage in actions that impact institutions. In contrast to the sometimes heroic tone of the institutional entrepreneurship literature (Suddaby and Viale, 2011), the concept of institutional work highlights how social actors are simultaneously constrained by institutions and able to shape them (Emirbayer and Mische, 1998). Drawing on the sociology of practice (e.g., Bourdieu, 1977; Giddens, 1984), actors are viewed as having both the ability to engage with their institutional environment and to exercise some degree of agency relative to institutional reproduction or change. Institutional work consequently highlights the purposeful activities of social actors that affect the institutional order in which they are embedded.

The concept of institutional work is just beginning to be fruitfully applied in studies of health care. To date, there has been more attention to "institutional maintenance" with a focus on the constraints that powerful actors can place on the possibility of fundamental change. For example, McCann et al. (2013) studied how the realities of paramedics' everyday work in the UK's National Health Service set limits on the efficacy of professionalization strategies. They showed that efforts by the College of Paramedics to engage in institutional creation (to create professional status for paramedics) were thwarted by the institutional maintenance work of paramedics "on the ground" who reproduced existing power differentials in the field between the paramedics, ambulance trust managers, regulating bodies, and other NHS clinical professionals. In another study of institutional maintenance, Currie et al. (2012) analyzed how specialist doctors used their professional power to take actions that maintained the status quo in spite of a government initiative to introduce new nursing and medical roles in genetic counseling. They detail how specialists invoked the concept of risk which resonated with contemporary concerns about patient safety and quality to constrain radical change in health care. Instead of transferring responsibility to general practitioners and nurses, as intended in the change initiative, the specialists reverted to the established practice of delegating professional tasks. In doing so, they reproduced current institutional arrangements and thus maintained their status and power.

Notions of institutional entrepreneurship and work provide an agentic perspective for both resistance and change. And institutional work, in particular, deals with the embedded nature of institutional agents. Professionalization is a particularly strong aspect of embeddedness, especially in health care, because most of the professions involved are relatively particular to the field of health care. Unlike accountants, lawyers, engineers, and management consultants, who can work in a wide variety of fields (including health care), doctors, nurses, physiotherapists, and so on, are primarily located in health care. Health care professionals, therefore, have virtually no knowledge of how work is accomplished outside the health care system, further strengthening the commonly held views of the "right" way to do things. Embeddedness, then, is very important, but it is from such embeddedness that action is possible and that power is exercised. In examining the issues of work, embeddedness, resistance, and change it is necessary to think about the nature of work and how the actions of professionals at the front line are important to our understanding of change and stability.

Bringing Work (and the Meaning of Work) Back into Health Care Studies

There have been ongoing appeals for organizational researchers to bring "work" back into organizational studies (Barley and Kunda, 2001; Phillips and Lawrence, 2012). We see that the topic of organizational change in health care is one of the places where attention to everyday work is perhaps most needed, but where there has so far still been insufficient attention. Since health care is both highly institutionalized and professionalized, established practices rely on interlinked professional and organizational activities that tend to reinforce "the way that things have always been done." These established routines have been orchestrated to suit the most powerful actors (usually physicians in the health care context) (Fligstein and McAdam, 2012), however these routines are also sustained by the integrated relationships and power dynamics of all participants. There are many studies showing that organizational change designed by top managers often fails to reach the level of everyday work (e.g., Westphal, Gulati, and Shortell, 1997; Zbaracki, 1998). In short, front line workers (especially professionals) can be particularly adept at avoiding changes in what they actually do.

When researchers focus on the nature of everyday work in health care and try to understand the associated meanings of that work, they find that successful change initiatives rely on new ways of thinking that somehow become embedded in new work practices (Reay et al., 2013). Of course, the important question is *how* such new ways of thinking can be developed. Grant et al. (2009) reported on their ethnographic study of changes in professional practice resulting from a new physician contract with government that included financial incentives intended to "improve the quality of patient care and reduce variation between practices" (2009, 230). They found that new working arrangements were developed, but the way in which change occurred recreated "well-worn professional boundaries and clinical hierarchies" (2009, 240) sustaining most of the previously existing power dynamics. Somewhat similarly, Waring and Currie (2009) engaged in an ethnographic study of a UK hospital's experience in implementing patient safety systems. Their findings suggest that change can only occur through the dynamic mediation of influences from the professional (physician) and management perspectives, and point to the need for managerial dexterity in facilitating practice level change.

Some studies have investigated change in the work of health professionals by considering how work practices are embedded within the institutional context. Reay et al. (2013) studied change initiatives designed to shift from a model of "autonomous professional care" to a model of "interprofessional team based care." They focused on changes in work at the front line (delivery of services) and found that the role of managers was critical in accomplishing this transition; the most effective managers were able to engage with professionals by helping to disrupt institutional pressures that perpetuated the old ways of working. This study showed that managers encouraged professionals to try new work routines, thus assisting in the creation of new meanings to support new (sustainable) ways of accomplishing work. A second study that takes this general approach is by Chreim, Williams, and Hinings (2007). They focused on changes in physician role identity by engaging in a longitudinal study with attention to the ways in which physicians accomplished work and how they made meaning of new work arrangements. In this study, physicians provided the original leadership for change, however, their efforts were both enabled and constrained by the institutional environment. In order to achieve the desired changes, physicians adopted and adapted interpretive, legitimating and material resources in the institutional context that impacted organizational arrangements. These two studies (Chreim, Williams, and Hinings, 2007; Reay et al., 2013) are important because they highlight the tight connection between established work practices and the institutional context within which they exist. They suggest that change in institutionalized practices relies on actors' use of power to disrupt institutional forces perpetuating the status quo.

Other studies have also investigated changes in health professionals' practice, but instead of analyzing the connection between practices and the institutional environment, they focused on the practices themselves. For example, Nicolini (2011) studied workplace practice in his study of telemedicine in northern Italy. This longitudinal ethnographic study suggested that professional "knowings" are woven together in established practice, and that power exists within the practice itself. That is, professionals' taken-for-granted knowledge about how work should be accomplished means that practice is the site of knowing and therefore the key to understanding either change or stability. Kellogg's (2011, 2012) studies of health care practice provided further insights into changes in everyday work. She highlighted the way in which "reformers" (change agents) took action or were dissuaded from participating in a change initiative. She found that the nature of the established power dynamics among people in the workplace was critical to understanding processes of change; professionals were particularly motivated by threats to status or loss of privilege. Therefore the meaning of the change initiative at the level of work was much different than anticipated by top management. Kellogg (2012) showed that change could only be accomplished when that meaning and the power dynamics sustaining that meaning were taken seriously. These studies focusing particularly on workplace practice suggest that changes in how work is accomplished must recognize the established power dynamics either surrounding practice or inherent in the practice itself.

Overall, we see that research focused on the level of work holds excellent potential to improve our understanding of change and the power dynamics involved in change. The key point in health care reform is often to make changes in the way services are provided, and yet research attention to this level has been lacking. Highly institutionalized practices take on a life of their own. Health professionals interact with each other in long established and taken-for-granted ways that show incredible resiliency. Studies that reveal the underlying meaning of these patterns can help to identify power dynamics that can either enable or constrain desired change.

Conclusions and Future Directions

We see that all three approaches outlined above bring institutionalization and professionalization together in ways that hold significant promise for improving our understanding of power dynamics and change in health care. Consequently we encourage researchers to continue on the paths set out in these studies utilizing an institutional logics, institutional entrepreneurship/institutional work, or workplace practice approach. In conducting our review of the literature, we observed that some studies combined aspects of two or more approaches (e.g., McCann et al., 2013; Kellogg, 2012) and we suggest that even more integration would benefit the field. We agree with Zilber (2013) who proposed that instead of segregating studies by either a framing of institutional logics or institutional work, researchers could generate a "more fruitful conversation" by bringing the core arguments of each together (2013: 77). Particularly in health care studies where a key goal is to develop actionable knowledge that will improve delivery of services and potentially health care outcomes, it is important to maintain a focus on understanding reality. Therefore, we see that studies grounded in the literature on multiple institutional logics and institutional complexity could provide even better insights into change initiatives by considering the "institutional work" of professionals in terms of creating, maintaining, or disrupting existing institutions. The reverse is also true. Studies focused only on institutional work tend to miss the importance of guiding logics that may be competitive or complementary, and help to explain behavior that we label as taken-for-granted. In addition, we see that there is significant potential value for studies framed either as institutional logics or institutional work to be more attentive to the nature and meaning of work at the front line. Without attention to the highly institutionalized practices and routines that characterize professional health care work, it is difficult to develop meaningful health care research. So our first suggestion for further research is that scholars should attempt to combine aspects of theory about guiding logics, agency of key actors, and attention to everyday work in order to further improve our understanding of successful (or unsuccessful) change initiatives in health care.

Our second direction for future research is for scholars to more clearly focus on the power dynamics inherent in health care settings, and how these dynamics play out in different types of change initiatives. We have given attention to the underlying assumptions about power in each of the research approaches identified above—noting that (1) an institutional logics approach tends to present battlefield imagery where logics either compete or strategies are developed to avoid battle, (2) an institutional work (or entrepreneurship) approach tends to highlight the ability of powerful professionals to resist change or sometimes shows how savvy lower-status actors can use alternate sources of power to achieve desired changes, and (3) the meaning of work can reveal power dynamics that are embedded in professional workplace relationships or professional practices—these power dynamics can facilitate or impede change. We encourage researchers to go further in overtly studying the sources of power held by different professions and how different types of power are employed. This might involve a return to earlier research on the sociology of professions that focused particularly on the importance of hierarchical relationships and how different professions resisted or enabled system changes. If combined with attention to everyday work, a more clear focus on power dynamics might help to reveal how professionals continue established routines—sometimes in spite of good reason for change. Pfeffer (2010) points out that if people ignore power plays, they are unlikely to achieve important workplace goals. Similarly, we suggest that if health care researchers ignore power dynamics, they are likely to miss critical aspects of the system they hope to understand.

A third suggestion for future work is that we encourage much more multi-level research. Several studies we discussed above employ multi-level methodology (e.g., Chreim, Williams, and Hinings, 2007; Reay et al., 2013). However, such studies are still too rare in our view. We certainly know that multi-level studies involve significant time and effort, but we believe that such research is absolutely essential to improving our knowledge of health care because of its highly institutionalized and professionalized nature. Change initiatives at one level can rarely be successful without specific consideration and attention to other levels. For example, changes in public policy are highly unlikely to be reflected in practice change without significant work from a variety of well-positioned and engaged actors at mid- and lower organizational levels. Institutionalized practices rely on institutionalized approaches to policy, in addition to the well-established ways of doing developed within all health professions. Further research that investigates these interconnections is essential.

Overall, in terms of research directions, we believe that all of these previous suggestions, but especially research that deals with relationships between logics, work, and meaning, will provide purchase on identifying when change will be difficult, if not impossible, and when it is likely to occur with relative ease. It is in examining the ways in which actors are aligned with respect to particular issues and how the power dynamics play out in different situations that we will gain a better understanding of successful and unsuccessful change.

In closing, we want to reiterate that health care is a setting where understanding the processes of institutionalization and professionalization and their interrelationship is essential. Stability in the system is critical to the ongoing reliability and predictability of high quality services. However, the tightly connected roles and responsibilities of highly professionalized providers together with taken-for-granted assumptions about what health care services should look like, means that resiliency can triumph over change that is needed and desired. Our review of the literature shows that the topics of institutionalization and professionalization have received significant attention separately, and are gaining increasing attention in combination. We encourage more research that advances this approach, and hope that with more focus on power dynamics and multilevel interactions we can increase our understanding of how successful change processes in health care can occur.

REFERENCES

Abbott, A. (1988). *The system of professions: An essay on the division of expert labor*. Chicago: University of Chicago Press.

Adams, T. L. (2015) Sociology of professions: International divergences and research directions. *Work, Employment and Society*, 29(1): 154–165.

Adler, P. S. and Kwon, S. W. (2013). The mutation of professionalism as a contested diffusion process: Clinical guidelines as carriers of institutional change in medicine. *Journal of Management Studies*, 50(5): 930–962.

Alexander, J. A. and Amburgey, T. L. (1987). The dynamics of change in the American hospital industry: Transformation or selection? *Medical Care Review*, 44(2): 279–321.

Alexander, J. A. and D'Aunno, T. A. (1990). Transformation of institutional environments: Perspectives on the corporatization of U.S. health care. In *Innovations in health care delivery*, ed. Stephen M. Mick and Associates, pp. 53–85. San Francisco, CA: Jossey-Bass.

Barley, S. R. (1986). Technology as an occasion for structuring: Observations on CT scanners and the social order of radiology departments. *Administrative Science Quarterly*, 31: 78–108.

Barley, S. R. and Kunda, G. (2001). Bringing work back in. *Organization Science*, 12(1): 76–95.

Battilana, J. (2011). The enabling role of social position in diverging from the institutional status quo: Evidence from the U.K. National Health Service. *Organization Science*, 22(4): 817–834.

Battilana, J. and Casciaro, T. (2012). Change agents, networks, and institutions: A contingency theory of organizational change. *Academy of Management Journal*, 55(2): 381–398.

Battilana, J. and D'Aunno, T. (2009). Institutional work and the paradox of embedded agency. In *Institutional work: Actors and agency in institutional studies of organizations*, ed. Lawrence, T. B., Suddaby, R., and Leca, B., pp. 31–58. Cambridge: Cambridge University Press.

Becker, H. S., Geer, B., Hughes, E. C., and Strauss, A. L. (1961). *Boys in white*. Chicago: University of Chicago Press.

Borum, F. (1995). *Organization, power and change* [English translation]. Copenhagen: Handelshøjskolens Forlag.

Borum, F. (2004). Means-End Frames and the politics and myths of organizational fields. *Organization Studies*, 25(6): 897–921.

Bourdieu, P. (1977). *Outline of a theory of practice*. Cambridge: Cambridge University Press.

Burns, L. R. (1982). The diffusion of unit management among United States hospitals. *Hospital and Health Services Administration*, 27(2): 43–57.

Burns, L. R. and Wholey, D. R. (1993). Adoption and abandonment of matrix management programs: Effects of organizational characteristics and interorganizational networks. *Academy of Management Journal*, 36: 106–138.

Carr-Saunders, A. M. and Wilson, P. A. (1933). *The professions*. Oxford: Clarendon Press.

Castel, P. and Friedberg, E. (2010). Institutional change as an interactive process: The case of the modernization of the French cancer centers. *Organization Science*, 21(2): 311–330.

Chreim, S., Williams, B. E., and Hinings, C. R. (2007). Inter-level influences on the reconstruction of professional role identity. *Academy of Management Journal*, 50: 1515–1539.

Clegg, S., Courpasson, D., and Phillips, N. (2006). *Power and organizations*. Thousand Oaks, CA: Sage.

Coburn, D. (1999). Professional autonomy and the problematic nature of self-regulation: Medicine, nursing and the state. *Health and Canadian Society*, 5: 25–53.

Currie, G., Lockett, A., Finn, R., Martin, G., and Waring, J. (2012). Institutional work to maintain professional power: Recreating the model of medical professionalism. *Organizational Studies*, 33: 937–962.

D'Aunno, T., Succi, M., and Alexander, J. (2000). The role of institutional and market forces in divergent organizational change. *Administrative Science Quarterly*, 45: 679–703.

D'Aunno, T., Sutton, R. I., and Price, R. H. (1991). Isomorphism and external support in conflicting institutional environments: A study of drug abuse treatment units. *Academy of Management Journal*, 34: 636–661.

DiMaggio, P. and Powell, W. W. (1983). The iron cage revisited: Institutional isomorphism and collective rationality in organizational fields. *American Sociological Review*, 48(2): 147–160.

Doolin, B. (2002). Enterprise discourse, professional identity and the organizational control of hospital clinicians. *Organization Studies*, 23(3): 369–390.

Dunn, M. B. and Jones, C. (2010). Institutional logics and institutional pluralism: The contestation of care and science logics in medical education, 1967—2005. *Administrative Science Quarterly*, 55(1): 114–149.

Durkheim, E. (1957). *Professional ethics and civil morals*. London: Routledge & Kegan Paul.

Emirbayer, M. and Mische, A. (1998). What is agency? *American Journal of Sociology*, 103(4): 962–1023.

Everts, J. (2011). A new professionalism? Challenges and opportunities. *Current Sociology*, 59(4): 406–422.

Fennell, M. L. and Warnecke, R. B. (1988). *The diffusion of medical innovations: An applied network analysis.* New York: Plenum.

Ferlie, E., Fitzgerald, L., Wood, M., and Hawkins, C. (2005). The (non) diffusion of innovations: The mediating role of professional groups. *Academy of Management Journal*, 48: 117–134.

Fisher, E. S., Shortell, S. M., Kreindler, S. A., Van Citters, A. D., and Larson, B. K. (2012). A framework for evaluating the formation, implementation, and performance of accountable care organizations. *Health Affairs*, 31 (11): 2368–2378.

Fligstein, N. (2001). Social skill and the theory of fields. *Sociological Theory*, 19(2): 105–125.

Fligstein, N. and McAdam, D. (2012). *A theory of fields.* Oxford: Oxford University Press.

Fournier, V. (2000). Boundary work and the (un)making of the professions. In *Professionalism, boundaries and the workplace*, ed. Malin, N., pp. 67–86. London: Routledge.

Freidson, E. (1970). *Professional dominance: The social structure of medical care.* New York: Atherton Press.

Freidson, E. (1988). *The profession of medicine: A study in the sociology of applied knowledge.* Chicago: University of Chicago Press.

Freidson, E. (2001). *Professionalism: The third logic.* Chicago: University of Chicago Press.

Friedland, R. and Alford, R. R. (1991). Bringing society back in: Symbols, practices, and institutional contradictions. In *The new institutionalism in organizational analysis*, ed. Powell, W. W. and DiMaggio, P. J., pp. 232–263. Chicago: University of Chicago Press.

Garud, R., Hardy, C., and Maguire, S. (2007). Institutional entrepreneurship as embedded agency: An introduction to the special issue. *Organization Studies*, 28(7): 957–969.

Giddens, A. (1984). *The constitution of society: Outline of the theory of structuration* (Berkeley: University of California Press).

Goodrick, E. and Reay, T. (2011). Constellations of institutional logics: Changes in the professional work of pharmacists. *Work and Occupations*, 38(3): 372–416.

Grant, S., Huby, G., Watkins, F., Checkland, K., McDonald, R., Davies, H., and Guthrie, B. (2009). The impact of pay-for-performance on professional boundaries in UK general practice: An ethnographic study. *Sociology of Health & Illness*, 31(2): 229–245.

Greenwood, R. and Hinings, C. R. (1996). Understanding radical organizational change: Bringing together the old and the new institutionalism. *Academy of Management Review*, 21(4): 1022–1054.

Haland, E. (2012). Introducing the electronic patient record (EPR) in a hospital setting: Boundary work and shifting constructions of professional identities. *Sociology of Health & Illness*, 34(5): 761–775.

Hinings, C. R., Casebeer, A., Reay, T., Golden-Biddle, K., Pablo, A., and Greenwood, R. (2003). Regionalizing health care in Alberta: Legislated change, uncertainty and loose coupling. *British Journal of Management*, 13: S15–S30.

Johnson, T. J. (1972). *Professions and power.* London: Macmillan.

Kellogg, K. C. (2011). Hot lights and cold steel: Cultural and political toolkits for practice change in surgery. *Organization Science*, 22(2): 482–502.

Kellogg, K. C. (2012). Making the cut: Using status-based countertactics to block social movement implementation and microinstitutional change in surgery. *Organization Science*, 23(6): 1546–1570.

Kimberly, J. R. (1978). Hospital adoption of innovation: The role of integration into external informational environments. *Journal of Health and Social Behavior*, 19: 361–373.

Kitchener, M. (2002). Mobilizing the logic of managerialism in professional fields: The case of academic health centre mergers. *Organization Studies*, 21: 487–513.

Larson, M. S. (1977). *The rise of professionalism: A sociological analysis*. Berkeley: University of California Press.

Lawrence, T. B., Malhotra, N., and Morris, T. (2012). Episodic and systemic power in the transformation of professional service firms. *Journal of Management Studies*, 49: 102–143.

Lawrence, T. B. and Suddaby, R. (2006). Institutions and institutional work. In *Handbook of organization studies*, ed. Clegg, S. R., Hardy, C., Lawrence, T. B., and Nord, W. R., 2nd edition, pp. 215–254. London: Sage.

Lawrence, T. B., Suddaby, R., and Leca, B. (2009). Introduction: Theorizing and studying institutional work. In *Institutional work: Actors and agency in institutional studies of organizations*, ed. Lawrence, T. B., Suddaby, R., and Leca, B., pp. 1–27. Cambridge: Cambridge University Press.

Light, D. W. (1993). Countervailing power? The changing character of the medical profession in the United States. In *The changing medical profession: An international perspective*, ed. Hafferty, F. W. and McKinlay, J. B., pp. 69–80. New York: Oxford University Press.

Light, D. W. (1995). Countervailing powers: A framework for professions in transition. In *Health professions and the state in Europe*, ed. Johnson, T., Lakin, G., and Saks, M., pp. 25–41. London and New York: Routledge.

Light, D. W. (2001). Managed competition, governentality and institutional response in the United Kingdom. *Social Science & Medicine*, 52: 1167–1181.

Lockett, A., Currie, G., Waring, J., Finn, R., and Martin, G. (2012). The role of institutional entrepreneurs in reforming healthcare. *Social Science & Medicine*, 74(3): 356–363.

McCann, L., Granter, E., Hyde, P., and Hassard, J. (2013). Still blue-collar after all these years? An ethnography of the professionalization of emergency ambulance work. *Journal of Management Studies*, 50(5): 750–776.

McDonald, R., Cheraghi-Sohi, S., Bayes, S., Morriss, R., and Kai, J. (2013). Competing and coexisting logics in the changing field of English general medicine practice. *Social Science & Medicine*, 93: 47–54.

McNulty, T. and Ferlie, E. (2002). *Reengineering health care: The complexities of organizational transformation*. Oxford: Oxford University Press.

Maguire, S., Hardy, C., and Lawrence, T. B. (2004). Institutional entrepreneurship in emerging fields: HIV/AIDS treatment advocacy in Canada. *Academy of Management Journal*, 47(5): 657–679.

Meyer, J. W. and Rowan, B. (1977). Institutionalized organizations: Formal structure as myth and ceremony. *American Journal of Sociology*, 83: 340–363.

Muzio, D., Brock, D., and Suddaby, R. (2013). Professions and institutional change: Towards an institutionalist sociology of the professions. *Journal of Management Studies*, 50(5): 699–721.

Nancarrow, S. A. and Borthwick, A. M. (2005). Dynamic professional boundaries in the healthcare workforce. *Sociology of Health & Illness*, 27(7): 897–919.

Nicolini, D. (2011). Practice as the site of knowing: Insights from the field of telemedicine. *Organization Science*, 22(3): 602–620.

Nigam, A. (2013). How institutional change and individual researchers helped advance clinical guidelines in American health care. *Social Science & Medicine*, 87: 16–22.

Parsons, T. (1951). *The social system*. New York: The Free Press.

Pettigrew, A., Ferlie, E., and McKee, L. (1992). *Shaping strategic change: Making change in large organizations—the case of the National Health Service*. London: Sage.

Pettigrew, A., McKee, L., and Ferlie, E. (1988). Understanding change in the NHS. *Public Administration*, 66(3): 297–317.

Pfeffer, J. (2010). Power play. *Harvard Business Review*, July–August: 84–92.

Phillips, N. and Lawrence, T. B. (2012). The turn to work in organization and management theory: Some implications for strategic organization. *Strategic Organization*, 10(3): 223–230.

Rao, H., Monin, P., and Durand, R. (2003). Institutional change in Toque Ville: Nouvelle cuisine as an identity movement in French gastronomy. *American Journal of Sociology*, 108(4): 795–843.

Reay, T., Chreim, S., Golden-Biddle, K., Goodrick, E., Williams, B. E., Casebeer, A., Pablo, A., and Hinings, C. R. (2013). Transforming new ideas into practice: An activity based perspective on the institutionalization of practices. *Journal of Management Studies*, 50(6): 963–990.

Reay, T., Golden-Biddle, K., and GermAnn, K. (2006). Legitimizing a new role: Small wins and micro-processes of change. *Academy of Management Journal*, 49(4): 977–998.

Reay, T. and Hinings, C. R. (2005). The recomposition of an organizational field: Health care in Alberta. *Organization Studies*, 26(3): 351–384.

Reay, T. and Hinings, C. R. (2009). Managing the rivalry of competing institutional logics. *Organization Studies*, 30(6): 629–652.

Scott, J. R. (2001). *Power*. Oxford: Blackwell.

Scott, W. R. (1965). Reactions to supervision in a heteronomous professional organization. *Administrative Science Quarterly*, 10: 65–81.

Scott, W. R. (2008). Lords of the dance: Professionals as institutional agents. *Organization Studies*, 29(2): 219–238.

Scott, W. R. (2014). *Institutions and organizations*. Thousand Oaks, CA: Sage.

Scott, W. R., Ruef, M., Mendel, P. J., and Caronna, C. A. (2000). *Institutional change and healthcare organizations: From professional dominance to managed care*. Chicago: Chicago University Press.

Selznick, P. (1949). *TVA and the grass roots*. Berkeley: University of California Press.

Shortell, S. M. (1988). The evolution of hospital systems: Unfulfilled promises and self fulfilling prophesies. *Medical Care Review*, 45(2): 177–214.

Starr, P. (1982). *The social transformation of American medicine: The rise of a sovereign profession and the making of a vast industry*. New York: Basic Books.

Suddaby, R. and Viale, T. (2011). Professionals and field level change: Institutional work and the professional project. *Current Sociology*, 59: 423–442.

Waldorff, S. B., Reay, T., and Goodrick, E. (2013). A tale of two countries: How different constellations of logics impact action. In *Institutional Logics in Action, Part A. Research in the Sociology of Organizations*, ed. Lounsbury, M. and Boxenbaum, E., Vol. 39, pp. 99–129. Bingley: Emerald.

Waring, J. and Currie, G. (2009). Managing expert knowledge: Organizational challenges and managerial futures for the UK medical profession. *Organization Studies*, 30(7): 755–778.

Weber, M. (1978). *Economy and society*. Berkeley: University of California Press.

Westphal, J. D., Gulati, R., and Shortell, S. M. (1997). Customization or conformity? An institutional and network perspective on the content and consequences of TQM adoption. *Administrative Science Quarterly*, 42: 366–394.

White, K. (2000). The state, the market and general practice: The Australian case. *International Journal of Health Services*, 30(2): 285–308.

Witz, A. (1992) *Professions and patriarchy.* London: Routledge.

Zbaracki, M. (1998). The rhetoric and reality of total quality management. *Administrative Science Quarterly*, 43: 602–636.

Zilber, T. B. (2013). Institutional logics and institutional work: Should they be agreed? In *Institutional Logics in Action, Part A. Research in the Sociology of Organizations*, ed. Lounsbury, M. and Boxenbaum, E., Vol. 39, pp. 77–96. Bingley: Emerald.

CHAPTER 2

....

A NEW LENS ON ORGANIZATIONAL INNOVATIONS IN HEALTH CARE

Forms and Functions

....

STEPHEN M. SHORTELL AND RACHAEL ADDICOTT

A confluence of forces, including the need to control costs and improve the quality of care while simultaneously incorporating new biomedical advances, is reshaping health systems across the globe (McClellan et al., 2014). These forces are giving rise to new types of health care organizations, modifications of existing types, and development of many innovations in care delivery and payment. This chapter addresses the overarching question of whether existing theories of organizational change and innovation can adequately explain the tumultuous changes occurring in the health care sector worldwide (Allen et al., 2011; Blumenthal and Dixon, 2012; Klein et al., 2013; Lee and Mongan, 2009; Porter and Teisberg, 2006). We focus primarily on England and the United States (US) but also note developments in Australia, Canada, New Zealand, and Singapore.

Our primary contribution is to question the sacred cow and long "received wisdom" that "form follows function" in making changes or introducing innovations to improve organizational performance. We define form as a macro-level concept involving the overall structure of the organization in terms of its size, ownership, governance, and arrangement of divisions and departments. We define function as a micro level concept involving the activities carried out that constitute the work of the organization to achieve its goals. Rather than form following function, we suggest a new possibility in which organizational forms emerge first followed by functions that are enabled by the newly emerged organizational forms. In brief, new organizational forms are needed in order to implement the innovations in functions. We suggest that this may be a more accurate and useful framing for understanding the seminal innovations occurring in the health care sector now and in the future.

We organize our assessment around four sets of questions. First, what are the internal and external conditions under which new organizations or new arrangements of existing organizations emerge? Second, does form always follow function as current theories suggest or are there examples where changes or innovations in organizational forms occur first before changes or innovations in functions? Third, are some organizational forms more conducive for making changes or innovations in functions than other forms? If so, what are these? Fourth, can you change forms without also changing functions and vice versa? What might be the consequences of changing one without the other? What might be some examples? We do not question that form may also follow function but suggest that this is most likely to occur in situations of small or modest change where existing forms can "absorb" the changes in functions or can be altered after the fact to fit the changing circumstances. But changes involving more complex interdependent functions are less likely to be accommodated by existing forms. Rather, they require changes in form prior to attempting to implement the changes in functions.

CONDITIONS UNDER WHICH NEW ORGANIZATIONAL FORMS/ ARRANGEMENTS EMERGE

A number of economic, political, clinical, and demographic challenges are driving innovations in the development of new organizational forms in the health care sector. All countries face economic pressures on their health care systems. In England, the National Health Service (NHS) budget has been effectively frozen—although there is increasing demand for services from an ageing population. The NHS has struggled both to keep within budget and to hit key targets for patient care. In the US there is continuing pressure to constrain the rate of growth in costs which currently comprise 18% of the gross domestic product (GDP). These expenditures are likely to increase as the population over age 65 is growing in all countries and, in many countries, becoming more diverse and further increasing health inequalities. These factors have resulted in increased pressure on the health care workforce which is also influencing the development of new ways of organizing.

The past seven years have given rise to significant legislative reform in both England and the US. In England, the Health and Social Care Act of 2010 triggered a major structural reform with the abolition of existing regional health authorities and purchasers, and the development of new organizations with responsibility for strategic commissioning. These new bodies (Clinical Commissioning Groups, or CCGs) were intended to be more clinically led, and work with partners across other public services to meet the needs of the population into the future. In the US, the Affordable Care Act of 2010 expanded health insurance coverage for the uninsured and created Accountable Care Organizations (ACOs) that would share in payment savings for providing more cost-effective care to defined populations of patients, Penalties for hospital re-admissions were also implemented.

These pressures and political reforms in both the US and England but also in other countries such as Australia, Canada, New Zealand, and Singapore have triggered a movement towards more accountable and integrated forms of delivering health ser-vices (Donato and Segal, 2010; Gauld, 2014; Vedel, Monette, and Bergman, 2011; Stukel et al., 2013; Cheah, Kirk-Chuan, W., and Lim, 2012). Service providers collectively take responsibility (across organizations) for the health and well-being of a defined popula-tion to improve the quality and patient experience of care, as well as the overall health of the population, and to reduce the rate at which costs are rising. These have led to a cor-responding shift in governance structures and mechanisms of accountability.

THE ENGLISH CONTEXT

Decades of regulatory restrictions and fragmentation between and within organi-zations has left a legacy, with barriers to achieving significant organizational change. Organizational fragmentation is compounded by fragmentation of payment mecha-nisms. Local, regional, and national commissioners all take financial responsibility for different parts of health and social care and rely on different currencies and contracts. This payment fragmentation is one of the main "wicked problems" facing the NHS, rep-resenting a misalignment of purpose and incentives.

The increasing dissatisfaction and fragmentation has led to efforts to develop differ-ent organizational models and to pool budgets across commissioners. For example, the Better Care Fund has been established as a single pooled budget combining £3.8 billion of existing funding to support health and social care services to work more closely together. In many places this will require a significant expansion of care services in a community setting and could act as a catalyst for introducing significant changes. Recently, national agencies have joined together to promote a selection of integration archetypes through the *Five Year Forward View*—these archetypes represent interorganizational models where providers integrate either horizontally or vertically (National Health Service, 2014). There are various pilot schemes to support these "vanguards," regions which dem-onstrate the capabilities to develop into these archetypes. The intent is to support plans to develop integrated care across the continuum.

THE US CONTEXT

The demand for greater value in terms of better health outcomes for the 18% of GDP investment has been a major motivator for change in the US. Health status outcome measures in the US are generally in the middle or bottom quartiles in international comparisons (Davis et al., 2014).With rare exceptions, the rate of growth in health care expenditures on an annual basis has been greater than the increase in GDP—usually by several percentage points—with little demonstrable gains in quality a or outcomes of care. There is also widespread variation in health care spending with no correlation with quality of care (Aaron and Ginsburg, 2009; Wennberg, Fisher, and Skinner, 2002).

The third party fee-for-service (FFS) payment system which rewards providers for providing more services contributes to the greater health care spending. Thus, new payment policies in the Medicare program and among private commercial insurers are moving toward paying for value; paying for outcomes and results; paying for keeping well. These include bundled payments that pay one amount for all care (e.g., inpatient and outpatient) for given conditions such as hip and knee replacements; episode of care payments which proved a fixed amount over a fixed period of time for a given condition episode such as for diabetes; partial capitation which pays a provider a set amount per member patient per month for defined services (e.g., ambulatory care); full capitation which covers all services provided; and global budgets in which providers assume full risk for all services provided to a defined group of patients over time. In the latter case any savings achieved are then shared between the payer and the provider on a predetermined percentage basis, generally 50/50. Losses can be fully absorbed by the payer; shared between the payer and provider; or totally absorbed by the provider.

A third major factor driving change in the US is public demand for greater transparency of data and accountability for results. The ACA has extended health insurance coverage to approximately 25 to 32 million more Americans but to select wisely they need information not only on benefits and price but also on the cost and quality of the provider networks associated with each health plan. Employers are also increasingly demanding such information. These pressures are likely to grow with the increase in consumer cost sharing evident in most of the insurance plans being offered.

A fourth motivator for change is the recognition that the current fragmentation of the system is not capable of responding to the new payment models and incentives. While slowly changing, most physicians in the US still practice in groups of nine physicians or fewer (Burns, Goldsmith, and Sen, 2013). While there has been growing horizontal consolidation of hospitals with each other over many years, vertical integration between hospitals and physician organizations has been slower to develop although is now gaining momentum. Combined with the above forces—the demand for greater value for the money spent, a concerted movement away from FFS payment, and the demand for greater transparency and accountability—the push for greater integration has given rise to several new organizational forms with ACOs and Patient-Centered Medical Homes (PCMHs) being among the most prominent.

FORMS AND FUNCTIONS—WHO LEADS?

What is different about the reforms now taking place in both countries is the increasing recognition that policy goals of achieving "greater value for the money spent" will not be achieved without major changes in organizational forms for paying for and delivering care. They cannot be accomplished within existing organizations. To succeed, changes in organizational forms will need to precede changes in functions. In England they include the creation of Clinical Commissioning Groups (CCGs), GP Federations, and various forms of integrated care organizations and new contractual models. In the US they include Accountable Care Organizations (ACOs), Patient-Centered Medical Homes (PCMHs) and Accountable Communities for Health (ACHs) (Shortell, Gillies, and Wu, 2010b). These models all seek to change the boundaries of existing organizations.

In England, many commissioners and providers have arguably reached the limits of what they can conceivably achieve through functional changes within existing organizational boundaries and informal relationships. They are now driving through fundamental shifts in form in order to trigger the desired functional changes. The combination of large-scale contractual procurements and pooled or capitated budgets requires a new organizational form to emerge in order to successfully deliver the services. In the US efforts to expand team-based care and the use of evidence-based processes to care for patients with chronic illness have proceeded slowly (Friedberg et al., 2014; Rodriguez et al., 2014; Wiley et al., 2015). For the most part, they have been grafted on to an existing delivery system comprised of small physician practices loosely linked to other care settings and with almost no linkage to community and social services. As a result there is growing recognition of the need for new organizational forms better equipped to develop and implement new innovations in care delivery. These include the earlier noted ACOs and PCMHs (Edwards et al., 2014; Rittenhouse and Shortell, 2009; Scholle et al., 2011).

To some extent, the above developments might be explained by coercive, mimetic, and normative pressures based on institutional theories of isomorphic change (DiMaggio and Powell, 1983; Tolbert and Zucker, 1983; Zucker, 1987). Coercive pressures to adopt specific features or practices include mechanisms of political influence, power relationships, demands of the state, and other large actors. Both the Affordable Care Act in the US and the Health and Social Act in England represent significant examples of such coercive political influence. Mimetic pressures are characterized as those encountered by organizations that when faced with uncertainty, will then tend to imitate their peers that are seen to be more successful or influential. In England, many new organizational forms have developed in response to early initiatives elsewhere in the country, and from international examples such as the ACOs in the US and the alliance contracts in New Zealand and England.

Normative pressures are also operating and are changing the very nature of how health care services are delivered over time. For example, there is growing acceptance of health care team approaches (Grace et al., 2014; Rodriguez et al., 2014), delegation of tasks to nurse practitioners and others, and more attention being given to the need to engage patients and families in their care (Carman et al., 2013; Hibbard and Greene, 2013). For instance, advances in drug therapies and diagnostic services mean that more people can receive treatment in their own home. Similarly, non-invasive treatments mean less concern for infection control and other follow-up activities. When accompanied with other remote monitoring devices and new forms of communication (such as electronic health records, mobile applications, and telecommunications), these new ways of interacting are becoming normalized by health professionals and patients.

On the other hand, normative levers also recognize that there are fundamental principles or norms that are untouchable. In England, such norms center on free health care at the point of use and a dominance of public funding and provision. In the US, these enduring norms are reflected in preserving patient choice and pluralism in financing and delivery. These normative levers both drive organizational change but restrict the direction of change, as innovations must work around these untouchables—and thus develop imperfect and compromised organizational solutions.

These developing forms involving the relational properties of organizations have been largely ignored by existing organizational theories (Baum and Amburgey, 2002). The markets, hierarchies, and networks framework has made significant contributions to explaining archetypical organizational forms in many sectors (Greenwood and Hinings, 1988; Greenwood and Hinings, 1993; Jung and Lake, 2011; Powell, 1990). These perspectives acknowledge change over time in response to both internal and external forces but typically suggest that the hybrid states that emerge from such changes are temporary and that organizations gravitate towards a stable state. The question that emerges, however, is at what point "temporary" becomes "enduring"? The hybrid state becomes the new state representing a new organizational form itself and not a temporary response to the various forces? The ongoing alliances, enduring networks, and other arrangements in the health care sector do not fit neatly within existing frameworks of organizational forms or change. Across both integrated care models in England and ACOs in the US and similar arrangements in other countries we are witnessing the creation and adaptation of seemingly enduring organizational forms. We suggest that these forms are emerging a priori to provide a platform for future changes in innovative care delivery models and related functions.

Within the above context, and following many others, we suggest that organizations exist to solve the twin problems of differentiation and integration (Galbraith, 1973; Lawrence and Lorsch, 1967; Mintzberg, 1979). Differentiation involves the division of tasks and specialization of functions needed to achieve the organization's goals. Integration involves the unity of effort needed to coordinate the functions and tasks needed to achieve the goals. The greater the division of labor and specialization of functions, the greater the need for coordination and for more sophisticated forms of coordination (Thompson, 1967). Where tasks are only loosely linked to each other, centralized "pooled" mechanisms can be used. Where tasks are sequential (i.e., one way directional) transactional coordination mechanisms can be used such as written routines. But where tasks are reciprocally interdependent with much back and forth communication required, more flexible relational coordination mechanisms are needed.

We suggest that these foundational concepts and theories of organizations and organizing (Weick 1969, 1974) are key building blocks for understanding the new forms of organizations emerging in the health care sector. Further, we suggest that they can help explain why it is that *forms* (i.e., organizations) often precede functions (i.e., organizing).

The problems for health care organizations to solve have changed dramatically without, for the most part, a corresponding change in the organizations needed to solve them. In many respects, the growing demands of an increasing chronically ill population have overwhelmed a health care system designed to primarily treat episodic acute illnesses. The systems of care are roughly a century behind the needs of the population. Attempts to change the division of labor (e.g., develop primary care teams or consider more flexible workforce models) or develop new types of integration (e.g., care transition teams) have been largely ineffective because they have been tried largely within existing organizational forms. Forms have not followed functions; largely due to the cultural, institutional, and professional forces deeply embedded with each country's health system. Taking care of people with chronic illness, and often with multiple chronic illnesses, requires a very different form of organizing. In particular, patients themselves become a key member of the health care team challenging the traditional doctor–patient relationship. Coordination is now needed across different providers, teams, and settings over time. The traditional flow of physician work is disrupted (Bodenheimer, Chen, and Bennett, 2009; Hoff, 2010). Meeting these challenges is difficult to do without first changing the organization in which the functions are performed.

England: Examples and Challenges

In England, the last several years have seen new organizational forms developing across the bodies that both pay for and provide health care services. . Many of these initiatives are driven by a highly technocratic approach, relying on contracts and performance measures to drive new partnerships.

Clinical Commissioning Groups

Clinical commissioning groups (CCGs) are a core part of the government's reforms to the health and social care system. They have replaced primary care trusts as the commissioners of most services funded by the NHS in England. They now control around two-thirds of the NHS budget and have a legal duty to support quality improvement in general practice, although national bodies have retained responsibility for commissioning most primary care provision and specialized services. All GP practices were required to be members of a clinical CCG and 211 groups became operational in April 2013. The aim was to give GPs and other clinicians the power to influence commissioning decisions for their patients.

Each CCG has a constitution and is run by its governing body. Each CCG typically has geographical boundaries that are coterminous with those of local authorities, though one authority may contain several CCGs. Although all GPs must be a member of a CCG, in practice CCG boards comprise a range of people from different backgrounds, with GPs in a minority among accountable officers.

To promote integration, CCGs have developed complex governance arrangements that vary significantly. The majority have some form of locality structure to support GP engagement and local priority-setting. Partnership arrangements and alliances of varying degrees of formality are also common between CCGs, often including sharing senior management posts and development of joint commissioning plans. These partnerships are necessary so that smaller CCGs can operate at scale, but they do further complicate governance arrangements and can create additional barriers to engagement if decision-making at partnership level is seen as remote from local GPs.

GP Federations

In addition to their changing role as commissioners, there has been some change in the way GPs work as providers. GP Federations see groups of practices and their primary care teams working together, sharing responsibility for developing and delivering high quality, patient-focused services for their local communities. Practices within a GP Federation may share responsibility for a range of functions, including developing, providing, or commissioning services, training and education, back office functions, safety, and clinical governance.

There are a range of Federation structures, from a relatively loose alliance to a highly managed model. Federations are typically structured through a collective legal entity such as a social enterprise, limited company, or charity. Their intention is to help ensure the continued viability of primary care—and the personal link between the patient and the GP—in a period when small or single handed practices, operating in isolation, are finding it increasingly difficult to provide a full range of clinical services, alongside ongoing operational practices and increasing commissioning responsibilities.

GP Federations intend to increase the range of primary care services by moving services from hospital settings and developing as many services as possible within the community, including enhanced diagnostic services and minor surgery. GP Federations would offer advantages to GPs and their staff, not least of which would be the freedom to deliver a more professional and comprehensive service and allow them to operate at a scale necessary to deliver a broader range of services. But the greatest advantages are those that improve services for patients, including: better access to GP services with opening hours that reflect the needs of the local community; different ways of accessing services with booked appointments and unscheduled "walk in" clinics; services in familiar GP settings rather than in hospitals or hi-tech health centers; strong patient involvement with patient representation on Federation boards; tailored services specifically designed to address very local needs; a greater emphasis upon health promotion; and continuity of care with shared patient records and integrated care pathways.

Similar examples exist in other countries. In the Quebec province of Canada, family medical groups and network clinics have formed to improve the integration of care for older persons and people with chronic illness (Vedel, Monette, and Bergman, 2011). Similar developments have occurred in British Columbia and Ontario to facilitate quality improvement, access to care, and to create economies of scale (Hutchison et. al., 2011). In Australia, primary care organizations (PCOs) have emerged using a needs-based capitation budget to better manage the delivery of health care services to a defined population (Donato and Segal, 2010). In New Zealand, district health boards that fund regional hospitals have formed an alliance with corresponding primary health organizations (PHOs) to better integrate services across levels of care (Gauld, 2014).

Integrated Care Organizations

In contrast to some of the more specified interorganizational partnerships in the US described below, many integrated care organizations in England have not thus far adhered to a single or series of specific models. However, more recent local and national initiatives suggest that there are movements towards a set of overarching interorganizational models. The *Five Year Forward View* sets out a national blueprint for a series of partnership models. Amongst other models, the vision describes integrated approaches such as multi-specialty community providers (based around general practice) and primary and acute care systems (focusing on vertical integration). Local regions can "choose" which of these models they are to operate, and then apply to a pilot program.

In 2014, the British government selected 14 pioneering local areas to act as exemplars (or "vanguards") of integrated care, demonstrating the use of ambitious and innovative approaches to efficiently deliver person-centered and coordinated care across the whole of their local health, public health, and care and support system for the benefit of patients and service users. More recently, the government announced 29 vanguard communities to take forward the models described in the *Five Year Forward View*.

Alongside these models, there is an array of different forms being discussed, promoted and implemented—prime contractor, prime provider, integrator, lead provider, accountable provider, accountable care organization, and alliance are some of these models (Addicott, 2014). All of these can then be administered within various structures—legal contract, an agreement, or a memorandum of understanding. Providers then establish an organizational and/or governance model to deliver care according to the terms of the contract.

Much of what is being seen in England is an attempt to use organizational form to stimulate changes in function, based on a theory by commissioners that a new innovative contract will drive providers to work together. These ideas tend to be adapted from initiatives from other countries such as Australia, New Zealand, or the US or other sectors, which are then reconceptualized for the NHS. Implementation tends to be highly technocratic, often ignoring relational aspects. Consequently, any relational conflicts eventually re-emerge, and can override the contractual or organizational form if they are strong enough. For example, a hospital can refuse to sign a sub-contract with a new overarching "integrator"—and the entire process grinds to a halt and the system defaults to inertia or business as usual. Furthermore, there are concerns about the "compatibility" in the governance of the different organizations that make up these alliances or new organizational forms. For instance, provider alliances in England can easily comprise voluntary/not for profit, private, NHS, local council organizations. The alliance itself typically forms its own governance arrangements, but the organizations within it have very different "governance cultures" and realms of accountability (i.e., to shareholders, the public/taxpayers, an electorate).There is need to study these hybrid governance structures.

US: Examples and Challenges

Two of the "new" organizational forms emerging in the US are based largely on alliance and partnership formation involving pre-existing organizations. These are the Accountable Care Organizations (ACOs) and Patient-Centered Medical Homes (PCMHs). The third, the Accountable Communities for Health (ACHs), is new but still based largely on organizations that pre-existed in sectors outside of health care such as education, housing, and transportation. We consider each in turn examining their formation and potential to meet the twin challenges of differentiation and integration.

Accountable Care Organizations

ACOs are entities that accept responsibility and accountability for both the cost and quality of care provided to a defined population of patients (Shortell and Casalino, 2008). They typically include a physician organization and hospital and may also include nursing homes, skilled nursing facilities, home health agencies, and related providers. They may be organized around an integrated delivery system (IDS), a multi-specialty group practice, a physician-hospital organization, an independent practice association (IPA) or even a network of loosely organized practices (Shortell, Casalino, and Fisher, 2010c). They enter into contracts with the Federal Government for Medicare patients and with private commercial insurers for other patients to accept a given amount of funds to care for a group of patients. Once various quality measures are met, they are eligible to share in any savings that may have been generated by staying within the agreed upon allotment of funds. Thus they have an economic incentive to better coordinate care and reduce unnecessary hospitalization, re-admissions, emergency department visits, and repeat testing.

There are currently over 700 ACOs in the United States with approximately half having primarily Medicare contracts and half private commercial contracts with some having both (Lewis et al., 2013; Muhlestein, 2013). They vary in the extent to which they are differentiated in regard to the services they provide and the number of different types of organizations that are ACO members (Colla et al., 2014; Shortell et al., 2014). Fifty-four per cent are members of integrated delivery systems.

The key aspect of this new payment/organizational model is that it creates a platform for functional innovation to occur. This is particularly true where payment moves away from fee-for-service to include bundled payments, capitated payments, and global budgets that create incentives for providers to collaborate. In these settings one observes innovations in care redesign, care transition programs, medication management, delegation of more functions to other health care professionals, and new ways of engaging patients and their families. The ACO "form" precedes and allows the adoption and implementation of these innovations in functions in care delivery that are particularly important for people with chronic illness.

Evidence on the performance of ACOs in regard to costs, quality, and patient experience is still emerging (Centers for Medicare & Medicaid Services, 2014; Colla et al., 2012; Epstein et al., 2014; Song et al., 2012; Song et al., 2014). There are many challenges including the presence of still large numbers of small and independent physician practices that may not have the resources to accept accountability for cost, the need for strong physician leadership, the need for more timely data feedback from payers, the need for more interoperable electronic health records (EHRs), the need for greater change management skills, the need to develop more effective teams, the need for effective partnership development, and the need to effectively engage patients and their families in their care (Burns and Pauly, 2012; Goldsmith, 2011; Larson et al., 2012; Mechanic and Zinner, 2012).

Primary Care Medical Homes

PCMHs have emerged primarily to provide more comprehensive coordinated care for people with multiple chronic illnesses. The basic concepts have been around for several decades. These include an emphasis on personalized, whole person, coordinated care across conditions, episodes of care, providers, and settings over time organized by a primary care provider (Primary Care Collaborative, 2014). What is new is the emphasis on "new model" practice involving use of electronic health records, implementation of the chronic care model, and participation in continuous quality improvement initiatives (Friedberg et al., 2009; Rittenhouse and Shortell, 2009; Wagner et al., 2001). Most important, there are payment incentives for coordinating care and practices are eligible for additional income from participating in pay for performance and related programs. In many cases PCMHs are the building block for ACOs at the individual clinic practice site level. There are currently over 1,000 PCMHs in the US (Edwards et al., 2014).

PCMHs primarily provide an organizational form for physician practices to better address the integration function; specifically, the coordination of care. Examples include the addition of pharmacists and social workers on care teams, timely communication with patients following hospital discharge or an emergency department visit, giving patients access to their electronic health record through portals, and using decision-making videos describing treatment options for elective procedures. The PCMH enables these functional innovations to occur by providing a conducive organizational structure and payment model.

The evidence to date on the impact of PCMHs on quality of care, cost, and patient experience is mixed. Some have found positive associations with improved quality and decreased emergency department use, and reduced costs while others have found no such relationships (Friedberg et al., 2014; Hoff, Weller, and DePuccio, 2012; Kern, Edwards, and Kaushal, 2014; Reid et al., 2009; Werner, Canamucio, and True, 2014). The PCMH model is primarily aimed at increasing the capabilities of mostly smaller practices to provide care under risk-based financial models of payment. Given the many cultural and structural changes needed for this to occur, they are unlikely to spread rapidly without considerable technical assistance and support. For example, data exist showing that even larger physician practices use on average less than half of twenty recommended elements of an index measuring PCMH functions (Rittenhouse et al., 2008). Thus, it is likely that the PCMH organizational form will need to be coupled with other forms such as ACOs to create the needed infrastructure and scale to address the challenges of differentiation and integration needed to improve care and reduce the rate of growth in costs.

Accountable Communities for Health

In both England and the US there is increasing recognition that in order to improve population health while constraining costs it is necessary to integrate health care services with public health and community/social services. This requires the development of new organizational forms that can transcend sectors. For example, in the US ACOs are charged with the responsibility for improving population health but it is limited to the health of its own population of patients and not of the broader community. To address community-wide issues that also involve the underlying social determinants of health, the health sector and its organizations need to engage with organizations in the education, housing, transportation, and other sectors that also influence population health (Halfon et al., 2014; Noble and Casalino, 2013; Shortell, 2013). Given new payment models that are rewarding providers for keeping people well and growing recognition of the role played by community-based social determinants of health there is increased interest in developing what have been variously called Accountable Care Communities (ACCs) or Accountable Communities for Health (ACHs). The ACH is a cross sector alliance or partnership of all relevant sectors that influence the health of the entire community. Among its key functions are to: 1) conduct a health needs assessment of the community; 2) develop shared goals based on the health needs assessment; 3) allocate resources aligned with strategies and action plans to meet the goals; 4) develop data and information systems to measure costs, quality, and related metrics to assess progress toward the goal; 5) hold the various entities involved accountable for results; and 6) develop a system for fairly allocating shared savings among the parties involved. This new organizational form is essentially a population health management system

(Shortell, Gillies, and Anderson, 2010a) based on paying for health (Kindig, 1999). Key to its success is whether there exists sufficient cross-sector leadership in the community to come together to form such an entity; sometimes referred to as an "integrator."

The ACH recognizes that to address population health places increased demands on both differentiation of tasks and integration of effort to coordinate those tasks as the challenge is not only to do so within sector organizations but across them. There is an extensive literature on alliances and partnerships in both the health and non-health sectors (see for example Conrad et al., 2003; Gulati, 1998; Kaluzny, Zuckerman, and Ricketts, 2002; Zajac, D'Aunno, and Burns, 2011; Zuckerman and D'Aunno, 1990). It emphasizes the importance of developing shared goals from the outset, perceived value for the parties involved, frequent communication, skilled leadership with the ability to manage conflict, and visible data to monitor progress, among other needs. There are some emerging examples in the US including Akron, Ohio (Austen BioInnovation Institute in Akron, 2012) which has brought together 70 different groups to focus on type 2 diabetes. Early results suggest a reduction in costs of (US)$3,185 per person per year; a decline in emergency room visits; and improved self-rated health. Participating organizations receive a share of the cost savings with the remainder re-invested into the ACC to sustain and expand efforts. Based, in part, on Akron's early success, some states such as California and Minnesota are including the ACH concept in State Innovation Model proposals to the Federal government for development funds. Creating such cross-sector organizational entities is challenging given each sector's own goals and objectives. The key lies in creating sufficient shared goals in which each sector organization involved realizes it cannot achieve its goals without close collaboration and coordination with organizations in other sectors. In brief, a high degree of interdependence is needed (Shortell, Gillies, and Wu, 2010b). Once again, a new organizational form is needed in order to take on the many functions involved in improving population health. Organizational innovation precedes or enables functional innovations.

Similar organizational arrangements are emerging in other countries. For example, in Quebec, Canada, the earlier noted family medical groups (*Groupe de médecine de famille*, or GMFs) composed of 6 to 12 physicians are being formed to provide greater access and continuity of care including linkages to health and social services (Vedel, Monette, and Bergman, 2011). In Ontario, Canada, research has identified multi-specialty physician networks which might become the basis for more formal organizations to provide more efficient, integrated, and accountable care (Stukel et al., 2013). In Singapore, the development of the Agency for Integrated Care (AIC) has facilitated the linkage of primary care physicians with home care, day care centers, and social service agencies (Cheah, Kirk-Chuan, and Lim, 2012).

FORM-FUNCTION ALIGNMENT

Are some forms of organization more conducive for making changes in functions and processes than others? If so, what are they and why do they provide for greater innovations in functions and processes than other forms? A related question is: to what extent does there need to be alignment between a given organizational form and given functions or processes? We suggest that the key to answering these questions lies in assessing the degree of change or innovation in functions and processes needed to achieve the organization's goals. This, in turn, is related to the organization's degree of differentiation/specialization in the tasks to be performed on the one hand and its need for integration and coordination of effort on the other hand. Differentiation can occur without a corresponding change or very little change in integration and vice versa in addition to changes in both. The major challenge to the health care systems of England and the US is that the delivery of health care has become so much more complex requiring increased levels of differentiation reflected in increased specialization of tasks and services. The integrating mechanisms have been largely absent or weakly applied within the existing organizational forms. Long-standing efforts in both countries to attempt this within the current historical organizational forms have had limited success, such as small physician practices and independent hospitals in the US and GP practices delivering a wider range of more traditionally acute care services in England (Imison, Naylor, and Maybin, 2008; Porter and Teisberg, 2006). Thus, there is a growing recognition of the need for changes in forms to serve as a foundation or platform to make changes in functions and processes to provide more integrated cost/effective care in the face of the increased specialization of tasks and services. We suggest some of the forms that might be most conducive to making these changes.

Examples from England

Many initiatives in England are being designed by commissioners and policy makers, in partnership with providers. Many of these use contractual mechanisms to stimulate new organizational forms.

An emergent form sees a set of providers enter into a single agreement with a commissioner to deliver services through an alliance contract. The commissioner(s) and all providers within the alliance share risk and responsibility for meeting the terms of a single contract. They are not coordinated by a single leader or integrator and there are no sub-contractual arrangements. Everyone within the alliance is an equal partner and they must instead rely on internal governance arrangements to manage their relationships and delivery of care. Alliance contracting is a fairly recent development in the NHS and most examples come from the construction industry in Australia or from health partnerships in New Zealand (Gauld, 2014; Timmins and Ham, 2013).

Alliance contracts rely on the strength of interpersonal relationships, requiring high trust. If the members of the alliance are not in alignment, then they are unlikely to reach their overarching objectives or outcomes. The intention of this approach is that integration and collaboration are formalized through the contract, as commissioners and providers within the alliance are legally bound together to deliver the specific contracted service. As such, they should be incentivized to innovate and identify efficiencies across the system—rather than solely within their organization. This is distinct from an alliance of providers that might come together informally for a time-limited period on a particular project. An alliance contract legally binds commissioners and providers together to deliver services for a population on an ongoing basis.

A contract of this type carries greater financial and clinical risk for providers, who are accountable for their own performance and that of other providers within the alliance. The provider members of the alliance will need to decide a formal "agreement" and governance framework through which money can flow and decisions can be made, as well as a model of service delivery. Providers establish an alliance leadership board where all members have an equal vote. Given the mutual dependencies, an alliance contract might be most suited where there are well-established provider relationships.

While the provider members of the alliance are accountable to the CCG, those within the alliance must determine the mechanisms and vehicle by which they will hold each other to account. The alliance may decide to establish a special purpose vehicle (e.g., joint venture, community interest company or other legal structure) to govern the alliance and stipulate the necessary safeguards around issues such as individual provider failure or malpractice. Alternatively, providers can collectively govern the alliance through an alliance leadership board with an agreed membership and terms of reference. The commissioner will have a direct relationship and single line of accountability to this special purpose vehicle or leadership board.

Alternative interorganizational forms are emerging in areas where there is less history of collaboration and lower trust between partners. In these prime contractor approaches, a commissioner contracts with a single organization (or consortia) which then takes responsibility for the day-to-day management of other providers that deliver care within the contracted scope or pathway. The prime contractor manages this supply chain through individual sub-contracts with each of the providers to deliver the specific contracted service.

The commissioner retains overall accountability for the commissioned services through their direct relationship with the prime contractor, while the prime contractor holds each of the sub-contractors individually to account. The prime contractor takes responsibility for designing a delivery model and patient pathway that will most effectively meet the terms of the contract. They use the terms of the sub-contracts to stimulate the necessary behaviors and performance they wish to see across other providers.

The prime contractor carries a great deal of risk for the population it covers, and must be comfortable that it has the skills and knowledge to be ultimately responsible for the performance of the sub-contracted providers. The prime contractor manages this risk through the terms of the sub-contracts and how it holds those within the supply chain to account. The terms of the sub-contracts intend to stimulate providers to work together and with the prime contractor to deliver care across the pathway. There is no necessity for providers to design a separate interorganizational form outside of these sub-contracts.

Typically—but not exclusively—the prime contractor is allocated a capitated budget to manage all care for the specific population or disease group. To varying extents, a proportion of this budget is "at risk," dependent upon the prime contractor (through its supply chain) meeting stipulated outcome measures. The model is based on the premise that these measures are more likely to be achieved if the prime contractor manages the pathway and encourages providers to work together more efficiently. In this sense, the commissioner contracts the prime contractor to be the service integrator.

In variations of the model, the prime contractor additionally provides services. This alternative is often referred to as a prime provider model. While a prime contractor will not deliver care as part of the agreement, a prime provider would deliver some or all care within the contract. In situations where this approach has been employed, the intention is to limit further fragmentation that could be caused by introducing a new organization into the landscape (i.e., the integrator). Instead, the intention is that the prime provider has greater leverage for transformation by directly building their provider capacity and delivery model to meet the terms of the contract.

Examples from the US

It is important to recognize that ACOs, PCMHs, and ACHs are broad categories or types of organizational forms within which different models or sub-types exist. Since ACOs often contain PCMHs and, in turn, are becoming a part of ACHs they serve as a good example for examining whether some specific types or forms encourage greater innovation than other forms or types. While, as previously noted, there are over 700 ACOs in the US, research has identified three dominant largely distinct sub-types or forms (Shortell et al., 2014). These are large Integrated Delivery System (IDS) linked forms offering a broad scope of services; small physician-led organizations offering a relatively narrow array of services; and hybrid joint hospital-physician or coalition led forms offering an intermediate scope of services. For purposes of illustration, we consider how conducive each of these forms might be for adopting and implementing three functional/process innovations influencing the delivery of care—use of complex case managers; electronic health records; and patient activation and engagement (PAE) approaches.

Given the growing number of patients with multiple complex chronic illness, many providers are introducing complex case or care managers (typically nurses) who lead teams overseeing the care of these patients. We suggest that the IDS and hybrid ACO forms may offer the best platform for making such changes due to their experience with offering a broader scope of services (including post-acute care facilities) that patients with multiple chronic illnesses may need. Between the IDS and hybrid form one might favor the IDS given their more integrated structure and likely greater resources to initiate such changes. Their larger size alone provides economies of scale and scope to spread resource investments in hiring and training the complex care managers. The smaller physician-led practices are less likely to be successful in implementing complex case managers due to offering a more narrow scope of services and being less able to create economies of scale and scope in resource investments.

The adoption and implementation of electronic health records (EHRs) in the US has increased significantly in recent years (Adler-Milstein et al., 2014; Furukawa et al., 2014; Hsiao et al., 2013), although there is considerable variability in regard to full use of its various functions and, in particular, in regard to inter-operability between hospitals, physicians, other providers, and payers (Adler-Milstein and Jha, 2012; Adler-Milstein et al., 2014; Hsiao et al., 2013; McClellan et al., 2013; Vest, Campion, and Kaushal, 2013; Williams et al., 2012). The IDSs and physician-led ACOs are more likely to be the form to promote the continued evolution and innovation in use of the EHR rather than the hybrid ACOs. Many IDSs have a long history of EHR use that can be drawn on, in addition to having the resources to invest. Physician-led ACOs tend to score high on performance monitoring and accountability using measures such as individual physician feedback reports on the quality of care provided to patients and, thus, have strong incentives to invest in EHRs to generate the needed data for the reports. They can also receive financial assistance through the Meaningful Use program (DesRoches et al., 2013) and technical assistance support for implementing EHRs through the Regional Extension Center and other state and federally funded programs (Lynch et al., 2014). In contrast, hybrid hospital-physician ACOs must typically confront different IT platforms and systems used by each party, making implementing EHR innovations difficult.

Some examples of PAE innovations are the use of surveys to measure how activated patients are to participate in their care (Hibbard et al., 2004; Hibbard et al. 2007); training physicians and nurses in motivational interviewing focusing on soliciting information on what really matters to patients; and the use of shared decision-making videos to help patients and family members to make decisions about elective procedures consistent with their values and preferences (Arterburn et al., 2012; Elwyn et al., 2013). We suggest that the IDS and physician-led ACO forms may be the best platforms to implement these innovations. The IDS because of their ability to spread learning from one practice to another using their more integrated communication and coordination structures and the physician-led approach because of their greater ability to reach the front line clinicians to make the changes needed to incorporate these innovations in PAE. The hybrid hospital-physician-led ACOs may have a more difficult time securing agreement among the parties involved given a greater variety of viewpoints on the pros and cons of these innovations.

The above examples are intended only to illustrate how various organizational forms may be more or less conducive to facilitating internal innovations in care delivery functions and processes. They do so by offering different degrees of differentiation and integration within which functional innovations can occur. It is in this sense that one can consider the extent to which a given organizational form "fits" or "matches up" with a given function or process innovation. There are many opportunities in both countries to further explore Form-Function relationships that can inform theory, policy, and practice.

CHANGES IN FORM AND FUNCTION

The themes discussed in this chapter raise the questions of whether an organization can change form without a corresponding shift in function, or vice versa. And what the consequences might be of changing one without the other.

Figure 2.1 provides a framework for considering this issue. As shown, theoretically all four combinations are possible. But, as indicated, we suggest that a priori changes in form will be most useful when significant changes in functions are needed (cell 1). When the functional changes are minor or moderate, there is less need to change organizational form as the existing structure can absorb or accommodate the new or altered function (cell 2). When organizational forms are changed without any apparent need to do so then there is either a waste of resources or the organization is making the change in anticipation of a future substantial change in function (cell 3). Finally, cell 4 depicts the status quo steady state situation where there is no need for either a change in function or form. Empirically, one could measure whether the changes in functions are minor, moderate, or major by such characteristics as whether the change involves reciprocally interdependent activities, the number of different people affected by the change, the extent to which the change affects different levels of the organization, the amount of resources involved, and the economics and other consequences of failure.

In summary, there have been numerous efforts to change various functions and introduce innovations in health care delivery, without giving sufficient attention to building a supportive organizational form. In England, existing institutions have been asked to take on additional commissioning and performance management responsibilities without a corresponding shift in form or governance. As indicated, this is now changing. In the US there have been long-standing efforts to implement clinical guidelines and protocols, disease registries, care transition models, and continuous quality improvement

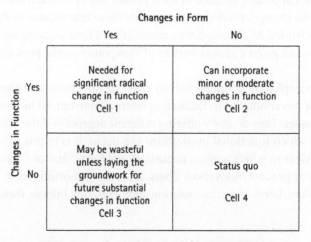

FIGURE 2.1 Form-Function Alignment Matrix

approaches and related changes in functions, with highly varying success due, we argue, to failing to take into account the larger organizational setting or form in which these changes were embedded. This, too, is now changing.

But aside from considerations of whether form should precede function, perhaps the more significant consideration is the presence of a corresponding governance structure—across form and function—that either supports transformation, or actively or passively works against the ambitions of change. New organizational forms will likely require changes in governance and accountability.

Over time, we have seen a movement in how those delivering health services have been held to account. There has been a move away from an agency model of accountability, where the accountability relationship is principal–agent or doctor–patient. This form of accountability is characterized by a lack of information, which can lead to uncertainty or trust issues. The movement was then to a contract model of accountability, reliant on credible information and systems to override professional regulation and autonomy. The move has since been to a governance model through loosely coupled networks. It is this model of accountability that might characterize current movements in the organization of health care in England and the US. This approach requires leadership rather than authority, bargaining, negotiation, guidance, and facilitation (Tuohy, 2003). However, across examples in England and the US at the moment, it appears that the thinking on governance has not caught up. The approach to governing loosely coupled networks is not adequate for addressing the high-risk interdependent relationships described in these new organizational forms (Addicott and Shortell, 2014).

It is also important to recognize that some new organizational forms might be an enduring legacy of unsuccessful attempts at radical organizational change. Cancer networks in England serve as an example. Although initially conceived as a novel approach to managing knowledge across organizational and professional boundaries in cancer services, the model was eventually distorted by a prevailing emphasis on centrally driven performance management and structural reforms. The result was an enduring, hybrid configuration possessing characteristics of a market, a hierarchy, and a network form. In the US the Physician–Hospital Organization (PHO) model of delivering care met with highly variable success due to the challenge of overcoming historically very different incentives and cultures between hospitals and physicians. Nonetheless, elements of it can still be found as part of an enduring legacy in the development of some ACOs.

An interesting question is whether these patchwork organizational forms are more adaptable. Various organizational forms have a "carrying capacity" or "absorptive capacity" for accommodating change in functions while maintaining essentially the same organizational form (Cohen and Levinthal, 1990). In England, these patchwork organizations can be seen where there are pockets of money all funding a single service, or with varying accountability mechanisms. In the US they can be found in the different models of ACOs and related forms as payment models evolve. Through the externally changing environment, the function shifts and the organizational form "makes do." The absorptive capacity of organizations is largely untested, representing an area for further research. It is unclear whether there could be an external trigger such as a new technological advancement, a sudden economic downturn, or more slowly evolving demographic changes that would stimulate the need for changes in both forms and functions that might create a new entity. For example, an innovation in musculoskeletal care that focuses on building a pathway to encourage more community care might be challenged by a new simple/cost-effective surgical treatment that changes the pathway (function). The question then becomes—does the structure (form) allow for this adaptability?

CONCLUSION

We have proposed that in the face of volatile significant change in the external environment—such as that occurring in the health sectors of England, the US, Australia, Canada, New Zealand, Singapore, and many other countries across the globe—one is likely to observe that changes in organizational form will precede changes in functions. Function follows form rather than the received wisdom of form following function. This is because the complex external drivers require new forms or platforms for introducing new functions or making significant changes in existing functions. The demand for greater value in England and the US and, indeed, in many countries has been a major stimulant for the development of new organizational forms. While coercive, mimetic, and normative factors may explain why the new forms may share some commonalities over time and begin to look alike (e.g., ACOs in the US, integrated care models in England, primary care organizations in Australia, and primary health organizations in New Zealand) existing theories are challenged to account for many of the new developments. The new forms such as clinical commissioning groups, GP federations, and integrated care organizations in England and ACOs, PCMHs, and Accountable Communities for Health in the US and the arrangements in other countries do not fit neatly within existing frameworks. They have emerged, however, to deal with the fundamental organizational dual challenges of differentiation and integration

Recognizing that the new forms may precede changes in or the development of new functions alters the way of thinking about form–function alignment or "fit." Instead of trying to post-hoc fit form to functions one is placed in an a priori position of selecting an organizational form that can best accommodate or facilitate changes or innovations in functions to be adopted and implemented. The decision choice is anticipatory. In England the hope is that the CCGs participating in new payment and contracting arrangements will be able to support changes such as discharge planning innovations, use of community and social services, and patient follow-up and feedback. In the US it is hoped that ACOs, for example, will support further implementation of electronic health records, care coordination programs, and various patient/family engagement activities. In both countries the extent to which this occurs will depend importantly on the quality of management and governance of the new forms.

The re-framing of the "form follows function" paradigm opens up several new areas for research. For example prospective studies involving the introduction of new innovations can be examined to see if they are preceded by changes in organizational forms or if such changes are made concurrently or sequentially. Given sufficient historical data, retrospective analysis could also be done involving the dates of past changes in organizational form relative to past changes in organizational functions linked to various measures of organizational performance. Where the external demands are such that they are likely to have a major pervasive impact on the organization then one would hypothesize that form preceding functional changes will be associated with better performance outcomes, while the reverse might be hypothesized where the changes involved are minor. Significant contributions could also be made by comparative qualitative case study research to further develop the typology we set out in figure 2.1, and characterize the conditions that affect the interplay between form and function. Such studies could provide a rich understanding of what organizational leaders consider in making "form-function" decisions and the implications of those decisions for organizational performance

ACKNOWLEDGMENTS

The authors acknowledge the helpful assistance of Zosha Kandel, Laura Spautz, and Jennifer Wong, UC Berkeley School of Public Health, in the preparation of this chapter.

REFERENCES

Aaron, H. J. and Ginsburg, P. B. (2009). Is health spending excessive? If so, what can we do about it? *Health Affairs*, 28(5): 1260–1275.

Addicott, R. (2014). *Commissioning and contracting for integrated care*. London: The King's Fund.

Addicott, R. and Shortell, S. M. (2014). How 'accountable' are accountable care organizations? *Health Care Management Review*, 39(4): 270–278.

Adler-Milstein, J., DesRoches, C. M., Furukawa, M. F., Worzala, C., Charles, D., Kravolec, P., Stalley, S., and Jha, A. (2014). More than half of US hospitals have at least a basic EHR, but stage 2 criteria remain challenging for most. *Health Affairs*, 33(9): 1664–1671.

Adler-Milstein, J. and Jha, A. K. (2012). Sharing clinical data electronically: A critical challenge for fixing the health care system. *JAMA*, 307(16): 1695–1696.

Allen, C. R., Fontaine, J. J., Pope, K. L., and Garmenstani, A. S. (2011). Adaptive management for a turbulent future. *Journal of Environmental Management*, 92(5): 1339–1345.

Arterburn, D., Wellman, R., Westbrook, E., Rutter, C., Ross, T., McCulloch, D., Handley, M., and Jung, C. (2012). Introducing decision aids at Group Health was linked to sharply lower hip and knee surgery rates and costs. *Health Affairs*, 31(9): 2094–2104.

Austen BioInnovation Institute in Akron (2012). Healthier by design: Creating accountable care communities (Akron, OH).

Baum, J. A. C. and Amburgey, T. L. (2002). Organizational Ecology. In *The Blackwell Companion to Organizations*, ed. Baum, J. A. C., pp. 304–326. Oxford: Blackwell.

Blumenthal, D. and Dixon, J. (2012). Health-care reforms in the USA and England: Areas for useful learning. *The Lancet*, 380(9850): 1352–1357.

Bodenheimer, T., Chen, E., and Bennett, H. D. (2009). Confronting the growing burden of chronic disease: Can the US health care workforce do the job? *Health Affairs*, 28(1): 64–74.

Burns, L. R., Goldsmith, J. C., and Sen, A. (2013). Horizontal and vertical integration of physicians: A tale of two tails. *Advances in Health Care Management*, 15: 39–117.

Burns, L. R. and Pauly, M. V. (2012). Accountable care organizations may have difficulty avoiding the failures of integrated delivery networks of the 1990s. *Health Affairs*, 31(11): 2407–2416.

Carman, K. L., Dardess, P., Maurer, M., Sofaer, S., Adams, K., Bechtel, C., and Sweeney, J. (2013). Patient and family engagement: A framework for understanding the elements and developing interventions and policies. *Health Affairs*, 32(2): 223–231.

Centers for Medicare and Medicaid Services (2014). Quality Measures and Performance Standards (updated 7 July 2014). Available at: <http://www.cms.gov/Medicare/Medicare-Fee-for-Service-Payment/sharedsavingsprogram/Quality_Measures_Standards.html> (accessed October 13, 2014).

Cheah, J., Kirk-Chuan, W., and Lim, H. (2012). Integrated care: From policy to implementation—The Singapore story. *International Journal of Integrated Care*, 12(4): 1–2.

Cohen, W. M. and Levinthal, D. A. (1990). Absorptive capacity: A new perspective on learning and innovation. *Administrative Science Quarterly*, 35(1): 128–152.

Colla, C. H., Lewis, V. A., Shortell, S. M., and Fisher, E. S. (2014). First national survey of ACOs finds that physicians are playing strong leadership and ownership roles. *Health Affairs*, 33(6): 964–971.

Colla, C. H., Wennberg, D. E., Meara, E., Skinner, J. S., Gottlieb, D., Lewis, V., Snyder, C., and Fisher, E. S. (2012). Spending differences associated with the Medicare physician group practice demonstration. *JAMA*, 308(10): 1015–1023.

Conrad, D. A., Cave, S. H., Lucas, M., Harville, J., Shortell, S. M., Bazzoli, G. J., Hasnain-Wynia, R., Sofaer, S., Casey, E., and Margolin, F. (2003). Community care networks: Linking vision to outcomes for community health improvement. *Medical Care Research and Review*, 60 (4 suppl), 95S–129S.

Davis, K., Stremikis, K., Squires, D., and Schoen, K. (2014). Mirror, mirror on the wall: How the performance of the US health care system compares internationally, 2014 update. New York: Commonwealth Fund.

DesRoches, C. M., Charles, D., Furukawa, M. F., Joshi, M. S., Kralovec, P., Mostashari, F., Worzala, C., and Jha, A. K. (2013). Adoption of electronic health records grows rapidly, but fewer than half of US hospitals had at least a basic system in 2012. *Health Affairs*, 32(8): 1478–1485.

DiMaggio, P. J. and Powell, W. W. (1983). The iron cage revisited: Institutional isomorphism and collective rationality in organizational fields. *American Sociological Review*, 48(2): 147–160.

Donato, R. and Segal, L. (2010). The economics of primary healthcare reform in Australia: Towards single fundholding through development of primary care organisations. *Australian and New Zealand Journal of Public Health*, 34(6): 613–619.

Edwards, S. T., Bitton, A., Hong, J., and Landon, B. E. (2014). Patient-centered medical home initiatives expanded in 2009–13: Providers, patients, and payment incentives increased. *Health Affairs*, 33(10) (October): 1823–1831.

Elwyn, G., Scholl, I., Tietbohl, C., Edwards, A., Clay, C., Legare, F., Van der Weijden, T., Lewis, C. L., Wexler, R. M., and Frosch, D. L. (2013). "Many miles to go …": A systematic review of the implementation of patient decision support interventions into routine clinical practice. *BMC Medical Informatics and Decision Making*, 13(Suppl 2): S14.

Epstein, A. M., Jha, A. K., Orav, E. J., Liebman, D. L., Audet, A. J., Zezza, M. A., and Guterman, S. (2014). Analysis of early accountable care organizations defines patient, structural, cost, and quality-of-care characteristics. *Health Affairs*, 33(1): 95–102.

Friedberg, M. W., Lai, D. J., Hussey, P. S., and Schneider, E. C. (2009). A guide to the medical home as a practice-level intervention. *American Journal of Managed Care*, 15(Suppl 10): S291–S299.

Friedberg, M. W., Schneider, E. C., Rosenthal, M. B., Volpp, K. G., and Werner, R. M. (2014). Association between participation in a multipayer medical home intervention and changes in quality, utilization, and costs of care. *JAMA*, 311(8): 815–825.

Furukawa, M. F., King, J., Patel, V., Hsiao, C.-J., Adler-Milstein, J., and Jha, A. (2014). Despite substantial progress in EHR adoption, health information exchange and patient engagement remain low in office settings. *Health Affairs*, 33(9): 1672–1679.

Galbraith, J. R. (1973). *Designing complex organizations*. Boston, MA: Addison-Wesley Longman Publishing Co., Inc.

Gauld, R. (2014). What should governance for integrated care look like? New Zealand's alliances provide some pointers. *The Medical Journal of Australia*, 201(3): S67–S68.

Goldsmith, J. (2011). Accountable care organizations: The case for flexible partnerships between health plans and providers. *Health Affairs*, 30(1): 32–40.

Grace, S. M., Rich, J., Chin, W., and Rodriguez, H. P. (2014). Implementing interdisciplinary teams does not necessarily improve primary care practice climate. *American Journal of Medical Quality*. September 12: 1–8.

Greenwood, R. and Hinings, C. R. (1988). Organizational design types, tracks and the dynamics of strategic change. *Organization Studies*, 9(3): 293–316.

Greenwood, R. and Hinings, C. R. (1993). Understanding strategic change: The contribution of archetypes. *The Academy of Management Journal*, 36(5): 1052–1081.

Gulati, R. (1998). Alliances and networks. *Strategic Management Journal*, 19(4): 293–317.

Halfon, N., Long, P., Chang, D. I., Hester, J., Inkelas, M., and Rodgers, A. (2014). Applying a 3.0 transformation framework to guide large-scale health system reform. *Health Affairs*, 33(11): 2003–2011.

Hibbard, J. H. and Greene, J. (2013). What the evidence shows about patient activation: Better health outcomes and care experiences; fewer data on costs. *Health Affairs*, 32(2): 207–214.

Hibbard, J. H., Mahoney, E. R., Stock, R., and Tusler, M. (2007). Do increases in patient activation result in improved self-management behaviors? *Health Services Research*, 42(4): 1443–1463.

Hibbard, J. H., Stockard, J., Mahoney, E. R., and Tusler, M. (2004). Development of the patient activation measure (PAM): Conceptualizing and measuring activation in patients and consumers. *Health Services Research*, 39(4): 1005–1026.

Hoff, T. (2010). *Practice under pressure: Primary care physicians and their medicine in the twenty-first century*. Brunswick, NJ: Rutgers University Press.

Hoff, T., Weller, W., and DePuccio, M. (2012). The patient-centered medical home: A review of recent research. *Medical Care Research and Review*, 69(6): 619–644.

Hsiao, C.-J., Jhas, A. K., King, J., Patel, V., Furukawa, M. F., and Mostashari, F. (2013). Office-based physicians are responding to incentives and assistance by adopting and using electronic health records. *Health Affairs*, 32(8): 1470–1477.

Hutchison, B., Levesque, J.-F., Strumpf, E., and Coyle, N. (2011). Primary healthcare in Canada: Systems in motion. *The Milbank Quarterly*, 89(2), 256–288.

Imison, C., Naylor, C., and Maybin, J. (2008). *Under one roof: Will polyclinics deliver integrated care?* London: King's Fund.

Jung, D. F. and Lake, D. A. (2011). Markets, hierarchies, and networks: An agent-based organizational ecology. *American Journal of Political Science*, 55(4): 972–990.

Kaluzny, A. D., Zuckerman, H., S., and Ricketts, T. C. (2002). *Partners: Forming strategic alliances in health care*. Washington, D.C: Beard Books.

Kern, L. M., Edwards, A., and Kaushal, R. (2014). The patient-centered medical home, electronic health records, and quality of care. *Annals of Internal Medicine*, 160(11): 741–749.

Kindig, D. A. (1999). Purchasing population health: Aligning financial incentives to improve health outcomes. *Nursing Outlook*, 47(1): 15–22.

Klein, P. G., Mahoney, J. T., McGahan, A. M., and Pitelis, C. N. (2013). Capabilities and strategic entrepreneurship in public organizations. *Strategic Entrepreneurship Journal*, 7(1): 70–91.

Larson, B. K., Van Citter, A. D., Kreindler, S. A., Carluzzo, K. L., Gbemudu, J. N., Wu, F. M., Nelson, E. C., Shortell, S. M., and Fisher, E. S. (2012). Insights from transformations under way at four Brookings-Dartmouth accountable care organization pilot sites. *Health Affairs*, 31(11): 2395–2406.

Lawrence, P. R. and Lorsch, J. W. (1967). Differentiation and integration in complex organizations. *Administrative Science Quarterly*, 12(1) (June): 1–47

Lee, T. H. and Mongan, J. J. (2009). *Chaos and Organization in Healthcare*. Cambridge, MA: The MIT Press.

Lewis, V. A., Colla, C. H., Carluzzo, K. L., Kler, S. E., and Fisher, E. S. (2013). Accountable care organizations in the United States: Market and demographic factors associated with formation. *Health Services Research*, 48 (6pt1): 1840–1858.

Lynch, K., Kendall, M., Shanks, K., Haque, A., Jones, E., Wanis, M. G., Furukawa, M., and Mostashari, F. (2014). The health IT regional extension center program: Evolution and lessons for health care transformation. *Health Services Research*, 49(1pt2): 421–437.

McClellan, M., Kent, J., Beales, S. J., Cohen, S. L. A., Macdonnell, M., Thoumi, A., Abdulmalik, M., and Darzi, A. (2014). Accountable care around the world: A framework to guide reform strategies. *Health Affairs*, 33(9): 1507–1515.

McClellan, S. R., Casalino, L. P., Shortell, S. M., and Rittenhourse, D. R. (2013). When does adoption of health information technology by physician practices lead to use by physicians within the practice? *Journal of the American Informatics Association*, 20(e1): 2012–001271.

Mechanic, R. and Zinner, D. E. (2012). Many large medical groups will need to acquire new skills and tools to be ready for payment reform. *Health Affairs*, 31(9): 1984–1992.

Mintzberg, H. (1979). *The structuring of organizations: A synthesis of the research*. Englewood Cliffs, NJ: Prentice-Hall.

Muhlestein, D. (2013). Continued growth of public and private accountable care organizations. *Health Affairs Blog*, February 19, 2013. Available at: <http://healthaffairs.org/blog/2013/02/19/continued-growth-of-public-and-private-accountable-care-organizations/> (accessed October 2, 2015).

National Health Service (2014). *NHS five year forward view*. London: NHS England.

Noble, D. J. and Casalino, L. P. (2013). Can accountable care organizations improve population health?: Should they try? *JAMA*, 309(11): 1119–1120.

Porter, M. E. and Teisberg, E. O. (2006). *Redefining health care: Creating value-based competition on results*. Cambridge, MA: Harvard Business Press.

Powell, W. W. (1990). Neither market nor hierarchy: Network forms of organizations. In *Research in organizational behavior*, ed. Staw, B. M. and Cummings, L. L., Vol. 12, pp. 295–336. Greenwich, CT: JAI Press Inc.

Primary Care Collaborative (2014). Defining the medical home: A patient-centered philosophy that drives primary care excellence. Available at: <https://www.pcpcc.org/about/medical-home> (accessed September 25, 2015).

Reid, R. J., Fishman, P. A., Yu, O., Ross, T. R., Tufano, J. T., Soman, M. P., and Larson, E. B. (2009). Patient-centered medical home demonstration: A prospective, quasi-experimental, before and after evaluation. *The American Journal of Managed Care*, 15(9): e71–e87.

Rittenhouse, D. R., Casalino, L. P., Gillies, R. R., Shortell, S. M., and Lau, B. (2008). Measuring the medical home infrastructure in large medical groups. *Health Affairs*, 27(5): 1246–1258.

Rittenhouse, D. R. and Shortell, S. M. (2009). The patient-centered medical home. *JAMA*, 301(19): 2038–2040.

Rodriguez, H. P., Giannitrapani, K. F., Stockdale, S., Hamilton, A. B., Yano, E. M., and Rubenstein, L. V. (2014). Teamlet structure and early experiences of medical home implementation for veterans. *Journal of General Internal Medicine*: 29(Suppl 2) (July): S623–31.

Rodriguez, H. P., Meredith, L. S., Hamilton, A. B., Yano, E. M., and Rubenstein, L. V. (2015). Huddle up!: The adoption and use of structured team communication for VA medical home implementation. *Health Care Management Review*, 404(4) (October/December): 1–14.

Scholle, S. H., Saunders, R. C., Tirodkar, M. A., Torda, P., Pawlson, L. G. (2011). Patient-centered medical homes in the United States. *The Journal of Ambulatory Care Management*, 34(1): 20–32.

Shortell, S. M. (2013). A Bold Proposal for Advancing Population Health. Discussion Paper, Institute of Medicine, Washington, D. C. Available at: <http://www.iom.edu/Global/Perspectives/2013/BoldProposal> (accessed September 25, 2015).

Shortell, S. M. and Casalino, L. P. (2008). Health care reform requires accountable care systems. *JAMA*, 300(1): 95–97.

Shortell, S. M., Casalino, L. P., and Fisher, E. S. (2010c). Achieving the vision—structural change. In *Partners in health: How physicians and hospitals can be accountable together*, ed. Crosson, F. J. and Tollen, L. A., pp. 46–71. San Francisco, CA: Jossey-Bass.

Shortell, S. M., Gillies, R. R., and Anderson, D. A. (2010a). *Remaking healthcare in America: The evolution of organized delivery systems*, 2nd edition. San Francisco, CA: Jossey-Bass.

Shortell, S. M., Gillies, R. R., and Wu, F. (2010b). United States innovations in healthcare delivery. *Public Health Reviews*, 32(1): 190–212.

Shortell, S. M., Wu, F. M., Lewis, V. A., Colla, C. H., and Fisher, E. S. (2014). A taxonomy of accountable care organizations for policy and practice. *Health Services Research*, 49(6): 1883–1899.

Song, Z., Rose, S., Safran, D. G., Landon, B. E., Day, M. P., and Chernew, M. E. (2014). Changes in health care spending and quality 4 years into global payment. *New England Journal of Medicine*, 371(18): 1704–1714.

Song, Z., Safran, D. G., Landon, B. E., Landrum, M. B., He, Y., Mechanic, R. E., Day, M. P., and Chernew, M. E. (2012). The "alternative quality contract", based on a global budget, lowered medical spending and improved quality. *Health Affairs*, 31(8): 1885–1894.

Stukel, T. A., Glazier, R. H., Schultz, S. E., Guan, J., Zagorski, B. M., Gozdyra, P., and Henry, D. A. (2013). Multispecialty physician networks in Ontario. *Open Medicine*, 7(2): e40–e55.

Thompson, J. D. (1967). Organizations in action: Social science bases of administrative theory. Classics in organization and management series. *Trans. Publishers*.

Timmins, N. and and Ham, C. (2013). *The quest for integrated health and social care: A case study in Canterbury, New Zealand*. London: The King's Fund.

Tolbert, P. S. and Zucker, L. G. (1983). Institutional sources of change in the formal structure of organizations: The diffusion of civil service reform, 1880–1935. *Administrative Science Quarterly*, 28(1): 22–39.

Tuohy, C. H. (2003). Agency, contract and governance: Shifting shapes of accountability in the health care arena. *Journal of Health Politics, Policy and Law*, 28(2–3): 195–215.

Vedel, I., Monette, M., and Bergman, H. (2011). Ten years of integrated care: backwards and forwards: The case of the province of Québec, Canada. *International Journal of Integrated Care*, 11(Special 10th Anniversary Edition): e004.

Vest, J. R., Campion, T. R., Jr., and Kaushal, R. (2013). Challenges, alternatives, and paths to sustainability for health information exchange efforts. *Journal of Medical Systems*, 37(6): 9987.

Wagner, E. H., Austin, B. T., Davis, C., Hindmarsh, M., Schaefer, J., and Bonomi, A. (2001). Improving chronic illness care: Translating evidence into action. *Health Affairs*, 20(6): 64–78.

Weick, K. E. (1969). Interlocked behaviors: The elements of organizing. In *The social psychology of organizing*, pp. 43–53. Reading, MA: Addison-Wesley.

Weick, K. E. (1974). Amendments to organizational theorizing. *Academy of Management Journal*, 17(3): 487–502.

Wennberg, J. E., Fisher, E. S., and Skinner, J. S. (2002). Geography and the debate over Medicare reform. *Health Affairs*, 21(2): w96–w113.

Werner, R. M., Canamucio, A., and True, G. (2014). The medical home transformation in the veterans health administration: An evaluation of early changes in primary care delivery. *Health Services Research*, 49(4) (August): 1329–1347.

Wiley, J. A., Rittenhouse, D. R., Shortell, S. M., Casalino, L. P., Ramsay, P. P., Bibi, S., Ryan, A. M., Copeland, K. R., and Alexander, J. A. (2015). Managing chronic illness: Physician practices increased the use of care management and medical home. *Health Affairs*, 34(1): 1–9.

Williams, C., Mostashari, F., Mertz, K., Hogin, E., and Atwal, P. (2012). From the office of the national coordinator: The strategy for advancing the exchange of health information. *Health Affairs*, 31(3): 527–536.

Zajac, E. J., D'Aunno, T. A., and Burns, L. R. (2011). Managing strategic alliances. In *Shortell and Kaluzny's Healthcare Management: Organization Design and Behavior* 6th edition, pp. 321–346. Clifton Park, NY: Delmar Cengage Learning.

Zucker, L. G. (1987). Institutional theories of organization. *Annual Review of Sociology*, 13: 443–464.

Zuckerman, H. S. and D'Aunno, T. A. (1990). Hospital alliances: Cooperative strategy in a competitive environment. *Health Care Management Review*, 15(2): 21–30.

CHAPTER 3

··

NARRATIVES OF HEALTH POLICY

··

GRAEME CURRIE AND GRAHAM MARTIN

INTRODUCTION

REGARDING dimensions and the effect of policy in health care systems, we note the following terms as influential, at least in the Anglo-American context: "new public management" (Hood, 1991), in the development of which the United Kingdom has played a central role, and, within the United States, "Reinventing Government" (Osborne and Gaebler, 1992). However, readers should note the impact of new public management (NPM) and Reinventing Government has spread beyond the United Kingdom and United States, particularly across North America, Australasia, and the Pacific Rim, with both the World Bank and the Organisation for Economic Co-operation and Development (OECD) acting as conduits for the diffusion of reform (McLaughlin and Osborne, 2002; Pollitt, 2002).

As with a limited number of studies within the public administration domain before us, we seek to undertake a narrative analysis of health policy reform (Bevir and Rhodes, 1999, 2006; Borins, 2011a, 2011b; Ferlie, Musselin, and Andresani, 2008; Pollitt, 2013). However, in contrast to Ferlie, Musselin, and Andresani (2008), who compared and contrasted two narratives of policy reform of NPM (Hood, 1991) and network governance (Skelcher, 2000), we consider them together, notably under one of our three narrative themes, "markets" (our other two themes are "management" and "measurement"). As Ferlie, Musselin, and Andresani (2008) note, the two reform narratives are not mutually exclusive and may well co-exist within the same country. A narrative analysis takes a long view and looks for both change and continuity over time. By examining health policy reform as a narrative underpinned by three themes, we highlight its intention to persuade its intended audience of the likelihood of a better future, assured by government intervention, at the same time as it sets that imagined future. To do so, a policy reform narrative encompasses the structure of any story or tale. Thus, we have villains, for example, protectionist professionals or administrative bureaucrats, whom heroes, such as market forces, inspirational leaders, and external democratic accountability, will counter. The broad long-term narrative within such structuring of the story is that governments are doing too much and must step down, displaced by a "steering" role achieved through external performance management as markets are instituted. So a policy narrative exhibits a beguiling and rhetorical quality meant to underpin the push for change.

In setting out our narrative analysis, we note a mixture of strategies, priorities, styles, and methods have been adopted by different governments across the world, dependent upon their tradition regarding the role of the state (Pollitt, 2002). From the 1980s forward, however, a number of commonalities are notable, reflecting the rise of "New Right" governments with neoliberal policy agendas across much of the developed world. Accordingly, commentators characterize contemporary policy reform as exhibiting a number of themes. As a starting point, Ferlie et al. (1996) note three broad themes, which cohere around the "3Ms" of management, measurement, and markets, around which other characterizations of policy can be considered, though we note emphasis has waxed and waned upon each of these themes. Such characterization of policy by Ferlie et al. (1996) is consistent with Hood's (1991) emphasis upon management and measurement of professionals, with greater emphasis on assuring quality of outputs, disaggregation of organizational divisions (often into units that compete for resource via market or other mechanisms), greater competition, the rise of styles of management modeled on the private sector (for a critique, see the following section, "The Management Theme"), and discipline and parsimony in resource use. Similarly in the American context, Osborne and Gaebler (1992), in their description of entrepreneurial governments, highlight competition and management by markets rather than bureaucracy, customers and choice, empowerment of citizens, focus upon outcomes not inputs, that organizations should be driven by their mission not rules and regulations, service delivery geared towards prevention rather than after problems emerge, revenue generation rather than spending, decentralization, and participatory management. In their more radical critique of policy, Currie and Learmonth (2010) highlight: professional-management relations; relationship between social and economic ends; policy desire for distributed governance; tensions between centralization and decentralization of government; increased emphasis upon leadership and other management apparatuses. Meanwhile, specific to health care policy, and discussing a possible transition to Post-NPM, Ferlie et al. (2013) identify a cluster of strands of policy, particularly evident in the United Kingdom, such as clinical governance, patient safety, and evidence-based practice, and trace changing interactions between network, market, and hierarchical forms of organization and governance. Such shifts mirrored wider academic and policy challenges to the efficiency and efficacy of public bureaucracies as a means of achieving policy objectives and meeting client needs, and concerns about the extent to which professionals could be entrusted to put patients' interests above their own (Le Grand, 1997). Responses to these concerns have manifested both in efforts to increase managerial power, and more particularly in the proliferation of markets and choice as a means of allocating resources within public services, including health care.

Our critique of policy is framed taking account of all these characterizations of policy reform, set out above, as applied to health care settings. Such reforms might be set in the context of wider political and economic change. The rise of NPM was driven (principally) by right-wing governments with economically liberal agendas, whose policies were formulated as the decades of post-war growth came to an end, and with them the Keynesian consensus on the role and remit of the state in providing for its citizens. Facing fiscal pressures, and seeking to address what had come to be seen as "overloaded" states with excessive burdens and inefficient operating models, the governments of Thatcher in the United Kingdom, Reagan in the United States, and others implemented reforms that sought to cut expenditure, increase contracting out of services to non-state bodies, and challenge the monopoly and autonomy of state-employed professionals over services they delivered, whose integrity and ethos was increasingly challenged (Le Grand, 1997). Though led by "New Right" governments in particular, it is important to note that this "hollowing out" of the state (Skelcher, 2000) through the introduction of NPM and associated reforms was not just the product of neoliberal ideology. Among the early movers was the traditionally socially democratic Labour government of New Zealand led by David Lange (Whitcombe, 2008); government deficits, weakening growth, and increasingly globalization were arguably at least as important as anti-state neoliberalism in driving reform. Regardless of their source, such political-economic shifts had profound implications for the governance and organization of health care, as Scott et al. (2000) highlight in their examination of the shift from an "era of federal involvement" in health care in the United States to an "era of managerial control and market mechanisms" in the early 1980s.

What some have termed "post-" NPM should also be understood in terms of its wider political-economic context. The rise of more networked forms of governance, that differ from both the bureaucratic-hierarchical forms of the traditional Keynesian welfare state and the contracts and performance management regimes of the NPM, can be explained in part by the phenomenon of what Skelcher (1998) calls the "congested" or "appointed" state. As Skelcher (2000, 8) puts it, the hollowing out of the state associated with NPM "produces an environment of organizational and political fragmentation in which the old certainties about the location of responsibility, accountability and authority for public action are lost." This, along with the protracted challenges caused by "wicked" issues that cross policy boundaries, has led to the proliferation of partnerships, networks, and quasi-governmental organizations in which increasing levels of responsibility and authority are invested (Kickert, Klijn, and Koppenjan, 1997). The consequence is complicated relationships of accountability and oversight that involve multiple stakeholder groups, responsible for governing, coordinating, and holding to account the agencies involved in service delivery. As with the reforms of the 1980s, the emergence of this era of "organizational fragmentation combined with plural modes of governance" (Skelcher, 2000, 12) in the 1990s and 2000s can be seen partly as a consequence of political ideology and partly as an "historical inevitability." Skelcher (2000) argues that the hollowed-out state resulted in something of a vacuum that had to be filled by some form of alternative, non-hierarchical governance arrangements to ensure accountability and authority, but the inclusion of wider stakeholder groups—notably, in the UK, representatives of the public, and of the public-service professions—might also be seen as explicit efforts on the part of governments since 1997 to foster democratic renewal (Barnes, Newman, and Sullivan, 2007), and to re-enfranchise professionals who had been sidelined by the original incarnation of NPM (Martin and Learmonth, 2012).

While taking a global view in this chapter, we draw upon particular examples from the NHS in England. The NHS provides an exemplar for both policy reform and its effects since it might be seen as a "fast mover" regarding changes in management, measurement, and markets (Martin, Currie, and Finn, 2009a), including both the emergence of the "hollowed-out" state during the Thatcher years of the 1980s, and the development of the "congested" state of partnerships, non-governmental agencies and complex relationships of accountability from the late 1990s onward (Skelcher, 2000). On the one hand, we suggest that England represents an illuminating case that exhibits general features. On the other hand, NPM is a general structural prescription spreading from Anglo-American countries, which represents a "loose collection of ideas." Dependent upon the institutional context, these prescriptions are translated in national settings beyond England so that some of our narrative themes presented below—management, measurement, markets—are of greater or lesser significance outside their Anglo-American origins (Barzelay, 2001; Christensen and Laegreid, 1999; Pollitt and Bouckaert, 2000).

THE MANAGEMENT THEME

Management (including both managers and management principles), as a policy strand within health care systems, has increased in importance, beyond the idea that managers are merely agents for translation of policy intent. Until the 1980s, health care organizations in most countries can be seen as a Weberian bureaucracy, with a standard administrative hierarchy from national government, through regional or more local government, to operating units. The stance of management was neutral, with a well-defined administrative cadre, which "valued probity, stability and due process" (Ferlie et al., 2013, 6), and was often characterized as offering a "diplomat" role (Giaimo, 2002). This was manifested in "professional bureaucracy" arrangements (Mintzberg, 1979), where doctors were "first amongst equals" in taking on managerial roles. Commonly, regarded as the "senior" professional by their peers, they would manage colleagues, as a representative that buffered them from external intrusion from the civil service and politicians. In contrast, under the new policy doctrine encompassed within NPM (Hood, 1991) and Reinventing Government (Osborne and Gaebler, 1992), such arrangements were challenged as ineffective and inefficient, and markets, general management, and performance measurement were introduced within policy reforms (Ferlie et al., 2013).

Encompassed within the management theme of policy, we highlight sustained emphasis upon the type of proactive management evident in more vigorous private sector organizations, what commentators describe as generic transfer of management models and practices, derived from private sector settings, to the health care system setting. A warning about a need for contextualization of private sector models and practices of management, when applied to health care, was offered by Pettigrew, Ferlie, and McKee (1992). At the same time, Pettigrew, Ferlie, and McKee (1992) argued we should not "throw the baby out with the bathwater" in rejecting private sector models and practices of management. It was not the management principle that was flawed, but rather often-crude application of those principles without concern for implementation, which led to their general lack of effectiveness. As such, we need to more carefully examine the contextualization of specific models and practices of management, as encompassed within health care policy, noteworthy examples being culture change, leadership, knowledge mobilization, and workforce development, which all need to take account of professional organization.

It is useful for analytical purposes to consider culture management and leadership together as exemplifying policy makers' orientation toward interventions to address health service delivery problems, often focused upon a drive for greater integration or collaboration across constituent organizations and professions. Together, culture management and leadership exemplify attempts at generic transfer of management models and practices from the private sector, and associated failings of crude transfer, as managerial attempts at re-organization are imposed upon professional organization (Pettigrew, Ferlie, and McKee, 1992). Despite critique, culture management and leadership interventions, imposed from policy makers, remain very visible currently. On the one hand, we might be somewhat supportive of such solutions for failure, on the basis at least they diverge from the large-scale organizational restructuring that policy makers sometimes tend toward when faced with service delivery problems (Pettigrew, Ferlie, and McKee, 1992). On the other hand, the effectiveness of cultural and leadership interventions have suffered from their top-down imposition. It has been too readily assumed that poorly performing health care organizations could be transformed or "turned around" by managing the culture and parachuting in charismatic leaders. Yet culture is something an organization "is," rather than "has" (Smircich, 1983), nowhere more so than in health care where long-standing, differentiated professional cultures are all-pervasive (Ferlie et al., 2005). Meanwhile, rather than the individualistic variant of leadership associated with transformation, professional organization may demand distributed leadership aligned with the collegial tradition of professional organization (Currie and Lockett, 2011). So, culture and leadership interventions represent a classical contemporary response of policymakers toward improving the performance of health care organizations, but also the seeds of failure that result in a policy implementation gap. In short, culture and leadership interventions exemplify both the generic transfer solution and the problems of implementation, and highlight the need for a more reflexive use of management models by policy makers.

A drive for more effective mobilization of knowledge has also been encompassed within the management policy theme (Canadian Health Research Foundation, 2003; Clark and Kelly, 2005; Davies and Nutley, 2000; Dobbins et al., 2009; Lomas, 2007; Van Kammen, de Savigny, and Sewankambo, 2006; Verona, Prandelli, and Sawhney, 2006; Ward, House, and Hamer, 2009a, 2009b), to address "wicked issues" (complex social problems, which are ill-defined and where any solution lies beyond the remit of any organization of professional group: Rittel and Webber, 1973). Recent policy toward knowledge mobilization has been focused upon accelerating, broadening, and deepening the translation of evidence to the frontline of service delivery, with concern for evidence-based health care (Dopson and Fitzgerald, 2006), or more narrowly, evidence-based medicine (EBM) (Sackett et al., 1996). Attempts to mobilize knowledge are also evident in workforce development, as new or changed roles are introduced, which impact existing professional jurisdiction. Such policy aims to highlight the effect of, and upon, a significant institution in health care settings, that of professional organization, which can be characterized as "medical professionalism" (Battilana, 2011). In particular, the interaction of macro-level influences (i.e., the institutionalized relationship between doctors and the state, and the dominance of the biomedical model that privileges doctors in health care delivery) and micro-level practice (which gives rise to professional autonomy) frame the implementation of new health care professional roles (Bourgeault and Mulvale, 2006; Bourgeault et al., 2008; Harrison and McDonald, 2008; Reay and Hinings, 2009; Martin et al., in press). Regarding this, long-standing literature on the sociology of professions highlights the importance of policing of occupational boundaries by professional associations, claiming exclusivity over knowledge that underpins their jurisdiction (Freidson, 1988, 1994; Nancarrow and Borthwick, 2005; Sanders and Harrison, 2008). Professional institutions however do not act in isolation to determine roles, but are influenced by relationships with the state and other professions within an interdependent system. Global policy focused upon workforce reconfiguration represents a response to workforce shortages and the need to better utilize resources, serving as the means to accomplish patient-centered care (see, in the NHS: Department of Health, 2000a, 2000b, 2000c, 2002). Importantly, Nancarrow and Borthwick (2005) argue that this has resulted in dynamic boundaries between the professions, whereby opportunities for changes in jurisdictions of work are opened up; for example, nurses taking on responsibilities previously the domain of doctors. This then represents state endorsement of challenges to medical dominance, with possibilities for some professions to extend their remit by taking up new areas of work, while others engage in processes of diversification, specialization, and substitution. However, policy makers arguably fail to adequately understand the social structures that underpin the introduction of new roles for health care professionals within the existing division of labor (Currie, Martin, and Finn, 2009). Professions operate as part of an interdependent system (Abbott, 1988), where the activities and developments of one group necessarily impact upon, and are constrained by, other groups within the system. Thus, workforce modernization remains a contested area, nowhere more so than in health care, where it works against pre-existing, but dynamic, professional systems (Currie, Martin, and Finn, 2009; Hyde et al., 2005; Martin, Currie, and Finn, 2009b).

As well as the management themes above, we also need to consider the production of managers themselves within health care policy. Policy has exhibited a desire to bring generic or general managers, as well as generic or general management models and practices, into health care organizations. However, the significance of the former can be over-estimated. Walshe and Smith (2011) noted that the general manager cadre in any English hospital constitutes only 3% of the workforce, whereas hybrid managers, fusing managerial and clinical roles, can constitute up to a third of the hospital workforce, many of whom come from the ranks of nursing (Burgess and Currie, 2013). Meanwhile, in the US, it is not uncommon (unlike the UK) for doctors to head up hospital organizations (Montgomery, 2001). Thus, we need to focus upon the development of hybrid clinical managers as a significant policy theme, with clinicians in hybrid managerial roles now expected to proactively manage their colleagues toward organizational aims (Ferlie et al., 2013; Thomas and Linstead, 2002). Rather than controlling professionals through managers, the policy intent is to convert professionals into managers, reconstituting clinicians' subjectivities through their co-option into such roles, enabling professional governance from a distance (Martin and Learmonth, 2012). Despite policy intent, the general management cadre has not gained power from professionals, as those moving into hybrid roles have drawn upon professional and caring values to drive managerial actions, enhancing their control and influence over key budgetary decisions. For example, McGivern et al. (2015) showed doctors moving into hybrid managerial roles did not merely resist managerial intrusion, but buffered their clinical colleagues from such intrusion, and co-opted managerial structures and processes to pursue clinical self-interest. In taking account of professional organization, we should note, however, that such opportunities may not be available to all professionals, with Croft, Currie, and Lockett (2015) describing how nurses struggled to adapt to, and legitimize, hybrid manager roles with other managers and their peers. Again, professional organization, both its inter-professional and intra-professional dimension, appears significant (Lockett et al., 2014).

THE MEASUREMENT THEME

The issue of managerial control over professionals is a long-standing one that predates contemporary policy emphasis (Colvard, 1961; Engel, 1970; Hall, 1967; Mintzberg, 1979; Raelin, 1984, 1985, 1995; Scott, 1965, 1982), which is exemplified in health care organizations (Argote, 1982; Hawkes, 1961). Professional organization cuts across managerial organization, the latter privileging calculability, predictability, and standardization for resource allocation and control purposes (Ackroyd, Hughes, and Soothill, 1989; Freidson, 1994; Light and Levine, 1988; Scott, 1982), and the desire of policy makers to maintain control over professional jurisdiction (Lerner and Tetlock, 1999; Power, 1997). Thus, we see more "hands-on," directive management of professionals, and increased use of explicit standards and measures of performance (Hood, 1991), but resisted or co-opted by professionals.

In general, contemporary policy seeks to curb the powers of professionals. "Old fashioned" Weberian bureaucracy was deemed unable to mediate professional power, but also unable to mediate managerial expansion of bureaucracy. Meanwhile, health care professionals on the front line cannot be trusted to engage in self-regulation in the public and patient interest. As a consequence, recent health care reforms illustrate a transition in the management of professional work exemplified by the introduction of more dynamic systems of governance, based on the use of evidence-based guidelines to direct professional practice and audit systems to assure compliance (Dopson and Fitzgerald, 2006; Power, 2007). Harrison (2004) characterizes this as the emergence of Scientific-Bureaucratic Medicine whereby medical practice becomes rationalized and standardized through "cook-book" guidelines, indicative of a shift toward more "encoded" and bureaucratic knowledge (Lam, 2000). Flynn (2004) suggests, however, this also highlights an example of "soft bureaucracy," as managerial expectations around service quality are more closely aligned with the performance expectations of doctors. Specifically, medical leaders become integral to the creation and monitoring of best-practice guidelines, indicative of "flexible corporatism" (Courpasson, 2000), while the responsibility for assuring adherence and performance becomes shared across professional networks (Sheaff et al., 2004).

We also see an increasing pre-occupation with governance, specifically more surveillance and regulation (Dent, Van Gestel, and Teelken, 2007; Hood et al., 1999). This is particularly pronounced in England where the values and institutions of public sector professionals are increasingly questioned, none more so than the medical profession (Ackroyd, Kirkpatrick, and Walker, 2007; Harrison, 2009). Specifically, in response to concerns over the quality and outcomes of health care, policy makers have promoted clinical governance in the NHS as a way of engendering service improvement (Ferlie and Shortell, 2001; Scally and Donaldson, 1998). The example of clinical governance in the English NHS is also reflected in new forms of governance for health care professionals evident in other countries (Burau and Vrangbæk, 2008). Globally, the effect appears the same. Policy makers are so pre-occupied with inspection and performance management (Hood et al., 1999), that clinical governance becomes orientated toward the accountability demands placed upon senior management. In the process, clinical governance becomes removed from day-to-day clinical staff concerns and viewed by clinical staff as a managerially driven exercise to extend control over the front line, rather than toward service improvement (Degeling et al., 2004; Nicolini, Waring, and Mengis, 2011). As Power (1997) argues, performance management and audit mechanisms (such as clinical governance) offer reassurance or "comfort" that performance is being measured, but may not result in service improvement.

Beyond an increasing focus on outcomes, performance, and ranking at the organizational level, the rise of clinical governance and audit has also made possible an increasingly forensic examination of specialist units' and even individual clinicians' performance. In the United States, the marketized health care system has long driven demand for detailed data on activity to assist billing and reimbursement by insurance companies, and in recent years such management information has come to focus increasingly on compliance with evidence-based standards of care, with a view to reducing avoidable costs from misuse, overuse, and under-use of care. This has also led to the identification of certain "never events"—interventions that are claimed to be entirely preventable, and which thus should never happen, such as wrong-site surgery—which have been deemed non-reimbursable by Medicare, Medicaid, and many private insurers in the US (i.e., they carry a financial penalty for providers). Publication of individual-level data on the performance of physicians and surgeons is also relatively well established in the United States, through what are known as "physician (or surgeon) report cards," although this has been on a piecemeal basis, resulting in variation in content and quality (Marshall et al., 2000). Again, these feed into insurer and managed care organization decision making. In England, similar efforts have been made to use the commissioning (purchasing) system as a means of incentivizing evidence-based practice and high-quality care. This of course relies on reliable data on provider activity, open to commissioner scrutiny. There are increasing moves toward disaggregating and publishing data to the level of the individual clinician, which bear similarities to the transparency movement in the United States.

However, the power of the medical and surgical professions remains critical. While these professions have undoubtedly been opened up to greater managerial, government, and public scrutiny than ever used to be the case, in England this has been a process in which they themselves have actively participated, and retained influence, rather than a subjection to oversight on managerial terms. As such, transparency (particularly individual-level transparency) in health care has taken the form of what Gabe et al. (2012) label a "disclosure game," in which, surgeons for example, have arguably gained the upper hand by self-disclosure, maintaining autonomy and control over the rules of the game and avoiding more punitive use of outcomes data by managers. Thus doctors have to some extent been successful in co-opting managerial technologies to their own ends, rather than being subservient to them (Waring and Currie, 2009). An added complication in health care, of course, is knowledge asymmetry, and the complexities added by individual patient heterogeneity and case-mix adjustment. Given these complications—and despite the shifts toward individual patient choice as part of marketization noted above—it seems likely that outcomes data will be used more by purchasers, insurers, and by other professionals such as referring doctors in primary care (General Practitioners in the NHS), than by patients themselves (again, in contrast to some other fields of public service, such as education, where client choice has been pursued with more vigor). To this extent, the realization of the NPM appears to have resulted more in a reordering of the relationships among professionals rather than a subjugation of professionals to management (Harrison and Ahmad, 2000).

Finally, linking the management theme to that of external measurement and control of professionals, another policy priority relates to quality improvement (QI) and associated QI interventions. Approaches and interventions cohere under the notion that QI is an important value, all have similar underlying concepts, which Berwick (2008) claims can be similarly applied across private sector and health care organizations. First, all QI interventions hold a systems view regarding health care comprising a network of organizations, underpinned by a series of processes. Second, they focus upon the value of the customer (i.e., the patient). Third, approaches and interventions are concerned with managing flows across different parts of the system. Fourth, they hold some concern with variation, although different interventions might seek to reduce variation or merely accommodate this. Finally, approaches and interventions seek to manage capacity so that supply and demand balance (Boaden et al., 2008). Others, however, highlight challenge associated with generic transfer of QI from private to public sector, which has resulted in fragmented intervention, with different labels being used for similar interventions, or vice-versa, and where implementation is insensitive to context (Robertson and Seneviratne, 1995).

THE MARKETS THEME

Traditionally, health care systems worldwide have shown much heterogeneity in their organization. The United States is usually characterized as representing one extreme, with no nationalized system and with even many poorer groups falling outside the safety-net state-purchased provision of health care via Medicare and Medicaid—though it is worth noting that even here, the state, via systems such as Medicare, Medicaid, and the Veterans' Health Administration, is responsible for a substantial proportion of health care expenditure. Providers in the United States are, though, by and large, in the private or not-for-profit sectors, and most physicians are self-employed private contractors who contract for services with hospital organizations rather than being employed by them. Many European systems, notably Germany and France, have traditionally operated a mixed economy, which includes a variety of private-sector and state-sector hospitals, and social and private insurance schemes, with both social and private insurers purchasing services from public and private hospitals, albeit with state regulation to ensure comprehensive coverage (Mattei et al., 2013; Palier and Davesne, 2013). Worldwide, there has been a trend across OECD countries toward greater use of co-payment mechanisms, with responsibility shifted from private or state insurers toward individuals, resulting in greater out-of-pocket expenses for patients (Hossein and Gerard, 2013). With its integrated, fully nationalized system, in which private insurance played a minimal role, the UK has traditionally represented the other extreme of a state-run and state-funded health care system, but as noted above critiques of public bureaucracies from the 1970s forward precipitated change in this regard. Consequently, the UK offers a particularly rich example of the growing significance of markets under NPM, with splitting of purchasers and providers following a rapid trajectory toward a more mixed economy that has arguably accelerated further in the last 5-10 years. That said, while England has often been characterized as a "fast mover" in terms of NPM-style reforms in general (Martin, Currie, and Finn, 2009a), within health care greater competition became a prominent feature of reforms somewhat later than other aspects of NPM, perhaps in part due to concerns about the privatization of the NHS in a context where several formerly nationalized assets had been sold off. So, even in those countries characterized as "fast movers" in response to the NPM narrative, we see the mediating effect of distinctive institutional context (Christensen and Laegreid, 1999). Such aversion to marketization is not limited to England: Palier and Davesne (2013) similarly note very limited privatization of health care services in France due to its political sensitivity, but accompanied by a much greater privatization of health risks, with reduced insurance coverage and increased use of co-payment in relation to many health care services (which so far has not happened to any significant degree in the UK). Nevertheless, over time, the basic format of marketization in health care in England and France is broadly in line with what might be expected from the predictions of the NPM scholars of the 1990s. As later discussed, distinctive institutional contexts may mediate the onslaught of the NPM narrative, but eventually its themes catch hold, even if somewhat translated (Christensen and Laegreid, 1999).

We emphasize that it is not that markets have supplanted other forms of organizing health care systems, but that markets, hierarchies, and networks co-exist (Currie, Grubnic, and Hodges, 2011). Alongside the development of markets has been a parallel increase in the role of networked forms of organization in the governance of health care systems. The network "solution" encompasses four aims, consistent with the contemporary health care policy narrative. First, network forms of organizing are expected to result in cost efficiencies as constituent stakeholders pool resources (Entwhistle and Martin, 2005). Second, they encompass a social aim to assist in addressing "wicked" problems that defy the efforts of a single agency (Rhodes, 1997). Third, they aim to mediate the democratic deficit in society through inclusion of users, carers and public voice (McQuaid, 2000). Finally, they encompass an organizational learning aim to promote service development as knowledge is more effectively exchanged in a context of reciprocal and co-operative relationships within networks (Thompson et al., 1991). Again using the example of the English NHS, a continuum of network forms are in evidence, from managed forms of network, focused upon knowledge mobilization and service development (Bate and Robert, 2002), to those whose service delivery is subject to centralized performance management, such as cancer networks (Addicott, McGivern, and Ferlie, 2007), to more voluntaristic, self-organized forms of networks, such as communities of practice (Tagliaventi and Mattarelli, 2006).

The third aim above—the involvement of patients and the public in networks with the aim of mediating any democratic deficit—is worthy of further discussion, since again it represents an aspect of the development of policy in health care that was perhaps not anticipated by those who theorized NPM in the 1990s. Patient and public involvement has gone beyond market-oriented initiatives, for example, encompassing in England a "duty to involve" patients and the public in any major decision to introduce, discontinue, or reconfigure health care services. Ostensibly, this commitment to patient and public involvement might seem to reflect a push toward democratization of public services, and undoubtedly it has been driven in part by the desire of patient groups, notably in the mental health sector, to challenge professional domination of decisions affecting them. Yet policy rationales seem confused about exactly what it is they wish to derive from patient and public involvement (Martin, 2008). Often, it seems to be a further form of expertise that is required from patient and public involvement initiatives, one that is seen to lack from existing sources of knowledge in health care governance. To this extent, whereas the drive toward individual-level patient participation might be seen as the latest iteration of marketization, the movement toward greater collective-level patient and public involvement might be understood as further pluralization of the stakeholders involved in networks aimed at addressing wicked issues (Martin, 2011).

CONCLUSION

In this chapter, drawing particular inspiration from illustrations within the English NHS, we have undertaken narrative analysis to present a longer-term retrospective look at the last 30 years of development of NPM policy in health care. Drawing upon a burgeoning narrative tradition that examines policy reform (Bevir and Rhodes, 1999, 2006; Borins, 2011a, 2011b; Ferlie, Musselin, and Andresani, 2008; Pollitt, 2013) allows us to derive novel insight in two ways. First, we draw attention to politics and ideology underpinning reform beyond the more technical approaches to evaluation often evident in studies within health services research. Second, such a narrative analysis highlights the beguiling and rhetorical quality of policy reform meant to underpin the push for change. Following this, we have examined whether its realization corresponds with the rhetoric of change embedded in the policy narrative.

The themes we identify, while illustrated through the English NHS, are ones that are evident in other NPM-based health care systems. Doolin's (2002) analysis of reforms in New Zealand, for example, highlights the significance of our three narrative themes of management, measurement, and markets in another national context. Similarly, Reay and Hinings (2005) reflect our narrative analysis, albeit themed by institutional logics, particularly reflecting our management and measurement themes in Canada. Even in countries falling outside the NPM doctrine, as earlier detailed, narrative analysis of policy in the US reveals that the management, measurement, and market themes are particularly significant (also see Kitchener, 2002, and Kitchener, Caronna, and Shortell, 2005, for an institutional policy narrative focused on these themes). So, we argue that national health care systems converge in terms of narrative themes identified in English health care policy, although their details in the face of distinctive institutional contexts may vary when examined "on the ground"—and in some cases may deviate substantially from what early theorists of NPM and even post-NPM predicted. In considering the translation of our narrative themes from the English setting, the Nordic countries represent an interesting example, which highlight our need to consider the institutional setting in any narrative analysis. For example, Norway exhibits a close relationship between political and administrative leadership that favors more incremental reform, and this has been accompanied by much less of an economic crisis of the kind that generated interest in NPM reform in much of the rest of the world (Christensen and Laegreid, 1999). Consequently, Nordic countries in particular have been characterized as moderate and reluctant NPM countries (Pollitt and Bouckaert, 2000). Framed by their distinctive institutional contexts, countries such as Denmark and Norway have adopted the management theme of the NPM narrative much more than the market theme (Christensen and Laegreid, 1999; Greve, 2006). Other European countries, such as Germany and Switzerland, might also be seen in a similar light (Kickert, 1997; Naschold, 1996; Wright, 1994), although all are affected by NPM reform in different ways, supplementing established procedures and work methods rather than replacing them (Christensen and Laegreid, 1999).

In considering whether the policy narrative has indeed proved beguiling, our conclusion is one that suggests the aspirations of policy makers toward general management models and practices, markets, and measurement, have to some extent been realized. However, across all three policy domains, aspirations of policy makers for change have been somewhat stymied, or at least moderated, by the significant influence of professional culture and power. This too has its own narrative linked to jurisdiction and autonomy, which beguiles regulatory bodies and clients to put their trust in the experts (Ackroyd, 1996; Raelin, 1985), and has made change slow to realize in some areas, even when mandated "hard" by government. We also note that, buttressing the effect of professional culture and power, policy sometimes exhibits inconsistency, so that one policy intervention has an unintended effect of countering another (Currie and Suhomlinova, 2006). Policy gains have been made, but this takes time. The "overnight" transformation that policy makers often seek for their health care systems in the face of increasing pressures are unlikely to happen. Furthermore, changes in direction at the level of national politics (changes of government and changes of minister) add further complication. Although we witness an overarching trend in the direction of reduced professional autonomy, pluralization of stakeholder networks, and greater use of markets, the pace of travel has varied, and individual policy changes have sometimes deviated from this direction. We therefore see a rather more heterogeneous set of policies and initiatives in co-existence than perhaps uni-linear accounts of NPM would suggest. The NHS was characterized by the Griffiths Report (Department of Health and Social Services, 1983), which drove managerial reform in the UK NHS in the 1980s, in the following terms: "To the outsider, it appears that when change of any kind is required, the NHS is so structured as to resemble a 'mobile': designed to move with any breath of 'air,' but which in fact never changes its position and gives no clear indication of direction" (para 8, 12). This may overstate the effectiveness of professional resistance to policy-driven change, since we have seen significant change in the English NHS and beyond over the time period examined within this chapter. As such, in analyzing the narrative of policy reform, a long time span must be considered. Changes on the front line as a consequence of policy reform may be incremental and represent "small wins" for policy makers, but over a longer period they can accumulate, and may come to achieve the type of institutional change desired by policy makers (Reay, Golden-Biddle, and Germann, 2006).

Finally, in considering narratives that run in opposition to the dominant NPM reform narrative, we should not just consider the effect of a professional narrative above, but also one that seeks to reclaim space for bureaucracy (Byrkjeflot and du Gay, 2012). As evident in Currie and Brown's (2003) study of managerial reform in the NHS, over time narratives may blend, so producing unintended, as well as intended policy effects. The NPM narrative presents values of Weberian public sector bureaucracy as an anachronism (Peters, 2003), associated with a failed past. For example, Osborne and Gaebler's (1992) narrative of policy reform presents bureaucracy as out of tune, and entrepreneurial governance as much more in tune with needs of history (Byrkjeflot and du Gay, 2012). Countering such epochal narratives, we note renewed interest in bureaucratic public sector organizations, and a growing critique of the "post bureaucratic organization" by commentators such as Pollitt (2008, 2009; see also Suleiman, 2003). Following which we argue that critical attention should be directed toward totalizing accounts of the "failure" of bureaucracy within the NPM narrative. For those wishing to maintain the narrative of Weberian bureaucracy, the need for flexibility, adaptability, and the emphasis upon delivery within the NPM narrative show little appreciation for the important principles of democracy embedded in Weberian bureaucracy. As Byrkjeflot and du Gay (2012) suggest, "costs of alternatives to bureaucracy far outweigh what critics see as the intolerable costs of bureaucracy" (105). We thus draw attention to the political and ideological underpinnings of any policy narrative, pro- or anti-NPM. Indeed the policy narrative around Weberian bureaucracy may yet prove the most beguiling of all narratives, so that rather than bureaucracy being seen as out of tune with the times, the NPM policy narrative that underpins contemporary health service reform ultimately comes to be seen as anachronistic (Byrkjeflot and du Gay, 2012).

REFERENCES

Abbott, A. (1988). *The system of professions: A study in the division of expert labour.* London: University of Chicago Press.

Ackroyd, S. (1996). Organization contra organizations: Professionals and organizational change in the United Kingdom. *Organization Studies,* 17(4): 599–622.

Ackroyd, S., Hughes, J. A., and Soothill, K. (1989). Public services and their management. *Journal of Management Studies,* 26(6): 603–619.

Ackroyd, S., Kirkpatrick, I., and Walker, R. M. (2007). Public management reform in the UK and its consequences for professional organisation: A comparative analysis. *Public Administration,* 85(1): 9–26.

Addicott, R., McGivern, G., and Ferlie, E. (2007). The distortion of a managerial technique? The case of clinical networks in UK health care. *British Journal of Management*, 18(1): 93–105.

Argote, L. (1982). Input uncertainty and organizational coordination in hospital emergency units. *Administrative Science Quarterly*, 27(3): 420–434.

Barnes, M., Newman, J., and Sullivan, H. (2007). *Power, participation and political renewal: Case studies in public participation*. Bristol: Policy Press.

Barzelay, M. (2001). *The new public management: Improving research and policy dialogue*. Berkeley: University of California Press.

Bate, S. P. and Robert, G. (2002). Knowledge management and CoPs in the private sector: Lessons for modernizing the National Health Service in England and Wales. *Public Administration*, 80(4): 643–663.

Battilana, J. (2011). The enabling role of social position in diverging from the institutional status quo: Evidence from the U.K. National Health Service. *Organization Science*, 22(4): 817–834.

Berwick, D. M. (2008). The science of improvement. *JAMA*, 299 (10): 1182–1184.

Bevir, M. and Rhodes, R. (1999). Studying British government: Reconstructing the research agenda. *British Journal of Politics and International Relations*, 1(2): 215–239.

Bevir, M. and Rhodes, R. (2006). *Governance stories*. London: Routledge.

Boaden, R., Harvey, G., Moxham, C., and Proudlove, N. (2008). *Quality improvement: Theory and practice in healthcare*. Warwick: NHS Institute of Innovation and Improvement.

Borins, S. (2011a). *Governing fables: Learning from public sector narratives*. Charlotte, NC: Information Age Publishing.

Borins, S. (2011b). Making narrative count: A narratological approach to public management innovation. *Journal of Public Administration Research and Theory*, 22(1): 165–189.

Bourgeault, I. L., Kulhman, E., Neiterman, E., and Wrede, S. (2008). *How can optimal skill mix be effectively implemented and why?* Tallinn: WHO European Ministerial Conference on Health Systems. Available at: <http://www.euro.who.int/document/hsm/8_ hsco8_ePB_ 11.pdf> (accessed October 28, 2009).

Bourgeault, I. L. and Mulvale, G. (2006). Collaborative health care teams in Canada and the U.S.: Confronting the structural embeddedness of medical dominance. *Health Sociology Review*, 15(5): 481–495.

Burau, V. and Vrangbæk, K. (2008). Global markets and national pathways of medical re-regulation. In *Rethinking professional governance: International directions in healthcare*, ed. Kuhlmann, E. and Saks, M., pp. 29–45. Bristol: Policy Press.

Burgess, N. and Currie, G. (2013). The knowledge brokering role of the hybrid middle manager: The case of healthcare. *British Journal of Management*, 24(S1): S132–SS142.

Byrkjeflot, H. and du Gay, P. (2012). Bureaucracy: An idea whose time has come (again)? *Research in the Sociology of Organization*, 35: 85–109.

Canadian Health Research Foundation. (2003). *The theory and practice of knowledge brokering in Canada's health system*. Ottawa: Canadian Health Services Research Foundation. Available at: <http://www.chsrf.ca/brokering/pdf/Theory_and_Practice_e.pdf> (accessed April 1, 2015).

Christensen, T. and Laegreid, P. (1999). New public management; Design, resistance or transformation—A study of how modern reforms are received in a civil service system. *Public Productivity and Management Review*, 23(2): 169–193.

Clark, G. and Kelly, E. (2005). *New directions for knowledge transfer and knowledge brokerage in Scotland*. Edinburgh: Scottish Executive, Office of the Chief Researcher. Available at: <http://www.scotland.gov.uk/Resource/Doc/69582/00018002.pdf> (accessed April 1, 2015).

Colvard, R. (1961). Foundations and professions: The organizational defense of autonomy. *Administrative Science Quarterly*, 6(2): 167–184.

Courpasson, D. (2000). Managerial strategies of domination: Power in soft bureaucracies. *Organization Studies*, 21(1): 141–161.

Croft, C., Currie, G., and Lockett, A. (2015). Broken "two way windows"? An exploration of professional hybrids. *Public Administration*, 93(2): 380–394.

Currie, G. and Brown, A. D. (2003). A narratological approach to understanding processes of organizing in a UK hospital. *Human Relations*, 56(5): 563–586.

Currie, G., Grubnic, S., and Hodges, R. (2011). Leadership in public services networks: Antecedents, process and outcome. *Public Administration*, 89(2): 242–264.

Currie, G. and Learmonth, M. (2010). Introduction: Making public services management critical. In *Making public services management critical*, ed. Currie, G. Ford, J., Harding, N., and Learmonth, M., pp. 1–10. New York: Routledge.

Currie, G. and Lockett, A. (2011). Distributing leadership in health and social care: Collective, concertive and conjoint? *International Journal of Management Reviews*, 13(3): 286–300.

Currie, G., Martin, G., and Finn, R. (2009). Professional competition and modernizing the clinical workforce in the NHS: Possibilities and limits to the development of the specialist generalist in primary care. *Work, Employment and Society*, 23(2): 267–284.

Currie, G. and Suhomlinova, O. (2006). The impact of institutional forces upon knowledge sharing in the UK NHS: The triumph of professional power and the inconsistency of policy. *Public Administration*, 84(1): 1–30.

Davies, H. T .O. and Nutley, S. M. (2000). Developing learning organisations in the new NHS. *British Medical Journal*, 320: 998–1001.

Degeling, P. J., Maxwell, S., Iedema, R., and Hunter, D. J. (2004). Making clinical governance work. *British Medical Journal*, 329: 679–682.

Dent, M., Van Gestel, N., and Teelken, C. (2007). Introduction to symposium on changing modes of governance in public sector organisations: Action and rhetoric. *Public Administration*, 85(1): 1–8.

Department of Health (2000a). *A health service of all the talents: Developing the NHS workforce. Consultation document on the review of workforce planning*. London: NHS Executive.

Department of Health (2000b). *The NHS plan*. London: Department of Health.

Department of Health (2000c). *Shifting the balance of power: The next steps*. London: Department of Health.

Department of Health (2002). *HR in the NHS plan: More staff working differently*. London: Department of Health.

Department of Health and Social Services (1983). *NHS management inquiry (Griffith's Report)*. London: HMSO.

Dobbins, M., Robeson, P., Ciliska, D., Hanna, S., Cameron, R., O'Mara, L., DeCorby, K., and Mercer, S. (2009). A description of a knowledge broker role implemented as part of a randomized trial evaluating three knowledge translation strategies. *Implementation Science*, 4: 23–27.

Doolin, B. (2002). Enterprise discourse, professional ideology and organizational control of hospital clinicians. *Organization Studies*, 23(3): 369–390.

Dopson, S. and Fitzgerald, L. (2006). *Knowledge in action: Evidence-based healthcare in context*. Oxford: Oxford University Press.

Engel, G. V. (1970). Professional autonomy and bureaucratic organization. *Administrative Science Quarterly*, 15(1): 12–21.

Entwhistle, T. and Martin, S. (2005). From competition to collaboration in public services delivery: A new agenda for research. *Public Administration*, 83(1): 233–242.

Ferlie, E., Ashburner, L., Fitzgerald, L., and Pettigrew, A. M. (1996). *The new public management in action*. Oxford: Oxford University Press.

Ferlie, E., Fitzgerald, L., Wood, M., and Hawkins, C. (2005). The non-spread of innovations: The mediating role of professionals. *Academy of Management Journal*, 48(1): 117–134.

Ferlie, E., Fitzgerald, L., McGivern, G., Dopson, S., and Bennett, C. (2013). *Making wicked problems governable? The case of managed networks in healthcare*. Oxford: Oxford University Press.

Ferlie, E., Musselin, C., and Andresani, G. (2008). The steering of higher education systems: A public management perspective. *Higher Education*, 56(3): 325–348.

Ferlie, E. and Shortell, S. (2001). Improving the quality of health care in the United Kingdom and the United States: A framework for change. *The Milbank Quarterly*, 79(2): 281–315.

Flynn, R. (2004). Soft-bureaucracy, governmentality and clinical governance: Theoretical approaches to emergent policy. In *Governing medicine*, ed. Gray, A. and Harrison, S., pp. 11–26. Maidenhead: Open University Press.

Freidson, E. (1988). *Profession of medicine: A study of the sociology of applied knowledge*. Chicago: University of Chicago Press.

Freidson, E. (1994). *Professionalism re-born: Theory, prophesy and policy*. Cambridge: Polity Press.

Gabe, J., Exworthy, M., Rees Jones, I., and Smith, G. (2012). Towards a sociology of disclosure: The case of surgical performance. *Sociology Compass*, 6(11): 908–922.

Giaimo, S. (2002). *Markets and medicine: The politics of health care reform in Britain, Germany, and the United States*. Ann Arbor, MI: University of Michigan Press.

Greve, C. (2006). Public management reform in Denmark. *Public Management Review*, 8(1): 161–169.

Hall. R. H. (1967). Some organizational considerations in the professional-organizational relationship. *Administrative Science Quarterly*, 12(3): 461–478.

Harrison, S. (2004). Governing medicine: Governance, science and practice. In *Governing medicine*, ed. Gray, A. and Harrison, S., pp. 180–187. Maidenhead: Open University Press.

Harrison, S. (2009). Co-optation, commodification and the medical model: Governing UK medicine since 1991. *Public Administration*, 87(2): 184–197.

Harrison, S. and Ahmad, W. I. U. (2000). Medical autonomy and the UK state, 1975 to 2025. *Sociology*, 34(1): 129–146.

Harrison, S. and McDonald, R. (2008). *The politics of healthcare in Britain*. London: Sage.

Hawkes, R. W. (1961). The role of the psychiatric administrator. *Administrative Science Quarterly*, 6(1): 89–106.

Hood, C. (1991). A public management for all seasons? *Public Administration*, 69(1): 3–19.

Hood, C., Scott, C., James, O., Jones, G. W., and Travers, T. (1999). *Regulation inside government: Waste watchers, quality police and sleazebusters*. Oxford: Oxford University Press.

Hossein, Z. and Gerard, A. (2013) Trends in cost sharing among selected high income countries, 2000–2010. *Health Policy*, 112(1–2): 35–44.

Hyde, P., McBride, A., Young, R., and Walshe, K. (2005). Role design: New ways of working in the NHS. *Personnel Review*, 34(6): 697–712.

Kickert, W. (1997). Public management in the United States and Europe. In *Public management and administrative reform in Western Europe*, ed. Kickert, W., pp. 15–40. Cheltenham: Edward Elgar.

Kickert, W., Klijn, E.-H., and Koppenjan, J. (1997). *Managing complex networks: Strategies for the public sector*. London: Sage.

Kitchener, M. (2002). Mobilizing the logic of managerialism in professional fields: The case of academic health centre mergers. *Organization Studies*, 23(3): 391–420.

Kitchener, M., Caronna, C. A., and Shortell, S. M. (2005). From the doctor's workshop to the iron cage? Evolving modes of physician control in US health systems. *Social Science and Medicine*, 60: 1311–1322.

Lam, A. (2000). Tacit knowledge, organizational learning and societal institutions: An integrated framework. *Organization Studies*, 21(3): 487–513.

Le Grand, J. (1997). Knights, knaves or pawns: Human behaviour and social policy. *Journal of Social Policy*, 26(2): 149–169.

Lerner, J. S. and Tetlock, P. E. (1999). Accounting for the effects of accountability. *Psychological Bulletin*, 125(2): 255–275.

Light, D. and Levine, S. (1988).The changing character of the medical profession: A theoretical overview. *Milbank Quarterly*, 66(S2): 10–32.

Lockett, A., Currie, G., Waring, J., Finn, R., and Martin, G. (2014). Institutional entrepreneurship in healthcare: Developing pathways of care in cancer treatment. *Academy of Management Journal*, 57: 1102–1129.

Lomas, J. (2007). The in-between world of knowledge brokering. *British Medical Journal*, 334: 129–132.

McGivern, G., Currie, G., Ferlie, E., Fitzgerald, L., and Waring, J. (2015). Hybrid manager-professionals' identity work: The maintenance and hybridization of professionalism in managerial contexts. *Public Administration*, 93(2): 413–432.

McLaughlin, K. and Osbourne, S. P. (2002). Current trends and future prospects of public management: A guide. In *New public management: Current trends and future prospects*, ed. McLaughlin, K., Osborne, S. P., and Ferlie, E., pp. 1–4. London: Routledge.

McQuaid, R. (2000). The theory of partnership: Why have partnerships? In *Public-private partnerships for public services: An international perspective*, ed. Osborne, S., pp. 9–35. London: Routledge.

Marshall, M., Shekelle, P. G., Leatherman, S., and Brook, R. H. (2000). Public disclosure of performance data: Learning from the US experience. *Quality in Health Care*, 9(1): 53–57.

Martin, G. (2008). "Ordinary people only": Knowledge, representativeness, and the publics of public participation in healthcare. *Sociology of Health & Illness*, 30(1): 35–54.

Martin, G. (2011). The third sector, user involvement and public-service reform: A case study in the co-governance of health-service provision. *Public Administration*, 89(3): 909–932.

Martin, G., Armstrong, N., Aveling, E.-L., Herbert, G., and Dixon-Woods, M. (in press). Professionalism redundant, reshaped, or reinvigorated? Realizing the "third logic" in contemporary healthcare. *Journal of Health and Social Behavior*.

Martin, G., Currie, G., and Finn, R. (2009a). Leadership, service reform, and public-service networks: The case of cancer-genetics pilots in the English NHS. *Journal of Public Administration Research and Theory*, 19(4): 769–794.

Martin, G., Currie, G., and Finn, R. (2009b). Reconfiguring or reproducing intra-professional boundaries? Specialist expertise, generalist knowledge and the "modernization" of the medical workforce. *Social Science and Medicine*, 68(7): 1191–1198.

Martin, G. and Learmonth, M. (2012). A critical account of the rise and spread of "leadership": The case of UK healthcare. *Social Science and Medicine*, 74(3): 281–288.

Mattei, P., Mitra, M., Vrangbæk, K., Neby, S., and Byrkjeflot, H. (2013). Reshaping public accountability: Hospital reforms in Germany, Norway and Denmark. *International Review of Administrative Sciences*, 79(2): 249–270.

Mintzberg, H. (1979). *The structuring of organization: A synthesis of the research.* New York: Prentice-Hall.

Montgomery, K. (2001). Physician executives: The evolution and impact of a hybrid profession. *Advances in Health Care Management*, 2: 215–241.

Nancarrow, S. A. and Borthwick, A. M. (2005). Dynamic professional boundaries in the health care workforce. *Sociology of Health and Illness*, 27(7): 897–919.

Naschold, F. (1996). *New frontiers in public sector management.* Berlin: De Gruyter.

Nicolini, D., Waring, J., and Mengis, J. (2011). Policy and practice in the use of root cause analysis to investigate clinical adverse events: Mind the gap. *Social Science and Medicine*, 73(2): 217–225.

Osborne, D. and Gaebler, T. (1992). *Reinventing government.* Reading, MA: Addison Wesley.

Palier, B. and Davesne, A. (2013). France: Squaring the health spending circle? In *Health care systems in Europe under austerity: Institutional reforms and performance*, ed. Pavolini, E. and Guillén, A. M., pp. 102–125. Basingstoke: Palgrave Macmillan.

Peters, B. G. (2003). Dismantling and rebuilding the Weberian state. In *Governing Europe*, ed. Hayward, J. and Menon, A., pp. 113–127. Oxford: Oxford University Press.

Pettigrew, A. M., Ferlie, E., and McKee, L. (1992). *Shaping strategic change: Making change in large organizations: Case of the National Health Service.* London: Sage.

Pollitt, C. (2002). The new public management in international perspective: An analysis of impacts and effects. In *New public management: Current trends and future prospects*, ed. McLaughlin, K., Osborne, S. P., and Ferlie, E., pp. 274–292. London: Routledge.

Pollitt, C. (2008). *Time, policy, management: Governing with the past.* Oxford: Oxford University Press.

Pollitt, C. (2009). Bureaucracies remember, post-bureaucratic organizations forget? *Public Administration*, 87(2): 198–218.

Pollitt, C. (2013). The evolving narratives of public management reform: 40 years of reform white papers in the UK. *Public Management Review*, 15(6): 899–922.

Pollitt, C. and Bouckaert, G. (2000). *Public management reform: A comparative analysis.* Oxford: Oxford University Press.

Power, M. (1997). *The audit society: Rituals of verification.* Oxford: Oxford University Press.

Raelin, J. A. (1984). An examination of deviant/adaptive behaviors in the organizational careers of professionals. *Academy of Management Review*, 9(3): 413–427.

Raelin, J. A. (1985). The basis for professionals' resistance to managerial control. *Human Resource Management*, 24(2): 147–175.

Raelin, J. A. (1995). *The clash of cultures: Managers managing professionals.* Boston, MA: Harvard University Press.

Reay, T., Golden-Biddle, K., and Germann, K. (2006). Legitimizing a new role: Small wins and microprocesses of change. *Academy of Management Journal*, 49(5): 977–998.

Reay, T. and Hinings, C. R. (2005). The recomposition of an organizational field: Healthcare in Alberta. *Organization Studies*, 26(3): 351–384.

Reay, T. and Hinings, C. R. (2009). Managing the rivalry of competing institutional logics. *Organization Studies*, 30(6): 629–652.

Rhodes, R. (1997). *Understanding governance: Policy networks, governance, reflexivity, and accountability.* Buckingham: Open University Press.

Rittel, H. W. J. and Webber, M. M. (1973). Dilemmas in a general theory of planning. *Policy Sciences*, 4: 155–169.

Robertson, P. J. and Seneviratne, S. J. (1995). Outcomes of planned organisational change in the public sector: A meta analytic comparison to the private sector. *Public Administration Review*, 55(6): 547–558.

Sackett, D. L., Rosenberg, W. M. C., Muir Gray, J. A., Haynes, R. B., and Richardson, W. S. (1996). Evidence based medicine: What it is and what it isn't. *British Medical Journal*, 312: 71.

Sanders, T. and Harrison, S. (2008). Professional legitimacy claims in the multidisciplinary workplace: The case of heart failure care. *Sociology of Health and Illness*, 30(2): 289–308.

Scally, G. and Donaldson, L. (1998). Clinical governance and the drive for quality improvement in the New NHS in England. *British Medical Journal*, 317: 61–65.

Scott, R. W. (1965). Reactions to supervision in a heteronomous professional organization. *Administrative Science Quarterly*, 10(1): 65–81.

Scott, R. W. (1982). Managing professional work: Three models of control for health organizations. *Health Services Research*, 17(3): 213–240.

Scott, R. W., Ruef, M., Mendel, P. J., and Caronna, C. A. (2000). *Institutional change and healthcare organizations: From professional dominance to managed care*. London: University of Chicago Press.

Sheaff, R., Marshall, M., Rogers, A., Roland, M., Sibbald, B., and Pickard, S. (2004). Governmentality by network in English primary healthcare. *Social Policy and Administration*, 38(1): 89–103.

Skelcher, C. (1998). *The appointed state: Quasi-governmental organisations and democracy*. Buckingham: Open University Press.

Skelcher, C. (2000). Changing images of the state: Overloaded, hollowed-out, congested. *Public Policy & Administration*, 15(3): 3–19.

Smircich, L. (1983). Concepts of culture and organisational analysis. *Administrative Science Quarterly*, 28(3): 339–358.

Suleiman, E. N. (2003). *Dismantling democratic states*. Princeton, NJ: Princeton University Press.

Tagliaventi, M. R. and E. Mattarelli (2006). The roles of networks of practice, value sharing, and operational proximity in knowledge flows between professional groups. *Human Relations*, 59(3): 267–290.

Thomas R. and Linstead A. (2002). Losing the plot? Middle managers and identity. *Organization*, 9(1): 71–93.

Thompson, G., Frances, J., Levacic, R., and Mitchell, J. (1991). *Markets, hierarchies and networks: The co-ordination of social life*. London: Sage.

Van Kammen, J., de Savigny, D., and Sewankambo, N. (2006). Using knowledge brokering to promote evidence-based policy-making: The need for support structures. *Bulletin World Health Organization*, 84: 608–612.

Verona, G., Prandelli, E., and Sawhney, M. (2006). Innovation and virtual environments: Towards virtual knowledge brokers. *Organization Studies*, 27(6): 765–788.

Walshe. K. and Smith, L. (2011). *The NHS management workforce*. London: The King's Fund.

Ward, V., House, A., and Hamer, S. (2009a). Developing a framework for transferring knowledge into action: A thematic analysis of the literature. *Journal of Health Services Research & Policy*, 14: 156–164.

Ward, V., House, A., and Hamer, S. (2009b). Knowledge brokering: The missing link in the evidence to action chain? *Evidence & Policy*, 5: 267–279.

Waring, J. and Currie, G. (2009). Managing expert knowledge: Organizational challenges and managerial futures for the UK medical profession. *Organization Studies*, 30(7): 755–778.

Whitcombe, J. (2008). Contributions and challenges of "new public management": New Zealand since 1984. *Policy Quarterly*, 4(3): 7–13.

Wright, V. (1994). Reshaping the state: The implications for public administration. *West European Politics*, 17(3): 102–137.

CHAPTER 4

......

CULTURE IN HEALTH CARE ORGANIZATIONS

......

RUSSELL MANNION AND HUW DAVIES

INTRODUCTION

......

THOSE with an interest in health care policy and health care management use many lenses or framings for understanding the nature of health care organizations and the forces at work on and within them. Sometimes the emphasis is on the structural configurations, exploring various organizational forms and the command and control structures that enable coordination of work effort. At other times, the focus is more contractual and economic, drawing attention to differentiation of roles and responsibilities within and between organizations, and highlighting the importance of contractual obligations, finance flows, and incentives for shaping service delivery. And always, in health care policy and management, there is a detailed concern with policy and procedural stipulations, with edicts, formal policy, guidance, and guidelines supporting, shaping, and constraining organizational life. Alongside these perennial concerns however, the past two decades has seen increasing interest in exploring the softer, social and cultural aspects of organizations, drawing on social anthropological rather than structural, procedural, or economic framings.

A key concern in these explorations of organizational culture have been attempts either to explain the undergirds of organizational failings, or to fashion cultural reorientations that (it is hoped) will lever turnaround and/or performance improvement. Nowhere are these cultural concerns more to the fore than in discussions of health care quality and safety (Lamont and Waring, 2015; Waring et al., 2010). Over a decade ago landmark reports published in the United States (IOM, 1999) and the UK (Department of Health, 2000) highlighted the scale of medical error and harm to patients in a range of health care settings and proved influential in developing the notion that organizational culture is a key component of health care quality and safety. With public inquiries and official reports into recent hospital scandals in the English National Health Service

(NHS) alighting on culture as both the key culprit and core remedy for widespread failings in quality and safety in the health care system (Francis, 2013; Berwick, 2013):

> Aspects of a negative culture have emerged at all levels of the NHS system. These include: a lack of consideration of risks to patients, defensiveness, looking inwards not outwards, secrecy, misplaced assumptions of trust, acceptance of poor standards and, above all, a failure to put the patient first in everything done. (Francis, 2013, 1357)

The policy and managerial rhetoric of culture as either villain in manifest failings, or magic ingredient in service improvement, is based on a number of implicit assumptions. First, it assumes that health care organizations have discernible cultures that exist with a degree of stability. That is, talk of culture in organizations presupposes that there are empirical regularities in the organizational setting that are describable in anthropological terms. Second, the logic of purposive cultural change suggests that, at least to some extent, such regularities or organizational characteristics are malleable even if not fully manageable. Third, this logic also suggests that it may be possible to identify particular cultural attributes that facilitate or inhibit performance (however defined). While such characteristics may not be universal, there must at least be hope that they can be assessed for their functionality within given contexts and in the light of certain goals. Finally, the interest in the cultural underpinnings of success and failure only makes sense if we can reassure ourselves that interventions here (however well-intentioned) will likely produce benefits that outweigh any (inevitable) dysfunctional consequences.

Such a wide range of assumptions and the careful logic that links these require a good deal of critical examination. In this chapter then we focus on unpacking what is meant by organizational culture in a health care context. We introduce some of the sources of the ideas and the conceptual underpinnings of organizational culture, and examine some of the processes (unguided or instrumental) that underpin cultural change. We then go further to address theory and evidence on the relationship between organizational culture and health care performance and quality. In so doing we hope to offer insights and understandings that strengthen the armoury of the health care analyst, while avoiding the charge that culture change "explains everything and nothing" (Alvesson, 2002).

ORGANIZATIONAL CULTURE—ORIGINS AND DEVELOPMENT

The term "culture" is derived from the Latin *cultura*, meaning to tend crops or attend to animals (Williams, 1983). Its use dates back to Roman times, and by the mid-modern era it was being applied to ideas of the betterment of the self (through education and social refinement) and further (by the nineteenth century) as a means of discussing common and shared attributes and ideals of peoples and nations. Early in the twentieth century social anthropologists applied this culture metaphor to describe processes of socialization of (often indigenous) peoples and societies through an examination of family, community, educational, religious, and other institutions (Williams, 1983).

Transference of these ideas about studying peoples into the study of organizations happened early, if initially at least only tangentially and haphazardly. The idea that an organization's effectiveness varied as a function of its culture can be traced back at least as far as the Hawthorne studies and related work in the 1930s and 1940s (Roethlisberger and Dixon, 1947). These studies observed how the informal, social dimension of human interactions mediated between organizational structures and performance and how these dimensions could be manipulated and managed to affect employee effort, commitment, and productivity. In the post-war period a number of researchers, including industrial sociologists and organizational psychologists, emphasized the importance of culture in shaping organizational behavior. However, it was not until the early 1980s that the concept entered mainstream management thinking through the influence of a number of bestselling—if controversial—management handbooks by US authors which popularized the notion that culture was a critical determinant of organizational performance (e.g., Peters and Waterman, 1982; Deal and Kennedy, 1982; Ouchi, 1981).

Perhaps the most influential of these 1980s writings was Peter and Waterman's *In Search of Excellence: Lessons from America's Best Run Companies* (1982). The book summarized research on the organizational attributes that distinguished "excellent" companies from less excellent companies (a differentiation that became problematic later on when some of these so-called excellent companies suffered manifest problems). A key theme running through that book, and other popular management books at the time, was the apparent need for "strong" cultures as a critical factor of organizational success, and various approaches were put forward as to how managers should diagnose, manage, and shape their company's culture (Ehrhart, Schneider, and Macey, 2014). While subsequently criticized extensively on various methodological, practical, empirical, and political grounds, such work was very influential in drawing attention to the importance of shared ideas and shared patterns of behavior in an organizational setting. There became then more of a focus in analysis and managerial action on the symbolic aspects of organizational life and the importance of creating shared values throughout all levels of the organization.

CONCEPTUALIZING ORGANIZATIONAL CULTURE

"Organizational culture" relates to the shared social aspects of organizations, but has been described as one of the most difficult organizational concepts to define (Hatch and Schultz, 1997). It has been elaborated in a wide range of overlapping and competing ways making it a rather elusive construct. For example, Van der Post, de Coning, and Smit (1997) dentified over 100 dimensions associated with the concept of organizational culture. Such definitional problems are compounded by the fact that there is little agreement on the meaning of either of the underlying components, "organization" and "culture." For example the American anthropologists, Kroeber and Kluckhohn (1963) critically reviewed concepts and definitions of culture, and compiled a list of 164 unique definitions of the term, the overall (sometimes repeated and overlapping) number of definitions reaching 300.

Given the plethora of dimensions and approaches it is unlikely that there will ever be an accepted universal definition of organizational culture (Ott, 1989). The problem then becomes that the concept faces the danger of being too all-encompassing and so vacuous, with accusation that it can easily be used to cover everything and consequently explains nothing (Alvesson, 2002).

In order to address this issue several approaches present themselves. First, when scrutinizing the content of definitions it is apparent that many cover similar ground, and therefore some clustering of views as to the core components of organizational culture is possible. Second, the nature and role of organizational culture can be clarified by reference to other metaphors commonly used to paraphrase its role in the organizational setting (Alvesson, 2002, 38–39). And third, we can clarify the analyst's intent in studying culture, and the basic ontological and epistemological assumptions they make in so doing. Such approaches reveal both a common core and a diversity of view around that core.

CORE COMPONENTS OF DEFINITIONS OF ORGANIZATIONAL CULTURE

Taking the first of these approaches to understanding organizational culture, we can seek to discover what is common among the many definitions proposed through commentary and empirical work in this field. One early definition, based on an examination of factory work in the immediate post-war period (Jacques, 1951), describes it thus: "The culture of a factory is its customary and traditional way of thinking and of doing things, which is shared to a greater or lesser extent by all its members, and which new members must learn, and at least partially accept, in order to be accepted into service in the firm." Thirty years later, and in probably the most cited definition of organizational culture, Schein (1985, 9) defines it similarly as "a pattern of basic assumptions invented, discovered, or developed by a given group as it learns to cope with its problems of external adaptation and internal integration ... [a pattern of assumptions] that has worked well enough to be considered valid, and therefore, to be taught to new members as the correct way to perceive, think, and feel in relation to those problems."

As can be seen, both of these definitions (and many others) cover similar aspects about the shared and taken-for-granted aspects of organizational life, covering both patterns of thinking and patterns of behavior, and the ways in which these are maintained and reinforced. More colloquially then, organizational culture is often expressed as being "the way things are done around here" and the shared ways of thinking that enable and constrain these ways of doing (Davies and Mannion, 2013).

THE METAPHORICAL UNDERPINNINGS OF CULTURE IN ORGANIZATIONS

Digging a little deeper, Alvesson (2002) enumerated eight distinctive contributions that "organizational culture" may make to organizational life. Each of these highlights the potential for understanding how shared cognitions and behaviors can contribute to shared patterns of behavior and other visible manifestations. Alvesson's eight possible sub-metaphors that collectively define "organizational culture" are as follows:

Exchange regulator: Culture operates as a control mechanism in which the informal contract and the long-term rewards are regulated. This is aided by common values and reference systems, and by corporate memory.

Compass: Culture gives a sense of direction and provides guidance for priorities.

Social glue: Culture, made up of common ideas, symbols, and values, is a source of identification for the group/organization, and so counteracts fragmentation.

Sacred cow: Culture helps articulate the basic assumptions and values at the organizational core to which people are strongly committed.

Affect regulator: Culture provides guidelines and scripts for emotions and their expression.

Explanation of disorder: Culture is defined by disorder, ambiguity, and fragmentation as well as commonality and so provides potential for disruption as well as conforming.

Blinders: Culture has un- or non-conscious aspects (such as taken-for-granted ideas and unexamined assumptions) that lead to blind spots in organizational understanding and unseen structures, motivations, and drivers for organizational behaviors.

World closure: Culture, its ideas and meanings, creates a fixed world within which people adjust, and are unable to critically explore and transcend existing social constructions.

Each of these sub-metaphors highlights a distinctive role for culture that arises from the shared-ness of thinking and acting in the organizational setting. Such an elaboration, when considered in the context of health care organizations, brings to the fore many issues and concerns that would seem to have a natural connection to health care organizational performance, patient experience, (un)safe systems and patient outcomes—reinforcing the logic around an interest in organizational culture in health care with which we introduced this chapter.

ONTOLOGICAL AND EPISTEMOLOGICAL CONSIDERATIONS IN ORGANIZATIONAL CULTURE

For all the overlap in definitions, especially when colloquially expressed, and for all the intuitive appeal of the roles for culture elaborated by Alvesson (2002), we have so far left unexplored the very nature of the phenomena of interest (its ontology) and the means by which we might know more (its epistemology). It is to these philosophical underpinnings that we now turn.

Conventionally the culture literature is divided into two broad streams (Smircich, 1983). One stream approaches culture as an *attribute*, something an organization *has*, alongside other attributes such as size, structure, and strategy. Here one can consider culture in relatively (albeit sometimes critically) realist terms, that is, culture is considered as simply another organizational variable, notwithstanding frequently a multidimensional one. Of course, operationalizing that variable, or set of variables, is fraught with practical and conceptual difficulty (Jung et al., 2009).

A second stream of literature regards culture more holistically as a *root metaphor*, simply something that an organization *is*. Here the view taken is that while the internal dynamics of an organization are describable, and perhaps even assessable in terms of their functionality vis-a-vis the organization's goals, they are not, as such, amenable to measurement. Narratives and situated accounts of the social dynamics suggest a more socially constructed or interpretivist understanding, one that asserts that cultural dynamics are less readily separated from their organizational time and place than is suggested by a measurement approach. Insights gained from such a framing may only be fleeting, partial, and contingent.

Those advocating the view that culture is a variable may consider the concept to serve four main functions (Smircich, 1983): it provides members of an organization with a sense of identity; it facilitates the commitment to a larger whole; it enhances social system stability; and it serves as a sense-making device which can guide and shape the behavior of organizational members. As such, culture is just one further aspect (alongside structure, policy, incentives, etc.) that can be used strategically to influence and satisfy organizational objectives. Culture change therefore is directed at "reengineering" an organization's value system for instrumental gain. Much popular management literature adopts this approach (e.g., Peters and Waterman, 1982).

The perspective that sees culture as a root metaphor goes beyond the instrumental view put forward in the "culture as variable" approach. Here organizations are perceived as cultural systems, with culture something that penetrates every aspect and layer of an organization. Thus managers are offered fewer levers to influence and shape the formation of beneficial cultures. While managers might be able to change some outward manifestations of culture, the basic assumptions held by organizational members may remain or change unseen and unpredictably (Buchanan and Huczynski, 1997). The attention therefore shifts from concerns about what organizations do and how they can do this more efficiently, to how organization is accomplished and what it means to be organized (Smircich, 1983).

When trying to sub-divide the field along the lines of either "culture as variable" or "culture as root metaphor" though, it soon becomes apparent that in a lot of cases no clear distinction can be made. Much research does not easily fit into either category, or may fall somewhere in between the two: researchers may refrain from reducing culture to a variable without fully viewing organizations as cultures either (Alvesson, 2002). This compromise appears to be rooted in the difficulty that the notion of culture as variable is weakened by the fact that cultural concepts frequently do not lend themselves to ready quantification or strict variable thinking. Conversely, the notion of culture as a root metaphor, with its focus on symbols and meaning, neglects the economic and other non-symbolic dimensions of organization (Alvesson, 2002).

The conceptual diversity underpinning organizational culture has been matched by some detailed elaborations of the concept that we now explore further. That organizational culture is often conceived of in layered terms—with surface manifestations being underpinned by deeper psychological processes—allows some differentiation between culture and the related metaphor of climate. Moreover, the application of different lenses that emphasize integration, differentiation, or fragmentation leads naturally into a discussion of sub-cultures and the ways in which sub-cultures and subgroup identities are related. Finally, this section offers a few observations of the challenges and opportunities of measuring and assessing organizational culture.

LAYERED COMPONENTS
TO ORGANIZATIONAL CULTURE

For all the discussion about diverse theories and definitions of culture, most researchers agree that it is layered in nature with the number of layers generally conceived as ranging from two to five (Ehrhart, Schneider, and Macey, 2014). Examples of those identifying two levels include espoused values *versus* values in use (Ott, 1989), observable manifestations *versus* underlying interpreted meanings, and espoused values *versus* enacted content themes (Siehl and Martin, 1990). A clear distinction made by these perspectives is between those aspects of culture that are observable and can be espoused and what is "really" going on at the deeper level cognitive or even subconscious level (Ehrhardt, Schneider, and Macey, 2014).

One of the most commonly used and cited examination of layers is that proposed by Schein (1985). Here he identifies three levels of cultural analysis of ascending importance, which provides a useful and widely acknowledged framework for practical application. Taking examples from health care (Mannion, Davies, and Marshall, 2005a; Davies and Mannion, 2013), these three levels can be described as follows:

Level 1: artifacts—the most visible manifestations of culture, including the physical layout of services, established processes of care, staff rotas and reporting arrangements, dress codes, rituals, reward structures, and ceremonies. Artefacts are especially concerned with the observable patterns of behavior within organizations. This would include, for example, standard care processes seen as normal working patterns, the agenda and processes of hospital Board meetings, the practices around sharing data on clinical and financial performance, and the arrangements and processes (both formal and informal) for handling patient complaints and staff concerns.

Level 2: beliefs and values—espoused beliefs and values may be used to justify particular behaviors, provide a rationale for choosing between alternate courses of action, and distinguish "right" from "wrong." Relevant health care examples here would include respect for patient autonomy and dignity, the prevailing views on current individual and collective clinical performance, and the beliefs that guide actions on apparent poor practice.

Level 3: assumptions—the unspoken, largely unconscious, expectations and presuppositions that underpin day-to-day work (e.g., assumptions about the nature of the caring role; respect or otherwise for the knowledge and perspectives of patients and relatives; and assumptions about the relative role and power of doctors, nurses, and managers in clinical settings).

In this schema, the observable patterns of behavior are explicitly linked to deeper levels of shared cognitions and (harder to access) assumptions, unconscious beliefs and precognition biases. Unsurprisingly, empirical work to date has focused more on levels 1 and 2 than on these harder-to-reach aspects of organizational culture outlined under level 3.

ORGANIZATIONAL CULTURE OR ORGANIZATIONAL CLIMATE?

At this point it makes sense to acknowledge that organizational culture is related to—but conceptually rather distinct from—another metaphor in common use: that of organizational climate. Although culture and climate have much in common, and are often used with unclear delineation, studies of culture attempt to assess deeper values and assumptions rather than the surface perceptions that are the focus of climate studies. Traditionally the two concepts were distinguished on the basis of the research approach applied—with culture research being generally qualitative and climate research more quantitative. However, since the rise of quantitative research approaches within the domain of organizational culture it has been argued that the two concepts have become virtually indistinguishable (Braithwaite, Hyde, and Pope, 2010).

Nevertheless, despite there being some overlaps between the two concepts, in our view there remain important differences and it is a mistake to use the two concepts interchangeably. First, the two metaphors are borrowed from two distinct domains: culture is anthropological while climate is meteorological in origin. Second, as noted above they tend to address different levels: climate focuses on organization members' perceptions of behavior, policies, practices, goals, and other methods of goal attainment at their workplace; culture is concerned not just with the surface orientations but the deeper cognitive and subconscious dynamics that drive these orientations. As such organizational climate might be perceived as a subsection of the broader area of organizational culture, and while organizational climate is thus influenced and influences organizational culture it is perhaps best considered as more of an index than a causative factor of an organization's health.

STABILITY, FLUX, AND FRAGMENTATION

It is tempting, in articulating a view of an organization's culture, to emphasise that which is shared and *stable* within the organization. Yet many scholars have drawn attention to the uncertain and shifting nature of these softer and social aspects of organizational dynamics. A helpful framework for understanding this aspect of culture was put forward by Martin (1992), which outlines three general perspectives on organizational culture.

The *integration* perspective (Martin, 1992) describes cultures in terms of a broad-based consensus and consistency about the values, beliefs, and appropriateness of behavior within the organization. The *differentiation* perspective emphasis allows for multiple groups or sub-cultures (elaborated further below) and posits the presence of diverse and possibly incompatible norms. The third, a *fragmentation* perspective, highlights ambiguities in an organization's culture where, at the extreme, differentiated cultures may diverge and fragment to such an extent that cross-organizational consensus and norms are either fleeting or absent.

Even within specific organizational subgroups, differentiation may be more marked than commonality, and agreements that are seen may be partial, temporary, and tied to specific issues. Thus the organization may be characterized by shifting alliances and allegiances, considerable uncertainty and ambiguity, and possibly a high degree of overt or covert conflict. Crucially, Martin (1992) does not suggest that organizations can reliably be categorized into one of these three perspectives. Instead, he argues that all three perspectives can elicit insights from within the same organization. There are, he suggests, likely to be aspects of culture that have strong agreement across the organization and aspects where there are clear sub-cultures (and indeed other aspects on which there is no discernible consensus at all). Each of these perspectives may be applied to the same organization to reveal, rather than hide, an overall lack of coherence.

ORGANIZATIONAL SUB-CULTURES

As will be clear thus far, organizational culture posits that there are at least some aspects of organizational life—in how people think and in what they do—that are shared and, to a degree, stable. Crucially, such shared-ness need not (although it sometimes may) extend right across an organization. Instead it may be seen, or better analyzed, in sub-groups defined by, for example, organizational sub-unit, professional role, service line, seniority, and so on. Thus the culture found within an organization may be far from homogenous or coherent, and although some cultural attributes may be represented across the organization others may be prevalent only in particular sub-cultures of the organization (Martin and Siehl, 1983). Van Maanen and Barley (1985) define an organizational sub-culture as "a sub-set of an organization's members who interact regularly with one another, identify themselves as a distinct group within the organization, share a set of problems commonly defined to be the problems of all, and routinely take action on the basis of collective understandings unique to the group" (38).

Researchers have (broadly) adopted two complementary frameworks for studying organizational cultures. The first defines sub-cultures relative to an organization's overall cultural patterns, especially its dominant values (Van Maanen and Barley, 1985). From this perspective sub-cultures may, at different times, be driving forces for change, overt defenders of the status quo, or covert counter-cultures quietly undermining new initiatives. Thus sub-cultures can be classified in terms of whether they support, deny or simply co-exist alongside the values of the dominant culture. An elaboration of this in health care (taken from Mannion, Davies, and Marshall, 2005a, and Davies and Mannion, 2013) leads to the following groupings:

Enhancing sub-cultures can develop in specialist teams or units. Here the core values and behaviors are a more fervent exemplification of the desired values/behaviors at whole organization level. Such enhancing sub-cultures can arise when special teams are created and resourced, tasked with transformational change, and shaped by charismatic local leadership.

Orthogonal sub-cultures arise in organizational subgroups whose members passively accept the dominant organizational culture but are themselves primarily animated by cultural influences from outside of that organization. Many medical specialties and subspecialties in health care can be characterized in this way, especially when physicians having admitting privilege at multiple organizational sites.

Counter cultures may emerge that challenge, either overtly or covertly, the dominant cultural logic of the overarching organization. For example, clinical resistance to management initiatives, the persistence of blame in the face of attempts to inculcate learning, and the maintenance of traditional patterns of care alongside reformed protocols. Counter cultures may be relatively small in number, scale, and scope, or pervasive, highly visible, and vociferous.

The second framework acknowledges that sub-cultures in health care organizations relate to department, ward, speciality, clinical network and, most obviously, occupational group. Occupational groups may, in turn be sub-divided into specialisms and services (e.g., ophthalmology, oncology, cardiology, gynaecology, etc.) and overlaying the basic occupational sub-culture we might expect each specialism to elaborate its own distinctive sub-culture based on the diseases, complications, procedures, technologies, and therapies with which it deals. These professional subgroups may seek to differentiate themselves from one another by their cultural artefacts or values. At times then, understanding cultural divergences becomes a case of understanding professional and sub-professional identities (Powell and Davies, 2012).

Such sub-cultures, so described, may be associated with very different levels of power and influence within the organization, whose dynamics may vary over time—witness, for example, the traditional dominance of the medical culture and the more recent rise of management culture in many health systems. Doctors and managers differ on many different cultural dimensions, which can lead to misunderstandings and tensions in working relationships and approaches to improving patient care (Davies and Harrison, 2003) and such tensions can be understood as (sub-) cultural manifestations. Thus deep-seated resistance by powerful clinical groupings to management-instigated changes (such as structural reorganizations, mergers, etc.) can help to explain the failure of such initiatives to take root (e.g., Kitchener, 2002; Reah and Hinings, 2009).

Measuring and Assessing Organizational Culture

The growing interest in understanding and shaping cultures in health care has generated a need for instruments and tools to measure and assess organizational culture in health care contexts. The most up-to-date review of the area identified 70 instruments and approaches that are available for exploring and assessing organizational culture and 48 of these were subject to detailed psychometric assessment (Mannion, Davies, and Marshall, 2005b; Jung et al., 2009). A variety of methodological approaches and research designs can be identified among the instruments, perhaps unsurprising given the methodological and conceptual diversity outlined above. These range from structured questionnaires to comparatively unstructured and emergent ethnographic approaches. Despite such methodological variety, the predominant approach taken by instruments is questionnaires, usually of a self-reported nature. Only rarely have these undergone any extensive testing, validation, or structural confirmation.

The perhaps inarguable conclusion of this review was that there is no such thing as an ideal instrument or approach to assess organizational cultures: an instrument that works well in one case may be inappropriate in another. Different instruments offer different insights: they reveal some areas and aspects of an organization's culture, but obscure others. Crucially, there are important differences in the required attributes of tools that are being used for formative purposes (e.g., as part of improvement processes) or summative purposes (e.g., as part of regulatory processes). In addition, tools that may offer informal diagnostic insights have very different characteristics from those used as part of formal research programs linking organizational dynamics to organizational outcomes.

ORGANIZATIONAL CULTURE AND HEALTH CARE PERFORMANCE

As elaborated at the opening of this chapter, a driving force in the interest shown in organizational cultures in health care is the belief that cultures of different kinds and types (however assessed) may be *causally* important in shaping important organizational and patient outcomes. It is to this issue that we now turn.

Linking Organizational Culture to Health Care Performance

The proposition that organizational culture (however defined) and health care performance (in all its variety) are linked has enduring intuitive appeal among policy makers and managers (as well as researchers). But research seeking to link organizational culture to health care performance needs to first clarify what is meant by organizational culture (as discussed above) *and* what is meant by performance: health care "performance" is surprisingly under-articulated and inherently complex.

In health care, there is a wide range of possible "accounts" (i.e., both measures and more informal, qualitative, or discursive assessments) of performance, across a wide range of domains including clinical processes, health outcomes, care efficiency, and unit productivity, as well as aggregate measures of patient experience, quality, and safety, alongside a variety of employee variables (such as commitment, satisfaction, and confidence). In addition different channels of assessment and communication may convey different performance information. For example, the apparent "hard" information conveyed in published performance measures may differ from the "softer" intelligence which circulates around informal and professional networks. Understanding this clarifies that we should expect to see no clear or simple relationships between "culture" and "performance."

That said, research has persistently sought to tease out detailed relationships between culture and performance in health care (and, indeed, within other organizational settings). Within the literature four key views on the relationship between organizational culture and performance can be discerned (Alvesson, 1992; Brown, 1995; Ehrhart Schneider, and Macey, 2014). While these are expressed as declarative statements, it is important to be clear that they are more hypotheses in want of testing than empirically-established facts. Indeed, the empirical evidence that does exist thus far is decidedly mixed on all counts.

Strong culture thesis: Here "strong" is usually linked to consistency and refers to organizations where beliefs, values, and norms are shared consistently at all levels of the organization. The assumption is that strong organizational cultures help facilitate agreement and a consensus on common goals as well as the best ways of achieving them. As a result, employee motivation energy and enthusiasm are all channeled in the same direction with few resources wasted on addressing internal conflicts. It is also argued that strong cultures enhance employee motivation because of the intrinsic appeal of working in an organization with a distinctive ethos and ways of working, and that this ultimately translates into higher organizational performance.

Reverse causality: Although most approaches seek a causal link whereby organizational culture influences performance, some researcher suggest the reverse relationship whereby high performance leads to strong (or at least, distinctive) organizational cultures. In this sense a history of organizational success may engender a common cultural orientation and value conformism. In situations where radical change is required this cultural conservatism may inhibit beneficial change. Others have argued that the relationship is non-linear, mutually constitutive, and recursive (Mannion, Davies, and Marshall, 2005a). For example, a particular set of cultural values may give rise to high performance and over time the continued organizational success may have an impact on the ways of working that are valued within an organization.

Contingency approach: This perspective assumes that different cultures are appropriate in different environments and that those cultures that "fit" the environment will perform better than those whose fit is poor (Davies, Nutley, and Mannion, 2000; Mannion, Davies, and Marshall, 2005a). From this perspective therefore, there is no single "best" culture which always leads to success as the key to success will depend on the how well the internal organizational culture aligns with its external environment and some cultures will be better or worse depending on the particular context. This means that as the context changes high performing organizations may have to modify their cultures to fit the new environment, and those that do not are likely to see—to some, unexpected—diminutions in performance.

Adaptability: This approach assumes that for an organizational culture to be continually successful it needs to be constantly adapting and responding to changes in its environment. Such cultures are characterized by risk taking, high trust, and a proactive and flexible approach to change management and the promotion of innovative working. Of course, in situations where an organization operates within an environment which is relatively stable, then risk taking and innovation are not necessarily desirable cultural attributes as they may lead to instability and a loss of sense of direction.

What these vignettes have in common is that they draw attention to the likely partial, contingent, and recursive nature of any relationships between aspects of culture and aspects of performance. Thus simplistic ideas of "line up the cultural values" and high performance will follow can be seen as naïve (although frequently policy stipulations and enquiry recommendations can be seen in this light (Davies and Mannion, 2013).

Evidencing Linkages between Culture and Performance

Much empirical work outside of health care has attempted to make linkages between organizational or ("corporate") culture and subsequent organizational performance. Several popular texts of the 1980s expounded these links. For example, Peters and Waterman (1982) claimed to have uncovered the corporate cultural characteristics leading to "excellence," Ouchi and Wilkins (1985) sought to explain links between culture and productivity, and various authors argued for the importance of "strong cultures" as a way of ensuring high corporate performance (e.g., Denison, 1990). Similarly, other work has investigated whether there is a contingent relationship between culture and performance. In the seminal work in this area Kotter and Heskett (1992) conducted a detailed study of 22 firms and concluded that those firms which fitted their environment were likely to perform better than those whose fit was less good. This "excellence" literature however, has not been without its critics (Alvesson, 1992; Ehrhart, Schneider, and Macey, 2014) and a review of ten major quantitative studies which sought to substantiate a culture-performance link came to a somewhat more cautious conclusion about any causal relationships (Wildercom, Glunk, and Mazlowski, 2000).

Specifically within health care there is a small but growing body of empirical work exploring the relationship between organizational culture and performance along a range of dimensions. In a review of the then available literature, Scott et al. (2003) assessed ten empirical studies across a range of health care contexts which met the inclusion criteria. They found that only four of the studies claimed to have uncovered evidence to support the hypotheses that culture and performance are linked. All the other studies failed to find a link although for the remainder it was more a case of absence of evidence rather than evidence of absence. The authors concluded that considerably greater methodological ingenuity will be required to unravel the relationships between organizational culture and performance.

Working internationally, empirical research by Gerowitz et al. (1996) explored the senior management team culture in 265 hospitals located in Canada, the UK, and the US. The Competing Values Framework (CVF)—a frequently used and partially validated instrument for measuring organizational culture in health care (Cameron and Quinn, 1998)—was used to identify orientations towards Clan, Open, Hierarchical, and (so-called) Rational cultures. The study found that the political economy of each country influenced the distribution of culture types: hospital senior management teams in the UK were frequently oriented towards Clan and Hierarchical cultures; hospital senior management teams in the US were more frequently tilted towards Rational and Open cultures, and hospital senior management teams in Canada more frequently leaned towards Clan and Rational cultures.

The study by Gerowitz et al. (1996) provides considerable support for the hypotheses that culture is linked to performance, but in a contingent manner. A key finding was that the dominant culture of the hospital management team was positively and significantly related to organizational performance in the case of Clan, Open, and Rational cultures, but only in the performance domains valued by that culture. For example, hospitals with predominantly Clan cultures performed significantly above average on measures of employee loyalty and commitment, those with dominant Open cultures performed better on measures of external stakeholder satisfaction.

More recently, large scale empirical longitudinal research in the English NHS hospital trusts between 2001 and 2008 (Jacobs et al., 2013), also using the CVF, similarly found that management cultures were linked to performance along a range of dimensions and provided further support for the hypothesis that specific domains of performance that are valued within a dominant culture are those in which the organization performed best. Further research has demonstrated that it is not only cultural types as measured by the CVF that is important but also the balance between different cultures. Shortell et al. (2004) for example found that that in a sample of chronic illness teams found that cultural balance among team members was associated with both the number and depth of changes aimed at improving the quality of care.

In contrast to such correlational approaches, Mannion, Davies, and Marshall (2005b) adopted a qualitative case study approach to understand the key cultural differences between "high" and "low" performing hospitals in the English NHS. In the six hospitals studied they found that there were clear differences in the cultural profile of the high and low performing hospitals in terms of: leadership style and management orientation; accountability and information systems; human resource policies; and relationships with other organizations within the local health economy. The authors concluded that the relationship between culture and performance is not necessarily simple, stable, or unidirectional, but is nonetheless important. Moreover, while high quality and performance may arise from facilitative cultures, it is equally possible that certain cultures develop or are enhanced because of the organization's historic performance record. In this sense culture and performance are likely to be mutually constituted in recursive fashion.

Despite a growing body of work seeking to identify culture-performance linkages, as well as the evaluation of interventions designed to create and nurture beneficial cultures in health care contexts, a recent systematic review of intervention studies "did not identify any effective strategies to change organizational culture" (Parmelli et al., 2011). Current policy prescriptions to improve health care performance through cultural transformation are therefore in need of a more secure evidence base underpinned by a more sophisticated understanding of the nature of relationships between culture and performance and how these might be explored empirically.

CULTURAL CHANGE

The final piece of the interlinking logic explaining the preoccupation with health care cultures is the sense that policy and managerial intervention can reshape organizational cultures for the better. This final section explores this in more detail.

The Possibilities of Cultural Change

A wide range of models for understanding organizational culture change have been developed and applied, but as with organizational culture none have received wide acceptance as the definitive means of modeling cultural change processes (Brown, 1995; Mannion, Davies, and Marshall, 2005a). Indeed the diversity of models for understanding organizational culture change reflects a lack of theoretical consensus surrounding definitions of organizational culture and processes of organizational change (Scott et al., 2003). Different conceptualizations of culture (as outlined above) generate rival claims as to the nature and feasibility of planned culture change: those who conceive of culture as a *variable* may view it as capable of being manipulated and managed to meet organizational ends. Whereas, those who view organizations more holistically *as* cultures more often tend to see it as something that is difficult or even impossible to manage purposefully towards specific ends. In both cases of course, unintended and dysfunctional consequences remain a risk (Brown, 1995).

Some commentators have prescribed a middle path between these two dominant approaches by treating an organization's culture as an emergent property (Mannion, Davies, and Marshall, 2005a). From this perspective culture is not assumed a priori to be controllable. Instead it is assumed that its key characteristics can at least be described and assessed in terms of their functional contributions to broader managerial and organizational objectives; and moreover, that once an understanding of these characteristics is attained, some shaping and influencing of these dynamics is possible.

First and Second Order Change

Different models of culture change differ in terms of the scale of change to which they apply (Brown, 1995). A distinction can be made in terms of whether culture change strategies are targeted at first- or second-order change (Bate, 1999). During "first-order" change the objective is to "do what you do better." According to the influential authors Deal and Kennedy (1982) many commercial organizations have maintained a competitive advantage by pursuing a policy of "cultural continuity," capitalizing on the lessons, traditions, and working practices that have served the organization well over a period of years. Thus the focus is on evolutionary growth or effective repetition (more of the same, but better). In contrast, "second-order," qualitative growth (something different, a radical break with the past) is more appropriate if an existing culture has begun to stagnate and a complete overhaul is required. Second-order change is often invoked in response to a growing crisis or acknowledged deficiency in the existing culture, which cannot be addressed adequately by a change *in* culture but rather demands a fundamental change *of* culture. This "second-order" change focuses on instilling *new* behaviors and values throughout the organization, whereas in first-order change the emphasis is more on adapting and refining the *extant* culture and traditional modes of working.

In practice, and especially in health care settings, such sharp distinctions between first- and second-order change may be overstated. Most change requires a balance between transformation and continuity, while avoiding the introduction of new dysfunctions. Moreover, an overemphasis on cultural change may neglect the necessity of parallel change in structures, processes, and incentives, for example.

Modeling the Cultural Change Process

In summarizing a wide range of models of culture change drawn from the literature (Brown, 1995; Scott et al., 2003) it can be seen that, despite some significant differences between the models reviewed, they all share some common foci. In particular, most models pay some attention to the following factors:

Crises: as a trigger for significant organizational change;
Leadership: in detecting the need for change and in shaping that change;
Success: to consolidate the new order and counter natural resistance to change (as one of the key functions of organizational culture is to establish and stabilize ways of organizing and interacting, resistance is inherent to any culture change efforts);
Relearning and re-education: as a means of embedding and helping explain the assimilation of new cultures.

Health care in particular seems to be beset by regular scandals and crises for which the diagnosis is often solely or in part "cultural failures" and the solution proposed is "cultural renewal." What is less often discussed is the role played by external policy and regulatory framings, pressures, and stipulations that contribute to the organizational dysfunctions that underpin these crises (Davies and Mannion, 2013). Thus while we might argue that cultural underpinnings of unwanted behavior patterns are likely, organizational change internal to the organization (whether focused on culture alone, or as part of a broader package of reforms) may be insufficient in the absence of wider policy and system reform.

Targets for Cultural Change

Supposing that cultural reorientation within organizations is warranted and desirable (notwithstanding the arguments above), Bate (1999) has highlighted the key dimensions to be targeted in a culture change strategy. These include:

The structural dimension: To be successful a culture change program must take account of the culture to be changed. Only after an effective diagnosis or cultural audit has revealed how the current order is sustained through existing structural arrangements can effective change management strategies be deployed. Such a diagnosis would proceed by first acquiring an appreciation of the currently prevailing culture (which links to notions of culture measurement or assessment discussed earlier).

The process dimension: If cultures develop spontaneously, as an emergent model suggests, how they change is a key question. Bate (1999) has applied a sailing metaphor based on wave movements to illustrate spontaneous change. If the latest cultural wave appears to be going in the right direction (a virtuous momentum) then it may be possible to ride the wave using its own energy to deliver the organization to its desired destination. If the prevailing wave is not going in the desired direction, at least three alternative strategies are possible: first, to deflect waves using their own momentum (re-framing strategies); second, to wait until the most powerful waves have subsided and then create new ones (new-wave strategies); and, third, to wait until a new wave is going in the desired direction and only then "hitch a ride" (opportunistic strategies).

The contextual dimension: It is important to assess the "fit" or alignment between a culture and the wider environment. As the external environment changes so must the internal culture to avoid obsolescence. More likely, if the external environment that has produced some unwanted organizational dynamics remains unchanged then change strategies need to address the likely dissonance from reformed positions. This adaptive approach involves an assessment of "cultural lag" or strategic drift to gauge the gap between the culture in use and the required culture.

These dimensions offer alternative ways for thinking about and enacting cultural change in health care systems and organizations. Yet as we discuss below there are many other issues that need to be addressed when seeking to purposefully shape culture in health care organizations to beneficial effect.

Overcoming Barriers to Planned Culture Change

Strategies of culture change need to be mindful of the possible barriers to that serve to block or attenuate managed change. These include:

Lack of ownership: A change often invokes a sense of loss and the reactions of individuals and professional groups can be unpredictable. Even a few disaffected individuals can cause disruption. The implication is that unless a critical mass of employees "buy into" a culture change program, such initiatives are likely to fail.

Complexity: Organization culture is transmitted and embedded via a wide range of media, including established working procedures and practices (e.g., rewards, ceremonies, physical spaces, shift patterns, etc.). It is unrealistic to expect culture change strategies to be effective on a ll these simultaneously.

External influence: The influence of outside interests may cut across and sometimes work against efforts towards internal reform. Culture change strategies need to heed the constraints posed by external stakeholders in determining the values and behavior of health professionals (e.g., professional bodies, regulatory agencies, etc.)

Managing Cultural Diversity, Mergers, and Partnership Working

As noted earlier, health care organizations are likely to comprise competing and overlapping professional subgroups. Thus a key challenge to culture change programs is to consider carefully the impact of change on specific groups within a health care organization (e.g., doctors, nurses and other health professionals, and managers) and to design appropriate policies to accommodate this. Child and Faulkner (1998) have developed a useful typology to assess approaches to managing organizational culture change in the face of organizational cultural diversity. Their analysis is structured according to two fundamental choices. The first concerns whether one subgroup's culture should dominate. The second relates to the decision either to integrate different sub-cultures (in order to derive synergy between them) or to segregate the various sub-cultures (with the aim of avoiding conflict or efforts devoted to cultural management). These strategic choices give rise to four possible bases for accommodating cultural diversity within an organization (see Figure 4.1). The first three offer some scope for establishing a cultural fits, whilst the fourth gives rise to serious dysfunctional consequences.

Any attempts at culture change in complex multi-professional organizations such as hospitals will need to address explicitly the importance of managing cultural diversity in order to achieve accommodation between a myriad of competing and overlapping organizational sub-cultures. Frameworks such as that elaborated above may aid that process, both analytically and practically.

One recent analytic application of this framework explored a common theme in many countries over recent years: the increase in partnership working and formal mergers between health care providers (Peck and Dickinson, 2008). Mannion et al. (2011) examined cultural diversity issues in relation to joint working between public and private providers as part of the Local Improvement Finance Trust (LIFT) initiative in the English NHS. Based on in-depth case studies of three LIFT partnerships the study found disconnect between the rather optimistic perspective on cultural integration within LIFT partnerships held by senior policy makers, and the reality on the ground. Different assumed value orientations and motives had created a degree of suspicion between LIFT partners, with public organizations often uncomfortable with the (assumed) profit motive of private sector partners, and private sector partners worried about the (assumed) lack of financial acumen and political interference associated with public providers. The espoused aspiration of all three LIFT partnerships was one of Synergy (see Figure 4.1);

| | Integration between cultural groups? | |
	Yes	No
Domination by one sub-culture?	1) *Synergy*	2) *Segregation*
No	Here the objective of collaboration is to meld both partners' cultures and to achieve the best possible fit between the two. The best elements are combined with the objective of making the whole greater than the sum of its parts.	Here the aim is to strike an acceptable balance between different cultures by virtue of maintaining separation rather than seeking integration.
Yes	3) *Domination* This is based on recognition that integrating organizational cultures may prove impossible and accepts the right of dominance of one sub-group's culture.	4) *Breakdown* This occurs when one culture seeks domination, integration, or mutually acceptable segregation but fails to secure the acquiescence of the other organizational culture.

Derived and expanded from a classificatory scheme on strategic alliances developed by Child and Faulkner (1998)

FIGURE 4.1 The meeting of cultures: achieving a "cultural fit"

however, in practice existing inter-organizational relations were not fully integrated and could be best described as being Segregated (see Figure 4.1). Perhaps encouragingly, none of the LIFT partnership relationships could be characterized as either Domination of Breakdown in the schema.

Several studies have also highlighted cultural compatibility and deep-seated resistance as key issues for post-merger integration in health care organizations, and in particular hospital organizations (Fulop et al., 2005). Indeed, a review of hospital mergers in Europe and North America concluded that "almost all consolidations fall short, since those in leadership positions lack the necessary understanding and appreciation of the differences in culture, values and goals of the existing facilities" (Weil, 2010). For example, in exploring the cultural issues associated with the merger of two hospital Trusts in the English NHS, Ovsieko et al. (2015) used mixed-method case-study approaches, drawing on the Competing Values Framework. They concluded that cultural issues relating to the relative size, identities, and clinical services were a key factor in mediating successful on-going post-merger integration of the two organizations. Similarly, in the US, and drawing on Institutional theory and political science, Kitchener (2002) highlights the cultural issues and "institutional logics" associated with the merger of two academic health centres in California, and in particular the problems of promoting adaptive change in multi-professional health care organizations. In an extension of this, Reah and Hinings (2009) identify the cultural issues and institutional logics associated with managing changes in the health system in Alberta and in particular highlight the importance of providing a way for different cultures and their competing logics to co-exist and separately guide the behavior of different actors involved in health care transformation. Accommodation across cultural subgroups remains a potent challenge to effective health care reform and reconfiguration.

Concluding Remarks

Health care policy and management in many countries frequently invoke notions of "culture" and "culture change" as key levers for delivering good quality health care. However, such notions of organizational culture are often under-specified, and unpacking these and exploring the nature of any linkages between cultures and quality remain an important task. The diversity and contested nature of understanding about culture will necessarily mean that there will be diverse and contested ways of seeking to harness the power of culture to deliver the desired improvements in health care quality and performance. In this chapter we have tried to sharpen thinking around the theory and feasibility of culture and culture change in health care settings by setting out some of the key conceptual and practical challenges that need to be addressed by policy makers, health care managers, researchers, and by others seeking to understand, assess, and change cultures in health care organizations. What is clear is attempting to enact culture change to improve performance is a difficult, uncertain, and risky enterprise and may not always generate the anticipated outcomes. As in many other areas of management we are in need of a more secure evidence base that is underpinned by a more sophisticated understanding of these complex and dynamic organizational phenomena.

REFERENCES

Alvesson, M. (2002). *Understanding organizational culture*. London: Sage.

Bate, P. (1999). *Strategies for cultural change*. Oxford: Butterworth-Heinemann.

Berwick, D. (2013). *A promise to learn-a commitment to act: Improving the safety of patient safety in England*. London: HSMO.

Braithwaite, J., Hyde, P., and Pope, C. (2010). *Culture and climate in health care organizations*. Basingstoke: Palgrave Macmillan.

Brown, A. (1995). *Organizational culture*. London: Pitman.

Buchanan, A. and Huczynski, D. (1997). *Organizational behaviour: An introductory text*. 3rd ed. Hemel Hempstead: Prentice-Hall.

Cameron, K. S. and Quinn, R. E. (1998). *Diagnosing and changing organizational culture: Based on the competing values framework*. Reading, MA: Addison-Wesley.

Child, J. and Faulkner, D. (1998). *Strategies of cooperation: Managing alliances, networks, and joint ventures*. Oxford: Oxford University Press.

Davies, H. and Mannion, R. (2013). Will prescriptions for cultural change improve the NHS? *British Medical Journal*, 346: f1305.

Davies, H., Nutley, S., and Mannion, R. (2000). Organizational culture and quality of health care. *Quality in Health Care*, 9: 111–119.

Davies, H. T. O., and Harrison, S. (2003). Trends in doctor–manager relationships. *British Medical Journal*, 326: 646–649.

Deal, T. E. and Kennedy, A. A. (1982). *Corporate cultures: The rites and rituals of corporate life*. Harmondsworth: Penguin.

Denison, D. R. (1990). *Corporate culture and organizational effectiveness*. New York: Wiley.

Department of Health. (2000). *An organization with a memory*. London: HMSO.

Ehrhart, M., Schneider, B., and Macey, W. (2014). *Organizational climate and culture: An introduction to theory, research and practice*. New York: Routledge.

Francis, R. (2013). *The Mid Staffordshire NHS Foundation Trust Public Inquiry*. London: HMSO.

Fulop, N., Protopsaltis, G., King, A., Allen, P., Hutchings, A., and Normand, C. (2005). Changing organizations: A study of the context and process of mergers of health care providers in England. *Social Science and Medicine*, 60: 119–130.

Gerowitz, M., Lemieux-Charles, L. Heginbothan, C., and Johnson, B. (1996). Top management culture and performance in Canadian, UK and US hospitals. *Health Services Management Research*, 9: 69–78.

Hatch, M. and Schultz, M. (1997). Relations between organization culture, identity and image. *European Journal of Marketing*, 31: 356–365.

Institute of Medicine (IOM) (1999). *To err is human: Building a safer health system*. Washington, D. C.: National Academy Press.

Jacobs, R., Mannion, R., Davies, H., Harrison, S., Konteh, F., and Walshe, K. (2013). The relationship between organizational culture and performance in acute hospitals. *Social Science and Medicine*, 76: 115–125.

Jacques, E. (1951). *The changing culture of a factory*. London: Tavistock Publications.

Jung, T., Scott, T., Davies, H., Bower, P., and Mannion, R. (2009). Instruments for the exploration of organizational culture. *Public Administration Review*, 69(6): 1987–1096.

Kitchener, M. (2002). Mobilizing the logic of managerialism in professional fields: The case of academic health centre mergers. *Organization Studies*, 23: 391–420.

Kotter, J. and Heskett, L. (1992). *Corporate culture and performance*. New York: Macmillan.

Kroeber, A. L. and Kluckhohn, C. (1963). *Culture: A critical review of concepts and definitions*. New York: Vintage Books.

Lamont, T. and Waring, J. (2015). Safety lessons: Shifting paradigms and new directions for patient safety research. *Journal of Health Services Research and Policy*, 20(9): 1–4.

Mannion, R., Davies, H., and Marshall, M. (2005a). *Cultures for performance in health care*. Buckingham: Open University Press.

Mannion, R., Davies, H., and Marshall, M. (2005b). Cultural attributes of "high" and "low" performing hospitals. *Journal of Health Organization and Management*, 19(6): 431–439.

Mannion, R., Brown, S., Beck, M., and Lunt, N. (2011). Managing cultural diversity in health care partnerships: The case of LIFT. *Journal of Health Organization and Management*, 25(6): 645–657.

Mannion, R., Konteh, H., McMurray, R., Davies, H., Scott, T., Bower, P., and Whalley, D. (2008). *Measuring and assessing organizational culture in the NHS* (report to the National Institute for Health Research Service Delivery and Organization Programme), p. 283.

Martin, J. (1992). *Cultures in organizations: Three perspectives*. Oxford: Oxford University Press.

Martin, J. and Siehl, C. (1983). Organizational culture and counterculture: An uneasy symbiosis. *Organizational Dynamics*, 12(92): 52–64.

Ott, J. S. (1989). *The organizational culture perspective*. Pacific Grove, CA: Brooks/Cole Publishing Company.

Ouchi, W. (1981). *Theory Z: How American business can meet the Japanese challenge*. Reading, MA: Addison Wesley.

Ouchi, W. G. and Wilkins, A. L. (1985). Organizational Culture. *Annual Review of Sociology*, 11: 457–483.

Ovsieko, P., Melham, K., Fowler, J., and Buchan, A. (2015). Organizational culture and post-merger integration in an academic health centre: A mixed methods study. *BMC Health Services Research*, 15(25): 201–209.

Parmelli, E., Flodgren, G., Beyer, F., Baillie, N., Schaafsma, M., and Eccles, M. (2011). The effectiveness of strategies to change organizational culture to improve healthcare performance: A systematic review. *Implementation Science*, 6(1): 33.

Peck, E. and Dickinson, H. (2008). *Managing and leading in inter-agency settings*. Bristol: Policy Press.

Peters, T. and Waterman, R. H. (1982). *In search of excellence: Lessons from America's best-run companies*. New York: Harper and Row.

Powell, A. and Davies, H. (2012). The struggle to improve professional boundaries. *Social Science and Medicine*, 75(5): 807–814.

Reah, T. and Hinings, C. (2009). Managing the rivalry of competing institutional logics. *Organization Studies*, 30(6): 629–652.

Roethlisberger, F. J. and Dickson, W. J. (1947). *Management and the worker*. Cambridge, MA: Harvard University Press.

Schein, E. H. (1985). *Organizational culture and leadership*. San Francisco, CA: Jossey Bass.

Scott, T., Mannion, R., Marshall, M., and Davies, H. (2003). Does organizational influence health care performance? A review of the evidence. *Journal of Health Services Research and Policy*, 8(2): 105–117.

Shortell, S. M., Marsteller, J. A., Lin, M., Pearson, M. L., Wu, S. Y., Mendel, P., Cretin, S., and Rosen, M. (2004). The role of perceived team effectiveness in improving chronic illness care. *Medical Care*, 42(11): 1040–1048.

Siehl, C. and Martin, J. (1990). Organizational culture: A key to financial performance? In *Organizational climate and culture*, ed. Schneider, B., pp. 146–155. San Francisco, CA: Jossey-Bass.

Smircich, L. (1983). Concepts of culture and organizational analysis. *Administrative Science Quarterly*, 28: 339–358.

Van der Post, W., de Coning, J., and Smit, E. (1997). An instrument to measure organizational culture. *South African Journal of Business Management*, 28(4): 147–168.

Van Maanen, J. and Barley, S. (1985). Cultural organization: Fragments of a theory. In *Organizational culture*, ed. Frost, P., Moore, M., and Louis, C., pp. 31–35. Beverley Hills, CA: Sage.

Waring, J., Rowley, E., Dingwall, R., Palmer, C., and Murcott, T. (2010). A narrative review of the UK patient safety research portfolio. *Journal of Health Services Research and Policy*, 15(1): 26–32.

Weil, T. (2010). Hospital mergers: A panacea? *Journal of Health Services Research and Policy*, 15(4): 251–253.

Wildercom, C., Glunk, U., and Mazlowski, R. (2000). Organizational culture as a predictor of organizational performance. In *Handbook of organizational culture and climate*, ed. Ashkanasey, C., Wilderom, J., and Peterson, M., pp. 193–209. Thousand Oaks, CA: Sage.

Williams, R. (1983). *Keywords: A vocabulary of culture and society*. New York: Oxford University Press.

CHAPTER 5

THE CRITICAL HEALTH CARE MANAGEMENT DOMAIN

MARTIN KITCHENER AND RICHARD THOMAS

INTRODUCTION

THE management of health care organizations faces an unprecedented set of challenges. These include state fiscal crises, demographic shifts, and rising demand for services stemming, in part, from the increased prevalence of chronic conditions. In response, many governments have encouraged health care organizations to adopt the discourse, strategies, and practices of the so-called "new public management" (NPM). The ensuing "reform" and "modernization" programs have included combinations of: privatization, corporatization, performance management, marketization, and changing roles for professionals, managers, and patients (Hujala, Laulainen, and Lindberg, 2014). This set of conditions has created both the need for critical scholarship (teaching and research) in health care management, and a fertile context within which it can be can be conducted.

Despite the promising context, and a history of notable achievements, health care management scholarship suffers from two main weaknesses. First, it is generally conservative in its objectives, its definitions of appropriate subjects, and in the knowledge that is produced. With attention directed towards finding ways of getting more work done for less money, as in other management fields a "booming silence" has shrouded significant organizational phenomena such as: exploitation, surveillance, manipulation, subordination, and sexuality (Hearn and Parkin, 1995, 4). Second, the relevance of health care management scholarship is questioned both by academics, and by the practitioners who are generally the focus of the work (Alexander et al., 2007).

Blame for the twin weaknesses of health care management scholarship must be shared amongst its sponsors, publishers, and producers. Its sponsors (researcher funders and the employers of teachers) have, as in other areas of management enquiry, tended to privilege theoretical perspectives that "support dominant discourses that are: prescriptive, positivist, managerial, functionalist and strategic" (Keegan and

Boselie, 2006, 1506). Globally, the major funders of health care management research, and the general approach to research and development are both oriented towards uncritical acceptance of managerialist literature (Learmonth, 2003). At the same time, although the primary purpose of social scientific scholarship in health care management should be to *explain* focal phenomena, many (journalistic) qualitative and (under-theorized) quantitative studies have contented themselves with description (Schofield, 2001). It is possible, here, only to speculate that the causes of this condition may include some combination of: failures to appreciate the potential of critical perspectives, acceptance of managerial ideology (Anthony, 1986), and acceptance of the role researchers as "servants of power" (Baritz, 1960). Whatever the causes, while the problems have been recognized for more than ten years (Learmonth, 2003), less progress is evident in health care management than in proximate fields such as general management and public sector management (Currie, Lockett, and Suhomlinova, 2009; Hujala, Laulainen, and Lindberg, 2014).

To address these problems, this chapter outlines the development of a domain of critical health care management (CHMS) scholarship, offers an articulating framework, and specifies an agenda for its development. The chapter is presented in three main parts. We begin by arguing that a more critical approach to health care management scholarship is required in order to shift mainstream work from its currently narrow, managerialist and performance-obsessed state towards a more vibrant, diverse, and relevant condition. In the second part, we extend the work of Delbridge (2010) and Burawoy (2004) to develop an articulation of CHMS as a distinctive domain within health care management scholarship. We then review progress in developing CHMS in terms of the four main concerns of critical management enquiry: (a) questioning the taken-for-granted, (b) moving beyond instrumentalism and assumptions of performativity, (c) a concern for reflexivity and meanings in research, and (d) challenging structures of domination. We conclude by discussing barriers to progress and presenting an agenda for the development of the CHMS domain.

THE MURMUR OF CRITICAL HEALTH CARE MANAGEMENT SCHOLARSHIP

Over the last 15 years, critical approaches have flourished in many areas of social scientific scholarship, including general management, to the extent that they have now become a "fully-fledged tradition" (Clegg, Dany, and Grey, 2011, 272). While the pace of development might have slowed recently, the upward trajectory is reflected in the burgeoning size of the annual Critical Management Studies Conference. To explore the state of health care management scholarship we conducted two sets of internet searches. The first addressed the outputs of research scholarship in terms of published papers, books, and conference presentations. The second concerned the impact of critical perspectives within health care management teaching in terms of the content of leading taught programs and textbooks.

Our search of research outputs was conducted in four stages: (i) health services journals, (ii) leading management journals, (iii) research books, and (iv) conference papers. The first search comprised 18 leading health care research journals including: *Health Services Management Research, Health Affairs, Social Science and Medicine, and Milbank Quarterly.*[1] We used a range of search terms including: "critical management," "critical research," and "critical investigation."[2] Disregarding papers on themes such as critical care, we identified a pool of 329 papers that contained elements of critical health care management. This represents less than 1% of total scholarship within the field, which we estimate to comprise around 42,000 articles published over the last 25 years, and even longer in the case of some journals. Perhaps most surprisingly, we found only nine critical health care management papers within the *International Journal of Health Services*, which exists to stimulate "debates about the most controversial issues of the day."

Our second search of research outputs comprised nine leading organization and management journals (e.g., *Organizational Studies, Academy of Management Journal*).[3] This surfaced fewer than a dozen examples of critical health care management papers. In both this and the first search category, most contributions came from the UK, with Nordic countries supplying a growing contribution. In our third search, for books, among the few on critical health care management we identified the most notable as Learmonth and Harding's (2004) ground-breaking edited collection, and Currie et al.'s (2009) edited collection of critical approaches in public services, which includes four cases from health care.

Our finding of very limited published research in critical health care management is supported by Ferlie et al.'s (2012) systematic review of the health care knowledge mobilization literature which found that critical perspectives were displayed in only 6% of relevant papers in management journals, 2% of papers in health journals and 1% of sources in health databases (within a total of 684 sources). Despite the limited development of critical approaches in health care management research, Ferlie et al. (2012, 1302) contend that:

---

[1] The full list of journal titles searched was *Health Care Management Review, Journal of Health Organization and Management, Journal of Health Services Research & Policy, Health Services Research, Social Science & Medicine, Sociology of Health & Illness, International Journal of Health Services, Milbank Quarterly, British Medical Journal, Critical Social Policy, Health Care Analysis, Health Policy, Health Services Management Research, International Journal of Health Planning and Management, Journal of Management in Medicine, Policy and Politics, Public Administration,* and *Public Money and Management.*

[2] The full list of search terms was. ... "critical management," "critical discourse," "critical lens," "critical research," "critical inquiry"/"critical enquiry," "critical investigation," "critical study," "critical scrutiny," "critical exploration," "critical examination," and "critical reflection."

[3] These journal titles were: *Academy of Management Review, Administrative Science Quarterly, The Academy of Management Journal, British Journal of Management, Human Relations, Journal of Management Studies, Organization, Organization Studies,* and *Sociology.*

Critical perspectives—especially labor process and Foucauldian perspectives—explain why many knowledge management systems fail in health care. The importance of power contests among occupational groups in health systems makes it appropriate to temper positivistic and technical approaches to knowledge management with scepticism.

Given the infancy of critical health care management scholarship, work of this type may be currently under refinement as conference presentations. To assess this in our final examination of research outputs, we searched abstracts from the biennial International Organization Behavior in Health Care Conferences (OBHC) for 2010, 2012, and 2014. We found fewer than 20 papers with a critical management approach. It is interesting to note that critical perspectives in health management were first given a dedicated plat-form, not at a health services conference, but rather at a stream of the 2013 annual Critical Management Studies Conference, from which selected papers later formed a special edi-tion of *Journal of Health Organization and Management* (Hujala, Laulainen, and Lindberg, 2014). A similar stream was planned for the 2015 CMS conference, but it did not occur.

It is in the classroom "that CMS meets actual, future or aspiring managers" (Clegg, Dany, and Grey, 2011, 272). Consequently, in order to assess the extent to which such approaches have influenced scholarship within health care management teaching pro-grams, we searched the online course descriptors for 23 specialist postgraduate pro-grams in leading academic providers in North America and the UK. Our main finding was that the word "critical" appeared only in relation to only four courses: MSc Health Management (City University, UK); MSc Health Policy, Planning and Financing (London School Hygiene & Tropical Medicine, UK); MRes Applied Health Research (Leicester University, UK); MSc Health & Social Care (Nottingham University, UK). Beyond the leading providers, an innovative example is the MSc management devel-opment program based on a critical (empowerment culture) perspective at Bangor University, UK (Sambrook, 2010). On the basis that Master's programs may often be taught by textbooks, our scrutiny of the indexes of 35 leading textbooks from the UK (e.g., Walshe and Smith, 2011) and USA (e.g., Burns, Bradley, and Weiner, 2012) revealed that "critical" in the appropriate context appeared only appeared once in a relevant con-text in any index. Indeed, the passage referenced as "critical reflection" by Walshe and Smith (2011, 407) resonates strongly with our understanding of critical management studies, but remains the only example we identified.

Overall, however, whilst the booming silence around critical approaches to health care management teaching and research has been punctuated, it is only by a murmur.

CRITICAL SCHOLARSHIP AS A DOMAIN OF HEALTH CARE MANAGEMENT

Just as we are concerned here with the conservatism and limited relevance of health care management scholarship, Burawoy's (2004) analysis of sociology focused on the divide between "ivory tower" professionals and their publics. As a means of framing this tension, Burawoy constructed a typology of disciplinary "domains." The domains emerge from answers to two fundamental questions through which researchers "can problematize our place in society": First, for whom is knowledge produced? And second, to what ends will that knowledge be used? Burawoy specifies the first question as, "If we are going to talk to others, which others and how shall we do it?" and differentiates between academic and extra-academic audiences (Burawoy, 2004, 1606). In addressing the second question, Burawoy draws on Weber to distinguish between technical rationality and value rationality, either or both of which might underpin the production of knowledge. Burawoy (2004, 1606) explains:

> Do we take the values and goals of our research for granted, handed down to us by some external (funding or policy) agency? Should we only concentrate on providing solutions to predefined problems, focusing on the means to achieve predetermined ends, on what Weber called technical rationality and what I shall call instrumental knowledge? In other words, should we repress the question of ends and pretend that knowledge and laws spring spontaneously from the data, if only we can develop the right methods? Or should we be concerned explicitly with the goals for which our research may be mobilized, and with the values that underpin and guide our research? ... Like Weber, I believe that without value commitments there can be no sociology, no basis for the questions that guide our research programs. Without values social science is blind. We should try to be clear about those values by engaging in what Weber called value discussion, leading to what I will refer to as reflexive knowledge.

Following Delbridge's (2010) work in the field of critical human resource management, we believe that: (a) Burawoy's identification of the values of research presents a useful starting point in the articulation of a domain of critical health care management, and (b) it is productive to use Burawoy's distinctions between types of knowledge (instrumental/reflexive) and different audiences (academic/extra-academic) to elaborate a typology of health care management scholarship. Whilst we represent our typology in Table 5.1, it is important to remember that Burawoy stresses that each of the resulting four domains will have sub-components ("fractals"), and they are not distinct. Rather, they are reciprocally interdependent and the "the flourishing of each depends on the flourishing of all."

It makes sense in explaining our typology to begin with the domain of professional studies of health care management (top right quadrant) because it: (a) provides the basis for the other forms, and (b) is the domain of mainstream academic enterprise. As in proximate fields, such as sociology and human resource management, the professional domain of health care management is shaped by norms of socially constructed "scientific legitimacy" and peer influence. In health care management, this mainstream tends to assume superordinate, managerially-determined corporate goals, and the autonomy of managers in individual organizations. Two leading US researchers illustrate this domain perfectly in one of the field's leading journals:

Table 5.1 Domains of Health Care Management Studies

	Academic audience	Extra-academic audience
Instrumental knowledge	Professional studies	Policy studies
• Knowledge	Theoretical/empirical	Concrete
• Legitimacy	Scientific norms	Effectiveness
• Accountability	Peers	Clients/patrons
• Pathology	Self-referentiality	Servility
• Politics	Professional self interest	Policy intervention
• Exemplar	Blumenthal and Their (2003)	Clarke et al. (2007)
Reflexive knowledge	Critical studies	Public studies
• Knowledge	Foundational	Communicative
• Legitimacy	Moral vision	Relevance
• Accountability	Critical intellectuals	Designated publics
• Pathology	Dogmatism	Faddishness
• Politics	Internal debate	Public dialogue
• Exemplar	Learmonth (2003)	Pollock (2004)

Developed from Burawoy (2004) and Delbridge (2010)

we assume that managers (and indeed other employees) in most health care organizations seek to improve the performance of those organizations and that they generally value and try to use valid information on ways to enhance that performance. In other words, managers behave, within limits, as rational decision-makers with goals in mind.... Consistent with this perspective, we define management research to be "systematic inquiry that is designed to affect decisions, actions, and results of organizational leaders, that uses recognized scientific methods, and that results in peer-reviewed publications or work of comparable quality (Blumenthal and Their, 2003, 366).

This mainstream approach of the professional domain typically gives limited attention to the contests and contexts of health care settings. Instead, it concentrates on demonstrating the performance effects of management practices such as quality improvement initiatives. Learmonth (2003) identified (what can be seen as) two main fractals of this professional domain. The first is labeled "for management" and comprises studies of the introduction of "new" managerial practices into health care such as business process re-engineering (Packwood, Pollitt, and Roberts, 1998). Some of this work, whilst not adopting a critical lens explicitly, does take context more seriously than is typical within managerial texts (Pettigrew, Ferlie, and McKee, 1992). The second fractal of the professional health care management domain can be labeled "about management" and comprises explorations of health care managers' worlds. Some of this work has drawn from social theory, rather than management theory. A classic example is Schofield's (2001) application of labor process theory within an ethnographic analysis of bureaucrats' obedient behavior. Sitting somewhere between these two fractals of the professional health care management domain, a distinct body of work examines the ongoing power struggle between management and the medical profession. The contribution of sociologists to this work has ensured a critical flavor and it is in this area of health care research that Marxian analyses have possibly had their greatest influence in the US and Europe (McKinlay and Arches, 1985; Harrison, 2009; Adler and Kwon, 2013; Andri and Kyriakidou, 2014).

In contrast to the domain of professional health care management scholarship, the public and policy domains speak explicitly to audiences beyond academia. Policy studies typically arise from specific "problems" defined by a client. Here, the relationship can be seen as "instrumental" in cases where the researcher does not define the research. In a distinctive health care fractal that overlaps with the proximate field of public administration scholarship, considerable attention has been given to the development and implications of the NPM agenda that brought more private sector management practices into health care settings (Pollitt, 1993). The work of John Clarke and Janet Newman has provided a critical dimension to this fractal through their exploration of themes including: changing professional-management relations; alterations to the relationship between social (equity) and economic (efficiency) ends; (re)casting citizens as consumers; and the increasing emphasis on leadership (Clarke et al., 2007).

A second fractal of the health care management policy domain comprises inductive "policy ethnographies" in which health service managers and policy makers are approached as experts on management, rather than as sources of data for theory building (Strong and Robinson, 1990, 8). Whilst less managerialist in approach than much of the professional health care management domain, the policy ethnographies fractal tends to be based on a priori assumptions about what managers and policy makers do, or should do, rather than from empirical work. In contrast, Aldrich, Zwi, and Short (2007) employ critical discourse analysis to examine how values and beliefs communicated by Australian politicians have shaped decades of policies and outcomes for Aboriginals.

Public studies of health care management operate in the domain of "public intellectualism" and engage audiences beyond the academy in dialogue on matters of political and moral concern. Allyson Pollock—the very epitome of the public intellectual—has adopted a radical approach in her writing and broadcasting on the privatization of the National Health Service (NHS) (e.g., Pollock, 2004). Her powerful analyses explains to a wide audience how the speed and direction of change is concealed by the rhetoric of "modernization" and "choice," and by the complexity of privatization mechanisms such as Private Finance Initiative (PFI). As Burawoy warns, such "public" forms of academic work must be relevant without falling into the trap of faddishness and subservience to publics (Burawoy, 2004).

Acknowledging the achievements of sociological scholarship across the other three domains, Burawoy argues that it is the public domain that sociologists need to develop. In contrast, we believe that health care management scholarship needs to develop the critical domain to reduce its conservatism and improve relevance. Critical studies in health care management, as in other fields, should provide the critique that is necessary to counterbalance the pathologies of the other forms of studies. In acting as "the conscience" of professional studies (Burawoy, 2004, 1609), the critical domain should examine the implicit and explicit, normative and descriptive foundations of professional studies. It should also consider the values under which policy studies are conducted, and the moral commitments of public research. Early contributions to this domain are reviewed in the next section.

Following Delbridge (2010), we argue that Burawoy's domains of intellectual labor give a framework through which the twin weaknesses of health care management research—conservatism and limited relevance—can be assessed and suggestions developed for how they might be addressed. His explicit reference to the audience for which knowledge is produced provides a basis for evaluating the engagement of researchers with the various stakeholders in health care management. The issue of the ends to which health care management teaching and research is put raises the further question of what has become termed "impact," particularly in higher education and in debates about the "value" of research. While distinct from the focus of Burawoy's primary concerns, his expectation that knowledge will be used anticipates that it will have impact in some form. This speaks directly to our charge of the irrelevance of much health care management research. Beyond the twin concerns of for whom knowledge is produced and to what purposes it may be used, we can extend our consideration to build further reflection on related matters regarding the assumptions that underpin research, the types of research conducted, the topics under investigation, and the forms of knowledge that are produced. For inspiration on how this agenda might be developed in health care management, the next section draws from the proximate field of critical management studies.

Building CHMS from Critical Management Studies

Whilst we acknowledge that the development of the critical health care management domain could benefit from the intellectual resources of multiple social science fields (including policy studies, the sociology of work and organizations, and industrial relations), we concentrate here on the work conducted under the label "critical management studies" (CMS).

CMS is a broad church that has an agenda that directly confronts health care management scholarship's weaknesses of conservatism and irrelevance (Adler, Forbes, and Willmott, 2007). At base, CMS aims to offer alternative ways to see the world by questioning and re-imagining management (Lancione and Clegg, 2014, 1). Research in this tradition is typically undertaken with the intention to alter management practices and organizational systems. Although that aspiration has rarely been achieved, CMS exists, in part, to "show that the world does not have to be the way it is" (Burawoy, 2004, 1612). As a result, critical management research seeks to provide analysis and explanation that connects questions of power with issues of "efficiency" that extend beyond standard managerial definitions. Beyond this (largely) shared mission of CMS scholars, the church houses a wide (and sometimes competing) range of ontological and epistemological approaches. Celebrating this plurality, Delbridge (2010) identifies four key themes within CMS: (a) the questioning of the taken-for-granted; (b) moving beyond instrumentalism and assumptions of performativity; (c) the concern for reflexivity, and meanings in research; (d) and the challenging of structures of domination. Below, we briefly introduce these themes and review extant contributions within health care management scholarship.

Questioning the Taken-for-Granted

CMS exists to challenge the assumptions and conventions of managerialist thinking (Fotaki and Hyde, 2014). In this regard, it meets the defining criterion of Burawoy's critical domain, it questions the purpose and effects of management, and it problematizes assumptions of managers as experts holding legitimate positions of authority. By challenging unitarist assumptions of shared corporate goals and functionalist concerns with efficiency, CMS focuses on the power relations in organizations, making transparent the inequalities of such roles, and questioning the rationales and consequences of such conventions. From the outset of this tradition, scholars such as Fox (1974) rejected conventional views that technologies and organizations develop in ways that are necessary or appropriate to the demands of the "neutral" economic conditions of the time. Fournier and Grey (2000, 18) describe this as the "unmasking" of mainstream management theory, which has constructed particular versions of appropriateness while obscuring these in a language of science, rationality, and "naturalness."

CMS challenges the *apparent* neutrality of the language and value bases of mainstream management theory and practice (Hasselbladh and Kallinikos, 2000; Adler, Forbes, and Willmott, 2007). Just as Burawoy's (2004, 1609) typology advocates discussions of "knowledge for whom and knowledge for what?," critical theorists hold that knowledge and its creation is not neutral. Moreover, the CMS project of "denaturalization" includes surfacing the partiality of managers and researchers (Jermier, 1998). In a rare example in health care, Learmonth (2005a) follows Derrida to reflect on the use of language within contests between health care managers and administrators, by viewing language as the grounds, the objects, and the means through which all power struggles are fought. He later reflects on how his experience as a NHS manager leads him to challenge the received wisdom that better management is, by definition, a good thing. Instead, he argues that better management may be only unconditionally "better" for a few people. Such considerations are particularly prescient in current policy contexts where academic researchers are expected to show the value of their research to society on the basis of its (economic) impact. As Burawoy's framework helps make explicit, researchers must work hard to ensure that their agendas are not captured/diverted by sponsors.

Whilst the CMS theme of "Questioning the Taken-for-Granted" has been given limited attention within health care management research, three lines of enquiry have been opened up. First, some authors have challenged assumptions including the "inevitabil-ity" of globalization and its consequences, and the dominance of "market forces." The lead was taken in the pioneering work of Pollitt (1993) whose neo-Marxist argument surfaces ideological aspects of managerialism in health care. For him, the transfer of managerialism from private sector corporations to welfare state services:

> sounds sober, neutral, as unopposable as virtue itself ... better management provides the label under which private sector disciplines can be introduced to the public ser-vices, political control can be strengthened, budgets trimmed professional auton-omy reduced, public service unions weakened and a quasi-competitive framework erected to flush out the 'natural' inefficiencies of bureaucracies (Pollitt, 1993, 49).

This theme has been pursued in Currie, Waring, and Finn's (2008, 382) empirical work which finds that "inappropriately imported models of private sector manage-ment ... are ill suited for the complexities and cultures of the NHS." Dickinson and Sullivan (2014) also follow this tradition of challenging the taken-for-granted by applying a critical approach to the issue of collaborative performance; a topic that is most commonly assumed to be "good." A parallel line of work adopts a Foucauldian approach to concentrate on dynamics among organizational power relations, profes-sional autonomy, and workforce resistance. A good example is provided by Doolin's (2004) examination of electronic knowledge management systems in health care organizations as they extend central surveillance over clinical work practices, pro-voking clinical resistance.

Among the few studies that have challenged the assumption of the political neutral-ity of health care organizations, Kitchener and Leca's (2009) empirical analysis explains how US nursing home corporations strategically used the institutional logic of share-holder value to help create a new organizational form (the large chain). Using a critical realist framework, they identified five mechanisms employed and justified by the insti-tutional logic of shareholder value: rapid growth of large chains through debt-financed mergers, labor cost control through low nurse staffing levels, creative financing, view-ing legal sanctions as a cost of business, and intense political activity. In sharp contrast to mainstream accounts of health care corporate behavior, this analysis poses serious questions about the relationship between the public good and private health care cor-porations that provide care to the some of the frailest and most vulnerable members of society (Kitchener et al., 2008).

In the second stream of "more questioning" health care management scholarship, work has begun to problematize dominant research conventions including those of apparent value and language neutrality and objectivity. In an early example, McDonald (2004) shows how the deployment of the term "empowerment" within managerial discourse could be seen as a form of oppression while masquerading as liberation. Similarly, MacEachen, Polzer, and Clarke (2008) employ critical discourse analysis to challenge mainstream accounts of "workforce flexibility" initiatives as improving the work-life balance of subordinates. Interviews with managers and subordinates reveal how the discourse of flexibility and the work practices it fosters makes possible and reinforce work intensification.

Third, some researchers have sought to evaluate and explain the implications of managerial "best practices," such as Lean and re-engineering, by unpacking and interrogating the objectives of managers and providing an understanding of the contextual circumstances of the introduction and operation. This again requires the recognition of the plurality of interests and potential for conflict within health care organizations, and it places control at the centre of understanding and explaining health care management. In an early example, McLaughlin (2004) examines evidence-based medicine (EBM) as a previously unquestionable mantra of health professionals. In her analysis, she deconstructs "evidence" and "knowledge" as discursive constructions to show that EBM is not a neutral tool to direct change. Rather, it should be seen as a social product whose meanings are embedded in power relations. In a similar vein, but drawing on a rare ethnographic study of a German hospital, Beil-Hilderbrand (2005) applies labor process theory to challenge the taken-for-granted nature of a corporate culture change initiative amongst nurses. In contrast to mainstream accounts of the managerial objectives of cultural change process being realized through shared values and employee participation, this study demonstrates features of increased managerial control and work intensification. The key message is that health care management researchers should make better use of critical approaches such as labor process theory to challenge the way that cultural change initiatives are explored and described by researchers and practitioners.

Waring and Bishop (2010) present an analysis of the implementation of Lean service redesign methodologies in one NHS hospital's operating department. Mainstream accounts emphasize that Lean, as a popular management "technology," is useful in pursuing the espoused managerial goals of reducing waste in health care. In contrast, this ethnographic study examines the way Lean is: (a) interpreted and articulated (rhetoric), (b) enacted in social practice (ritual), and (c) experienced in the context of prevailing lines of power and resistance. The findings illustrate how, contra the espoused goals, Lean follows a line of service improvements that bring to the fore tensions between clinicians and service leaders around the social organization of health care work.

In a similar vein, Finn, Learmonth, and Reedy (2010) draw on ethnographic studies of an operating theatre and a medical-records department to explore teamwork practices of NHS staff. In contrast to the evangelical exaltation of teamworking as "essential" for safe, efficient, and patient-centered care, this research examines how teamwork plays out in practice as an "identity discourse." Inspired by Fox's (1966) argument that teamworking may form an aspect of managerial ideology that can be used to dupe workers (through association with notions of belonging and membership) into aligning with elite interests, this work reveals how NHS teamwork discourse is instrumentally co-opted in the reproduction of the very occupational divisions it is espoused to ameliorate. In a similar fashion, Martin and Learmonth's (2012) study of managerial attempts to introduce dispersed leadership and networks into the NHS shows how endemic organizational and professional boundaries mean that managerial ideology can be just as much an impediment as a virtue to the spread of service reforms.

Beyond Instrumentalism and Performative Intent

A second distinctive contribution of CMS arises from the way in which it has taken the wider field of management studies to task for instrumental and performative predilections. A critical domain in health care management would challenge the emphasis given to material, and in particular, financial measurements of inputs and outputs and encourage a wider range of issues and outcomes to be considered. Dixon-Woods et al. (2012) illustrate the value of this approach in their ethnographic study of data reported to a managerialist patient safety program. Similarly, Waring's (2009) study shows how the definition and control of risks in patient safety has steadily moved from the localized and tacit domains of professional practice, to become an explicit and rationalized feature of management intervention that seeks to establish objective knowledge around clinical risk. This critical approach concludes that rather than seeing this managerial system as purely an objective and instrumental method of raising quality and controlling risk, it also has the capacity to re-order and better control the work of health care professionals.

Neo-Marxist accounts have also been offered on specific issues such as the commodification of health care in Western nations (Henderson and Petersen, 2002), and Turkish dentistry (Ocek and Vatansever, 2014). Typically this stream of research concentrates on ways on which the imposition of market mechanisms into health care systems produces outcomes including the loss of professional autonomy and the adoption of business-like practices by health care professionals.

Reflexivity, Meaning, and Difference

It was noted earlier that CMS houses a broad collection of researchers with assorted interests, research methods, philosophical assumptions about the nature of the social world they are researching (ontology), and ideas about how knowledge of that world may be acquired (epistemology). As Burawoy (2004) notes, such plurality, and even its attendant conflicts, can be a productive source of advances in theorizing and understanding. CMS has shown that for this to be achieved, however, explicit and reflexive (taking account of itself) consideration must be given to researchers' epistemological, methodological, and ontological positions. Herepath and Kitchener (2015) present one of the first major funded studies of health care management to apply a critical realist philosophy of social science across study inception, design, fieldwork, analysis, and writing. In conceptual terms, they develop an innovative framework that harnesses realist social theory and institutional theory to forward a view of "situated context" as stratified, conditioned, relational, and temporally dynamic. In empirical terms, this frames an explication of the fundamental role of beliefs and values—*institutional logics*—within contested processes of practice elaboration or reproduction.

In a rare journal paper in which health care management researchers consider reflexivity, Greenhalgh et al. (2009) illuminate and challenge the way that researchers think about the introduction of a managerial innovation; in their case, electronic patient records (EPR). Using a meta-narrative method, they show that the apparently conflicting findings of previous EPR research can be usefully expressed as tensions and paradoxes relating to the nature of the EPR initiative, the context in which it is implemented and used, and the way "success" is defined and pursued.

This theme of "reflexivity, meaning and difference" within CMS has clear relevance for health care management research. In this field, whilst some critics have bemoaned the dominance of positivism and quantitative research methods (see Greenhalgh et al., 2009), there is no necessary assumption that any particular approaches and methods might be found in the critical domain outlined here. Rather, what will be required is an explicit reflection upon the limitations and implications of any research approach and the recognition that the currently dominant paradigm presents a naturalizing discourse around positivism and "scientific methods" that must be unpacked and examined. That said, much CMS is founded on qualitative research approaches that seek to get close to a subject of study and make sense of the social phenomena under investigation on the terms of the research participants. This allows greater access to understanding of the historical and context of management practices and their unpredictable and emergent properties. Dar (2008) advocates and illustrates how poststructuralist and discursive approaches can be of value in understanding the development of health care management as a social construct. Kreindler et al. (2012) illustrate the use of social identity theory as a way of understanding and overcoming divisions among occupational groups in health care. Meanwhile, in revealing the socioeconomic conditions of health care organizations and through describing aggregate patterns of developments, survey work will have its place. CHRM researchers will also become familiar with the challenges of interpreting micro-level observational data in their wider contexts and in seeking to explain more macro levels of activity on the basis of the analysis of micro-data.

While CMS is imbued with self-reflection (Clegg, Dany, and Grey, 2011), the issue of reflexivity has typically been neglected within the field of health care management education. As Davies (2006) argues, academic and vocation programs should increasingly include reflexive consideration of the context for practice, research awareness, and managerial ideology and skills. Sambrook (2010) reports on an early response to Davies' call with an evaluation of an MSc management development program based on a critical (empowerment culture) perspective. Early participant evaluations from the program suggest that the critical pedagogy employed does help NHS managers to better understand issues of power and to challenge dominant cultures.

Challenging Structures of Domination

Because mainstream health care management research tends to decontextualize, a critical domain is required to situate analysis in context and history. Jermier (1998) suggests that contextual/historical themes worthy of study include the misuse of power in society, and the resulting mistreatment of some individuals and groups. Within CMS, two approaches have emerged to deal with this issue. In the first, scholars advocate a radical commitment to change, which is expressly "anti-management." At its most radical, this perspective rejects engagement and discussion with managers and seeks to undermine and destabilize management through critique. From this perspective, notions of "better management" are rejected because: "the argument is that management is irredeemably corrupt since its activity is inscribed within performative principles which CMS seeks to challenge" (Fournier and Grey, 2000, 24). For some, this will display the dogmatic pathology of the critical domain as suggested by Burawoy (2004).

The second approach accepts notions of "better management"; generally understood in terms of it and its effects becoming less oppressive or socially divisive (Alvesson and Willmott, 1996). In this approach, there is a commitment to engagement *with* management practitioners in order to seek change and some form of transformation of systems and structures. For some, this view of management is inappropriate to certain managerial forms. For example, Harrington et al.'s (2011) study of the ten largest US for-profit nursing home chains demonstrates how they have systematically worked to maximize shareholder value through tactics including increasing occupancy rates, developing real estate investment trusts, reducing corporate taxes, and reducing liability risk. These findings demonstrate, at a minimum, the need for greater transparency in ownership and financial reporting, and for more government oversight.

Within the "better management approach," there is also recognition of the heterogeneity of "management" and that managers are themselves managed and thus subject to control and potential exploitation. The latter, often over-looked, issue is the subject of Macfarlane et al.'s (2011) study of senior NHS managers, which shows how they weather successive structural reorganizations through their emotional attachment to the ideals of NHS. For those health care management researchers who opt to engage with managers, the search for better management may provide the platform and orientation from which CHMS can aspire to relevance, "whilst simultaneously throwing off the conservative cloak of the mainstream" (Delbridge, 2010).

Contributing to the study of groups that are mistreated by health care management, Ford (2005) applies a feminist lens to examine the development of leadership in the NHS. She describes patriarchy as being at the heart of dominant thinking about leadership and suggests how shared ideas about leadership reinforce pervasive associations between men, power, and authority in health care organizations. Specifically, she shows how the technique of personality profiling perpetuates masculine ideals. For her, better management would require a wider range of workplace behaviors to be valued in the activities of senior managers.

Traynor (2004) adopts a poststructuralist approach to explore ways in which certain readings of organizational phenomenon become normalized and therefore dominant. Taking the nursing profession as another group that has been mistreated by health care management, Traynor argues that its recent history can be understood as a struggle for influence and credibility that has been pursued through the adoption of managerialism and evidenced-based practices. After surfacing the paradoxes in this story, he suggests alternative possibilities for the nursing profession to seek influence through, for example, building an intellectual identity based on feminist ideas. Ford's (2005) work suggests this may be optimistic under current conditions.

Homosexuals are shown to be a third group to be mistreated by health care organizations. Lee (2004) describes how: (a) ideals of the "good manager" are constructed around heterosexual norms, and (b) how such norms are pervasive, even among those gay managers and managers who provide services targeted to gay men. For Lee, better health care management would involve the de-coupling of ideals of good management from heterosexual norms.

Fotaki (2011) concentrates on patients as another marginalized group within mainstream health care management research. She argues that increased concern for economic efficiency under austerity has led health care management practice and research to emphasize issues of patient choice. Whilst some argue that this may redress power balances and help develop better services, it may also turn service users into customers or co-producers of care.

TOWARDS A LESS CONSERVATIVE AND MORE RELEVANT FUTURE

In this chapter we have reviewed the development of a critical domain of health care management scholarship, offered an articulating framework, and reviewed existing work. Following Delbridge (2010), we argue that Burawoy's typology of intellectual labor gives a framework through which the twin weaknesses of health care management scholarship—conservatism and irrelevance—can be assessed and addressed. Concern for the audience for which health care management knowledge is produced provides a useful basis for evaluating the engagement of scholars (researchers and teachers) with the various stakeholder groups including researchers, patients, and students. Concern for the ends to which the scholarship is put speaks to our charge of the irrelevance of much health care management scholarship. Beyond our articulating framework's twin concerns of for whom knowledge is produced and to what purposes it may be used, we now use it as a basis from which to reflect on related matters regarding the assumptions that underpin health care management scholarship, the types of work conducted, the topics under investigation, and the forms of knowledge that are produced.

Our review of the murmurs within the critical health care management domain recognizes that it will never provide a neat set of alternative ideas. However, for those who wish to establish a different political and intellectual domain, it presents a basis for less conservative and more relevant scholarship. Further development will require a more reflexive and constructive engagement between health care management practitioners, scholars, and others with related interests across the social science spectrum, in particular critical management studies. In our view, this will have implications for *both* mainstream and critical health care management scholars in terms of the work that they conduct and the manner in which they engage with various audiences.

Establishing a vibrant critical domain within health care management has not been, and is unlikely to be, straightforward. This may be in part because evidence from CMS indicates that scholars often feel that engagement comes at the expense of critique (Delbridge, 2014). Too much of the debate regarding academic relevance and the "impact of research" is currently being conducted in ignorance of Burawoy's crucial distinction between the policy domain—where researchers attend to a problem that has been defined by the sponsor—and the public domain which seeks to be relevant without subservience to any particular sponsor or interest group. In advocating that research be rigorous and relevant, it is important not to be seen to provide the context wherein only research projects deemed of "economic value" and conducted in response to the concerns of societal elites are considered legitimate. In pursuing engagement and relevance, critical health care management researchers must try to avoid being captured by their sponsors.

It must, however, be recognized that there are risks associated with speaking the truth to power. As Allyson Pollock (2004, 202–213) explains, research in health care management that is critical of elite interests (especially the State and large corporations) is hard to get financed, difficult to get published, and can expect systematic and vigorous challenge. Whilst it might be possible to withstand these pressures from the position of senior professor, there will continue to be safer career paths for junior academics. It is, therefore, necessary for the Academy (especially senior academics) to create safe havens for this activity to occur through, for example, funded research posts and dedicated conferences and tracks. In this spirit, the first author, as host, will chair a dedicated critical health care management track at the next biennial Organizational Behavior in Health Care (OBHC) Conference to be held in Cardiff in 2016.

For others in a position to help develop the critical domain of health care management, emphasis should be placed on the analysis and explanation of managerial practices, but in ways that acknowledge the multiple interests of public, policy, and professional stakeholders. This research agenda will require researchers and teachers to engage with a wider variety of organizational and institutional actors than is currently the case in mainstream research. These include: trade unionists, policy makers, charities and non-governmental organizations, professional bodies and associations, and lobbyists. In turn, the new challenges implied in this approach will require a diversity of theoretical lenses and a much broader range of topics will need to be studied. For example, whilst some analysts have explored the political activity of health care entities (Kitchener and Leca, 2009), developments including growth in the size and number of for-profit operators in fields such as UK elderly care present a real need for studies of corporate power and political influence in contemporary health care (Currie et al., 2012).

The required plurality in the critical health care management domain will need to be matched by new ways of engaging and debating within academic circles to ensure that positions do not remain fragmented and polarized. Put simply, CHMS will require changes in both whom health care management researchers talk with, and the form of reflexive engagement that is pursued. Rather than attempting synthesis or proposing a radical alternative—with the attendant danger that the debates are polarized and nothing productive emerges—Delbridge (2010) suggests following Janssens and Steyaert's (2009) R(econstructive)-reflexivity approach. This stands for reconstructing and reframing by bringing in alternative issues, perspectives, paradigms, and political values in order to illuminate the domain, and in particular draw attention to what has been marginalized or left out. From this view, in only resisting, the critical domain of health care management runs the risk of remaining within the existing frame and reinforcing the positivist research agenda in a reactive way. This may result in a failure to re-set that agenda and a concomitant inability to meaningfully contribute to the development of that field. In contrast, R-reflexivity "provides alternative descriptions, interpretations, vocabularies and voices that could be taken into account, aiming to open up new avenues, paths and lines of interpretations that produce 'better' research ethically, politically, empirically and theoretically" (Janssens and Steyaert, 2009, 144). This approach thus seeks to connect different perspectives rather than synthesizing or displacing one with another.

A key aspect of communicating the findings of critical health care management research must be their incorporation in educational programs ranging from the vocational to the academic. These are the vehicles that currently promote the dominant managerialist discourse. Thus, critical health care management scholars will need to disseminate their ideas and findings through educational materials in order to influence the normative development of both students and health care management professionals (Sambrook, 2010). Approaches to doing this may include publishing beyond traditional academic vehicles, dedicated textbooks and case studies, which are a particularly valuable way of bringing critical issues to life within "real-life" scenarios. Too often, the ways researchers engage with student and other stakeholders is overlooked or trivialized in discussions of how theoretically-informed research can have impact beyond academic audiences. Broader engagement with the full range of stakeholders in health care management is necessary for the development of a critical domain that is less conservative and more relevant.

REFERENCES

Adler, P., Forbes, L., and Willmott, H. (2007). Critical management studies: Premises, practices, problems and prospects. *Annals of the Academy of Management*, 1: 119–180.

Adler, P. and Kwon, S.-W. (2013). The mutation of professionalism as a contested diffusion process: Clinical guidelines as carriers of institutional change in medicine. *Journal of Management Studies*, 50(5): 930–962.

Aldrich, R., Zwi, A., and Short, S. (2007). Advance Australia fair: Social democratic and conservative politicians' discourses concerning Aboriginal and Torres Strait Islander peoples and their health, 1972–2001. *Social Science and Medicine*, 64: 125–137.

Alexander, J., Hearld, L., Jiang, J., and Fraser, I. (2007). Increasing the relevance of research to health care managers: Hospital CEO imperatives for improving quality and lowering costs. *Health Care Management Review*, 32(2): 150–159.

Alvesson, M. and Willmott, H. (eds) (1992). *Critical management studies.* London: Sage.

Alvesson, M. and Willmott, H. (1996). *Making sense of management: A critical introduction.* London: Sage.

Andri, M. and Kyriakidou, O. (2014). Professional autonomy under pressure: Towards a dialectical approach. *Journal of Health Organization and Management*, 28(5): 635–652.

Anthony, P. (1986) *The foundation of management.* London: Tavistock.

Baritz, L. (1960). *The servants of power: A history of the use of social science in American industry.* Middletown, CT: Wesleyan University Press.

Beil-Hilderbrand, M. (2005). Instilling and distilling a reputation for institutional excellence. *Journal of Health Organization and Management*, 19(6): 440–465.

Blumenthal, D. and Their, S. (2003). Improving the generation, dissemination and use of management research. *Health Care Management Review*, 28(4): 366–375.

Burawoy, M. (2004). Public sociologies: Contradictions, dilemmas, and possibilities. *Social Forces*, 82(4): 1603–1618.

Burns, L., Bradley, E., and Weiner, B. (2012). *Shortell and Kaluzny's Health Care Management: Organization Design and Behavior.* New York: Delmar.

Clarke, J., Newman, J., Smith N., Vidler, E., and Westmarland, L. (2007). *Creating citizen-consumers: Changing publics and changing public services.* London: Sage.

Clegg, S., Dany, F., and Grey, C. (2011). Introduction to the special issue critical management studies and managerial education: New contexts? New agenda? *M@n@gement*, 14(5): 271–279.

Currie, G., Ford, J., Harding, N., and Learmonth, M (eds) (2009). *Making public services management critical.* London: Routledge.

Currie, G., Dingwall, R., Kitchener, M., and Waring, J. (2012). Let's dance: Organizational studies, medical sociology and health policy. *Social Science and Medicine*, 74: 273–280.

Currie, G., Lockett, A., and Suhomlinova, O. (2009). The institutionalization of distributed leadership: A "Catch-22" in English public services. *Human Relations*, 62(11): 1735–1761.

Currie, G., Waring, J., and Finn, R. (2008). The limits of knowledge management for UK public services modernization: The case of patient safety and service quality. *Public Administration*, 86(2): 363–385.

Dar, S. (2008). Re-connecting histories, modernity, managerialism and development. *Journal of Health Organization and Management*, 22(2): 93–110.

Davies, S. (2006). Health services management education: Why and what? *Journal of Health Organization and Management*, 20(4): 325–334.

Delbridge, R. (2010). The critical future of HRM. In *Reassessing the employment relationship*, ed. Blyton, P., Heery, E., and Turnbull, P., pp. 21–42. Basingstoke: Palgrave Macmillan.

Delbridge, R. (2014). Promising futures: CMS, post-disciplinarity, and the new public social science. *Journal of Management Studies*, 51(1): 95–117.

Dickinson, H. and Sullivan, H. (2014). Towards a general theory of collaborative performance: The importance of efficacy and agency. *Public Administration*, (92)1: 161–177.

Dixon-Woods, M., Leslie, M., Bion, J., and Tarrant, C. (2012). What counts? An ethnographic study of infection data reported to a patient safety program. *Milbank Quarterly*, 90(3): 548–591.

Doolin, B. (2004). Power and resistance in the implementation of a medical management information system. *Information Systems Journal*, 14(4): 343–363.

Ferlie, E., Crilly, T., Jashapara, A., and Peckham, A. (2012). Knowledge mobilization in health care: A critical review of health sector and generic management literature. *Social Science and Medicine*, 74: 1297–1304.

Finn, R., Learmonth, M., and Reedy, P. (2010). Some unintended effects of teamwork in health care. *Social Science and Medicine*, 70(8): 1148–1154.

Ford, J. (2005). Examining leadership through critical feminist readings. *Journal of Health Organization and Management*, 19(3): 236–251.

Fotaki, M. (2011). Towards developing new partnerships in public services: Users as consumers, citizens and/or co-producers in health and social care in England and Wales. *Public Administration*, 89(3): 933–955.

Fotaki, M. and Hyde, P. (2014). Organizational blindspots: Counteracting splitting, idealization and blame in public health services. *Human Relations*, 68(3): 441–462.

Fournier, V. and Grey, C. (2000). At the critical moment: Conditions and prospects for critical management studies. *Human Relations*, 53(1): 7–32.

Fox, A. (1966). *Research papers 3: Industrial sociology and industrial relations*. London: HMSO.

Fox, A. (1974). *Beyond contract*. London: Faber and Faber.

Greenhalgh, T., Potts, H., Wong, G., Bark, P., and Swinglehurst, D. (2009). Tensions and paradoxes in electronic patient record research: A systematic literature review using the meta-narrative method. *The Milbank Quarterly*, 87(4): 729–788.

Harrington, C., Hauser, C., Olney, B., and Vallancourt-Roseau, P. (2011). Ownership, financing, and management strategies of the ten largest for-profit nursing home chains in the United States. *International Journal of Health Services*, 41(4): 725–746.

Harrison, S. (2009). Co-optation, commodification and the medical model: Governing UK medicine since 1991. *Public Administration*, 87(2): 184–197.

Hasselbladh, H. and Kallinikos, J. (2000). The project of rationalization: A critique and reappraisal of neo-institutionalism in organization studies. *Organization Studies*, 21(4): 697–720.

Hearn, J. and Parkin, W. (1995) *"Sex" at "work": The power and paradox of organizational sexuality*. London: Prentice Hall.

Henderson, S. and Petersen, A. (2002), Introduction. Consumerism in Health Care. In *Consuming health: The commodification of health care*, ed. Henderson, S. and Petersen, A., pp. 1–10. London: Routledge.

Herepath, A. and Kitchener, M. (2015). *Hospital patient safety: A realist analysis*. Southampton: National Institute for Health Research.

Hujala, A., Laulainen, S., and Lindberg, K. (2014). Powerless positions, silenced voices? Critical views on health and social care management. *Journal of Health Organization and Management*, 285: 590–600.

Janssens, M. and Steyaert, C. (2009). HRM and performance: A plea for reflexivity in HRM studies. *Journal of Management Studies*, 46(1): 143–155.

Jermier, J. (1998). Introduction: Critical perspectives on organizational control. *Administrative Science Quarterly*, 43: 235–256.

Keegan, A. and Boselie, P. (2006). The lack of impact of dissensus inspired analysis on developments in the field of human resource management. *Journal of Management Studies*, 43(7): 1492–1511.

Kitchener, M. and Leca, B. (2009). A critical realist analysis of change in the field of US nursing homes. In *Making public services management critical*, ed. Currie, G., Ford, J., Harding, N., and Learmont, M., pp. 148–172. London: Routledge.

Kitchener, M., O'Meara, J., Brody, A., Lee, H., and Harrington, C. (2008). Shareholder value and the performance of a large nursing home chain. *Health Services Research*, 43(3): 1062–1084.

Kreindler, S., Dowd, D., Star, N., and Gottschalk, T. (2012). Silos and social identity: The social identity approach as a framework for understanding and overcoming divisions in health care. *Milbank Quarterly*, 90(2): 347–374

Lancione, M. and Clegg, S. (2014). The lightness of management learning. *Management Learning*. Available at: <http://mlq.sagepub.com/content/early/2014/03/17/1350507614526533> (accessed February 9, 2015).

Learmonth, M. (2003). Making health services management research critical: A review and suggestion. *Sociology of Health and Illness*, 25(1): 93–119.

Learmonth, M. (2005a). Doing things with words: The case of "management" and Administration. *Public Administration*, 83(3): 617–637.

Learmonth, M. (2005b). Tales of the unexpected? Stirring things up in health care management. *Journal of Health Organization and Management*, 19(3): 181–188.

Learmonth, M. and Harding, N. (eds). (2004). *Unmasking health management: A critical text*. New York: Nova.

Lee, H. (2004). The public and private manager: Queer(y)ing health management. In *Unmasking health management: A critical text*, ed. Learmonth, M. and Harding, N., pp. 129–142. New York: Nova.

McDonald, R. (2004). Empowerment, modernisation and ethics: The shaping of individual identity in an English primary care trust. In *Unmasking health management: A critical text*, ed. Learmonth, M. and Harding, N., pp. 155–170. New York: Nova.

MacEachen, E., Polzer, J., and Clarke, J. (2008). You are free to set your own hours: Governing worker productivity and health through flexibility and resilience. *Social Science and Medicine*, 66: 1019–1033.

Macfarlane, F., Exworthy, M., Willmott, M., and Greenhalgh, T. (2011). Plus ca change, plus c'est la meme chose: Senior NHS managers' narratives of restructuring. *Sociology of Health and Illness*, 33(6): 914–929.

McKinlay, J. and Arches, J. (1985). Towards the proletarianization of physicians. *International Journal of Health Services*, 15(2): 161–195.

McLaughlin, J. (2004). Professional translations of evidence based medicine. In *Unmasking health management: A critical text*, ed. Learmonth, M. and Harding, N., pp. 75–91. New York: Nova.

Martin, G. and Learmonth, M. (2012). A critical account of the rise and spread of "leadership": The case of UK health care. *Social Science and Medicine*, 74(3): 281–288.

Ocek, Z. and Vatansever, K. (2014). Perceptions of Turkish dentists of their professional identity in a market-oriented system. *International Journal of Health Services*, 44(3): 593–613.

Packwood, T., Pollitt, C., and Roberts, S. (1998). Good medicine? A case study of business process re-engineering in a hospital. *Policy and Politics*, 26(4): 141–155.

Pettigrew, A., Ferlie, E., and McKee, L. (1992). *Shaping strategic change: Making change in large organizations: The case of the NHS*. London: Sage.

Pollitt, C. (1993). *Managerialism and the public services: Cuts or cultural change in the 1990s?*, 2nd edition. Oxford: Blackwell.

Pollock, A. (2004). *NHS PLC: The privatisation of our health care*. London: Verso.

Sambrook S. (2010). Critical pedagogy in a health service management development programme: Can "critically thinking" managers change the NHS management culture? *Journal of Health Organisation and Management*, 23 (6): 656–671.

Schofield, J. (2001). The old ways are the best? The durability and usefulness of bureaucracy in public sector management. *Organization*, 8(1): 77–96.

Strong, P. and Robinson, J. (1990) *The NHS under new management*. Milton Keynes: Open University.

Traynor, M. (2004). Nursing, managerialism and evidence based practice: The constant struggle for influence. In *Unmasking health management: A critical text*, ed. Learmonth, M. and Harding, N., pp. 117–128. New York: Nova.

Walshe, K. and Smith, J. (eds) (2011). *Health care management*. Maidenhead: Open University Press.

Waring, J. (2009). Critical risk management: Moral entrepreneurship in the management of patient safety. In *Making public services management critical*, ed. Currie, G., Ford, J., Harding, N., and Learmonth, M., pp. 95–113. London: Routledge.

Waring, J. and Bishop, S. (2010). Lean health care: Rhetoric, ritual and resistance. *Social Science and Medicine*, 71: 1332–1340.

PART II

PEOPLE IN HEALTH CARE ORGANIZATIONS: PATIENTS, PROFESSIONALS, AND LEADERS

CHAPTER 6

RE-HUMANIZING HEALTH CARE

Facilitating "Caring" for Patient-centered Care

CHERYL RATHERT, TIMOTHY J. VOGUS,
AND LAURA E. McCLELLAND

BACKGROUND

PATIENT-CENTERED care (PCC) has been emphasized by scholars and practitioners across the globe for decades, with interest ranging from policy at national and health system levels, to individual care at the bedside. Although there is no consensus on its specific definition, the concept seems to transcend national boundaries. While issues on the ground may vary by health system, most cultures across the globe aim to improve quality of care, patient safety, patient experiences, and as well, health care worker experiences and outcomes (Buttigieg et al., 2015). Although the majority of published PCC research originated in the West, we see a growing interest in PCC research worldwide as evidenced by the number of recent PCC studies from Asia, Australia, and Africa. A recent systematic review of PCC definitions (Scholl et al., 2014), examined 417 PCC studies and found that 54% of studies were conducted in the US, 15% in Canada, 15% in Europe, 4% in Australia or New Zealand, 3% in Asian countries, and 1% in South Africa. The authors conducting this study were from Germany. Further, some of the most influential work on the concept was conducted by authors in the United Kingdom (UK) (Mead and Bower, 2000). This global trend suggests that there may be something about therapeutic, caring relationships between patients and care providers that is inherently human, and should be kept in mind as health systems face the challenges of sustaining efficiency and quality while managing costs.

   As noted, there is no consensus on PCC's definition; however, it generally means that each patient should be treated with his or her values, preferences, and unique needs taken into consideration. Even with this emphasis, there has been no significant overall improvement in how patients and family members perceive the quality and patient-centeredness of the care they receive (Entwistle and Watt, 2013). Nor have objective indicators of patient safety (i.e., freedom from harm) improved in the 15 years since publication of the famous Institute of Medicine report, *To Err is Human* (IOM, 1999). This chapter will assess the current state of research on PCC. The major research question underpinning our review is, given all the focus on improving PCC, patient experiences, and patient safety, why do we observe so little improvement in patient health care experiences? What must be done to bring about sustainable PCC? This chapter will illustrate two key problems and identify two emerging solutions. First, there is little scholarly or practitioner consensus regarding what PCC is. Without a clear definition, it is virtually impossible to build a coherent body of research that contains valid, generalizable measures, clear linkages to outcomes, consistent processes by which PCC works, and appropriate recommendations for practice. Second, many organizations seek to implement a list of behaviors and processes that are "patient-centered," apparently in name only. We suggest two potential remedies evident in emerging work. First, refocus PCC from a specific set of tasks toward cultivating the development of healing relationships between patients and their care providers.[1] Second, move beyond expecting care providers to develop specific kinds of patient-centered skills, to providing the right kind of environment, one that supports both patients and care providers in developing and maintaining compassionate, therapeutic relationships.

THE PATIENT-CENTERED CARE CONCEPT

Here we discuss how PCC has been defined in the empirical literature. The Institute of Medicine (IOM) asserted PCC as a key aim for improving health care (IOM, 2001), and its definition has been one of the most widely adopted. It defined PCC as patients being informed decision-makers; care should be empathetic and compassionate; and should be responsive to the preferences, values, and needs of each patient. After years of scholars and practitioners studying and trying to implement PCC, Berwick (2009) went further and defined it as, "The experience (to the extent the individual patient desires it) of transparency, individualization, recognition, respect, dignity, and choice in all matters, without exception, related to one's person, circumstances, and relationships in health care" (w560). Unfortunately, few patients would likely say that their experiences have met these ideals. Historically, the idea of PCC came about as a way of deviating from

---

[1] In this chapter we use the term "care provider" to indicate any clinical professional who provides direct care to patients. We recognize that the medical, nursing, and allied health professionals have preferred terms for their own professions. In the interest of developing shared meaning for a wide audience, we have selected the term care provider to encompass all who provide clinical care to patients.

disease-, task-, and/or profession-centered approaches. However, in practice, implementation of PCC often simply individualizes the existing system for each patient, rather than actually transforming systems to become truly patient-centered (Epstein and Street, 2011; Hobbs, 2009).

PCC Concept Reviews

Several recent studies and literature reviews have examined how PCC has been defined in the empirical literature (Bergman and Connaughton, 2013; Hobbs, 2009; Robinson et al., 2008; Scholl et al., 2014). In an especially influential conceptual paper, Mead and Bower (2000) articulated the *therapeutic alliance* as being central to PCC. This alliance is based on the *relationship* between the care provider and patient, and emphasized a biopsychosocial perspective, that is, care providers considering the patient's full life in the patient–care provider relationship and in treatment plans. This includes socio-emotional connections, including communication of caring, empathy, and reassurance. The therapeutic alliance necessitates "empathy, congruence, and unconditional positive regard" (1090) on the part of care providers. While the traditional biomedical model of health care does not preclude a therapeutic alliance, it is not considered essential to quality care, as is proper diagnosis and treatment. Further, Mead and Bower (2000) emphasized that the care provider–patient relationship is dependent on attributes of the care provider as well, given that true patient-centeredness is a sharing of power and responsibility. In contrast, the traditional biomedical model assumes care providers are interchangeable, in that well-trained providers should be able to make an accurate diagnosis and treatment plan, and thus, education and training should remediate any variability across providers.

Later, Robinson et al.'s review (2008) examining the relationship between PCC and treatment adherence identified four perspectives: (1) public policy; (2) economic; (3) clinical; and (4) patient. The *public policy* perspective promotes the vision of what PCC should be, and is mostly based on the IOM's definitions. The *economic* perspective focuses on the idea of "consumerism" in health care; that is, consumers are now able to make much more informed choices for their care. The *clinical* perspective focuses specifically on the patient–provider relationship. With PCC, patients are more empowered in their interactions with health care providers, and their needs and goals are considered in treatment plans. A clear definition of the patient perception of PCC was not identified in the literature at that time in relation to adherence.

Hobbs conducted a systematic review (2009) that included 69 peer reviewed articles, with the aim of clarifying the PCC concept. She used "dimensional analysis," a sociological approach for clarifying phenomena and concepts. The studies were analyzed in terms of: (1) perspective; (2) context; (3) condition; (4) process; and (5) consequences. A key finding from Hobbs' (2009) analysis was that the most prominent *perspective* in the literature was that PCC involves "alleviating vulnerabilities experienced by the patient ..."(55). From patients' perspectives, an injury or illness not only involves physical and/or medical problems; but submitting to the health care system also threatens their individual identities. Some type of vulnerability is the whole reason patients seek care. Getting appropriate care in a timely manner can reduce vulnerabilities. In contrast, problems with access, inappropriate services, and being treated as a diagnosis instead of a person can exacerbate vulnerabilities (Entwistle and Watt, 2013). The top patient themes in Hobbs' (2009) analysis were "feeling alienated" and "lack of control" (55). An important point about the *conditions* dimension is the recognition that patients are heterogeneous in how they manifest a particular illness. The heterogeneity stems from demographic characteristics, culture, lifestyle choices, access to care, and other unique circumstances, consistent with the biopsychosocial dimension asserted by Mead and Bower (2000) and others. Accordingly, appropriate PCC requires practitioners to maintain a "therapeutic engagement" with each patient (Hobbs, 2009, 55). This includes: a caring presence; approaching the patient as an experiencing individual; and alleviating patient vulnerabilities.

Scholl et al. (2014) conducted a systematic review specifically to analyze definitions of PCC in the peer reviewed literature (417 studies through 2012). Their review found 15 dimensions, which they divided into three categories: (1) principles; (2) enablers; and (3) activities. *Principles* lay the foundations from which PCC can occur and include characteristics of clinicians; clinician–patient relationships; the patient as a unique person; and the biopsychosocial perspective. The researchers found that PCC requires clinicians to be respectful, empathetic, tolerant, compassionate, and they must build a committed, collaborative relationship with patients. Thus, clinicians need to get to know each patient. *Enablers* are "elements that foster PCC" (3) and include: (1) clinician–patient communication; (2) integration of medical and non-medical care; (3) teamwork and team building; (4) access to care; and (5) coordination and continuity of care. Finally, the *activities* category includes behaviors that produce PCC: (1) patient information; (2) patient involvement in care; (3) involvement of family and friends; (4) patient empowerment; (5) physical support; and (6) emotional support. This systematic review highlights how PCC has been defined, studied, and why there continues to be conceptual and implementation problems. Specifically, part of the conceptual problem with PCC is that different studies have labeled PCC based on these different categories. For example, sometimes an "enabler" of PCC is studied as PCC itself.

Another recent systematic review analyzed empirical studies that examined the relationship between PCC and outcomes (Rathert, Wywrich, and Boren, 2013). The study aimed to find out if PCC is significantly related to important patient outcomes. This study did not analyze conceptual definitions of PCC, focusing instead on empirical studies that purported to measure PCC and their operational definitions of PCC. This review organized the studies based on the IOM dimensions (IOM, 2001). These dimensions were based on findings from interviews the Picker Institute conducted with patients in the 1980s and early 1990s (Gerteis et al., 2002). Overall, this study found mixed results regarding the use of PCC and improved clinical outcomes. Some randomized trials found no differences between PCC intervention and control groups (Wolf et al., 2008), while others found significant improvements in some outcomes but not in others (Kinmonth et al., 1998). Nearly all the studies found positive relationships between PCC and satisfaction and well-being. While there may be several reasons for the mixed findings, one key reason is likely not only the variety of definitions used under the umbrella term of PCC, but also the type of concept used, as noted above (e.g., enablers vs. activities vs. principles) (Scholl et al., 2014).

Hobbs (2009) noted that most of the published studies were conducted in the acute care context, thus, much of how we define PCC is based on this setting. Similarly, the systematic review by Rathert, Wyrwich, and Boren (2013) suggested that different dimensions of PCC may be more or less important depending on the patient population and service setting. Thus, implementing PCC processes that were developed in an acute care setting, in an ambulatory setting, may bring about different results, or have no impact. This finding has implications for how we develop PCC in practice. PCC may be more dependent on the particular care setting than has been previously recognized.

Summary of Systematic Reviews

A key finding from this literature as a whole is that the term "patient-centered care" is defined and understood in a variety of ways. This is likely one reason why we lack conceptual and empirical clarity, and why, despite years of trials, health care organizations have had a difficult time implementing and sustaining PCC. This might also help explain why some scholars have chosen to instead adopt standardized patient experience measures such as the U.S. Centers for Medicare and Medicaid Services (CMS) Hospital Consumer Assessment of Health Providers and Systems (HCAHPS) survey as proxies for PCC measures; we review this work next. Based on the existing body of research though, PCC is rooted in a therapeutic *relationship* between the care provider and patient. Unfortunately, many PCC studies and strategies have focused on relatively general *processes* (Hobbs, 2009) or *enablers* and *activities* (Scholl et al., 2014) that facilitate PCC. While enablers and activities are important in terms of management, the conceptual core of PCC is the *relationship* that reduces patient vulnerabilities, and thus, health care organizations must learn what types of activities best support a patient-centered relationship in different contexts. The focus on patients in relation to others also helps keep the compromised, *vulnerable* states of patients in mind. Thus, certain experiences may actually "harm" patients by leading to increased stress, fear, and anxieties (Entwistle and Watt, 2013). For example, an experience that results in a low rating for "communication" on a standardized survey may have resulted in a negative experience far worse than the rating captures, due to fears and even life-changing decisions and outcomes that may come from a poor communication experience. Therefore, as we will argue below, facilitating such a therapeutic relationship requires that health care organizations focus on creating and maintaining practices that specifically facilitate *caring* and *compassion*. This means care providers must practice in environments that are psychologically safe (Nembhard et al., 2009) and conducive to developing the skills and authenticity necessary for building and executing therapeutic relationships with patients.

However, therapeutic relationships are a tall task. Across service sectors in the US and the UK, patients still generally perceive that they are being treated as a disease, a number, or a "lump of meat or a thing on a conveyor belt" (Entwistle and Watt, 2013, 32). The 2013 UK *Francis Report* decried the poor state of health care delivery as a failure of not only processes and systems, but also of humanity (Stoddart et al., 2014). As noted, it is not enough to simply individualize processes in a system that continues to be disease- or provider-centered (Epstein et al., 2010; Hobbs, 2009). The emphasis in recent years on patient-centeredness has mostly meant that practitioners are expected to capture information about patient preferences, when what is really needed is *therapeutic engagement*: "knowing the patient and developing a relationship" (Hobbs, 2009, 58). Yet there seems to be an inescapable tension between PCC and value (i.e., high quality health care provided at the lowest cost) with its emphasis on efficiency, standardization, and quantitative performance metrics. Thus, any research or process change with the aim of understanding or improving PCC must include a dual focus on *patient vulnerabilities* and care provider–patient *relationships*.

THE PATIENT EXPERIENCE OF CARE DELIVERY

There has been a flurry of research recently among US scholars to understand the patient experience of health care delivery, much of it inspired because of the US CMS Value Based Purchasing (VBP) reimbursement program (Stein et al., 2014). The VBP incentive aims to improve the quality of health care in the US by aligning government-sponsored Medicare reimbursement payments to acute care hospital outcome metrics that include specific clinical outcomes and patient perception measures of health care delivery. Patient experience is measured with the HCAHPS survey, an instrument developed by CMS and the Agency for Healthcare Research & Quality (AHRQ) as a standard measure of patient experiences (CMS, 2014a). VBP also uses other patient data reported by hospitals in its calculations; however, patient experience data make up a significant proportion (30%) of the score utilized to calculate reimbursement. Currently 1.5% of hospital Medicare reimbursement is tied to VBP scores, and this is scheduled to increase over time up to 2% (CMS, 2014b). Ambulatory surgery centers are now mandated to participate in VBP as well, and other service settings such as outpatient clinics and primary care providers may soon be held accountable for their scores (CMS, 2014b). Therefore, and not surprisingly, hospitals and health systems are concerned with their patient experience scores.

The mandated HCAHPS surveying also has made hospital-level patient perception data available to scholars and the public. Although VBP affects Medicare reimbursement, all discharged patients are eligible for the survey sampling frame, not just Medicare patients. The data are used not only by practitioners who are expected to improve their patient experience scores, but also by researchers trying to gain generalizable information about experiences that influence patient satisfaction and other outcomes. Recent studies utilizing HCAHPS data have enabled scholars to examine relationships among variables at the hospital-level of analysis. By focusing on the hospital- or organization-level of analysis, we can identify factors that are amenable to manipulation to improve care on a large scale. Weiner (2009) argued that in order for health care delivery to improve, it is necessary to motivate "collective behavior change" (1) by redesigning systems involved in care delivery. In theory, use of valid, generalizable patient perception tools should be useful for identifying opportunities for improvement, and the evidence provided should be useful for motivating collective behavior change, especially when financial incentives are tied to results.

Organization-Level Findings

So far, scholars have used HCAHPS data to identify common features among hospitals providing high quality patient experiences. For example, Jha et al. (2008) found that hospitals with higher nurse-to-patient-days ratios were significantly more likely to score higher on HCAHPS measures. In addition, patients rated their care significantly higher in not-for-profit hospitals than in for-profit hospitals. Similarly, Smith (2014) found that hospitals either with Magnet® status, or those working on attaining it, had higher HCAHPS scores.[2] Another study used a hospital-level analysis of HCAHPS data to identify organizational characteristics related to positive patient experiences (Manary et al., 2015). This study found that both the methods of communicating HCAHPS results to employees, and organizations with more collaborative cultures had significantly higher HCAHPS scores. Weech-Maldonado et al. (2012) found that hospitals that focused on improving their cultural competence had higher HCAHPS scores and reduced disparities among minority patients (Weech-Maldonado et al., 2012). And importantly, as will be discussed in more detail below, one study that examined workplace compassion found that hospitals with practices that supported and incentivized workplace compassion had significantly higher HCAHPS scores (McClelland and Vogus, 2014). HCAHPS scores also have been shown to be predictive of patient safety. Specifically, significantly fewer hospital acquired infections (HACs) were found among patients discharged from hospitals with higher HCAHPS ratings (Stein et al., 2014). Thus, it appears that organizational factors like culture, decentralization, nurse-to-patient-days ratios, and compassion practices influence an important indicator of patient experience (i.e., HCAHPS ratings) and potentially provide guidance

---

[2] Magnet® status is an accreditation designation granted by the American Nurses Credentialing Center (ANCC, 2014) that indicates the hospital is an attractive workplace for high quality nurses. It takes approximately five years for a hospital to attain Magnet® status once it begins the process.

to practitioners in terms of organizational practices they might implement to improve patient perceptions of the care they receive.

Many practitioners, administrators, and scholars accept patient experience measures as proxies for PCC; yet, there may be important PCC attributes missing from such measures. For example, a recent systematic review of the literature examined empirical studies in which patient perceptions of quality were assessed (Mohammed et al., 2014). The study inferred that patient perceptions of quality are the same as PCC, yet it made no linkages to the PCC concept; it simply assumed that patients who reported high quality care received PCC. Others have found that even though patient experience surveys tend to find that patients are satisfied with their care (i.e., they give positive ratings on questionnaires), many, if not most, still report numerous problems with the care they received (Jenkinson et al., 2002). Furthermore, relying on patient ratings alone may be insufficient, as patients who have always received suboptimal care may be satisfied with care that falls far short of being patient-centered (Epstein et al., 2010).

Summary of Patient Experience Literature

The recent literature on patient perceptions follows two trajectories. First, in many countries, patient experience measures and studies are front and center, and such measures are often assumed to measure PCC. In the US, acute care hospitals are now being held financially accountable for their patient experience scores. Some empirical studies suggest that such metrics correlate with quality metrics and patient satisfaction (Luxford, 2012; Manary et al., 2013; Price et al., 2014). Yet, a focus on standardized measures may result in organizations taking their "eyes off the ball" when it comes to PCC. Patients may respond positively to questions about communication and amenities, yet deeper concerns regarding poorly coordinated care, being treated like a number, and medical errors remain (Entwistle and Watt, 2013; Epstein et al., 2010; Jenkinson et al., 2002). Second, and most importantly, we argue that patient experience measures need to embrace PCC's inherently relational nature (Entwistle and Watt, 2013; Hobbs, 2009; Mead and Bower, 2000) as well as the quality of the provider-patient relationship, especially in terms of caring and compassion. Yet, current measures of patient experience capture some *indicators* of PCC, in terms of communication and amenities, but other important indicators are missing. We need measures and research that better capture caring or therapeutic relationships. Only then will we move beyond implementations of PCC that merely individualize the existing system for each patient, rather than actually transforming systems to become truly patient-centered (Epstein and Street, 2011; Hobbs, 2009). We turn now to scholarship that begins to build this approach—research on the patient perspective, caring, and compassion.

PATIENT-CENTERED CARE FROM THE PATIENT PERSPECTIVE

The patient perspective of PCC has been studied extensively, but important patient perspectives are often not subsequently woven into the conceptual underpinnings or measures of PCC. Interestingly, in patient perspective studies, patients don't use the words "therapeutic alliance," "therapeutic relationship," or most other terms related to a healing relationship, as do patient care scholars. Yet, they do consistently speak of "caring," or lack thereof, shown by care providers (Jakimowicz, Stirling, and Duddle, 2014). This section discusses aspects of PCC most frequently reported in studies that have directly asked patients what PCC means to them.

Individualized Care

Most research and intervention work on PCC has focused on involving patients in decisions about their care, eliciting their preferences, and individualizing treatment plans for their specific needs. One systematic review on PCC and outcomes, noted above, found that of 40 empirical studies, 19 focused primarily on individualized treatment planning, particularly among studies that involved testing interventions in randomized controlled trials (Rathert, Wyrwich, and Boren, 2013). Yet, eliciting patient preferences and individualizing care is complex. It may be that patients can clearly articulate their concerns in some situations, but in unexpected, emotionally-charged situations, patient preferences may be unstable and hard to discern (Epstein and Street, 2011). In fact, some research has demonstrated that care providers can subtly influence patient preferences (Epstein and Peters, 2009). Other work has found that patients not only exercise agency, but also are affected by others' agency, and patient agency may change over time and through the course of illness (Montgomery and Little, 2011). This means that PCC cannot rely on patients articulating preferences based on "stable guiding principles or values" (Epstein and Street, 2011, 195). Checklists that elicit preferences at one point in time may only touch the surface of patients' preferences. The majority of empirical studies on individualizing care have found increased patient satisfaction and well-being, although there have been mixed results in terms of clinical outcomes (Rathert, Wyrwich, and Boren, 2013). As noted, individualizing treatment plans, and eliciting patient preferences can still occur in systems that are disease-centered, system-centered, or provider-centered (Entwistle and Watt, 2013). Thus, such studies may not be measuring PCC. As one patient noted (Ferguson et al., 2013):

> you can have input and tell them, but they just go ahead with protocol anyways. Most of the time your opinions don't mean nothing (286).

Beyond the acute care setting, many patients with serious life-limiting illness express that their stated preferences are not honored as they move across service settings. For example, frequently an elderly person with a life-limiting illness goes to the emergency department, then is admitted to the inpatient setting, then gets discharged to a rehabilitation or long-term care facility. The patient may have stated preferences or signed a "do not resuscitate" (DNR) order in the acute care setting or primary care, but often documentation of the preferences does not follow the patient into other care settings. Some patients who express end-of-life care preferences for palliative ("comfort") care rather than aggressive treatment say they still get more aggressive treatment than what they wanted (Teno et al., 2002). These examples illustrate that individualizing treatment plans is necessary, but not sufficient, for patient-centeredness.

COMMUNICATION

Patients consistently express that they want effective communication, and when they don't experience it, they are not only dissatisfied, but also concerned about their safety (Rathert, Brandt, and Williams, 2012). Delays in communicating important news about diagnosis and prognosis can exacerbate patient anxieties and fears (Mazor et al., 2013). Other issues around communication in health care settings include: allowing patients to talk during the health care encounter, hospital discharge and self-care instructions, and care provider honesty or disclosure to patients. Each of these communication topics is important and all are covered in their own right elsewhere. Here the focus is on patient perceptions of general communication during their health care experiences.

Communication is one area that many measures, including HCAHPS, emphasize. Many organizations have worked hard to implement improved communication policies and practices, and researchers have worked hard to link improved communication with better patient experiences and outcomes. However, patients not only want effective communication between themselves and their providers, they also express concern about communication among care staff, communication that is reflected in the coordination of their care, or the lack thereof. A notable perception among patients in the acute care setting is that care providers often do not review their "charts" (Ferguson et al., 2013; Rathert, Brandt, and Williams, 2012). This finding emerged in qualitative studies of discharged patients from 12 hospitals in the Midwestern US and in interviews with admitted acute care patients in Saskatchewan, Canada. Patients in several studies have said that given the large numbers of clinicians they encounter, especially in the acute care setting, if care providers do not "know" their patients' "stories," it makes them feel that care providers are not reviewing their charts. After all, the patients have provided all this information to someone, likely several times. According to one patient (Rathert, Brandt, and Williams, 2012):

[it's] knowing about the patient before you walk in the room. If I was going into an interview, or to a client, and I said, "okay, now who are you and what's going on?" I just don't understand that, because that should be their main focus (5).

Indeed, such a perception harkens back to the nursing literature which defines PCC and caring as "knowing the patient" (Dewar and Nolan, 2013). Furthermore, electronic medical records (EMRs) were implemented so that every clinician would have patients' up-to-date information at their fingertips. Yet, implementing an EMR is not necessarily patient-centered unless it enables care providers to develop and maintain therapeutic relationships with patients (Epstein and Street, 2011). In the zeal to improve quality, many organizations implemented EMRs without considering how they can ensure the type of preparation and informed communication that would enhance PCC rather than act as a substitute for interaction. One opinion article illustrated this risk to the delivery of PCC (Toll, 2012). In it, a physician describes a picture that a young child drew of her recent visit to her pediatrician:[3]

> *The drawing was unmistakable. It showed the artist—a 7-year-old girl—on the examining table. Her older sister was seated nearby in a chair, as was her mother, cradling her baby sister. The doctor sat staring at the computer, his back to the patient—and everyone else (2497).*

In sum, patients appear concerned about many facets of communication. Despite managerial emphasis on care providers communicating appropriate and important information, and eliciting appropriate information from patients, emerging research shows that there are additional communication matters that patients include in PCC, such as communication between care providers and interactions with information technology.

Involving Families and Significant Others

One of the initial IOM (2001) dimensions of PCC, involvement of families and significant others, has not received much empirical attention. This is surprising given that the early Picker Institute studies found that patients considered involving family, part of PCC (Gerteis et al., 2002), and qualitative studies continue to find that patients think family involvement is important (Rathert, Brandt, and Williams, 2012). Although health care has traditionally involved families in pediatric care, it is now starting to consider families in adult care too. Conceptually, this means involving family members, as defined by the patient, as respected members of the care team (Piper, 2011). Many acute care hospitals in the US have incorporated sleeping areas for families who want to

---

[3] The article and picture can be found at: <http://jama.jamanetwork.com/article.aspx?articleid=1187932> (accessed May 20, 2015).

stay with their loved ones (Bush, 2012; Mikesell and Bromley, 2012). Involving families is particularly important for debilitating long-term illnesses such as cancer, as family members tend to take on essential caregiving roles (Ewart et al., 2014; Mazor et al., 2013). During critical care and end-of-life care, patients and families often merge psychologically to the extent that they almost become a single "unit" that must be considered by care providers (Fleming et al., 2006). In such cases, if care is not delivered appropriately in the eyes of the patient's loved ones, conflicts can arise and the bereavement process can be prolonged when the patient dies (Fleming et al., 2006). Thus, care providers not only have the responsibility of managing patient expectations of PCC, they also must consider the family or significant loved ones.

Yet, family involvement can be a double-edged sword. Family members want efficient communication, just as patients do, and in addition, they also want their own therapeutic relationships with care providers (Mazor et al., 2013). At a health system level, engaging families could help reduce overall health care costs. Having family caregivers can mean the difference for some patients in whether they are discharged to their home, or to a rehabilitation or skilled nursing center. On a large scale, this could have a significant impact on Medicare and other insurance costs; that is, if patients can be discharged to the care of a family member as opposed to transferring to another facility such as long term care. In one qualitative study that interviewed patients and family members after a hospital increased its number of visiting hours, family members expressed that being in the hospital more helped them learn how to provide care for their loved ones (Ewart et al., 2014). According to one husband:

> Mainly for me to see first-hand what the staff had to do in caring for my wife which helped me no end when she became my responsibility on returning home (215).

On the other hand, some families believe that over-worked nurses rely on them to deliver care to their patients while in the hospital, and other family members express concerns that they need to be with their patients in order to get safe, adequate care (Rathert, Brandt, and Williams, 2012). According to one family member's hospital experience:

> I was a babysitter to them. It was like, 'Oh, you're there, you take care of it' (6).

In situations like that above, it is possible that nurses and other staff were aware of the patient's condition, and knew the patient was in no real danger. On the other hand, the family member is not privy to all of the clinical information. Thus, family members can easily feel that they are being relied upon to monitor and care for their patients. Yet, the requirement that staff develop relationships and provide "customer service" to family and other loved ones adds significantly to their workload (Mikesell and Bromley, 2012). This means that as involvement of families and significant others increases, organizations must be mindful, and this increased involvement must be managed appropriately.

It is not sufficient to expect nurses and other care providers to automatically adapt to increases in family members wanting to be present and expecting therapeutic relationships (Davidson et al., 2007).

Emotional Support

A notable attribute overlooked by many patient experience measures (including HCAHPS) is emotional support. The Picker Institute's early open-ended patient interviews identified a number of important attributes that were categorized as emotional support (addressing patient fears and concerns; helping to reduce anxiety; having confidence and trust in care providers; Gerteis et al., 2002). Patients tend to highly value emotional support, but find it is often lacking, particularly in acute care. Indeed, emotional support could, in patients' eyes, be a sign of "caring." Prior research has quantitatively linked emotional support and patient satisfaction (Flach et al., 2004; Rathert et al., 2012). For example, some longitudinal empirical studies suggest that acute care patients experiencing better emotional support may have better long-term outcomes because such support inspires trust in their care providers and treatment plans both of which increase adherence to plans (Kahn et al., 2007; Meterko et al., 2010). More specifically, one study found that breast cancer patients who felt emotionally supported by their care providers were significantly more likely to continue their Tamoxifen use than those who felt less supported (Kahn et al., 2007). Research further shows that diabetic patients who experience empathy from their physicians have better clinical outcomes including better control of their diabetes and lower cholesterol (Hojat et al., 2011). Interestingly, patients' concerns about emotional support come up consistently in qualitative studies. One study found that acute care patients were more likely to trust care providers who showed caring and support, and trust led to better patient engagement (Ferguson et al., 2013). Research into patient preferences and decision-making has found that emotions are essential for sound decision-making, for care providers and patients alike (Epstein and Peters, 2009). These findings should not be surprising given the conceptual definitions of PCC. As noted, it is the situation of being physically vulnerable (sick or injured) that motivates patients to seek care in the first place. Thus, if reducing vulnerabilities is constitutive of PCC, emotional support is likely to play a key role.

To summarize, the body of research taking the perspective of the patient and family further refines some of the defining characteristics of PCC. Specifically, it formulates how care should be individualized, the preparation needed for effective communication, how families can constructively be engaged, and the emotional support needed. Overall, it reaffirms the central premise of our review, that PCC needs to embed all care activities within the framework of a therapeutic relationship seeking to manage vulnerability. This relies on the nature of the interaction and the organizational practices that shape it. We next discuss each in turn.

PATIENT- OR PERSON-CENTERED
RELATIONSHIPS

The therapeutic relationship between providers and patients makes the delivery of health care different from almost any other relationship. However, cost pressures have increasingly put the relational in tension with efficiency. This challenge is exacerbated by incentives by organizations and payers (e.g., insurers) to treat patients quickly ("through-put") and efficiently (i.e., diagnosis-based or treatment-based) rather than in a patient-centered way that recognizes a patient is a human being who has a life, a job, and a family (Epstein and Street, 2011). Providers are often required to utilize expensive technologies to meet administrative requirements when they know a "hands-on" approach may be more effective. Thus, we argue that any health care environment that truly wants to adopt PCC must focus on that relationship between the care provider and patient, and, such an environment needs to consider the care provider's needs to effectively guide the relationship. Indeed, Entwistle and Watt (2013) and others (Rathert, Ishqaidef, and May, 2009) have suggested that true patient- or person-centeredness must consider the care provider as a "person" as well and create the support structures and compassionate environments that best facilitate true PCC (McClelland and Vogus, 2014). This idea will be discussed further below.

The negative and unintended consequences of a less relational implementation of PCC are evident in a recent qualitative study of nursing (Mikesell and Bromley, 2012). This study interviewed nurses working in a new hospital that was intentionally designed to be "patient-centered" in terms of its focus on amenities and customer service, that is, patient experience. Nursing work was reorganized in this setting in terms of which tasks were "visible" and which were "invisible." Importantly, the design of this new hospital, with its private patient rooms, clearly separated the public areas from the staff-only work areas such as equipment and supply areas. Additionally, the hospital included a number of patient and family amenities, such as satellite television, large windows with views, and space for families to stay overnight. Staff members were trained on communicating with a "customer service" orientation. The study found that staff could tell patients and their families enjoyed the space and amenities, and they believed this was important. However, nurses noted a number of problems, many of which challenged their ability to relate to and care for patients in a true patient-centered way.

Specifically, many nurses indicated that "the caring culture had been re-defined as a service culture" (Mikesell and Bromley, 2012, 1664) which some believed violated their professional identities. For example, in the new service culture, nurses found that they were expected to address patient requests, many that were not health care related, as quickly as possible. They found that in order to fulfill the "customer service" objectives, they were running non-medical errands for patients and families, such as dealing with parking problems and rounding up extra chairs for visitors. Such errands were in addition to their normal clinical workload. As well, survey cards intended to capture patient and family perceptions of service quality were placed throughout the hospital's public areas, and nurses thus felt their professional status was de-valued because they were being evaluated on non-clinical and non-caring tasks, such as how they greeted family members. Some expressed that they felt more like hotel service workers than clinicians in this new environment. Making nursing work invisible to patients and their families unintentionally impeded workflow and gave the appearance to patients and families that nurses were highly available to run errands for them. Nurses complained that with this new service model, they actually had less time to develop the types of relationships with patients and families that lead to better care. They also were more isolated from other clinicians and patients, which cut down on the amount of informal information and learning they had previously obtained that helped them better deliver care. Furthermore, they felt this hindered coordination and teamwork (Mikesell and Bromley, 2012).

The care delivery environment may make developing and nurturing therapeutic relationships more difficult. Unfortunately, improving the appearance of the physical environment and infusing nursing staff with a customer service orientation may make developing the necessary relational bonds between provider and patient even more elusive. We next examine recent research on practices that rebalance these efforts by organizing to foster greater caring and compassion.

CARING AND COMPASSION

"Care" is a defining characteristic of the health care experience in general, and of PCC in particular. Traditionally, most care providers have entered their professions due to a "calling" to care for others (Beck, 1993). True caring under conditions of patient vulnerability and suffering necessarily involves *compassion*. Given the emphasis in the literature on therapeutic relationships as the key to PCC, a management focus on caring and compassion, as opposed to customer service, scripts, and checklists, may be the best way to improve PCC and patient experiences. In this section we discuss emerging research on caring and compassion.

Caring and the *patient as central* are ideas that have traditionally been the foundation of nursing education and practice (Ewart et al., 2014; Grilo et al., 2014). Yet, modern health care systems are "organized around care rather than caring" (Chochinov, 2013, 757). Several studies have focused on identifying the attributes of caring in the nursing profession. Generally, a caring nurse starts with an "authentic presence" (Beck, 1993, 30) which means the nurse listens, shares, and senses patient needs. The caring nurse is also competent, provides emotional support, encouragement, and physical touching when necessary. Others have conceptualized caring to include honoring the dignity and autonomy of each patient; recognizing that each person has a unique response to illness; and helping each patient to reach her or his healing potential (Grilo et al., 2014).

One component of caring is *compassion*. Compassion has been defined as the "intersection between empathy ... and sympathy" (Lown, Rosen, and Marttila, 2011, 1772). *Empathy* involves hearing and understanding concerns of patients. *Sympathy* is the ability to feel patients' emotions. Compassion also includes an action or *behavior* that responds to the patient's relationship needs, based on an understanding of the patient's context and perspective (Lown, Rosen, and Marttila, 2011). Scholars of workplace compassion define it as, "noticing another person's suffering, empathically feeling that person's pain, and acting in a manner intended to ease the suffering" (Lilius et al., 2008, 194–195). The concept of workplace compassion is particularly relevant for health care, given that patients travel to health care workplaces in order to receive care and alleviate their suffering. Further, a focus on workplace compassion necessarily leads back to PCC. Given these definitions of caring and compassion, we argue that compassion lies at the heart of the therapeutic relationship, and therefore, patient-centeredness. Yet, one of the few studies that examined patient perceptions of compassion found that only about half of patients believed their recent health care experience was compassionate (Lown, Rosen, and Marttila, 2011). It is not enough to simply expect compassion from care providers; health care organizations must provide work environments that allow compassion to flourish. A compassionate environment exhibits compassion for care providers as well as patients, and therefore, is truly *person*-centered.

Several studies have examined and articulated models of workplace compassion. When the organization shows compassion toward care providers, it supports them in developing better relationships with their patients (Kahn, 1998; McClelland and Vogus, 2014), which as we've seen, is the essence of PCC. Compassionate work environments lead to better interpersonal relationships among workers and positive feelings, and help workers who have experienced suffering either on or off the job (Lilius et al., 2008). Compassion in the workplace has been shown to influence job satisfaction and commitment, and may have financial implications for organizations (Lilius et al., 2011). Indeed, a recent study that examined the extent to which acute care hospitals supported and rewarded compassion through organizational practices found a significant positive relationship between compassion practices and HCAHPS scores (McClelland and Vogus, 2014). When hospitals recognize and reward acts of compassion not only toward patients and family members but also among care providers, compassion becomes an expected and integrated aspect of care delivery. Organizational practices that provide support to employees who are suffering or experiencing hardship, often times from the strain of the work itself (i.e., burnout, stress, compassion fatigue), directly attend to employee suffering that can compromise the delivery of high-quality PCC. Examples of compassionate organizational resources include: pastoral care, Schwartz Rounds, and Code Lavenders (Lown and Manning, 2010).[4] Recognition and rewards for employees who compassionately support one another further legitimate the appropriateness of

---

[4] An article on "Code Lavenders" can be found at: <http://www.huffingtonpost.com/2013/12/02/the-amazing-way-this-hosp_n_4337849.html> (accessed May 20, 2015).

compassion. These practices enable and sustain a capacity for compassion (Lilius et al., 2011) in the workplace and in caregiving. It's no surprise then that patients rate their care higher at hospitals that utilize compassion practices—employees are more likely to have the capacity for showing compassion and are encouraged to do so, and patients are more likely to receive the compassion they expect in their own care (Lown, Rosen, and Marttila, 2011).

WORK ENVIRONMENTS FOR CARING AND COMPASSION

Many health care organizations are attempting to improve organizational attributes to better support the delivery of PCC. Many hospitals have adopted a customer service model in which patient and family amenities are central (Epstein and Street, 2011; Mikesell and Bromley, 2012). However, at least in some cases, focusing exclusively on patients and concierge services may actually detract from the caring work nurses and other clinicians have been called to provide (Epstein and Street, 2011). Next we review some evidence-based facilitators and barriers to organizational attempts to change their cultures to support PCC.

One study interviewed senior staff and patient representatives in eight US organizations that have been recognized for their success in providing PCC (Luxford, Safran, and Delbanco, 2011). A top facilitator identified was strong, committed leadership. In many of the successful organizations, top leadership meetings devoted as much time to discussing how to improve care quality as they did to discussing financial matters. Interestingly, many of the leaders in these organizations had had personal experiences themselves or with a loved one in which the care they experienced was less than patient-centered, and this motivated them to improve PCC in their organizations. Interviewees indicated that staff satisfaction was a top priority as well. These organizations emphasized maintaining work environments and cultures that embodied a "Caring for the caregivers" philosophy (512). Each of the organizations also consistently reported specific patient experience data to front line staff. In addition, each organization had a long history of using a variety of tools for obtaining patient feedback, and had focused on being continually responsive to patient feedback. Another notable facilitator was promoting organizational cultures of learning and change, and many of the organizations felt communicating a strong PCC strategic vision was critical.

Several PCC barriers also were identified by organizations. Changing from a provider-focused organization to a PCC organization was much harder, and took much longer, than anticipated (Luxford, Safran, and Delbanco, 2011). Consequently, successful organizations had leaders who framed the culture change as a "journey" rather than a short-term pilot project. Some of those interviewed indicated that one of the barriers was insufficient resources devoted to the change. Interestingly, two factors the research team expected to have notably contributed to better PCC were not mentioned as key factors in the interviews. These were: physical environment quality and information technology (IT). The absence of these two factors in facilitating transformation is curious, and should give pause for concern, given that in recent years health care organizations have devoted billions of dollars toward renovating to improve their physical facilities and implementing IT systems. Clearly, more research is needed on these factors. Upgrading facilities and implementing IT systems may be important for other reasons; but more evidence is needed before we can unequivocally say it is important to invest in these activities in the name of PCC. As noted in several studies, these systems might actually impose new barriers to PCC (Mikesell and Bromley, 2012; Toll, 2012). Perhaps we should, instead, refocus efforts on practices and activities that build therapeutic relationships, a hallmark of truly patient-centered care.

SUMMARY AND CONCLUSION

In this chapter we presented some recent PCC findings, identified two major challenges for PCC, and discussed two promising solutions. First, although PCC receives significant attention from scholars and practitioners, there is a lack of conceptual clarity in the literature and no consensus on how PCC should be measured. Conceptual clarity is important because only when we agree on PCC's definition can we develop valid measures and implementation strategies (Hobbs, 2009). Organizations and practitioners have tried a variety of strategies in the aim to implement PCC. Some were successful, others were not. Although some organizations share best practices (Bush, 2012; Hayward, Endo, and Rutherford, 2014), we still find that many patients report bad experiences (Entwistle and Watt, 2013; Epstein et al., 2010) and that they do not experience compassion in their health care (Lown, Rosen, and Martilla, 2011). Further, because there are no clear definitions and measures, some scholars and practitioners have turned to validated patient experience surveys as proxy measures for PCC. While such surveys may prove useful, and researchers have found significant linkages between patient experience ratings and certain outcomes, these instruments may lack the measures that appear most important for gauging and improving PCC: patient perceptions of therapeutic relationships, caring, and compassion.

One factor influencing the lack of consensus may be that PCC may manifest differently in different service settings and patient populations. Aside from one of the few agreed upon notions, that individual patient preferences and values must be incorporated into treatment plans, there may be elements of PCC that are more important under certain conditions. As noted above, research shows that patients with long-term debilitating conditions such as cancer may have greater needs for emotional support, whereas, patients with chronic conditions such as diabetes may have better outcomes with individualized treatment and life management plans (Rathert, Wyrwich, and Boren, 2013). Therefore, PCC processes that have been developed in an acute care setting may not be as effective in an ambulatory setting; processes that are effective in critical care settings may have little to no impact for chronically ill patients in primary care settings. Future research should examine different PCC attributes among different types of patients in a variety of service settings.

While the focus on patient preferences and values is essential for PCC, research should continue to examine the complexities of identifying preferences, given that recent research has found that this is not a straight-forward process that can be done effectively with scripts and checklists (Epstein and Peters 2009; Montgomery and Little, 2011). Enabling care providers to develop and maintain relationships with patients may be the fertile ground from which accurate identification of preferences can appropriately grow. Further, if PCC varies across service settings, relationships may be the key for eliciting preferences in different patient populations. This is an important area for continuing research.

While nursing leaders, scholars, and educators have traditionally focused on caring and compassion, organizational focus on PCC has often overlooked these important aspects that patients consistently say they want but are lacking (Entwistle and Watt, 2013). Recently some scholars have called for caring and compassion to become more central in patient care. A growing body of research finds that caring and compassion should be directed at care providers as well as patients (Goodrich, 2012; Hennessy et al., 2013; McClelland and Vogus, 2014; Rathert, Ishqaidef, and May, 2009). Promising research in this area, known as practice theory, has emerged in the organizational literature (Lillius et al., 2011; McClelland and Vogus, 2014). Practice theory supports building of organizational capabilities through implementation of recurring patterns of actions and routines within organizations (Lillius et al., 2011). Identification of practices that build compassion capability has begun in health care, and we propose that such capability will support holistic work environments and PCC. We see this research and policy trajectory as the next important direction for health care as we "re-humanize" care delivery, for patients and care providers alike.

REFERENCES

American Nurses Credentialing Center (ANCC) (2014). ANCC magnet recognition program. Available at:<http://www.nursecredentialing.org/Magnet> (accessed December 1, 2014).

Beck, C. T. (1993). Caring relationships between nursing students and their patients. *Nurse Educator*, 18(5): 28–32.

Bergman, A. A. and Connaughton, S. L. (2013). What is patient-centered care really? Voices of Hispanic prenatal patients. *Health Communication*, 28: 789–799.

Berwick, D. M. (2009). What "patient-centered" should mean: Confessions of an extremist. *Health Affairs*, 28(4): w555–w565.

Bush, H. (2012 February). Action plans for better care. *Hospitals and Health Networks*, 65(2): 12–14.

Buttigieg, S., Rathert, C., D'Aunno, T., and Savage, G. (2015). International research in health care management: Its need in the 21st Century, methodological challenges, ethical issues, pitfalls and practicalities. *Advances in Health Care Management*, 17: 3–22.

Center for Medicare and Medicaid Services (CMS) (2014a). HCAHPS: Patients' perspectives of care survey. Available at: <http://www.cms.gov/Medicare/Quality-Initiatives-Patient-Assessment-Instruments/HospitalQualityInits/HospitalHCAHPS.html> (accessed December 1, 2014).

Center for Medicare and Medicaid Services (CMS) (2014b). Hospital value based purchasing: The official website for the medicare value based purchasing program. Available at: <http://www.cms.gov/Medicare/Quality-Initiatives-Patient-Assessment-Instruments/hospital-value-based-purchasing/index.html?redirect=/Hospital-Value-Based-Purchasing/> (accessed December 1, 2014).

Chochinov, H. M. (2013). Dignity in care: Time to take action. *Journal of Pain and Symptom Management*, 46(5): 756–759.

Davidson, J. E., Hedavat, K. M., Tieszen, M., Kon, A. A., Sheppard, E., Spuhler, V., Todres, I. D., Levy, M., Barr, J., Ghandi, R., Hirsch, G., and Armstrong, D. (2007). Clinical practice guidelines for support of the family in the patient-centered intensive care unit: American College of Critical Care Medicine Task Force 2004–2005. *Critical Care Medicine*, 35(2): 605–622.

Dewar, B. and Nolan, M. (2013). Caring about caring: Developing a model to implement compassionate relationship centred care in an older people care setting. *International Journal of Nursing Studies*, 50: 1247–1258.

Entwistle, V. A. and Watt, I. S. (2013). Treating patients as persons: A capabilities approach to support delivery of person-centered care. *The American Journal of Bioethics*, 13(8), 29–39, doi: 10.1080/15265161.2013.802060.

Epstein, R. M., Fiscella, K., Lesser, C. S., and Stange, K. C. (2010). Why the nation needs a policy push on patient-centered health care. *Health Affairs*, 29(8): 1489–1495.

Epstein, R. M. and Peters, E. (2009). Beyond information: Exploring patients' preferences. *Journal of the American Medical Association*, 302(2): 195–197.

Epstein, R. M. and Street, R. L. (2011). The values and value of patient-centered care. *Annals of Family Medicine*, 9(2): 100–103.

Ewart, L., Moore, J., Gibbs, C., and Crozier, K. (2014). Patient- and family-centered care on an acute adult cardiac ward. *British Journal of Nursing*, 23(4): 213–218.

Ferguson, L. M., Ward, H., Card, S., Sheppard, S., and McMurty, J. (2013). Putting the "patient" back into patient-centered care: An education perspective. *Nurse Education in Practice*, 13: 283–287.

Flach, S. D., McCoy, K. D., Vaughn, T. E., Ward, M. M., Bootsmiller, B. J., and Doebbling, B. N. (2004). Does patient-centered care improve provision of preventive services? *Journal of General Internal Medicine*, 19: 1019–1026.

Fleming D. A., Sheppard V. B., Mangan P. A., Taylor, K. L., Tallarico, M., Adams, I., and Ingham, J. (2006). Caregiving at the end of life: Perceptions of health care quality and quality of life among patients and caregivers. *Journal of Pain Symptom Management*, 31(5): 407–420.

Gerteis, M., Edgman-Levitan, S., Daley, J., and Delbanco, T. L. (2002). *Through the patients' eyes: Understanding and promoting patient-centered care*. 2nd edition. San Francisco, CA: Jossey-Bass.

Goodrich, J. (2012). Supporting hospital staff to provide compassionate care: Do Schwartz Center Rounds work in English hospitals? *Journal of the Royal Society of Medicine*, 105(3): 117–122.

Grilo, A. M., Santos, M. C., Ritat, J. S., and Gomes, A. I. (2014). Assessment of nursing students and nurses' orientation towards patient-centeredness. *Nurse Education Today*, 34: 35–39.

Hayward, M., Endo, J. A., and Rutherford, P. (2014). A focus on "always events." Strategy ensures patient-centered care and a better patient experience. *Healthcare Executive*, 29(1) (Jan/Feb): 78–80.

Hennessy, J. E., Lown, B. A., Landzaat, L., and Porter-Williamson, K. (2013). Practical issues in palliative and quality-of-life care. *Journal of Oncology Practice*, 9(2): 78–80.

Hobbs, J. L. (2009). A dimensional analysis of patient-centered care. *Nursing Research*, 58: 52–62.

Hojat, M., Louis, D. Z., Markham, F. W., Wender, R., Rabinowitz, C., and Gonnella, J. S. (2011). Physicians' empathy and clinical outcomes for diabetic patients. *Academic Medicine*, 86(3): 359–364.

Institute of Medicine (IOM) (1999). *To err is human: Building a better health system*. Washington, D.C.: National Academy Press.

Institute of Medicine (IOM) (2001). *Crossing the quality chasm: A new health system for the 21st century*. Washington, D. C.: National Academy Press.

Jakimowicz, S., Stirling, C., and Duddle, M. (2014). An investigation of factors that impact patients' subjective experience of nurse-led clinics: A qualitative systematic review. *Journal of Clinical Nursing*, doi: 10.1111/jocn.12676.

Jenkinson, C., Coulter, A., Bruster, S., Richards, N., and Chandola, T. (2002). Patients' experiences and satisfaction with health care: Results of a questionnaire study of specific aspects of care. *Quality and Safety in Health Care*, 11: 335–339.

Jha, A. K., Orav, E. J., Zheng, J., and Epstein, A. M. (2008). Patients' perception of hospital care in the U.S. *New England Journal of Medicine*, 359: 1921–1931.

Kahn, W. A. (1998). Relational systems at work. In *Research in organizational behavior: An annual series of analytical essays and critical reviews*, ed. Staw, B. M. and Cummings, L. L., pp. 39–76. Grennwich, CT: Elsevier Science/JAI Press.

Kahn, K. L., Schneider, E. C., Malin, J. L., Adams, J. L., and Epstein, A. M. (2007). Patient centered experiences in breast cancer: predicting long-term adherence to tamoxifen use. *Medical Care*, 45(5): 431–439.

Kinmonth, A. L., Woodcock, A., Griffin, S., Spiegal, N., and Campbell, M. J. (1998). Randomised controlled trial of patient centred care of diabetes in general practice: Impact on current wellbeing and future disease risk. The Diabetes Care from Diagnosis Research Team. *British Medical Journal*, 317(7167): 1202–1208.

Lilius, J. M., Worline, M. C., Dutton, J. E., Kanov, J. M., and Maitlis, S. (2011). Understanding compassion capability. *Human Relations*, 64(7): 873–899.

Lilius, J. M., Worline, M. C., Maitlis, S., Kanov, J., Dutton, J. E., and Frost, P. (2008). The contours and consequences of compassion at work. *Journal of Organizational Behavior*, 29: 193–218.

Lown, B. A. and Manning, C. F. (2010). The Schwartz Center Rounds: Evaluation of an interdisciplinary approach to enhancing patient-centered communication, teamwork, and provider support. *Academic Medicine*, 85(6): 1073–1081.

Lown, B. A., Rosen, J., and Marttila, J. (2011). An agenda for improving compassionate care: A survey shows about half of patients say such care is missing. *Health Affairs*, 30(9): 1772–1778.

Luxford, K. (2012). What does the patient know about quality? *International Journal for Quality in Health Care*, 24(5): 439–440.

Luxford, K, Safran, D. G., and Delbanco, T. (2011). Promoting patient-centered care: A qualitative study of facilitators and barriers in the healthcare organizations with a reputation for improving the patient experience. *International Journal for Quality in Health Care*, 23(5): 510–515.

McClelland, L. E. and Vogus, T. J. (2014). Compassion practices and HCAHPS: Does rewarding and supporting workplace compassion influence patient perceptions? *Health Services Research*, 49(5): 1670–1683.

Manary, M. P., Boulding, W., Staelin, R., and Glickman, S. W. (2013). The patient experience and health outcomes. *New England Journal of Medicine*, 368(3): 201–203.

Manary, M., Staelin, R., Kosel, K., Schulman, K. A., and Glickman, S. W. (2015). Organizational characteristics and patient experiences with hospital care: A survey study of hospital chief patient experience officers. *American Journal of Medical Quality*, 30(5): 432–440, doi: 10.1177/1062860614539994.

Mazor, K. M., Beard, R. L., Alexander, G. L., Arora, N. K., Firnemo, C., Gaglio, B., Greene, S. M., Lemayh, C. A., Robinson, B. E., Roblin, D. W., Walsh, K., Street, R. L., and Gallagher, T. H. (2013). Patients' and family members' views on patient-centered communication during cancer care. *Psycho-Oncology*, 22: 2487–2495.

Mead, N. and Bower, P. (2000). Patient-centredness: A conceptual framework and review of the empirical literature. *Social Science & Medicine*, 51: 1087–1110.

Meterko, M., Wright, S., Lin, H., Lowy, E., and Cleary, P. D. (2010). Mortality among patients with acute myocardial infarction: The influences of patient-centered care and evidence-based medicine. *Health Services Research*, 45(5pt 1): 1188–1204.

Mikesell, L. and Bromley, E. (2012). Patient centered, nurse averse? Nurses' care experiences in a 21st Century hospital. *Qualitative Health Research*, 22(12): 1659–1671.

Mohammed, K., Nolan, M. B., Rajjo, T. R., Shah, N. D., Prokop, L. J., Varkey, P., and Murad, M. H. (2014). Creating a patient-centered health care delivery system: A systematic review of health care quality from the patient perspective. *American Journal of Medical Quality* (online), doi: 10.1177/1062860614545124.

Montgomery, K. and Little, M. (2011). Enhancing patient-centered care in serious illness: A focus on patients' experiences of agency. *The Milbank Quarterly*, 89(3): 381–398.

Nembhard, I. M., Alexander, J. A., Hoff, T., and Ramanujam, R. (2009). Understanding implementation failure in health care delivery: A role for organizational research and theory. *Academy of Management Perspectives*, 23(1): 1–27.

Piper, L. E. (2011). The ethical leadership challenge: Creating a culture of patient- and family-centered care in the hospital setting. *The Health Care Manager*, 30(2): 125–132.

Price, R. A., Elliott, M. N., Zaslavsky, A. M., Hays, R. D., Lehrman, W. G., Rybowski, L., and Cleary, P. D. (2014). Examining the role of patient experience surveys in measuring health care quality. *Medical Care Research and Review*, 71(5): 522–554.

Rathert, C., Brandt, J., and Williams, E. S. (2012). Putting the "patient" in patient safety: A qualitative study of consumer experiences. *Health Expectations*, 15: 327–336.

Rathert, C., Ishqaidef, G., and May, D. R. (2009). Improving work environments in health care: Test of a theoretical framework. *Health Care Management Review*, 34(4): 334–343.

Rathert, C., Williams, E. S., McCaughey, D., and Ishqaidef, G. (2012). Patient perceptions of patient-centered care: Empirical test of a theoretical model. *Health Expectations*, doi: 10.1111/hex.12020.

Rathert, C., Wyrwich, M. D., and Boren, S. A. (2013). Patient-centered care and outcomes: A systematic review of the literature. *Medical Care Research and Review*, 70(4): 351–379.

Robinson, J. H., Callister, L. C., Berry, J. A., and Dearing, K. A. (2008). Patient-centered care and adherence: Definitions and applications to improve outcomes. *Journal of the American Academy of Nurse Practitioners*, 20: 600–607.

Scholl, I., Zill, J. M., Harter, M., and Dirmaier, J. (2014). An integrative model of patient-centeredness: A systematic review and concept analysis. *PLoS One*, doi: 10.1371/journal.pone.0107828. eCollection 2014.

Smith, S. A. (2014). Magnet hospitals: Higher rates of patient satisfaction. *Policy Politics Nursing Practice*, 15 (1–2): 30–41.

Stein, S. M., Day, M., Karia, R., Hutzler, L., and Bosco III, J. A. (2014). Patients' perceptions of care are associated with quality of hospital care: A survey of 4605 hospitals. *American Journal of Medical Quality* (online), doi: 10.1177/1062860614530773.

Stoddart, K., Ciccu-Moore, R., Grant, F., Niven, B., and Paterson, H. (2014). Care and comfort rounds: Improving standards. *Nursing Management*, 20(9): 18–23.

Teno, J. M., Fisher, E. S., Hamel, M. B., Coppola, K., and Dawson, N. V. (2002). Medical care inconsistent with patients' treatment goals: Association with 1 year Medicare resource use and survival. *Journal of American Geriatric Society*, 50(3): 496–500.

Toll, E. (2012). The cost of technology. *Journal of the American Medical Association*, 307(23): 2497–2498.

Weech-Maldonado, R., Elliott, M. N., Pradhan, R., Schiller, C., Hall, A., and Hays, R. D. (2012). Can hospital cultural competency reduce disparities in patient experiences with care? *Medical Care*, 50: S48.

Weiner, B. J. (2009). A theory of organizational readiness for change. *Implementation Science*, 4(67), doi: 10.1186/1748-5908-4-67.

Wolf, D. M., Lehman, L., Quinlin, R., Zullo, T., and Hoffman, L. (2008). Effect of patient-centered care on patient satisfaction and quality of care. *Journal of Nursing Care Quality*, 23(4): 316–321.

CHAPTER 7

CLINICAL ETHICS SUPPORT IN CONTEMPORARY HEALTH CARE

Origins, Practices, and Evaluation

EVAN DORAN, IAN KERRIDGE, CHRISTOPHER
JORDENS, AND AINSLEY J. NEWSON

INTRODUCTION

THIS chapter concerns current initiatives to create and maintain specialized services to help respond to ethical issues that arise in the practice of health care. These initiatives, the obstacles they face, and the controversies they engender should be of considerable interest to those concerned with the management of health care organizations. This is because ethics is and should be intrinsic to routine health care practice. Also, no less, it is because ethical disputes and controversies, even if they seldom occur, can severely disrupt the complex organizations that deliver health care in modern societies.

Clinical ethics support services (CES services) are comprised of an individual or group, usually in an organization, who can provide a suite of services to support all stakeholders in identifying and managing the ethical issues that inevitably arise in the design and delivery of health care. While there is a degree of consensus about the potential value of such services, they are also the focus of ongoing theoretical, methodological, and political debates. This chapter does not aim to resolve these debates. Rather, our aim is to provide health care managers with an account of how and why CES services are becoming a part of the contemporary organizational landscape of health care, and describe the concerns that bioethicists and observers and critics of bioethics have raised regarding their role, function, and dissemination.

We first describe the origins of CES services, to provide a context for the following discussion about the goals, functions, and models of support that exist across this discipline—drawing on some relevant examples. We then describe how CES services can be evaluated. Third, we discuss initiatives that aim to optimize quality of CES services and some of the criticisms and suspicions that these initiatives have engendered. Finally, we offer some reflections on the direction that CES services may take in the future.

THE ORIGINS OF CES SERVICES

Clinical ethics support is derived from the discipline of bioethics, which, at least as it applies to the health care sector, can be defined as the study and critical appraisal of ethical, legal, social, and political issues arising in the delivery and management of health care and research. Bioethics operates in three distinct spheres: academic, policy, and clinical. The incorporation of bioethics into clinical practice to improve patient care (clinical ethics) may be seen as a continuation of the tradition of medical ethics—the means by which the medical profession itself has attended to ethical problems that arise in practice (Dzur, 2002; Pellegrino, 1988; Moreno, 2009). However it can also be seen as a significant departure from that tradition. Bioethics is an interdisciplinary enterprise in which philosophers, lawyers, social scientists, and the public engage with biomedical researchers and clinicians. Bioethics has thus opened up the ethics of medical encounters and biomedical research to external ethical scrutiny and critique and so represents a break in the tradition of medical ethics (Dzur, 2002).

Histories of bioethics offer a variety of explanations for its emergence during the twentieth century. In some accounts (e.g., Callahan, 1999), bioethics emerged from biomedical researchers and clinicians reaching out to non-medical disciplines such as philosophy and law for support with the perplexing moral choices imposed by new medical technologies. In other accounts (e.g., Rothman, 1992; Bosk, 1999) bioethics emerged as a response to medical scandals such as the infamous Tuskegee Syphilis Experiment, with critics both within and outside medicine concerned to more closely monitor biomedical research and practice. Bioethics is also seen to emerge (e.g., Jonsen, 1993) from increased secularism and greater awareness of moral pluralism. Intellectual histories of bioethics have also associated it with the rise of new social movements of the 1960s, such as the civil rights movement, feminism, and environmentalism, which questioned all forms of authority and called for the public to have a greater say in institutional decision-making (Dzur, 2002).

Similarly, accounts of the emergence of CES services point to the technological and social changes that have increased the ethical complexities of patient care (Aulisio, Arnold, and Youngner, 2000; Agich, 2005; Larcher, Slowther, and Watson, 2010). Advances in specialties such as critical care, reproductive medicine, fetal medicine, and genetic testing have led to new treatments that blur important boundaries (e.g., between life and death) and create unprecedented ethical and legal dilemmas around issues such as withdrawing/withholding care. Diversity of values in society is reflected in the clinical setting; also compounded by differences between the health professions, and institutional and systemic imperatives (Aulisio, Arnold, and Youngner, 2000). As a number of authors (e.g., Zussman, 1997; Royal College of Physicians, 2005) have noted, clinical relationships have changed: medicine has lost some of its authority; paternalism is yielding to "partnership" and shared decision-making with better educated patients and more assertive "consumers"; nursing is more professionalized. The medical encounter is increasingly crowded with competing interests and influences. Clinical transactions usually involve third party payers such as governments or private insurers, making clinical work increasingly subject to scrutiny from these and related institutions. The ethical issues that arise as a result are not confined to the clinic, but often attract intense scrutiny from the media, from religious authorities, and from the law. As a result, clinical decisions (such as a withholding treatment) can become the focus of far-ranging public debates.

CES services first emerged in a few hospitals in the US in the 1960s and 1970s (Moreno, 2009; Tapper, 2013). According to several scholars (e.g., Cranford and Doudera, 1984; Rosner, 1985; Jonsen, 1993; Rubin and Zoloth, 2004), the catalyst for the growth of CES services was the judgment of the New Jersey Supreme Court in the case of Karen Quinlan in 1976. This case was prompted by a disagreement about whether to withdraw ventilation support from a young woman who was in what would now be called a minimally conscious state. Quinlan's parents asked her doctors to cease ventilation, but her doctors refused to do so, due to concerns about their legal liability. The case was the first legal adjudication on life-support in the US and it generated intense public interest (Jonsen, 1993). In a landmark decision, the Court found in favor of extubation, drawing on a paper by Teel (1975) which argued that doctors frequently face difficult ethical and legal decisions in end-of-life care, which they are ill-equipped to deal with. Teel argued for greater access to mechanisms for support such as the then novel hospital ethics committees (Tapper, 2013; Engelhardt, 1999). The judgment in the Quinlan case included a recommendation that clinical ethics committees be established to offer doctors guidance in such cases.

The Quinlan case is significant as it is frequently cast as emblematic of the factors that precipitated the spread of CES services. The case is often cited to show how physicians reached out for assistance with the perplexing choices created by advances in medical technology. Tapper (2013) uses the case to argue that the advent of extreme life-prolonging measures created a yearning among clinicians to share the responsibility for the tough decisions these technologies imposed. ECs were "[b]orn to serve the dual and reinforcing fears of futile care and medicolegal liability" (Tapper, 2013, 417). In other histories, the Quinlan case represents the moment medical ethics became a more public affair and the "internal morality" of medicine opened up to the norms and values of the wider community (Pellegrino, 1988; Bosk, 1999; Dzur, 2002; Rubin and Zoloth, 2004). For Engelhardt (1999) the Quinlan judgment represents the point at which moral authority within health care could, and *should*, be transferred from clinicians, patients and their families to CES services "in the name of oversight and the protection of patients" (Engelhardt, 1999, 92). For Jonsen (1993) the Quinlan case heralded a "culture sensitive ... to the rights of individuals and their abuse of powerful institutions" and stimulated a movement committed to vigorously asserting the "needs and preferences of patients" (1993, S3).

The Quinlan case and a later series of Baby Doe cases (also involving the withdrawal of life supporting interventions) gave momentum to the idea that clinical ethics committees provided an alternative to resolving medico-ethical disputes in courts of law.

The idea of CES services was taken up by the President's Commission for the Study of Ethical Problems in Medicine and Biomedical and Behavioral Research, which recommended that health care institutions explore the use of ethics committees for decisions regarding incapacitated patients (Agich, 2009a; Dzur, 2002). Momentum grew to effective mandate when in 1992 having an institutional means of addressing the ethics of patient care was made a requirement of hospital accreditation by the Joint Commission on Accreditation of Health Care Organisations (Agich, 2009a, 2009b; Pope, 2009). This event, more than any other, induced the rapid spread of CES services in the US, to the extent that they have become an almost ubiquitous feature of health care organizations in this country. The most recent US national data indicated that 81% of general hospitals have an ethics consultation service and a further 14% are in the process of establishing a service (Fox, Myers, and Pearlman, 2007).

Following these early US developments, CES services have now become established in many other nations—with the experience and knowledge gained in the US motivating the creation of services elsewhere (Slowther, Hill, and McMillan, 2002; Pfafflin, Kobert, and Reiter-Theil, 2009). CES support is now a feature of at least some hospitals in Australia, Belgium, Bulgaria, Canada, Croatia, Finland, France, Germany, Israel, Italy, Japan, Lithuania, Netherlands, New Zealand, Switzerland, and the United Kingdom, to name just a few (McNeill, 2001; Meulenbergs, Vermylen, and Schotsmans, 2005; Aleksandrova, 2008; Gaudine et al., 2010; Frikovic and Gosic, 2006; Guerrier, 2006; Louhiala et al., 2011; Wenger et al., 2002; Hurst et al., 2007a; Akabayashi et al., 2008; Bankauskaite and Jakusovaite, 2006; Dauwerse et al., 2011; Macdonald and Worthington, 2012; Hurst et al., 2008; Slowther, McClimans, and Price, 2012).

Accounts of the emergence of CES in these nations (e.g., Beyleveld, Brownsword, and Wallace, 2002; Dorries et al., 2011) are similar to US histories in attributing their emergence to factors such as advances in biomedical technologies, moral pluralism (there being more than one view on an issue that could be said to be reasonably held), the rise in patient rights, and medical scandals. The developmental trajectory has been quite different, however. With the exception of Norway, Belgium, Greece (where they have legal status), and Spain, most nations have not made CES services mandatory for hospitals (Lebeer, 2005). Rather, CES services have developed in an ad hoc and sporadic way; usually led by motivated clinicians (Beyleveld, Brownsword, and Wallace, 2002). Even here, however, most countries have witnessed the gradual emergence of CES services. In Canada, a survey by Gaudine and colleagues found that in 2008 85% of hospitals had an ethics committee compared to 58% in 1989 and 18% in 1984 (Gaudine et al., 2010).

A recent survey of clinical ethics committees in the UK showed the number of identified committees to have risen from 20 in 2001 to 82 in 2010 (Slowther, McClimans, and Price, 2012). Clinical ethics networks have also been established in Europe with the European Clinical Ethics Network (Fournier et al., 2009) and in the UK with the United Kingdom Clinical Ethics Network (UKCEN) in an attempt to embed clinical ethics as a core element of health care systems (Slowther, 2008).

The spread of CES services internationally shows that the idea of having available some manner of expert ethical support, has clearly taken hold (Aulisio, Arnold, and Youngner, 2000; Gill et al., 2004; Agich, 2005; Royal College of Physicians, 2005; Williamson, McLean, and Connell, 2007; Larcher, Slowther, and Watson, 2010; Dorries et al., 2011). In the next section we will describe some of the major, common features of CES services. We start, however, by noting that there is continuing debate on foundational issue of CES services—what goals can and should a service strive to meet. This issue partly explains the somewhat precarious institutional existence of such services, at least in some jurisdictions.

GOALS, FUNCTIONS, AND MODELS OF CES SUPPORT

Goals

The commonly stated or implied goals of support services include: minimizing the distress and conflict that clinicians and patients experience when faced with ethically difficult clinical decisions (Yen and Schneiderman, 1999); improving the quality of patient care (Slowther, 2008); controlling health care costs; reducing complaints; reducing litigation and the costs associated with it; reducing the fear of litigation; increasing trust in health care professions and institutions; creating better decision-making processes; facilitating decision-making where there is disagreement; creating a greater focus on patient-centered outcomes; reducing the frequency of intractable or unresolved disputes; improving staff morale; developing policies and practices that reduce risks to health care organizations, and promoting greater understanding of ethics (Nelson et al., 2010a).

Whilst there is broad acceptance of the potential value of CES services, the characteristics of existing services reflect a plurality of visions and values. For CES services can be envisaged as a service accessible to clinicians (and perhaps patients as well); or as a watchdog for the ethical quality of patient care; or as a champion of patient rights, or as a means of risk management and legal cover for their institutions. These various visions of CES services can be classified in different ways. Beyleveld, Brownsword, and Wallace (2002), for example, identify two main categories. The first is "bottom-up" and clinician-oriented, while the second is "top-down" and managerial. The first category describes settings where enthusiasts for clinical ethics are likely to have established a

CES service; while the second describes those in which CES support has been encouraged or mandated by an entity other than those who form the service itself.

These categories highlight the fact that CES services can serve different purposes: they can help clinicians to deal with ethically complex issues; and/or they can help health care organizations manage risks and crises (Beyleveld, Brownsword, and Wallace, 2002). While these different goals are not mutually exclusive, sometimes they conflict. Thus questions about what CES services can and should do are political as well as theoretical and technical. Clinical ethics support is not politically innocent (Dzur, 2002; Brecher, 2006; Engelhardt, 2009); there are always partisan ideas, interests and agendas at work and it is possible for CES services to be "captured" in the interests of some at the expense of others.

Functions

There are three main functions typically associated with CES: education, policy development, and case consultation (Singer, Pellegrino, and Siegler, 1990; Blake, 1992), although a fourth—providing assistance with organizational ethics—is gaining increasing prominence. Different services emphasise different functions (Mills, Rorty, and Spencer, 2006). Of these three functions, case consultation, the "driving force" of clinical ethical infrastructure (Mills, Tereskerz, and Davis, 2005, 57), has received the most scholarly attention. It is "the most potentially volatile and the most labor-intensive" function (Moreno, 2009, 577).

The CES function of education is considered by some clinical ethicists to be its most important and efficient function (Moreno, 2009). However it is relatively underrepresented in the literature and there are few detailed descriptions and recommendations for the educative role of ethics support services (Chidwick et al., 2010). In most discussions, description of a service's educational activity is limited to enumerating the types of ethics teaching activities that are commonly undertaken such as presenting a case or an issue at a Grand Rounds seminar, or conducting in-service training sessions for clinical staff. An exception to this is the educational method called "moral case deliberation" employed in some Dutch health care institutions (Weidema et al., 2012).

The policy development function of ethics services is also not usually discussed in the literature at length. More typically it is limited to stating that an institution's ethicist or committee frequently provides input into policies and guidelines. The neglect of the policy function of CES support has recently been noted elsewhere (Frolic et al., 2012), although exceptions to this are the descriptions of policy work by Ells (2006) and McDonald, Simpson, and O'Brien (2008).

Further, there does not appear to have been any systematic evaluation of the process and impact of the educational and policy functions of CES services. Frolic et al. seek to redress the policy development knowledge gap, arguing that the policy review function is a distinctive practice requiring its own metrics, which the authors have developed (Frolic et al., 2012).

In contrast to the education and policy functions, case consultation has been the subject of considerable debate and also significant attempts at reaching consensus on what best practice might look like. In a case consultation, clinicians, patients or their carers who are uncertain or troubled by a particular issue or decision may consult with a CES service much as they might seek the opinion and advice of colleagues with expertise in other specialty areas. The CES service (individual or committee) assists by clarifying the values and conflicts involved, advising on the ethical implications of the available courses of action and *facilitating* an ethically justified consensus on what should be done (Tarzian and the ABSH Core Competencies Update Task Force, 2013). Case consultation appears to be a central function of many CES services in the US but is less so in the UK (Slowther, McClimans, and Price, 2012) and other European nations (Lebeer, 2005; Pfafflin, Kobert, and Reiter-Theil, 2009) where CES services are seen more as a "body for reflection" provided primarily to clinicians (Lebeer, 2005).

There are differing approaches to both the role and method of clinical ethics consultation (Dzur, 2002) but the most commonly accepted approach is facilitation. CES services have previously tended to lean towards one of two approaches: *authoritarian* or *pure facilitation*, both of which are argued to be inadequate (Aulisio, Arnold, and Youngner, 2000; American Society for Bioethics and Humanities, 2009). In the authoritarian approach, the ethicist (or clinical ethics committee) becomes the central figure in the deliberation; the expert making decisions and issuing binding recommendations. The obvious concern here for critics of CES is that the ethicist assumes decision-making authority—usurping the authority of the patient and the clinical team.

In contrast, in the pure facilitation approach the ethicist's role is to broker consensus. While superficially this seems less problematic, even here the focus on consensus can compromise patient autonomy, for example where consensus between clinicians and the patient's family overrides the wishes of the patient and thereby diminishes patient self-determination (Aulisio, Arnold, and Youngner, 2000; American Society for Bioethics and Humanities, 2009).

A third and now most widely adopted approach to CES services is "ethics facilitation"—where consultation involves clarifying the value uncertainty or conflict involved and facilitating consensus—"agreement by all involved parties, whether that agreement concerns the substantively morally optimal solution or, more typically, who should be allowed to make the decision" (Aulisio, Arnold, and Youngner, 2000, 61). The ethics facilitation approach differs from the pure facilitation approach in that it considers whether the consensus decision reached is ethically justified (Tarzian and the ABSH Core Competencies Task Force, 2013).

A fourth function of CES services is to provide assistance with ethics at the level of the organization as opposed to the level of patient care. This usually entails working through the ethical issues involved in areas such as health care management, resource allocation, and quality improvement (Dorries et al., 2011; McClimans, Slowther, and Parker, 2012). This development reflects the rise in a "systems" approach which seeks to integrate clinical ethics into the institution and wider health care system. But while some of the field's most influential scholars and practitioners have advocated for this model (Singer, Pellegrino, and Siegler, 2001; MacRae et al., 2005; Fox, 2010) a systems approach to clinical ethics remains to be widely adopted (MacRae et al., 2005). There are, however, a number of well-developed frameworks for implementing systems thinking in ethics support (Fox, 2010; MacRae et al., 2005; Nelson et al., 2010a). All posit the mutual dependence of quality care and ethical principles. With reference to ethics, "quality" means that practices throughout an organization are consistent with the accepted ethical standards, norms, or expectations for the organization and its staff (Fox, 2010). Drawing on theoretical developments in disciplines such as organizational studies and social, cognitive, and cultural psychology, all share a commitment to ethics services having a more proactive role in the continuous *quality improvement* effort of the organization and system within which it operates. In a systems approach, ethics support moves "upstream" to address systemic and structural elements that produce value conflict rather than remaining only at the level of the particulars of the issue or case at hand. This encourages a more proactive and preventative (the approach is some time labeled "preventive ethics") form of ethics support (Fox, 2010; MacRae et al., 2005; Nelson et al., 2010a).

Service Models

"The ethics consultation team is ideally composed of individuals who bring a balance of the knowledge and skills requisite for effectively providing ethics consultation services. Although it is an open and empirical question whether such skills and knowledge are best delivered by teams or individual ethics consultants, it is certainly evident that both formats are thriving in a wide variety of health care settings" (Agich, 2009a, 14).

As Agich indicates, there is considerable uncertainty about how best to deliver CES services. Three models are currently prevalent: the "ethicist" model of an individual with specialist training in ethics; the "clinical ethics committee" model—a multi-disciplinary group convened on a regular basis; and a small team model, often convened as a sub-group of the larger ethics committee. The individual ethicist model is more prevalent in the United States and Canada, while the committee model appears to be favored in the UK, Europe, and elsewhere (Larcher, Slowther, and Watson, 2010).

Both models have strengths and weaknesses. The consultant model, for example, may be more flexibile and responsive (Aulisio, Arnold, and Youngner, 2000; Slowther, Hope, and Ashcroft, 2001), but also relies on the perspective of a single individual. In contrast, the major strength of the committee model of ethics support, which appears to be the most widely adopted model internationally, is that it brings multiple disciplines, professions, and perspectives to bear in consideration of the issues or problem under debate (American Society for Bioethics and Humanities, 2009). But while a larger group may provide better procedural practice, with it comes more constraints, such as meeting times and responsiveness to requests for case consultation. The ethics team model, which has been widely adopted in the US and elsewhere, attempts to address philosophical issues raised by single ethicists operating as expert ethics consultants and practical issues associated with large ethics committees performing contemporaneous case consultation (Fox, Myers, and Pearlman, 2007). In this model, a small number of members of the larger committee undertake consultation work, thereby allowing for a more timely response to a request for advice than is possible for the full committee. While a quicker response comes at the cost of the greater range of views offered by a multi-disciplinary committee, the ethics team can also contact members of the larger committee for advice.

To date, few studies have systematically compared the different models of CES support. Increasingly, those engaged in ethics consultation advocate for a support service to combine all three models in order to maximize the strengths and minimize the weaknesses of each (American Society for Bioethics and Humanities, 2009; Fox, 2010). Fox (2010) recommended that the consultation task itself should determine which model is utilized.

While there is no consensus, there are a number of well-developed approaches. In the following section we briefly describe two with a systems-oriented approach.

Integrated Ethics

The *IntegratedEthics* program was developed by the National Center for Ethics in Health Care of the United States Government's Department of Veterans Affairs (VA) which operates the largest integrated health care system in the United States (Fox, 2010). The IntegratedEthics approach was developed to address some of the perceived shortcomings of traditional approaches to CES services such as the lack of integration of CES into its host organization, lack of defined purpose and lack of standards and accountability for quality. The IntegratedEthics program is a standardized approach designed to help individual health care facilities improve "ethics quality" at three levels: decisions and actions, systems and processes, and environment and culture. The need to recognize levels is illustrated using an iceberg analogy; at the tip of the iceberg are ethically problematic decisions and practices; below these are the organizational systems and process that inform decisions and practices; and below these are the organizations' ethical environment and culture which through values and norms almost imperceptibly shape ethics practices.

The approach is structured around three core functions associated with each of the levels: *ethics consultation* targets ethics quality at the level of decisions and actions; *preventive ethics* targets the level of systems and processes; and *ethical leadership* targets the level of environment and culture. The IntegratedEthics approach to consultation, which is closely aligned with the ABSH Core Competencies approach, is captured in the acronym CASES: Clarify the consultation request, Assemble the relevant information, Synthesize the information, Explain the synthesis, Support the consultation process. The acronym ISSUES is used for preventive ethics at the systems level: Identify an issue, Study the issue, Select a strategy, Undertake a plan, Evaluate and adjust, Sustain and spread. At the environmental and cultural level, ethical leadership involves demonstrating that ethics is a priority, communicating clear expectations for ethical practice, practicing ethical decision-making and supporting institutional ethics programs.

THE HUB AND SPOKES MODEL

A more recent innovation for providing ethics support is the "hub and spokes" strategy developed by the Joint Centre for Bioethics (JCB) at the University of Toronto, Canada in conjunction with ten affiliated hospitals (MacRae et al., 2005). The core approach of the strategy is to provide decentralized resources, with the "spokes," coordinated by the centralized "hub." The hub provides the bioethics expertise and leadership to the spokes. Clinicians and others organized along professional or departmental lines throughout the organization then act as a local ethics resource.

The Hub and Spokes model tries to create an "ethics infrastructure" within health care organizations. The goal is for ethics support services to become fully integrated into the life of the organization it serves over time (MacRae et al., 2005). The model aims to foster an ethical climate where the responsibility to be ethically engaged and aware is recognized from "those in the boardroom to those at the bedside" (MacRae et al., 2005, 257). The core innovation of the strategy is that builds capacity through ethical expertise "radiating" from the Hub, through the Spokes and to the clinical and general staff (MacRae et al., 2005).

This diffusion of knowledge and skills is intended to overcome some of the limitations of the typical static model of ethics support where expertise remains concentrated in the individual consultant or committee. The Spokes reach out to all parts of the organization generating ethics awareness and competence and thereby minimizing the perennial challenges of workload, peer support and isolation facing the lone ethicist (or committee). The strategy establishes an infrastructure of relationships within an organization which serves to both formalize previously implicit responsibilities and generate a commitment (or "buy-in") to ethics at all levels; this helps address the problem of poor sustainability and limited accountability of traditional models of support.

EVALUATION OF CES SERVICES

The proliferation of clinical ethics support has seen a rapidly growing literature, but there has been less by way of empirical research and evaluation of the CES process and outcomes. Empirical studies of clinical ethics support services are overwhelmingly descriptive in nature, with only a few attempting systematic evaluation. There is also no consensus in the literature as to how CES services should be evaluated (Schildmann et al., 2013).

Most studies of ethics support services have sought to establish aspects such as: the prevalence of support services, their type, structure, composition, main functions, activities, and processes (see for example McGee et al., 2001; Slowther et al., 2001, 2004; Slowther, McClimans, and Price, 2012; Godkin et al., 2005; Milmore, 2006; Fox, Myers, and Pearlman, 2007; Frewer and Fahr, 2007; Swetz et al., 2007; Pedersen, Akre, and Førde, 2009; Romano et al., 2009; Whitehead et al., 2009; Kesselheim, Johnson, and Joffe, 2010; Gaudine et al., 2010; Nelson et al., 2010b; Tapper et al., 2010; Moeller et al., 2012). What these studies mostly show is the diversity of CES services. Many CES services provide all three of the core functions of education, policy review and development and consultation; but usually focus on one function. Some services are provided by a single ethicist; some by committees; others use both. Regarding consultations, many issue non-binding recommendations, a small number issue binding recommendations and some do not make any recommendations at all. Most ethics committees are multi-disciplinary but vary in their membership mix and their mode of recruitment. Some committees have members with formal ethics training, many do not; legal expertise is represented on some committee but not on others. Some committees actively educate their members, while others do not or are unable to. Some services involve patients and families directly in their deliberative process and allow them to refer to the service, in many others support is primarily if not exclusively for clinicians (Fournier et al., 2009). Some committees have adopted systematic means of documenting their activities, others do not. Some services undertake to evaluate their activities, many do not.

A small number of studies have focussed on the interaction between a service and clinicians. Studies have looked at the types of ethical issues (variously referred to as *inter alia*—problems, dilemmas, difficulties) that clinicians face; what issues prompt clinicians to seek ethical support; what enables or impedes access to support; clinician's perceptions of the adequacy of ethics support available to them and their preferences for types of ethics support. Studies such as that by Du Val et al. (2001, 2004) and the Royal College of Physicians (2005) show ethics consultations are mostly requested for end-of-life issues, decisions about withdrawing "futile" treatments, and late-term abortions. Other frequently occurring issues include disagreement among clinicians, professional misconduct, and concerns related to truth-telling and confidentiality. Dilemmas about justice, such as lack of insurance or limited resources, were rarely referred (Du Val, 2004).

Many of these studies have investigated why clinicians do or do not seek ethics support. Findings suggest that clinicians tend to seek support for conflict resolution, reassurance about a decision, clarification of issues, new insights on a case and emotional support (Du Val et al., 2001). Clinicians with ethics training appear to be more likely to request ethics support, although it is unclear whether this represents greater awareness of CES services, greater support for CES services, or greater willingness to seek external review of clinical decisions or difficulties (Du Val et al., 2004; Hurst et al., 2007b). Clinicians often do not seek support because consultations are difficult to access, the process is time consuming or intimidating, the outcomes may be unhelpful, they may fear being scrutinized, fear loss of autonomy, or they may fear retaliation (Du Val et al.,

2004; Førde, Pedersen, and Akre, 2008; Gaudine et al., 2011). Other possible reasons for underutilization include clinicians not being aware that a clinical support service exists, fear that a committee will worsen the situation (Gaudine et al., 2011) and placing a low value on shared decision making (Orlowski et al., 2006).

Two prospective studies by La Puma et al. (1988, 1992) collected descriptive information on consultations including the reason(s) for consultation, the characteristics of the patients involved, the clinicians' satisfaction with the service and whether they would use it again. In both studies large majorities of clinicians found consultation helpful and nearly all indicated they would use the service in the future. Similar findings on the perceived helpfulness of consultations have been found in other studies of clinicians (Orr and Moon, 1993; McClung et al., 1996; Yen and Schneiderman, 1999). Interestingly, in those studies that have compared clinician with patient satisfaction, patients have been found to be less satisfied with ethics consultation (McClung et al., 1996; Yen and Schneiderman, 1999).

A few studies have assessed clinical ethics support service using an experimental design. The best-known are a series of studies by Schneiderman and colleagues looking at the impact of ethics consultation in intensive care settings (Schneiderman, Gilmer, and Teetze, 2000; Schneiderman et al., 2003). These trials examined consultations involving parents who had "value laden" treatment conflicts as identified by clinicians. A single-centre trial and a multi-centre trial were conducted, with patients randomized to the intervention (offer of ethics consultation) or control (not offered). Both trials found that ethics consultation was associated with shorter hospital ICU stays, reduced use of services, and less cost among those who did not survive to discharge. There were, however, no statistically significant differences between the intervention and control arms for those who survived to discharge. The results of these studies suggest that the intervention of ethics consultation was beneficial to patients who did not survive to hospital discharge and was not harmful to patients who did survive. The authors' conclusion was that consultations "seem to be useful in resolving conflicts that may be inappropriately prolonging nonbeneficial or unwanted treatments at the end of life" (Schneiderman et al., 2003, 1172). A later cost analysis of data from the multi-centre trial confirmed the finding that ethics consultation was associated with a reduction in hospital days and treatment costs (Gilmer et al., 2005).

To summarize, there has been extensive uptake of CES services, most widely in the US but with increasing numbers in many other nations. Empirical studies (as well as more general reports) indicate that CES services vary considerably in form, function, and activity. The limited and contested nature of evaluation of performance means the overall value of CES, its effectiveness, costs and benefits, cannot be precisely determined. And as we discuss below, the heterogeneity of CES and the paucity of evaluation have raised considerable concern about the quality and impact of CES services.

Two particular concerns regarding case consultations arise from studies of CES services—the often low utilization by clinicians and lack of patient involvement in consultations. Empirical evidence suggests that many CES services have low rates of referral. According to the most recent data for the US (Fox, Myers, and Pearlman,

2007) the median number of consultations for the year prior to the survey was three. In the UK, Slowther, McClimans, and Price (2012) found half of the committees they survey had between one and five consultations in the previous year. Another relatively recent study of clinical ethics services in the United Kingdom led the researchers to conclude "At the moment, the stark reality about CECs in the UK is that clinicians are not using them" (Whitehead et al., 2009, 454). While this is an important observation, these data are limited in that they are not recent and where CES services are flourishing, rates of consultation are likely to be higher.

It is widely acknowledged that there has been mixed success with establishing and maintaining CES support services. Some flourish, others fail to thrive (Conrad, 2006). Failure to thrive can arise from: a lack of clear purpose or lack of institutional support (Mills, Rorty, and Spencer, 2006); clinician reluctance to seek support because of factors such as fear of scrutiny or loss of authority; because they are not found to be helpful; because they are not trusted or simply because clinicians are not aware of them (DeRenzo, Mokwunye, and Lynch, 2006; UNESCO, 2005; Slowther, McClimans, and Price, 2012). No particular model appears to be any more likely to flourish or fail to thrive than any other.

The low rates of consultation experienced by many services might indicate that what is being offered is seen by many clinicians as neither desirable nor warranted. A low rate of referral could mean that clinicians do not perceive a need for ethics support. Neither the "bottom-up" development nor increased prevalence of support services show how widely the need for ethics support is shared among clinicians. With only a small number of studies attempting to empirically establish need among clinicians (Larcher, Lask, and McCarthy, 1997; Slowther, 1998; Racine and Hayes, 2006), need for formal clinical ethics support appears more assumed than systematically, empirically established (Williamson, 2007; Dauwerse et al., 2011).

Many CES services do not appear to facilitate the direct participation of patients and their families in the consultation process (e.g., Newson, Neitzke, and Reiter-Theil, 2009). There has also been contention in the literature as to whether patients *should* be involved in ethics case consultations and if so, to what degree. Some have claimed that where consultations have a direct bearing on care, the lodestars of clinical ethics support are potentially undermined, namely, patient autonomy and self-determination (Wolf, 1992), raising important questions about *due process* (McLean, 2007, 2009). This concern has been expressed most forcefully in the US, with critics of CES fearing that a creeping quasi-legal status may become attached to the deliberations of committees and consultants (Pope, 2009), reflecting the possibility that, as McLean (2008) has observed, it is "all-too-easy move from advice to authority and from commentary to decision-making" (2008, 101). Even if the consultant (or committee) issues non-binding advice, this may still impact on subsequent actions (McLean, 2007). In cases where a consultation involves a dispute between the patient (and family) and the clinical team, there is a need to ensure some degree of procedural fairness; all parties in a dispute have the right to a fair hearing. Attention to formal justice and due process is considered particularly important (McLean, 2007).

OPTIMIZING THE QUALITY OF CES SERVICES

The heterogeneity of CES and the paucity of evaluation have given rise to concerns about the quality of CES services. Tulsky and Fox have claimed, for example, that: "Despite all that has been written about this field, two fundamental questions remain unanswered. First, does ethics consultation offer measurable benefits worthy of the current investment of time and money? Second, if it is effective, which models are the most effective and under what conditions are different models more or less effective?" (1996, 111).

According to Magill (2013), quality has become the preeminent discourse on CES services in the US (and elsewhere). The heterogeneity of CES services, given a lack of standards of practice, oversight, and accountability, is likely to be matched by variation in service quality (Aulisio, Arnold, and Youngner, 2000; Slowther, 2008; Frolic and PHEEP Steering Committee, 2012; Schiedermayer and La Puma, 2012). Quality, particularly in regards to case consultation, is predominantly concerned with the competence of CES services—that is, whether they command the necessary knowledge and skills in ethics and health law. Given that the evidence indicates many people involved in CES have only rudimentary training in philosophical ethics (e.g., Fox, Myers, and Pearlman, 2007; Slowther, McClimans, and Price, 2012), claims to ethics expertise are often questionable. Claims to moral expertise are also subject to critique on more theoretical grounds, such as debate over what moral expertise is. We discuss this further below.

For some, this worryingly indicates that well-meaning but inexpert consultants or committees are having a potentially decisive influence on decisions about patient care (Fletcher and Hoffmann, 1994; Dubler and Blustein, 2007; Courtwright et al., 2014). Clinical ethicists have responded by devoting significant intellectual and material effort to develop standards of practice for CES and develop appropriate and rigorous methods to evaluate quality (e.g., Tarzian and ABSH Core Competencies Update Taskforce, 2013; Larcher, Slowther, and Watson, 2010).

The most significant development in practice standards has been the *Core Competencies* developed by the American Society of Bioethics and Humanities, first issued in 1998 (Society for Health and Human Values–Society for Bioethics Consultation, 1998) and more recently updated (Tarzian and ASBH Core Competencies Update Taskforce, 2013). The foundational assertion of the Core Competencies is "that HCEC done well by competent HCE consultants benefits stakeholders, and HCEC done poorly by unqualified HCE consultants either fails to benefit or harms stakeholders" (Tarzian and ASBH Core Competencies Update Task Force, 2013, 3). The *Core Competencies* focus on the knowledge, skills, and character traits that any service (consultant or committee) must have to adequately perform as an ethical consultation service. The knowledge required is wide-ranging and calls for targeted recruitment of suitable members or co-opting relevant expertise as it is needed. The values required of a committee are described as "aspirations" to be acquired over time similar to professional development. While there is limited evidence on the extent to which the Core

Competencies are applied by individual services, and whilst there is some concern that emphasis on competencies reflects the malign influence of managerialism and may divert CES from the primary goal of moral inquiry towards more institutional or bureaucratic goals (King, 1999; Bishop, Fanning, and Bliton, 2009), there is little doubt that debate about the competencies of CES has had a significant impact on the establishment of standards for CES services (Adams, 2009; Bishop, Fanning, and Bliton, 2009).

A parallel development to developing practice standards to enhance quality has been the push to professionalise clinical ethics expertise (Tarzian, 2009; Childs, 2009; Frolic and PHEEP Steering Committee, 2012; Acres et al., 2012; Reel, 2012). For some, professionalization is not only necessary and desirable but also inevitable given the increasing emphasis on standards, quality and accountability, concerns about medical liability and the emergence of the patient safety movement (Acres et al., 2012). More generally, both advocates and critics of CES agree that in order to fulfil their function and meet the expectations and needs of relevant stakeholders the people doing the work of clinical ethics consultation (CEC) should be able to demonstrate at least minimal levels of competence (Tarzian, 2009).

On our reading, the predominant theme in the literature addressing quality is that CES services are too often *underpowered*; they lack ethics expertise, standards, and evaluable outcomes; they engage consultants who lack professional standing; they are poorly integrated into their organization and consequently are under-used; they are frequently under-resourced, and they have unproven benefits. The main solution offered is further institutionalization, through the standardization of consultation, the professionalization of consultants, a thorough integration into its host organization and having CES more generally incorporated into a particular health care system. The influence of the Core Competencies, the accelerating push to professionalise consultants (at least in the US) and the prominence of integrated approaches such as the VA's IntegratedEthics model suggest that institutionalization is well under way.

Institutionalization, however, has its critics. The concern is that standardization and professionalization risks *overpowering* the very clinicians and patients it is meant to serve. Institutionalization can inflate the authority of CES at the expense of patients, may homogenize practice, diminish moral inquiry, and result in CES being co-opted as a tool for risk-management and saving money. Others are concerned that standardization forces ethics consultation towards procedural efficiency and metrics and away from the substantive goods of the case at hand. A focus on standardized, measurable process can limit the capacity of a CES service to reveal, clarify, and perhaps challenge the various understandings, of all parties, of what is a medical good, an institutional good, and what a patient holds as good (Bishop, Fanning, and Bliton, 2009).

There has also been resistance to the notion of an ethics "expert" from the inception of CES services (Bishop, Fanning, and Bliton, 2009) and this has been a significant obstacle for establishing CES and gaining patronage (Rasmussen, 2011a). The notion of expertise in ethics is a complicated matter that involves both metaphysical and epistemological questions of whether expertise in ethics is actually possible and moral and normative questions of whether such expertise and the authority it brings is desirable (Noble, 1982;

Yoder, 1998; Rasmussen, 2011a). Critics of ethics expertise such as Scofield (2008) and Smith (2001) argue that *expertise* presumes access to facts or consensus among practitioners. In the absence of any moral consensus among ethicists, holding actual "expertise" on moral issues simply isn't possible (Engelhardt, 2009; Scofield, 2008). As Shalit argues, "[t]he philosopher's recommendation depends on a set of criteria that is not agreed upon, but varies from culture to culture and, more and more, from individual to individual" (1997, 24). For some critics (e.g., Noble, 1982), even if ethics expertise is possible, it may not be desirable because it shifts moral authority from the patient, and their carer, to the ethics expert, thereby undermining the agency and autonomy of both and challenging the very principles of democracy upon which the idea of CES is based (Scofield, 2008).

Advocates of CES argue that ethics expertise need not involve any metaphysical claim regarding moral truths or the claim that clinical ethicists have epistemic access to such truths (Yoder, 1998; Steinkamp, Gordijn, and ten Have, 2008; Rasmussen, 2011a, 2011b). According to Rasmussen (2011a), metaphysical objections largely stem from the ambiguity of the term "moral expertise." She claims that expertise here should be conceived as a "facility with moral arguments" (2011a, 649) rather than "possession of moral truth" (2011a, 649). Ethics expertise involves a "superior familiarity with context" (2011a, 651) where the consultant uses her training and knowledge to guide the parties involved through the relevant "facts" (laws, policies, norms, cultural values) to a more informed understanding of the situation (Rasmussen, 2011a). Ethics expertise, as opposed to moral expertise, involves making "non-normatively binding recommendations grounded in a pervasive ethos or practice within a particular context" (Rasmussen, 2011a, 650). Steinkamp, Gordijn, and ten Have (2008) use a similar definition of ethics expertise, that is, the capacity to provide "strong justifications" to argue that the dialogue between the expert ethicist and clinicians is a cogently democratic means of reaching consensus on the moral norms at hand (Steinkamp, Gordijn, and ten Have, 2008). In this dialogue, the expertise of the ethicist complements and enhances the moral competence of the non-ethicists, clinicians (and patients) by clarifying what is ethically at stake (Steinkamp, Gordijn, and ten Have, 2008). Conceived as such, ethics expertise does not make a metaphysical claim that there are moral truths and that clinical ethicists have epistemic access to such truths, does not usurp the autonomy and agency of the non-expert, and offers expertise but does not assume authority (Rasmussen, 2011a).

Evaluating the quality of a clinical ethics services is therefore an area of considerable uncertainty and debate. Major criticism has been voiced at evaluating clinical ethics services using outcome measurements more suitable for standard clinical interventions. It is not clear to some observers that quantitative measures, such as tallying the tasks performed by a service, measuring user satisfaction or calculating cost savings are appropriate for assessing the quality of a clinical ethics service (Mills, Tereskerz, and Davis, 2005; Gordon, 2007; Williamson, 2007; Pfafflin, Kobert, and Reiter-Theil, 2009). The number of consultations a service provides is clearly not a proxy for quality. One ethics committee may conduct a large number of consultations but be a little more than a rubber stamp; another committee may conduct fewer consultations but provide rigorous ethical analysis (Williamson, 2007). While user satisfaction with an ethics service may be helpful in assessing service quality, there are some difficulties with it. Williamson (2007) advises caution in using satisfaction, firstly because its validity as a measure of quality is suspect given its inherent subjectivity, and secondly because often only clinicians and not patients are asked to participate.

A number of authors have voiced concern at the use of cost-savings to evaluate the effectiveness of CES (e.g., Mills, Tereskerz, and Davis, 2005; Rasmussen, 2006, 2011b). Rasmussen (2006) argues that if cost saving is the measure by which an ethics service is evaluated, there could be significant pressure on CES services to achieve savings, such as providing advice that encourages less costly decisions. Mills, Tereskerz, and Davis (2005) similarly argue that savings may come to rival if not dominate the integral goals of consultation resulting not only in consultation emphasising the least costly options but in making consultation mandatory for cases where costs may be saved, for example end-of-life care decisions. The potential for co-optation of CES services as a cost-saving measure (which Rasmussen (2006) labels as a "sinister innovation") could result in a profound loss of trust among clinicians (and patients) if they come to perceive this as the primary objective of consultation "If the 'quality' or effectiveness of an outcome has any relationship to trust, as it should in healthcare-related activities, then quality will be eroded, as stakeholders understand that cost savings may be one of the reasons for initiating a consultation" (Mills, Tereskerz, and Davis, 2005, 60).

CONCLUSION

The story of CES services is one of increasing expansion and advocacy for its potential benefits. It is also a cautionary tale about the challenges involved in ensuring competency and viability. A review of the literature and the international experience with CES services suggests that they have considerable potential to prevent and resolve moral conflicts, minimize moral distress, support patient autonomy, and enhance institutional efficiency and cost-effectiveness. But while these benefits are highly plausible, the ad hoc development and heterogeneity of CES services and the lack of consensus over the evaluation of their performance raises some doubts about how often they are achieved. Many questions remain to be answered regarding the structure, function, and organizational model for CES support. Where should CES services be located within hospital structures? How independent should they be? Should CES provide contemporaneous case consultation or retrospective case review? Should case consultation be provided by "experts"? Should the deliberations of CES services be advisory or binding (or neither)? Who should be the primary beneficiary of CES support? How should potential conflicts of interest be managed? While it is crucial that institutions seeking to establish CES services and those working in clinical ethics confront these issues, questions about CES should not obscure the fact that CES services have primarily spread because those involved in patient care have recognized the need for support. These questions should also not diminish the significant intellectual effort devoted to thinking through the appropriate purposes and best practices of CES services. There are now decades of collective experience and scholarship, well-established approaches and detailed models and guidelines from which those seeking to establish a CES service can draw.

Experience suggests that to be active and sustainable, a CES service must be visible, accessible, understood, and trusted. These in turn require the service to be clear in purpose; fully integrated into the life of the organization; adequately resourced; appropriately constituted and competent; accountable (transparent and assessable); and independent. Ongoing evaluative research should be a core component of the development of CES services. This will have three distinct benefits: it will enable evaluation of clinical ethics services; it will strengthen the culture of ethical inquiry and ethical practice within the health service; and it will provide opportunities to increase understanding of issues of ethical and legal importance in the design and delivery of health care. It is crucial that ongoing research into clinical ethics is conducted in order to establish what is necessary for clinical ethics services to work.

REFERENCES

Acres, C. A., Prager, K., Hardart, G. E., and Fins, J. J. (2012). Credentialing the clinical ethics consultant: An academic medical center affirms professionalism and practice. *The Journal of Clinical Ethics*, 23(2): 156–164.

Adams, D. M. (2009). Ethics consultation and 'facilitated' consensus. *The Journal of Clinical Ethics*, 20(1): 44–55.

Agich, G. (2005). What kind of doing is ethics consultation? *Theoretical Medicine and Bioethics*, 26(1): 7–24.

Agich, G. J. (2009a). The issue of expertise in clinical ethics. *Diametros*, 22: 3–20.

Agich, G. J. (2009b). Understanding criticisms of clinical ethics and ethics consultation. *Formosan Journal of Medical Humanities*, 10(1 and 2): 8–19.

Akabayashi, A., Taylor-Slingsby, B., Nagao, N., Kai, I., and Sato, H. (2008). A five year follow-up national study of ethics committees in medical organizations in Japan. *HEC Forum*, 20(1): 49–60.

Aleksandrova, S. (2008). Survey on the experience in ethical decision-making and attitude of Pleven university hospital physicians towards ethics consultation. *Medicine, Health Care and Philosophy*, 11(1): 35–42.

American Society for Bioethics and Humanities (2009). The report of the American society for bioethics and humanities core competencies for health care ethics consultation (Online). Available at: <http://asbh.org/publications/content/asbhpublications.html> (accessed October 9, 2015).

Aulisio, M. P., Arnold, R. M., and Youngner, S. J. (2000). Health care ethics consultation: Nature, goals and competencies. A position paper from the society for health and human values society for bioethics consultation task force on standards for bioethics consultation. *Annals of Internal Medicine*, 33(1): 9–69.

Bankauskaite, V. and Jakusovaite, I. (2006). Dealing with ethical problems in the health care system in Lithuania: Achievements and challenges. *Journal of Medical Ethics*, 32(10): 584–587.

Beyleveld, D., Brownsword, R., and Wallace, S. (2002). Clinical ethics committees: Clinician support or crisis management? *HEC Forum*, 14(1): 13–25.

Bishop, J. P., Fanning, J. B., and Bliton, M. J. (2009). Of goals and goods and floundering about: A dissensus report on clinical ethics consultation. *HEC Forum* 21(3): 275–291.

Blake, D. C. (1992). The hospital ethics committee: Health care's moral conscience or white elephant? *Hastings Centre Report*, 22(1): 6–11.

Bosk, C. L. (1999). Professional ethicist available: Logical, secular, friendly. *Daedalus*, 128(4): 47–68.

Brecher, B. (2006). The politics of medical and health ethics: Collapsing goods and the moral climate. *The Journal of Value Inquiry*, 40(2): 359–370.

Callahan, D. (1999). The social sciences and the task of bioethics. *Daedalus*, 128(4): 275–294.

Chidwick, P., Bell, J., Connolly, E., Coughlin, M. D., Frolic, A., Hardingham, L., and Zlotnik Shaul, R. (2010). Exploring a model role description for ethicists. *HEC Forum*, 22(1): 31–40.

Childs, B. H. (2009). Credentialing clinical ethics consultants: Lessons to be learned. *HEC Forum*, 21(3): 231–240.

Conrad, E. (2006). Terminal success. *HEC Forum*, 18(4): 287–290.

Courtwright, A., Brackett, S., Cist, A., Cremens, M. C., Krakauer, E. L., and Robinson, E. M. (2014). The changing composition of a hospital ethics committee: A tertiary care center's experience. *HEC Forum*, 26(1): 59–68.

Cranford, R. E. and Doudera, A. E. (1984). The emergence of institutional ethics committees. *Medicine and Health Care*, 12(1): 13–20.

Dauwerse, L., Abma, T., Molewijk, B., and Widdershoven, G. (2011). Need for ethics support in health care institutions: Views of Dutch board members and ethics support staff. *Journal of Medical Ethics*, 37(8): 456–460.

DeRenzo, E. G., Mokwunye, N., and Lynch, J. L. (2006). Rounding: How everyday ethics can invigorate a hospital's ethics committee. *HEC Forum*, 18(4): 319–331.

Dorries, A., Boitte, P., Borovecki, A., Cobbaut, J-P., Reiter-Theilv S., and Slowther, A. (2011). Institutional challenges for clinical ethics committees. *HEC Forum*, 23(3): 193–205.

Dubler, N. N. and Blustein, J. (2007). Credentialing ethics consultants: An invitation to collaboration. *The American Journal of Bioethics*, 7(2): 35–37.

Du Val, G., Clarridge, B., Gensler, G., and Danis, M. (2004). A national survey of U.S. internists' experiences with ethical dilemmas and ethics consultation. *Journal of General Internal Medicine*, 19(3): 251–258.

Du Val, G., Sartorius, L., Clarridge., B., Gensler, G., and Danis, M. (2001). What triggers requests for ethics consultations? *Journal of Medical Ethics* 27(Suppl 1): 24–9.

Dzur, A. W. (2002). Democratizing the hospital: Deliberative-democratic bioethics. *Journal of Health Politics, Policy and Law*, 27(2): 177–212.

Ells, C. (2006). Healthcare ethics committee's contribution to review of institutional policy. *HEC Forum*, 18(3): 265–275.

Engelhardt, H. T. (1999). Healthcare ethics committees: Re-examining their social and moral functions. *HEC Forum*, 11(2): 87–100.

Engelhardt, H. T. (2009). Credentialing strategically ambiguous and heterogeneous social skills: The emperor without clothes. *HEC Forum*, 21(3): 293–306.

Fletcher, J. C. and Hoffmann, D. E. (1994). Ethics committees: Time to experiment with standards. *Annals of Internal Medicine*, 120(4): 335–338.

Førde, R., Pedersen, R., and Akre, V. (2008). Clinicians' evaluation of clinical ethics consultations in Norway: A qualitative study. *Medicine, Health Care and Philosophy*, 11(1): 17–25.

Fournier, V., Rari, E., Førde, R., Neitzke, G., Pegoraro, R., and Newson, A. J. (2009). Clinical
ethics consultation in Europe: A comparative and ethical review of the role of patients.
Clinical Ethics, 4(3): 131–138.

Fox, E. (2010). IntegratedEthics: An innovative program to improve ethics quality in health
care. *The Innovation Journal: The Public Sector Innovation Journal*, 15(2) (article 8) (online).
Available at: < http://www.innovation.cc/scholarly-style/fox_integrated8ethics_8_final.pdf
> (accessed October 9, 2015).

Fox, E., Myers, S., and Pearlman, R. A. (2007). Ethics consultation in United States hospitals: A national survey. *American Journal of Bioethics*, 7(2): 13–25.

Frewer, A. and Fahr, U. (2007). Clinical ethics and confidentiality: Opinions of experts and ethics committees. *HEC Forum*, 19(4): 277–291.

Frikovic, A. and Gosic, P. (2006). Practical experiences in the work of institutional ethics committees in Croatia on the example of the ethics committee at clinical hospital center Rijeka
(Croatia). *HEC Forum*, 18(1): 37–48.

Frolic, A., Drolet, K., Bryanton, K., Caron, C., Cupido, C., Flaherty, B., Fung, S., and McCall,
L. (2012). Opening the black box of ethics policy work: Evaluating a covert practice. *The
American Journal of Bioethics*, 12(11): 3–15.

Frolic, A. and Practicing Healthcare Ethicists Exploring Professionalization (PHEEP) Steering
Committee (2012). Grassroots origins, national engagement: Exploring the professionalization of practicing health care ethicists in Canada. *HEC Forum*, 24(3): 153–164.

Gaudine, A., Lamb, M., LeFort, S. M., and Thorne, L. (2011). Barriers and facilitators to consulting hospital clinical ethics committees. *Nursing Ethics*, 18(6): 767–780.

Gaudine, A., Thorne, L., LeFort, S., and Lamb, M. (2010). Evolution of hospital clinical ethics
committees in Canada. *Journal of Medical Ethics*, 36(3): 132–137.

Gill, A. W., Saul, P., McPhee, J., and Kerridge, I. (2004). Acute clinical ethics consultation: The
practicalities. *Medical Journal of Australia*, 181: 204–206.

Gilmer, T., Schneiderman, L. J., Teetzel, H., Blustein, J., Briggs, K., Cohn, F., Cranford, R.,
Dugan, D., Komatsu, G., and Young, E. (2005). The costs of non-beneficial treatment in the
intensive care setting. *Health Affairs*, 24(4): 961–971.

Godkin, M. D., Faith, K., Upshur, R. E., McRae, S. K., and Tracy, C. S. (2005). Project examining effectiveness in clinical ethics (PEECE): Phase 1 descriptive analysis of nine clinical ethics services. *Journal of Medical Ethics*, 31(9): 501–512.

Gordon, E. J. (2007). A better way to evaluate clinical ethics consultations? an ecological
approach. *The American Journal of Bioethics*, 7(2): 26–29.

Guerrier, M. (2006). Hospital based ethics, current situation in France: Between "Espaces" and
committees. *Journal of Medical Ethics*, 32(9): 503–506.

Hurst, S. A., Reiter-Theil, S., Slowther, A., Pegoraro, R., Foerde, R., and Danis, M. (2007a).
Physicians' access to ethics support services in four European countries. *Health Care
Analysis*, 15(4): 321–335.

Hurst, S. A., Perrier, A., Pegoraro, R., Reiter-Theil, S., Forde, R., Slowther, A. M., Garret-Mayer,
E., and Danis, M. (2007b). Ethical difficulties in clinical practice: experiences of European
doctors. *Journal of Medical Ethics*, 33(1): 51–57.

Hurst, S. A., Reiter-Theil, S., Baumann-Hölzle, R., Foppa, C., Malacrida, R., Bosshard, G.,
Salonth, M., and Mauron, A. (2008). The growth of clinical ethics in a multilingual country: Challenges and opportunities. *Bioethica Forum*, 1(1): 15–24.

Jonsen, A. R. (1993). The birth of bioethics. *Hastings Center Report*, 23(6): S1–S15.

Kesselheim, J. C., Johnson, J., and Joffe, S. (2010). Ethics consultation in children's hospitals: Results from a survey of pediatric clinical ethicists. *Pediatrics*, 125(4): 742–746.

King, N. M. (1999). Who ate the apple? A commentary on the core competencies report. *HEC Forum*, 11(2): 170–175.

La Puma, J., Stocking, C. B., Darling, C. M., and Siegler, M. (1992). Community hospital ethics consultation: Evaluation and comparison with a university hospital service. *American Journal of Medicine*, 92(4): 346–351.

La Puma, J., Stocking, C. B., Silverstein, M. D., Di Martini, D., and Siegler, M. (1988). An ethics consultation service in a teaching hospital: Utilization and evaluation. *JAMA*, 260(6): 808–811.

Larcher, V. F., Lask, B., and McCarthy, J. M. (1997). Paediatrics at the cutting edge: Do we need clinical ethics committees? *Journal of Medical Ethics*, 23(4): 245–249.

Larcher, V., Slowther, A. M., and Watson, A. (2010). Core competencies for clinical ethics committees. *Clinical Medicine*, 10(1): 30–33.

Lebeer, G. (2005). Clinical ethics committees in Europe: Assistance in medical decisions, fora for democratic debates or bodies to monitor basic rights? In *Ethics, law and society*, ed. Gunning, J. and Holm, S., Vol. 1, pp. 65–73. Aldershot: Ashgate Publishing Ltd.

Louhiala, P., Saarni, S., Hietala., K., and Pasternack, A. (2011). Physicians' Ethics Forum: A web-based ethics consultation service. *Journal of Medical Ethics*, 38(2): 83–86.

McClimans, L., Slowther, A., and Parker, M. (2012). Can UK clinical ethics committees improve quality of care? *HEC Forum*, 24(2): 1–9.

McClung, J. A., Russell, S. K., DeLuca, M., and Harlan, J. (1996). Evaluation of a medical ethics consultation service: Opinions of patients and health care providers. *American Journal of Medicine*, 100(4): 456–460.

McDonald, F., Simpson, C., and O'Brien, F. (2008). Including organizational ethics in policy review processes in health care institutions: A view from Canada. *HEC Forum*, 20(2): 137–153.

McGee, G., Spanogle, J. P., Caplan, A. L., and Asch, D. A. (2001). A national study of ethics committees. *American Journal of Bioethics*, 1(4): 60–64.

McLean, S. A. (2007). What and who are clinical ethics committees for? *Journal of Medical Ethics*, 33(9): 497–500.

McLean, S. A. (2008). Clinical ethics committees: A due process wasteland? *Clinical Ethics*, 3: 99–104.

McLean, S. A. (2009). Clinical ethics consultation in the United Kingdom. *Diametros*, 22: 76–89.

McNeill, P. M. (2001). A critical analysis of Australian clinical ethics committees and the functions they serve. *Bioethics*, 15(5/6): 443–460.

Macdonald, A. and Worthington, R. (2012). The role of clinical ethics in the health care system of New Zealand. Health Quality and Safety Commission (NZ) and Capital and Coast District Health Board, New Zealand, Auckland.

MacRae, S., Chidwick, P., Berry, S., Secker, B. P., Zlotnik, H., Shaul, R., Faith, K., and Singer, P. A. (2005). Clinical bioethics integration, sustainability, and accountability: The hub and spokes strategy. *Journal of Medical Ethics*, 31(5): 256–261.

Magill, G. (2013). Quality in ethics consultations. *Medicine, Health Care and Philosophy*, 16(4): 761–774.

Meulenbergs, T., Vermylen, J., and Schotsmans, P. T. (2005). The current state of clinical ethics and health care ethics committees in Belgium. *Journal of Medical Ethics*, 31(6): 318–321.

Mills, A. E., Rorty, M. V., and Spencer, E. W. (2006). Introduction: Ethics committees and failure to thrive. *HEC Forum*, 18(4): 279–286.

Mills, A. E., Tereskerz, P., and Davis, W. (2005) Is evaluating ethics consultation on the basis of cost a good idea? *Cambridge Quarterly of Healthcare Ethics*, 4: 57–64.

Milmore, D. (2006). Hospital ethics committees: A survey in upstate New York. *HEC Forum*, 18(3): 222–244.

Moeller, J. R., Albanese, T. H., Garchar, K., Aultman, J. M., Radwany, S., and Frate, D. (2012). Functions and outcomes of a clinical medical ethics committee: A review of 100 consults. *HEC Forum*, 24(2): 99–114.

Moreno, J. D. (2009). Ethics committees and ethics consultants. In *A Companion to Bioethics*, 2nd edition, ed. Kuhse, H. and Singer, P., pp. 573–583. Oxford: Blackwell.

Nelson, W. A., Gardent, P. B., Shulman. E., and Plaine, M. E. (2010a). Preventing ethics conflicts and improving health care quality through system redesign. *Quality and Safety in Health Care*, 19(6): 526–530.

Nelson, W. A., Rosenberg, M. C., Mackenzie, T., and Weeks, W. B. (2010b). The presence of ethics programs in critical access hospitals. *HEC Forum*, 22(4): 267–274.

Newson, A. J., Neitzke, G., and Reiter-Theil, S. (2009). The role of patients in European clinical ethics. *Clinical Ethics*, 4(3): 109–110.

Noble, C. N. (1982). Ethics and experts. *Hastings Center Report*, 12(3): 7–15.

Orlowski, J. P., Hein, S., Christensen, J. A., Meinke, R., and Sincich, T. (2006). Why doctors use or do not use ethics consultation. *Journal of Medical Ethics*, 32(9): 499–502.

Orr, R. D. and Moon, E. (1993). Effectiveness of an ethics consultation service. *The Journal of Family Practice*, 36(1): 49–53.

Pedersen, R., Akre, V., and Førde, R. (2009). What is happening during case deliberations in clinical ethics committees? A pilot study. *Journal of Medical Ethics*, 35(3): 147–152.

Pellegrino, E. (1988). Clinical ethics: Biomedical ethics at the bedside. *JAMA*, 206(6): 837–839.

Pfafflin, M., Kobert, K., and Reiter-Theil, S. (2009). Evaluating clinical ethics consultation: A European perspective. *Cambridge Quarterly of Healthcare Ethics*, 18: 406–419.

Pope, T. M. (2009). Multi-institutional health care ethics committees: The procedurally fair internal dispute resolution mechanism. *Campbell Law Review*, 31: 257–332.

Racine, E. and Hayes, K. (2006). The need for a clinical ethics service and its goals in a community health care service centre: A survey. *Journal of Medical Ethics*, 32(10): 564–566.

Rasmussen, L. M. (2006). Sinister innovations: Beware the co-optation of clinical ethics consultation. *The Journal of Value Inquiry*, 40(2): 235–242.

Rasmussen, L. M. (2011a). An ethics expertise for clinical ethics consultation. *The Journal of Law, Medicine and Ethics*, 39(4): 649–661.

Rasmussen, L. M. (2011b). Clinical ethics consultation's dilemma, and a solution. *The Journal of Clinical Ethics*, 22(4): 380–392.

Reel, K. (2012). The benefits of practice standards and other practice-defining texts: And why health care ethicists ought to explore them. *HEC Forum*, 24(3): 203–217.

Romano, M. E., Wahlander, S. B., Lang, B. H., Li, G., and Prager, K. M. (2009). Mandatory ethics consultation policy. *Mayo Clinic Proceedings*, 84(7): 581–585.

Rosner, F. (1985). Hospital medical ethics committees: A review of their development. *JAMA*, 253(19): 2693–2697.

Rothman, D. (1992). *Strangers at the bedside: A history of how law and bioethics transformed medical decision making*. New York: Basic Books.

Royal College of Physicians (2005). *Ethics in practice: Background and recommendations for enhanced support.* London: Royal College of Physicians.

Rubin, S. B. and Zoloth, L. (2004). Clinical ethics and the road less taken: Mapping the future by tracking the past. *Journal of Law Medicine and Ethics,* 32(2): 218–225.

Schiedermayer, D. and La Puma, J. (2012). Credentialing and certification in ethics consultation: Lessons from palliative care. *The Journal of Clinical Ethics,* 23(2): 172–174.

Schildmann. J., Molewijk, B., Benaroyo, L., Forde, R., and Neitzke, G. (2013). Evaluation of clinical ethics support services clinical and its normativity. *Journal of Medical Ethics,* 39(11): 681–685.

Schneiderman, L. J., Gilmer, T., Teetzel, H. D., Dugan, D. O., Blustein, J., Cranford, R., Briggs, K. B., Komatsu, G. I., Goodman-Crews, P, Cohn, F., and Young, E. W. (2003). Effect of ethics consultations on nonbeneficial life-sustaining treatments in the intensive care setting: a randomized controlled trial. *JAMA,* 290(9): 1166–1172.

Schneiderman, I., Gilmer, T., and Teetze, H. (2000). Impact of ethics consultations in the intensive care setting: A randomized, controlled trial. *Critical Care Medicine,* 28(12): 3920–3924.

Scofield, G. R. (2008). Speaking of ethical expertise. ... *Kennedy Institute of Ethics Journal,* 18(4): 369–384.

Shalit, R. (1997). When we were philosopher kings: The rise of the medical ethicist. *New Republic,* 216(17): 24–28.

Singer, P. A., Pellegrino, E. D., and Siegler, M. (1990). Ethics committees and consultants. *Journal of Clinical Ethics,* 1(4): 263–267.

Singer, P. A, Pellegrino, E. D., and Siegler, M, (2001). Clinical ethics revisited. *BMC Medical Ethics,* 2(1): 1.

Slowther, A. (1998). Is there a demand for a clinical ethics advisory service in the UK? *Journal of Medical Ethics,* 24(3): 207.

Slowther, A. (2008). Embedding clinical ethics in a health care system: The experience of the UK clinical ethics network. *Bioethica Forum,* 1(1): 40–44.

Slowther, A., Bunch, C., Woolnough, B., and Hope, T. (2001). Clinical ethics support services in the UK: An investigation of the current provision of ethics support to health professionals in the UK. *Journal of Medical Ethics,* 27(supp), i2–i8.

Slowther, A., Hill, D., and McMillan, J. (2002). Clinical ethics committees: Opportunity or threat? *HEC Forum,* 14(1): 4–12.

Slowther, A., Hope, T., and Ashcroft, R. (2001). Clinical ethics committees: A worldwide development. *Journal of Medical Ethics,* 27(Suppl 1): i1.

Slowther, A., Johnston, C., Goodall, J., and Hope, T. (2004). Development of clinical ethics committees. *BMJ,* 328(7445): 950.

Slowther, A., McClimans, L., and Price, C. (2012). Development of clinical ethics services in the UK: A national survey. *Journal of Medical Ethics,* 38(4): 210–214.

Smith, W. J. (2001). The question of method in ethics consultation: Transforming a career into a profession? *The American Journal of Bioethics,* 1(4): 42–43.

Society for Health and Human Values–Society for Bioethics Consultation (1998). *Core competencies for health care ethics consultation: The report of the american society for bioethics and humanities.* Glenview, IL: American Society for Bioethics Consultation.

Steinkamp, N. L., Gordijn, B., and ten Have H. A. M. J. (2008). Debating ethical expertise. *Kennedy Institute of Ethics Journal,* 18(2): 173–192.

Swetz, K. M., Crowley, M. E., Hook, C. C., and Mueller, P. S. (2007). Report of 255 clinical ethics consultations and review of the literature. *Mayo Clinic Proceedings,* 82(6): 686–691.

Tapper, E. B. (2013). Consults for conflict: The history of ethics consultation. *Proceedings (Baylor University Medical Center)*, 26(4): 417–422.

Tapper, E. B., Vercler, C. J., Cruze, D., and Sexson, W. (2010). Ethics consultation at a large urban public teaching hospital. *Mayo Clinic Proceedings*, 85(5): 433–438.

Tarzian, A. J. (2009). Credentials for clinical ethics consultation – are we there yet? *HEC Forum*, 21(3): 241–248.

Tarzian, A. J. and ASBH Core Competencies Update Task Force (2013). Health care ethics consultation: An update on core competencies and emerging standards from the American Society for Bioethics and Humanities' core competencies update task force. *The American Journal of Bioethics*, 13(2): 3–13.

Teel, K. (1975). Physician's dilemma—A doctor's view: What the law should be. *Baylor Law Review*, 27: 6–10.

Tulsky J. A. and Fox, E. (1996). Evaluating ethics consultation: Framing the questions. *The Journal of Clinical Ethics*, 7(2): 109–115.

UNESCO (2005). *Establishing Bioethics Committees. Guide No. 1.* Paris: UNESCO.

Wenger, N. S., Golan, O., Shalev, C., and Glick, S. (2002). Hospital ethics committees in Israel: Structure, function and heterogeneity in the setting of statutory ethics committees. *Journal of Medical Ethics*, 28(3): 177–182.

Weidema, F. C., Molewijk, A. C., Widdershoven, G. A. M., and Abma, T. A. (2012). Enacting ethics: Bottom-up involvement in implementing moral case deliberation. *Health Care Analysis*, 20(1): 1–19.

Whitehead, J. M., Sokol, D. K., Bowman, D., and Sedgwick, P. (2009). Consultation activities of clinical ethics committees in the United Kingdom: An empirical study and wake-up call. *Postgraduate Medical Journal*, 85(1007): 451–454.

Williamson, L. (2007). Empirical assessments of clinical ethics services: Implications for clinical ethics committees. *Clinical Ethics*, 2(4): 187–192.

Williamson, L., McLean, S., and Connell, J. (2007). Clinical ethics committees in the United Kingdom: Towards evaluation. *Medical Law International*, 8: 221–237.

Wolf, S. M. (1992). Due process in ethics committee case review. *HEC Forum*, 4(2): 83–96.

Yen, B. and Schneiderman, L. J. (1999). Impact of pediatric ethics consultations on patients, families, social workers, and physicians. *Journal of Perinatology*, 19(5): 373–378.

Yoder, S. D. (1998). The nature of ethical expertise. *Hastings Center Report*, 28(6): 11–19.

Zussman, R. (1997). Sociological perspectives on medical ethics and decision-making. *Annual Review of Sociology*, 23: 171–189.

CHAPTER 8

INTERPROFESSIONAL INTERACTIONS AND THEIR IMPACT ON PROFESSIONAL BOUNDARIES

LOUISE FITZGERALD

INTRODUCTION

THIS chapter explores research on the interactions occurring between actors in the health care system and how they impact professional boundaries. Abbott (1995) stated that social entities come into existence when actors tie social boundaries together, so boundaries came first, then entities. We argue here that a focus on interactions between professions remains an underdeveloped area of research.

The chapter begins with a brief historical overview of key themes emerging from the sociology of the professions and alludes to boundaries and professional jurisdictions. The major, central sections of the chapter discuss the empirical data on professional interactions and two key themes emerge—role blurring, and role merging through the development of professional hybrids. The final section draws together some concluding themes.

HISTORICAL PERSPECTIVES ON THE HEALTH CARE PROFESSIONS AND DOMINANT PARADIGMS IN THEIR STUDY

Authors have articulated the "traits," the distinguishing characteristics of professions, including an advanced body of knowledge and an esoteric theoretical base, which enable autonomy over tasks, an elevated ethical sensibility, an altruistic orientation, and a sense of professional community (Goode, 1957; Parsons, 1939). Parsons' (1951) book provided a theoretical base and a structural-functionalist model of society, which included the function of medicine. Cockerham (2004) argues that structural-functionalism, with its emphasis on value consensus, social order, and functional processes at the macro level of society had a short life as the leading theoretical paradigm. Symbolic interactionists challenged the structural-functionalist perspective and the relatively passive role assigned to individuals, maintaining that social reality was constructed at the micro level by interacting individuals. Studies in this period, Becker et al. (1961) on medical school socialization and Goffman (1961) on asylums as total institutions offered novel approaches to research methods. Annandale (1998) suggested symbolic interactionism still offers powerful explanations of small group interactions.

Conflict or power-based theories offered a radically different perspective. Authors proffered less altruistic views of professions, debated the concept of autonomy and introduced the concepts of professional dominance and closure. Freidson's (1970) book argued that only certain professions, like medicine, had been deliberately granted autonomy, state sanctioned, thus institutionalizing expectations of societal trust. His early work proposed that the dominance of the medical profession over other professions was dependent on professional autonomy. He delineated differing types of autonomy: technical, political, and economic. Comparing the complex positions of hospital doctors in the UK and the US, he illustrated the contextual and historical influences on autonomy. Elston (1991) reviewed the classifications of autonomy by Freidson (1970), Ovreteit (1985) and Schultz and Harrison (1986) concluding that the evidence supported three forms of autonomy: political autonomy—the profession's right to make policy decisions as the legitimate expert; economic autonomy—the right of the profession to determine remuneration (or restrict entry numbers); and technical autonomy—the right of the profession and the individual to set its own standards and control performance. Conflict theory examined the role of competing interests in health care delivery and policy and the sources of illness in work and society (McKinlay, 1984; Navarro, 1986). Closure theory (Berlant, 1975; Collins, 1979) focused on the strategies adopted by professions to achieve control through limiting entry.

One major poststructuralist contribution was Foucault's (1973) analysis of the social functions of the medical profession, including the use of medical knowledge as a means of social control and regulation, through studies of madness, clinics, and sexuality.

From the 1980s onwards, within power-based perspectives, research argued that the loss of medical autonomy or "de-professionalization" was due to the shifts in society (McKinlay, 1988; Ritzer and Walczak, 1988). Elston and Gabe (2013) noted a substantial literature linked shifts in medical autonomy to broader societal changes. So autonomy might decline, but relative dominance might remain unchanged. A complementary argument (Hafferty, 1988) suggested a loss of collective power by the medical profession due to internal competition. Freidson's later work (1994, 2001) argued that internal re-stratification was more important than loss of autonomy. Abbott (1988) and Crompton's work (1990) accounted for the wider societal influences, perceiving the position of a profession as situated in a culture and a period of time. Professions, Abbott stated, could only be understood as part of a broader interacting, competitive system of occupations and professions. He suggested attention to a profession's task and knowledge base since he maintained that only knowledge abstraction enabled survival in the competitive system. Crompton argued that the concept of "profession" did not describe a generic occupational group, but a mode of regulation of expert labor. She examined an era in which the government was attempting to deregulate the occupational market, yet despite this, professional regulation persisted. Research (Ferlie et al., 1996; Shortell, Morrison, and Friedman, 1990) recorded the nuanced impact of societal changes and the resilience of the medical profession in adapting and retaining its position and jurisdiction. Social constructionists sought to explain the position of the professions in relation to interacting institutional and societal influences. Research imbalance is underlined with limited research on professions other than medicine (Allen, 1997; Navarro, 1986; Wicks, 1998).

Professions in the Twenty-First Century

Many of these themes continue as research topics today, albeit in different forms. Bourgeault, Benoit, and Hurschkorn (2009) documented the shift towards comparative analysis exploring the influences shaping professions within and across cultures, but noted the continuing focus on a single profession.

McKinlay and Marceau (2002) developed the de-professionalization and proletarianization debate by proposing that the latter has been enhanced in the US through a process of corporatization of the medical profession and in the UK by a process of privatization of health care. Continuing research accounts for and analyses the position of the health care professions in a context of new public management (NPM) and the introduction of market-like mechanisms (Braithwaite et al., 2013; Buchanan and Fitzgerald, 2011; Ferlie and Fitzgerald, 2002; Reay and Hinings, 2005). Osborne (2010) predicted the transition to "new public governance" drawing on ideas of relational markets and suggesting that a pluralist state will have multiple independent actors. There emerged an emphasis on a consumer driven society with a stronger voice for patients and the public (Clarke et al., 2007). Fotaki (2007) described forms of a revival of market and competitive mechanisms. In an overview, Reed (2011) subscribed to the notion of a neo-bureaucratic health care system and was skeptical of the emergence of a post-bureaucratic system.

Novel models are evidenced. Freidson's (2001) later work argued that professionalism offered a third and different logic of organizing compared with markets and hierarchies. He proposed a general model of professionalism as a set of institutions which permit an occupation control over their work. Noordegraaf (2007) presented "professionalism" as under threat and weakened. He perceived the terms profession and professionalism as applied to specific occupational practices, with particular forms of occupational regulation, in a specific era. He mapped adapted forms of professionalism as "situated" professionalism and "hybridized" professionalism. Such models have to be empirically tested. Using data, Fitzgerald and Ferlie (2000) argued that improved systems of professional control over tasks may offer organizational benefits and Noordegraaf (2011) postulated that amended education could re-connect professionalism and organizations. Using data on the development of a novel role offering potential for greater autonomy, Potsma, Oldenhof, and Putters (2014) used articulation theory to demonstrate the potential to incorporate organizational and professional work. Authors adopted institutional theory to analyze the changing relationships in health care, with Muzio, Brock, and Suddaby (2013) proffering a broad re-theorizing of contemporary professionalism. Leicht et al. (2009) display country specific responses which are highly path-dependent.

Foucault's (2002a, 2002b, 2013) work on the power/knowledge nexus interconnected the individual professional and their task to the institutional and societal culture. His distinctive approach to the sociology of knowledge emphasized how practices are formed by the complex interrelations between contexts, actors, and forms of knowledge. These ideas have been applied to suggest that some developed health care systems have moved towards "soft" governance (Ferlie et al., 2013; Newman, 2001).

So some consistent themes are evidenced in the literature, but the scope of research has broadened, is more comparative, examines more professions, and debates the issues of professions as part of a context. Empirical data on inter-professional interactions and the development of novel roles is discussed in the following sections. Applying this lens enables the clarification of task shifting and the potential alteration of professional boundaries.

BOUNDARIES OF PROFESSIONS AND PROFESSIONAL JURISDICTION

Examining Boundaries

This section alludes briefly to definition and then to boundaries and jurisdiction. Heracleous (2004) proposed a focus on the boundaries themselves, as social structures. Sturdy et al. (2009) reviewed typologies of boundaries, and outlined organizational boundaries of competence, identity, and power. Montgomery and Oliver (2007) emphasized that symbolic boundaries are a precursor to the development of socially constructed boundaries, whilst serving to reinforce a sense of identity once the grouping is established. We define boundaries as recurring "distinctions and differences between and within activity systems that are created and agreed on by groups and individual actors over a long period of time while they are involved in those activities" (Kerosuo, 2006, 4).

Boundaries and Claims of Professional Jurisdiction

Abbott (1988) suggested professional jurisdiction claims were made: in the legal arena, public opinion, and the workplace. Legal jurisdictional claims are considerably more specific than in the public arena, they may include monopoly of certain activities and payments. Legal jurisdictions are the most durable. He argued that relationships in these arenas have changed over time and the balance of power has tipped towards the public arena. But, he suggested, it was in the workplace where boundaries were most fluid and negotiable (as we hope to illustrate). Claims made in the workplace might blur publically established jurisdictions. Under pressure of work, a talented subordinate may replace an untalented professional, a process Abbott described as "workplace assimilation." These ideas suggest that boundaries may have differing meanings in differing arenas. One can postulate that in the UK medical claims to legal jurisdiction over self-regulation have lost ground, and the public, shocked by scandals leading to public enquiries (e.g., Francis Enquiry into Mid-Staffs NHS Foundation Trust, 2010; Shipman Enquiry, 2002) have lost faith in the ethics of the nursing and medical professions. Such public reactions may make the medical and nursing professions more vulnerable to jurisdictional attacks. A focus on processes of assimilation is warranted if this reveals the dilemmas facing professionals about how their legal responsibilities may clash with reality in the workplace.

Boundary building processes illuminate the interplay between public and institutional arenas. Abbott (1988) stated that each profession is bound to a set of tasks by ties of jurisdiction, but since none of these links are permanent, the professions make up an interacting, competitive system. Larger social forces may reshape tasks and thus impact on individual professions. Using empirical data, Oliver and Montgomery (2005) and Montgomery and Oliver (2007) illustrated the importance of social networking activities which predate boundaries and the political and legal processes which confer jurisdiction. Thus legally acknowledged jurisdictions have strong political elements and the data stresses professions as social groupings.

There remains debate concerning what boundaries are primarily bounding. The historic argument that jurisdiction is built around the knowledge base and tasks of a profession may be contested. Abbott (1988) maintained that professional tasks have both objective and subjective aspects, with these activities tied to a formal academic knowledge base. But the knowledge base of a profession will develop through research over time and he claimed that only abstraction (of knowledge) enabled survival in the competitive system of the professions. Authors (Gorman and Sandefur, 2011; Young and Muller, 2014;) have debated the nature of professional knowledge and maintained that there are two principal kinds of knowledge that make up professional knowledge: knowledge specialized to develop conceptually; and knowledge specialized to a contextual purpose. Young and Muller suggested that the demarcation criteria for a profession remain unclear.

Professional associations have perceived the importance of policing state sanctioned boundaries with the term "professional" represented as a much sought after identity (Nancarrow and Borthwick, 2005; Sanders and Harrison, 2008). Professions may act as self-interested groups who have negotiated with the state to control and set entry standards; thus maintaining status and income and excluding others. Self-regulation may lead to a lack of transparency which may hide poor performance by some individuals.

The Processes of Interaction between Professions in the Current Context: Role Blurring?

From the preceding discussion, the argument unfolds that a relevant approach to examining professional boundaries would be to focus on the processes of interaction between professions. Discussion and research has centered on medicine's interactions with nursing and to a lesser extent with allied health professionals (AHPs). However health care professionals have a wider range of everyday interactions and attention to the interactions between core professionals such as doctors, AHPs; pharmacists and health care assistants might yield interesting perspectives. A more inclusive approach would observe that professionals' interactions with management and social care are critical, but difficult interactions. In part, this is because clinicians, managers, and social care professionals have differing knowledge bases and differential power. This section therefore maps out the changing terrain and in particular explores the outer boundary of the professional domain or system of the professions.

Professional Interactions and Role Blurring?

There have been international changes in health care delivery systems over the last fifteen years which impact on all inter-professional interactions. For example, nursing became a graduate profession in many countries; the European Working Hours Directive in 1998 limited junior doctors' hours; and specialist nurse roles were instigated. Other influences have impacted on the professions, such as technical advances, increased day surgeries, and cost pressures which have meant quality targets for acute hospitals and extended auditing.

Research highlights the continuing distance between professional groups and between professionals and managers, with doctors communicating most with doctors, nurses with nurses, and managers with managers (Fitzgerald et al., 2006; McDermott et al., 2015). Topics which address professional interactions—multi-disciplinary teams and coordination between professionals—provide further evidence. West and Lyubovnikova's (2013a, 2013b) work illustrated that many "teams" in hospital settings were pseudo teams which did not agree common objectives or have accepted leaders. Whereas some groups were relatively stable over time, such as multi-disciplinary groups; others only collaborated briefly, such as a surgical team and were not able to form relationships of trust. Bourgeault and Mulvale (2006) illustrated similar comparative findings in Canada and the US. Montgomery's (2013) overview of professional role changes in the US suggested limited changes in the professional hierarchy. But research findings have demonstrated that the quality of teamwork in health care is crucial and is related to patient mortality in hospitals (West et al., 2001), lower staff absenteeism, effective use of resources, and greater patient satisfaction (West et al., 2011). Gittell's extensive research on relational co-ordination proved the importance of lateral relationships in health care and reinforced these findings in a US setting (Gittell, 2009, 2013). And Gittell et al. (2008) explored the inter-relationships around a new role of "hospitalists" in the US, physicians who operate full time within the hospital. The results uniformly show that nurses' relational co-ordination is stronger with nurses, physicians with physicians, and therapists with therapists. Additionally, the results demonstrated that those who are co-located and working in the same stage of care have an improved chance of building robust relationships.

Thus we can see that the professional boundaries continue to create "silos" of communication, whereas patient care in many settings requires inter-professional and inter-departmental collaboration of activities to deliver effective care.

Blurring of Roles in the Interactions between Doctors and Nurses?

Possibly the most prevalent, and undoubtedly one of the most important sets of relationships are between doctors and nurses. Despite this, there have been relatively few studies of the work based interactions of doctors and nurses. In European countries, the US, Canada, and Australia, nursing has for many years been accepted as a regulated and accredited occupation or profession, yet in the UK, nursing has not been able to negotiate with the state for exclusive rights to a defined area of knowledge. Ongoing disputes suggest that establishing the boundary of a knowledge base is difficult and acceptance by the state and other groups is a highly political and competitive process. Etzioni (1969) described the relationships between doctors and nurses, with doctors being the "guardians" of knowledge and the patient, and nurses being non-questioning of doctors. Nurses provided tender loving care; doctors provided the "science." This perspective remains relevant today, when there is a massive debate in the UK about the perceived lack of compassion in nursing (Francis Enquiry, 2010).

Wicks' (1998) study displayed insights into the conflictual interactions between doctors and nurses and demonstrated that doctors imposed on both nurses and patients! However, most nurses expressed pleasure in their work. Doctors continued to restrict nurses' activities even though this inhibited good patient care. Empirical studies of the interactions between nurses and doctors evidence both "traditional" attitudes to the boundaries between roles and simultaneously, the blurring of some role boundaries (Allen, 1997; Snelgrove and Hughes, 2000). Role blurring was apparent in four arenas: work pressures and contingencies, the distinctive situation of special locales, the changing health policy climate, and nurses' growing preoccupation with patient advocacy. Snelgrove and Hughes detailed instances of doctors "downloading" tasks to nurses to reduce their workload and noted that in specialized locales, for example renal units with smaller teams and more specialist nurses, there was more shared decision making. The introduction of higher qualifications for specialist nurses has blurred boundaries (and this is explored next). Finally, nurses were more assertive and questioning when they acted as patient advocates. Allen (2001) made the illuminating observation that interactions differed at institutional and ward levels. At the hospital level, there was a "sustained negotiation and jurisdictional dispute." But at ward level, there was a realignment of doctors' and nurses' roles with minimal negotiation and low conflict. Allen (2007) argued that medical hegemony in decision-making was a barrier to the full use of nurses' knowledge. Goodrick and Reay (2010) examined the means by which a new professional role identity was established for registered nurses. This analysis mirrors themes already noted— the subservience of nurses, and nurses' caring role versus the science of medicine. They concluded that developing a new professional identity was a slow, evolutionary process, but did change significantly over time (37 years). They highlighted the importance of the interactions between professional tasks and the wider institutional environment. Compared with the nursing profession's self-identity, ten Hoeve, Jansen, and Roodbol (2014) illustrated that the public image of nursing was somewhat diverse. They argued that nurses needed to improve the professionalism of their public image and obtain senior positions in health care organizations. An empirical study by Currie, Finn, and Martin (2010) explored the tensions and nuances of establishing this new role identity for nurses in the workplace featuring nurses moving into potentially more autonomous roles in genetics. Their findings showed nurses' autonomy was constrained by the attitudes and behavior of doctors, but interestingly, at times lacked support from senior nurses.

Specialist Nursing Roles and Role Blurring

Among several potentially influential changes in health care systems, the introduction of "hospitalists" in the US (Gittell et al., 2008) and community matrons in the UK (Currie, Koteyko, and Nerlich, 2009), this section focuses on one novel exemplar role—the introduction of Nurse Practitioners (NPs). The development of NPs worldwide is one example of the current shifts in the roles of nurses and doctors. Standards and a validation framework for NPs exist in many countries (e.g., the US, American College of Nurse Practitioners, 2009; Netherlands, Zwijnenberg and Bours, 2012; and the UK, Royal College of Nursing, 2005). Zwijenberg and Bours showed that NPs in the Netherlands spent 57.8% of their time on patient care and 14.2% of their time on medical activities. All the NPs in the study reported substitution of tasks from doctors. They reported some legal issues concerning, for example, the lack of legal framework to prescribe. Frequently, it was recognized that NPs combine some practice features of medicine with the fundamental aspects of nursing, but remain nursing oriented (Gould, Johnstone, and Wasylkiw, 2007; Reay, Golden-Biddle, and Germann, 2003).

Reay, Golden-Biddle, and Germann (2006) illustrate the agency of individual actors in establishing a role and delineate a three stage process of using opportunities, fitting the role to current systems and then demonstrating its value. However, Currie, Finn, and Martin (2010) and McDonnell et al. (2015) show that establishing novel roles may be a tenuous process, and involve substitution more than blurring.

Role Interactions between Nurses, Doctors, and AHPs

Reeves and Lewin's (2004) study of ward interactions examined interactions between doctors, nurses, and AHPs and reinforced and extended findings already discussed. They noted that professional collaboration frequently consisted of short, unstructured, and opportunistic interactions, suggesting professionals formed loose transient "working groups" and not teams. Most interactions (75%) were initiated by doctors with nurses and interactions with therapists and social workers were less common. Doctors' interactions with nurses were task based and terse and on occasions, doctors ignored other team members, like health care assistants. On the other hand, nurses' interactions with other professionals, for example therapists were friendlier, less rushed, and contained detailed discussion of patients. The explanation may lie in the fact that there is less power differential between nurses and therapists, compared to doctors and nurses. Another reason mirrors previous findings on co-location, since nurses and therapists spend time together on the ward. The main formal meeting, the weekly multi-disciplinary meeting (MDT) was perceived as an important forum, but was inconsistently attended by senior doctors and nurses. As previously reported, doctors viewed collaboration as an activity to be undertaken with other medics, whereas nurses, therapists, and social workers viewed collaboration as an inter-professional activity. Zwarenstein et al. (2013) reported similar Canadian findings. Additionally, they noted that in their research setting of General Internal Medicine with complex patients, the necessity for inter-professional decision-making was apparent.

A few single studies look beyond doctors and nurses to examine other professions (Kitchener and Merse, 2012; McCann et al., 2013). Goodrick and Reay (2011) and Kitchener and Merse (2012) examine the process of professionalization of pharmacists and dental hygienists in the US, exploring the development pathways. But both studies focused within the profession, rather than on professional interactions.

The Outer Reaches of the System of Professions: Health Care Assistants

Beyond nurses and therapists, the outer reaches of the system of professions is now populated by health care assistants (HCAs). The growth in employment of HCAs is one of the most significant changes in health care and possibly the most ignored. Accurate figures of the numbers of those employed in HCAs roles in the UK are hard to discover, but Saks and Allsop (2007) estimated 1 million, whilst the Nursing and Midwifery Council (NMC) (2006) suggested there had been a 26% increase over ten years. The growth in the numbers of HCAs, particularly in hospital settings, may be traced to the downward cost pressures noted earlier. A research focus on the acute hospital sector masks the other important fields of HCA's employment in the largely private nursing and residential home sector and the care of the disabled and the elderly in their own homes. There are few empirical studies which document the interactions of clinicians and health care assistants. Yet it is blatantly apparent that the system of health care in many countries would not survive without the work of HCAs. Cross-national comparisons illustrate the extent of employment of HCAs across national domains (Kessler, Heron, and Dopson, 2012). In some countries—South Africa, Australia, New Zealand, the US, Canada, Japan, Sweden, and Brazil—there is a three-tiered system with nurses, enrolled nurses (accredited), and HCAs. The tasks of HCAs focus on "hands-on" care, with some technical tasks, these being more complex in countries such as Sweden. Across the world, the role is mostly unregulated with the exceptions of Japan, Germany and the US.

In the UK, the HCA role is formally unregulated, but critically, the NMC Code of Practice states that the registered nurse is accountable for delegating tasks to the HCA but not for their performance. Where HCAs are qualified, they normally hold National Vocational Qualifications (NVQ) at either Level 2 or Level 3. Empirical data on the enactment of the role in hospital settings (Kessler, Heron, and Dopson, 2012, 2013; Spilsbury and Meyer, 2004) shows poor alignment between grades and qualifications, with qualifications only loosely associated with tasks. Thus HCAs with no or low qualifications were performing technical and extended roles. The range of tasks performed by HCAs varied widely. Kessler, Heron, and Dopson (2012, 2013) distinguished five "types" in the HCA role. These were labeled bedside technician, ancillary, citizen, all-rounder, and expert, thus underlining the "fuzzy" boundaries of the role. The variations were, in part, dependent on the shift worked as well as the range of other professionals working on the ward and the degree to which the HCAs' roles overlapped with theirs. But the major influence on the boundaries of the HCAs role was the Ward Manager and that individual's attitude to the HCA role. With a supportive Ward Manager, the HCA might extend their range of activities, but with a less supportive manager, the tasks of the HCA were restricted. It was observed that some individuals crafted the role, as some HCAs were keen to "develop" and take on tasks, such as cannulation. This might be a double edged sword since the individuals were not necessarily trained in these procedures. HCAs described their interactions with doctors as "tense," "conflictual," "patronizing," and sometimes "nasty." On the other hand, the interactions with nurses were generally described positively as supportive. For nurses, the main source of tension was the issue of accountability. Kessler, Heron, and Dopson (2015) supported the view that nurses are "off-loading" tasks to HCAs. They distinguished between two logics in nursing: one of specialist expertise, encouraging the profession to discard routine tasks; and one of holistic expertise, nurturing the hoarding of tasks, and described off-loading as specialist-discard logic.

In summary, there is limited evidence of role blurring in the workplace, though some tasks have undoubtedly moved across the prior, demarcated professional boundaries. The data presented evidenced "off-loading" of tasks from doctors to mainly specialist nurses and substitution of junior doctors by specialist nurses. The limited available evidence illustrated virtually no change in the boundaries between medicine and Allied Health professions. There is significant growth in the employment of HCAs which alters the overall form of the system of the professions. The data demonstrated more substantive evidence of role blurring between nurses and HCAs.

The Processes of Interaction between Professions in the Current Context: Role Merging

Relationships between managers and doctors are frequently portrayed as conflictual (Farrell and Morris, 2003; Pollitt, 1990; Raelin, 1986). However, levels of conflict are difficult to scale overall. It may depend on the unit of analysis and whether one is referring to individual relationships and interactions, or collective organizational and inter-organizational relations, or formal relationships at the national level. Many of the sources of tension, sometimes attributed by clinicians to management in an organization, do not originate from managers but from policy changes. But managers are required to implement the policy. Another source of tension lies in the acknowledged, differing objectives of managers and doctors. Managers are responsible for the effective and efficient organization and delivery of care to a population, whilst doctors are responsible for the quality and delivery of care to an individual patient (McDermott et al., 2015). Previously quoted research has portrayed the distance between doctors and managers. Managers were reluctant to intervene in clinical disputes, even when they were aware of the impact on patient care (Fitzgerald et al., 2006). Research on middle and junior managers in the NHS (Hyde et al., 2013) displayed conflicts over cost control. Yet collaborative working between clinicians and managers has been identified as a key activity for effective health care delivery (Ferlie et al., 2013; Gittell, Godfrey, and Thistlethwaite, 2013; Pettigrew, Ferlie, and McKee, 1992; Shortell, Morrison, and Friedman, 1990).

Role Merging: "Hybrid" Clinicians as Managers

The focus of this section is on "hybrids," clinical managers who are practicing clinicians holding a part-time management role. The development of hybrid roles may be labeled as role merging. The adoption of clinical manager roles by doctors in the UK is an interesting example of a profession adapting to policy driven organizational changes. With the formation of clinical directorates, doctors rapidly colonized the key posts of Clinical Director (Fitzgerald, 1994). Clinicians wished to continue to practice and this has emerged as a crucial dimension of their continued credibility (Hyde et al., 2013).

Indeed research has illustrated the similarity of doctors' views and attitudes concerning their role, over a period of time, and across countries (Denis, Lamothe, and Langley, 2001; Fitzgerald and Dufour, 1997; Hoff, 2000; Iedema et al., 2004; Llewellyn, 2001).

From the start, clinical managers performed a critical role in bridging between professions and between professions and management. Unlike general managers, it was noted that clinical managers (CMs) were capable (though not always willing) of dealing with clinical issues and problems with consultant colleagues. CMs exercised "control" via processes of management by reciprocation and invoking collegial relations. However, the role could be isolating, since other consultants sometimes perceived CMs as having "gone over to the enemy" by taking up a management position (Fitzgerald, 1996; Llewellyn, 2001). Researchers noted CMs had unmet training needs and their organizational support was limited (Fitzgerald and Dufour, 1997; McDermott et al., 2015). In some locales, for example, Canada, clinical director posts had existed over a longer period and CMs had more developed strategies for engagement of other clinical colleagues. Llewellyn (2001) underlined that CMs utilized ideas from both clinical practice and management and thus potentially created a new area of expertise—medical management. She argued that CMs can appropriate management ideas and incorporate them into their work, but that it is more difficult for general managers to acquire clinical expertise. Thus CMs gained a privileged position. In several studies, (Fitzgerald, 1996; Llewellyn, 2001; Thorne, 1997) clinical managers portrayed a degree of suspicion of managers' intellectual abilities and occasionally their motives, maintaining that managers were profit orientated. Equally, CMs were aware of the suspicions of their clinical colleagues. In all the quoted studies, CMs recognized the political and sensitive nature of their decisions. Longitudinal data (Fitzgerald and Ferlie, 2000) on the impact of the quasi-market in health care in the UK illustrated no uni-dimensional shift of power to managers, but rather a set of nuanced shifts and adaptations with individual actors responding to events and shaping the context. Thus the picture emerged of a more interactive process between the dimensions of the context, unfolding events *and* the reactions of the professionals. Currie et al. (2012) used 11 cases of the introduction of novel clinical roles, which threatened the power and status of specialist doctors to illustrate how the medical elite responded and adapted. Essentially, they circumvented the threats by delegating routine tasks to other actors whilst retaining control.

The data has evidenced that some CMs were reluctant to adopt the role (Dopson, 1995). McGivern et al. (2015) described these individuals as "incidental" hybrids. Other individuals were "willing hybrids," who developed hybrid professional-managerial identities aligning professionalism with their personal identity, and regulating and auditing other professionals. Thus extant research across national domains suggests that medical hybrids are able to adapt or align their professional identity with a hybrid role, mediating a critical boundary between general managers and their professional peers (Llewellyn, 2001; Montgomery, 2001; Denis, Lamothe, and Langley, 2001; Iedema et al., 2004). However, Croft, Currie, and Lockett (2015) questioned whether nurse "hybrids" could so readily make this crucial adaptation. All nurse respondents suggested that they experienced identity conflict in their hybrid roles and struggled to resolve this conflict. Some medical hybrids experienced identity conflict, but they appeared to adapt better, continued in clinical practice, and derived satisfaction through exercising influence.

Research has illuminated key differences internationally, in the development of medical management collectively if one compares physician managers in the US and medical managers the UK. There is substantial evidence of the development of academic, accredited qualifications for physician managers in the US (Montgomery, 2001; Montgomery and Oliver, 2007; Schneller and Singh, 2000). Physician managers are more embedded and accreditation processes have progressed, but this process is less developed in the UK. Thus there is evidence of the slow development of a new, elite hybrid professional group.

Increasingly, health care systems are developing inter-organizational networks to address complex problems, such as the delivery of specialist cancer care and the care of older people. Managing a network and complex care pathways is a demanding role. One notes the presence of hybrids in the management of networks. Where networks were effectively managed, this was accomplished by a tight, collective management group of two or three individuals (Ferlie et al., 2013). Intriguingly, medical hybrids holding senior management roles in networks were seen to employ sophisticated influencing and managerial strategies. They used "soft" governance and invoked a complex mix of professional standards, evidence-based medical data and nationally led regulatory pressures to persuade and implement improvements (Ferlie, McGivern, and Fitzgerald, 2012).

In summary, potentially, medical and clinical hybrids are a positive development which could prove a powerful mechanism to aid improved inter- and intra-professional collaboration and effective delivery of care. The activities of hybrids illustrate the power of agency to effect change. If the potential for improvement is to be adequately supported, the selection of hybrids needs greater care. In particular, there is considerable scope for expansion in the numbers and roles of clinical hybrids from nursing, and the AHPs. But to effectively deliver collaboration and service improvements, more training is required in the UK, as in the US.

Organizationally, hybrids have begun to form elite of medical managers, advantaged by their clinical and management knowledge base, thus forming new sub-boundaries within and between professional and general management boundaries.

Concluding Themes

This section begins by reviewing the substantive findings emerging from the central sections of the chapter. The chapter has highlighted a lack of interchange and collaboration, especially laterally between differing professions and between clinical professionals and managers. Low levels of collaboration threaten quality and safety in health care systems. The findings display two key themes—*role blurring* and the extent to which blurring has altered professional boundaries and *role merging* between doctors and managers and its impact on boundaries and accountability.

Role Blurring and Boundary Interactions

In analyzing the interactions of professionals, the chapter explored the question of whether numerous tasks have moved across professional boundaries. We detected only slight evidence of role blurring, predominantly, between doctors and NPs. But the data did not support the view that role blurring had occurred between doctors and any other clinical groups, especially AHPs, such as physiotherapists. At the lower levels of qualifications, role blurring appeared more extensive. There are greater numbers of HCAs employed and the extent of assimilation of nurses' roles in the workplace was more widespread. It is debatable whether this process might not be more accurately described as the "off-loading" of tasks, rather than "role blurring." "Off-loading" does not produce partnership or collaboration. Nor does this term imply respect for the contribution of other occupations. Moreover, the majority of empirical data on HCAs relates to acute hospitals, but many HCAs are employed in settings such as nursing homes. In these settings, jurisdictions between nurses and HCAs may be even "fuzzier."

Essentially, the medical profession has selected and retained the core of high class, specialized knowledge and tasks, as well as status and the dominant position in the clinical team. Their status in the public arena has barely altered, though individual scandals have dinted the public's trust. And shifts in the formal, legal arena have been severely limited. Nurse practitioners appear to have made the most progress in shifting tasks across boundaries, but their numbers remain relatively small. So in this process, it cannot be stated that doctors have "lost out" to nurses, or that nurses have "encroached" on the tasks of the doctors. One might argue that the doctors have "off-loaded" the less specialized tasks to nurses and the nurses have similarly "off-loaded" some tasks to HCAs, in order to retain the technical aspects of nursing. The evidence illustrated that the system of the professions has changed most significantly at the lower boundary.

Doctors maintain (and society supports this maintenance) the critical tasks and decisions and indeed their dominance of other professions. The record demonstrates that the boundaries that distinguish the medical profession from other health care and non-health care professions have remained particularly stable over time, despite concerted efforts by, for example, nurses and physician assistants to shift these boundaries.

Role Merging, Boundaries, and Governance

The chapter provides evidence on role merging between doctors and managers with the growth of hybrid medical manager roles across different countries. As a result, there is interesting evidence of the development of processes of professional control of professionals, using a "soft" governance approach to management and leadership (Ferlie et al., 2013; Currie et al., 2012; McGivern et al., 2015). Data on the positive influence of hybrids indicates that increasingly tight audit by general managers may be counter-productive. One might hypothesize that hybrid professionals holding positions of authority in hospitals and networks represent a novel and more effective nexus of control—of professionals by professionals (Freidson, 2001; Fitzgerald and Ferlie, 2000).

There remain issues concerning the appropriate and effective form of managing professional expertise and professional accountability (Raelin, 2011; Montgomery, 2001). Around the jurisdiction of medical managers, one sees the early stages of a process of boundary construction underway (Montgomery and Oliver, 2007). The enactment of the boundary is partially accomplished by "others" underlining difference and making distinctions. The formation of an elite group of medical managers is progressing at differing rates in differing countries. Thus the identification of a knowledge base and accreditation processes has developed faster in the US than in the UK. Following Oliver and Montgomery (2005), one may speculate that this has occurred because the networking activities of the physician managers in the US have enabled them to identify priority actions, whereas this has not occurred in the UK. Individual actors engage in complex interactions between policy directions, the contextual dimensions of institutions and the form of social groups and have varying interpretations of all of these. A process of restratification is distinguished with doctors responded to changes by adaption, amending existing collegial systems to reflect policy aspirations and circumventing management systems by emphasizing the superiority of their own (Ferlie et al., 1996; Fitzgerald and Ferlie, 2000; Waring and Currie, 2009).

Professional Interactions and Professional Boundaries

This section considers whether historically debated themes of professional autonomy, professional dominance, and professional jurisdictions are influenced by these data.

There is a diminutive volume of evidence to suggest the medical profession has suffered major losses of formal, political autonomy when compared with other professions. The medical profession has ceded some tasks to other professions such as nursing which may be considered a selected loss of task autonomy. One might more accurately suggest that a degree of task autonomy has been lost to the state due to performance management and monitoring requirements, especially in hospitals. In terms of professional dominance, there may be some intriguing hints of change here. But this is mainly from the perspective of professions other than medicine. Nurses appear to be gradually less willing to accept the dominance of doctors and to perceive their roles in terms of a partnership with doctors.

In considering professional boundaries and jurisdiction, there is no evidence of substantial shifts in the legal acknowledgment of extended jurisdictions for non-medical professions. There is some illuminating evidence that the knowledge base of a profession is important to the maintenance of status. The medical profession has sought to enclave higher levels of knowledge through specialization and inclusion (the expansion of power via the merging of clinical and management knowledge). Throughout the system of the clinical professions, there are strong downward pressures creating governance and supervision issues at the lower levels of the hierarchy. Instead of a focus on the medical profession, here it is argued that the most critical issues of governance and accountability in health care lie at the lower levels in the system of the professions. In many countries, society and the state have allowed changes to produce a situation where a large group of HCAs are employed, but this role is unregulated and unaccredited. Crucially, there is a lack of formal responsibility for the supervision of HCAs and for a line of accountability for their work.

In conclusion, the chapter argues that an analysis of professional interactions provides a potentially significant perspective on the system of professions and is revealing. It illuminates the extent of autonomy of individual professions; and one discovers novel issues of power, professional control, and accountability. It challenges normative debates on professional jurisdiction or those based on a narrow empirical foundation. This inclusive perspective illustrates that significant change has occurred through intra-professional restratification in medicine and through the off-loading of tasks from nurses to HCAs. We suggest that a research agenda exploring professional interactions through comparative, longitudinal studies to include a broader range of occupations and professions, such as pharmacy, and physiotherapy, is warranted.

References

Abbott, A. (1988). *The system of professions*. Chicago: University of Chicago Press.

Abbott, A. (1995). Things of boundaries. *Social Research*, 62 (4): 857–882.

Allen, D. (1997). The nursing-medical boundary: A negotiated order? *Sociology of Health and Illness*, 19: 498–520.

Allen, D. (2001). *The changing shape of nursing practice: The role of nurses in the hospital division of labour*. London and New York: Routledge.

Allen, D. (2007). What do you do at work? Profession building and doing nursing. *International Nursing Review*, 54(1): 41–48.

American College of Nurse Practitioners (2009). Frequently asked questions about nurse practitioners. Available at: <http://www.acnpweb.org/files/public/FAQ_about_NPs_May06.pdf> (accessed November 10, 2009).

Annandale, E. (1998). *The sociology of health and medicine: A critical introduction*. Cambridge: Polity Press.

Becker, H. S., Greer, B., Hughes, E., and Strauss, A. (1961). *Boys in white: Student culture in medical school*. Chicago: University of Chicago Press.

Berlant, J. L. (1975). *Profession and monopoly: A study of medicine in the United States and Great Britain*. Berkeley: University of California Press.

Bourgeault, I., Benoit, C., and Hurschkorn, K. (2009). Introducing comparative perspectives. *Current Sociology*, 57(4): 475–485.

Bourgeault, I. and Mulvale, G. (2006). Collaborative health care teams in Canada and the U.S.: Confronting the structural embeddedness of medical dominance. *Health Sociology Review*, 15(5): 481–495.

Braithwaite, J., Westbrook, M., Nugus, P., Greenfield, D., Travaglia, J., Runciman, W., Foxwell, A. R., Boyce, R. A., Devinney, T., and Westbrook, J. (2013). Continuing differences between health professions' attitudes: The saga of accomplishing systems-wide interprofessionalism. *International Journal for Quality in Health Care*, 25(1): 8–15.

Buchanan, D. and Fitzgerald, L. (2011). New lock, new stock, new barrel, same gun: The accessorized bureaucracy of healthcare. In *Managing modernity: Beyond bureaucracy?*, ed. Clegg, S., Harris, M., and Höpfl, H., pp. 56–80. Oxford: Oxford University Press.

Clarke, J., Newman, J., Smith, N., Vidler, E., and Westmorland, L. (2007). *Creating citizen consumers*. London: Sage.

Cockerham, W. C. (2004). Medical Sociology and Sociological Theory. In *The Blackwell companion to medical sociology*, ed. Cockerham, W. C. Oxford: Blackwell Publishing. Available at: <http://www.blackwellreference.com/subscriber/tocnode.html?id=g9781405122665_chunk_g97814051226653> (accessed October 7, 2015).

Collins, R. (1979). *The credential society*. New York: Academic Press.

Croft, C., Currie, G., and Lockett, A. (2015). Broken "two-way windows"? An exploration of professional hybrids. *Public Administration*, 93(2): 380–394.

Crompton, R. (1990). Professions in the current context. *Work, Employment and Society*, Special Issue, 4: 147–66.

Currie, G., Finn, R., and Martin, G. (2010). Role transition and the interaction of relational and social identity: New nursing roles in the English NHS. *Organization Studies*, 31(07): 941–961.

Currie, G., Koteyko N., and Nerlich, B. (2009). The dynamics of professions and development of new roles in public services organizations: The case of modern matrons in the English NHS. *Public Administration*, 87: 295–311.

Currie, G., Lockett, A., Finn, R., Martin, G., and Waring, J. (2012). Institutional work to maintain professional power: Recreating the model of medical professionalism. *Organization Studies*, 33: 937–962.

Denis, J.-L., Lamothe, L., and A. Langley, A. (2001). The dynamics of collective leadership and strategic change in pluralistic organizations. *Academy of Management Journal*, 44(4): 809–837.

Dopson, S. (1995). Management: The one disease consultants did not think existed. *Journal of Management in Medicine*, 8(5): 25–36.

Elston, M. A. (1991). The politics of professional power: Medicine in a changing health service. In *The sociology of the health service*, ed. Gabe, J., Calnan, M., and Bury, M., pp. 58–88. London: Routledge.

Elston, M. A. and Gabe. J. (2013). Medical autonomy, dominance and decline. In *Key concepts in medical sociology*, 2nd edition, ed. Gabe, J. and Monaghan, L. F., pp. 151–156. London, California, New Delhi, and Singapore: Sage.

Etzioni, A. (ed.) (1969). *Semi-professions and their organization*. London: Free Press.

Farrell, C. and Morris, J. (2003). The "neo-bureaucratic" state: Professionals, managers and professional managers in schools, general practices and social work. *Organization*, 10: 129–156.

Ferlie, E., Ashburner, L., Fitzgerald, L., and Pettigrew, A. M. (1996). *The new public management in action*. Oxford: Oxford University Press.

Ferlie, E. and Fitzgerald, L. (2002). The sustainability of the new public management in the UK. In *Trends in new public management*, ed. Osbourne, S., pp. 341–353. London: Routledge.

Ferlie, E., Fitzgerald, L., McGivern. G., Dopson, S., and Bennett, C. (2013). *Making wicked problems governable? The case of managed networks in health care*. Oxford: Oxford University Press.

Ferlie, E., McGivern, G., and Fitzgerald, L. (2012). A new mode of organizing in health care?: Governmentality and managed cancer networks in England. *Social Science & Medicine*, 74(3): 340–347.

Fitzgerald, L. (1994). Moving clinicians into management: A professional challenge or threat? *Journal of Management in Medicine*, 8(6): 32–44.

Fitzgerald, L. (1996). Clinical management: The impact of a changing context on a changing profession. In *Beyond reason? The national health service and the limits of management*, ed. Leopold, J., Hughes, M., and Glover, I., pp. 189–203. Averbury and Brookfield, VT: Ashgate.

Fitzgerald, L. and Dufour, Y. (1997). Clinical management as boundary management: A comparative analysis of Canadian and UK healthcare institutions. *International Journal of Public Sector Management*, 10(1/2): 5–20.

Fitzgerald, L. and Ferlie, E. (2000) Professionals: Back to the future?" *Human Relations*, 53(5): 713–739.

Fitzgerald, L., Lilley, C., Ferlie, E., Addicott, R., McGivern, G., and Buchanan, D. (2006). Managing change and role enactment in the professionalized organization. Final Report to the SDO R and D Programme, Department of Health, February 2006. Available at: <http://www.sdo.nihr.ac.uk/sdo212002.html> (accessed May 28, 2015).

Fotaki, M. (2007). Patient choice in health care in England and Sweden: From quasi-market and back to market? A comparative analysis of failure in unlearning. *Public Administration*, 85(4): 1059–1075.

Foucault, M. (1973). *The birth of the clinic*. London: Tavistock.

Foucault, M. (2002a). *The order of things: An archaeology of the human sciences*. London: Routledge.

Foucault, M. (2002b). *The archaeology of knowledge*. London: Routledge.

Foucault, M. (2013). *Lectures on the will to know: Lectures at the College de France 1970–1971, and Oedipal knowledge*. Basingstoke: Palgrave Macmillan.

Francis Enquiry (2010). *Independent Inquiry into care provided by mid-Staffordshire NHS foundation trust January 2005–March 2009*, Vol. I. London: HMSO.

Freidson, E. (1970). *Profession of medicine: A study of the sociology of applied knowledge*. New York: Dodd, Mead.

Freidson, E. (1994). *Professionalism reborn: Theory, prophecy and policy*. Chicago: University of Chicago Press.

Freidson, E. (2001). *Professionalism: The third logic*. Chicago: University of Chicago Press.

Gittell, J. H. (2009). *High performance healthcare: Using the power of relationships to achieve quality, efficiency and resilience*. New York and London: McGraw-Hill.

Gittell, J. H., Godfrey, M., and Thistlethwaite, J. (2013). Interprofessional collaborative practice and relational coordination: Improving healthcare through relationships. *Journal of Interprofessional Care*, 27(3): 210–213.

Gittell, J. H., Weinberg, D. B., Bennett, A. L., and Miller, J. A. (2008). Is the doctor in? A relational approach to job design and the coordination of work. *Human Resource Management*, 47(4): 729–755.

Goffman, E. (1961). *Asylums*. New York: Anchor.

Goode, W. (1957). Community within a community: The professions. *American Sociological Review*, 22: 194–200.

Goodrick, E. and Reay, T. (2010). Florence Nightingale endures: Legitimizing a new professional role identity. *Journal of Management Studies*, 47: 55–84.

Goodrick, E. and Reay, T. (2011). Constellations of institutional logics: Changes in the professional work of pharmacists. *Work and Occupations*, 38(3): 372–416.

Gorman, E. H. and Sandefur, R. L. (2011). "Golden age," quiescence, and revival: How the sociology of professions became the study of knowledge-based work. *Work and Occupations*, 38: 275–302.

Gould, O., Johnstone, D., and Wasylkiw, L. (2007). Nurse practitioners in Canada: Beginnings, benefits, and barriers. *Journal of the American Academy of Nurse Practitioners*, 19: 165–171.

Hafferty, F. (1988). Theories at the crossroads: A discussion of evolving views of medicine as a profession. *Milbank Quarterly*, 66(2): 202–225.

Heracleous, L. (2004). Boundaries in the Study of Organization. *Human Relations*, 57 (1): 95–103.

Hoff, T. J. (2000). Professional commitment among US physician executives in managed care. *Social Science and Medicine*, 50(10): 1433–1444.

Hyde, P., Granter, E., Hassard, J., McCann, L., and Morris, J. (2013). Roles and behaviours of middle and junior managers: Managing new organizational forms of healthcare. Project Report to the NIHR SDO Programme.

Iedema, R., Degeling, P., Braithwaite, J., and White, L. (2004). "It's an Interesting Conversation I'm Hearing": The Doctor as Manager. *Organization Studies*, 25(1): 15–33.

Kerosuo, H. (2006). *Boundaries in action: An activity-theoretical study of development, learning and change in health care for patients with multiple and chronic illnesses*. Helsinki: Helsinki University Press.

Kessler, I., Heron, P., and Dopson, S. (2012). *The modernization of the nursing workforce: Valuing the healthcare assistant*. Oxford: Oxford University Press.

Kessler, I., Heron, P., and Dopson, S. (2013). Indeterminacy and the regulation of task allocation: The shape of support roles in healthcare. *British Journal of Industrial Relations*, 51(2): 310–332.

Kessler, I., Heron, P., and Dopson, S. (2015). Professionalization and expertise in care work: The hoarding and discarding of tasks in nursing. *Human Resource Management*, 54(5): 737–752.

Kitchener, M. and Mertz, E. (2012). Professional projects and institutional change in healthcare: The case of American dentistry. *Social Science & Medicine*, 74: 372–380.

Leicht, K., Walter, T., Sainsaulieu, I., and Davies, S. (2009). New public management and new professionalism across nations and contexts. *Current Sociology*, 57(4): 581–605.

Llewellyn, S. (2001). "Two-way windows": Clinicians as medical managers. *Organization Studies*, 22: 593–623.

McCann, L., Granter, E., Hyde, P., and Hassard, J. (2013). Still blue-collar after all these years? An ethnography of the professionalization of emergency ambulance work. *Journal of Management Studies*, 50: 750–776.

McDermott, A., Fitzgerald, L., and Buchanan, D. (2013). Beyond acceptance and resistance: Entrepreneurial change agency responses in policy implementation. *British Journal of Management*, 24: S93–S115.

McDermott, A., Fitzgerald, L., Van Gestel, N., and Keating, M. (2015). From bipartite to tripartite devolved HRM in professional service contexts: Evidence from hospitals in three countries. *Human Resource Management, SI*, 54(4): 813–831.

McDonnell A., Goodwin, E., Kennedy, F., Hawley, K., Gerrish, K., and Smith, C. (2015). An evaluation of the implementation of advanced nurse practitioner (ANP) roles in an acute hospital setting. *Journal of Advanced Nursing*, 71(4): 789–799.

McGivern, G., Currie, G., Ferlie, E., Fitzgerald, L., and Waring, J. (2015). Hybrid manager-professionals' identity work: The maintenance and hybridisation of professionalism in managerial contexts. *Public Administration*, 93(2): 412–432.

McKinlay, J. (ed.) (1984). *Issues in the political economy of health care.* London: Tavistock.

McKinlay, J. (1988). Introduction: The changing character of the medical profession. *Milbank Quarterly*, 66(2): 1–9.

McKinlay, J. and Marceau L. D. (2002). The end of the golden age of doctoring. *International Journal of Health Services*, 32(2): 379–416.

Montgomery, K. (2001). Physician executives: The evolution and impact of a hybrid profession. *Advances in Health Care Management*, 2: 215–241.

Montgomery, K. (2013). Health care professions. In *Sociology of work, an encyclopedia*, ed. Smith, V., pp. 361–364. Thousand Oaks, CA: Sage.

Montgomery, K. and Oliver, A. (2007). A fresh look at how professions take shape: Dual-directed networking dynamics and social boundaries. *Organization Studies*, 28: 661–687.

Muzio, D., Brock, D., and Suddaby, R. (2013). Professions and institutional change: Towards an institutionalist sociology of the professions. *Journal of Management Studies*, 50: 699–721.

Nancarrow, S. and Borthwick, A. (2005). Dynamic professional boundaries in the healthcare workforce. *Sociology of Health and Illness*, 27: 897–919.

Navarro, V. (1986). *Crisis, health, and medicine: A social critique.* London: Tavistock.

Newman, J. (2001). *Modernizing governance.* London: Sage.

Noordegraaf, M. (2007). From "pure" to "hybrid" professionalism: Present-day professionalism in ambiguous public domains. *Administration & Society*, 39(6): 761–785.

Noordegraaf, M. (2011). Remaking professionals? How associations and professional education. *Current Sociology*, 59(4): 465–488.

Nursing and Midwifery Council (2006). The regulation of health care support workers: A scoping paper. London: NMC.

Oliver, A. and Montgomery, K. (2005). Toward the construction of a profession's boundaries: Creating a networking agenda. *Human Relations*, 58: 1167–1184.

Osborne, S. (2010). The (new) public governance: A suitable case for treatment? In *The new public governance*, ed. Osborne, S., pp. 1–16. London: Routledge.

Ovreteit, J. (1985). Medical dominance and the development of professional autonomy in physiotherapy. *Sociology of Health and Illness*, 7: 76–93.

Parsons, T. (1939). The professions and social structure. *Social Forces*, 17: 457–467.

Parsons, T. (1951). *The social system.* New York: Free Press.

Pettigrew, A. M., Ferlie, E., and McKee, L. (1992). *Shaping strategic change: Making change in large organizations.* London: Sage.

Pollitt, C. (1990). *Managerialism and the public services*, 2nd edition. Oxford: Basil Blackwell.

Potsma, J., Oldenhof, L., and Putters, K. (2014). Organized professionalism in healthcare: Articulation work by neighbourhood nurses. *Journal of Professions and Organization*, 1: 1–17.

Raelin, J. A. (1986). *The clash of cultures, managers and professionals.* Boston: Harvard Business School Press.

Raelin, J. A. (2011). The end of managerial control? *Group and Organization Management*, 36(2): 135–160

Reay, T., Golden-Biddle, K., and Germann, K. (2003). Challenges and leadership strategies for managers of nurse practitioners. *Journal of Nursing Management*, 11(6): 396–403.

Reay, T., Golden-Biddle, K., and Germann, K. (2006). Legitimizing a new role: Small wins and micro processes of change. *Academy of Management Journal*, 49: 977–998.

Reay, T. and Hinings, C. R. (2005). The recomposition of an organizational field: Health care in Alberta. *Organization Studies*, 26(3): 351–384.

Reed, M. (2011). The post bureaucratic organization and the control revolution. In *Managing modernity: Beyond bureaucracy?*, ed. Clegg, S., Harris, M., and Hopfl, H., pp. 230–256. Oxford: Oxford University Press.

Reeves, S. and Lewin, S. (2004). Interprofessional collaboration in the hospital: Strategies and meanings. *Journal of Health Services Research and Policy*, 9(4): 218–225.

Ritzer, G. and Walczak, D. (1988). Rationalization and the deprofessionalization of physicians. *Social Forces*, 67: 1–22.

Royal College of Nursing (2005). *Maxi nurses: Advanced and specialist nursing roles.* London: RCN.

Sanders, T. and Harrison, S. (2008). Professional legitimacy claims in the multidisciplinary workplace: The case of heart failure care. *Sociology of Health and Illness*, 30: 289–308.

Saks, M. and Allsop, J. (2007). Social policy, professional regulation and health support workers in the UK. *Social Policy and Society*, 6(2): 165–177.

Schneller, E. and Singh, A. (2000). The role of the physician executive in managing the health care value chain. *Hospital Quarterly*, Fall: 38–43.

Schultz, R. and Harrison, S. (1986). Physician autonomy in the federal republic of Germany, Great Britain and the United States. *International Journal of Health Planning and Management*, 2: 335–355.

Shipman Enquiry (2002). *Death disguised*, Vol. 1. Norwich: HMSO.

Shortell, S., Morrison, E., and Friedman, B. (1990). *Strategic choices for America's hospitals.* San Francisco, CA, and Oxford: Jossey Bass.

Snelgrove S. and Hughes, S. D. (2000). Interprofessional relations between doctors and nurses: Perspectives from South Wales. *Journal of Advanced Nursing*, 31(3): 661–667.

Spilsbury, K. and Meyer, J. (2004). Use, misuse, and non-use of health care assistants in a hospital setting. *Journal of Nursing Management*, 12: 411–418.

Sturdy, A., Clark, T., Fincham, R., and Handley, K. (2009). Between innovation and legitimation-boundaries and knowledge flow in management consultancy. *Organization*, 16(5): 627–653.

Ten Hoeve, Y., Jansen, G., and Roodbol, P. (2014). The nursing profession: Public image, self-concept and professional identity. A discussion paper. *Journal of Advanced Nursing*, 70(2): 295–309.

Thorne, M. (1997). Being a clinical director: First among equals or just a go-between? *Health Services Management Journal*, 10: 205–215.

Waring, J. and Currie, G. (2009). Managing expert knowledge: Organizational challenges and managerial futures for the UK medical profession. *Organization Studies*, 30(7): 755–778.

West, M. A., Borrill, C., Dawson, J., Scully, J., Carter, M., Anelay, S., Patterson, M., and Waring, J. (2001). The link between the management of employees and patient mortality in acute hospitals. *The International Journal of Human Resource Management*, 13(8): 1299–1310.

West, M. A., Dawson, J. F., Admasachew, L., and Topakas, A. (2011). NHS staff management and health service quality: Results from the NHS staff survey and related data". Available at: <http://www.dh.gov.uk/health/2011/08/nhs-staff-management/> (accessed May 28, 2015).

West, M. and Lyubovnikova, J. (2013a). Illusions of team working in health care. *Journal of Health Organization and Management*, 27(1): 134–142.

West, M. and Lyubovnikova, J. (2013b). Why teamwork matters: Enabling health care team effectiveness for the delivery of high quality patient care. In *Developing and enhancing teamwork in organizations*, ed. Salas, E., Tannenbaum, S., Cohen, D., and Latham, G., pp. 331–372. (San Francisco, CA: Jossey Bass).

Wicks, D. (1998). *Nurses and doctors at work: Rethinking professional boundaries.* Buckingham: Open University Press.

Young, M. and Muller, J. (2014). From the sociology of professions to the sociology of professional knowledge. In *Knowledge, expertise and the professions*, ed. Young, M. and Muller, J., pp. 3–17. Abingdon and New York: Routledge.

Zwarenstein, M., Rice, K., Gotlib-Conn, L., Kenaszchuk, C., and Reeves, S. (2013). Disengaged: A qualitative study of communication and collaboration between physicians and other professions on general internal medicine wards. *BMC Health Services Research*, 13(1): 494. ISSN (online) 1472–6963.

Zwijnenberg, N. C. and Bours, G. J. J. W. (2012). Nurse practitioners and physician assistants in Dutch hospitals: Their role, extent of substitution and facilitators and barriers experienced in the reallocation of tasks. *Journal of Advanced Nursing*, 68(6): 1235–1246.

CHAPTER 9

PLURAL LEADERSHIP IN HEALTH CARE ORGANIZATIONS

Forms, Potential, and Challenges

VIVIANE SERGI, MARILINE COMEAU-VALLÉE,
MARIA LUSIANI, JEAN-LOUIS DENIS,
AND ANN LANGLEY

INTRODUCTION: LEADERSHIP IN HEALTH CARE ORGANIZATIONS

HEALTH care organizations present a number of characteristics that render them interesting to study when it comes to leadership. Especially with regards to change initiatives and strategic direction, health care organizations pose specific, and often complex challenges due to their structure and constitution. Indeed, they are quintessential "pluralistic organizations" (Denis, Langley, and Rouleau, 2007) characterized by diffuse power and authority, diverse value systems, and expert knowledge work. In health care specifically, power, authority, and legitimacy are diffused between managers, clinicians, and other organized groups such as unions and external bodies including the government in most countries (Glouberman and Mintzberg, 2001a, 2001b). Decision-making in these organizations may involve long and sometimes arduous negotiation processes, processes that are nonetheless necessary in order to obtain the required consensus between actors who do not share a priori the same priorities and concerns. The issues to be addressed by health care organizations also tend to be complex, multi-dimensional, and thorny, combining considerations that cannot be simply associated solely with managerial or medical concerns; as such, these issues may generate tensions, paradoxes, or "catch-22" situations between the diverse priorities pursued.

Moreover, in recent years, many health care organizations and systems around the world have confronted the need to adapt to a range of innovations in both their management and in the delivery of services (Denis and Forest, 2012; Maynard, 2013). Changes include new technologies, new more integrated forms of care, and the implementation of managerial techniques such as lean management. At the same time, health care organizations, especially public ones, are experiencing growing pressures on their finances, forcing them to operate under increasingly difficult conditions. In addition, health care organizations around the world have been for some time in a seemingly continual state of structural reform, embracing new incentive schemes, new tools and techniques, and engaged in re-engineering processes or facing mergers and restructuring. This contemporary context, combining the specific challenges associated with these organizations' distinctive characteristics and the current global economic situation, complicates the challenges of leadership in these organizations, making it more challenging than ever to navigate.

The investigation of leadership in health care organizations is not new (Hodgson, Levinson, and Zaleznik, 1965), but, as Gilmartin and D'Aunno (2007) note in their review, many dimensions of this topic still need further study. Along these lines, we argue that with all of the challenges mentioned above, the need for leadership is experienced both at the top management team level and at levels closer to operations where multiple groups with different sources of expertise need to coordinate among themselves, sometimes across organizational boundaries. Such coordination is today more than ever necessary, and lies at the heart of leadership practices themselves. Indeed, the managerial and clinical sides of the health care organization need to come together at multiple levels in order to allow change to happen. In such a context, forms of collective leadership in which influence is shared or distributed among different individuals playing complementary roles seems to offer a solution to the challenges of achieving collaboration, coordination and strategic direction (Currie and Lockett, 2011).

In this respect, plural or collective forms of leadership emerge as particularly relevant in the context of health care organizations, because they match these organizations' inherent complexity. Health care organizations have also long been identified as an organizational context where shared and collective forms of leadership are not only accepted, but well recognized as relevant and appropriate to better face the inherent variety of perspectives and challenges (Denis, Lamothe, and Langley, 2001; Currie and Lockett, 2011; Chreim et al., 2010). In the current context, the possibility of sharing leadership roles and responsibilities may even become a necessity, as a way of practicing leadership that ensures that better-informed decisions are taken, and that stronger consensus and commitment from various actors is attained (Fitzgerald et al., 2013; Ferlie et al., 2013). Sharing leadership may also be in itself a source of innovation, by offering the possibility for actors to jointly create and carry out initiatives that could not have been imagined by a single individual associated only with a specific set of concerns (either managerial or clinical).

Without being the only form leadership adopted in this context, plural forms of leadership appear more common in health care organizations, as well as in other professional and knowledge-based settings, than in other settings in the public and private sectors (Denis, Langley, and Sergi, 2012). Yet, it should be noted that leadership is not *de facto* shared in health care organizations. Leadership has been studied following more traditional, individual-centric approaches in health care settings as well (for a review, see Gilmartin and D'Aunno, 2007). In other words, empirically, leadership in health care organizations lends itself particularly well to plural forms; and theoretically, there are a variety of conceptualizations of plural leadership in the literature that can be mobilized. But how does such a collective approach to leadership happen? What forms can it take, and what kind of results can it produce? In this chapter, we will first discuss plural forms of leadership in general, untangling the various labels and ideas associated with the main forms that have been identified in the literature, building on previous conceptual work (Denis, Langley, and Sergi, 2012; Sergi, Denis, and Langley, 2012). We will then illustrate these different forms drawing on specific examples from health care organizations. These illustrations show how different situations may call for different modalities in terms of plural forms of leadership, operating both inside and across these organizations.

Conceptualizing Plural Leadership

Despite the counter-intuitive nature of the idea that more than one person might occupy leadership positions as head of a team, a unit, or an organization, the possibility that leadership might be shared or distributed among multiple individuals is not new. In various forms, traces of this idea can be found in the work of Follett (1924), Gibb (1950), Hollander (1961), Etzioni (1965), and Hodgson, Levinson, and Zaleznik (1965). After remaining relatively marginal for decades, the literature on this topic has grown exponentially since the end of the 1990s. Notwithstanding the distinctions that exist between its various strands, this literature as a whole challenges the assumption that leadership is or should be practiced by a sole individual; by doing so, these studies call into question and try to transcend what some researchers have identified as the "heroic" and "romantic" view of leaders (e.g., Meindl, Ehrlich, and Dukerich, 1985; Fletcher, 2004). However, this recent increase in interest for plural forms of leadership has also given rise to a proliferation of labels (such as shared, distributed, collective, relational, post-heroic, or dual leadership) used to identify this phenomenon, and to a multiplicity of definitions. Moreover, the same phenomenon of multiple individuals sharing a leadership role has been studied from many different theoretical, epistemological, and methodological positions. Literature on the topic is thus heterogeneous and scattered. This observation has prompted a number of reviews of this body of work (see the recent reviews by Yammarino et al., 2012; Contractor et al., 2012; and Denis, Langley, and Sergi, 2012). The review by Denis, Langley, and Sergi (2012) on which we draw here identified four main forms of plural leadership. This variety in plural forms of leadership found in the literature not only indicates that this approach to leadership can be conceptualized differently; more interestingly, this variety also indicates that there are multiple ways to organize and to practice leadership in the plural.

Hence, not only do multiple forms of plural leadership exist when it comes to having many individuals in leadership positions, but varying contexts and situations may call for and even require different forms. Yet, until now, empirical studies of plural forms of leadership have tended to focus on a single particular form. For example, many contexts have been looked at through the prism of distributed leadership (e.g., for schools, see Gronn, 2002; Spillane, Halverson, and Diamond, 2001; for health care, Chreim et al., 2010; Currie and Lockett, 2011; for higher education, Bolden, Petrov, and Gosling, 2009). While this approach has helped shed light on this phenomenon, it also tends to fragment our understanding of it. As we have argued elsewhere (Denis, Langley, and Sergi, 2012), a more global understanding of plural forms of leadership is needed. The first step in developing such an understanding is to distinguish the different forms that have been proposed and studied in organizations. In the following section, we present the typology organized around four distinct forms of plural leadership drawing on Denis, Langley, and Sergi's (2012) analysis of the existing literature on the topic; we then illustrate each of these forms with empirical examples from the health care context, discussing where each of them can be found in these organizations, when each may be especially productive, and some of the issues and challenges associated with it.

Figure 9.1 presents the four forms of plural leadership in the typology. As the figure shows, the forms can be distinguished along two dimensions. First, plural leadership forms can be distinguished based on their formality: leadership can formally be defined as practiced by many individuals, thus being decided upon and structured; or it can emerge out of the recurrent patterns of interactions between actors, thus being a localized phenomenon resulting from individuals ongoing ways of working. Second, plural leadership forms can differ depending on toward whom influence is mainly exercised. In some forms, we note that the plural form adopted involves group members leading each other (what we call mutual leadership), whereas in other forms, we note the presence of a team of leaders who collectively lead other organizational actors (coalitional leadership). Combined, these two axes organize the four forms of plural leadership identified (Denis, Langley, and Sergi, 2012).

We have deliberately labeled these forms with verbs to indicate that despite their differences, all of these forms require active work on the part of the actors involved in making leadership a collective, rather than individual phenomenon and practice. In the next sections, we successively present these four forms based on the stream of literature that has proposed and studied each. Following these descriptions, we illustrate each form with empirical examples, either by showcasing material taken from our own fieldwork in health care organizations, or by mobilizing situations described in already published articles.

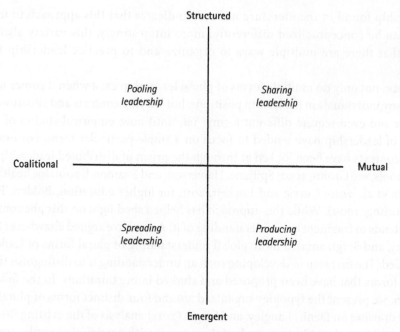

FIGURE 9.1 Typology of plural leadership forms

FORMS OF PLURAL LEADERSHIP
WITH ILLUSTRATIONS FROM HEALTH CARE
SETTINGS

Sharing Leadership

We have called the first configuration of plural leadership "sharing leadership." This configuration is defined by Pearce and Conger as follows: "A dynamic, interactive influence process among individuals in groups for which the objective is to lead one another to the achievement of group or organizational goals or both" (Pearce and Conger, 2003, 1). Anchored in organizational behavior and clearly influenced by psychology, this conception of plural leadership highlights the behavioral dimensions of leadership, as shared in teams. Research in this line of inquiry is mainly concerned with the effectiveness of team processes, and suggests that where leadership roles and responsibilities are shared, effectiveness and performance are enhanced because people feel more committed to joint goals and work harder to accomplish them. Research from this perspective underlines that individuals' motivation and capacity for self-leadership are key to the development of this form. Nevertheless, individual leaders may also exist and be clearly identified. For example, authors within this stream have suggested that "vertical leaders" play a key role in laying the foundations for shared functioning. Vertical leaders are also crucial in insuring that these teams attain the results expected of them (Ensley, Hmieleski, and Pearce, 2006; Pearce and Sims, 2002)

Based on this line of research, this form appears most appropriate when the work is complex and knowledge-based, when tasks are naturally interdependent and when the team's responsibilities require a high degree of involvement from leaders. Given the rise in the number of organizations that fit with this description, some researchers have suggested that sharing leadership might become more common (Pearce, 2004; Pearce and Manz, 2005). This configuration is thus proposed as being especially relevant for today's knowledge-intensive settings, such as health care, as we see next.

Health Care Illustration: Sharing Leadership in Interprofessional Collaboration

Emphasizing the activities of teams where people "lead one another to the achievement of team or organizational goals," the notion of "sharing leadership" appears particularly suited to a phenomenon that is of increasing importance and prevalence in health care settings today: that of interprofessional collaboration in which professionals with different backgrounds work together in multi-disciplinary teams to the benefit of clients.

Multi-disciplinary or interprofessional teams are designed to improve process efficiency and address complex clinical cases (Heinemann, 2002; Leathard, 2003; Gaboury et al., 2009). Defined as the gathering together of people from different disciplines around a common objective, multi-disciplinary teams inherently embed the idea of sharing and the values of mutuality and community (D'Amour et al., 2005). These teams are usually formed on the principle that all members can contribute to the mission of the team because of their distinctive expertise. In this sense, leadership should ideally rotate within these teams; everyone is called upon to take the lead at one time or another, to assert his or her unique skills and to participate in the development of a new and shared understanding of the goal. This sharing process constitutes the strength of the team (Pearce, 2004; Pearce, Manz, and Sims, 2009).

To illustrate this phenomenon in a health care setting, we draw on data from an empirical study of interprofessional collaboration in multi-disciplinary mental health care teams carried out from 2012 to 2014 (Chreim et al., 2013). The study was based on interviews with team members and observations of team meetings. We refer in particular to observations of two multi-disciplinary teams composed of psychiatrists, psychologists, social workers, and nurses. Sharing leadership can first be observed in the alternation of roles and responsibilities of professionals composing the team. For example, we saw that during the clinical process of the same case, different professionals were expected to take charge of the treatment, depending on the particular client's needs. As one member noted: "Sometimes, it could be the social worker who takes up more space; at other times, it could be the psychologist or the doctor. Everyone will be leader for a period of time." Similarly, another member told us: "Everyone has their moment of being leader, when their professional skills become necessary." We see that leadership circulates from one profession to another. In addition, it also appears in the interdependence and lateral influence among members (Pearce, Manz, and Sims, 2009). Indeed, how a member chooses to intervene with a client will undoubtedly have an influence on how other professionals will position themselves vis-à-vis the client thereafter.

These empirical observations, however, do not mean that shared leadership unfolds in exactly the same way in all multi-disciplinary teams. Indeed, in our study, we found significant variations that seemed to depend on the distinctive style of the psychiatrist involved in the team. The influence of the latter became especially noticeable in one of the teams we studied, which was split during the course of our study into four multiple inter-professional sub-teams, each one with its own psychiatrist. With a psychiatrist whose style was very democratic (e.g., who adopted suggestive rather than authoritative instructions), members strongly and equally engaged in clinical discussions. Collectively, they participated in the development of innovative therapeutic processes. Indeed, this psychiatrist rejected the traditional dominance of medical treatment in psychiatric care, and encouraged professionals to question his diagnostic hypotheses and to show creativity and initiative in the development of alternative treatments. Thus, through his particular behavioral style and through the sharing of a unique vision, this psychiatrist, as a vertical leader, enabled shared leadership. He encouraged the idea that the strength of the team does not stem from his power, but from the involvement and the relationships among all team members.

In contrast, another team we studied was dominated by a psychiatrist with a completely different style: he was authoritarian and radical in his demands vis-à-vis the other professionals. In this case, the professionals functioned in execution mode and tended to draw up treatment plans in parallel rather than together. When they occasionally sought to exercise their leadership, the psychiatrist impeded this by interfering in their decision-making and taking control of the direction of treatment. One member compared the two vertical leaders as follows: "He [the first one] has considerable expertise in the management of the team. He does his share of the work and trusts us to do ours. While with [the second one], we can build a clinical plan as a team and suddenly he forgets, or does not take into account the plan that we all built together. Then, everything we have done is scrapped … That is a strange type of leadership."

Although briefly reported, the two cases described above reveal the importance of vertical leaders (here represented by psychiatrists) in enabling the sharing of leadership roles so that different types of expertise can effectively be brought to bear on crucial client-oriented decisions. This confirms the more general findings from the leadership literature described above, but also underlines how existing professional dominance hierarchies may be a double-edged sword in attempting to implement more collaborative forms of health care. It is interesting to note that in a study of the implementation of new surgical technologies that required teamwork, Edmondson, Bohmer, and Pisano (2001) found that the more effective surgical teams were those in which the surgeon (as hierarchical leader) was willing to "allow himself to become a partner, not a dictator" as one respondent in the study put it (Edmondson, Bohmer, and Pisano, 2001, 699).

Pooling Leadership

The second form of plural leadership described above is labeled "pooling leadership." As in all forms of plural leadership, this configuration is based on a collection of individuals, but here, these individuals (usually a dyad, triad, or small group) are conceived as jointly leading other members of the organization, occupying what Gronn and Hamilton (2004) called a "shared role space" often located at the highest levels of the organization. Contrary to the first configuration, in this form the individuals that make up the team assume together the responsibility of leading. Moreover, this form of co-leadership is often formally inscribed in the organization's structure demanding connections between these people and structurally linking domains of expertise that would otherwise remain separated. Each member of these dyads or triads then represent a side of the organization or a particular logic of action, such as the artistic and administrative sides of an artistic organizations (Reid and Karambayya, 2009), or the clinical and managerial perspectives in health care contexts (e.g., Denis, Lamothe, and Langley, 2001). With their idea of *constellation*, Hodgson, Levinson, and Zaleznik (1965) were among the first to describe this approach to practicing leadership. A constellation is a group composed of a few individuals (usually two or three) in which leadership roles and positions are occupied jointly, but which exhibits specialization, differentiation, and complementarity of the roles these individuals play among themselves.

Empirical studies of pooling leadership have found this configuration in contexts as different as newspapers, entrepreneurial ventures, and technology firms. These studies underline in particular that creating fully conjoined positions within the organization's structure may be especially relevant in pluralistic and/or professional contexts, marked by internal complexity where different competing logics co-exist. In such contexts, a combination of viewpoints may be indispensable to establish and maintain legitimacy, and to facilitate decision-making (Alvarez and Svejenova, 2005; Fjellvaer, 2010). Again, health care organizations appear as a "natural" for such an approach to practicing plural leadership. However, the fact that this form of plural leadership can often be found in these organizations does not imply that it is necessarily widely appreciated: for example, in health care organizations, it is not uncommon that while people recognize the validity and the relevance of this form, they see it at the same time as a "necessary evil." It is thus not surprising that empirical studies of this form of plural leadership tend to show that the question of boundaries between individuals occupying such joint position might be sensitive, and might over time become problematic or contested, either from the inside or from the outside of the group, in part because they are pursuing disparate goals and responding to different constituencies. Also, clarifying the roles of each individual involved in this form of plural leadership is key. These studies also reveal that the satisfactory functioning of this configuration is based on a delicate balance between the

individuals involved in it, and that this balance can be affected by organizational decisions or changes (Denis, Lamothe, and Langley, 2001). Finally, studies of pooling leadership tend to show that establishing and maintaining this form requires time and effort
of all organizational actors involved. In sum, as these studies suggest, this form of plural
leadership may be particularly fragile: one of the central challenges of this form may
thus be to hold it together over time.

Health Care Illustration: Pooling Leadership in the Co-Management of Clinical Programs

To illustrate this form of leadership, we turn to another of our empirical studies, this
time of the functioning of an organizational structure in which two people (one a doctor and the other a professional with managerial training and experience) share the
management of clinical programs in a formalized co-management dyadic arrangement.
We focus in particular on Omega, a Canadian health centre and social services centre
including an acute care hospital, nursing homes, home care, and social services. This
organization formally adopted a co-management structure with doctor-administrator
dyads formally inscribed in Omega's organization chart. This approach clearly exemplifies the constellation model proposed by Hodgson, Levinson, and Zaleznik (1965),
as the leadership roles are defined de facto as joint, but where the roles played by the
members of the dyads are at the same time specialized, differentiated, but complementary. One of these dyads was locally recognized as high performing with this co-management approach. At the time of our study, this pair, composed of two women, had
been collaborating for five years, and enjoyed the experience. They shared a similar
task-oriented and responsive approach, and a common conception of their co-management dyad: they viewed it as a close collaboration and developed a bilateral way of
working stemming from a shared concern for the patients' well-being. Both described
their way of working together as relying on intense information sharing. Over time,
they also developed the practice of meeting in person at least once a week. They both
talked about their shared decision-making process, in which each of them relied on the
other to arrive at the decision both felt appropriate, because these decisions combined
their respective viewpoints or concerns.

Interestingly, both have declared that being involved and committed to co-management led them to learn to think differently: the physician commented that this close
relationship helped her better understand better the functioning of the administrative
side of Omega while the administrator fine-tuned her way of dealing with physicians
and their demands. Asked about the success of their collaboration, both underlined
how information—and processes to share it—were crucial. Not surprisingly, they
also talked about the necessity of trusting the other member of the dyad, but they
also extended this trust to the co-management form itself. In other words, not only
did they see that they had found a good way of deciding on various matters, solving

issues together and ultimately leading, but they were both convinced of the relevance of this form. Both underlined that working in such a dyad requires flexibility to adapt to change, transparency in the process of sharing information, and also that key decisions be taken jointly, which is how they themselves operate.

The description of this dyad highlights several of the characteristics that Gronn (1999) discussed when he introduced the idea of the leadership couple: in this case, we see a dyad that is closely working together, that has found over time a way of functioning that suits them and helps them in leading their clinical program, who fit well together and who exhibit reciprocity, especially in terms of information sharing. This example corresponds to what can be described as the ideal situation, based on a symmetrical and egalitarian relationship between members of the dyad. However, in an extensive study of four Québec health care organizations that had adopted this form of plural leadership, Langley et al. (2014) found that other kinds of pairings were possible between members of such dyads. They describe the egalitarian dyad at Omega as horizontally organized, where leadership is shared on all (or most) of the issues encountered and which operates in an integrated way. They consider that this form represents the purest form of pooling. However, they also found that other dyads that were still horizontally organized functioned in a less obviously symbiotic way. In these teams, leadership roles were more strongly differentiated between individuals, leading the dyad to work closely together while having very distinct territories. In other words, in these dyads, leadership responsibilities were separated between members, who respected each other's territory while keeping the other well-informed of the issues and decisions taken. In addition, Langley et al. (2014) found instances of dyads that were ostensibly intended to be equal within the formal organizational structure, but who organized themselves in a vertical, more hierarchical way. In these dyads, the relationship between members was asymmetrical, as one of them—either the physician or the administrator (and they found examples of both possibilities)—had a preponderant role, holding more responsibilities, while the other acted more as an expert or as an assistant. All of these ways of allocating the leadership roles and responsibilities inside a same structural form, the dyad, underlines that many of the expected benefits of such a joint leadership position rest on how the individuals inside these pairs work with each other. However, as Langley et al. (2014) stress, the success of such a form of plural leadership does not solely lie on the shoulders of the individuals within the dyads themselves, but will be influenced by wider organizational elements and dynamics. For example, they found that the credibility of both members of the dyad could be either supported or undermined by managers and physicians at other levels who might include them or not in the discussions of organization-wide issues.

Spreading Leadership

In the third form of plural leadership that we call "spreading leadership," we see leadership as being practiced in a more dispersed way across different levels and functions. In this configuration, leadership is shared across time and space, sometimes inside organizations and in other instances between organizations, and it functions in relay mode. This form of leadership has been recognized as occurring for many successful change projects (see for example Buchanan et al., 2007; Chreim et al., 2010; Zhang and Faerman, 2007). Indeed, the relaying of leadership over time between different people is viewed as a productive approach to meeting the objectives of a complex project, especially one involving inter-organizational initiatives. The approach has also been found to impact innovation performance in high technology alliances (Davis and Eisenhardt, 2011). In this form, the group of people involved in leadership is organized as a chain. Individuals sequentially take on leadership roles in realizing one phase of the joint project. However, while studies have shown that the success of collaborative projects often involves this form of leadership, the conditions enabling the creation of such a productive combination are not entirely clear.

Indeed, the spreading of leadership roles across departments or organizations does not automatically *guarantee* success given the potential for ambiguity, discord, and confusion among individuals who are not necessarily linked hierarchically. Crosby and Bryson (2010) suggest that deliberately creating this form of plural leadership requires powerful sponsors or clear champions. Huxham and Vangen (2000) argue that collaborative leadership of this kind is constructed not only through the activities of particular individuals but also through the structures that are put in place to enable collaboration and the routines and procedures that govern them. Thus, these studies have begun to suggest that leadership may need to be spread not only between individuals but also between human and non-human components in order to produce results (Crosby and Bryson, 2010; Huxham and Vangen, 2000; Mailhot et al., 2014).

Health Care Illustrations: Spreading Leadership in the Implementation of Integrated Care

To illustrate this form of plural leadership, we draw on two different case studies, both involving the implementation of integrated forms of care, and detailed separately in articles by Buchanan et al. (2007) and Chreim et al. (2010). These cases deal with health care settings in which leadership was distributed and spread across organizational boundaries. However, they differ significantly in the degree of formality shown in the distribution of leadership roles and responsibilities.

Buchanan et al. (2007) report on a case of an English health care organization that along with its network partners implemented a series of change initiatives in prostate cancer services delivery over a period of five years. Not only was this series of changes successful in terms of the performance targets, but it was also—and intriguingly—brought about by a wide network of different organizational actors (in lieu of an officially designated team), without any formal plan or project management driving the process. Buchanan et al. (2007) title their article "Nobody in Charge," clearly indicating that no specific individual or group of individuals assumed the leadership of the change. Leadership was rather seen as shifting between different individuals depending on the priorities or issues to be tackled. This network of individuals included a number of "change champions" that were keen on taking the lead whenever their leadership was needed; these individuals were also encouraged by the hospital's top management, which had not only decided to make cancer services a top priority of the hospital, but also wanted to promote a participative organizational culture. Buchanan et al. (2007) show that such a distributed, fluid, and evolving way of rotating leadership in this change initiative (which itself was not conceived as a single project, but as an array of various projects all needed to modify and improve the delivery of cancer services) rested on a combination of factors that together created a favorable context for it to emerge and develop over time. These factors included granting autonomy to the individuals involved in the process of improving the services, relationships between the clinical and the administrative sides of the hospital that were deemed good, and support for top management in the form of priority given to this initiative. Buchanan et al. also underline that there was a widespread understanding of the performance targets that had to be met. Moreover, they argue that the absence of a single, formally-defined initiative to which each project would have had to converge was in fact beneficial for the overall change initiative as it gave more autonomy to individuals. Finally, they suggest that the broader health care context was another element that enabled this distributed form of plural leadership, which was also in the process of evolving toward a more networked form at the time of the study.

The case documented by Buchanan et al. (2007) sounds exceptional in many respects. While it was highly successful, it is difficult to see how it can be easily replicated. Indeed, the shifting network of leadership they describe appears to be the result of the concatenation of multiple factors that were largely fortuitous. This exceptional case is nonetheless interesting as it reveals an extreme case of spreading leadership quite different from more traditional patterns, and even from some of the other plural leadership forms we identified in the literature.

While sharing some commonalities with Buchanan et al.'s case, the form of plural leadership described by Chreim et al. (2010) might offer a more realistic understanding of what such a form requires to function and what its management challenges might be. Chreim et al.'s case revolves around the development of multi-disciplinary primary health teams, dispersed across a number of health care organizations, an initiative that also revealed a form of plural leadership spread across organizations. Bringing about this initiative over a period of three years required changes on several levels, and thus involved a variety of actors, such as physicians, regional health care agency managers, and government. Significantly, a project coordinator was hired to facilitate the overall process. A team of key individuals, labeled the integration team, was also created, and acted as the main decision-making body for the initiative, linking the various actors associated with the project. In this case, multiple individuals assumed leadership roles over time. Some of these roles also emerged out of the initiative, and were not clearly defined from the start. Following Chreim et al.'s analysis of this case, and given the complexity of implementing the multi-disciplinary teams, we see that a complex network of leadership roles spread across the integration team, the regional agency managers, the physicians, the project coordinator, and the government was both deliberately set up and emerged out of the process of making this project come about. Their analysis highlights the importance of trust and the quality of relationships between all individuals in the project, and also draws attention to the project coordinator as a central actor in this network, playing a linking role.

Producing Leadership

The final form of plural leadership that we have identified views leadership as produced through the connections between and interactions among organizational actors, clearly decentering leadership from individuals. In contrast to the previous forms, this one starts from a different definition of leadership: instead of being associated to specific individuals (either single actors or a plurality), this form conceives of leadership as a collective product, resulting from the active involvement of actors as they are together trying to create a sense of direction (Collinson, 2005; Crevani, Lindgren, and Packendorff, 2010; Drath et al., 2008; Uhl-Bien, 2006). Leadership does not therefore reside *in* people, but transcends individuals, emerging *out* of the dynamic interactions between them. Studies in this vein emphasize the communicational nature of leadership practice (Fairhurst and Connaughton, 2014; Tourish, 2014; Vine et al., 2008).

Notably, some of the studies associated with this form of plural leadership have been inspired by complexity theory (e.g., Lichtenstein and Plowman, 2009; Lichtenstein et al., 2006; Uhl-Bien and Marion, 2009). For example, Uhl-Bien and Marion (2009) suggest that direction emerges in complex organizations based on three forms of leadership that they label "administrative leadership" (concerned with top-down control functions), "adaptive leadership" (concerned with entrepreneurial initiative), and "enabling leadership" that integrates the other forms and enables them to function together. Our illustration below draws in particular on this conception of how overall strategic leadership might be produced in complex organizations.

Health Care Illustration: Producing Strategic Direction across a Large Health Care Organization

In this form, leadership is produced through interactions that emerge organically as different actors collectively take part in the decision-making and priority setting processes, and as a a shared sense of direction comes to be created. We illustrate this with a study of the case of Salute, a large public health care organization located in Northern Italy (Lusiani, 2011). Salute runs the main city hospital, a subsidiary provincial hospital, and community health and social services in the four districts that compose its territory. At the time of the study, hospital activity was organized into twelve medical departments, each under the direction of a clinical director supported by a nurse coordinator. A growing role was played by the administrative staff units, in particular the Planning Office and Management Control unit. Over time, the hospital underwent a significant change. In the past, there had been a neater separation between the administrative and the clinical sides of the hospital: the administration was in charge of providing administrative support by producing rules, plans, and reports, whereas medical clinicians took local decisions and influenced organizational decisions virtually ignoring budget constraints, organizational goals, performance targets, or even what was happening in other units. However, in the late 1990s things started to change. As elsewhere in the world, the Italian health care sector was reformed under pressures for increased cost control and quality of services. This implied, amongst other, more transparent planning and more accountable clinical behavior: because doctors are the main decision-makers in their clinical practice, they are the main cost drivers within the organization. There was therefore a push to formalize and render more transparent their role in the organization's leadership and to render them accountable for the organizational impact of their clinical decisions. Put differently, it was felt that clinical professionals' informal leadership needed to be explicitly integrated into the formal organizational system.

Salute's General Director attempted to achieve this by establishing a somewhat "participative" system of strategic planning, budgeting, and project management practice, and by establishing a Planning Office as a technical support function to "coach" clinical professionals in these activities. Specifically, the system involved three components. First, *strategic planning* was conducted by the top management team, but involved the reception, adjustment, and alignment of "inputs" to the plan from clinical professionals and other stakeholders, as well as a process of consultation of clinical directors on provisional versions. Second, *budgeting* involved the definition of annual activity targets and related resources by hospital units to meet the strategic goals, and was negotiated yearly at ad hoc meetings between the top management team, on one side, and each clinical director and nurse coordinator for every department, on the other side. Finally, through *project management*, any clinical professional at any organizational level was given the opportunity to structure project proposals to improve an activity or propose innovative initiatives, if connected to specific goals of the strategic plan. The top management team, assisted by planning officers, reviewed all project proposals and selected, revised, or approved their implementation.

Taken together, strategic planning, budgeting, and project management tools are designed to work in a systemic way as a platform to integrate clinicians' contributions and top managers' inputs in decision-making and priority setting. A crucial role is here played by Planning Officers who, by assisting both top managers and clinicians throughout these activities, happen to perform indispensable boundary work, as they bridge these different social spheres and translate between administrative and clinical values. Overall, this system appears in our study to enable some kind of coherent strategic direction to emerge while incorporating multiple perspectives.

The question remains: where does leadership in such a structure lie, and where exactly does it happen? It would be limiting or misleading to see leadership as a property of some individuals at Salute. Rather, leadership is produced as actors interact in the entanglement of heterogeneous dynamics that Uhl-Bien and Marion (2009) defined as "adaptive," "administrative," and "enabling." *Adaptive leadership* is defined as a complexity dynamic of self-organizing processes that govern the behavior of agents (Uhl-Bien and Marion, 2009). This can be seen in the informal decisions of clinical practice, as clinicians interact to generate and advance novel solutions addressing the adaptive needs of the system. Second, we can see that there is also a place for *administrative leadership* represented by the formal hierarchy of top managers' work: top managers set the broad strategic goals and, although they open up these goals for discussion with stakeholders within the strategic planning process, they retain the final word on what is included and what is silenced. Similarly, they also manage budget negotiations with clinical directors and make the final selection of the projects proposed by professionals. As Uhl-Bien and Marion (2009) note, administrative leadership tends to standardize and normalize activity.

However in order to realize change, innovation, and learning, the informal (or adaptive, representing the need for "creative chaos") and the formal (or administrative, representing the "desire for structure") need to be entangled and integrated. The incorporation of adaptive initiatives into the formal organizational system is something that rarely happens spontaneously. Generally, *enabling leadership* mechanisms are needed for this purpose. One enabling mechanism involves the creation of conditions for the emergence of adaptive leadership (Uhl-Bien and Marion, 2009). In the case of Salute, this occurs through the overall planning platform with its three components: the strategic planning practice inasmuch as it is open to including clinicians' contributions; the budgeting practice inasmuch as it works as a locus for dialogue and negotiation between top managers and clinicians; the project management practice inasmuch as clinicians formalize their initiatives in the form of organizational projects. But our study suggested that none of this could happen without another enabling mechanism: mediation work between administrative and adaptive leadership (Uhl-Bien and Marion, 2009). At Salute this "enabling leadership" function appears through the work of the Planning Officers as they interface between top managers and clinicians. Planning Officers were ostensibly there to accomplish a prescribed technical support role. However, we observed that they accomplished much more than this. Besides their assistance function, and through that, they also translated between otherwise disconnected bodies of knowledge that often remained opaque to each other like two foreign languages: management/accounting logics and clinical professional logics. At the same time, Planning Officers bridged different and often conflicting parts of the organization by connecting the professional base and top management in part through their ability to maintain credibility in both worlds due to combined clinical and managerial experience. They were thus able to reduce both cognitive and social distance between managerial and clinical worlds, thus mediating between the need for control (administrative leadership) and the need for innovation and entrepreneurship (adaptive leadership).

In sum, this is a case where the emergent informal decisions and influential acts by professionals (adaptive leadership) interact with the top managers' priorities and are eventually channeled into a formal system in the form of inputs to the plan, agreed-upon budget targets and projects (administrative leadership) through the existence of the overall planning platform that creates the conditions for interaction, and, even more importantly, through the mediating work of Planning Officers (enabling leadership). In other words, strategic leadership here is not possessed by any individual or group, but something that is produced through a system of interactions. It involves a dose of emergence, but it also requires effort and continuous maintenance activity.

DISCUSSION AND CONCLUSION

As this conceptual and empirical overview of plural forms of leadership has shown, this practice does not refer to a single configuration, but rather to a family of forms, each corresponding to different patterns and modes of interaction. In complex settings such as health care organizations, this opens the door to a reflection on the choice of the most appropriate form depending on the specific set of responsibilities or on the project that might benefit from the presence of multiple leaders sharing leadership roles and responsibilities. As suggested by our analysis of a large body of literature, in the situations where they succeed and work well, these plural forms can have significant and positive consequences for health organizations. Generally speaking, these forms have been associated with a number of beneficial effects, such as promoting better engagement from physicians who, by taking an active part in leadership and decision-making processes, gain a finer understanding of administrative realities and constraints. These forms have also been associated with improved relationships between the administrative and clinical sides of the health care organizations, and have been found to improve the flow of information and coordination. Also, these forms have been associated in some instances with organizational and clinical innovations, such as the development of better solutions in terms of patient care (Langley et al., 2014).

However, as Langley et al. (2014) have underlined, moving towards plural forms of leadership is more than a structural choice, as it often requires a cultural change on all sides. Also, these forms need to be legitimated both by the people who will be taking part in them and by employees who will be subjected to them, as well as being supported by top management. Despite all of their differences, the four forms of plural leadership we have discussed in this chapter imply changes in how authority is negotiated and established, how information circulates, how decisions are made and communicated, how coordination is achieved, and how, ultimately, leadership roles and responsibilities are conceived and practiced.

When considering the literature around the four forms we discussed, we identified several issues associated with each form that still require further research (Denis, Langley, and Sergi, 2012). For the sharing leadership form, we noted that the tension between the notion of sharing which presupposes egalitarian relationships, and the apparently still important role of vertical leadership in sustaining the potential for such relationships to occur in an effective manner; for the pooling leadership form, several authors have noted its fragility (Denis, Langley, and Cazale, 1996; Denis, Langley, and Pineault, 2000; Denis, Lamothe, and Langley 2001; Alvarez and Svejenova, 2005), suggesting that the conditions for its sustainability over time need further study; for the spreading leadership form, the underlying mechanisms mobilized to create such networks of leadership could be more finely explored. Finally, for the producing leadership form, more research is needed on how this pattern might be created and maintained.

Beyond these specific areas for further research, we note a few more general underlying issues that are relevant to all of them, and require attention from researchers and practitioners alike. First, when considering any of these forms of plural leadership, one should not be blinded by their collective nature: in all of the four forms we have discussed, the individual dimension of leadership has not disappeared. Rather, there are individual *and* collective elements simultaneously at play in the dynamics of these plural forms. Indeed, we suggest that all these forms of plural leadership require "pockets" of individual agency to nurture, drive, and sustain the collective processes associated with them. Our suggestion highlights that, both conceptually and empirically, plural forms of leadership should not be considered in direct opposition with more individualistic views of leadership. There is thus a duality deeply inscribed in plural leadership, and one that may not always be recognized, either in research or by practitioners. Such a duality opens the door to a stimulating line of inquiry, one that would address simultaneously the collective and the individual aspects of leadership practice. In this regard, health care organizations may not only be especially well-suited to pursue such studies, but may be at the forefront of new developments in leadership theory and practice.

Moreover, further research is needed to understand more precisely the conditions required for all forms to flourish. Various empirical studies, including some of our own, indicate—sometimes implicitly rather than explicitly—that there might be individual and material dimensions that promote these various forms of plural leadership. In addition to the varying degrees of agency and influence individuals possess, relational factors such as personal compatibility, experience of working together, and mutual respect of discretionary spaces for action (Gronn, 1999) may impact how plural leadership evolves. On the material side, the organizational structures in place, how committees are constituted and function, and the routines developed to channel decision-making and the distribution of leadership roles are all elements that contribute to making plural leadership possible (see also Huxham and Vangen, 2000). Therefore, alongside individual agency and influence, plural forms of leadership need dedicated spaces and places to thrive.

These considerations lead to an important question with regards to plural leadership: to what point can any of these forms be deliberately implemented and used instrumentally in health care organizations? As we indicated at the beginning, health care is naturally pluralistic, so influence is de facto diffused and distributed. As such, they appear as natural sites for plural forms of leadership, which all aim at combining various interests, expertise, and logics. Viewed in this light, health care organizations appear as contexts where the main issue is not so much to make leadership more plural (because in any case, no single individual has the authority, expertise, and legitimacy to lead alone). Rather, it is a question of channeling existing pluralism in ways that are likely to be productive (Denis, Langley, and Sergi, 2012). Couched in terms of leadership, this latter challenge emerges out of the necessity to find ways to accommodate the variety of viewpoints that often need to be harmonized in decision-making processes. Although positive cases (such as those described in many of our illustrations) indicate that plural leadership can be highly effective and beneficial when it works, we still have very little research on how, very concretely, these forms can be put in place in health care organizations to generate these positive consequences. In health care organizations, channeling plurality may hence be at the same time a fundamental challenge, and a crucial necessity—one that various forms of plural leadership may answer, but we need further research to assess how they are deployed and sustained over time. Moreover, the agency of individual actors probably impacts on the ability to sustain these plural forms of leadership through time. There may also be a tendency to see more the positive side of plural forms of leadership. Like any social arrangement, these forms are subject to contradictions and can also be a source of inertia. We have also come across and studied situations where the aggregate impact of a network of leaders was more on the side of inertia rather than of change and innovation (Denis et al., 2011).

Finally, the expansion of various organizational forms such as inter-organizational networks in health care may present new challenges for the development of plural forms of leadership. More and more policy, organizational, and clinical issues in health care are dealt with in highly distributed environments (Ferlie et al., 2013) which means that plural forms of leadership have to develop in a much less structured context and cover a wider range of actors at multiple levels. In the computing and communication industries, Davis and Eisenhardt (2011) observed that rotating leadership plays a key role in strategic alliances across firms. The fluidity of strategic objectives and leadership roles may become more central to understanding how joint action becomes possible. This may mean that in such contexts, approaches based on the producing leadership perspective will be more and more important in shaping the leadership phenomenon. In addition, related to the environment and dynamic of health care systems, the connections between pockets of leadership and agency at various levels of governance from central government to sub-national authorities, to organizations, and to clinical work may play a crucial role in driving system changes (Denis and Van Gestel, 2015). The conditions and process for developing joint action and plural forms of leadership across these levels represents fertile ground for further research.

REFERENCES

Alvarez, J. L. and Svejenova, S. (2005). *Sharing executive power: Roles and relationships at the top.* Cambridge: Cambridge University Press.

Bolden, R., Petrov, G., and Gosling, J. (2009). Distributed leadership in higher education: Rhetoric and reality. *Educational Management Administration and Leadership*, 37(2): 257–277.

Buchanan, D. A., Addicott, R., Fitzgerald, L., Ferlie, E., and Baeza, J. I. (2007). Nobody in charge: Distributed change agency in healthcare. *Human Relations*, 60(7): 1065–1090.

Chreim, S., Langley, A., Comeau-Vallée, M., Huq, J.-L., and Reay, T. (2013). Leadership as boundary work in healthcare teams. *Leadership*, 9(2): 201–228.

Chreim, S., Williams, B. E. B., Janz, L., and Dastmalchian, A. (2010). Change agency in a primary health care context: The case of distributed leadership. *Health Care Management Review*, 35(2): 187–199.

Collinson, D. (2005). Dialectics of leadership. *Human Relations*, 58(11): 1419–1442.

Contractor, N. S., DeChurch, L. A., Carson, J., Carter, D. R., and Keegan, B. (2012). The topology of collective leadership. *The Leadership Quarterly*, 23(6): 994–1011.

Crevani, L., Lindgren, M., and Packendorff, J. (2010). Leadership, not leaders: On the study of leadership as practices and interactions. *Scandinavian Journal of Management*, 26(1): 77–86.

Crosby, B. C. and Bryson, J. M. (2010). Integrative leadership and the creation and maintenance of cross-sector collaborations. *Leadership Quarterly*, 21: 211–230.

Currie, G. and Lockett, A. (2011). Distributing leadership in health and social care: Concertive, conjoint or collective? *International Journal of Management Reviews*, 13(3): 286–300.

D'Amour, D., Ferrada-Videla, M., Rodriguez, L. S. M., and Beaulieu, M.-D. (2005). The conceptual basis for interprofessional collaboration: Core concepts and theoretical frameworks. *Journal of Interprofessional Care*, 19(S1): 116–131.

Davis, J. P. and Eisenhardt, K. M. (2011). Rotating leadership and collaborative innovation: Recombination processes in symbiotic relationships. *Administrative Science Quarterly*, 56(2): 159–201.

Denis, J.-L., Dompierre, G., Langley, A., and Rouleau, L. (2011) Escalating indecision: Between reification and strategic ambiguity. *Organization Science*, 22(1): 225–244.

Denis, J.-L. and Forest, P.-G. (2012). Real reform begins within: An organizational approach to health care reform. *Journal of Health Politics, Policy and Law*, 37(4): 633–645.

Denis, J.-L., Lamothe, L., and Langley, A. (2001). The dynamics of collective leadership and strategic change in pluralistic organizations. *Academy of Management Journal*, 44(4): 809–837.

Denis, J.-L., Langley, A., and Cazale, L. (1996). Leadership and strategic change under ambiguity. *Organization Studies*, 17(4):673–699.

Denis, J.-L., Langley, A., and Pineault, M. (2000). Becoming a leader in a complex organization. *Journal of Management Studies*, 37(8):1063–1099.

Denis, J.-L., Langley, A., and Rouleau, L. (2007). Strategizing in pluralistic contexts: Rethinking theoretical frames. *Human Relations*, 60(1): 179–215.

Denis, J.-L., Langley, A., and Sergi, V. (2012). Leadership in the plural. *The Academy of Management Annals*, 6(1): 211–283.

Denis, J.-L. and Van Gestel, N. (2015). Leadership and innovation in healthcare governance. In *The Palgrave international handbook of health care policy and governance*, ed. Kuhlmann, E., Blank, R. H., Bourgeault, I. L., and Wendt, C., pp. 425–440. Basingstoke: Palgrave Macmillan.

Drath, W., McCauley, C., Palus, C., Van Velsor, E., O'Connor, P., and McGuire, J. (2008). Direction, alignment, commitment: Toward a more integrative ontology of leadership. *Leadership Quarterly*, 19(6): 635–653.

Edmondson, A. C., Bohmer, R. M., and Pisano, G. P. (2001). Disrupted routines: Team learning and new technology implementation in hospitals. *Administrative Science Quarterly*, 46(4): 685–716.

Ensley, M., Hmieleski, K., and Pearce, C. (2006). The importance of vertical and shared leadership within new venture top management teams: Implications for the performance of startups. *Leadership Quarterly*, 17(3): 217–231.

Etzioni, A. (1965). Dual leadership in complex organizations. *American Sociological Review*, 30(5): 688–698.

Fairhurst, G. T. and Connaughton, S. L. (2014). Leadership: A communicative perspective. *Leadership*, 10(1): 7–35.

Ferlie, E., Fitzgerald, L., McGivern, G., Dopson, S., and Bennett, C. (2013). *Making wicked problems governable?: The case of managed networks in health care.* Oxford: Oxford University Press.

Fitzgerald, L., Ferlie, E., McGivern, G., and Buchanan, D. (2013). Distributed leadership patterns and service improvement: Evidence and argument from English healthcare. *The Leadership Quarterly*, 24(1): 227–239.

Fjellvaer, H. (2010). Dual and unitary leadership: Managing ambiguity in pluralistic organizations. Unpublished doctoral thesis, Norwegian School of Economics and Business Administration.

Fletcher, J. K. (2004). The paradox of postheroic leadership: An essay on gender, power, and transformational change. *Leadership Quarterly*, 15(5): 647–661.

Follett, M. P. (1924). *Creative experience*. New York: Longmans, Green and Co.

Gaboury, I., Bujold, M., Boon, H., and Moher, D. (2009). Interprofessional collaboration within Canadian integrative healthcare clinics: Key components. *Social Science and Medicine*, 69(5): 707–715.

Gibb, C. A. (1950). The sociometry of leadership in temporary groups. *Sociometry*, 13(3): 226–243.

Gilmartin, M. J. and D'Aunno, T. A. (2007). Leadership research in healthcare. *Academy of Management Annals*, 1(1): 387–438.

Glouberman, S. and Mintzberg, H. (2001a). Managing the care of health and the cure of disease, part I: Differentiation. *Health Care Management Review*, 26(1): 56–69.

Glouberman, S. and Mintzberg, H. (2001b). Managing the care of health and the cure of disease, part II: Integration. *Health Care Management Review*, 26(1): 70–84.

Gronn, P. (1999). Substituting for leadership: the neglected role of the leadership couple. *The Leadership Quarterly*, 10: 141–162.

Gronn, P. (2002). Distributed leadership as a unit of analysis. *Leadership Quarterly*, 13(4): 423–451.

Gronn, P. and Hamilton, A. (2004). "A bit more life in the leadership": Co-principalship as distributed leadership practice. *Leadership and Policy in Schools*, 3(1): 3–35.

Heinemann, G. D. (2002). Teams in health care settings. In *Team performance in health care: Assessment and development*, ed. Heinemann, G. D. and Zeiss, A. M., pp. 3–18. New York: Springer.

Hodgson, R. C., Levinson, D. J., and Zaleznik, A. (1965). *The executive role constellation*. Boston, MA: Harvard Business School Press.

Hollander, E. P. (1961). Emergent leadership and social influence. In *Leadership and interpersonal behavior*, ed. Petrullo, L. and Bass, B. M., pp. 30–47. New York: Holt, Rinehardt and Winston.

Huxham, C. and Vangen, S. (2000). Leadership in the shaping and implementation of collaboration agendas: How things happen in a (not quite) joined-up world. *Academy of Management Journal*, 43(6): 1159–1175.

Langley, A., Gibeau, E., Van Schendel, N., Denis, J.-L., and Pomey, M.-P. (2014). *Vers de nouvelles pistes de partenariat medico-administratif*. Association Québécoise d'établissements de santé et de services sociaux. Final Report, available at: <http://www.aqesss.qc.ca/docs/public_html/document/Documents_deposes/Part_Med_Adm_Rapport%20Final_20141118.pdf> (accessed October 1, 2015).

Leathard, A. (2003). Models of Interprofessional Collaboration. In *Interprofessional collaboration: From policy to practice*, ed. Leathard, A., pp. 93–117. New York: Routledge.

Lichtenstein, B. B. and Plowman, D. A. (2009). The leadership of emergence: A complex systems leadership theory of emergence at successive organizational levels. *Leadership Quarterly*, 20(4): 617–630.

Lichtenstein, B. B., Seers, A., Uhl-Bien, M., Orton, J. D., Marion, R., and Schreiber, C. (2006). Complexity leadership theory: An interactive perspective on leading in complex adaptive systems. *Emergence: Complexity and Organization*, 8(4): 2–12.

Lusiani, M. (2011). Formal planning rationality in public sector professional work: Between discourse and practice. Dissertation thesis, Alma Mater Studiorum Università di Bologna. Dottorato di ricerca in Direzione aziendale, 23. Ciclo.

Mailhot, C., Gagnon, S., Langley, A., and Binette, L.-F. (2014). Distributing leadership across people and objects in a collaborative research project. *Leadership*, <http://lea.sagepub.com/content/early/2014/07/25/1742715014543578.full.pdf+html> (accessed October 1, 2015).

Maynard, A. (2013). Health care rationing: Doing it better in public and private health care systems. *Journal of Health Politics, Policy and Law*, 38(6): 1103–1127.

Meindl, J. R., Ehrlich, S. B., and Dukerich, J. M. (1985). The romance of leadership. *Administrative Science Quarterly*, 30(1): 78–102.

Pearce, C. L. (2004). The future of leadership: Combining vertical and shared leadership to transform knowledge work. *Academy of Management Executive*, 18(1): 47–59.

Pearce, C. L. and Conger, J. A. (2003). *Shared leadership: Reframing the hows and whys of leadership*. Thousand Oaks, CA: Sage.

Pearce, C. and Manz, C. (2005). The new silver bullets of leadership: The importance of self- and shared leadership in knowledge work. *Organizational Dynamics*, 34(2): 130–140.

Pearce, C. L., Manz, C., and Sims Jr, H. P. (2009). Where do we go from here?: Is shared leadership the key to team success?" *Organizational Dynamics*, 38(3): 234–235.

Pearce, C. L. and Sims Jr., H. P. (2002). The relative influence of vertical vs. shared leadership on the longitudinal effectiveness of change management teams. *Group Dynamics: Theory, Research and Practice*, 6(2): 172–197.

Reid, W. and Karambayya, R. (2009). Impact of dual executive leadership dynamics in creative organizations. *Human Relations*, 62(7): 1073–1112.

Sergi, V., Denis, J.-L., and Langley, A. (2012). Opening up perspectives on plural leadership. *Industrial and Organizational Psychology*, 5(4): 403–407.

Spillane, J. P., Halverson, R., and Diamond, J. B. (2001). Investigating school leadership practice: A distributed perspective. *Educational Researcher*, 30(3): 23–28.

Tourish, D. (2014). Leadership, more or less? A processual, communication perspective on the role of agency in leadership theory. *Leadership*, 10(1): 79–98.

Uhl-Bien, M. (2006). Relational leadership theory: Exploring the social processes of leadership and organizing. *Leadership Quarterly*, 17(6): 654–676.

Uhl-Bien, M. and Marion, R. (2009). Complexity leadership in bureaucratic forms of organizing: A meso model. *Leadership Quarterly*, 20(4): 631–650.

Vine, B., Holmes, J., Marra, M., Pfeifer, D., and Jackson, B. (2008). Exploring co-leadership talk through interactional sociolinguistics. *Leadership*, 4(3): 339–360.

Yammarino, F. J., Salas, E., Serban, A., Shirreffs, K., and Shuffler, M. L. (2012). Collectivistic leadership approaches: Putting the "we" in leadership science and practice. *Industrial and Organizational Psychology*, 5(4): 382–402.

Zhang, J. and Faerman, S. R. (2007). Distributed leadership in the development of a knowledge sharing system. *European Journal of Information Systems*, 16(4): 479–493.

CHAPTER 10

··

EFFECTIVE TEAM WORKING IN HEALTH CARE

··

MICHAEL A. WEST AND LYNN MARKIEWICZ

INTRODUCTION

··

TEAM working in health care is a taken-for-granted good. Teams of people must work interdependently to provide high quality care for patients. They have to combine their varied expertise to deliver the best possible care. Uni-professional, lone practitioner working cannot deliver the care patients need to the same extent as multi-professional team working. Teams of health care practitioners working together is therefore the context of health care in both developing and developed countries. The vast majority of health care staff work in teams and deliver care in teams. In this chapter, we explore this taken-for-granted assumption and argue that, though team working is vital for high quality health care, the quality of team working in this sector is often poor. Such poor team working leads to errors that harm both staff and patients; injuries to staff; poor staff well-being; lower levels of patient satisfaction; poorer quality of care; and higher patient mortality. We describe how team working and, equally importantly, team-based working as an organizational form, can be developed within and across organizations to ensure continually improving, high quality, and compassionate patient care.

We begin by asking "what is a team?" Our definition of team working is based on the research on team working across sectors (not just health) and across countries. It has some important implications for the way we then address questions about team working in health care. We ask why work in teams in health care? Drawing on research evidence across health care sectors we show the relationships between team working and health care outcomes and how these are powerfully mediated by the quality and extent of team working in health care organizations. We also provide evidence to show that the quality of team working in the English National Health Service (NHS) is, for the most part, poor with consequent dangers to patients and relative ineffectiveness of the system.

Such an analysis begs questions about how to improve team working and team-based working in health care and we draw on a range of evidence from research conducted over the last 30 years to answer these questions. In particular, we identify the central importance of team objectives and team leadership to team effectiveness. But there are specific challenges for team working and team-based working in health care, because of the complexity of the context and the historical legacy of separate professional development and status hierarchies. We explore how these challenges can be overcome, arguing that ensuring effective team working in health care is as critical to performance as dealing with infections in hospitals and medication errors in primary care. Finally, we conclude by reinforcing the fundamental importance of good team working to the delivery of high quality, continually improving, and compassionate care and urge practitioners and policy makers to take account of the prescriptions we offer in this chapter.

WHY HAVE TEAMS IN HEALTH CARE?

Humans have worked in teams over at least 150,000 years to cope with complex tasks, whether herding prey into canyons, or performing complex surgery. Homo sapiens developed hunting techniques that involved groups cooperating and herding animals such as wild horses into narrow gorges where they could be easily slaughtered (Harari, 2014). We have developed the skills of team working as a species because, quite simply, by combining skills and delineating differentiated roles we accomplish more than we possible could working alone. Health care is complex, whether it involves treating a patient with diabetes, dealing with accident and emergency cases, providing supports for severely depressed adolescents, supporting frail and elderly patients, or ensuring the delivery of nursing care on a busy ward. The level of complexity requires team working. That complexity also implies the probability of error and errors can lead to patient harm and death (Sharit, 2006). Below we consider the research evidence on the value or otherwise of working in teams at the level of individual team members, team level outcomes (particularly in relation to patient care), and at the organizational level (is more widespread team working in health care organizations associated with better outcomes for patients?).

Individual Level Outcomes: Health care is a stressful sector to work within. Nurses are the most stressed group in the UK working population, according to the Health and Safety Executive in 2014 (<http://www.hse.gov.uk/statistics/causdis/stress/>). This alarming observation reveals how the service delivery and organization of caring for people in society incurs damage to the very people who provide that care. Does team working make a difference? Carter and West (1999) showed that team working was associated with lower stress levels among health care workers as a result of greater role clarity, social support, and being buffered by their teams from negative organizational factors. Moreover, Richter, Dawson, and West (2011), in a meta-analysis of 35 studies of the implementation team working in health care, found an overall positive effect on employee satisfaction and well-being. The effects in health care were significantly larger than those found in 23 studies in non-health care environments. The research suggests that this is dependent on the quality of team functioning. In a study of 400 health care teams (Borrill et al., 2000), researchers found that quality of team functioning was associated with lower team member stress levels. Team functioning was measured as clarity of team objectives, levels of participation of team members in decision-making, emphasis on quality of task performance, and support for innovation within the teams. Buttigieg, West, and Dawson (2011) gathered data from 65,142 hospital staff in the NHS in England and found that those working in well-structured teams had the highest levels of job satisfaction. Again, levels of social support and role clarity appeared to account for these differences.

A consistent, though happily reducing phenomenon within the English NHS is violence against staff by patients, carers, or other members of the public. There is evidence that violence is less likely to be perpetrated against staff working in well-functioning teams (Borrill et al., 2000; Buttigieg, West, and Dawson, 2011; Carter and West, 1999). One explanation for these findings is that the positivity of effective teams influences patients and carers via emotional contagion. This in turn builds confidence and positivity in the affective environment, thereby reducing the likelihood of hostility and frustration.

Team Level Outcomes: Does effective team working lead to better patient care and patient outcomes? A recent review of the literature (West and Lyubovnikova, 2013) suggests that team working in health care is associated with a range of patient outcomes. This review echoed the conclusions of earlier review that concluded that good team working reduced errors in patient care and improved quality (Firth-Cozens, 2001) and a review of team working in intensive care settings. The latter review concluded that working in teams can significantly reduce the level of error and promote learning and quality improvement in intensive care units (Richardson, West, and Cuthbertson, 2010).

But quality of team working matters. There is evidence also that poor team working leads to medical errors while good team working prevents them. Nembhard and Edmondson (2006) found that medical errors were often a result of poor team working and status hierarchies. Such hierarchies are associated with reluctance on the part of lower status team members to challenge the decisions of more senior team members, even when they believe those decisions to be wrong. In an analysis of 193 critical prescribing incidents (Lewis and Tully, 2009), one-third were attributed to team-related problems such as hierarchies, prescribing etiquette (failure to challenge), ignoring hospital regulations, and neglecting best practices in the interests of team relationships. Team working in health care should not be a taken-for-granted good; it is the quality of team working that counts in ensuring high quality care.

Research also shows that quality of team working predicts the extent to which teams develop and implement innovation in health care—introducing new and improved treatments for patients and new and improved methods of delivering care. Fay et al. (2006) found in two samples of health care teams (66 and 95 teams respectively) that multi-disciplinary teams did produce higher quality innovation than less diverse teams, but only when the teams functioned effectively. Effective team working included clear team objectives, high levels of team member participation in decision-making, commitment to high quality work, and practical support for innovation.

In a study of community health teams over a six-year period in Sweden, Jansson, Isacsson, and Lindhom (1992) found that where team working was introduced, regions reported reductions in emergency visits. Again, quality of team working was important and accessibility and continuity of care were particularly important factors. Similar findings emerged from a study of community mental health teams in England. Jackson, Sullivan, and Hodge found positive effects 12 months after the introduction of teams upon both treatment and service rates.

Organizational Level Outcomes: Recent research has begun to examine the impact of team working in health care by examining the extent of team-based working in organizations and exploring the relationships with outcomes such as patient satisfaction, quality of care, efficiency of use of resources, innovation, staff engagement and well-being, and (in the acute sector) patient mortality.

A study of the links between human resource management practices in hospitals (West et al., 2001) found that the extent and quality of team working had a significant negative relationship with patient mortality = the more and better the team working, the lower the levels of patient mortality. Where more than 60% of staff reported working in teams, mortality was 5% lower than expected and this result held after controlling for the number of doctors per 100 beds, GP facilities per 100,000 population, and local health and socio-economic profiles. An analysis of the NHS staff survey data over eight years suggested that quality of team working in health care organizations (across primary care, mental health care, ambulance services, and acute care) was associated with patient satisfaction, quality of patient care, efficiency of use of resources, staff absenteeism, staff turnover, and financial performance (West et al., 2011; Lyubovnikova et al., 2015). Studies of team working in primary care in the United States suggest greater use and higher quality is associated with reduced hospitalization and physician visits (Sommers et al., 2000).

Overall, the research suggests that team working and team-based working in health care have positive outcomes for staff, for patients, and for organizations. But a consistent finding is that quality of team working is important and that there is a need to clarify in health care both what is meant by the concept of "team" and what constitutes effective team functioning or team working. Calling a group of people who work in health care a team is not a guarantee that their combined efforts will prove beneficial for patients, as the research above confirms. What then is a "team"?

WHAT IS A TEAM?

When our ancestors formed teams, they did so for a purpose. There was a task to be accomplished that was best confronted by individuals working towards a shared goal.

Herding the horses into the gorge in order to kill them and feed the community was a clear task. Similarly, in surgery for fractured neck of femur, a group of individuals work together to carry out the task; or a primary care team screening the local population for cholesterol levels; or a mental health team providing support and treatment for drug addicts; or a team of ambulance staff ensuring good first-responder services for people in a defined geographical area. The assumption that teams are a good thing is supported by these examples. But increasingly in health care the term "team" is applied to all sorts of groupings where it is somewhat difficult to identify what the task is. Do all the nurses working on a ward over the course of a week constitute a team? What is their collective task? Does a committee that meets regularly to review patient complaints constitute a team? Are they working together, as a team, to fulfill a task or do they simply sit in a room, have some discussions, and make decisions that the most expert of them could have done more effectively working alone? Are the 16 members of the board of a hospital a team and to what extent are non-executive members part of the team? And does it matter if we call all sorts of health care entities teams, whether they correspond to a definition or not?

If we consult the wider literature (not just in health care) on what we mean by a team, key characteristics include that teams have a clear task, shared objectives, the necessary authority, autonomy, and resources to have a good shot at completing the task; team members work interdependently and have to rely on each other's task performance to enable individual and shared success (goal interdependence and task interdependence) (Hackman, 2002; West, 2012). Team members see themselves as part of the team and have expectations therefore about how other team members will behave (e.g., backing them up when workloads are high, being cooperative); team members have relatively clear roles in the team and understand the roles others in the team play in achieving the task; and, in organizations, others are aware of the team as an entity. In practice, effective teams are rarely any bigger than 10–15 people and, to function most effectively, have the minimum number of members necessary to complete the task. The ideal maximum is probably around 6–8 members. At a minimum, teams should have a clearly stated task, clear objectives, relatively clear roles, and work interdependently, and members should meet regularly to review and (consequently) adjust their performance.

A standard definition of a team is: "A team is a relatively small group of people working on a clearly defined, challenging task that is most efficiently completed by a group working together, rather than individuals working alone or in parallel; who have clear, shared, challenging, team level objectives derived directly from the task; who have to work closely and interdependently to achieve those objectives; whose members work in distinct roles within the team; and who have the necessary authority, autonomy and resources to enable them to meet the team objectives" (Woods and West, 2014, 423).

In practice, in our work in the English National Health Service, we encounter the use of the title "team" for many entities that abrogate many of these definitional requirements. We repeatedly encounter "teams" whose members are not clear about their team's task; who do not have clear team objectives; they do not agree on who their fellow team members are; do not understand others' roles; and these teams do not have the authority, autonomy, or resources to complete their work effectively. Moreover, some teams do not sufficiently (if ever) take time out to review their performance and adjust their work accordingly in order to improve. Too often team boundaries are unclear—team members are not clear who is and is not a member of the team. Increasingly complex tasks and environments have led to the growth in requirement for multi-disciplinary team working which has contributed to an already confused picture of "the team" in many organizations. In our work in health care organizations we find many individuals who perceive the boundaries of the team differently from their colleagues and certainly from their line management. This confusion leads to less effective decision-making and communication which inhibits the team's ability to achieve its aims and objectives.

This is not to require that the term "team" only be applied to some academically stipulated narrow range of entities—it is to recognize that "teams" are created to perform a task that individuals working alone could not achieve (or at least not so effectively); that teams are entities where people work interdependently towards shared goals; and where there is clarity among team members about their roles and the roles of others in the team. And there appear to be serious consequences of varying team working from these fundamental properties which endanger both patients and staff.

In a large-scale study of team working in health care, involving responses from 62,000 staff from 147 hospitals in the English NHS, Lyubovnikova et al. (2015) distinguished between what we called "real" teams and "pseudo" health care teams (or co-acting groups). Respondents were asked whether they worked in a team and, if so, did their team have shared objectives, did team members work interdependently, and did they meet regularly to review their performance in order to improve this performance. These three criteria, we argued, are fundamental to team work—without one of more of them, the entity is not truly a task-performing team—it is simply a co-acting group. The results revealed that individuals who reported working in real teams, in comparison with those working in pseudo teams, witnessed fewer errors in the previous three months that could have harmed patients or staff. They also reported fewer work-related injuries (needle-stick and back injuries for example) and work-related illnesses and were less likely to be victims of violence and harassment. Perhaps not surprisingly, they were also less likely to be considering or intending to leave their current employment.

Of course other factors might account for these findings, so the analysis controlled for background and demographic factors such as age, gender, organizational tenure, occupational group of the respondent, and patient contact. The research also took account of hospital size and whether the hospital was a "teaching" hospital, given that teaching hospitals might have more advanced medical practices and technologies that could influence the research outcomes. The research also took account of the extent to which staff members felt valued and trusted in their work as a proxy measure of general affect towards the organization. Moreover, staff sickness absence was significantly lower in these hospitals, indicating considerable financial savings also for the organizations where real team working was well developed.

What might account for these findings? We suggest that pseudo teams are more dangerous because their members will see themselves as working independently with more distinct discrete roles, and lack understanding about how their work is interrelated with that of their colleagues. Work is likely to be duplicated unnecessarily and team members are less able to understand and adapt to the needs of their team colleagues in carrying out their tasks. Mistakes are likely to happen because of lack of clarity about team roles and responsibilities. Lack of shared objectives will be associated with more confusion over the focus of the team's work. Pseudo teams also fail to take time out to review and improve their performance so collective learning is inhibited, and errors are more likely (West and Lyubovnikova, 2013; Lyubovnikova and West, 2013).

Most strikingly, in those hospitals with higher proportions of staff reporting that they worked in real teams, patient mortality levels were significantly lower. The relationship was such that 5% more staff working in real teams would be associated with 40 deaths per year (assuming this was a causal association), in the average hospital equivalent to 5,880 across the entire sample. The research showed that around 9% of staff reported not working in a team, around 40% were categorized as working in real teams and a substantial 50% as working in pseudo teams. By extension, if the percentage of staff working in real teams could be increased by 25%, and the relationship with mortality was direct and causal, this would be associated with a reduction of just under 30,000 hospital deaths per year.

Even without such speculation, the results clearly suggest there is considerable valuable work to be done to ensure that health care staff are working in teams with the basic structural and process characteristics of what is meant by a team and that this lack of effective team working is damaging to quality of care.

This research makes a strong case for developing health care team working with these basic characteristics, though it is worth reinforcing that within these fundamental properties there can be considerable variation.

VARIATIONS IN TEAM WORKING

Hollenbeck, Beeersma, and Shouten (2012) identify three important dimensions along which teams vary: skill differentiation, temporal stability, and authority differentiation. We consider each of these in turn below.

A team of pediatric nurses working together in a ward of children suffering from whooping cough will have relatively low skill differentiation whereas a multi-disciplinary community mental health team offering early intervention for people with acute mental health problems will have higher skill differentiation (psychologists, psychiatrists, social workers, psychiatric nurses all working in the team). And we have good evidence of the value of high skill differentiation in health care where the task requires this (Edmondson, Roberto, and Watkins, 2003; Xyrichis and Ream, 2008).

Temporal stability is low in a surgical team that works together just for one day but high for the community mental health team we described. The advantage of stability is that it enables the team to develop "shared mental models" of their work, enabling them to work more effectively together (Hackman, 2002; Mathieu et al., 2000). Moreover, there is evidence that stability leads to team psychological safety in health care teams, leading to higher levels of innovation and less of a risk of errors (Edmondson, 1996, 1999).

Authority differentiation refers to the extent to which team members have different status that inhibits the open exchange of ideas, opinions, and contributions. If senior medical staff, for example, seek to exert authority by imposing their decisions and opinions, safety, high quality decision-making, and innovation will all be jeopardized (Leape and Berwick, 2005; West, 2012). There is considerable evidence that health care teams are more effective where there is mutual respect, responsiveness, empathy, and communication among team members, irrespective of professional group or any other characteristics (Smith and Cole, 2009). It is clear also that effective teamwork is characterized by a constantly swirling mix of changes in leadership and followership, dependent on the task at hand or the unfolding situational challenges. Of course, there is still a formal hierarchy with dedicated positions but the ebb and flow of power is situationally dependent on who has the expertise at each moment. The literature on team work demonstrates that shared leadership in teams consistently predicts team effectiveness, particularly but not exclusively within health care (Aime et al., 2014; Carson, Tesluk, and Marrone, 2007). Yet many teams in health care are characterized by unhelpful status hierarchies and professional rivalry that lead to failures detrimentally affecting patients, sometimes with fatal consequences as successive reviews have shown (Berwick, 2013; Francis, 2013).

Another model that has proved useful in our work with health care teams is Casey's teamwork framework (Casey, 1993). Casey argues that the way in which team work is organized should be determined by two features: the task need for interdependence and the amount of complexity and dynamism in the environment. High levels of both need for interdependence and environmental complexity and dynamism create challenges for teams which require more sophisticated levels of team working which enable teams to innovate. Low levels of need for both interdependence and environmental complexity and dynamism create team tasks which require little more than basically effective interpersonal relationships such that, these entities could even be termed work groups rather than teams. In practice we believe that the establishment of different levels of skill differentiation and temporal stability should be a result of the task and environmental need for effective team working. More attention needs to be given to the design of teams to reflect these features in health and social care settings.

We have established that team working in health care cannot be a taken-for-granted good. Much depends on the quality of team working. If we want to create high quality team working delivering high quality and continually improving and compassionate care, how do we do it?

KEY FACTORS IN ENSURING HIGH QUALITY HEALTH CARE TEAM WORKING

Nurturing effective team working in health care requires attention to five key domains: team task and objectives; team member roles and interactions; quality improvement and innovation; leadership; and reflexivity. Each is considered in turn below.

Task and objectives: We need to create teams when there is a task that can best be undertaken by teams. So the starting point is defining the task. Appropriate team tasks have the following characteristics: they are complete tasks rather than a narrow component; the task creates varied demands that require interdependent working by people with differing skills; the task requires innovation and quality improvement; team members are enabled to grow and develop through working on the task; and they have a high degree of autonomy—they have the freedom to decide how best to do the task within sensible limits. The more of these characteristics a task exhibits, the more appropriate it is for a team. Two examples are conducting surgery for people who have broken hips; and providing treatment and support for young people with learning disabilities and emotional difficulties, in collaboration with their carers. Team members are particularly motivated and more likely to work well as a team if they are able to articulate a clear inspiring statement about the purpose of the team's work, for example, to positively transform the quality of life of people with learning disabilities through constantly improving and compassionate support in a way that positively transforms their quality of life.

Such tasks and associated mission statements must then be translated into clear objectives. Clarity of objectives of health care teams is the most consistent predictor of team performance across many studies (West and Anderson, 1996; Goñi, 1999; Poulton and West, 1999; Borrill et al., 2000; Cashman et al., 2004; Dixon-Woods et al., 2013). Yet few health care teams in our experience take the time to set clear objectives. Team objectives (and individual objectives) should be clear and specific, challenging, agreed, measureable, and they should identify reliable measures to provide the team with regular and timely feedback on its performance. This is not simply empty management rhetoric. The research cited above shows that those health care teams that have such objectives and ensure they seek feedback on performance deliver safer and higher quality health care than other health care teams. Team objectives should be limited in number (around 5–7) and include: providing high quality care; continually improving that care; ensuring that it is delivered compassionately; ensuring the well-being, growth, and development of team members; and ensuring that working relationships and practices with other teams within the organization are of high quality and continually improving. And the team's objectives should be aligned with and derived from the organization's overall objectives. (For a fuller discussion of these requirements for team objectives see chapter 6 in West 2012.)

Team member roles and interactions: Team working is at the heart of how individuals interact, cooperate, engage, and "dance" teamworking together to make significant progress towards achieving team objectives. It is about interaction, information sharing, and influencing decision-making. It is dependent on shared understanding of tasks; clarity about what role each person will play; effective listening, questioning, and disagreeing; and trust. These interactions are crucial to effective team performance. Team members have to interact sufficiently frequently to be effective as a whole team and too often people rely on impoverished mechanisms for interaction such as emails and telephone calls rather than face-to-face interaction. Team members must play a full role in decision-making. After all, they are part of the team because they have skills that are necessary to complete the task. And at different points all team members will be the leading expert if team member selection has been effective. In high performing teams, "air time" and expertise are correlated (team members with relevant expertise at that point are listened to most). Status hierarchies and dominant individuals hinder effective decision-making, thereby jeopardizing patient care (Koslowski and Bell, 2003; Mathieu et al., 2008).

Conflict in teams is generally damaging. Interpersonal conflict is particularly damaging to team effectiveness (De Dreu and Weingart, 2003; De Wit, Greer, and Jehn, 2012; Tjosvold, 1998). Aggressive, intimidating, and otherwise confrontational behaviors undermine effective team functioning and those who often exhibit these behaviors require coaching to change them. Rude or intimidating behaviors by team members are a direct threat to safe patient care because they can prevent team members from speaking up when they see unsafe practice. There is a cultural norm within the English NHS that accepts intimidating or aggressive behavior, particularly by a small number of senior medical staff, despite the threat to patient safety. This norm must be challenged and changed to make such behavior unacceptable.

Health care is a high stress environment, yet health care staff are required to deliver care with compassion. Compassion can be understood as having three components: paying attention to the other; allowing an empathic response; and taking intelligent action to help the other. If teams are to model compassionate care for patients, it seems obvious their compassion should begin with fellow team members, given the level of stress health care staff experience. Social support for fellow team members therefore requires that team members pay attention to each other (Nancy Kline calls it "listening with fascination" (Kline, 1999, 37); are empathic in reactions to fellow team members; and take intelligent action to help each other. When team members are overloaded, stressed, or distressed they cannot pay sufficient attention to patients; have less emotional capacity to be empathic; and are less likely to make intelligent decisions to help patients when under stress. Team members can promote compassionate care by creating a compassionate team environment that supports team members (Atkins and Parker, 2012; Gilbert and Choden, 2013)

Quality improvement and innovation: Teams are powerhouses of innovation—or should be. When we bring together a diverse group of individuals in health care, with varying skills and experiences, and we identify a task with a clear set of associated objectives, innovation is inevitable. With good team processes, such teams will be sparkling fountains of innovation, developing and applying new and improved ways of delivering patient care (West, 2003). And that capacity is ideal in a context where quality improvement must be part of the texture of working since quality improvement leads to better health and well-being for the community. Effective health care team working therefore involves a commitment to continually improving quality of care such that quality improvement is the way teams work. In addition, team members should be equipped with and empowered to adapt appropriate suites of tools from the quality improvement movements in the private sector (and increasingly in health care) (Plsek, 2013). Health care teams must have objectives focused on improving quality and developing new and improved ways of delivering care but organizational leaders must also find ways to support teams to do that. This includes providing resources and leadership support for innovation; reducing work that does not add value to patient care; freeing up innovation time for teams; and removing systems blockages that prevent teams from innovating (Dixon-Woods et al., 2013).

Leadership: The leadership of health care teams has a significant influence on their effectiveness—this is a statement of the obvious. Poor leadership hinders teams from delivering continually improving, high quality, and compassionate care. When teams have leaders who are interfering, controlling, aggressive, unfair, or focused on meeting their own needs rather than those of their followers, team work suffers. What is required then from the leadership of health care teams?

Leadership is about providing clarity of direction and purpose and helping to articulate an inspiring view of the team's work. It is about ensuring that the core human values of wisdom, humanity, courage, prudence, justice, and gratitude are embodied in the work of the team. The wisdom to learn and develop knowledge to improve quality of health care; the courage to pursue a vision, to persevere, to deal with difficult challenges, conflicts, or colleagues; the humanity to model kindness and compassion; the justice to treat people fairly and to be honest and transparent; the prudence to manage initiatives in ways that do not overburden and relationships in ways that resolve rather than escalate conflict; and the gratitude and wonder to celebrate the work of health care in communities.

Research evidence increasingly suggests that effective teams have shared leadership (Aime et al., 2014; Carson, Tesluk, and Marrone, 2007). There may well be a designated leader but *leadership* is shared. Leadership shifts between team members as expertise needs and motivational orientations vary with the task at hand. Effective teams develop their *leadership* to ensure they deliver high quality care; moving away from the notion of a single heroic leader is a key part of that development. That requires a recognition that top-down, hierarchical, command and control leadership is inimical to effective teamwork. For many readers it will be surprising to learn that the military was one of the first sectors to understand the need for shared leadership in teams, despite its formal hierarchical structure. Platoons need the expertise and good decision-making of all their

This requires that formal leaders see their role as helping to clarify direction, facilitating the participation of all team members in decision-making, valuing the contributions of all (because not regardless of the diversity of team members), and building supportive relationships with the rest of the organization and its leaders. A key skill for a team leader is listening to team members rather than talking themselves, summarizing understanding, and ensuring all voices are heard by all members. Research on the "hidden profile" phenomenon reinforces this perspective: team members spend more time discussing information held in common and tend to ignore information known only to one member, even when that is critical information (Stasser and Stewart, 1992). In health care the threat to quality of care of this weakness in team decision-making is as real as the threat posed by "groupthink." Team leaders who listen and summarize are far more effective than those who talk and direct. The only caveat to this is that in a crisis, someone needs to lead the team rather than initiate extended consultation but it is not necessarily the hierarchical leader. In surgery, it will sometimes be the anesthetist who leads in a crisis and sometimes the surgeon, depending on the nature of the crisis.

And leaders should not exhibit favoritism in teams. This is obvious, but a particularly influential theory of leadership exposes an endemic problem that is little understood outside of academia. Leader Member Exchange (LMX) Theory describes how virtually all leaders have different reactions to each of those they lead and this particularly depends on similarity and liking between them (Graen and Cashman, 1975). The greater the personal compatibility with followers, the more time leaders spend with them and the more likely they are to attribute follower success to ability; conversely, the lower the compatibility, the less time they spend with particular followers and the more they are likely to attribute success to situational factors. And of course, followers quickly realize whether they are "in-group" or "out-group" members, with consequent effects on trust, commitment, and engagement. As transformational leadership theory suggests, team leaders who offer a high degree of individual consideration and support for each of their followers, ensure more effective team work, cooperation, and quality of care (Howell and Avolio, 1993; Gilmartin and D'Aunno, 2007).

If we are to develop cultures in which those seeking health care are treated with compassion, teams should also have norms of compassion. Formal leaders can play a key role in modeling compassion in working with team members and thereby reduce the degree of favoritism that is implied by LMX theory and supported by research evidence (Martinko, Harvey, and Douglas, 2007). This would be enacted by team leaders paying careful attention to each of their team members and their needs and challenges at work; responding empathically in each case; and then taking intelligent action to help and support them. Modeling compassion in this way helps to create norms of compassion within the team which will extend, via emotional contagion, to interactions with those seeking health care. And in the process it may help to reduce the very high levels of stress, described earlier, that health care workers suffer. Although shared leadership is important, we know that the behaviors, values, and orientations of formal hierarchical leaders exert a disproportionately strong effect on team climate.

Reflexivity: A visit to almost any health care institution will often reveal teams engaged in high levels of activity, overwhelming workloads for team members, noise, complexity, emotional tension, and a hum of frenetic busyness. These are not great circumstances in which to deliver compassionate care, to make complex team decisions, to communicate confidence, and to think creatively as a team about how to improve care. The response to high demands by teams is often to work harder and faster, leading to errors and more stress (West, 2000). For more than 25 years we have been amassing evidence showing that teams that take time out on a regular basis to review what it is they are trying to achieve and how they are going about it, and then adapting their objectives and processes accordingly are much more effective and much more innovative in delivering patient care (Widmer, Schippers, and West, 2009; Schippers, Edmondson, and West, 2014). For example, a study of 98 primary health care teams showed that teams with high workloads (patient to doctor ratio) or with poor premises whose members took more time out to review their working methods, were significantly more innovative than other teams. Health care teams should pause in their work from time to time and reflect on team objectives, working methods, challenges, conflicts, innovations, and team functioning generally to discover how to improve health care methods and processes (see Schippers, Edmondson, and West, 2014, for a discussion of how this can prevent medical errors). This might be at the end of a shift, in the middle of day, or in quarterly team away days. The evidence suggests that such "team reflexivity" leads to much higher levels of team effectiveness, quality of patient care, and to continually improving care (Widmer, Schippers, and West, 2009).

Team-Based Working in Health Care Organizations

To understand and improve team working in modern organizations, we have to address the wider organizational context within which teams work. Nurturing teams in hierarchical, directive, antagonistic, or aggressively competitive environments is unlikely to be highly successful. Team work is about listening, cooperation, shared objectives, and engagement. It is important to focus, not so much on individual team building, as on building organizations which are truly "team-based." Such organizations will have structures, processes, and behaviors which enable teams to produce the synergy required to provide high quality outcomes.

Developing effective team-based working involves all teams prioritizing patient care overall, not only in their individual areas, supporting, cooperating, and engaging with other teams with which they interact to provide that overall care. And every health care team should therefore have, as one of its five or six objectives, a commitment to improving the effectiveness with which the team works with other teams in the organization. Indeed,

be vital for intergroup cooperation and support and therefore for patient care (Richter et al., 2006).

Team-based health care organizations describe their structures as team communities, identified as a number of teams that need to work together to achieve a shared goal such as delivering high quality care for patients on a particular pathway such as fractured neck of femur. This is different in nature from the description of organizational areas as "directorates," or, worse, "divisions" which suggest siloed and separately focused rather than integrated sets of operations. A team community may well include teams outside the organization, such as GP practices, suppliers, and regulators. All team members need to know how their team relates to all the other teams that need to work together to achieve the overall purpose. Mapping the team community helps to ensure the alignment of goals and objectives within and between teams to ensure achievement of the overall goal of delivering high quality, continually improving, and compassionate care.

Building team-based organizations requires consideration of supporting processes. For example, team-based organizations are likely to employ team-level appraisals to support teams in setting, reviewing, and delivering against their team objectives. Team members then appraise individuals within the team collectively. Such organizations also invest in team training, developing team leaders, training team coaches, and ensuring individual teams make the journey from start-up to fully-fledged team working (West and Markiewicz, 2004).

Given the findings reported above about the poor development of team working in the English NHS and the significant consequences, it is clear that there is much to be gained from improving team working and team-based working in health care. Other challenges face teams working in health care and we briefly identify some of these and potential solutions.

CHALLENGING ISSUES IN THE CURRENT CONTEXT

A challenge but also an opportunity for team working is the need for different professional groups to work effectively together in teams: "a key characteristic of health care organizations is the range of distinctive and vivid occupational subcultures which provide the 'raw' material for its organizational culture" (Scott et al., 2003, 25). Health care professionals have unusually strong professional affiliations (both broadly, such as doctors' or nurses' professional identification, and also more narrowly in terms of particular specialisms such as pediatrics, obstetrics, accident and emergency). The socialization of professionals in health care takes place over long periods of time, ensuring a deep sense of professional identity and distinctiveness. This is one consequence of occupational groups organizing themselves into associations and institutions that enjoy status and recognition from the general public and governments (Bloor and Dawson, 1994).

Members of such professions tend to share schemas for the way they make sense of their work, their professional encounters, the technologies they employ, individuals (such as patients and other professions) they interact with, and the organizations they are a part of. They develop a distinctive discourse as well as distinctive identities. Their shared values, beliefs, understanding, and identity lead to the development of strong professional (sub-) cultures. Associated with this is the tendency of such groups to accumulate power and decision-making influence, such as the medical cohort in hospitals (Tolbert and Barley, 1991). This then becomes a powerful cause of intra- and inter-team conflict.

These conflicts between professional staff groups (e.g., doctors, nurses, radiologists) and between agencies in health care lead to inter-professional rivalries or schisms that produce interaction processes inimical to the sharing of knowledge and skills, instead protecting professional identities by hoarding knowledge to the detriment of patient care. For example, a study of 16 Canadian hospitals revealed that disagreement over patient treatment goals was the most common source of conflict in the Intensive Care Unit (Meth, Lawless, and Hawryluck, 2009). Professional sub-cultures therefore embody differences in values, despite all professions in health care being focused on providing high quality care for patients, and these value differences are a source of team and inter-team conflict.

The evidence also points to deeply rooted tensions in relationships between doctors and managers, especially when they work in the same team and especially when managers' actions result in perceived restrictions to doctors' autonomy and authority (Martinussen and Magnussen, 2011). Such tensions lead to frequent conflicts between doctors and managers and teams which is detrimental to team performance (De Dreu and Weingart, 2003). But there is also evidence that these differences can be overcome depending on other contextual factors. Martinussen and Magnussen (2011) investigated the attitudes of doctors in managerial positions and doctors directly involved in patient care, four years after a market-driven reform in the Norwegian health care system. Doctors involved in management had positive attitudes, while those directly involved in patient care were more negative to the reforms. There was considerable evidence that managers with medical backgrounds had adopted managerial values and tools, when they made the transition across professional sub-cultures.

Health care teams tend to be highly diverse on a number of dimensions. A community mental health team, for example, typically comprises a consultant psychiatrist, a clinical psychologist, several mental health nurses, an occupational therapist, a social worker, and other support workers. As a result, health care teams are often characterized by status inequalities based on professional groupings or disciplines. Such status hierarchies inhibit open communication and information sharing across professional groups, which can in turn affect decision-making quality, innovation, and the quality of patient care (Edmondson, Roberto, and Watkins, 2003). For example, low status groups such as nursing assistants or administrative staff may have difficulty speaking up or challenging high status groups such as physicians. Furthermore, team member status can inhibit

professional diversity judged their overall effectiveness and their effectiveness in delivering patient focused care as better than teams low in such diversity. Moreover, diverse teams introduced more innovations focused on improving quality of patient care, reinforcing the value of professional diversity.

What the research evidence does clearly indicate, is that teams with clear objectives and high levels of participation (in terms of interaction frequency, information sharing, and influence over decision-making) benefit rather than suffer from such diversity. Where teams are structured in the ways suggested in this chapter, diversity becomes a source of creativity, a spur for innovation, and is associated with higher levels of productivity. We turn now to consider other challenges in the current context.

One often stated challenge is that health care workers are often members of more than one team and may have different roles in different teams. The more teams they are a part of, the more difficult it can be to function as an effective member of any of them. One way of helping individuals to manage the inevitable stresses of working in multiple teams is to utilize the "home team" concept (Aston Team Journey: Aston Organization Development, 2009). The home team is defined as the team whose objectives determine how the individual works in all other teams they are a member of. Thus the medical oncologist may be a part of one or more multi-disciplinary cancer care teams, a multi-agency project team to improve services, a clinical specialist team, and a service management team. It is helpful if the oncologist in this example can identify which of these teams is the one whose objectives determine how they work in all the other teams they are part of; that is the team from which they derive their aligning objectives. This does not mean that the work they do in teams other than their home team is any less valuable or engaging, but it will be informed by the home team's goals and objectives. Another example is the Medical Director who is a member of the Hospital Executive Team, the Medical Management Team, a Specialist Surgery Team, and the regional Cardiology Services Review Team. Which of these is her home team? She spends more time in her Specialist Surgery Team where she is a valued senior Surgeon; she feels she has most support from her colleagues in the Medical Management Team; and she feels least comfortable in the Executive Team. In our experience many Medical Directors would like to think of their speciality team as their home team rather than the Executive Team, which may be more appropriate. The consequences of poor definition of the "home team" at all levels of the organization can be significant, but particularly at Senior Management levels. We often see Executive Teams comprised of team members who all regard their Divisional or Directorate Management Teams as their "home team". As a consequence many Executive Teams function as un-focused committees, with individual competing interests, rather than as integrated, collaborative, supportive teams.

The "home team" concept suggests that usually the "home team" should be the most senior team that the individual is a member of—in large, hierarchically arranged, organizations this enables alignment of objectives and is critical to the achievement of organizational goals. For individuals, the ability to describe their "home team" is likely to increase role clarity and reduce levels of stress. At the team level, the discussion of the "home team" concept amongst team members increases understanding about different team members' motivations and decision-making criteria and this increases role clarity within the team and aids identification of opportunities for improved inter-team influence.

In some areas there is structural complexity, created by the need for large numbers of people to work in "action teams" for a short time (e.g., a shift on an acute hospital ward) to carry out the same role but with different team members on a daily basis. And there are particular pressures on team work when some members are rotated after only a short time working with the team—for example, junior doctors on rotation must cope with such rapid and repeated changes. The challenges of working in teams where multiple professional groups are represented have been referred to above, particularly where these reinforce status hierarchies. And there is lack of clarity about the extent to which patients and their carers should be seen as part of teams, partly because there is limited understanding of how the role of patient might be effectively enacted in a health care team.

One solution is to augment our understanding of team by using it also as a verb "to team" (Edmondson, 2012, 2014). In our work in health care organizations, we encourage leaders to think about how the, often large, group of people they lead, will "team." This allows them to develop a visual depiction of all the different work groups; uni-disciplinary and multi-disciplinary teams; within function, cross-functional and cross agency project teams; management teams; and so on, which the people they lead will work in at different times during their work. For each of these different types of "team" there will still be a requirement for the basic features of effective real team working. For example, even a shift team which forms at 8am and disperses at 4pm, never to work together again in the same formation, will need to know what it is there to achieve during the shift (clear, shared objectives), who will do what and how they will work together (role clarity and interdependence), and the shift will be more likely to carry out its work effectively if at some point near the middle of the shift the team members meet to review if they are achieving what they set out to do and, if not, to adapt their approach to ensure success.

Amy Edmondson (Edmondson, 2012, 2014) has described the increased importance for employees at all levels to develop the skills of "teaming." The key skills Edmondson believes that all individuals need to demonstrate in highly flexible teaming environments are: asking questions, sharing information, seeking help, identifying potential errors, suggesting improvements, discussing mistakes, and seeking feedback. However, there is still a requirement for each team, as in the shift team example above, to have a "hard frame" of objectives, clarity about team membership and mutual role understanding, to enable individuals to utilize these softer skills, not least because these structural features help to create the necessary levels of safety which will enable individuals to feel confident to use their skills. This need to develop participative safety is particularly important in health care settings where the ghosts of traditional power hierarchies may still be alive in the memories of staff. With the changing demands in health care nation-

housing, and police services to ensure integrated care for the community. There is also an increasing need to work across sectors. No longer is health care a purely public service and the creation of effective team-based working with private and third sector providers is vital for the provision of high quality care in future. Such cross boundary working requires that teams work together across service areas and organizations to identify the superordinate, shared goals they can commit to together—such as supporting the health and well-being of all those in their community. Our understanding of cross-boundary working and relationships also emphasizes a joint commitment to long-term stability and continuity in the relationship (not just another short-lived initiative between agencies); the importance of sufficiency of regular face-to-face contact between teams that must work together across boundaries; a commitment to dealing swiftly, fairly, openly, and creatively with the inevitable conflicts that arise; and a commitment to understanding and prioritizing the needs of the other teams they are working with to ensure high quality care and support for the community. Applying our understanding of these principles in cross-boundary contexts is essential if we are to respond to the current challenges faced by health care systems internationally.

Conclusions

The evidence of the importance and value of team and team-based working in health care is convincing. Equally convincing is the evidence that quality of team working in health care is often poor and that there are errors, near misses, inefficiencies, wastage of resources, and lack of responsiveness to patients as a consequence. Clinical effectiveness, patient safety, and patient experience are all jeopardized on a scale just as (if not more) damaging as infections and medication errors. This chapter described the methods by which we can develop effective team working in health care. We end by urging practitioners and policy makers to focus their efforts on improving the quality of team-based working in order to improve quality of care. It is team working that ultimately determines whether or not patients receive high quality, continually improving, and compassionate care. And so the leadership of health care organizations must ensure high quality and continually improving team-based working.

References

Aime, F., Humphrey, S., DeRue, D. S., and Paul, J. B. (2014). The riddle of heterarchy: Power transitions in cross-functional teams. *Academy of Management Journal*, 57(2): 327–352.

Aston Organization Development. (2003). *Aston Team Facilitation Programme.* Farnham: Aston Organization Development.

Atkins P. W. B. and Parker, S. K. (2012). Understanding individual compassion in organizations: The role of appraisals and psychological flexibility. *Academy of Management Review*, 37: 524–546.

Berwick, D. (2013). *A promise to learn—a commitment to act: Improving the safety of patients in England*. London: Department of Health. Available at: <https://www.gov.uk/government/uploads/system/uploads/attachment_data/file/226703/Berwick_Report.pdf> (accessed June 25, 2013).

Bloor, G. and Dawson, P. (1994). Understanding professional culture in organizational context. *Organization Studies*, 15: 275–295.

Borrill, C., West, M. A., Shapiro, D., and Rees, A. (2000). Team working and effectiveness in the NHS. *British Journal of Health Care Management*, 6: 364–371.

Buttigieg, S. C., West, M. A., and Dawson, J. F. (2011). Well-structured teams and the buffering of hospital employees from stress. *Health Services Management Research*, 24(4): 203–212.

Carson, J. B., Tesluk, P. E., and Marrone, J. A. (2007). Shared leadership in teams: An investigation of antecedent conditions and performance. *Academy of Management Journal*, 50(5): 1217–1234.

Carter, S. M. and West, M. A. (1998). Reflexivity, effectiveness, and mental health in BBC-TV production teams. *Small Group Research*, 29(5): 583–601.

Carter, A. J. and West, M. A. (1999). Sharing the burden: Teamwork in health care settings. In *Stress in health professionals: Psychological causes and interventions*, ed. Firth-Cozens, J. and Payne, R., pp. 191–202. Chichester: John Wiley & Sons.

Casey, D. (1993). *Managing Learning in Organizations*. Buckingham: Open University Press.

Cashman, S., Reidy, P., Cody, K., and Lemay, C. (2004). Developing and measuring progress toward collaborative, integrated, interdisciplinary health care teams. *Journal of Interprofessional Care*, 18(2): 183–196.

De Dreu, C. K. W. and Weingart, L. R. (2003). Task versus relationship conflict, team performance, and team member satisfaction: A meta-analysis. *Journal of Applied Psychology*, 88(4): 741–749.

De Wit, F. R. C., Greer, L. L., and Jehn, K. A. (2012). The paradox of intragroup conflict: A meta-analysis. *Journal of Applied Psychology*, 97: 360–390.

Dixon-Woods, M., Baker, R., Charles, K., Dawson, J., Jerzembek, G., Martin, G., McCarthy, I., McKee, L., Minion, J., Ozieranski, P., Willars, J., Wilkie, P., and West, M. (2013). Culture and behaviour in the English National Health Service: Overview of lessons from a large multi-method study. *British Medical Journal Quality and Safety*, 23(2): 106–15.

Edmondson, A. C. (1996). Learning from mistakes is easier said than done: Group and organizational influences on the detection and correction of human error. *Journal of Applied Behavioral Science*, 32(1): 5–28.

Edmondson, A. C. (1999). Psychological safety and learning behavior in work teams. *Administrative Science Quarterly*, 44(2): 350.

Edmondson, A. C. (2012) *Teaming: How organizations learn, innovate, and compete in the knowledge economy*. San Francisco, CA: Wiley.

Edmondson, A. C. (2014). *Teaming to innovate*. San Francisco, CA: Wiley.

Edmondson, A. C., Roberto, M. A., and Watkins, M. D. (2003). A dynamic model of top management team effectiveness: Managing unstructured task streams. *The Leadership Quarterly*, 14(3): 297–325.

Fay, D., Borrill, C., Amir, Z., Haward, R., and West, M. A. (2006). Getting the most out of multidisciplinary teams: A multi-sample study of team innovation in health care. *Journal of Occupational and Organizational Psychology*, 79(4): 553–567.

Francis, R. (2013). *Report of the Mid Staffordshire NHS Foundation Trust Public Inquiry.* London: HMSO. Available at: <http://cdn.midstaffspublicinquiry.com/sites/default/files/report/Executive%20summary.pdf> (accessed July 4, 2014).

Gilbert, P. and Choden (2013). *Mindful Compassion.* London: Constable & Robinson.

Gilmartin, M. J. and D'Aunno, T. A. (2007). Leadership research in healthcare: A Review and Roadmap, *The Academy of Management Annals,* 1: 387–438.

Goñi, S. (1999). An analysis of the effectiveness of Spanish primary health care teams. *Health Policy,* 48(2): 107–117.

Graen, S. G. and Cashman, J. F. (1975). A role-making model of leadership in formal organizations: A development approach. *Organization and Administrative Sciences,* 6: 143–165.

Hackman, J. R. (2002). *Leading teams: Setting the stage for great performances.* Boston, MA: Harvard Business School Press.

Harari, Y. N. (2014). *Sapiens: A brief history of humankind.* London: Harvill Secker.

Hollenbeck, J. R., Beersma, B., and Shouten, M. E. (2012). Beyond team types and taxonomies: A dimensional scaling conceptualization for team description. *Academy of Management Review,* 37: 82–106.

Howell, J. M. and Avolio, B. J.(1993). Transformational leadership, transactional leadership, locus of control, and support for innovation: Key predictors of consolidated-business-unit performance. *Journal of Applied Psychology,* 78: 891–902.

Jansson, A., Isacsson, A., and Lindhom, L. H. (1992). Organization of health care teams and the population's contacts with primary care. *Scandivian Journal of Health Care,* 10: I257–I265.

Kline, N. (1999). *Time to think: Listening to ignite the human mind.* London: Ward Lock.

Koslowski, S. W. J. and Bell, B. S. (2003). Work groups and teams in organizations. In *Industrial/organizational psychology,* Vol. 12, ed. Borman, W. C., Ilgen, D. R., and Klimoski, R., pp. 333–375. London: John Wiley & Sons.

Leape, L. L. and Berwick, D. M. (2005). Five years after "to err is human": What have we learned? *Journal of the American Medical Association,* 293(19): 2384–2390.

Lewis, P. J. and Tully, M. P. (2009). Uncomfortable prescribing decisions in hospitals: The impact of teamwork. *Journal of the Royal Society of Medicine,* 102(11): 481–488.

Lyubovnikova, J. and West, M. A. (2013). Why teamwork matters: Enabling health care team effectiveness for the delivery of high quality patient care. In *Developing and enhancing teamwork in organizations,* ed. Salas, E., Tannenbaum, S. I., Cohen, D., and Latham, G., pp.331–372. San Francisco, CA: Jossey Bass.

Lyubovnikova, J., West, M. A., Dawson, J., and Carter, M. (2015). 24-Karat or fool's gold? Consequences of real team and co-acting group membership in healthcare organizations. *European Journal of Work and Organizational Psychology,* 24(6): 929–950.

Martinko, M., Harvey, P., and Douglas, S. C. (2007). The role, function, and contribution of attribution theory to leadership: A review. *Leadership Quarterly,* 18: 561–585.

Martinussen, P. E. and Magnussen, J. (2011). Resisting market-inspired reform in healthcare: The role of professional subcultures in medicine. *Social Science and Medicine,* 73: 193–200.

Mathieu, J. E., Heffner, T. S., Goodwin, G. F., Salas, E., and Cannon-Bowers, J. A. (2000). The influence of shared mental models on team process and performance. *The Journal of Applied Psychology,* 85(2): 273–283.

Mathieu, J. M., Maynard, T., Rapp, T., and Gilson, L. (2008). Team effectiveness 1997–2007: A review of recent advancements and a glimpse of the future. *Journal of Management,* 34: 410–476.

Meth, N. D., Lawless, B., and Hawryluck, L. (2009). Conflicts in the ICU: Perspectives of administrators and clinicians. *Intensive Care Medicine*, 35: 2068–2077.

Molyneux, J. (2001). Interprofessional teamworking: What makes teams work well? *Journal of Interprofessional Care*, 15(1): 30–35.

Nembhard, I. M. and Edmondson, A. C. (2006). Making it safe: The effects of leader inclusiveness and professional status on psychological safety and improvement efforts in health care teams. *Journal of Organizational Behavior*, 27(7): 941–966.

Plsek, P. (2013). *Accelerating health care transformation with lean and innovation: The Virginia Mason experience.* Boca Raton, FL: CRC Press.

Poulton, B. C. and West, M. A. (1999). The determinants of effectiveness in primary health care teams. *Journal of Interprofessional Care*, 13(1): 7–18.

Richardson, J., West, M. A., and Cuthbertson, B. H. (2010). Team working in intensive care: Current evidence and future endeavours. *Current Opinion in Critical Care*, 16(6): 643–648.

Richter, A., Dawson, J. F., and West, M. A. (2011). The effectiveness of teams in organizations: A meta-analysis. *The International Journal of Human Resource Management*, 13: 1–21.

Richter, A., West, M. A., Van Dick, R., and Dawson, J. F. (2006). Boundary spanners' identification, intergroup contact, and effective intergroup relations. *Journal of Applied Psychology*, 49(6): 1252–1269.

Schippers, M. C., Edmondson, A. C., and West, M. A. (2014). Team reflexivity as an antidote to team information-processing failures. *Small Group Research*, 45(6): 731–769.

Schippers, M. C., West, M. A., and Dawson, J. F. (in press). Team reflexivity and innovation: The moderating role of team context. *Journal of Management* (published online 17 April 2012), doi: 10.1177/0149206312441210.

Scott, T., Mannion, R., Davies, H., and Marshall, M. (2003). *Healthcare performance and organizational culture.* Oxon: Radcliffe Medical Press.

Sharit, J. (2006). Human error. In *Handbook of human factors and ergonomics*, ed. Salvendy, G., pp. 708–760. Hoboken, NJ: John Wiley & Sons.

Smith, J. R. and Cole, F. S. (2009). Patient safety: Effective interdisciplinary teamwork through simulation and debriefing in the neonatal ICU. *Critical Care Nursing Clinics of North America*, 21(2): 163–179.

Sommers, L. S., Marton, K. I., Barbaccia, J. C., and Randolph, J. (2000). Physician, nurse, and social worker collaboration in primary care for chronically ill seniors. *Archives of Internal Medicine*, 160(12): 1825–1833.

Stasser, G. and Stewart, D. (1992). Discovery of hidden profiles by decision-making groups: Solving a problem versus making a judgment. *Journal of Personality and Social Psychology*, 63: 426–434.

Tjosvold, D. (1998). Cooperative and competitive goal approaches to conflict: Accomplishments and challenges. *Applied Psychology: An International Review*, 47: 285–342.

Tolbert, P. S. and Barley, S. R. (eds) (1991). Professions and organizations. Special edition of *Research in the sociology of organizations: Organizations and professions*, Vol. 8, pp. 97–118. Greenwich, CT: JAI Press.

West, M. A. (2000). Reflexivity, revolution and innovation in work teams. In *Product development teams: Advances in interdisciplinary studies of work teams*, ed. Beyerlein, M., pp. 1–30. Greenwich, CT: JAI.

West, M. A. (2002). Leadership clarity and team innovation in health care. *The Leadership*

West, M. A. (2012). *Effective teamwork: Practical lessons from organizational research*, 3rd edition. Oxford: Blackwell Publishing.

West, M. A. and Anderson, N. R. (1996). Innovation in top management teams. *Journal of Applied Psychology*, 81(6): 680–693.

West, M. A., Alimo-Metcalfe, B., Dawson, J. F., El Ansari, W., Glasby, J., Hardy, G., Hartley, G., Lyubovnikova, J., Middleton, H., Naylor, P. B., Onyett, S., and Richter A. (2012). *Effectiveness of multi-professional team working (MPTW) in mental health care*. Final Report, NIHR Service Delivery and Organization Program.

West, M. A., Borrill, C. S., Dawson, J. F., Scully, J., Carter, M., Anelay, S., Patterson, M., and Waring, J. (2001). The link between the management of employees and patient mortality in acute hospitals. *The International Journal of Human Resource Management*, 13(8): 1299–1310.

West, M. A., Dawson, J. F., Admasachew, L., and Topakas, A. (2011). NHS staff management and health service quality: Results from the NHS staff survey and related data. Available at: <http://www.dh.gov.uk/health/2011/08/nhs-staff-management/> (accessed September 29, 2015).

West, M. A. and Lyubovnikova, J. R. (2013). Illusions of team working in health care. *Journal of Health Organization and Management*, 27(1): 134–142.

West, M. A. and Markiewicz, L. (2004). *Building Team Based Working: A Practical Guide to Organizational Transformation*. London: BPS Blackwell.

Widmer, P., Schippers, M., and West, M. A. (2009). Recent developments in reflexivity research: A review. *Psychology of Everyday Activity*, 2(2): 2–11.

Woods, S. and West, M. A. (2014). *The psychology of work and organizations*, 2nd edition. London: Sage

Xyrichis, A. and Ream, E. (2008). Teamwork: A concept analysis. *Journal of Advanced Nursing*, 61(2): 232–241.

PART III

ORGANIZATIONAL PROCESSES AND PRACTICES IN HEALTH CARE MANAGEMENT

CHAPTER 11

COMMUNITIES OF PRACTICE AND SITUATED LEARNING IN HEALTH CARE

DAVIDE NICOLINI, HARRY SCARBROUGH,
AND JULIA GRACHEVA

THIS chapter deals with an issue which goes to the heart of health care policy and management: how to reconcile an established structure based on professional expertise with the multi-disciplinary strategies that are increasingly needed to address chronic conditions, link research to practice, and improve processes? This tension between fundamentally different ways of organizing knowledge and expertise has been heightened by the challenge of delivering high quality and safe care within tight resource constraints. This has placed health care organizations under acute policy and managerial pressure to learn from their failures, and to support the rapid application of new knowledge and evidence in practice. In the US, for example, explicit calls to establish specific processes to learn from failures goes back at least to the Institute of Medicine report "To Err is Human" published at the turn of the millennium (Kohn, Corrigan, and Donaldson, 2000). In the UK context, these pressures have been highlighted most recently in the Francis Report on the failings of the Mid-Staffs hospital trust (Francis, 2013) and the Berwick report on patient safety (Berwick, 2013). In both cases the emphasis is on the need to "learn lessons" from and establish a "culture of learning."

The established professionalized role structure of the National Health Service (NHS) and other health care systems has consistently struggled to produce the kind of multi-disciplinary collaboration and organization-centered learning which these reports (and their precursors) so cogently advocate (Ferlie et al., 2005; Addicott, McGivern, and Ferlie, 2006; Battilana, 2011). As a result, in the last two decades a large number of health care organizations and funding bodies have developed initiatives around learning and knowledge sharing which congregate under the banner of "communities of practice." This notion has become widely used within the health care field as a way of talking about the many forms of knowledge and learning which fall outside the boundaries of established professional expertise. Communities of practice resonate with health care professional as they promise to foster mutual learning and knowledge sharing building on the affinities which stem from doing the same work. The idea of communities of practice has thus achieved widespread currency internationally, both as a tool for understanding how learning unfolds in health care settings and as a tool for promoting knowledge transfer and sharing, with studies or interventions reported in Australia, Canada, Denmark, the UK, and the US (Bentley, Browman, and Poole, 2010; Ranmuthugala et al., 2011).

In this chapter, we show how the "community of practice" concept helps to illuminate some of the challenges of creating a "learning culture" within health care systems. We also show how it has been applied in diverse ways by health care organizations and funders, how these experiments in new ways of knowing and learning have been inserted into the established institutional order, and the mixed, but sometimes promising, outcomes which have flowed from them. To do this, we examine the origins and nature of this broad family of interventions, discuss their characteristics, and summarize their key success factors. We begin, however, by clarifying some of the key concepts under discussion, starting with the concepts of situated learning and community of practice.

WHAT ARE SITUATED LEARNING AND COMMUNITIES OF PRACTICE?

The concept of situated learning, also known as situated learning theory, emerged in the late 1980s as an alternative to the traditional cognitive theory's understanding of learning as a process of knowledge transfer between teacher and learner, the acquisition of a stock of skill, and the development of mental structures. For situated learning theorists, learning is much more than the transfer and accumulation of information and should be rather conceived as a continuous active and social process arising from the involvement in the socially constructed practice and the interpretation of personal experiences associated with it (Elkjaer, 1999; Lave and Wenger, 1991, Brown and Duguid, 1991; Gherardi, Nicolini, and Odella, 1998). Learning has thus less to do with acquiring or accumulating information and is rather a process of becoming socialized in a particular way of doing and knowing:

> Absorbing and being absorbed in the "culture of practice" (....) might include (knowing) who is involved, what they do, what everyday life is like, how masters talk, walk, work, and generally conduct their lives, how people who are not part of the community of practice interact with it, what other learners are doing, and what learners need to learn to became full practitioners. It includes an increasing understanding

of how, when, and about what old-timers collaborate, collude, and collide, and what they enjoy, dislike, respect, and admire. In particular it offers exemplars (which are grounds and motivation for learning activity), including masters, finished products, and more advanced apprentices in the process of becoming full practitioners (Lave and Wenger, 1991, 95).

In short, situated learning is associated with engagement, belonging, inclusiveness, and developing identities rather than acquiring concepts and theories while sitting in a class. To explain the process of situated learning, Lave and Wenger (1991) introduced the two key notions: legitimate peripheral participation and communities of practice.

Legitimate peripheral participation refers to the progressive involvement of new arriv-als in the practice as they acquire growing competence in the ongoing activity. The term "legitimate" emphasizes that a necessary condition to learn anything at all is to become part of an activity; to learn one needs both to immerse oneself in what is going on, with all the risks and emotions that this implies. "Participation" indicates that learning always takes place because (and thanks) to the interaction with others. Learning can-not take place if participation is not possible. At the same time, the context of learning is shaped by historical conditions (learning how to become a nurse today and 20 or 80 years ago is very different) and articulated according to a specific division of influence and power (for example between teacher and knower but also advance learners and total novices). One of the consequences is that no matter how compliant and subservient the novice is, there is no such thing as learning without conflict; any modification of the knowledge distribution is perceived as a way of subverting the established knowledge/ power relations within a social context. One example is when advanced novices start to usurp the hierarchical position of other practitioners when they begin to acquire decisional discretion. For this reason, legitimate peripheral participation always entails some unresolved ambivalence, as between revealing trade secrets to novices to enable their socialization, against hiding them to preserve the status quo; and between attempts by novices to try to steal the knowledge with their eyes against their search for new and emancipating ways of doing things that may affirm their autonomy. Finally, the adjective "peripheral" suggests the existence of a variety of positions that members can occupy with respect to the activity carried out and the people involved in it. Peripherality, that is, sitting at the boundary of what is going on and simply making copies or serving tea, both exempts and empowers: "where" novices stand with respect to the responsibilities for the final product is highly significant both to them and to others. Peripherality, how-ever, is a key condition as it allows novices to make mistakes, experiment, and learn, and not only from their mentors (as in the traditional model), but also from other partici-pants in the practice, including other novices. Lave and Wenger (1991) clearly state that the notion of peripheral participation does not necessarily imply the existence of a cen-tre. The opposite of peripheral here is fully immersed and responsible for the ongoing accomplishment of a practice and its outcomes. The specific ways of interacting among those involved in the practice and the existing power relations (which in turn define the forms and conditions of participation) interact with characteristics of the individual learners to generate similar (but never identical) learning curricula and trajectories (Lave and Wenger, 1991; Gherardi, Nicolini, and Odella, 1998).

The term *Community of Practice* (CoP) was coined initially to describe the totality of the social learning systems that originates around any particular activity (Lave and Wenger, 1991). Defined broadly as "groups of people who share a passion for something that they know how to do, and who interact regularly in order to learn how to do it better" (Wenger, 2004, 2), CoPs represent social learning spaces in which commitment derives from identification with a shared domain of interest, a shared repertoire of tools and words, and specific modes of communication which emerge as a result of continuous collaboration (Wenger, 1998, 15). The shared domain or joint enterprise is the area of common interest that serves as the source of identity construction. Learning about and contributing to the shared domain of interest (from collecting stamps to midwifery) constitute the major source of cohesion. By virtue of working together, sharing knowledge and socializing newcomers, participants develop an internal social organization with different levels of influence and prestige. CoP is thus a descriptor for the set of interconnected people who stay in touch and kept together by the shared interest in the common task. Finally, by virtue of working together members of a CoP develop a common repertoire of artefacts, narrative practices, knowledge, and shared methods which itself becomes a further source of cohesion among members and differentiation from non-members.

In sum, the idea of community of practice shifts the attention from the learning process—which was the main object of situated learning theory—to the relationships and exchanges of those who are brought together by the desire or need to improve their practice. It emphasizes that people who have been socialized and carry out the same practice are often joined by a "complex [set of] relationships, self-organization, dynamic boundaries, ongoing negotiation of identity and cultural meaning" (Wenger, 1998, 1). Practitioners involved in a shared domain of knowing thus develop a number of commonalities, and in the right conditions they can constitute and recognize themselves as a community. In this sense CoPs are different from teams, which are artificially assembled to achieve a specified goal. They are also different from other forms of networks as the latter are usually kept together by mutual exchanges rather than a common identity, history, and joint enterprise.

Crucially, CoPs are first and foremost knowledge communities, in the sense that they exist because and for the sole purpose of perpetuating, sharing, and refining some form of expertise and mastery. Mutual bonds derive, in fact, from their passion about a topic and above all the desire "to deepen their knowledge and expertise in this area by interacting on an ongoing basis" (Wenger, McDermott, and Snyder, 2002, 4). As such, CoPs are powerful mechanisms of knowledge sharing, knowledge production, and mutual learning. CoPs are particularly effective in transferring best practices through social relations; they are also a powerful mechanism for solving problems and generating new solutions (members in a community know who and how to ask for help); and a mechanism to refine and update professional skills (Wenger and Snyder, 2000).

In sum, situated learning theory and CoP constitute two different faces of the same coin: one offers a new appreciation of the process of learning and socialization; the other foregrounds the community that is generated around this process and its capacity to operate as a mechanism of knowledge sharing and mutual learning. The two concepts are especially suitable to be applied in health care and, in fact, both were originally derived from the study of, amongst others, a group of traditional midwives (Lave and Wenger, 1991).

SITUATED LEARNING AND COMMUNITIES OF PRACTICE IN HEALTH CARE

Situated learning theory and CoPs have been enthusiastically embraced by the health care sector (Cope, Cuthbertson, and Stoddart, 2000; Li et al., 2009a, 2009b; le May, 2009; Ranmuthugala et al., 2011) as they offer the potential of new learning partnerships that are not hostage to professional silos and may facilitate the engagement with a variety of stakeholders including input from patient-led communities (le May, 2009). Such partnerships may take a variety of forms, ranging from more informal networks with loosely defined goals and agendas to more formalized support groups with clearer objectives and a pronounced focus on fostering workplace social interaction (Li et al, 2009a, 2009b).

As with other concepts that have emerged from industry, the adoption of situated learning, and especially CoPs, in health care followed a process of "translation" and "editing" rather than a mechanical transfer (Czarniawska-Joerges and Sevón, 1996). As health care organizations in certain countries have been pressured to become more business-like in their governance and operations, the innovations developed by private sector industry have become correspondingly more attractive (at least to managers and policy makers: see e.g. Chapters 16 and 23, this volume). Even if only in a totemic sense, such innovations are seen to promise greater efficiency and more streamlined processes within the health care setting.

This is no less the case with the CoP concept. This was initially adopted by a number of leading organizations in the private sector (notably BP), very often as a way of labeling and making sense of operational changes which had been introduced to share good practice across the functional and geographical boundaries of large multinational organizations (Collison and Parcell, 2004). The concept, and the associated ideas around "Knowledge Management" were then highlighted by the work of health service researchers. In part, the concept was drawn upon to better understand aspects of health care practice, which did not conform to the dominant, objectified view of knowledge associated with professional expertise. Thus, Gabbay and le May used the term to help explain the socially situated character of the use of evidence by GPs. "Mindlines," not guidelines, as they put it, were seen as being negotiated through "a range of informal interactions in fluid communities of practice" (Gabbay and le May, 2004). In part, however, the CoP idea was also introduced as a response to the limitations of existing attempts to introduce multi-disciplinary collaborative arrangements into health care practice. Bate and Robert, for example, argued that the limited effectiveness of new Cancer Services Collaboratives in the UK was attributable to their being constituted as "time-limited project teams," and not "linked and active communities of practice" (Bate and Robert, 2002).

Thus, both in conception and implementation, CoPs were not being slavishly imitated but were being *translated* to meet the particular needs of the health care setting. As we will discuss in more detail below, this meant that their application in practice encountered a different set of barriers to those found elsewhere. In the private sector particularly, CoPs sat rather uneasily within hierarchical organizations. Studies here found a contradiction between managerial attempts to direct them in a "top-down" fashion, and their organic, "bottom-up" engagement of community members (Agterberg et al., 2010). In contrast, in health care CoPs have been seen as most relevant to overcoming barriers to multi-disciplinary collaboration (Bate and Robert 2002; Oborn and Dawson, 2010; Kislov, Harvey, and Walshe, 2011). Indeed, a number of health care providers and researchers seem to have readily adopted CoP thinking for these reasons. Ranmuthugala et al. (2011), for example, noted a rapid increase in articles discussing CoPs in the period 2003–2009. One consequence of this process of translating and editing, rather than simple diffusion, was that the actual implementation of CoPs and situated learning in health care practice varied greatly between contexts. In that sense, the notion of using CoPs is more an umbrella term covering a variety of initiatives than a marker of a specific method or technique. Thus, previous analysis of CoP initiatives in health care found that initiatives differed greatly in their aims, design, mode of operation, and utilization of technology (Li et al., 2009a). While some units were dependent on virtual forms of communication, others invested heavily into traditional face-to-face interaction (Ranmuthugala et al., 2011). Likewise, the composition and geographical localization of CoPs was found to vary substantially: while some groups consist primarily of local members with identical professional backgrounds, others may be multi-disciplinary in nature and bring together practitioners from diverse geographical regions (Jiwa et al., 2009).

In a systematic review, Li et al. (2009a) identify a marked division in the literature on CoPs in health care. They distinguish between reports of initiatives concerned with the socialization of young professionals into health care, and accounts of how CoPs can be used to facilitate knowledge sharing, knowledge creation, skill development, and continuing professional education. The former group of studies, which often refer to situated learning theory and are inspired by the classical apprenticeship models, predominantly deal with issues concerning the development of professional identity and gradual skills acquisition. The latter tend to pay attention to knowledge creation and sharing among established professionals in the context of CoPs (Li et al., 2009a, 5). In the next two sections we examine these two strands of the literature more closely.

Supporting Socialization and Fostering Learning through Communities of Practice

Many of the initiatives that build on the insights of situated learning theory are aimed at addressing some of the shortcomings of the traditional methods used to train and support the continuous professional development of health care professionals. For example, studies often find that traditional medical education is preoccupied with familiarizing students with significant amounts of theoretical knowledge and frameworks. It is therefore often incapable of preparing practitioners for clinical work (McKenna and Green, 2004). Saturation with formulaic knowledge, however, does not lead directly to the development of skills directly applicable to practice, as medicine is not an exact science. Rather, the practice of medicine is a skill, a craft, constantly requiring personal judgment and heavily based on experience (Knight and Mattick, 2006). Comparing the art of medicine to a jazz improvisation, Haidet (2007) notes that being a successful physician requires

> [taking] recognition that all voices in the medical encounter have things to say that are as important as one's own statements. It takes listening aligned toward *understanding*, not just the collection of factual data. And it takes raising one's awareness to clues— nonverbal signals, fleeting glimpses of emotion, and key words (such as worried, concerned, and afraid)—and following up on these clues when they present themselves. The essence of ensemble, whether in jazz or in medicine, lies in looking beyond one's own perspective to see, understand, and respond to the perspectives of others (Haidet, 2007, 167).

Trying to bridge the gap between theoretical base and applied medical knowledge, educational programs for health care professionals usually include a clinical practice component that complements the standardized academic curriculum and is employed to prepare students for hands-on practice work. Egan and Jaye (2009) point out that these two types of educational settings, the latter being directly modeled according to the tenets of situated learning theory, differ significantly in their goals, requirements, and the structure of learning processes. While formal academic education stresses the traditional individual mastery of theoretical "textbook" knowledge, the latter shifts the emphasis to the importance of social forces, collaboration, contextual factors, and professional socialization at the workplace (Egan and Jaye, 2009; Cope, Cuthbertson, and Stoddart, 2000). Clinical placements thus become the situated training grounds in which students for the first time come into contact with various communities of medical practice. By following the routines of newly joined communities of clinical practice, novices develop their sense of professional identity and obtain valuable hands-on experience which can "support, augment, contradict, or even resist the teaching and learning objectives of the formal curriculum" (Egan and Jaye, 2009, 120). Jenkins and ⬛⬛⬛⬛⬛⬛⬛ observed, for example, that occupational therapists developed their ⬛⬛⬛⬛⬛⬛⬛ rather than a classroom setting.

Similar conclusions were obtained by Lindsay (2000); Cope, Cuthbertson, and Stoddart (2000); and Meagher-Stewart et al. (2012). These authors observed that regardless of the clinical setting, the acquisition and assimilation of skills such as clinical reasoning and evidence-utilization were significantly facilitated when novices were allowed to work in real situations under the mentorship of more experienced colleagues.

The transition from classroom to practice can be a very stressful experience. For example, Brown et al. (2005, 87) described nursing students' attitude to their first encounter with clinical practice as feeling abandoned and being left "in the dark" due to a very limited understanding of expected behaviors and a sudden lack of guidance in comparison with their previous educational experience. In this darkness, the support of colleagues and the development of a sense of belonging in relation to the team are crucially important factors affecting the well-being of students and their learning outcomes (Levitt-Jones et al., 2008). Being properly inducted to the practice, feeling welcomed, accepted as "a valid and legitimate learner" and having an access to a wide variety of experiences, allows students to build the sense of connectedness to the placement area and, thus, proceed smoothly with their learning process (Myall, Levett-Jones, and Lathlean, 2008, 1838; Nolan, 1998).

As social communities consolidating members around a common purpose and giving participants a sense of common identity, CoPs serve as supportive and integrative tools for novices allowing students to join practice as legitimate participants while they gradually develop relevant skills and "move through the zone of proximal development toward independent competence" (Cope, Cuthbertson, and Stoddart, 2000, 855). As the gradual acquisition of skills takes place, learners internalize values and cultural practices embedded in the discourse, as well as developing a tacit understanding of individuals and the community (Spouse, 1998). This process triggers the development of students' self-understanding in the context of their new profession. Socialized via practice, young professionals reach graduation not as *tabula rasa*, but as individuals with a well-defined sense of self and "carry with them tacit knowledge and shared social identities that only those who have experienced similar training can understand" (Bartunek, 2010).

While the literature is usually very optimistic about the value and benefits of utilizing a situated learning approach with regard to the socialization of health care professional, other authors suggest that some caution is in order. Egan and Jaye (2009), for instance, point out that while the general trajectory of a medical professionals in training is directed toward becoming a full participant of the professional community, the trajectories of students admitted to clinical practice may remain peripheral as they slide through their placements and develop temporary attachments to small teams or their particular members (112). Also, it should not also be presumed that students are automatically embraced by professional communities. Short placements (Cope, Cuthbertson, and Stoddart, 2000; Warne et al., 2010; Papastavrou et al., 2010), lack of meaningful supportive relationships at workplace (Konrad and Browning, 2012; Nolan, 1998), general deficit of busy personnel's attention and direction (Myall, Levett-Jones, and Lathlean, 2008; Löfmark and Wikblad, 2001) and the absence of effective introduction and guidance by a mentor or tutor (Spouse, 1998; Warne and McAndrew, 2008; Papastavrou et al., 2010;

Dimitriadis, Iyer, and Evgeniou, 2014) may make it difficult for students to participate effectively in the activities of the practical community.

Deliberating about the ways to improve the learning experience of students in clinical placements, it may be offered to include patient educators into the learning process in order to provide medical students with the access to a wider range of experiences, some of which challenge traditional formulaic wisdom of medical schools. Yet, as pointed out by Bleakley and Bligh (2008), despite the vivid rhetoric praising the benefits of a patient-centered approach to medical education, contemporary undergraduate curricula for medical students still lack a meaningful early access to patients and "incorporating deliberate practice" (95) that would allow learners to establish relationships with those they treat and, by doing so, engage in the process of joint knowledge construction via dialogue. From this point of view, case-specific experiential knowledge of patients and their families makes them valuable and valid contributors to the educational process who can not only communicate their first-hand experience, but also can raise awareness about their needs and initiate a sharing activity (Towle and Godolphin, 2011).

COMMUNITIES OF PRACTICE AS MECHANISMS FOR SHARING KNOWLEDGE AND FOSTERING INNOVATION AND CHANGE

As distinct from accounts of novice experiences in health care, another strand of the literature on CoPs discusses their role in continuing professional development, knowledge sharing, innovation, and knowledge translation. While clinical practice programs generally have the formation of a certain professional identity as their final goal (Li et al., 2009a), working groups consisting of professionals seeking further education, development, and innovation may emerge around a variety of goals. These include, for example: the promotion of a new measurement tool in child and youth mental care (Barwick, Peters, and Boydell, 2009); improvement of the quality of referral letters to specialty clinics (Jiwa et al., 2009); the improvement of dermatology outpatient services (Lathlean and Myall, 2009); the development and dissemination of national guidelines on breast cancer (Fung-Kee-Fung et al., 2009); and the promotion of provincial guidelines on laparoscopic surgery for colon cancer (Fung-Kee-Fung et al., 2008). Sometimes such groups, which are created for the solution of a particular problem, evolve over time and change their objectives (e.g., le May, 2009). Due to the flexibility and adaptability of CoPs, this model is generally considered to be well suited to meet the learning requirements of a wide and diverse group of health care professionals (Barwick, Peters, and Boydell, 2009).

The proliferation of clinical knowledge and the rapid pace of scientific advancement make it difficult even for seasoned practitioners to keep track of new discoveries. The process of transferring research findings to clinical practice often becomes slow and unpredictable (Eccles et al., 2009). The gravity of this problem is so substantial that the whole new field of implementation research has developed in recent decades to study scientific methods which seek "to promote the systematic uptake of clinical research findings and other evidence-based practices into routine practice, and hence to improve the quality (effectiveness, reliability, safety, appropriateness, equity, efficiency) of health care" (10). However, implementation and knowledge translation guidelines are typically based on an objective view of knowledge, and may therefore overlook the importance of such subjective dimensions as interactive knowledge construction, the role of context and unique interpretations rooted in personal practical experience (Oborn, Barrett, and Racko, 2012).

In clinical settings, however, personal experience, relationships, and unique contextual factors are inseparable from learning processes. A good example is provided by Edmondson, Bohmer, and Pisano (2001), who studied the experience of several cardiac surgical teams with regard to the implementation of a new technology. Despite general similarities between participating top-tier cardiac surgery departments, their experience with the adoption of innovative surgical technique were signficantly different and depended heavily on contextual factors and intragroup social processes. Successful implementers learned in situ as a team, invested heavily in ensuring the psychological safety of individual members and their involvement in communicative processes as well as the creation of shared meaning. In the organizations studied, the introduction of new technologies challenged existing power relations in teams as role boundaries blurred and the interdependency of group members increased. The teams that managed to adapt to the new organizational reality became successful implementers of the new technology, while those clinging to status quo routines eventually abandoned the effort to implement the new practice. Crucially important for the successful sites was the role played by the project leader in promoting meaningful communication and reflective discussions revolving around practice-related issues (Edmondson, Bohmer, and Pisano, 2001).

Reflective cardiac surgical teams analyzing their practical experience and encouraging in situ learning provide great examples of CoPs dealing with the disruption of existing routines. In such groups, new routines are mutually constructed via interaction and as "experience with the joint activity accumulates, each participant abstracts and generalizes, not simply from personal understandings and actions but from understandings and actions that have been jointly, intersubjectively established" (Dyonisiou and Tsoukas, 2013, 191).

The process of collective learning preceding the successful implementation of innovation, thus, must involve individuals "jointly analysing information, openly discussing concerns, sharing decision-making, and coordinating experimentation … [while also being] willing to challenge others' views, acknowledge their own errors, and openly discuss failed experiments" without fear of seeming incompetent (Nembhard, 2009, 30). CoPs, thus, become the ideal environment and medium for facilitating the translation of knowledge into practice (Thomson, Schneider, and Wright, 2013). As Gabbay and le May (2009) note, the assumption by advocates of evidence-based medicine that medical practitioners behave as purely rational and calculative decision makers is actually unwarranted. During their ethnographic study of a primary care practice in semi-rural England, the authors observed that clinicians rarely, if at all, follow the rational sequence of actions prescribed by official evidence-based guidelines. Despite the ability to access a wide variety of sources, including those available via sophisticated computer repositories, researchers rarely observed experienced health practitioners consult these databases in order to solve a problem related to clinical practice. Rather, clinicians participating in the study tended to "glean" what is thought to be the best practice from, for example, the way local consultants treat their patients, from snippets of reading, and from each other, especially "by means of partners with specific areas of expertise helping to keep each other up to date" (53). Participating physicians were, thus, disciplined to take evidence-based information with a pinch of salt as it often did not take into account essential aspects of the particular practice and, thus, did not easily match the particular discourse. It was though discussions and exchange of opinions with trusted colleagues that the new information was absorbed into physicians' "mindlines" and became a part of their practical knowledge. These discussions and reflective practices associated with them constituted the essence of CoPs at the primary care practice in the study and served as potent mechanisms for learning and the diffusion of practicable knowledge into the organizational reality. This in-depth study provides an example of the supportive environment in which the opinions of trusted colleagues help to validate individual absorption of information, and learning opportunities emerge as a natural extension of daily interactions with peers (see also Parboosingh, 2002; Thomson, Schneider, and Wright, 2013).

CoPs as Improvement Initiatives and Managerial Tools

From Emergent to Mandated

When they were first theorized, CoPs were considered mainly as emergent and self-organized phenomena in the sense that they emerged spontaneously in the interstices of organizations and under the radar of the formal organization (Brown and Duguid, 1991; Wenger, 1998). In this sense, managers were advised not to interfere or meddle with them lest the CoP could dissolve or go underground. In succeeding years, however, prompted by the adoption of the term by some leading companies (Collison and Parcell, 2004), there were increasing efforts to intentionally promote what can be termed "mandated" CoPs within formal organizations so as to enhance learning and foster collaboration (Li et al., 2009a; Barwick, Peters, and Boydell, 2009). Advocates argued that well-designed and carefully designed CoPs could in fact provide a favorable social context for the development and utilization of organizational knowledge (Wenger, McDermott, and Snyder, 2002). These CoPs were attractive to organizations because they were able to tap into individuals' intrinsic motivations to share knowledge and learning (Swan, Scarbrough, and Robertson, 2002).

However, the establishment of such mandated CoPs raises a number of new organizational and managerial challenges, including: designing, setting up, and legitimating CoPs; managing and making the CoPs sustainable; and making CoPs effective. The first challenge to be addressed is how to establish CoPs. Because of their dependence on shared knowledge and identity, CoPs cannot be artificially created or designed but need to build instead on existing commonalities and practice-driven relationships that need to be identified, foregrounded, and legitimated. In health care, this is facilitated by occupational specialisms that often cut across organizational boundaries and even hierarchical levels. Fung-Kee-Fung et al. (2009) for example, report the emergence and establishment of a CoP to improve surgical oncology that spanned different organizations and professions. The boundaries of the communities were designed to follow the natural contours of different health care professionals already working in surgical oncology. A critical role is played in this sense by recognized experts in the field that can act both as champions of the initiative and catalysts of interest, so that the CoPs can actually start operating. The literature in other sectors (Wenger, McDermott, and Snyder, 2002; McDermott and Archibald, 2010) suggests that in this phase it is critical that management provides support to the emerging CoP in terms of recognition (the activity must be legitimated); institutional support (a sponsor needs to be identified within the organization); governance (specific roles are allocated and leadership is clearly identified); resources (facilitators are appointed and leaders are given sufficient time); and infrastructure (access is provided to the necessary communication technologies).

A second main challenge in utilizing CoPs as a managerial intervention is finding ways to make such initiatives sustainable. Many of the initiatives reported in the health care literature (Gabbay and le May, 2009; Ranmuthugala et al., 2011) tend in fact to have a very limited time span. This contrasts with the view that CoPs evolve over time, display a typical life cycle (Wenger, 1998), and progress through stages of development (Wenger, McDermott, and Snyder, 2002) and that CoPs need time to produce benefits for the organization. It seems that a critical factor in making CoPs initiatives sustainable is the provision of adequate leadership and governance (McDermott and Archibald, 2010). In many industries, CoP leaders and facilitators are trained and supported in their professional development. They then ensure that participation is sustained, that contributions continue to flow, and that newcomers are not put off by the current group of core members. CoPs at the same time are helped to develop a sense of place and rhythm through periodic rituals (e.g., an annual CoP convention) and alignment with the natural cycle of the hosting organization (the successes of the CoP are included in the annual report). Health care organizations have been good at adopting some of these practices, although examples of the systematic and strategic use of CoPs in health care are still few and far between (Li et al., 2009a). For example, while the use of facilitation in health care CoPs seems to be widely accepted (5)—probably because working in facilitated groups is commonplace in many health care systems—other aspects mentioned above (e.g., institutional support, resources, and governance) are omitted in spite of being critical to help CoPs to move toward full maturity and produce value for the organization.

A third challenge in developing successful mandated CoPs is to prevent them from becoming inward looking. McDermott and Archibald (2010), for example, note that a critical role of CoP leaders is to establish clear goals and deliverables, and ensure that these are aligned with the goals of the organization. Goals and deliverables have been found, in fact, to energize communities. They provide a reason for members to meet and participate. More importantly, they establish the contribution of communities to the organization, thus making the value of the CoP visible. Important strides, in this sense, have been recently made especially in the UK, where CoPs have been successfully employed in a programmatic and strategic way to facilitate knowledge translation and the adoption of clinical innovations (Thomson, Schneider, and Wright, 2013). Rowley et al. (2012), for example, report how emergent communities of practice were enhanced and new ones created and fostered around specific themes that aligned with the strategic health care objectives of the hosting organizations.

Aligning the work of the CoP with the strategic intent of the organization also serves another critical purpose, that is, demonstrating value. This remains, in fact, an open question as the benefits of CoPs are notoriously difficult to pinpoint and measure. In their reviews of the literature, for example, both Li et al. (2009a) and Ranmuthugala et al. (2011) failed to find any study that tried to measure the effectiveness of CoPs or at least that met the traditional "eligibility criteria for quantitative analysis" (Li et al., 2009a, 7). While the issue of whether initiatives such as CoPs can be evaluated using traditional metrics goes beyond the scope of this chapter, it can be noted that demonstrating the value added to the organization, and thus justifying the resource investments required to establish and sustain a CoP programme, remains a pressing concern for all CoP practitioners (McDermott and Archibald, 2010). Wenger, Trayner, and de Laat (2011), for example, suggest that CoPs add value in five distinct ways: *immediate value* (interactions have value in and for themselves, for example, the capacity to finds information one needs though a community); *potential value* (e.g., the results of interactions yield new ideas or resources that still need to be applied); *applied value* (e.g., the knowledge obtained through the CoP as resulted in some demonstrable changes); *realized value* (the changes obtained thanks to the input by the CoP result in measurable improved performance); and *reframing value* (the interactions of the community leads to reframing the strategies, goals, values, and way of doing business). Aligning the activity of the CoP with the strategic goals of the organization may facilitate the demonstration of its value by generating applied and realized value in addition to the immediate value usually described by participants (Lathlean and le May, 2002; Chandler and Fry, 2009; Swift, 2014).

Beyond Face to Face: Virtual and Online CoPs

⋯⋯ above of emergent versus mandated CoPs, the distinction between ⋯⋯⋯⋯⋯ virtual or online CoPs based on electronically mediated interaction is often blurred. The latter type of CoP (henceforth we will simply use the term "virtual" since this also encompasses "online" forms) may often be linked to conventional face-to-face meetings (Chandler and Fry, 2009). Similarly, virtual CoPs may sometimes be difficult to distinguish from looser networks of individuals, being based as much, if not more, on mutual exchanges than on a shared history and identity.

Accepting these caveats, however, it is possible to recognize that virtual CoPs can have just as diverse a range of objectives and benefits as conventional CoPs. In particular, virtual CoPs have been used to address the two major themes of CoP development outlined earlier; namely socialization of (often new) health care staff (e.g., Jevack et al., 2014), and knowledge-sharing amongst existing staff. In the first category, a review of the literature relating to the role of CoPs in GP training in Australia found that such CoPs can help to generate social ties amongst participants (Barnett et al., 2012). Meanwhile, work in the UK context suggests that virtual CoPs can also help to create so-called "weak ties" across groups who are otherwise disconnected (Russell et al., 2004).

Compared to face-to-face communities, however, virtual CoPs may struggle to create social interaction and a genuine sense of participation amongst their members. This can apply even when sophisticated web tools are being employed. When a CoP was set up to promote improvements in discharge planning in Wales, for example, it was found that the online forum and website were the least successful elements (Chandler and Fry, 2009). This was attributed to limited computer access for social care staff, and that nurses and social workers were more comfortable with face-to-face or phone-based interaction.

On the other hand, studies suggest that, through the use of ICT and web tools, virtual communities can also help to create social ties amongst groups and individuals who are otherwise geographically or professionally isolated. Groups supported in this way include GPs in rural areas of Australia (Barnett et al., 2012) and nurses practicing mental health care in rural areas (Cassidy, 2011). This function of virtual CoPs may be as important as overcoming the disciplinary and professional boundaries which we discussed earlier in relation to conventional CoPs. One example of this in practice is the virtual community which emerged through use of an email tool (Listserv) for clinicians in intensive care units in Australia. This was seen as helping to decrease the professional isolation of specialists in rural areas (Rolls et al., 2008). The virtual community also supported networking amongst members with valued expertise, such that the CoP acted as an effective knowledge broker for a network of otherwise disconnected intensive care units.

In some cases, the apparent disadvantages of relying on ICT-mediated interactions may actually be beneficial to developing communities around specific domains. One example is the virtual community which developed in the North West of England around the sharing of adverse lessons from incidents in anesthetic departments (Sharma et al., 2006). Here, anonymity of the users allowed participating clinicians to share experiences while avoiding personal embarrassment and the stigmatization of particular departments Similarly, studies suggest that the greater social distance provided by virtual CoPs may overcome individuals' inhibitions about participating due to a lack of confidence in the value of their expertise, or a fear of losing face by admitting ignorance (Rolls et al., 2008; Ardichvili, Page, and Wentling, 2003).

In addition to overcoming professional and geographical boundaries, virtual CoPs can also help to overcome the institutional boundary between researchers in universities and practitioners in the health care system. One example of a virtual CoP being developed to span this research-practice boundary is provided by Friberger and Falkman (2013), who investigated the workings of a geographically dispersed "oral care" CoP that included both practitioners and academics. The CoP was established to give practitioners access to cases of low prevalence by combining data from various facilities and providing learning opportunities beyond the scope of one clinic's operation. Participating physicians presented cases via a virtual submission system in order to receive opinions regarding diagnosis, pose a general question, or educate other CoP members. In this situation, participants often became immediate beneficiaries of sharing by obtaining feedback on their cases, and the community as a whole benefited by gaining access to authentic data and aligning their models of treatment with others present in the discipline (Friberger and Falkman, 2013).

Given their diverse forms and outcomes, it is clearly difficult to generalize about what makes for an effective virtual CoP. Some studies have outlined critical success factors (e.g., Ho et al., 2010), but these tend to differ according to the community under review (cf. Barnett et al., 2012). Certain themes which emerge from the literature, however, include: the importance of voluntary and motivated participation on the part of members (Ho et al., 2010); the role played by leaders and facilitators (Nurani et al., 2012); and the provision of appropriate ICT infrastructure.

The virtual nature of these CoPs makes each of these issues especially challenging. First, discussion of participation in conventional CoPs differentiates between core and "peripheral" participants. Virtual communities tend to heighten the distinction between various forms of participation. It is important, for example, to differentiate between "nominal" and actual participation in virtual CoPs. This can be illustrated by a virtual CoP set up to promote innovation in primary care in the Basque Public Health Service in Spain (Mendizabal et al., 2013). Of the 1,627 registered "users" of this CoP, a survey found that only 4% had contributed ideas, and only 6% had commented on ideas. While these figures suggest that there may be a major disparity between the official membership of a virtual CoP, and the numbers actively participating, it also highlights the scope for large numbers of members to participate in a passive way—so-called "lurking"— by following the information exchanges supported by the CoP's IT infrastructure. This passive participation has been viewed as equivalent to the "legitimate peripheral participation" seen in more conventional CoPs, through which members can learn about a particular domain and be encultured into its discourse and forms of practice (Russell et al., 2004).

Second, facilitation and leadership take on particular forms in virtual CoPs where social interaction needs to be carefully "cultivated" online (Wenger, McDermott, and Snyder, 2002). This may involve facilitators engaging in a range of activities. In the case of the CHAIN network in the NHS, for example, such activities included: "ensuring that the database of members is up to date; targeting messages to appropriate subgroups based on members' interests; reminding members of the opportunities for networking; and affirming the principle of reciprocity" (Russell et al., 2004). Because virtual CoPs are less likely to arise spontaneously due to informal interaction, they may also require dedicated resources to develop and sustain them. A study of a virtual, inter-professional CoP in Canada concluded that a dedicated facilitator and associated funding for development of electronic tools and resources were key to sustaining virtual CoPs (Nurani et al., 2012).

Third, a critical element in any dedicated support given to virtual CoPs is likely to be its information and communications technology (ICT) infrastructure (Dube and Jacob, 2005). Choice of appropriate ICT is critical. This needs to be simple enough to allow widespread and easy access and use, but also to support content and dialogue rich enough to meet the community's needs. The technical aspect of infrastructure, however, should be viewed as secondary to the importance of "socializing" it within the community—that is, ensuring it is accepted as a legitimate and effective way of mediating social interaction (McDermott, 1999).

MAKING COPS WORK IN HEALTH CARE SETTINGS: FACILITATORS AND BARRIERS

Not every CoP initiative is successful. Initiating collaboration among health care practitioners is not an easy task. Strong occupational boundaries commonly exist between different groups of medical personnel (i.e., nurses, doctors, medical administrators, paramedics), which hinders the development of collaborative relationships and undermines trust (Bartunek, 2010; O'Leary et al., 2008; Sirota, 2007; Nicolini et al., 2008). The ability to establish interpersonal relationships, however, is crucially important at the initial stages of a CoP's existence (Chandler and Fry, 2009).

Speaking about the failures to establish a dynamic and healthy collaborative initiative, le May (2009, 14) points out that problems usually arise in CoPs at either structural or individual level. The structural subset of problems stems from the inability of CoPs to secure a steady following or their lack of necessary connections, while the source of individual problems resides in personal behaviors, such as tendency to monopolize knowledge or distrust peers (14–15).

Similarly, in a systematic review of CoP-based initiatives in the area of surgical oncology, Fung-Kee-Fung et al. (2009, 565) establish the following general factors influencing the implementation of collaborative projects: "(a) the formation of trust among health professionals and health institutions; (b) the availability of accurate, complete, relevant data; (c) clinical leadership; (d) institutional commitment; and (e) the infrastructure and methodological support for quality management." While infrastructural and organizational support factors can be conceptualized as structural in nature, the relational dimension belongs to the individual realm. Power relations deserve separate consideration.

Structural Factors

The structure of CoP meetings themselves seems to have a substantial impact on the willingness of practitioners to participate in discussion, as well as on their perceptions of value added by this activity. For example, Friberger and Falkman (2013) found that regular communication provides a necessary rhythm for distributed CoPs, and structured case-based meetings present a way to manage busy professionals' time more effectively. Similarly, in a dermatological CoP, members viewed pre-set agendas and structured meetings as a means to maintain focus and fight the frustration associated with a loss of purpose (Lathlean and Myall, 2009), and in a successful Canadian CoP for nurse practitioners, participants believed that regular agenda-driven face-to-face and email interactions created a sense of direction for future discussions, and ensured group cohesiveness (Sawchenko, 2009).

Structural factors affecting the activities of CoPs are not limited to the composition of the group and its modes of operation. Rather, often the ability of CoPs to introduce regular meetings and establish a following is constrained by the conditions of the larger health care system. For example, Chandler and Fry note that the NHS reality does not generally allow "time and head space to be creative and innovative" and, thus, having such a forum in this system may be considered an "unaffordable luxury" (Chandler and Fry, 2009, 45). Also, the establishment and promotion of CoPs among practicing clinicians may require the introduction of various incentives and feedback mechanisms, possibly tied to payment modalities that are currently not in place (Soubhi et al., 2010). In addition to the lack of systemic ability to accommodate motivating practices, common resistance to cross-institutional data sharing, often reflected in pre-existing policies, further hinders the ability of physicians to access and share data (Fung-Kee-Fung, 2009, 570).

Individual Factors

Trust is a fundamental element of CoPs. In relation to health care, the issue of trust has to be broken down to two dimensions: the formation of trusting relationships between members of CoPs and the establishment of trust between members and participating institutions (Fung-Kee-Fung et al., 2009).

Importantly, multi-disciplinary teams are inherently more susceptible to the perils of distrust and impaired communication. Fragmented and compartmentalized, contemporary medicine provides a fertile ground for the creation of narrow professional identities and, while all of them relate to the general field of health care, they often come into conflict with each other. Bartunek (2011) points out that because social identity bound-aries within health care CoPs often inhibit the spread of knowledge, in order to be success-ful these groups need to stimulate cross-occupational sharing and encourage the formation of second, superordinate identities as members of the larger health care community (164).

Further, Tagliaventi and Mattarelli (2006) suggest that the specificity of the practices of a given community and the strong collective identity of members constitute a criti-cal factor which creates barriers to knowledge sharing. Ferlie et al. (2005) corroborate this view suggesting that CoPs in health can be very insular, they tend to seal them-selves off from contiguous communities and can become highly institutionalized. This in turn creates stickiness of knowledge across boundaries, so that while learning circu-lates effectively among local members, circulation between and across communities and locales becomes difficult. To avoid these shortcomings, several authors suggest the need to identify and mobilize a series of boundary objects, boundary spanners, and knowl-edge brokers and to actively promote boundary crossing interactions which can bridge between and across neighboring CoPs (Lomas, 2007; Mitton et al., 2007; Currie and White, 2012; Chew, Armstrong, and Martin, 2013; Waring et al., 2013).

The role of institution is similarly important here. As collective bodies bring-ing together complete strangers, CoPs and benefiting institutions have to establish the norms of institution-based trust and sharing in order to initiate an open dialogue (Ardichvili, Page, and Wentling, 2003). The formation of trust between various CoP members and sponsoring institutions often involves political matters leading to the uneasy task of negotiating terms and the creation of shared vision between members of different clinical teams and disciplines (Fung-Kee-Fung et al., 2009).

Dealing with Power Relations

Cliques within CoPs may become another factor endangering the successful flow of knowledge among members. In some non-apprenticeship-based CoPs, learners may never become core participants and, thus, "learning and the negotiation of meaning may continue to be only a reflection of the dominant source of power" (Li et al., 2009a). To a large degree, the problems of full engagement stem from the highly hierarchical nature of medicine. Thus, Nembhardt (2009) reminds us that medical professionals are conditioned into a hierarchy in which certain professional groups rank higher than oth-ers, thus "the lower the professional rank, the less consideration is typically given to that individual in clinical decision making" (30). Yet, collaborative initiatives, such as CoPs, require a multitude of voices and opinions in order to be successful and sustainable.

Sustaining the membership in CoPs when participants become disillusioned or feel psychological discomfort is a very challenging task (Jiwa et al., 2009). It is, thus, criti-cally important not to alienate newcomers by authoritarian control or using excessively high standards benchmarking. Specialists coming from different professional commu-nities in diverse geographical localities will always vary in their skills sets and knowl-edge, but it is beneficial for an open dialogue not to attach labels of inferiority.

Conclusions

The notions of situated learning and communities of practice provide valuable insights into some of the challenges faced by health care organizations. Under increasing pressure to innovate, reduce costs, and improve services, these organizations need to find effective means of socializing highly training professional staff and encouraging them to share knowledge across professional, institutional, and geographical boundaries. The notion of situated learning, in effect, underscores the challenges of achieving these broad objectives by showing that the acquisition of knowledge is not reducible to information exchanges, but is bound up with social practices, relationships, and identities. The notion of "community of practice" has foregrounded this social dimension by showing the role that such CoPs can play in socializing new staff, and in encouraging the sharing of knowledge through reciprocity and motivated participation. This not only helps us to better understand the limitations of formal organization structures, and even "mandated networks" in supporting organization learning and knowledge mobilization (Bate and Robert, 2002; Ferlie et al., 2012), it also provides a template for the development of new CoP-based interventions better equipped to meet these challenges.

Health care organizations globally have been in the forefront of developing CoPs. However, this notion has often been translated in a piecemeal rather than systematic way, and has been expanded to encompass a wide range of initiatives including CoPs which are mandated, rather than emergent, and which apply ICT tools to engage looser networks made up of disparate groups and individuals rather than focal communities with a defined history and identity. This pattern of translation makes it difficult to generalize about the potential contribution of CoPs and situated learning theory to the problems facing health care management, as outlined in the Introduction to this chapter. However, the range of initiatives do throw up some new questions which may help us better understand that contribution. As highlighted by our analysis, the forms taken by mandated CoPs in health care settings are diverse and therefore demand much greater attention to the possibilities, and constraints, of more fluid, technologically-mediated forms. For example, CoPs were originally viewed as an expression of situated learning. Is it possible that mandated CoPs may become a vehicle for overcoming the limitations of such learning by overcoming organizational boundaries, and supporting more collaborative approaches to learning and knowledge mobilization?

Finally, in relation to our introductory question of how far CoPs can help to produce a shift toward a "learning culture" within health care organizations, it is clear from our analysis that CoPs may present themselves as both a barrier and an enabler to such a shift. As tacit social networks through which identity is formed and knowledge is shared, CoPs may actually reinforce the boundaries between groups, and thus undermine attempts to produce knowledge and learning as an organizational or systemic resource (Swan, Scarbrough, and Robertson, 2002). Conversely, the mixed outcomes achieved by mandated CoPs to date suggest that further research is needed on adapting their form to specific contexts if they are to properly fulfill their potential and support moves toward a learning culture.

References

Addicott, R., McGivern, G., and Ferlie, E. (2006). Networks, organizational learning and knowledge management: NHS cancer networks. *Public Money & Management*, 26(2): 87–94.

Agterberg, M., Van den Hooff, B., Huysman, M., and Soekijad, M. (2010). Keeping the Wheels Turning: The Dynamics of Managing Networks of Practice. *Journal of Management Studies*, 47(1): 85–108.

Ardichvili, A., Page, V., and Wentling, T. (2003). Motivation and barriers to participation in virtual knowledge-sharing communities of practice. *Journal of Knowledge Management*, 7(1): 64–77.

Barnett, S., Jones, S. C., Bennett, S., Iverson, D., and Bonney, A. (2012). General practice training and virtual communities of practice: A review of the literature. *BMC family practice*, 13(1): 87.

Bartunek, J. (2011). Intergroup relationships and quality improvement in health care. *BMJ Quality and Safety*, 20(Suppl 1): i62–i66.

Barwick, M. A., Peters, J., and Boydell, K., (2009). Getting to uptake: Do communities of practice support the implementation of evidence-based practice. *Journal of the Canadian Academy of Child and Adolescent Psychiatry*, 18(1): 16–29.

Bate, S. P. and Robert, G. (2002). Knowledge management and communities of practice in the private sector: Lessons for modernizing the National Health Service in England and Wales. *Public Administration*, 80(4): 643–663.

Battilana, J. (2011). The enabling role of social position in diverging from the institutional status quo: Evidence from the UK National Health Service. *Organization Science*, 22(4): 817–834.

Bentley, C., Browman, G. P., and Poole, B. (2010). Conceptual and practical challenges for implementing the communities of practice model on a national scale: A Canadian cancer control initiative. *BMC Health Services Research*, 10(3): 1–8.

Berwick, D. (2013). An independent report to the Department of Health. A promise to learn— a commitment to act. Improving the safety of patients in England. Available at <https://www.gov.uk/government/uploads/system/uploads/attachment_data/file/226703/Berwick_Report.pdf> (accessed January 29, 2015).

Bleakley, A. and Bligh, J. (2008). Students learning from patients: Let's get real in medical education. *Advances in Health Sciences Education*, 13(1): 89–107.

Brown, J. S. and Duguid, P. (1991). Organizational learning and communities-of-practice: Toward a unified view of working, learning, and innovation. *Organization Science*, 2(1): 40–57.

Brown, L., Herd, K., Humphries, G. and Paton, M. (2005). The role of the lecturer in practice placements: What do students think? *Nurse Education in Practice*, 5: 84–90.

Cassidy, L. (2011). Online communities of practice to support collaborative mental health practice in rural areas. *Issues in Mental Health Nursing*, 32(2): 98–107.

Chandler, L. and Fry, A. (2009). Can communities of practice make a meaningful contribution to sustainable improvement in health care and social care? *Journal of Integrated Care*, 17(2): 41–48.

Chew, S., Armstrong, N., and Martin, G. (2013). Institutionalising knowledge brokering as a sustainable knowledge translation solution in health care: How can it work in practice? *Evidence & Policy: A Journal of Research, Debate and Practice*, 9(3): 335–351.

Collison, C. and Parcell, G. (2004). *Learning to fly: Practical knowledge management from leading and learning organizations*. New York: John Wiley & Sons.

Cope, P., Cuthbertson, P., and Stoddart, B. (2000). Situated learning in the practice placement. *Journal of Advanced Nursing*, 31(4): 850–856.

Currie, G., Finn, R., and Martin, G. (2007). Spanning boundaries in pursuit of effective knowledge sharing within networks in the NHS. *Journal of Health Organization and Management*, 21(4/5): 406–417.

Currie, G. and White, L. (2012). Inter-professional barriers and knowledge brokering in an organizational context: The case of health care. *Organization Studies*, 33(10): 1333–1361.

Czarniawska-Joerges, B. and G. Sevón (1996). *Translating organizational change*. Berlin: Walter de Gruyter.

Dimitriadis, P. A., Iyer, S., and Evgeniou, E. (2014). Learning in the Surgical Community of Practice. *Medical Science Educator*, 24(2): 211–214.

Dionysiou, D. D. and Tsoukas, H. (2013). Understanding the (re) creation of routines from within: A symbolic interactionist perspective. *Academy of Management Review*, 38(2): 181–205.

Dube, A. and Jacob, R. 2005. The impact of structuring characteristics on the launching of virtual communities of practice. *Journal of Organizational Change Management*, 18(2): 145–166.

Eccles, M., Armstrong, D., Baker, R., Cleary, K., Davies, H., Davies, S., Glasziou, P., Ilott, I., Kinmonth, L., Leng, G., Logan, S., Marteau, T., Michie, S., Rogers, H., Rycroft-Malone, J., and Sibbald, B. (2009). An implementation research agenda. *Implementation Science*, 4(18): 1–7.

Edmondson, A. C., Bohmer, R. M., and Pisano, G. P. (2001). Disrupted routines: Team learning and new technology implementation in hospitals. *Administrative Science Quarterly*, 46(4): 685–716.

Egan, T. and Jaye, C. (2009). Communities of clinical practice: The social organization of clinical learning. *Health*, 13(1): 107–125.

Elkjaer, B. (1999). In search of a social learning theory. In *Organizational learning and the learning organisation*, ed. Easterby-Smith, M., Burgoyne, J., and Araujo, L., pp. 75–91. London: Sage.

Ferlie, E., Crilly, T., Jashapara, A., and Peckham, A. (2012). Knowledge mobilisation in health care: A critical review of health sector and generic management literature. *Social Science & Medicine*, 74(8): 1297–1304.

Ferlie, E., Fitzgerald, L., Wood, M., and Hawkins, C. (2005). The nonspread of innovations: The mediating role of professionals. *Academy of Management Journal*, 48(1): 117–134.

Francis, R. (2013). *Report of the Mid Staffordshire NHS Foundation Trust public inquiry: executive summary*, Vol. 947. London: HMSO.

Friberger, M. and Falkman, G. (2013). Collaboration processes, outcomes, challenges and enablers of distributed clinical communities of practice. *Behaviour & Information Technology*, 32(6): 519–531.

Fung-Kee-Fung, M., Goubanova, E., Sequeira, K., Abdulla, A., Cook, R., Crossley, C., Langer, B., Smith, A., and Stern, H. (2008). Development of communities of practice to facilitate quality improvement initiatives in surgical oncology. *Quality Management in Healthcare*, 17(2): 174–185.

Fung-Kee-Fung, M., Watters, J., Crossley, C., Goubanova, E., Abdulla, A., Stern, H., Oliver, T. (2009). Regional collaborations as a tool for quality improvements in surgery: A systematic review of the literature. *Annals of Surgery*, 249(4): 565–572.

Fung-Kee-Fung, M., Boushey, R. P., Watters, J., Morash, R., Smylie, J., Morash, C., DeGrasse, C., and Sundaresan, S. (2014). Piloting a regional collaborative in cancer surgery using a "community of practice" model. *Current Oncology*, 21(1): 27–33.

Gabbay, J. and le May, A. (2004). Evidence based guidelines or collectively constructed "mindlines?" Ethnographic study of knowledge management in primary care. *BMJ*, 329(7473): 1013.

Gabbay, J. and le May, A. (2009). Practice made perfect: Discovering the roles of a community of general practice. In *Communities of practice in health and social care*, ed. le May, A., pp. 49–65. Oxford: Blackwell Publishing.

Gherardi, S., Nicolini, D., and Odella, F. (1998). Toward a social understanding of how people learn in organizations: The notion of situated curriculum. *Management Learning*, 29(3): 273–297.

Haidet, P. (2007). Jazz and the "art" of medicine: Improvisation in the medical encounter. *Annals of Family Medicine*, 5 (2): 164–169.

Ho, K., Jarvis-Selinger, S., Norman, C. D., Li, L. C., Olatunbosun, T., Cressman, C., and Nguyen, A. (2010). Electronic communities of practice: Guidelines from a project. *Journal of Continuing Education in the Health Professions*, 30(2): 139–143.

Jenkins, M. and Brotherton, C. (1995) In search of a theoretical framework for practice, part 2. *British Journal of Occupational Therapy*, 58(8): 332–336.

Jevack, J. M., Tusaie, K. R., Jones, J. S., Purcell, P. J., and Huff, M. S. (2014). Integrating a Virtual Community of Practice (VCoP) into graduate psychiatric nursing curriculum. *Journal of Nursing Education and Practice*, 4(9): 100–110.

Jiwa, M., Deas, K., Ross, J., Shaw, T., Wilcox, H., and Spilsbury, K. (2009). An inclusive approach to raising standards in general practice: Working with a "community of practice" in Western Australia. *BMC Medical Research Methodology*, 9(1): 1–13.

Kislov, R., Harvey, G., and Walshe, K. (2011). Collaborations for Leadership in Applied Health Research and Care: Lessons from the theory of communities of practice. *Implementation Science*, 6(1): 64–74.

Knight, L. V. and Mattick, K. (2006). "When I first came here, I thought medicine was black and white": Making sense of medical students' ways of knowing. *Social Science & Medicine*, 63(4): 1084–1096.

Kohn, L. T., Corrigan, J. M., and Donaldson, M. S. (2000). *To err is human: Building a safer health system*. Washington, D. C.:National Academies Press.

Konrad, S. C. and Browning, D. M. (2012). Relational learning and interprofessional practice: Transforming health education for the 21st century. *Work: A Journal of Prevention, Assessment and Rehabilitation*, 41(3): 247–251.

Lathlean, J. and le May, A. (2002). Communities of practice: An opportunity for interagency working. *Journal of Clinical Nursing*, 11(3): 394–398.

Lathlean, J. and Myall, M. (2009). Developing dermatology outpatient services through a community of practice. In *Communities of practice in health and social care*, ed. le May, A., pp. 36–47. Oxford: Blackwell Publishing.

Lave, J. and Wenger, E. (1991). *Situated learning: Legitimate peripheral participation*. Cambridge: Cambridge University Press.

le May, A. (2009). Introducing communities of practice. In *Communities of practice in health and social care*, ed. le May, A. Oxford: Blackwell Publishing.

Levitt-Jones, T., Lathlean, J., Higgins, I., and McMillan, M. (2008). Staff–student relationships and their impact on nursing students' belongingness and learning. *Journal of Advanced Nursing*, 65: 316–324.

Li, L. C., Grimshaw, J. M., Nielsen, C., Judd, M., Coyte, P. C., and Graham, I. D. (2009a). Use of communities of practice in business and health care sectors: A systematic review. *Implementation Science*, 4(27): 16.

Li, L. C., Grimshaw, J. M., Nielsen, C., Judd, M., Coyte, P. C., and Graham, I. D. (2009b). Evolution of Wenger's concept of community of practice. *Implementation Science*, 4(1): 11.

Lindsay, L. N. (2000). Transformation of learners in a community of practice occupational therapy fieldwork environment. Doctoral dissertation, University of Georgia.

Löfmark, A. and Wikblad, K. (2001). Facilitating and obstructing factors for development of learning in clinical practice: a student perspective. *Journal of Advanced Nursing*, 34(1): 43–50.

Lomas, J. (2007). The in-between world of knowledge brokering. *British Medical Journal*, 334(7585): 129–132.

McDermott, R. (1999). Why information technology inspired but cannot deliver knowledge management. *California Management Review*, 41: 103–115.

McDermott, R. and Archibald, D. (2010). Harnessing your staff's informal networks. *Harvard Business Review*, 88(3): 82–89.

McKenna, L. G. and Green, C. (2004). Experiences and learning during a graduate nurse program: An examination using a focus group approach. *Nurse Education in Practice*, 4(4): 258–263.

Mayrhofer, A., Goodman, C., and Holman, C. (2014). Establishing a community of practice for dementia champions (innovative practice). *Dementia*, 14(2): 259–266.

Meagher-Stewart, D., Solberg, S. M., Warner, G., MacDonald, J. A., McPherson, C., and Seaman, P. (2012). Understanding the role of communities of practice in evidence-informed decision making in public health. *Qualitative Health Research*, 22(6): 723–739.

Mendizabal, G. A., Nuño-Solinís, R., and González, I. Z. (2013). HOBE+, A case study: A virtual community of practice to support innovation in primary care in Basque Public Health Service. *BMC Family Practice*, 14(1): 168.

Mitton, C., Adair, C. E., McKenzie, E., Patten, S. B., and Perry, B. W. (2007). Knowledge transfer and exchange: Review and synthesis of the literature. *Milbank Quarterly*, 85(4): 729–768.

Myall, M., Levett-Jones, T., and Lathlean, J. (2008). Mentorship in contemporary practice: The experiences of nursing students and practice mentors. *Journal of Clinical Nursing*, 17(14): 1834–1842.

Nembhard, I. M. (2009). Learning and improving in quality improvement collaboratives: Which collaborative features do participants value most? *Health Services Research*, 44(2p1): 359–378.

Nicolini, D., Powell, J., Conville, P., and Martinez-Solano, L. (2008). Managing knowledge in the health care sector: A review. *International Journal of Management Reviews*, 10(3): 245–263.

Nolan, C. A. (1998). Learning on clinical placement: The experience of six Australian student nurses. *Nurse Education Today*, 18(8): 622–629.

Nurani, Z., Suter, E., Bainbridge, L., Harrison, L., Grymonpre, R., and Achilles, S. (2012). Engaging people and strengthening partnerships through an eCoP: The Western Canadian Interprofessional Health Collaborative experience. In *Technology enabled knowledge translation for ehealth*, ed. Ho, K., Jarvis-Selinger, S., Novak Lauscher, H., Cordeiro, J., and Scott, R., pp. 133–152. New York: Springer.

Oborn, E., Barrett, M., and Racko, G. (2012). Knowledge translation in health care: Incorporating theories of learning and knowledge from the management literature. *Journal of Health Organization and Management*, 27(4): 412–431.

Oborn, E. and Dawson, S. (2010). Knowledge and practice in multidisciplinary teams: Struggle, accommodation and privilege. *Human Relations*, 63(12): 1835–1857.

O'Leary, K. J., Ritter, C. D., Wheeler, H., Szekendi, M. K., Brinton, T. S., and Williams, M. V. (2010). Teamwork on inpatient medical units: Assessing attitudes and barriers. *Quality and Safety in Health Care*, 19(2): 117–121.

Papastavrou, E., Lambrinou, E., Tsangari, H., Saarikoski, M., and Leino-Kilpi, H. (2010). Student nurses experience of learning in the clinical environment. *Nurse Education in Practice*, 10: 176–182.

Parboosingh, J. T. (2002). Physician communities of practice: Where learning and practice are inseparable. *Journal of Continuing Education in the Health Professions*, 22(4): 230–236.

Ranmuthugala, G., Plumb, J. J., Cunningham, F. C., Georgiou, A., Westbrook, J. I., and Braithwaite, J. (2011). How and why are communities of practice established in the health care sector? A systematic review of the literature. *BMC Health Services Research*, 11(1): 273.

Rolls, K., Kowal, D., Elliott, D., and Burrell, A. R. (2008). Building a statewide knowledge network for clinicians in intensive care units: Knowledge brokering and the NSW Intensive Care Coordination and Monitoring Unit (ICCMU). *Australian Critical Care*, 21(1): 29–37.

Rowley, E., Morris, R., Currie, G., and Schneider, J. (2012). Research into practice: Collaboration for leadership in applied health research and care (CLAHRC). *Implementation Science*, 7(1): 40.

Russell, J., Greenhalgh, T., Boynton, P., and Rigby, M. (2004). Soft networks for bridging the gap between research and practice: Illuminative evaluation of CHAIN. *BMJ*, 328(7449): 1174.

Sawchenko, L. (2009). The interior health nurse practitioner community of practice: Facilitating NP integration in a regional health authority. In *Communities of practice in health and social care*, ed. A. le May, pp. 28–35. Oxford: Basil Blackwell

Seibert, S. The meaning of a healthcare community of practice. *Nursing Forum*, 50(2): 69–74.

Sharma, S., Smith, A., Rooksby, J., and Gerry, B. (2006). Involving users in the design of a system for sharing lessons from adverse incidents in anaesthesia. *Anaesthesia*, 61: 350–354.

Sirota, T. (2007). Nurse/physician relationships: Improving or not? *Nursing*, 37(1): 52–56.

Soubhi, H., Bayliss, E. A., Fortin, M., Hudon, C., van den Akker, M., Thivierge, R., and Fleiszer, D. (2010). Learning and caring in communities of practice: Using relationships and collective learning to improve primary care for patients with multimorbidity. *The Annals of Family Medicine*, 8(2): 170–177.

Spouse, J. (1998). Learning to nurse through legitimate peripheral participation. *Nurse Education Today*, 18(5): 345–351.

Swan, J., Scarbrough, H., and Robertson, M. (2002). The construction of "communities of practice" in the management of innovation. *Management Learning*, 33(4): 477–496.

Swift, L. (2014). Online communities of practice and their role in educational development: A systematic appraisal. *Community Practitioner*, 87(4): 28–31.

Tagliaventi, M. R. and Mattarelli, E. (2006). The role of networks of practice, value sharing, and operational proximity in knowledge flows between professional groups. Human Relations, 59(3): 291–319.

Thomson, L., Schneider, J., and Wright, N. (2013). Developing communities of practice to support the implementation of research into clinical practice. *Leadership in Health Services*, 26(1): 20–33.

Towle, A. and Godolphin, W. (2011). A meeting of experts: The emerging roles of non-professionals in the education of health professionals. *Teaching in Higher Education*, 16(5): 495–504.

Waring, J., Currie, G., Crompton, A., and Bishop, S. (2013). An exploratory study of knowledge brokering in hospital settings: Facilitating knowledge sharing and learning for patient safety? *Social Science & Medicine*, 98: 79–86.

Warne, T., Johansson, U-B., Papastavrou, E., Tichelaar, E., Tomietto, M., Van den Bossche, K., Moreno, M., and Saarikoski, M. (2010). An exploration of the clinical learning experience of nursing students in nine European countries. *Nurse Education Today*, 30: 809–815.

Warne, T., and McAndrew, S. (2008). Painting the landscape of emotionality: Colouring in the emotional gaps between the theory and practice of mental health nursing. *International Journal of Mental Health Nursing*, 17(2): 108–115.

Wenger, E. (1998). *Communities of practice: Learning, meaning, and identity*. Cambridge: Cambridge University Press.

Wenger, E. (2004). Knowledge management as a doughnut: Shaping your knowledge strategy through communities of practice. *Ivey Business Journal*, 68: 1–8.

Wenger, E., McDermott, R. A., and Snyder, W. (2002). *Cultivating communities of practice: A guide to managing knowledge*. Cambridge, MA: Harvard Business Press.

Wenger, E. C. and Snyder, W. M. (2000). Communities of practice: The organizational frontier. *Harvard Business Review*, 78(1): 139–146.

Wenger, E., Trayner, B., and de Laat, M. (2011). Promoting and assessing value creation in communities and networks: A conceptual framework. *Rapport 18*, Open University of the Netherlands.

CHAPTER 12

....

MOBILIZING KNOWLEDGE IN HEALTH CARE

....

HUW DAVIES, ALISON POWELL, AND
SANDRA NUTLEY

INTRODUCTION

....

KNOWLEDGE of all kinds underpins the work of health care organizations, and the past 50 years or so have seen substantial increases in the creation, collation, and communication of diverse kinds of knowledge. In particular from the 1990s there has been a wide range of initiatives aimed at creating robust knowledge (often referred to as "evidence") and making sure that such knowledge is applied to best effect. In the UK recent initiatives have included the development of the Collaborations for Leadership in Applied Health Research and Care (CLAHRCs) and the Academic Health Science Networks (AHSNs), both of which aim to bring together health service and research organizations to increase the application of research in the provision of health services. Similar initiatives have been developed by organizations like the Canadian Institutes of Health Research, the Canadian Foundation for Healthcare Improvement, the Institute for Healthcare Improvement in the US, and the Sax Institute and the National Health and Medical Research Council in Australia. In parallel there has been growing interest in the potential for evidence-informed policy in health care, fueled both by the growth of evidence-based medicine and by wider public sector trends towards forging closer links between research and policy.

Knowledge is needed to underpin health care policy, to help shape organizational design and management, and to inform the day-to-day practices of health care practitioners. Of particular interest is the knowledge that comes from careful and replicable study, that is from research. However, research-based knowledge does not sit in isolation, but rather sits alongside other forms of knowledge, such as that derived from experience (sometimes called experiential knowledge, including aspects of tacit knowledge) and that derived from values (i.e., preferences and ideologies).

In this chapter we explore the nature, use, and flow of knowledge in health care organizations, focusing especially on the role of *research-based knowledge* and its interactions with other forms of knowing. Central to our concerns is the observation that knowledge "flows" are often slow, intermittent, and uncertain, and that active strategies to "mobilize knowledge" are needed if the latent power of research-based knowledge to inform services is to be realized. At this point we should acknowledge that there is a bewildering array of terminology in the field around "knowledge." Differences in terminology reflect widely differing assumptions and presumptions about the world, how it operates, and how (or indeed, whether) knowledge can be managed. For example, "dissemination," "research into practice," and "knowledge transfer" tend to be terms that reflect a more linear uni-directional conceptualization of knowledge use, whereas terms such as "knowledge translation," "knowledge-to-action," and "knowledge exchange" embody greater acknowledgment of non-linearity, multi-way knowledge interaction, and system complexity (these issues are unpacked in greater depth subsequently). For our purposes here we use the umbrella terms "knowledge mobilization" and "mobilizing knowledge" to cover any activities aimed at collating and communicating research-based knowledge within the health care system.

We begin by discussing the nature of knowledge, before exploring what it means to use research-based knowledge in health care policy and management. We then examine some of the models, theories, and frameworks that have been used as both descriptions and prescriptions for understanding knowledge in policy and organizations, showing the evolution of thinking from "rational, linear models" to ideas of knowledge being embedded in "complex adaptive systems." The second half of the chapter then explores the audiences and actors involved in knowledge mobilization, and assesses the nature of the supporting practices needed. Our focus here is more on how research-based knowledge informs health care policy and management, and on the organizational and managerial supporting arrangements for evidence-based (or evidence-informed) practice, than on the details of professional practice change per se. A strong emerging theme here is the need to have a clear sense of the context in which knowledge dynamics are playing out.

WHAT IS KNOWLEDGE?

There is no simple or singular definition of knowledge (Contandriopoulos et al., 2010). Even when the focus is on research-based knowledge, there is considerable complexity and nuance as to the nature of that knowledge. Different terminology around knowledge mobilization, and different models of the processes by which knowledge is created, flows, and influences (see later), make different assumptions about the nature of knowledge. The underpinning paradigms that lie behind these models embody different assumptions about both the nature of the reality being explored (the ontology) and how one might come to know that reality (the epistemology). For example, positivism assumes that knowledge can be uncovered and expressed in generalizable laws, constructivism holds that knowledge is socially constructed and that there are multiple truths, and critical theory analyzes the relationship between knowledge and power.

Such distinctions are often applied to the underpinning research whose findings are being mobilized. Yet these distinctions apply equally to the preconceptions about the organizational world within which such findings are intended to have effect. In other words, models of the knowledge mobilization process have paradigmatic assumptions (about, for example, the nature of organizational reality) as much as the research being mobilized does.

Varying types of knowledge have been identified in the literature, and these can be brought together and categorized in different ways. For example, types of knowledge can be grouped according to the source: does the knowledge arise from structured data gathering (empirical knowledge), from practical experience (experiential knowledge), or from abstract discourse and debate (theoretical knowledge)? Another grouping in the knowledge mobilization literature contrasts explicit knowledge (such as that which can be set down in declarative statements and embodied in instructional guidelines) and the less-codifiable "tacit" knowledge held by individuals and groups (Denis and Lehoux, 2013). Both types of knowledge may be used to inform decisions in policy, management, and practice settings but tacit knowledge may not be susceptible to clear definition and explicit description. Amalgamations of explicit and tacit knowledge in clinical contexts have been referred to as "mindlines" (Gabbay and le May, 2011).

Going further, one theory of knowledge creation (Nonaka, 1994) holds that there is a close relationship between tacit and explicit knowledge. It suggests that new knowledge is created most rapidly when conversion between different forms of knowledge occur continually (e.g., from tacit to explicit and from explicit to tacit). A related categorization, drawing on work by Aristotle, distinguishes between episteme (scientific knowledge), techne (craft knowledge), and phronesis (situation-specific practical wisdom and the ability to apply generic knowledge to the current case) (Greenhalgh and Wieringa, 2011). These differentiations of different types of knowledge highlight the complexity of the relationships between research findings and the knowledge needed to accomplish effective actions in health care.

Research-Based Knowledge

There are also many methodological categorizations of research-based knowledge (Nutley, Powell, and Davies, 2013). This is not just a distinction between quantitative and qualitative findings; there are also a variety of more-or-less hierarchical distinctions, often with implicit or explicit endorsements as to their validity (Bagshaw and Bellomo, 2008; Petticrew and Roberts, 2003). A further stream of literature distinguishes between knowledge as data and knowledge as ideas, asserting that data, information, and knowledge lie on a continuum and differ in the extent to which human processing and judgment are needed (Greenhalgh, 2010). Such literature also considers the extent to which knowledge has been processed, synthesized, "recycled," re-interpreted, or adapted and whether the knowledge is specific to a particular issue and context, or whether it is more general. Similar notions underpin the "knowledge to action" framework (Graham et al., 2006). Here, knowledge creation is composed of three phases, each involving a greater degree of processing: knowledge enquiry (first generation knowledge), knowledge synthesis (second generation knowledge), and the creation of knowledge tools such as practice guidelines and algorithms (third generation knowledge).

Knowledge or Knowing?

But should we even be talking of research-based knowledge as a separate isolatable "thing"? If knowledge is seen as socially embedded, then separating "it" from its context begins to look problematic. Perhaps, instead, we need to think more of knowledge-in-context—or "knowledge-in-practice-in-context," as Gabbay and le May describe "mindlines" (Gabbay and le May, 2011). Such considerations lead to a series of challenging questions about research knowledge, such as: who is (or should be) involved in setting the research agenda and in deciding what issues warrant the production or collation of research-based knowledge? Who is involved in producing that knowledge and what are the power dynamics around what is defined as knowledge (Fazekas and Burns, 2012; Oborn, 2012)? Is knowledge produced "elsewhere" by research specialists? Or is knowledge co-produced in situ by potential research users and researchers working collaboratively, and what are the benefits and disadvantages of this? Who defines who are the relevant stakeholders and by what processes are they involved? Many of these issues link to the discussions explored later in this chapter about the actors, audiences, and activities around mobilizing knowledge.

An Ecology of Knowledge

Several authors (Contandriopoulos et al., 2010; Gabbay and le May, 2004, 2011; Oborn, Barrett, and Racko, 2013) argue strongly from empirical study that research-based knowledge does not occupy a privileged position. Instead it sits alongside and competes with other forms of existing, structured, and contextualized knowledge (e.g., professional knowledge and professional judgment). It follows then that there is not a direct correlation between attributes of the knowledge (e.g., the internal validity of the research-based knowledge) and the likelihood of subsequent use (Contandriopoulos et al., 2010). For example, professional consensus-based guidelines may be valued more than research-based guidelines despite having a weaker evidence base. There is thus an ecology of knowledge, where research-based knowledge must compete with other ways of knowing for influence.

Implications for Knowledge Mobilization

Taken together then, these observations have a number of implications for knowledge mobilization. First they suggest that knowledge mobilization practices need to consist of mixed portfolios of activities that are heavily shaped by the types of knowledge under consideration. Second, the concern that actionable messages for decision-makers may more properly be seen to come from syntheses and systematic reviews rather than from single studies (Lavis et al., 2003; Wilson et al., 2010) would suggest that research and health care organizations should focus their mobilization efforts more on *bodies* of research-based knowledge than on the promulgation of individual pieces of work. Third, knowledge mobilization activities may need to differentiate more clearly between information (data) and knowledge (Holmes, Scarrow, and Schellenberg, 2012); these may require different kinds of interaction between researchers and users and hence different kinds of knowledge translation training and support. Fourth, knowledge mobilization leaders may need to consider how they can support the interaction and integration of different types of knowledge, including perhaps deliberative processes that seek to surface hidden assumptions and tacit knowledge.

Finally, although there may be no absolute correlation between the attributes of research-based knowledge and its subsequent use (as it competes with other forms of knowing in the local context), it is still important to consider the attributes of research that help to make it more conducive to uptake: for example, if the research-based knowledge is perceived by the potential users to be credible, accessible, relevant, based on strong evidence, legitimate, and endorsed by respected opinion leaders (Walter, Nutley, and Davies, 2005). Tailoring the format and presentation method of knowledge products to the intended users can also make the knowledge that they contain more accessible (Cordingley, 2008; Pentland et al., 2011).

WHAT IS KNOWLEDGE USE?

As well as there being no singular definition of knowledge in the literature (as discussed above) there are also multiple competing definitions of knowledge *use* in that literature, with no one definition dominating (Contandriopoulos et al., 2010).

Basic Types of Knowledge Use

Given our central concern with the use of research-based knowledge, it is appropriate to start with a common and recurring typology (Estabrooks et al., 2011; Lavis et al., 2003; Sudsawad, 2007) that suggests that there are three main types of research use: instrumental, conceptual, and symbolic:

- **Instrumental/direct use:** applying research findings in specific and direct ways to influence decision choices.
- **Conceptual/indirect use:** using research results for changing understanding or attitudes, including introducing new conceptual categories, terminology, or theories.
- **Symbolic/political/persuasive use:** using research findings to legitimize and maintain predetermined positions, including the "tactical use" of research, for example justifying inaction while awaiting further study.

These different types of use may be affected by many different factors. For example, direct use is associated with well-defined decision-taking; conceptual use may be longer-term and more percolative, and only readily discernible in retrospect; and symbolic use may be closely associated with political argument and the use of mass media. It is likely, however, that all three will be seen simultaneously (although perhaps differently weighted) in some settings and for some issues. The categorizations above are related to, and have some overlap with, the influential typology produced earlier by Weiss (Weiss, 1979) which maps the ways that research-based knowledge may be used into seven different categories:

1. **Knowledge-driven:** where research produces knowledge that might be relevant to public policy decisions. This is closely aligned with the direct and instrumental use noted above (and is central to strategies of research "push") but can also encompass more conceptual uses of research where the knowledge shared is more theoretical or conceptual in nature.
2. **Problem-solving:** where research is sought out that can provide empirical evidence to help solve contemporary policy problems. This again is most often associated with an instrumental approach (and with notions of research "pull"), but can also encompass some conceptual rethinking.
3. **Interactive:** where those engaged in policy, management, or practice seek information from a variety of sources to help make sense of their problems and develop solutions. This is associated with "linkage and exchange" approaches to knowledge mobilization (Lomas, 2000) and may encompass both direct and indirect uses of research.
4. **Political/symbolic:** policy makers and other high-status actors search for knowledge to help justify their positions, so research-based information becomes

ammunition for whichever side finds it most useful. Intermediary agencies with well-defined value sets may seek to exploit such opportunities.

5. **Tactical:** where those who could be (and perhaps should be) research-users fund or require new research to avoid taking action. Funders and research producers may each see opportunities here for longer-term gains in research-based knowledge.

6. **Enlightenment:** where research has gradual influence over time in shaping conceptualizations of the issues and framings of the policy agenda. Recognition of these slower percolative processes may lead agencies into planning for the longer term by focusing on social processes.

7. **Societal:** where policy interest, public concern, and professional interests are meshed and stimulated by new research findings. Such a broader view enlarges the scope of organizations and agencies to encompass much broader sets of stakeholders.

Knowledge use categorizations, like those above, can further be teased out by additional analysis *within* each category. For example, instrumental use may be concerned with decisions that impact on professional processes, individual patient outcomes or aggregate economic outcomes (Scott et al., 2012) and each of these can become targets or goals of knowledge mobilization activities. An alternative view (Lavis et al., 2003) might look for impacts on knowledge-use processes (such as knowledge being seen, discussed, and cited), intermediate outcomes (such as key actors' awareness and attitudes) and decision outcomes (evidence-supported change). Combinations and hybrids of these typologies of use and impact are of course possible, and a consideration of these may help to sharpen the strategic focus of knowledge mobilization.

The "Politics" of Research-Based Knowledge Use

Some commentators have sought to expose and critique the limited way in which the use of research-based knowledge is traditionally defined. Drawing on Habermas' framework of "knowledge-constitutive interests," Murphy and Fafard (2012) define three types of knowledge use: instrumental (i.e., problem-solving), hermeneutic (i.e., explanatory) and emancipatory (i.e., equity-seeking). The authors suggest that most conventional knowledge mobilization approaches focus on instrumental problem-solving and argue that social research has, or should have, other goals that are aimed at hermeneutic and emancipatory objectives. Such a reading brings to the fore political considerations as to whether knowledge mobilization strategies seek to work with the grain of existing policy and practice presumptions, or to challenge these from a values-based position (Brown, 2013; Nutley, Walter, and Davies, 2007; Weiss, 1995).

Implications for Knowledge Mobilization in Health Care

So, for health care managers developing knowledge mobilization work, it may be important to consider the types of "use" they are aiming to influence and to what end. The centrality or otherwise of research is a key consideration for knowledge mobilization strategies. That is, do we wish to see evidence-*based* actions, evidence-*informed* actions, or just activities that are evidence-*congruent* or simply evidence-*aware*?

MODELING KNOWLEDGE FLOWS WITHIN AND BETWEEN ORGANIZATIONS

Mobilizing knowledge is about making connections. Much of the literature on knowledge mobilization discusses the complex institutional, professional, and social environments within which knowledge is created and flows (or, more often, gets stuck). While some of these discussions lay heavy emphasis on "context" as a mediator (which we cover later) there is also more specific consideration of the role of specific networks of interests or the practical configurations of research and brokering agencies and health care organizations, and the relationships that they create.

A framework that is increasingly well known (and resonant with other framings) is the "three generations" framework (Best and Holmes, 2010). This proposes that there have been three stages or generations of thinking about knowledge to action processes: linear approaches, relationship approaches, and systems approaches. The authors set out the characteristics of each of these approaches and suggest conditions under which such approaches might be more or less appropriate (see subsections following). While these approaches are often linked to historical developments, with ideas of progression of thinking from "simple" linear models to "complex" systems thinking, it may be more helpful to think of these as parallel models of the knowledge mobilization system with contingent application and different strengths and weaknesses.

Linear Conceptualizations of Research Flow

Linear models of connectivity have dominated the literature, and such thinking can be seen underpinning many of the models and frameworks in use (Walter et al., 2004; Brown, 2012). Sitting within the linear conception (and, to a lesser extent, within the relational view) is the "two communities" perspective: the idea that there are two separate social worlds of knowledge production and knowledge application, and that there is limited interconnectivity between these. However, more expansive views of knowledge (see earlier discussions on the nature of knowledge) contribute to a weakening (sometimes considerable) of such neat categorizations.

Despite being very widely used in health care and elsewhere (Best and Holmes, 2010; Brown, 2012), linear models have received significant critique: they tend to see "knowledge" as a transferable product; they place much emphasis on individuals and their rational cognitions; and they fail to address notions that knowledge is translated into practice in a social, collective, and situated manner (Nutley, Walter, and Davies, 2007; Oborn, Barrett, and Racko, 2013). An additional concern is that the evaluation research around knowledge mobilization has tended to evaluate linear approaches rather than more complex forms (Oborn, Barrett, and Racko, 2013), providing both symbolic and practical encouragement to organizations to continue to use these approaches.

Relational Considerations in Research Connectivity

A shift from linear approaches to more relational approaches has been observed in the health sector and generic management literatures after 2000 (Ferlie et al., 2012). One of the underlying premises of relationship models is that learning is a social and situated process. This means that knowledge mobilization is political: there is negotiation around competing meanings of "knowledge" and "evidence," and around issue-framing and problem definitions.

In relationship models, the emphasis is on "linkage and exchange" (Lomas, 2000), suggesting more engagement with potential users than is implied with "push" or "pull" approaches (Tetroe et al., 2008). The degree of engagement ranges from dialogue between researchers and practitioners through to collaborative engagement in producing research evidence (co-production) and in working together to implement evidence (e.g., in action research approaches or quality collaboratives) (Mitton et al, 2007; Pentland et al, 2011; Ovretveit et al, 2014). A recent study (Cooper, 2014), which may be the first to map the work of knowledge brokering organizations, found that the organizations carried out a wide range of brokering functions including building partnerships, raising awareness, capacity building, implementation support, and policy influence. Relationship approaches draw on a range of theories including principal-agent theory; communities of practice; social capital; organizational learning; socio-cultural learning; and resource-dependence (Honig and Venkateswaran, 2012). Key features of relationship approaches to knowledge mobilization are an emphasis on accountability, reciprocity, and respect for the other party's knowledge.

A common critique of relationship approaches (Oborn, Barrett, and Racko, 2013) is that many models and approaches fail to fully acknowledge the implications of conflict over what constitutes knowledge, and give insufficient attention to meaning/power negotiations. Indeed Ferlie et al. (2012) suggest that post-modern accounts that emphasise power are a further stage on from relational models. An additional concern is that the relationships that are possible will depend on the skill-sets and personalities of those involved; many researchers may feel most confident in talking about research findings to their academic peers rather than to policy or managerial actors. Such relationships are also affected by organizational turbulence: if there is high turnover in policy, management, practice, or academic settings, then it will be more difficult to develop ongoing relationships (Ettelt, Mays, and Nolte, 2013). Some of these issues reappear when we discuss the actors, audiences, and actions needed for effective knowledge mobilization.

Systems Thinking in Knowledge Mobilization

There is no consistent use of the term "systems thinking," encapsulated by Best et al. (2009) as an approach that "recognises that relationships are shaped, embedded and organized through structures that mediate the types of interactions that occur among multiple agents with unique rhythms and dynamics, worldviews, priorities and processes, language, time scales, means of communication and expectations" (628). There is however increasing support for the idea that health systems need to be seen as complex assemblages of interlocking networks that cannot be understood in terms of linear and "rational" relationships but are instead conditional, contextual, and relational (Riley, 2012). Reviews suggest that although the knowledge mobilization literature is now beginning to embrace systems thinking, practical tools and strategies have yet to emerge (Best et al., 2009; Riley, 2012). In addition, reviewers suggest that there are many key aspects of a systems approach to knowledge that have not yet had sufficient attention, including the nature of evidence and knowledge, the role of leadership, and the role of networks (Best and Holmes, 2010). Exploring this further, Contandriopoulos et al. (2010) suggest that there are three core aspects of systems that influence knowledge use within that system: polarization (the extent to which the potential users share similar opinions and preferences or are widely divergent in their views); cost-sharing (the distribution between research producers, intermediaries and users of the resource costs associated with knowledge use); and social structures (e.g., formal and informal communication networks).

The evolution of thinking around the connections and configurations that support knowledge mobilization has highlighted the limitations of "two communities" thinking, suggesting that standard "push" approaches are unlikely to result in practice or policy change. Knowledge mobilization strategies that take a relational view, and that work within and through existing networks, or that seek to build new networks, can draw on a wide array of concepts and theories to help shape their actions. In doing so, they will need a nuanced understanding of the role of power, and insights from political science may be of some help here. Although there is increasing support for a systems approach in principle, a lack of practical tools and detailed guidance means that it has been difficult to operationalize these ideas into innovative knowledge mobilization strategies (Best et al., 2009; Riley, 2012; Willis et al., 2012, 2014).

A Plethora of Models, Theories, and Frameworks

Beyond these broad categorizations of thinking articulated by Best and Holmes (2010) (i.e., linear, relational, and systems thinking) the literature documents a bewildering variety of detailed models, theories, and frameworks. The models have diverse underpinnings and assumptions, and draw on distinct disciplinary concepts from psychology, sociology, organization studies, implementation science, and political science. They vary in the extent to which they draw narrow or more inclusive boundaries around what counts as knowledge, and some differ in their primary areas of application (e.g., being either policy or practice focused, with few being expressly directed at service management knowledge).

Many of these models are primarily descriptive of the processes around knowledge creation/flow/application, and they tend not to be explicit about the necessary configurations, actions, or resources that will underpin successful knowledge mobilization. That is, they do not readily provide prescriptions for a coherent knowledge mobilization strategy or effective action (Pentland et al., 2011). In addition, with a few notable exceptions, the models have received only limited empirical testing. The models that have been tested empirically to some degree include the PARIHS framework (Kitson, Harvey, and McCormack, 1998); the Knowledge to Action framework (Graham et al., 2006); the Ottawa Model of Research Use (Logan and Graham, 1998); the Consolidated Framework for Implementation Research (Damschroder et al., 2009) and the conceptual framework of the knowledge transfer process developed by Ward, House, and Hamer (2009).

The empirical studies provide useful accounts of these models in use, demonstrate the range of available frameworks, and illustrate the challenges of operationalizing these frameworks into prescriptions for knowledge mobilization strategies. However, none of the models listed have been comprehensively evaluated, and the majority of the other models in the literature have been subject to even less empirical testing. Indeed, given their descriptive rather than prescriptive orientations, verification and validation may be more realistic prospects for the future than evaluative testing.

Implications for Knowledge Mobilization

The sheer range and diversity of models, theories, and frameworks available for understanding knowledge mobilization in health care presents significant challenges for managers and researchers in the field. Drawing insights from multiple models, and adapting models before application is likely to be key, as is recognizing the assumptions inherent in different models about, for example, the nature of knowledge, or the nature of knowledge use.

AUDIENCES, ACTORS, AND ACTIONS FOR EFFECTIVE KNOWLEDGE MOBILIZATION

Audiences and Actors

The potential "audiences" for research-based knowledge fall into diverse categories (Lavis et al., 2003), including other researchers, members of the public and service users, professional practitioners, health service managers, and policy makers. Clearly none of these are discrete categories (Contandriopoulos et al., 2010), and individuals may belong to more than one group. Multiple identities and group memberships may constrain or facilitate actions around knowledge mobilization.

There has been relatively little empirical work on the actual or potential roles and responsibilities of different knowledge mobilization actors (Tetroe et al., 2008), but Lavis et al. (2003) suggest two key questions in defining a narrower group of stakeholders in a given situation: firstly, who can act on the basis of the research knowledge, and secondly, who can influence those who can act? These questions helpfully give prominence to the issue of power, which many authors (Ferlie et al., 2012; Oborn, Barrett, and Racko, 2013) suggest has been neglected in relation to understanding of knowledge mobilization.

Despite the general lack of attention paid to the role of different players in knowledge mobilization, there is a strong focus in the literature on "knowledge brokers" and other "mediator" roles. Indeed, a growing number of empirical studies (Cameron et al., 2011; Chew, Armstrong, and Martin, 2013; Cooper, 2010; Lightowler and Knight, 2013; Meagher, 2013) have investigated these roles. A range of functions have been suggested including: problem definition; research synthesis; facilitating access to research knowledge; developing outputs that are more accessible to users; and developing and brokering networks and other connections (Phipps and Morton, 2013; Sebba, 2013). Linking and mediator roles have been promoted in many organizational settings and are perceived by health organizations to be an important component of the organizational infrastructure to encourage evidence use (Ellen et al., 2013). However, one review (Contandriopoulos et al., 2010) suggests that the structural position of brokers within organizations may mean that they have most scope to intervene in contexts where there is low polarization of views (i.e., where actors already share similar views on key issues) and significant user investment in knowledge exchange, and that they may have limited ability to have an impact on the many existing networks that exist outside formal communication channels.

Conceptual uncertainty remains around who should perform knowledge broking and what activities should be encompassed by the role (Levin and Cooper, 2012; Sebba, 2013). For example, it is unclear whether and in what ways knowledge broker roles are different from other roles like opinion leaders, facilitators, champions, change agents, or linking agents (Thompson, Estabrooks, and Degner, 2006). Leadership (including endorsement of the evidence from expert and peer opinion leaders) is regarded in the literature as important in knowledge mobilization (Walter, Nutley, and Davies, 2005) but the requirements of roles here also remain under-specified. Although leadership has been addressed in other literatures, the precise nature of leadership and its defining qualities have not yet been fully addressed in the knowledge mobilization literature (Best and Holmes, 2010).

One final group that has largely been absent from the literature (and practice) of knowledge mobilization is the public or service users. While patient and public involvement has been strongly encouraged in research and service (re-) design, the literature has been largely silent on the potential knowledge mobilization role of these groups. One exception here is more recent work that has considered the evidence base on patient-direct and patient-mediated knowledge mobilization interventions (Grimshaw et al., 2012; Stacey and Hill, 2013). The challenges and opportunities of greater involvement of patients and the public are underexplored and, perhaps, underexploited.

While roles matter, some authors argue that there has been disproportionate emphasis on individuals and their roles in relation to knowledge mobilization. They argue that sustainable knowledge mobilization requires multi-level systemic changes (Holmes et al., 2012) alongside appropriate technological and organizational infrastructures (Grimshaw et al., 2012) and that greater attention needs to be paid to the organizational systems in which individuals work and which strongly affect what they are able to do (Levin, 2011). Such critiques draw attention to broader concerns about organizational design, control, and development, so that knowledge mobilization is seen in a more integrated way as part of broader organizational dynamics, rather than something separate to be "grafted on."

From Roles to Actions

To further their goals, knowledge mobilization strategies need not only to identify audiences and clarify roles, but they need also to develop action plans and commit resources. The actions taken will depend on the underlying model of knowledge mobilization being used (explicitly or implicitly), and the resource requirements differ for different models of knowledge mobilization. The wide variety of models discussed earlier have largely not yet been tested as prescriptions for practice, so it is not clear how suitable they are for planning and evaluating knowledge mobilization strategies (Ward, House, and Hamer, 2009). Many models provide a quite general overview of knowledge mobilization rather than analyzing the key features and intended effects of specific knowledge mobilization interventions (Boyko et al., 2012). They thus leave unaddressed the specific actions required and the resources needed. Indeed, many models seem more descriptive of how change occurs rather than directly addressing the planning of change initiatives (Graham, Tetroe, and the KT Theories Research Group, 2007).

Some sets of activities have been identified in the literature that might form the first step in operationalizing a knowledge mobilization strategy. For example, Walter, Nutley, and Davies (2003) highlight the key underlying mechanisms that can be used to build research impact, including: dissemination; interaction; social influence; facilitation; incentives; and reinforcements. A major review in 2012 (Powell et al., 2012) collated 68 specific implementation actions for knowledge mobilization, grouped according to six key implementation processes: planning; educating; financing; restructuring; managing quality; and attending to the policy context. In practice, many strategies will involve a judicious mix of these, and selecting the appropriate mix and emphases remains to be addressed.

Taking a holistic view of encouraging research use, one review in social care (Walter et al., 2004) sets out a collection of imperatives, each of which might suggest collections of (resourced) activities that need to be planned. These include: ensuring a relevant research base; ensuring access to research; making research comprehensible; drawing out the practice implications of research; developing best practice models (e.g., pilot or demonstration projects); requiring research-informed practice (e.g., through regulatory influence); and developing a culture that supports research use. Again, these broad categorizations leave much detail that needs to be fleshed-out in specific local contexts.

All the above suggest that actions are required across a number of spheres. This draws attention to the potential for balanced and multifaceted activities in knowledge mobilization. While some reviews suggest that multifaceted approaches are more effective than single interventions (Boaz et al., 2011), some authors suggest that multifaceted approaches may not always be appropriate: there is a risk of a "scattergun" approach, and the effectiveness of multi-component approaches will depend on the interaction of the different mechanisms within particular contexts (Nutley, Walter, and Davies, 2009). One review of strategies used in public health (LaRocca et al., 2012) found that simple or single strategies were in some cases as effective as complex multi-component interventions, and suggested that this was because key messages might be diluted or harder to comprehend in complex multiple interventions. Multifaceted approaches are also likely to be more costly than single interventions and consideration needs to be given to how the different components might interact (Grimshaw et al., 2012).

Implications for Knowledge Mobilization

This account of the actions and resources needed for effective knowledge mobilization has many implications. It draws attention to the wide array of actions needed, the breadth and diversity of actions available, the complex and vexed issue of resourcing these, and the need for coherent, interlocking, and mutually reinforcing actions within and across agencies. It also draws attention to the significant gap between the articulation of a *process* of knowledge mobilization (seen in many of the models, theories, and frameworks) and the *translation* of those accounts into workable, practicable, properly-resourced *strategies* within specific organizational contexts. That is, much of the conceptual background reviewed in this chapter does not readily lend itself to the creation of action plans for health care managers or actors in other parts of the health care system. At the heart of these difficulties lies an uncertainty about whose role it is to facilitate knowledge mobilization, with particular tensions between those seeking to "push" knowledge and those seeking to support "pull." In some senses, effective knowledge mobilization is a *system property*, and yet individual actors and agencies have to operate independently and are uncertain in coordination. Creating the conditions for shared goals, co-investment, and coordinated actions remains a major challenge.

The Importance of Context

Scholars of knowledge mobilization are usually sensitive to the potentially facilitating or (more usually) inhibiting effects of the local environment on knowledge flows (Contandriopoulos et al., 2010). As Greenhalgh et al. (2004) assert: "the multiple (and often unpredictable) interactions that arise in particular contexts and settings are precisely what determine the success or failure of a dissemination initiative."

The "context is important" strand in the knowledge mobilization literature has a long history in organizational research (The Health Foundation, 2014). The processual-contextual perspective (e.g., the content, context, and process framework) (Pettigrew, 1985; Pettigrew, McKee, and Ferlie, 1988) has informed a number of studies in the change literature in recent decades (Armenakis and Bedeian, 1999). It is reflected in Pawson and Tilley's well-known "CMO" configuration in realist evaluation (context, mechanism and outcome) (Pawson and Tilley, 1997) and in the PARIHS framework (Promoting Action on Research Implementation in Health Services) (Kitson, Harvey, and McCormack, 1998), which was developed in part to address the lack of attention to context in earlier models (Estabrooks et al., 2006). The importance of context in quality improvement in health care and the key empirical findings from the literature have recently been explored in a publication for the Health Foundation (The Health Foundation, 2014).

In relation to influencing policy, a recent review (Moat, Lavis, and Abelson, 2013) also emphasizes the importance of an analysis of context and refers to two frameworks: the "3is" of political science (institutions, interests, ideas) and to the framework proposed by Contandriopoulos et al. (2010) which considers issues in terms of their polarization, salience, and familiarity. Similar frameworks are available when looking at the uptake of policy interventions. For example, the RE-AIM framework (Reach; Effectiveness; Adoption; Implementation; Maintenance) (Best and Holmes, 2010) emphasises that it is the broader contextual factors that influence adoption, implementation, and maintenance and so decision-makers need to balance evidence on effectiveness against these factors.

Internal and External Context

Analytic approaches to context typically divide it into inner/internal and outer/external, although many authors emphasize that the interactions between these add to the challenges of assessing and addressing context.

Among the aspects of *internal* context suggested as being relevant to knowledge mobilization are: organizational structures and processes (e.g., the impact of modes of governance on research use, conditions that affect the facilitation and prioritization of research activity including incentives and levers, the degree to which service user preferences are accurately known and prioritized); organizational cultures (e.g., the distribution of power between different groups, perspectives on whose responsibility it is to encourage evidence use, current norms and practices, the climate for innovation); and organizational facilities and resources (e.g., time, equipment).

In relation to *external* context, the knowledge mobilization literature emphasizes three key related aspects: the social and political climate/culture; the degree of environmental stability; and the extent of inter-organizational communication and norm-setting. Analyzing all of these (internal and external) components should be a precursor to the development of knowledge mobilizing strategies.

Barriers and Facilitators

There is broad agreement then (Dopson, 2006; Fixsen et al., 2005; Levin, 2011) that context is an important (if poorly understood) mediator. It is a feature of many models of barriers to knowledge uptake (Bhattacharyya, Reeves, and Zwarenstein, 2009) and analysis of context is one of the five common components shared by the majority of models of the knowledge mobilization process (Ward, House, and Hamer, 2009). Indeed, a large proportion of the knowledge mobilization literature is made up of analyses of "barriers and facilitators" (Mitton et al., 2007). For example, there is strong evidence for a wide range of generic barriers to effective research impact, including, for researchers, a lack of resources, a lack of skills, and an absence of professional reward for research impact activities and, for research users, competing organizational pressures, an organizational culture that does not value research, a preference for other sources of evidence, and a suspicion that research may displace professional skills and experience (Walter, Nutley, and Davies, 2003). In similar vein, the Cochrane Effective Practice and Organization of Care (EPOC) group classifies barriers to change into nine categories (information management, clinical uncertainty, sense of competence, perceptions of liability, patient expectations, standards of practice, financial disincentives, administrative constraints, and a miscellaneous category) (Grimshaw et al., 2012).

Although identifying and addressing key barriers is recommended in many knowledge mobilization models as an important consideration when choosing a strategy, many important barriers affecting knowledge use (e.g., difficulties arising from working in multi-professional teams) are long-standing and complex and are not actually easily addressed (Grimshaw et al., 2012). Moreover, this marked emphasis in the literature on understanding barriers and facilitators has been critiqued for leading to a narrow "technicist" understanding of knowledge mobilization rather than one that is attentive to knowledge mobilization as an interactive, social, and deeply situated process (Ward et al., 2012).

In contrast, the contextual approach taken by Ward et al. (2012) proposes that a detailed understanding of local interpersonal interactions, shared experiences, and networks may be particularly useful in considering how opportunities for knowledge mobilization emerge or are constrained within an organizational setting. Thus they see context as playing a dynamic and interactive role with local actions, not simply existing as a passive and inhibiting backdrop. This perspective emphasises the importance of assessing the existing "naturalistic" knowledge exchange processes that are already occurring (for example in relation to other innovations or change programmes), and building on these when planning formal knowledge mobilization interventions.

Multiple and Layered Contexts

It has also been noted that contexts are multiple rather than singular. Levin's model of knowledge mobilization (Levin, 2011) refers to three types of contexts for the use of research: the context in which it is produced; the context in which it is used; and all the mediating processes between these two contexts. Emphasis is thus placed on the multiple dynamics at play within each context. Other authors (e.g., Nicolini et al., 2008) emphasize the extent to which any one sector (e.g., health care) will have different sub-sectors within it (e.g., clinical research, health services research, health policy) that may require different approaches to knowledge mobilization. In that sense, contexts are not just multiple, parallel, and perhaps overlapping, but are also nested. Indeed, the "complex adaptive systems" perspective (Best and Holmes, 2010; Holmes et al., 2012; Willis et al., 2014) emphasizes how the different levels of the system affect each other: interventions at one level are affected by, and affect, factors at other system levels (Davies and Edwards, 2013).

There are differing views about the extent to which and how contextual factors can be managed or even influenced. Many authors (e.g., Greenhalgh et al., 2004) emphasize that while context is important, it is also unpredictable and not easily controlled. Knowledge mobilization activities are embedded within a system and changes will only be sustained if attention is paid to the factors that influence that system (Best et al., 2009). This rules out simple prescriptions for approaches which will apply in a range of contexts and points to the need to design, tailor, refine, and evaluate any knowledge mobilization approach with reference to the particular setting and alongside those who will be responsible for implementing the changes (Best et al., 2009; Greenhalgh et al., 2004). Advocates for an integrated knowledge mobilization research approach (i.e., collaboration between researchers and knowledge users) emphasize that research knowledge has to be integrated with contextual knowledge (e.g., population data, local expertise, knowledge of the characteristics of the local setting) and that this integration is more likely to happen if the potential users are involved in the research process from the outset (Bowen and Graham, 2013).

Implications for Knowledge Mobilization

For organizations seeking to develop knowledge mobilization strategies then, a thoroughgoing and realistic evaluation of context remains central. However, while "context" is a key heading in many models and frameworks of the knowledge mobilization process, it is variably conceptualized and differentially understood. Moreover, there is divergence of view as to whether context is a passive (usually inhibitory) backdrop or a potentially modifiable and co-optable "resource" for the knowledge mobilization effort. What is clear is that it is inadequate to treat context as merely a catch-all term for all that is not modeled: such an approach will disguise vital issues such as goal misalignment, power disparities, and political practices. As yet however, tools to assess and disentangle the role of context in knowledge mobilization are insufficiently developed.

CONCLUDING REMARKS

The rapid development of research-based knowledge relevant to health care provides a major opportunity for more informed policy, management, and professional practice in health care. Yet the challenges of mobilizing this knowledge in complex political and social systems mean that such potential has not yet been fully realized.

This review has drawn attention to the many ways in which knowledge has been conceptualized, the diversity of understandings as to what constitutes "research use," and the complexity of the organizational context within which evidence-informed change is being sought. The profusion of terminology around these issues (with often unclear and unstated assumptions), and the proliferation of theories and frameworks purporting to model knowledge flows, have contributed to a rich literature that either appropriately reflects the challenges of understanding this complex phenomenon or needlessly complicates matters (readers may form their own opinions here). Translating these models for practical application and evaluating their use in health care policy and practice is certainly needed. Further research is also needed on approaches for assessing research use and impact, on sustaining and scaling up knowledge mobilization activities, and on applying systems theory to knowledge mobilization.

What is clear is that considerations of knowledge mobilization cannot neatly be separated from the wider political concerns of health care policy or the challenges of organizational dynamics. Issues of leadership, organizational culture, performance assessment and management, professional identity, and role socialization all impinge on how knowledge is seen, interpreted, and communicated. In that sense, the separate development of the knowledge mobilization literature, while fruitful in some senses, gives rise to a need for more effective reintegration into the wider health care management literature. Situating this account of knowledge mobilization in this collection of wider scholarly contributions on health care policy and management is a part of that process. The knowledge mobilization in health care field would also benefit from drawing on the wider range of emerging literatures outside health care management (e.g., cognitive psychology, behavioral economics) that show potential to enrich our understanding of how individuals and groups create and use knowledge.

References

Armenakis, A. A. and Bedeian, A. G. (1999). Organizational change: A review of theory and research in the 1990s (Yearly Review of Management). *Journal of Management*, 25(3): 293–307.

Bagshaw, S. and Bellomo, R. (2008). The need to reform our assessment of evidence from clinical trials: A commentary. *Philosophy, Ethics and Humanities in Medicine*, 3: 23.

Best, A. and Holmes, B. (2010). Systems thinking, knowledge and action: Towards better models and methods. *Evidence & Policy*, 6(2): 145–159.

Best, A., Terpstra, J., Moor, G., Riley, B., Norman, C., and Glasgow, R. (2009). Building knowledge integration systems for evidence-informed decisions. *Journal of Health Organization and Management*, 23(6): 627–641.

Bhattacharyya, O., Reeves, S., and Zwarenstein, M. (2009). What is implementation research? Rationale, concepts and practices. *Research on Social Work Practice*, 19(5): 491–502.

Boaz, A., Baeza, J., Fraser, A., and the European Implementation Score Collaborative Group (EIS) (2011). Effective implementation of research into practice: An overview of systematic reviews of the health literature. *BMC Research Notes*, 4(212), doi:10.1186/1756-0500-4-212.

Bowen, S. and Graham, I. D. (2013). Integrated knowledge translation. In *Knowledge translation in health care: Moving from evidence to practice*, 2nd edition, ed. Straus, S. E., Tetroe, J., and Graham, I. D., pp. 14–23. Chichester: John Wiley.

Boyko, J. A., Lavis, J. N., Abelson, J., Dobbins, M., and Carter, N. (2012). Deliberative dialogues as a mechanism for knowledge translation and exchange in health systems decision-making. *Social Science & Medicine*, 75: 1938–1945.

Brown, C. (2012). The 'policy preferences model': A new perspective on how researchers can facilitate the take-up of evidence by educational policy makers. *Evidence & Policy*, 8(4): 455–472.

Brown, C. (2013). The policy agora: How power inequalities affect the interaction between researchers and policy makers. *Evidence & Policy*, 10(3): 421–438.

Cameron, D., Russell, D. J., Rivard, L., Darrah, J., and Palisano, R. (2011). Knowledge brokering in children's rehabilitation organizations: Perspectives from administrators. *Journal of Continuing Education in the Health Professions*, 31 (1): 28–33.

Chew, S., Armstrong, N., and Martin, G. (2013). Institutionalising knowledge brokering as a sustainable knowledge translation solution in healthcare: How can it work in practice? *Evidence & Policy*, 9(3): 335–351.

Contandriopoulos, D., Lemire, M., Denis, J.-L., and Tremblay, E. (2010). Knowledge exchange processes in organizations and policy arenas: A narrative systematic review of the literature. *Milbank Quarterly*, 88(4): 444–483.

Cooper, A. (2010). Knowledge Mobilization Intermediaries in Education. Paper presented to the Canadian Society for the Study of Education (CSSE), Montreal.

Cooper, A. (2014). Knowledge mobilization in education across Canada: A cross case analysis of 44 research brokering organisations. *Evidence & Policy*, 10(1): 29–59.

Cordingley, P. (2008). Research and evidence-informed practice: Focusing on practice and practitioners. *Cambridge Journal of Education*, 38(1): 37–52.

Damschroder, L. J., Aron, D. C., Keith, R. E., Kirsh, S. R., Alexander, J. A., and Lowery, J. C. (2009). Fostering implementation of health services research findings into practice: A consolidated framework for advancing implementation science. *Implementation Science*, 4: 50.

Davies, B. and Edwards, N. (2013). Sustaining knowledge use. In *Knowledge translation in health care: Moving from evidence to practice*, 2nd edition, ed. Straus, S. E., Tetroe, J., and Graham, I. D., pp. 237–248. Chichester: John Wiley.

Denis, J.-L. and Lehoux, P. (2013). Organizational theories. In *Knowledge translation in health care: Moving from evidence to practice*, 2nd edition, ed. Straus, S. E., Tetroe, J., and Graham, I. D., pp. 308–319. Chichester: John Wiley.

Dopson, S. (2006). Debate: Why does knowledge stick? What we can learn from the case of evidence-based health care. *Public Money and Management*, 26(2): 85–86.

Ellen, M. E., Leon, G., Bouchard, G., Lavis, J. N., Ouimet, M., and Grimshaw, J. M. (2013). What supports do health system organizations have in place to facilitate evidence-informed decision-making? A qualitative study. *Implementation Science*, 8: 84.

Estabrooks, C. A., Squires, J. E., Strandberg, E., Nilsson-Kajermo, K., Scott, S. D., Profetto-McGrath, J., Harley, D., and Wallin, L. (2011). Towards better measures of research utilization: a collaborative study in Canada and Sweden. *Journal of Advanced Nursing*, 67(8): 1705–1718.

Estabrooks, C. A., Thompson, D. S., Lovely, J. E., and Hofmeyer, A. (2006). A guide to knowledge translation theory. *The Journal of Continuing Education in the Health Professions*, 26(1): 25–36.

Ettelt, S., Mays, N., and Nolte, E. (2013). Policy-research linkage: What we have learned from providing a rapid response facility for international healthcare comparisons to the Department of Health in England. *Evidence & Policy*, 9(2): 245–254.

Fazekas, M. and Burns, T. (2012). *Exploring the complex interaction between governance and knowledge in education*. OECD Education Working Paper, No.67, OECD Publishing.

Ferlie, E., Crilly, T., Jashapara, A. and Peckham, A. (2012). Knowledge mobilization in health-care: A critical review of health sector and generic management literature. *Social Science & Medicine*, 74: 1297–1304.

Fixsen, D. L., Naoom, S. F., Blase, K. A., Friedman, R. M., and Wallace, F. (2005). *Implementation research: A synthesis of the literature*. Tampa, FL: University of South Florida, Louis de la Parte Florida Mental Health Institute, The National Implementation Research Network (FMHI Publication #231).

Gabbay, J. and le May, A. (2004). Evidence-based guidelines or collectively constructed "mindlines"? Ethnographic study of knowledge management in primary care. *British Medical Journal*, 329: 1013–1017.

Gabbay, J. and le May, A. (2011). *Practice-based evidence for healthcare: Clinical mindlines*. Abingdon: Routledge.

Graham, I. D., Logan, J., Harrison, M. B., Straus, S. E., Tetroe, J., Caswell, W., and Robinson, N. (2006). Lost in knowledge translation: Time for a map? *The Journal of Continuing Education in the Health Professions*, 26(1): 13–24.

Graham, I. D., Tetroe, J., and the KT Theories Research Group (2007). Some Theoretical Underpinnings of Knowledge Translation. *Academic Emergency Medicine*, 14: 936–941.

Greenhalgh, T. (2010). What is this knowledge that we seek to "exchange"? *Milbank Quarterly*, 88(4): 492–499.

Greenhalgh, T., Robert, G., Macfarlane, F., Bate, P., and Kyriakidou, O. (2004). Diffusion of innovations in service organizations: Systematic review and recommendations. *The Milbank Quarterly*, 82(4): 581–629.

Greenhalgh, T. and Wieringa, S. (2011). Is it time to drop the "knowledge translation" metaphor? A critical literature review. *Journal of the Royal Society of Medicine*, 104: 501–509.

Grimshaw, J. M., Eccles, M. P., Lavis, J. N., Hill, S. J., and Squires, J. E. (2012). Knowledge translation of research findings. *Implementation Science*, 7(50), doi:10.1186/1748-5908-7-50.

Holmes, B., Scarrow, G., and Schellenberg, M. (2012). Translating evidence into practice: The role of health research funders. *Implementation Science*, 7: 39.

Holmes, B. J., Finegood, D. T., Riley, B. L., and Best, A. (2012). Systems thinking in dissemination and implementation research. In *Dissemination and implementation research in health: Translating science to practice*, ed. Brownson, R., Colditz, G., and Proctor, E., pp. 175–191. Oxford: Oxford University Press.

Honig, M. I. and Venkateswaran, N. (2012). School-central office relationships in evidence use: Understanding evidence use as a systems problem. *American Journal of Education*, 118(2): 199–222.

Kitson, A., Harvey, G., and McCormack, B. (1998). Enabling the implementation of evidence based practice: A conceptual framework. *Quality in Health Care*, 7: 149–158.

LaRocca, R., Yost, J., Dobbins, M., Ciliska, D., and Butt, M. (2012). The effectiveness of knowledge translation strategies used in public health: A systematic review. *BMC Public Health*, 12(751), doi:10.1186/1471-2458-12-751.

Lavis, J. N., Robertson, D., Woodside, J. M., McLeod, C. B., Abelson, J., and the Knowledge Transfer Study Group (2003). How can research organizations more effectively transfer research knowledge to decision makers? *The Milbank Quarterly*, 81(2): 221–248.

Levin, B. (2011). Mobilizing research knowledge in education. *London Review of Education*, 9(1): 15–26.

Levin, B. and Cooper, A. (2012). Theory, research and practice in mobilizing research knowledge in education. In *Knowledge mobilization and educational research: Politics, languages and responsibilities*, ed. Fenwick, T. and Farrell, L., pp. 17–29. London: Routledge.

Lightowler, C. and Knight, C. (2013). Sustaining knowledge exchange and research impact in the social sciences and humanities: Investing in knowledge broker roles in UK universities. *Evidence & Policy*, 9(3): 317–334.

Logan, J. and Graham, I. D. (1998). Towards a comprehensive model of health care research use. *Science Communication*, 20(2): 227–246.

Lomas, J. (2000). Using linkage and exchange to move research into policy at a Canadian foundation. *Health Affairs*, 19(3): 236–240.

Meagher, L. (2013). The invisible made visible: Using impact evaluations to illuminate and inform the role of knowledge intermediaries. *Evidence & Policy*, 9(3): 409–418.

Mitton, C., Adair, C. E., McKenzie, E., Patten, S. B., and Waye Perry, B. (2007). Knowledge transfer and exchange: Review and synthesis of the literature. *The Milbank Quarterly*, 85(4): 729–768.

Moat, K. A., Lavis, J. N., and Abelson, J. (2013). How contexts and issues influence the use of policy-relevant research syntheses: A critical interpretive synthesis. *Milbank Quarterly*, 91(3): 604–648.

Murphy, K. and Fafard, P. (2012). Knowledge translation and social epidemiology: Taking power, politics and values seriously. In *Rethinking social epidemiology: Towards a science of change*, ed. O'Campo, P. and Dunn, J. R., pp. 267–284. Dordrecht: Springer.

Nicolini, D., Powell, J., Conville, P., and Martinez-Solano, L. (2008). Managing knowledge in the healthcare sector: A review. *International Journal of Management Reviews*, 10(3): 245–263.

Nonaka, I. (1994). A dynamic theory of organizational knowledge creation. *Organization Science*, 5(1): 14–37.

Nutley, S. M., Powell, A. E., and Davies, H. T. O. (2013). *What counts as good evidence?* London: Alliance for Useful Evidence.

Nutley, S. M., Walter, I., and Davies, H. T. O. (2007). *Using evidence: How research can inform public services.* Bristol: Policy Press.

Nutley, S. M., Walter, I., and Davies, H. T. O. (2009). Promoting evidence-based practice: Models and mechanisms from cross-sector review. *Research on Social Work Practice,* 19(5): 552–559.

Oborn, E. (2012). Facilitating implementation of the translational research pipeline in neurological rehabilitation. *Current Opinion in Neurology,* 25(6): 676–681.

Oborn, E., Barrett, M., and Racko, G. (2013). Knowledge translation in healthcare: Incorporating theories of learning and knowledge from the management literature. *Journal of Health Organization and Management,* 27(4): 412–431.

Ovretveit, J., Hempel, S., Magnabosco, J. L., Mittman, B. S., Rubenstein, L. V., and Ganz, D. A. (2014). Guidance for research-practice partnerships (R-PPs) and collaborative research. *Journal of Health Organization and Management,* 28(1): 115–126.

Pawson, R. and Tilley, N. (1997). *Realistic evaluation.* London: Sage.

Pentland, D., Forsyth, K., Maciver, D., Walsh, M., Murray, R., Irvine, L., and Sikora, S. (2011). Key characteristics of knowledge transfer and exchange in healthcare: Integrative literature review. *Journal of Advanced Nursing,* 67(7): 1408–1425.

Pettigrew, A., McKee, L., and Ferlie, E. (1988). Understanding change in the NHS. *Public Administration,* 66: 297–317.

Pettigrew, A. M. (1985). *The awakening giant: Continuity and change in Imperial Chemical Industries.* Oxford: Basil Blackwell.

Petticrew, M. and Roberts, H. (2003). Evidence, hierarchies and typologies: Horses for courses. *Journal of Epidemiology and Community Health,* 57: 527–529.

Phipps, D. and Morton, S. (2013). Qualities of knowledge brokers: Reflections from practice. *Evidence & Policy,* 9(2): 255–265.

Powell, B. J., McMillen, J. C., Proctor, E. K., Carpenter, C. R., Griffey, R. T., Bunger, A. C., Glass, J. E., and York, J. L. (2012). A compilation of strategies for implementing clinical innovations in health and mental health. *Medical Care Research and Review,* 69(2): 123–157.

Riley, B. L. (2012). Knowledge integration in public health: A rapid review using systems thinking. *Evidence & Policy,* 8(4): 417–432.

Scott, S. D., Albrecht, L., O'Leary, K., Ball, G. D., Hartling, L., Hofmeyer, A., Jones, C. A. Klassen, T. P., Kovacs Burns, K., Newton, A. S., Thompson, D. S., and Dryden, D. M. (2012). Systematic review of knowledge translation strategies in the allied health professions. *Implementation Science,* 7(70), doi: 10.1186/1748-5908-7-70.

Sebba, J. (2013). An exploratory review of the role of research mediators in social science. *Evidence & Policy,* 9(3): 391–408.

Stacey, D. and Hill, S. (2013). Patient-directed and patient-mediated KT interventions. In *Knowledge translation in health care: Moving from evidence to practice,* 2nd edition, ed. Straus, S. E., Tetroe, J., and Graham, I. D. Chichester: John Wiley.

Sudsawad, P. (2007). *Knowledge translation: Introduction to models, strategies and measures.* Austin, TX: National Center for the Dissemination of Disability Research.

Tetroe, J., Graham, I. D., Foy, R., Robinson, N., Eccles, M. P., Wensing, M., Durieux, P., Legare, F., Palmhoj Nielson, C., Adily, A, Ward, J. E., Porter, C., Shea, B., and Grimshaw, J. M. (2008). Health research funding agencies' support and promotion of knowledge translation: An international study. *The Milbank Quarterly,* 86(1): 125–155.

The Health Foundation (2014). *Perspectives on context.* London: The Health Foundation.

Thompson, G. N., Estabrooks, C. A., and Degner, L. F. (2006). Clarifying the concepts in knowledge transfer: A literature review. *Journal of Advanced Nursing,* 53(6): 691–701.

Walter, I., Nutley, S., and Davies, H. (2003). *Research impact: A cross sector review.* St Andrews: Research Unit for Research Utilisation, University of St Andrews.

Walter, I., Nutley, S., and Davies, H. T. O. (2005). What works to promote evidence-based practice? A cross-sector review. *Evidence & Policy,* 1(3): 335–363.

Walter, I., Nutley, S. M., Percy-Smith, J., McNeish, D., and Frost, S. (2004). *Improving the use of research in social care. Knowledge Review 7.* Social Care Institute for Excellence and the Policy Press.

Ward, V., House, A., and Hamer, S. (2009). Developing a framework for transferring knowledge into action: A thematic analysis of the literature. *Journal of Health Services Research and Policy,* 14(3): 156–164.

Ward, V., Smith, S., House, A., and Hamer, S. (2012). Exploring knowledge exchange: A useful framework for practice and policy. *Social Science & Medicine,* 74: 297–304.

Weiss, C. H. (1979). The many meanings of research utilization. *Public Administration Review,* 39(5): 426–431.

Weiss, C. H. (1995). The haphazard connection: Social science and public policy. *International Journal of Educational Research,* 23(2): 137–150.

Willis, C. D., Best, A., Riley, B., Herbert, C. P., Millar, J., and Howland, D. (2014). Systems thinking for transformational change in health. *Evidence & Policy,* 10(1): 113–126.

Willis, C. D., Mitton, C., Gordon, J., and Best, A. (2012). System tools for system change. *BMJ Quality and Safety,* 21(3): 250–262.

Wilson, M. G., Lavis, J. N., Travers, R., and Rourke, S. B. (2010). Community-based knowledge transfer and exchange: Helping community-based organizations link research to action. *Implementation Science,* 5: 33.

CHAPTER 13

A DISCURSIVE APPROACH TO ORGANIZATIONAL HEALTH COMMUNICATION

PETER KJÆR, ANNE REFF PEDERSEN, AND ANJA
SVEJGAARD PORS

INTRODUCTION

COMMUNICATION is a key concern for health care organizations; both patients and health care practitioners now see communication as an indispensable aspect of the care continuum—in doctor–patient relations, clinical practice, hospital management, and health care governance. Indeed, it seems as if improved communication has become an almost universal prescription, whereby any issue in health care, such as quality, preventive care, costs, work environment, compliance, patient satisfaction, or waiting lists, can be articulated as problems in communication for which the solution is more or better communication. From a management perspective, improved communication seems an attractive tool, but it also carries a potentially limitless number of applications and interpretations. Similarly, from the perspective of health care professionals, communication constitutes a core dimension of the clinical encounter, but it also poses new challenges to professionalism. Finally, from a patient perspective, communication is pivotal to patient-centered health care, but it also involves new demands on patients. There is thus a need to develop a perspective on health communication that allows an evaluation of the wider implications of working with and improving communication.

The phenomenon of communication can be conceptualized in numerous ways, ranging from technical concepts of information transfer or linguistic concepts of language structure and use, to broader sociological concepts emphasizing interaction, interpretation, and shared meaning. Rather than seeking to elaborate a particular theoretical concept of communication, our chapter will discern the uses of ideas of communication in the health care field. It will present three types of communication ideas and practices within health care to illustrate communication as an organizational and managerial concern.

First, we describe *clinical communication* ideas and practices that focus on patient–doctor or patient–professional communication. Patient–doctor communication is a classical concern within health care, in many ways predating the current organizational and managerial preoccupation (Ong et al., 1995). Second, we describe *extra-clinical communication*, which includes communication ideas and practices in health care organizations—beyond immediate treatment and care. Human resource management communication in hospitals is an example of extra-clinical communication. Finally, we describe ideas and practices related to *corporate communication*, which is typically concerned with the relationship between health care organizations and the broader institutional or corporate environments in which they operate.

Our focus on the uses of communication ideas in various settings represents a *discursive perspective* on health care organization and management. Most work within the field of health communication has a strong instrumental focus on the ability to produce desired behavioral outcomes through communication. There is much less attention to the wider ramifications of communication work from the perspective of organizations, professions, and patients.

The ability to evaluate such implications requires moving current perspectives on health communication from a narrow focus on communication as a tool, towards a broader focus on how the introduction of new communication ideals and tools denotes particular worldviews and practices interacting with existing worldviews and practices in health care settings. We argue that this discursive perspective provides a richer understanding of the role of communication in health care organizations but, importantly, also a more adequate point of departure for health care managers and other health care actors in relation to communication. Thus a discursive perspective allows us to analyze and evaluate both the intended and unintended consequences of focusing on communication, establishing communication departments, creating communication policies and programs, and so on.

Our empirical focus within the broader field of health communication will be on *organizational health communication* (Apker, 2012, 3). Whereas health communication is defined as the use of information and communication to influence health outcomes, organizational health communication is more specific, emphasizing the use of communication to affect *organizational* processes and outcomes. Organizational health communication encompasses an array of practices and phenomena: interpersonal communication, written communication, aesthetic communication, public communication, and information and communications technology in a variety of concrete settings: the clinic, hospital support functions, health care teams, top management, and so on.

Our ambition is to describe the field of organizational health communication and present a set of analytical lenses, rooted in a discursive perspective on organization that allows us to understand organizational health communication in its context and to identify some of its intended and unintended consequences.

The chapter is structured as follows.

- First, we describe how communication has become a key concern within health care, outlining the drivers involved in the expansion of communication ideas and practices over the last four decades: health care reforms, marketization of health care, the rise of patient centered health care, and the advent of new technological opportunities.
- Second, we identify three distinct types of organizational health communication: clinical communication, that is communication in the clinical interaction between health care professionals and patients; extra-clinical communication, that is organizational communication activities seeking to qualify activities in and especially around the core tasks in health care; and corporate communication, that is communication activities addressing organizational stakeholders.
- Third, we challenge the theoretical approaches informing most contemporary organizational health communication research, introducing a discursive approach to communication that highlights the institutional history of communication, communication as management of meaning, and the performativity of communication tools, respectively illustrated by a small case story from Scandinavian health care.
- Fourth, we summarize our argument, highlighting the need for further investigation of the unintended consequences of modern organizational health communication and the need for health care managers to develop balanced and realistic expectations, limits, risks, and interests in managing organizational health communication.

THE COMMUNICATIVE TURN IN HEALTH CARE ORGANIZATIONS

In 2007 a Norwegian regional health enterprise in charge of a number of hospitals in western Norway proudly announced that, "reputation building has to be an integral part of the workday at all levels of the organization, ranging from the provision of services to patients and users to the very core of leadership" (cited from Byrkjeflot and Angell, 2011, our translation). This quote not only articulates the great expectations of health care managers with respect to communication but also exemplifies the institutionalization of organizational health communication since the 1990s in most developed countries. Today, most health care authorities, hospitals, and other health care providers employ communication professionals, have distinct communication units, formulate communication strategies and policies, and initiate projects or processes to, as it were, make communication "an integral part of the workday," from the offices of top management to clinics and even to the ongoing interaction with patients and citizens.

Informing this development—and answering to its demands—a distinct research field has emerged with dedicated journals, book series, handbooks, textbooks, and manuals for practitioners.

Organized communication efforts in a health care setting comprise several rationales, practices, and techniques (for an overview, see Apker, 2012; Thompson, Parrott, and Nussbaum, 2011; Hamilton and Chou, 2014). It involves conscious efforts to understand and change how patients experience clinical encounters while also involving strategic communication efforts *within* health care organizations in an attempt to shape staff beliefs, motivation, work practices, and routines and even attempts to influence policymaking, mass media coverage, and public perceptions. What is shared is a common expectation that communication matters, that individuals and organizations should work systematically and even strategically with communication, and that communication is an important management concern in health care organizations (Kjær and Pors, 2010).

The specific patterns of expansion and organization have still to be studied systematically but based on existing studies of organizational health communication we can point to at least four drivers for the development of the field: reforms, marketization, patient-centeredness, and technological innovation.

Organizational reforms have been an important driver in the expansion of organizational health communication since the 1970s. In both Europe and in North America several waves of organizational and legislative reforms have transformed the environment in which health care organizations operate, creating new organizational entities and relationships (Moran, 1999; Scott et al., 2000; Byrkjeflot and Angell, 2007). The creation of health maintenance organizations (HMOs), the rise of managed care in the United States—and efforts to merge hospitals or the creation of a new division of labor among health care providers in most other countries has increased both political and public attention to health care issues. This, in turn, resulted in a new generation of health care executives/managers who were increasingly concerned with the broader organizational and political environment. Similarly, hospital reforms in Western Europe, guided by the ambition of cost containment and productivity, emphasize management control, economies-of-scale, and the changing balance between political regulation and organizational/professional autonomy (Vrangbæk and Christiansen, 2005).

In this setting, the communication efforts of health care organizations can be seen as attempts to strategically manage new and more turbulent environments by engaging with key stakeholders. In other words, reforms and restructuring create a need for managers to communicate in order to maintain focus and legitimacy in a changing context. Some analysts have also suggested that reform processes can be seen as processes that aim to reconstitute health care providers as *proper* organizations and that the creation of professional communication units and the hiring of communication officers are symbolic signposts of the "modern organization" (Røvik, 2011).

The second driver of organizational health communication is *marketization*. Most countries have experienced processes of marketization and increased competition within health care. Whereas competition in the US context has often entailed the entry of new for-profit actors in the field (Loubeau and Jantzen, 1998), competition in many European contexts has tended to be an outcome of political decisions to selectively introduce market elements, such as purchaser-provider schemes, fee-for-service arrangements and diagnosis-related group, or DRG, reimbursement, into traditionally non-market environments (Lega, 2006). Health care reforms in most European countries have often been described as manifestations of a new public management (NPM) philosophy, aiming to restructure public services by highlighting market-like governance arrangements alongside an emphasis on organizational leadership, accountability, and entrepreneurship (Vrangbæk, 1999; see also Ferlie et al., 1996).

Increasing competition and trends towards marketization not only created new turbulence and uncertainty but has also challenged the very rationale of health care organizations. From concepts of specialized professional organizations dedicated to curing patients based on expert knowledge, health care organizations are increasingly seen as service providers, offering services to particular customers whose needs could not simply be stipulated a priori by the medical profession. Competition has become a question of identifying and meeting demands by engaging with health care consumers—through orchestrated communication processes.

The trend towards *patient-centered health care* (Gerteis et al., 1993; Nordgren, 2003; Kjær and Reff, 2010) is a third driver of organizational health communication. Initially, patient-centered health care emerged as a movement that challenged the authority of physicians and the supremacy of the biomedical paradigm during the 1970s. Modern health care practices, it was said, had reduced the patient to a passive object of biomedical intervention, creating a huge gap between the subjective experience of patients and the assumptions and requirements of modern medicine. From the 1990s the movement for the humanization of health care was linked to health policy debates on quality, coordination, and governance emphasizing how patients could be mobilized as resources in health care systems plagued by high costs, excessive demands, and increased specialization (Pedersen, 2010). Accordingly, mobilizing patients as an integral part of the care continuum was a result of political initiatives and the work of certain health care professions (especially nurses) and patient associations. In some cases, patient-centered health care merged with the ideals of marketization according to which the demands and choices of patient-cum-consumers could stimulate health care organizations to maximize efficiency (Kjær and Reff, 2010).

In relation to patient-centered health care, communication became a distinguishing feature of the relationship between patients and health care providers. Interactions were typically seen as communicative processes and, increasingly, the communicative capacity of health care professionals and organizations were seen as equally important as biomedical and technical capacity (Bensing, 2000).

Finally, *technological changes* have, increasingly, become an important driver of organizational health communication (Suggs, 2006; Mechanic, 2008). Information and communication technologies have affected health care organizations in several respects since the mid-1990s. Electronic patient records provided new ways of structuring professional communication as well as making that communication accessible to patients and next-of-kin (and across health care organizations or sectors). Similarly, the advent of the internet, email, and smartphones provided new and more flexible platforms for both official and personal communication. Finally, the development of new interactive and user-defined social media platforms has, as it were, moved communicative interactions out of formalized and controlled intra-organizational settings and into new networks, rendering health care professionals and health care organizations with only indirect influence on communication and information processes.

Technologically mediated communication is pervasive and partly uncontrollable. Patients and their networks are empowered in new and complex ways, driving health care organizations' constant attention to communication platforms, opportunities, and risks.

The rise and expansion of organizational health communication still needs to be documented in detail. There is a lack of comparative studies to describe the origins and trajectories of communication work in various contexts. In contrast to the case of patient safety or evidence-based medicine, the few existing studies (e.g., Kjær and Pors, 2010) suggest that organizational health communication does not entail a coherent set of ideas, programs, and practices that have spread uniformly across contexts. It is therefore important to keep in mind the diversity of the phenomenon of organizational health communication and to avoid seeing its emergence as unilinear or even necessary.

VARIETIES OF ORGANIZATIONAL HEALTH COMMUNICATION: CLINICAL, EXTRA-CLINICAL, AND CORPORATE

We will now focus on three varieties of organizational health communication that draw upon different theoretical sources of inspiration with different implications for practice.

Until recently, most research on communication in the health care context was preoccupied with health outcomes. A broad literature on *health communication* has emerged since the 1970s (Nussbaum, 1989). In this literature, health communication is first and foremost defined as a means to influence health behavior. Research contributions typically focus on how planned communication and information interventions, such as information campaigns, health education, and social media interaction can affect individual behavior. Quantitative analyses of mass media content and audience effects loom large, whereas other methods and studies of other types of communication are less prevalent (Freimuth, Massett, and Meltzer, 2006; Noar, 2006). Interestingly, research on health communication largely bypasses health care organizations and even interpersonal relations between patients and professionals, rather emphasizing a world in which medical expertise is mass-communicated to the general population or to particular audiences. Organizational issues only enter at the technical level as questions of how communication or information design and planning affect intended outcomes (Neuhauser and Kreps, 2003).

However, in the world of health care, public information campaigns constitute only a single type of communicative activity, one that is typically beyond the purview of the individual health care organization. Communication does play an important role within health care organizations but organizational health communication often differs from standard perceptions of health communication. Organization-level health communication addresses a variety of audiences, including individual patients (and kin) and also professionals, policy makers, and local communities. It may be one-way but often involves two-way communication; and the effects of organizational health communication may be both immediate and more indirect, in the sense that it affects roles and evaluations rather than (solely) behavior and knowledge. Finally, it draws on a wider set of theoretical sources of inspiration, beyond classical communication theory.

We distinguish between three varieties of organizational health communication: *Clinical communication* refers to communication in the clinical encounter between health care professionals and patients. *Extra-clinical communication* is a tentative term describing organization-level communication work, below the level of top management but typically outside the clinic, in the context of quality improvement programs, organizational development activities, and so on. *Corporate communication* refers to organizational health communication in the interface between the organization and its broader environment.

Clinical Communication

Clinical communication is communication that takes place between patients and health care professionals in everyday clinical practice. The interest in clinical communication evolved with the problematization of the clinical encounter from the late 1960s onward—in health care practice and in the sociology of medicine (Ong et al., 1995; Roter and Hall, 2011). The problematization of the clinical encounter addressed several aspects: doctor–patient communication, inter-professional communication among health care professionals concerning the care for and treatment of patients, and the impact of medical discourse on communication.

The interest in *doctor–patient communication* was inspired by in-depth studies of the interaction between patients and health care professionals. A number of influential studies (DiMatteo et al., 1980; Mishler, 1984; Kleinman, 1988) investigated how the medical interview is a particular type of conversation or textual exchange between the patient on one side and the doctor on the other. In clinical practice, this concern has entailed attempts to improve the quality of such conversations and to change particular health care behaviors (Hinyard and Kreuter, 2007). DiMatteo et al. investigated how physician communication skills, including non-verbal emotional communication skills, are positively correlated with patient compliance (DiMatteo et al., 1980; Zolnierek and DiMatteo, 2009). An important organizational outcome is the extension of the education of doctors to include a stronger focus on communication skills in medical training. Another practical outcome is the enhanced focus on patients, for example by hiring or training patient counselors to assist or empower patients with improved knowledge about options and rights. A final organizational outcome is patient education, sponsored by hospitals or patient associations, training patients for the medical interview.

Inter-professional communication is concerned with the communication among health care professionals in a variety of settings. Lingard et al. studied how inter-professional communication in teams influences clinical safety and effectiveness (Lingard et al., 2005; see also Real and Poole, 2011). Others (Pedersen and Johansen, 2012) have studied how clinical managers, physicians, and nurses dealing with organizational change initiatives create innovation narratives from polycentric and fragmented health care communication. Finally, the role of inter-professional communication in fostering individual and group identity and norms has been examined (Apker, 2012).

Medical discourse is the wider context of meaning in which clinical encounters occur. Research on medical discourse (or biomedical rationality) is concerned with the interplay of knowledge, power, and meaning in health care. Here, a number of sociological studies have described patient–doctor interaction as an outcome of the power of medical discourse that positions doctors and patients in a particular relationship of knowledge and power and privileges biomedical knowledge and the practices associated with it (Mishler, 1984). A parallel and critical approach toward medical discourse studies has been to examine "patient worlds" as an important part of the clinical communication. Several studies demonstrated how illness narratives may unfold the patient's perspective and articulate the experience of the patient with illness problems and symptoms in contrast to the medical discourse (Bury, 2001; Hydén, 1997; Charon, 2005; Kelly and Dickinson, 1997; Davenport, 2011). In practice this entails conscious work with patient narratives and the contrasting of patient and professionals narratives in the development of medical communication.

Common for most approaches to clinical communication is a focus on the clinical encounter as a communicative event situated in a unique context. Materiality (the places and spaces of the encounter) and the broader organizational setting also affect patient–doctor interaction, that is as a part of patient pathways or planned health care trajectories. In recent years interest in the wider context of the clinical encounter has even extended to the domestic situation of the patient, relations to next-of-kin and to technologically-mediated interaction. Thus, new information technologies provide new opportunities for patients to interact with medical knowledge and health care professionals via internet or social media platforms (Suggs, 2006; Kjær and Reff, 2010).

Extra-Clinical Communication

Extra-clinical communication is our tentative characterization of a second variety of organizational health communication. Extra-clinical communication can, somewhat misleadingly, be characterized as "internal communication," that, in a sense, unfolds at the boundaries of the organization, in contrast to the two other varieties of communication.

Internal communication such as staff newsletters, bulletin boards, or professionals meetings has been an inconspicuous aspect of most health care organizations for many years. However, in the course of the last two decades, a new variety of communication practice has gradually transformed the nature of internal communication. Extra-clinical communication denotes a range of attempts to work systematically with communication as an integral aspect of the internal organization of health care in hospitals, health clinics, home care, and hospice care settings (see Apker, 2012). The concept "extra-clinical communication" highlights the fact that, while such communication initiatives may ultimately seek to influence patient treatment and care, they are typically directed at shaping *professional* (or staff) behaviors, routines, and attitudes.

Extra-clinical communication draws on concepts and knowledge from outside the medical world, for example from industrial process management, risk management, and human resource management, translating them into new activities in health care settings. Extra-clinical communication is not linked directly to the expertise of the classical health care professions but draws on general models of interpersonal or organizational communication. Here communication tends to be conceptualized as a supplementary organizational task in the service of, for example, quality assurance, patient safety, workflow optimization, lean management, patient-centered trajectories, or human resource development. Typically, the optimization of communication is seen as a precondition for such organizational practices and interventions.

Communication is considered a key factor in patient satisfaction and evaluation of treatment quality as well as in patient safety and in the prevention of medical errors in health care (Duggan and Thompson, 2011; Kohn, Corrigan, and Donaldson, 2000). In the patient safety movement, communication is an integral tool to improve health care organizations or systems via safety regulation, information standards, and routines promoting organizational learning, in which co-collegial and organizational communication is granted an important role.

Concurrently, the focus on communication has been picked up in a range of occupational programs and in the post-graduate education of health care professionals and strategies of patient-centered health care, e-health, or local approaches developed specifically to improve organizational communication (Pors, 2012). As a result new extra-clinical sub-professions in communication have emerged within health care organizations: quality managers, risk managers, and patient safety consultants, communication managers and consultants, development consultants, and so on. These new extra-clinical professions all share communication as a central competence. Moreover, part of their task is to facilitate a communicative turn in the organization by putting communication on the agenda through programs and projects and by incorporating communication tools into the daily practices of health care professionals (Pors, forthcoming).

Corporate Communication

Corporate communication is communication at the executive level of organizations preoccupied with the management of the organization as a whole and its relationship to its environment. The notion of corporate communication comes from the field of strategic communication and denotes the ideal of integrating all communication activities under a shared strategic understanding of organizational identity and reputation (van Riel, 1995; Christensen, Morsing, and Cheney, 2008; Byrkjeflot and Angell, 2011; Waeraas, Byrkjeflot, and Angell, 2011). At least three types of corporate communication can be found in the health care field: management communication, marketing communication, and public relations.

Management communication is described by classical management theory as the role of "continuously persuading individual subordinates that the goals of the organization are desirable. Communication, therefore, is vitally necessary to an organization, not only to transmit authority, but also to achieve cooperation" (van Riel, 1995, 9). Case studies point to the role of organizational leadership and communication in hospitals and other health care organizations both at the executive or department level (Bentsen, 2003) and at the team level (Apker, 2012). Typically, management communication involves both the sharing of knowledge about organizational goals and the means and attempts to create a sense of organizational loyalty and belonging to forge shared organizational culture (Schein, 2010).

Health care marketing is preoccupied with an organization's management of its exchange relations with its various markets and publics and involves attending to the needs and demands of health care consumers and adopting services to market demands—or seeking to influence the market strategically. Health care marketing initially focused on advertising of hospitals or health care services (Loubeau and Jantzen, 1998). From the 1990s, health care marketing came to include a broader set of techniques and concepts, such as the analyses of consumer needs, market opportunities, patient satisfaction, and focus on adapting the service mix of hospitals to market demands (Thomas, 2006). While being a product of changes in the American health care market, health care marketing also plays a role in public health care systems (Lega, 2005). In public organizations health marketing is relevant, not because of the existence of actual markets or distinct for-profit health care actors, but because the marketing perspective offers an approach to health care organizations as consumer-oriented and well adapted to receptualizing health care organizations as more responsive, patient-oriented service providers.

Public relations communication (Grunig and Grunig, 1991; Gordon and Kelly, 1999; Aldoory and Austin, 2011) emphasizes the importance of strategically managing an organization's relations with relevant publics and stakeholders, especially when organizations are under threat. Relevant publics include consumers, government, the media, and employees. Public relations involve communication tools such as media management, organizational publications, and interpersonal persuasion. Public relations work within health care emerged in the United States, but has spread to most other countries. The public relations perspective posits health care providers as organizations embedded in complex environments on which they rely for resources and support. Public relations, and other forms of organizational communication, are thus to be seen as ways of orchestrating organizational interdependencies through processes of legitimization and impression management (Pfeffer and Salancik, 1978; Elsbach, 1994; Arndt and Bigelow, 2000; Kjær, 2009). In recent years, *reputation management* has become a key concern within health care public relations. The focus on reputation management is indicative of a more general shift toward an integrated, "total"/holistic or corporate communication perspective, intended to overcome the fragmentation of various types of communication (cf. Christensen, Morsing, and Cheney, 2008). Ideally, now, all communications of an organization should build on a shared holistic strategic framework describing an organization's desired identity and image (Byrkjeflot and Angell, 2007; see also the section entitled "Communication as Institutionalized Organizational Ideals").

A DISCURSIVE APPROACH TO COMMUNICATION IN HEALTH CARE ORGANIZATIONS

The literature on organizational health communication is primarily concerned with the determinants of effective or successful communication—that is the factors leading to desired behavioral, attitudinal, or reputational outcomes. In contrast, there are surprisingly few considerations of the organizational consequences of organizational health communication: What happens to health care practice and organizational relations when communication becomes the object of attention and intervention at all levels of organization?

Save for a few discussions of communicator roles and program implementation, health care organizations are oddly absent, both in the prescriptive and analytical literature (but see Apker, 2012). Likewise, there is little or no discussion of the values, worldviews, or constraints built into popular communication tools.

For the proponents of organizational health communication this may be an acceptable state but—especially for health care managers and other observers of health care organizations—there is a need for consideration of both the efficiency (or effectiveness) of communication interventions and broader organizational and managerial ramifications. To address these concerns, it is necessary to adopt a reflexive understanding of organizational health communication in and around organizations.

Discourse and Organization

In organization and management studies, discursive approaches offer useful entry-points into the reflexive examination of organizational tools and technologies. Discursive approaches pay particular attention to how social meanings are produced and how meanings prevail in society and organizations (Iedema, 2008) through language, social practice, and materiality.

Organizational knowledge, relationships, roles, and identities are defined by the language with which actors seek to represent organizational reality and relations (Deetz, 2003); by the ongoing interaction of organizational actors who draw upon positions of authority and legitimacy and employ particular power strategies to define situations, problems, and solutions (Vaara, 2008); and by the particular technologies and material opportunities that allow actors to engage in specific ways, while constraining from other types of engagement (Hardy and Thomas, 2015).

The analytical contribution of discursive analysis demonstrates how communication processes are embedded in particular discursive formations that are both reproduced and strategically reworked by organizational actors. Thus, organizational health communication shapes and is shaped by the discourses of health care organizations, institutions, and policy. Examining the relationship between organizational health communication and discourse enables the discernment of how particular communication practices, tools, and sociolects affect health care organizations while also being framed by the prevailing discourses within the health care field.

Within a general discursive perspective on organization and management, several specific approaches may be elaborated. Health care management researchers have often drawn upon discursive approaches in the analysis of health care policy to identify dominant framings of health care problems that have become institutionalized in health care policy making (Buse, Mays, and Walt, 2012). Likewise, students of culture and identity in health care organizations have often been inspired by discursive analysis as a means to arrive at more dynamic conceptions of culture that also recognize the power dimension of cultural phenomena (Czarniawska, 1998). Finally, research into organizational technologies has drawn on the notion of discourse when attempting to analyze the ways in which particular technologies and the rationalities they embody interact with social and organizational processes (Rose, 1989).

We now present three approaches to organizational health communication inspired by discursive analysis. The first approach focuses on the institutionalization of discourses of communication, that is the creation and stabilization of a particular communication perspective on health care organization within the broader field of health care. The second approach focuses on the narratives of organizational health communication and how they interact with broader meaning constructions. The third approach focuses on the tools of organizational health communication and how they discursively shape health care organizations, including the positions of professionals and patients. Each approach is illustrated by an example drawn from existing research.

Communication as Institutionalized Organizational Ideals

Discourse analysis implies an interest in textual or linguistic analysis and in the broader reconfiguration of discursive spaces in modern societies. With regard to the latter aspect, the recent focus on organizational health communication can be seen as an instance of discursive and institutional change within health care. To study such changes, a discursive history approach can be adopted, inspired by Michel Foucault's archaeology of knowledge and the neo-institutional approach within organization studies (Foucault, 1972; Scott et al., 2000). A discursive history analysis focuses on three moments in backwards mapping of a process of discursive change (Kjær, 2008; Pedersen, 2010; Kjær and Pors, 2010): First, a description of an organizational field and its institutional arrangements. In the case of organizational health communication, this would be a mapping of the degree to which organizational health communication has become formalized, that is characterized by distinct and recognizable functions, roles, and practices within health care organizations such as strategies, policies, programs, units, and dedicated staff. Second, a description of the discourses within which communication activities are deemed necessary and which outline the problems, solutions, means, and ends that legitimate an emphasis on communication. In the case of health care, this would involve mapping of the ways in which debates on communication define communication problems in hospitals and elsewhere, identify particular activities (meetings) or actors (trained nurses, communication specialists) as solutions, describe particular objectives and tools to be implemented, and so on. Third, identifying the ideal(s) of social organization that can be said to organize a particular discourse. In the case of organizational health communication, this could involve contrasting the ideal of the "communicative organization" with that of the hospital as a modern specialized medical institution.

Taken together, the three analytical steps allow for the consideration of how a particular discourse of communication emerges, becomes elaborated and gradually takes hold in hospitals and other health care organizations, and how that—in effect—introduces a new organizing logic in the health care field. The analysis, then, allows us to ascertain the context in which specific communication practices unfold and to understand how communication discourse also constitutes a distinct and "different" universe of health care.

Case: Reputation management in a changing hospital field[1]
    In 2002 Norway carried out a comprehensive health care reform that shifted the ownership of hospitals from the county level to the state, while at the same time establishing five regional and 28 local health enterprises. Among the many outcomes of the reform, the growth in organizational health communication was conspicuous. Prior to the reform, about 30% of the hospitals employed information managers. A few years later that figure had risen to more than 90%. Similarly, the share of information managers in top-management teams had increased from 20% to about 50%.

---

[1] The case builds on Byrkjeflot and Angell (2007, 2011).

Clearly, it would seem that a radical change had occurred and that strategic communication had been institutionalized in the health care field—as a response to changes in the overall governance system.

A discourse analysis of communication statements from hospitals and health care enterprises from 2002 to 2010 gives an indication of the emerging perspective on communication and health care. Three overall themes can be discerned: a marketing theme focusing on the expectation that there will be increased competition for patients and that health care organizations need to focus on advertising and profiling; a mediatization theme focusing on the need for professional and proactive media management in a period characterized by increase public focus on health care; and a reputation theme focusing on the need for hospitals to appear as unified and legitimate actors organized around a shared corporate identity or brand, shared symbols, and consistent communication. While there was a great deal of variation among the communication statements, they generally converged on a reputation-management discourse in the second half of the period under study.

It is impossible to extrapolate a general change in ideals of organization from a single discourse analysis, but it is possible to make a least three observations: First, health care management and strategic communication become mutually implicated in the course of the 2000s. Second, health care enterprises seem to develop mixed identities, referring to public institution and private enterprise values interchangeably. Third, health care institutions seem to become part of an "audit society" regime in which internal, and often implicit, professional standards are increasingly challenged by an ideal of performance control, monitoring, and strategic transparency.

The case illustrates how the expansion of organizational health communication is informed by particular discourses of communication that may potentially be indicative of new organizing ideals of health care. While the Norwegian case is far from conclusive in this respect, it does suggest the value of moving from a first-order focus on optimizing communication outcomes toward a second-order focus on the broader context of communication ideas. That move may in turn allow for a more critical reflection on some of the core assumptions drawn upon by communication professionals and managers alike (see Byrkjeflot, 2011).

Communication as Management of Meaning

A management of meaning perspective on communication perceives communication as a sense-making or meaning-creating tool. Communication and the discourses in which it is implicated can be seen as a narrative resource that allows individuals and organizations to create culturally accepted meanings in processes of interpretation. Bruner (1990) claimed that there are two modes of knowing: a logo-scientific and a narrative mode of knowing. In the latter mode we use stories in order to construct our conceptions of self and others in everyday life. An interpretative perspective on communication thus defines communication as a way to construct meaning. One implication is that a core task for organizational health communication in concrete organizational contexts is to translate "outside" reforms, policies, programs, and strategies into everyday practice by constructing local narratives that make sense of such generalized constructs.

Czarniawska (1999) described how management is a narrative discipline that aims to persuade, translate, and enact meanings. For management, health communication is a way to translate, meaning. In recent narratives studies of organizations, narratives are seen as interactive and relational phenomena that are co-products of interactions (Boje, 2001; Cunliffe and Coupland, 2012; Humle and Pedersen, 2014). In a health care management context, this implies that management must consider the fragmented work-stories of health care professionals as a management condition and that stories never are isolated, but are related to other stories (meta-stories or discourses). Communication is thus the act of reassembling discursive elements into potential narratives that can construct meaning and identity in fragmented situations.

Case: Narratives of a health care change[2]

An emergency ward in a hospital implemented the idea of using triage as a new digital visitation tool in the ward. Before the introduction of triage, a nurse selected the incoming patients based on her/his experience. Digital triage is a standardized visitation system using color codes to address symptoms and prioritize among the incoming patients in order to treat the most acute patients first. The system uses digitals boards and involves new standardized work practices for doctors and nurses. The staff in the ward translated the idea of triage by constructing two types of innovation narratives: A spokesperson narrative constructed by consultants and team leaders in the ward, which highlighted the advantages that the digital triage system has for the old patients. The narrative presented the change as a legitimized way to create qualitative improvement for the patients. This management narrative co-existed with a more "fragmented narrative" that was constructed by the staff, and conveyed the many problems of the implementation process. Some versions emphasized the stress and social control among the staff who became visible by means of the new digital boards, while other versions captured the unseen consequences of the implementation, for example in terms of how to handle a situation with two patients with identical color codes.

The case demonstrates that narratives are used to make sense of this change event. Local managers sought to construct coherent narratives, appealing to professional values of patient improvement, to persuade staff to adopt the digital triage system, while the more fragmented narratives of the staff sought to voice the unseen consequences of the process and ensure that new tools of work standardization still allowed for professionals to reflect and make professional choices. Thus, both local managers and staff created meanings of the new process of prioritizing incoming patients. The co-existing narratives were an organizing condition that allowed for conflicts, resistance, and a diverse everyday life at a hospital, but also made room for shared values and legitimized change and coordination practices (see also Pedersen, Sehested, and Sørensen, 2011).

---

[2] The case builds on Pedersen and Johansen (2012).

A narrative perspective in health care is only one of many interpretative approaches embracing the many voices in health care management and the unseen consequences of management. A common feature of many of these approaches is that the object of study is everyday practices in the local clinic or in meetings between both patients and health care professions. Everyday practices are defined as discursive practices, which cannot be separated from how local managers, health care professionals, and patients interact through talk, narrative, and conversation.

Communication as Organizing Technologies

The discursive perspective on organization is influenced by two important turns in social science: the *linguistic* turn, whereby language and discourse are studied as key objects of social analysis (Deetz, 2003) and the *performative* turn, whereby language is seen as performative and the world is a regarded as a performative field of practice (Pickering, 1995), in which human and material actors together engage in a continuous stabilization and reorganization of reality. These strands of thought are closely connected to the field science and technology studies (e.g., Latour, 1987, 1999, 2005; Law and Hassard, 1999; Law, 2004; Mol, 2002), suggesting that the effects of current organizing technologies such as global or local programs, standards, and perspectives that travel inside and across organizational borders be examined. Thus, organizational studies of health communication need to investigate how health care institutions deploy and manage communication as an organizational task. When communication becomes a focal point in visions, policies, and strategies of health care organizations, communication is turned into different practices that permeate the whole organization. Organizing communication work not only involves reputation management, branding, and marketing in relation to other health institutions, interest groups, and politicians but also constitutes a political arena inside health care organizations.

The emergence of communication units and communication-oriented sub-professions brings discursive organizing technologies such as programs, standards, and perspectives into health care institutions. Here, the professional bureaucracy and the established organizational order of most health care institutions are challenged by the arrival of communication experts and their approach to communication. Professionalization of communication is to a large degree concerned with public value management and views on how to facilitate organizational communication on the patients' terms. Medical rationales and professions have traditionally ruled the social and professional worlds of health care institutions with a focus on the content and specificity of knowledge. Communicative interventions in health care professionals' practices change routines, language, and culture. Such initiatives lead to discussions about valuable communication, focusing on form versus content of communication. These controversies often involve turf battles about jurisdiction and organizational terrain between different professional groups (Freidson, 1970; Cheney and Ashcraft, 2007; Real, Bramson, and Poole, 2009; Real, 2010). The effects of discursive organizing technologies can for example be explored in ethnographic studies of health care organizations (see Pors, 2012). Discursive organizing technologies, programs, standards, and perspectives enact expectations to patients and professionals in collaboration between different actors (e.g., professions, sub-professions, patients), discourses (language, diffusion of documents, orality versus standardization and documentation practices), and materialities (design of communication products such as leaflets and websites, setting, tools and concrete technologies used). As a discursive organizing technology, communication enacts a political arena that needs to be studied in detail, to examine the different ways it manages and reorganizes practices, roles, and relations in health care.

Case: Turf battles in implementing an organizational approach to health care communication[3]

The Perspective of the Patient is a communication program at a Danish university hospital. Since the late 1990s, the hospital has aimed to professionalize its communication with patients. The program targeted face-to-face communication and *all* communication activities in the hospital. In doing so, the program drew on two opposing discourses of communication: communication as a strategic management tool aimed at optimizing organizational and clinical efficiency and communication as the ethical commitment to dialogue, which levels out hierarchies and creates organizational coherence.

The documents and interventions in the program became sites in which these two discourses and the professions advocating them clashed. Thus, when physicians, nurses, and communication workers met to develop or revise communication policies or patient pamphlets, debates about, for example, good communication and patient needs became controversies over professional jurisdiction. In these controversies the patient was cast as a discursive figure enrolled by both sides. On the one hand, the program's documents and interventions articulated care-oriented understandings of the patient. Here, the patient was seen as an affective care recipient, as a citizen with rights and as user with individual needs. Yet, on the other hand, the documents and interventions also employed a market-oriented approach to patients, construed as homogeneous target groups to which information can be standardized, as resources for improved organizational performance and as customers which displayed particular types of (malleable) behavior. The various positions of the patient had different organizational implications, for example the 'target group' called for standardization, the 'care recipient' called for individualized approaches and 'the patient as resource' called for organizational adaptation.

The communication program has no single unifying rationale or logic. Rather, care and market were two co-existing and entangled ways of organizing contemporary health care, both of which are closely tied to the role of communication in the health care sector.

This case illustrates how a professionalized approach to communication is both organized by particular discourses of communication and has organizing effects on the way

---

[3] The case builds on Pors (2012).

that ideals of the patient are articulated and negotiated. The patient became a discursive figure—a space for the enactment of conflicting organizational interests—and also a political figure, through which the organization tried to manage and transform itself from the inside in order to meet pressures from outside. Thus, the program was performed as both *regulation of* patients and *management through* the patient. For example visions of communicative coherence, stronger internal management information, and increased patient satisfaction were ways of managing through the patient that mobilized employees via ideals of the patient.

CONCLUSION AND DISCUSSION

In this chapter we have sought to describe organizational health communication as a management concern.

Given that organizational health communication work has evolved into an organized and even professionalized practice in response to changes in the wider health care field, it is pivotal for health care managers to become aware of the potentials and challenges of organizational health communication. Debates on organizational health communication are first and foremost concerned with intended outcomes, measured in terms of patient or staff behavior and attitudes. However, it is also important to address the wider organizational implications and potentials of organizational health communication.

By first emphasizing the variety of practices and perspectives within the field of organizational health communication and then elaborating a discursive perspective on communication tools and practices, we have focused on the institutionalization of communication ideals, on the management of meaning in communication about organizational change, and on the performative effects of communication work on professional work. We have drawn on empirical examples from health care in Scandinavia but also on new Scandinavian research contributions using a discursive perspective on communication and organization.

The dominant instrumental or optimizing perspective on organizational health communication was supplemented by pointing to the political, strategic, and leadership implications of communication. The chapter is thus a call for a more critical examination of the phenomenon of organizational health communication. It is a field that a lot of resources and hopes have been invested in and it has become yet another field of professionalization within health care. New forms of expertise and new standards are being installed in a field that is already populated by a number of strong and resourceful professions.

The broader field of health communication has been characterized by waves of enthusiasm and skepticism in terms of the effectiveness of planned public communication interventions. This has led to what seems to be more balanced ideals of public health communication, where the media campaign is only one of several approaches of health promotion. In relation to organizational health communication, more studies on both the effectiveness of various communication practices and their unintended consequences are needed. Surely, "communication" is the answer, but not to every question. We need to continue the discussion about the organizational (and societal) ideals embodied in communication discourse, the strategic uses of communication within organizations, and the shifting professional landscape that is produced by new communication tools and practices.

Our contribution and recommendation to the field of health care communication is that communication is more than a tool and a structural condition for health care management. We argue that many studies of health care management can be nuanced by a focus on how talk, meaning, and communicative performance contributes to the management of health care organizations. Therefore, we encourage new micro-studies of health care communication practices to reveal how such practices are negotiated, enacted, and institutionalized in the everyday life of health care organizations.

There are several stakeholders in such a discussion. One stakeholder is clearly the health care manager, who not only needs to strengthen his or her communication competencies (as it is now commonplace to stress) but also needs to become a competent judge of communication practices, tools, and ideals and how they may gradually transform, or exert adverse effect on, health care organizations.

Another stakeholder is the health care professional, who is often cast in the role of an obstacle to change and as in need of new competencies and perspectives, but who may also need to maintain a critical awareness of the limits of the communication perspective in relation to the core values of medicine or nursing, apart from those articulated in the discourses of communication.

Finally, the patient's interests are also at stake. Patients are generally viewed as the key beneficiaries of the communicative turn in health care. Yet it is important to stress that patients are also reshaped by communication: patients are trained to communicate effectively with health care providers and there are high demands on communicative literacy on behalf of patients who are called upon to become involved in the production and improvement of health care services. It is easy to see how a more communicative health care system may benefit the patient. However, it is also a system that increasingly enrols the patient in reputation management processes, in health care governance, and in organizational change initiatives. These forms of enrolment are at one and the same time sincere attempts to communicate with and involve the patient—and complex strategic organizational initiatives in which patient voices and inputs are resources drawn upon by professionals and managers alike in an attempt to exercise control, redraw boundaries, or demonstrate one's legitimacy in highly complex professional, managerial, and political environments.

REFERENCES

Aldoory, L. and Austin, L. (2011). Relationship building and situational publics: Theoretical approaches guiding today's health public relations. In *The Routledge handbook of health communication*, ed. Thompson, T. L., Parrott, R., and Nussbaum, J. F., pp. 132–145. London: Routledge.

Apker, J. (2012). *Communication in health organizations*. Cambridge: Polity Press.

Arndt, M. and Bigelow, B. (2000). Presenting structural innovation in an institutional environment: Hospitals' use of impression management. *Administrative Science Quarterly*, 45(3): 494–522.

Bensing, J. (2000). Bridging the gap: The separate worlds of evidence-based medicine and patient-centered medicine. *Patient Education and Counselling*, 39: 17–25.

Bentsen, E. Z. (2003). Laegelige ledere som institutionelle entreprenører. In *Ledelse i sygehusvaesenet*, ed. Borum, F., pp. 169–207. Copenhagen: Handelshøjskolens Forlag.

Boje, D. M. (2001). *Narrative methods for organizational & communication research*. London: SAGE.

Bruner, J. S. (1990). *Acts of meaning*. Cambridge, MA: Harvard University Press.

Bury, M. (2001). Illness narratives: Fact or fiction? *Sociology of Health & Illness*, 23(3): 263–285.

Buse, K., Mays, N., and Walt, G. (2012). *Making health policy*. London: McGraw Hill Education.

Byrkjeflot, H. (2011). Et kritisk blikk på omdømmeblikket. In *Substans og framtreden: Omdømmehåndtering i offentlig sector*, ed. Waeraas, A., Byrkjeflot, H., and Angell, S. I., pp. 51–70. Oslo: Universitetsforlaget.

Byrkjeflot, H. and Angell, S. I. (2007). Dressing up hospitals as enterprises: The expansion and managerialization of communication in Norwegian hospitals. In *Mediating business: The expansion of business journalism*, ed. Kjær, P. and Slaatta, T., pp. 235–264. Copenhagen: Copenhagen Business School Press.

Byrkjeflot, H. and Angell S. I. (2011). Omdømmehåndtering og strategisk kommunikasjon i sykehus. In *Substans og framtreden: Omdømmehåndtering i offentlig sektor*, ed. Waeraas, A., Byrkjeflot, H., and Angell, S. I., pp.116–130. Oslo: Universitetsforlaget.

Charon, R. (2005). Narrative medicine: Attention, representation, affiliation. *Narrative*, 13(3): 261–270.

Cheney, G. and Ashcraft, K. L. (2007). Considering "the professional" in communication studies: Implications for theory and research within and beyond the boundaries of organizational communication. *Communication Theory*, 17: 146–175.

Christensen, L. T., Morsing, M., and Cheney, G. (2008). *Corporate communications: Convention, complexity and critique*. London: SAGE.

Cunliffe, A. and Coupland, C. (2012). From hero to villain to hero: Making experience sensible through embodied narrative sensemaking. *Human Relations*, 65(1): 63–88.

Czarniawska, B. (ed.) (1998). *A narrative approach to organization studies*, Vol. 43. London: SAGE.

Czarniawska, B. (1999). *Writing management*. Oxford: Oxford University Press.

Davenport, N. H. (2011). Medical residents' use of narrative templates in storytelling and diagnosis. *Social Science & Medicine*, 73(6): 873–881.

Deetz, S. (2003). Reclaiming the legacy of the linguistic turn. *Organization*, 10(3): 421–429.

DiMatteo, M. R., Taranta, A., Friedman, H. S., and Prince, L. M. (1980). Predicting patient satisfaction from physicians' nonverbal communication skills. *Medical Care*, 18(4): 376–387.

Duggan, A. P. and Thompson, T. L. (2011). Provider–patient interaction and related outcomes. In *The Routledge handbook of health communication*, ed. Thompson, T. L., Parrott, R., and Nussbaum, J. F., pp. 414–427. London: Routledge.

Elsbach, (1994). Managing organizational legitimacy in the California cattle industry: The construction of effectiveness and verbal accounts. *Administrative Science Quarterly*, 39: 57–88.

Ferlie, E., Pettigrew, A., Ashburner, L., and Fitzgerald, L. (1996). *The new public management in action*. Oxford: Oxford University Press.

Foucault, M. (1972). *The archaeology of knowledge*. London: Routledge.

Freidson, E. (1970). *Professional dominance: The social structure of medical care*. New York: Atherton Press, Inc.

Freimuth, V. S., Massett, H. A, and Meltzer, W. (2006). A descriptive analysis of 10 years of research public in the journal of health communication. *Journal of Health Communication*, 11: 11–20.

Gerteis, M., Edgman-Levitan, S., Daley, J., Delbanco, T. L. (eds) (1993). *Through the patient's eyes: Understanding and promoting patient-centered care*. San Francisco, CA: Jossey-Bass.

Gordon, C. G. and Kelly, K. S. (1999). Public relations expertise and organizational effectiveness. A study of U.S. hospitals. *Journal of Public Relations Research*, 11: 143–165.

Grunig J. E. and Grunig L. A. (1991). Conceptual differences in public relations and marketing: The case of health-care organizations. *Public Relations Review*, 17(3): 257–278.

Hamilton, H. and Chou, W. S. (2014). *The Routledge handbook of language and health communication*. London: Routledge.

Hardy, C. and Thomas, R. (2015). Discourse in a material world. *Journal of Management Studies*, 52(5): 680–696.

Hinyard, L. J. and Kreuter, M. W. (2007). Using narrative communication as a tool for health behavior change: A conceptual, theoretical, and empirical overview. *Health Education & Behavior*, 34(5): 777–792.

Humle, D. M. and Pedersen, A. R. (2014). Fragmented work stories: Developing an antenarrative approach by discontinuity, tensions and editing. *Management Learning* (online version, October). Available at: <http://mlq.sagepub.com/content/early/2014/10/16/1350507614553547.full.pdf+html> (accessed October 4, 2015).

Hydén, L. C. (1997). Illness and narrative. *Sociology of Health & Illness*, 19(1): 48–69.

Iedema, R. (2008). Discourse analysis. In *International encyclopedia of organization studies (Vol. I)*, ed. Clegg, S. R. and Bailey, J. R., pp. 389–393. London: SAGE.

Kelly, M. P. and Dickinson, H. (1997). The narrative self in autobiographical accounts of illness. *The Sociological Review*, 45(2): 254–278.

Kjær, P. (2008). Institutional History. In *Institutions and politics*, ed. Nedergaard, P. and Campbell, J. L., pp. 111–133. Copenhagen: DJØF.

Kjær, P. (2009). How mass media influence organizations. In *Exploring the worlds of mercury and minerva: Essays for Lars Engwall*, ed. Wedlin, L., Sahlin, K., and Grafström, M., pp. 179–197. Uppsala: Acta Universitatis Upsaliensis: Studia Oeconomiae Negotiorum No. 51.

Kjær, P. and Pors, A. S. (2010). Patienten og kommunikationsliggørelsen af sundhedsvaesenet. In *Ledelse gennem patienten: nye styringsformer i sundhedsvaesenet*, ed. Kjær, P. and Reff, A., pp. 47–74. Copenhagen: Handelshøjskolens forlag.

Kjær, P. and Reff, A. (eds) (2010). *Ledelse gennem patienten: nye styringsformer i sundhedsvaesenet*. Copenhagen: Handelshøjskolens forlag.

Kleinman, A. (1988). *The illness narratives: Suffering, healing, and the human condition*. New York: Basic Books.

Kohn, L. T., Corrigan, J. M., and Donaldson, M. S. (eds) (2000). *To err is human: Building a safer health system*. Washington, D.C.: National Academy Press.

Latour, B. (1987). *Science in action: How to follow scientists and engineers through society*. Cambridge, MA: Harvard University Press.

Latour, B. (1999). *Pandora's hope: Essays on the reality of science studies.* Cambridge, MA: Harvard University Press.

Latour, B. (2005). *Reassembling the social: An introduction to actor-network-theory.* Oxford: Oxford University Press.

Law, J. (2004). *After method: Mess in social science research.* London: Routledge.

Law, J. and Hassard, J. (eds) (1999). *Actor network theory and after.* Oxford: Blackwell Publishing.

Lega, F. (2006). Developing a marketing function in public health care systems: A framework for action. *Health Policy,* 78: 340–352.

Lingard, L., Espin, S., Rubin, B., Whyte, S., Colmenares, M., Baker, G. R., Doran, D., Grober, E., Orser, B., Bohnen, J., and Reznick, R. (2005). Getting teams to talk: Development and pilot implementation of a checklist to promote interprofessional communication in the OR. *Quality and Safety in Health Care,* 14(5): 340–346.

Loubeau, P. R. and Jantzen, R. (1998). The effect of managed care on hospital marketing orientation. *Journal of Healthcare Management,* 43(3): 229–239.

Mechanic, D. (2008). Rethinking medical professionalism: The role of information technology and practice innovations. *Milbank Quarterly,* 86: 137–152.

Mishler, E. G. (1984). *The discourse of medicine: Dialectics of medical interviews,* Vol. 3. Norwood, NJ: Greenwood Publishing Group.

Mol, A. (2002). *The body multiple: Ontology in medical practice.* Durham and London: Duke University Press.

Moran, M. (1999). *Governing the health care state: A comparative study of the United Kingdom, the United States, and Germany.* Manchester: Manchester University Press.

Neuhauser, L. and Kreps, G. L. (2003). Rethinking communication in the E-health era. *Journal of Health Psychology,* 8: 7–23.

Noar, S. M. (2006). A 10-year retrospective of research in health mass media campaigns: Where do we go from here? *Journal of Health Communication,* 11: 21–42.

Nordgren, L. (2003). *Från patient till kund.* Lund: Lund University Press.

Nussbaum, J. (1989). Directions for research within health communication. *Health Communication,* 1: 35–40.

Ong, L. M. L., de Haas, J. C. J. M., Hoos, A. M., and Lammes, F. B. (1995). Doctor–patient communication: A review of the literature. *Social Science & Medicine,* 40(7): 903–918.

Pedersen, A. R. and Johansen, M. B. (2012). Strategic and everyday innovative narratives: Translating ideas into everyday life in organizations. *The Innovation Journal: The Public Sector Innovation Journal,* 17(1): 2–18.

Pedersen, A. R., Sehested, K., and Sørensen, E. (2011). Emerging theoretical understanding of pluricentric coordination in public governance. *The American Review of Public Administration,* 41(4): 375–394.

Pedersen, K. Z. (2010). Patienten som diskurspolitisk styringsredskab. In *Ledelse gennem patienten: nye styringsformer i sundhedsvaesenet,* ed. Kjær, P. and Reff, A., pp. 27–45. Copenhagen: Handelshøjskolens forlag.

Pfeffer, J. and Salancik, G. R. (1978). *The external control of organizations.* New York: Harper & Row.

Pickering, A. (1995). *The mangle of practice: Time, agency, and science.* Chicago: University of Chicago Press.

Pors, A. S. (2012). Ivaerksaettelse af kommunikation: Patientfigurer i hospitalets strategiske kommunikation. PhD thesis, Copenhagen Business School.

Pors, A. S. (forthcoming). Constructions of the patient in healthcare communications *Journal of Health Organization and Management*.

Real, K. (2010). Health-related organizational communication: A general platform for interdisciplinary research. *Management Communication Quarterly*, 24: 457.

Real, K., Bramson, R., and Poole, M. S. (2009). The symbolic and material nature of physician identity: Implications for physician-patient communication. *Health Communication*, 24: 575–587.

Real, K. and Poole, M. S. (2011). Health care teams: Communication and effectiveness. In *The Routledge handbook of health communication*, ed. Thompson, T. L., Parrott, R., and Nussbaum, J. F., pp. 100–116. London: Routledge.

Rose, N. (1989). *Governing the soul: The shaping of the private self*. London: Routledge.

Roter, D. L. and Hall, J. A. (2011). How medical interaction shapes and reflects the physician-patient relationship. In *The Routledge handbook of health communication*, ed. Thompson, T. L., Parrott, R., and Nussbaum, J. F., pp. 55–68. London: Routledge.

Røvik, K. A. (2011). Analyse av kommunikatorenes innmarsj i offentlig sektor. In *Substans og framtreden: Omdømmehåndtering i offentlig sector*, ed. Waeraas, A., Byrkjeflot, H., and Angell, S. I., pp. 71–83. Oslo: Universitetsforlaget.

Schein, E. (2010). *Organizational culture and leadership*. San Francisco, CA: Jossey-Bass.

Scott, W. R., Ruef, M., Mendel P., and Caronna, C. A. (2000). *Institutional change and healthcare organizations: From professional dominance to managed care*. Chicago: University of Chicago Press.

Suggs, S. L. (2006). A 10-year retrospective of research in new technologies for health communication: International perspectives. *Health Communication: International Perspectives*, 11(1): 61–74.

Thomas, R. K. (2002). "How far have we come?" *Marketing Health Services*, 22(4): 36–41.

Thompson, T. L., Parrott, R., and Nussbaum, J. F. (eds) (2011). *The Routledge handbook of health communication*. London: Routledge.

Vaara, E. (2008). A discursive perspective on legitimation strategies in multinational corporations. *Academy of Management Review*, 33(4): 985–993.

Van Riel, C. B. M. (1995). *Principles of corporate communication*. New York: Prentice Hall.

Vrangbæk, K. (1999). *Markedsorientering i sygehussekoren: Opkomst, udformning og konsekvenser af frit sygehusvalg*. Copenhagen: Copenhagen University.

Vrangbæk, K. and Christiansen, T. (2005). Health policy in Denmark: Leaving the decentralized welfare path? *Journal of Health Politics, Policy, and Law*, 30(1/2): 29–52.

Waeraas, A., Byrkjeflot, H., and Angell, S. I. (eds) (2011). *Substans og framtreden: Omdømmehåndtering i offentlig sektor*. Oslo: Universitetsforlaget.

Zolnierek, K. B. H. and DiMatteo, M. R. (2009). Physician communication and patient adherence to treatment: A meta-analysis. *Medical Care*, 47(8): 826.

CHAPTER 14

··

PATIENT SAFETY
AND QUALITY

··

JEFFREY BRAITHWAITE AND LIAM DONALDSON

INTRODUCTION

··

THIS chapter is focused on reviewing attempts to address patient safety and quality issues through the lens of the organizational factors—collective social processes and practices—that operate to create good or bad care. The chapter is in four parts. We first discuss the nature of the challenges facing us; then, we move to key management and leadership responses; and we follow this up with a discussion. Finally, we conclude the chapter and offer ideas on what's next.

We aim in the chapter to illuminate what we know about organizational and institutional factors, and how we can use such knowledge to strengthen how we manage safety and quality. It is widely believed that patient safety and care quality can be improved by providing more accomplished leadership and management, addressing teamwork and culture, learning from things going wrong, and consequentially enhancing the systems delivering care to patients. Yet three decades of accelerating attention have shown how difficult it is to secure substantial gains, and how the original optimism has given way to hard-bitten realism.

On this point, perhaps surprisingly, despite there being notable successes associated with identifiable interventions such as to decrease catheter-related bloodstream infections in intensive care (Pronovost et al., 2006) and lower mortality and morbidity attributable to the use of checklists in operating theatres (Haynes et al., 2009), there has been no reduction in the overall rates of harm at the systems level. Thus managing safety and quality better, including improving the way services are led, coordinated, and organized, looms as a very important, albeit very challenging, endeavor. But before we can discuss remedies, we must first examine the scale and scope of the problem.

THE SCALE AND SCOPE OF THE PROBLEM

Underuse, Overuse, Misuse, Underutilization, Overutilization, Variation, and Appropriateness of Care

The aim of any health system is to provide the right care to the right patient in the right place at the right time for the right price. Another take on this is to ask: Are the health benefits expected by an intervention in excess of the anticipated risks by a sufficiently high margin? We have accumulated knowledge about underuse, overuse, misuse, variation, and inappropriate care, which suggests that while there is a great deal of sound care offered, there is work to do to advance these normative aims.

Underuse occurs when the system falls short of providing a service (care, or an intervention) that is indicated—that is, would have been beneficial to the patient. Common examples are untreated depression, failure to immunize children in a population, or treatment such as that for cancer or hypertension is not provided because the condition is undetected or the care is started too late. *Overuse* manifests as a service which is un-needed, or the harm it could invoke exceeds the benefit it might provide. Recurring examples are prescribing antibiotics for a viral infection, or performing procedures inappropriately. Elshaug and colleagues identified 156 ineffective or unsafe health care services, including arthroscopic surgery for knee osteoarthritis, chest x-ray for acute coronary syndrome and imaging in cases of low back pain (Elshaug et al., 2012). None of these is indicated, yet many procedures of this type are performed. *Misuse* is when the service is appropriate but a preventable complication or adverse event occurs, reducing any benefit. Injuries from poor quality care (e.g., injuries resulting from administration of medication) are typical examples (Chassin, Galvin, and the National Roundtable on Health Care Quality, 1998). This traditional tripartite "use" conceptualization has broadened into more modern thinking on patient safety.

In addition, work has shown repeatedly that there are unjustifiable *variations in costs, processes and outcomes* of care. Beginning with Wennberg and colleagues' landmark publication in 1973, the Dartmouth Institute for Health Policy and Clinical Practice has demonstrated variations of care over the last 40 years in its Atlas of geographical clinical studies (Wennberg and Gittelsohn, 1973; The Dartmouth Institute for Health Policy and Clinical Practice, 2014). Studies in other countries show that variation is widespread (Corallo et al., 2014). This means there are opportunities to alter utilization patterns across health care services and thereby improve health care efficiency and quality.

Compounding these problems, the proportion of care deemed *appropriate* or "recommended" (in line with level I evidence or clinical practice guidelines) runs on average at a little over half. Of the large-scale population studies showing this, the proportion of recommended care delivered to adults in the US is 54.9% (McGlynn et al.,

2003) and indicated care delivered in ambulatory settings to children in the US is 46.5% (Mangione-Smith et al., 2007); for Australian adults across 22 common conditions representing 40% of the burden of disease it is 57% (Runciman et al., 2012).

Enquiries and Reports, Studies of Harm and Adverse Events

Taking a different tack, there is direct harm as a result of deficits in systems of care. Various authoritative reports (e.g., *To err is human: Building a safer health system* (Kohn, Corrigan, and Donaldson, 2000), *An organisation with a memory* (Donaldson, 2002, 2000), and *Iatrogenic injury in Australia* (Runciman and Moller, 2001)), and systems-level studies such as in the US (Brennan et al., 1991; Leape et al., 1991), Australia (Wilson et al., 1995), and Britain (Vincent, Neale, and Woloshynowych, 2001), have shown that around 10% of acute care admissions suffer harm, of which a proportion—perhaps a third—is deemed preventable. There is a possibility that this is an underestimate (see Landrigan et al., 2010). Whether or not that is the case, most experts believe there are plenty of opportunities to make care safer for patients.

The most dramatic examples of systems deficits occur when there is a meltdown—where a health care organization (usually a hospital) exhibits across-the-board failures in standards of care and clinical governance. An inquiry of some form almost always ensues. Inquiry reports offer the opportunity to see deeply into organizations where clinical practice is poor, management falls short, or systems are deficient. Hindle and colleagues (2006) analyzed eight inquiries in six countries (in the UK, at Bristol Royal Infirmary, and Glasgow's Victoria Infirmary; in Australia, at King Edward Memorial Hospital, Royal Melbourne Hospital, and Campbelltown-Camden Hospitals; in Slovenia, at Celje Hospital; in New Zealand, in Southland DHB; and in Canada, at Winnipeg Health Sciences Centre). A recent inquiry worth taking note of is that presided over by Francis at Mid Staffordshire in the UK (Francis, 2013; Berwick, 2013). The recommendations from inquiry reports are remarkably similar: attention should be given to leadership, training, teamwork, and organizational culture; to be more patient-not business-focused; and to have improvement at the heart of all endeavors.

Responses

World Health Organization (WHO) World Alliance for Patient Safety and the Magnitude of the Challenges

Notwithstanding those lamentations about shortcomings in making progress, much work has been done to tackle these problems. For instance, there are several ways to conceptualize patient safety and quality in order to enable improvement activities. Donabedian, amongst the first to think systematically about this, indicated we should conceptualize quality of care in terms of structure, process, and outcomes (Donabedian, 1966). The World Health Organization (WHO) became sufficiently concerned about safety and quality shortcomings in the 2000s that it commissioned multiple international groups, projects, and initiatives, gathered together relevant expertise and established an international agenda for action and research. One, reporting in 2008 (Jha, 2008) developed a list of global patient safety research priorities for the future, mapped to Donabedian's framework (Table 14.1). This list is not exhaustive; nevertheless it is indicative of important research priorities. Thus, Donabedian's definition has given way to more recent thinking which says we should identify specific issues within these three categories to tackle harm (Table 14.1).

Table 14.1 WHO World Alliance for Patient Safety: key structural factors, processes, and outcomes of unsafe care

Key structures, processes and outcomes	Specific areas to be addressed
Key structural factors that contribute to unsafe care	• Organizational determinants and latent failures • Structural accountability: use of accreditation and regulation to ensure patient safety • Safety culture • Training, education, and human resources • Stress and fatigue • Production pressure • Lack of appropriate knowledge and its transfer • Devices and procedures with no human factors
Key processes that contribute to unsafe care	• Misdiagnosis • Poor test follow-up • Counterfeit and substandard drugs • Inadequate measures of patient safety • Lack of involvement of patients in patient safety
Key outcomes of unsafe medical care	• Adverse events due to drug treatment • Adverse events and injuries due to medical devices • Injuries due to surgical and anesthesia errors • Health care-associated infections • Unsafe injection practices • Unsafe blood products • Safety of pregnant women and newborns • Safety of the elderly • Falls in hospitals • Decubitus ulcers

Adapted from: Jha (2008)

World Health Organization (WHO) World Alliance for Patient Safety

A WHO workshop designed to learn from errors two years following the global patient safety priorities suggested five methods: develop standard operating procedures and guidelines; ensure valid and up-to-date training; encourage effective communication; focus on medication safety; and work towards greater patient engagement (World Health Organization, 2010). These are priority areas for attention in many health systems, but are easier said than done.

Tackling Harm and Improving Quality

Hierarchies of Harm

While there are multiple ways to tackle harm, it is common to look at it hierarchically. This leads to frameworks which conceptualize health care in micro, meso, and macro terms, and the design of implementation strategies targeted to these levels.

Adverse events can occur at the level of individual human error, in on-the-ground teams and via front-line interpersonal or communication errors. These are microsystems problems—the domain of localized clusters of clinicians who deliver care to identified groups of patients (Mohr and Batalden, 2002). Next, there are procedural, divisional, or pathway events beyond any one service, at the organizational level (Vincent, 2003). These are meso-level systems problems. There can also be widespread failures across multiple health care organizations as a result, for example, of policy or regulatory omissions or commissions (Kushniruk et al., 2013). These are macro-level systems problems.

Whichever is the focus, context is crucial. For example, the care that matters is delivered by clinicians on the front line. Local systems, and cultures and politics, all play a role in the environment, affecting behaviors and practice which can produce harm or levels of care quality (Øvretveit, 2011; Shekelle et al., 2011). Indeed, according to WHO, "It is often the situation rather than the person that is error-prone" (Jha, 2008). However, engineering safe and effective care is complex, and any particular adverse event can have multiple causes (e.g., education deficits, resources constraints, experience levels, production pressures, or lack of appropriate knowledge transfer) (Jha, 2008).

Taking a Systems Perspective

Holding to a perspective that argues that the situation and collective behaviors rather than the individual is at the root of harm has led to many thinkers taking a systems perspective on safety and quality. Under this logic, remedying the system by streamlining or re-engineering processes, making things more efficient, contributes to alleviating the problems. However, most systems of care have become highly-connected, complex, stretched, and very busy. They are often saturated with work, behaviors, technology, and events: what has been labeled "going solid" (Cook and Rasmussen, 2005). In such circumstances, people continuously make efficiency-thoroughness trade-offs, labeled the ETTO principle (Hollnagel, 2009), in tightly-bound organizational structures.

Ultimately, many health care settings have "gone solid" with people being obliged under production pressures to trade thoroughness for efficiency. The propensity for patients to be harmed or quality of care to be compromised in such circumstances is high.

A Systems-Level Campaign Approach

Another way to tackle harm and quality of care across the whole system is to consider the task as a social campaign rather than a service-level or within-institutional matter. The Institute for Healthcare Improvement's (IHI) 5 Million Lives Campaign, based on a mantra of "no needless deaths, pain, helplessness, unwanted waiting or waste for any-one" designed 12 "Campaign Interventions" (e.g., deploy rapid response systems; prevent central line infections) (McCannon, Hackbarth, and Griffin, 2007) which many health systems have taken up in varied forms.

However, these and other strategies such as using structured checklists in theatres have not been adopted universally despite evidence that if they were introduced successfully, care would likely improve. Among the reasons typically tendered are that health care might not be sufficiently well organized, leadership could be deficient, clinicians may be unreceptive, resources are not available or have not been prioritized to these initiatives, people may not have committed and involved clinicians adequately in these programs to implement them effectively, or that clinicians are not convinced of their benefits and have resisted implementation. It might also be the case that implementation is hard—much harder than prescribing what to do. The explanation for why systems fall short might reside in a mix of these factors, and is likely to be context-specific.

The Present State of Play

In essence, then, there has been a slow transfer of evidence of benefits derived from research into front-line practice. We have accumulated extensive knowledge about the extent of the safety and quality problem, and internationally, considerable work has been done in understanding the categories of harm, but the central problems of successfully tackling the issues, improving quality of care, and making things safer for patients has meant that progress has been painfully slow (Braithwaite and Coiera, 2010).

For example, there is underutilization of many organizational programs of proven effectiveness. There is good evidence for the use of medical emergency teams (METS) or rapid response systems (RSSs) in acute settings to manage deteriorating patients (Hillman et al., 2005; DeVita, Hillman, and Bellomo, 2011, 2006). There is also evidence that hand hygiene programs can enhance the levels of hand washing by clinicians, which feeds into reduced levels of infection (Pittet et al., 2000; Pittet and Donaldson, 2006). Yet take-up has often been slow and uneven.

All in all, most experts have expressed concern about the stickiness of the problems, with "relatively high levels of adverse outcomes arising from unsafe practices, incidents, and medical errors" (Donaldson, 2001) continuing over time. As far as we can ascertain, despite the growing capacity of medicine to treat many more people with a wider range of conditions at advanced age, levels of harm (at 1:10 acute admissions) and appropriateness of care (half of care in line with level I evidence or consensus-based guidelines) have flat-lined for at least 25 years. In part, this is because of the tightly-coupled nature of busy, high-production health settings (Cook and Rasmussen, 2005; Braithwaite et al., 2013), and the fact that health care complexity seems perennially to be pushing in the modern era just at the edge of chaos (Kauffman, 1995; Glynn and Scully, 2010).

Key Management and Leadership Concepts and Initiatives

Managing and Leading Improvements in Safety and Quality

Hand in hand with the efforts to describe and measure the extent of harm, the problems with quality of care and the context within which adverse events arise, have emerged multiple strategies to improve things. We have already seen some of these: WHO's categories (Table 14.1) and IHI's campaign targets represent entire agendas for improvement at macro-, meso-, and micro-levels. Taken together, recommended initiatives boil down to detecting, monitoring, addressing, and preventing harm; applying tools, techniques, programs, and approaches; and managing and leading improvements to the safety and quality of care. But we have already noted that gains are not easy, and any that have eventuated have been hard-won. Dixon-Woods, McNicol, and Martin (2012) have summarized what has to be addressed in improving care into ten challenges including convincing people that there is a problem on the first place, tribalism, and having excessive ambitions.

Ways of Tackling Harm and Improving Care

Given the principles and priorities of WHO and the multiplicity of efforts devoted to improving care, it is not surprising that there are many tools and approaches at the disposal of clinicians and managers through which they might tackle harm, boost health care quality, and enhance delivery systems. Table 14.2 lists and summarizes a range of the most popular improvement strategies drawn from an array of sources. We have assigned them to nine categories.

Table 14.2 Popular improvement strategies

Category	Examples
1. Philosophical, conceptual	• Accounts of causation • Theoretical domains framework • Quality improvement conceptual frameworks
2. Patient journey	• Clinical practice guidelines • Care pathways • Chronic disease management • System re-engineering (or business process redesign) • Lean productions cycles
3. Education, development	• Educational outreach • Continuing medical education • Professional development and self-directed learning • Extended professional roles • Specialty outreach programs • Continuous quality improvement programs
4. Specific tools	• Clinical governance • Audit and feedback • Risk and safety management • SBAR communication • Severity assessment systems • Causation analysis • Forcing functions • Failure modes and effects analysis • Functional resonance analysis method • Six Sigma • Plan-Do-Study-Act cycles (PDSA) • Managerial walkarounds • Checklists • Clinical decision support systems • Adjuvant models of care • Evidence-based medicine
5. Natural systems characteristics	• Local opinion leaders and champions • Physician practice profiling • Culture change • Political reframing
6. Reviews, evaluations	• Peer case reviews • Realistic evaluation • Formative and summative evaluation approaches • Clinical audit
7. Teamwork, collaboration	• Interdisciplinary collaboration and teamwork • Multi-site quality improvement collaborations • Clinical service networks • Influencing organizational culture • Social campaigns

(Continued)

Table 14.2 (Continued)

Category	Examples
8. Patient–led	• Patient-mediated quality improvement strategies • Patient reported outcomes measures • Patient-centered or patient-focused care
9. External stimulus, reporting	• Public scorecards and performance reporting • Pay for performance schemes • External accreditation and standards • Incident reporting • Market-based control mechanisms

Adapted from: Scott (2009); Braithwaite and Coiera (2010); Hughes (2008); Frankel et al. (2003)

This however is only a list, and an incomplete one at that, albeit that it might help in specifying the types of activities that can be operationalized to tackle safety and quality. Most commentators would agree that it is much easier to list the techniques, philosophies, and approaches that have been designed, adapted, or adopted than to make effective use of them.

Models for Successful Improvement

The received wisdom of the field, after this long gestation period of attempting to engineer more safety and higher quality of care, is that, because of the poor progress we need models to enhance the way people on-the-ground make change and succeed with evidence-based improvement activities. One stream of thinking about this has come to be called implementation science. An example drawn from this field is the Promoting Action on Research Implementation in Health Services (PARiHS) framework which says that successful implementation is a product (or function, f), of three factors: the quality of the evidence (E), the context (C) within which implementation will take place, and the caliber of the facilitation (F) (Kitson et al., 2008). This has been summarized as a formula: SI = f (E, C, F) (Kitson et al., 2008). The PARiHS investigators see their framework as best applied as a two-stage model: to diagnose and scope the evidence and context, and then to determine the optimum facilitation mechanisms.

An alternative (or perhaps complementary) mechanism is to take an evidence-based approach to the phases of localized implementation. A recent systematic review of targeted literature in implementation science laid the foundation for a model (called Harnessing Implementation), applied to quality and safety (Braithwaite, Marks, and Taylor, 2014). It describes a cycle of implementation activities including getting ready (phase 1), assessing capacity for change (phase 2), selecting the appropriate implementation type (phase 3), committing resources and creating leverage (phase 4), and ensuring and measuring sustainability of the implementation and its effect size (phase 5). Communicating well, providing incentives, and regular feedback as progress unfolds are key enabling strategies in the model.

Implementation Science—Getting Evidence into Practice

The PARiHS and Harnessing Implementation approaches are specific examples of implementation science—concerned with getting evidence into clinical practice. This is a rapidly growing academic endeavor aiming to promote the uptake of research findings. Others have called for more evidence-based policy and management practices (Walshe and Rundall, 2001). A key problem is to weigh the value of evidence being created and sort out the evidentiary wheat from the chaff. There are 23 million papers in Medline, a comprehensive data base, and 11 systematic reviews and 75 randomized trials published every day (Bastian, Glasziou, and Chalmers, 2010).

Clinical Leadership versus Top Down Strategies

PARiHS and Harnessing Implementation require local action and facilitation (PARiHS) and enabling mechanisms within the phases (Harnessing Implementation). Both inevitably require effective management and leadership in some form or another, to sponsor, resource, or support the accomplishment of the envisaged uptake and associated changes. A long-standing question is whether leaders and managers should seek to adopt a top-down, bottom-up or middle-out approach. The answer is that all are needed depending on the circumstances. A key target for improvement specialists' attention is clinical managers. These are hybrid middle-out positions which translate organizational requirements between the top-level corporate management ranks (the blunt end of the system) and the staff providing care (the sharp end). Donaldson (2001) suggests essential qualities of a clinical manager can be divided between insights (e.g., an appreciation of the organizational context), attributes (e.g., capacity to lead and inspire), and skills (e.g., being able to resolve complex problems and work across boundaries).

There is widespread support for the role and capacities of clinical leadership and management and how they can assist in change being managed productively (Braithwaite and Mannion, 2011). For example, according to some scholars, clinical leaders are well placed to overcome barriers to quality improvement (Kumar, 2013). For others, "as the custodians of the processes and micro-systems of health care, doctors are ideally placed to lead improvements" (Clark, 2012). Dowton calls for new forms of leadership in health care, by pointing to the need for the development of meaningful leadership identities, the necessity to link managers with other professionals and stakeholders in health care systems more effectively, and requiring leaders to act as ethical role models and interpreters of institutional complexity for followers (Dowton, 2004).

Middle-level clinical managers play an important role in diffusing and synthesizing information, and bridging macro- and micro-level concerns, that is mediating between the strategy and coalface clinical activities of health care organizations (Birken, Lee, and Weiner, 2012). Specifically, clinician-managers are not only subject to pressure from above (from blunt-end corporate-level managers, seeking efficiency, performance, and productivity) and below (from sharp-end coalface clinicians, seeking resources to provide better clinical care, but also asking the clinician-manager to advocate for them and not curtail their clinical autonomy). They are also in competition with clinician-managers at the same level—for organizational resources or senior management attention, for example.

Other commentators have sought to distinguish individual with collective, shared (distributed) leadership approaches. Greenfield and colleagues define distributed leadership as "an emergent property of a group or network of interacting individuals; there is an openness of boundaries of leadership; and leadership expertise is spread amongst those involved … [to] … realize a concerted dynamic that is greater than the sum of the parts." In their study of a research partnership, they found that distributed leadership was the key determinant in realizing successful collaborations. Relationship-building and reciprocity, along with a preparedness to persevere and engage in ongoing negotiations, emerged as factors of distributed leadership (Greenfield et al., 2009). Fitzgerald and her co-researchers agree, indicating that distributed change leadership included three stakeholder groups: competent senior leaders interested in and supportive of change; credible, middle level opinion leaders; and others with a willingness to embrace change efforts (Fitzgerald et al., 2013).

Distributed leadership is predicated on multiple stakeholders each playing a role, and good management-professional relationships. Multiple layers of coordination are needed, and responsibility for improvement is shared across senior, middle-level, and coalface-level roles (Fitzgerald et al., 2013).

Diagrams and models are always more neat and tidy than real life, and distributed leadership is not unproblematic. In an interview of 107 National Health Service (NHS) stakeholders, participants expressed the concern "that distributed leadership could mean confusion about who was in charge" (McKee et al., 2013). As always, coordination of the diverse suite of attitudes in health care is an important consideration, but presents both generic and localized challenges.

Teamwork

Most improvement programs include initiatives based on enhancing teamwork and communication between team members and across teams. Amongst a large literature Ezziane indicated: "Several factors appear to contribute to the development of successful teams, including effective communication, comprehensive decision making, safety awareness and the ability to resolve conflict. Not only is strong leadership important if teams are to function effectively but the concept and importance of followership is also vital" (Ezziane et al., 2012).

Providing care is of course a "team sport," and there are clear links between teamwork and patient outcomes (Sorbero et al., 2008). Salas and colleagues recommend principles for training teams including developing competencies, modifying training and teamwork to the circumstances, incorporating simulation in the package of educational measures, providing feedback, evaluating progress, and sustaining behaviors over time (Salas et al., 2008).

When Teamwork and Communication Fail

Teamwork and communication are clearly viewed as important, but what about when they fall short or fail? What, for example, about anti-social, self-interested, or troublesome individuals or groups? In a survey of disruptive behavior, physicians' and nurses' disruption of services was linked to adverse safety for patients; 67% of respondents' believed disruptive behaviors and adverse events were related, 71% that there was a linkage to medical errors, and 27% that there was a relationship with patient mortality. In addition, 18% of respondents could report a specific adverse event that occurred because of disruptive behavior, three-quarters of whom believed that the adverse event could have been prevented. Disruptive behaviors can create perturbations in the system affecting others' focus and concentration, and aspects of collaboration, communication, and information transfer. These in turn can result in preventable errors, compromised safety and quality, and patient morbidity and mortality (Rosenstein and O'Daniel, 2008).

Champions and Opinion Leaders

Champions are people who contribute to the facilitation of improvement strategies. Opinion leaders are those with an influential voice, regardless of them holding any managerial or leadership role, and who can disproportionally affect others. They are believed to be key in leveraging stakeholders to commit to improvement activities, and are a positive or negative force for change depending on their stance. Interviews with Veterans Health Administration stakeholders in the United States showed that participants believed that local champions were important for successful change. They can communicate about a project or program, draw people into it, be active as local experts and resource persons, and become information conduits, connecting local and external stakeholders (Kirchner et al., 2012). Participants suggested that champions must be well-respected, good communicators and exhibit leadership behaviors in order to be effective (Kirchner et al., 2012).

Organizational champions and opinion leaders are often most prominent in the early stages of adoption (Hendy and Barlow, 2012) in helping or hindering implementation. In unsuccessful implementation, opinion leaders' propensity to hold fast to their existing positions can have detrimental effects in anchoring progress to the status quo. In successful implementation, on the other hand, champions' management and people skills can be harnessed and leverage created from their valuable organizational connections (Hendy and Barlow, 2012; Flodgren et al., 2011).

Individual Diligence

Champions and opinion leaders are specific examples of the broader idea of individual diligence. Although it is unfashionable to lay the blame for things going wrong at the feet of individuals, it is hard to escape the role of the individual in being mindful, conscientious, and reflexive in improving care—or in holding fast to existing cultural characteristics. In their study of "sociological citizenship," Corbett and colleagues reminded us that at the heart of successful systems changes are diligent individuals (Corbett, Travaglia, and Braithwaite, 2011).

Diligent individuals are professionals who are aware of their role as actors in health care organizations, and who take responsibility for both their own and their colleagues' actions to initiate improvements to safety and quality (Corbett, Travaglia, and Braithwaite, 2011). Another facet of this is positive deviance (Lawton et al., 2014). Enabling individual diligence is an important consideration to safety and quality improvement programs, and may assist in overcoming the problem of turning policy into practice or implementing change (Corbett, Travaglia, and Braithwaite, 2011).

Systems Improvement

There are many strategies for systems improvement. Labels such as "systems redesign," "business process re-engineering," and "lean" come to mind. They share a common understanding—that processes of care can be streamlined, promoting efficiency (Carayon et al., 2006).

According to such conceptualizations, the organization consists of connected components (people, technology, departments) which concertedly provide care as it unfolds over time, operationalized by people executing distinctive roles. Clinicians are thus embedded in processes and work on tasks which contribute to the delivery of better or worse outputs and outcomes. Many examples of improvement activities based on this logic have been documented (e.g., DelliFraine, Langabeer, and Nembhard, 2010; Elkhuizen et al., 2006). In the wrong hands, however, they can become mechanistic, or fail to realize improvements, or both. They can also reduce flexibility by removing needed tasks and necessary redundancy.

Inter-Professional Care

Inter-professional care is seen as a way to conjoin the expertise of clinical professionals such that differing clinician groups (doctors, nurses, allied health staff) work together effectively and productively, with each member contributing uniquely to common goals. The logic is that in encouraging inter-professionalism, clinicians will enhance the way they relate, interact, communicate, and collaborate. This, in turn, will result in improved quality of care and patient safety.

It has proven hard to demonstrate this beyond specific or isolated examples. There are randomized studies which, depending on the context, show benefits from inter-professional ward rounds (Curley, McEachern, and Speroff, 1998), inter-professional meetings (Schmidt et al., 1998), and externally facilitated inter-professional audits (Cheater et al., 2005). However, Braithwaite and colleagues conducted a longitudinal, four-year action research study of inter-professional collaboration. Despite concerted efforts, including presiding over multiple projects to induce greater levels of inter-professionalism, it was difficult to measure gains. Levels of inter-professional collaboration and attitudes toward cross-disciplinary teamwork were no different at years two, three, and four of the study (Braithwaite et al., 2012a, 2012b).

Restructuring

Thinking about a health system as if it is able to be predicted, definitively analyzed, and calculated is equivalent to conceptualizing it as an inanimate object, as a "rock." However, health systems can more aptly be conceived as complex biological systems with minds of their own, as a "bird" that needs to be fed, nurtured, and developed. Mechanistic, "rock-like" thinking is pervasive. It seems to be associated with people taking the view that the system can be decomposed into parts, and that they are interchangeable. This sort of thinking all-too-often points the way to restructuring. When people in positions of authority take this stance they frequently reorganize people by changing the boxes on the organizational chart, imagining that this represents meaningful change or streamlining of the system. There have been many attempts to restructure health systems and refocus efforts in this way. Studies show the benefits are poor or non-existent, and depending on circumstances, restructuring puts back progress by eighteen months or more (Fulop et al., 2005). Yet it is clear that health care systems are better described as being organic rather than mechanistic; as birds not rocks. Thus, restructuring is not a solution (Braithwaite, 2005, 2007; Braithwaite, Westbrook, and Iedema, 2005; Braithwaite et al., 2006); and in any case, as we have argued earlier, top-down solutions are ineffective without bottom-up involvement (Braithwaite, 2006; Braithwaite et al., 2006). It is much more important to engage clinicians in decision-making processes rather than restructure them. In contradistinction, it is a more suitable solution to support naturally occurring networks of clinicians (Braithwaite, Runciman, and Merry, 2009) to deliver care rather than formal structures.

Essentially, instead of restructuring health systems in the vain hope of inducing a better focus on safety and quality, we need resilient and vigilant organizations which can cope with the unexpected as well as try to tackle the commonly occurring— the constant tide of patients coming for care. Indeed, there are increasing grounds for believing that organizations will be safer and less risky if they have an inclusive organizational climate (Svyantek and Bott, 2004), effective leadership (Øvretveit, 2009), a positive culture and sub-cultures (Boan and Funderburk, 2003; Braithwaite, Hyde, and Pope, 2010), features of resilience (Hollnagel, Braithwaite, and Wears, 2013) and an approach which involves patients in care processes (Lawton and Armitage, 2012).

The Challenge of the Health Care Complex Adaptive System

We have seen that it is very hard to make change in health care, and specifically difficult to make the kind of transformation we are seeking in safety and quality though structural thinking. One reason is because of systems complexity.

A complex adaptive system (CAS) is one which self-organizes (i.e., it requires limited external effort or management to propagate itself) (Mennin, 2010), is dynamic (i.e., change transpires over time) (Choi, Dooley, and Rungtusanatham, 2001), and it exhibits emergence (i.e., spontaneous behaviors occur, generated by relatively simple roles and interactions) (Ellis and Herbert, 2011), and herding (i.e., agents pay attention, to what others are doing, and cluster with them, or emulate or reject them) (Zhao et al., 2011). CASs are characterized by structures which combine features of hierarchy (with laddered, vertical layers) and heterarchy (with silo-like, horizontal divides) (Martin, 2002; Stark, 2011) but they manage to traverse and communicate across these boundaries. In essence, a CAS will have a range of agents interacting in complex ways, both within and across pervasive boundaries, vertically and horizontally (Eljiz, Fitzgerald, and Sloan, 2010; MacMahon, MacCurtain, and O'Sullivan, 2010).

Health care is a CAS, of course, and this means that there is, to a considerable extent, self-determination, with continuously emergent behaviors and practices. Tightly-coupled clinicians interface with each other, and occasionally interact with loosely-coupled managers and policy makers, in separate but related hierarchical and heterarchical configurations. In such complicated ecosystems, localized clinical behaviors will not be readily understood by others outside those localities. Because behaviors are always emergent, and reverberate through the system, they are not readily predictable, notwithstanding that clinical and managerial routines in broad outline are specifiable and normalized. As Braithwaite and colleagues indicate, "perturbations in one locale may propagate through the levels, or laterally, manifesting as outcomes in an area unrelated in time or place to the originating activity" (Braithwaite et al., 2013). In effect, there will be opaque, iterating behaviors in sub-systems emerging from a multiplicity of interacting agents and various formal and informal feedback loops of adaptive capacity, applied to accomplish goals.

In such an environment, it is not clear how effective leadership and management of services and entire organizations, let alone across whole systems, can accomplish much beyond nudging clinical behaviors in preferred directions, and shaping and influencing cultures and sub-cultures in subtle ways. In any case, it is clear that clinicians in CASs will not respond in a 1:1 correspondence to being told *what to do*, or *when*, and they will be almost completely unresponsive to being told *how to do* anything. Doctors, especially, in every health system we know, have relatively high levels of discretion and autonomy. If an external request or demand for compliance via an above-down policy, procedure, or standard does not make sense to them on their terms, or is not, according to their principles, values and logic, good for their patients, or aligned to their professional preferences or interests, or fails to make sense clinically, or is seen as excessively bureaucratic, they are likely to resist, neglect to accept what is being proposed, or just ignore it.

Seen in this light it is hard to make the case for anything less than having highly skilled and credible leadership engaging with clinicians in positive ways over time. Other more top-down styles will not likely have effects beyond the superficial. Engaging clinicians, and encouraging partnerships between clinicians and other stakeholder groups to realize mutually agreeable goals, is just about the only strategy in such circumstances that will count.

Health care comprises a diversity of interests and cultures, technology, and ecosystems, and is at least as complex as any other human system. So working with rather than against its CAS features is an important consideration.

Use of Clinical Networks and Communities of Practice

This brings us to the naturally-occurring properties at the heart of the CAS delivering health care: the clinical networks (Cunningham et al., 2012) and communities of practice (Ranmuthugala et al., 2011) that are the essential mechanisms for providing services at the sharp end, underpinning safety and quality activities. Clinical networks are clusters of health professionals whose enduring, repeated relationships deliver care to patients, and communities of practice are interactive platforms for groups to exchange information and learn together.

For every clinical problem there are networks and communities of clinicians that have not been engaged and harnessed to the extent they might (Braithwaite, Runciman, and Merry, 2009). We have not encouraged these naturally occurring characteristics of complex systems, instead often preferring to manage them. Current "normal" patient safety and quality initiatives, including mandating standards, releasing policies, prescribing when root cause analyses should be done, and sponsoring hand hygiene, handover, and associated projects, have proven insufficient—but they are imposed on clinical networks in formal ways. Thus we want to draw a distinction between mandated, formally structured, and authorized networks and communities—those enforced by someone from the top and sanctioned on an ongoing basis by those in authority—and self-selected, emergent, collaborative networks with which clinicians identify, and into which clinicians elect to join. Clinicians work best when their expertise is called on and they flourish in networks and communities of their own choosing, reflecting their interests and preferences.

The choice seems to us stark: more of the same, trying to regulate, manage, and prescribe behaviors more intensively, or inviting, empowering, and nurturing clinicians in their own configurations. Rather than directing, micro-managing, or controlling clinicians through a hierarchy, using the leverage of their natural groupings to provide better care might be a more sustainable option. The management and leadership style choice, inevitably, will be bottom-up rather than top-down if the latter choice is made. According to this logic, successful organizations are more likely to exhibit desired behaviors via approaches which *encourage, support, and nudge* than *command, control, and mandate*. Progress in this vein will be predicated on leadership rather than management, and with more emphasis on supporting the sharp end than putting resources into the blunt end.

Resilient Health Care

Based on this kind of logic, an alternative approach to the find-and-fix model that has prevailed until now is in its early days, but is starting to contribute to a sea-change in our thinking on safety and quality. Based on complexity thinking, it has become known as resilient health care (Hollnagel, Braithwaite, and Wears, 2013; Wears, Hollnagel, and Braithwaite, 2015). Most of the work on safety and quality to date has been predicated on a model which essentially says: *make as few errors as possible, and stamp out harm wherever it appears*. Focusing on things going wrong is reactive, and assumes that specific errors can be fixed, and the generic causes of harm can be found and remedied. Fixing and remedying involves standardizing procedures, streamlining the system, mandating or prescribing solutions, and introducing barriers to prevent future harmful occurrences. This Safety-I view has not spent much time considering that if harm occurs in 10% of cases, then health systems performance goes right in 90% of cases.

This alternative to Safety-I—focusing on things going right—is labeled Safety-II (Hollnagel, 2014). Things go right often even in CAS-like health care settings because people on the front line skillfully adjust their behaviors, practices, and performance to match the conditions. They do not slavishly follow guidelines, procedures, and policies in precise ways as prescribed by those at the blunt end, but make sensible, localized accommodations in order to deliver care in flexible, resilient ways at the sharp end. Clinicians in this model are seen positively—not as error-prone agents whose behaviors need to be decomposed into constituent parts, but as resources who already facilitate everyday solutions to complex situations.

Moving to a Safety-II perspective requires an underlying change to how we conceive of and do patient safety and quality. Adverse events will still be tackled by Safety-I methods, and rightly so where they are linear problems which can be decomposed into their constituent parts and then readily addressed. But there are many more cases where things go right and we do not understand the circumstances—or why. The Safety-II paradigm asks: *How is it that everyday, flexible work contributes so much to safe, effective care?* We will have to design new ways of appreciating this, and consider everyday clinical practice as underpinning the system rather than as a problem to be solved. Clinicians and their performance in this way of thinking are investments, and the task is to understand how resilient care manifests. The Safety-II paradigm suggests that we need to spend more time looking at what goes right, and as we learn how and under what circumstances, striving to spread effective practices, ideas and models across the systems of care. Encouraging what goes right and diffusing ideas, about how care mostly succeeds is a counterbalance to the current obsession with how care sometimes fails, mostly responding to things going wrong, and trying to stamp out errors.

Discussion: Patient Safety and Quality in Relation to Health Care Organizational Processes and Practices

The Long-Term Nature of the Problem

Patient safety and quality problems, then, are deeply etched into the organizational processes that make up the value chain delivering care to patients. For that reason most experts have been on a journey, and now see poor care not as an individual but a collective problem—a systems concern. The individual clinician, according to this rationale, is not to be blamed unless there is willful or reckless disregard for the patient's well-being. In any case, the complexity of modern care means that its production is never the result of one person's actions. For these reasons, patient safety and quality of care are viewed as systems and cultural issues, and improving them must take into account organizational and human factors. Traditionally, effective management, leadership, and coordination of care loom as important considerations in the improvement enterprise, but in the past, they have often manifested through relatively top-down managerial activities.

Although studies have demonstrated successful changes (for example through decreased catheter-related bloodstream infections (Pronovost et al., 2006); checklists in operating theatres (Haynes et al., 2009); hand hygiene programs (Pittet et al., 2000); handovers (Catchpole et al., 2007); and Root Cause Analyses (RCAs) (Percarpio, Watts, and Weeks, 2008)) they remain relatively isolated exemplars. No known study has shown a health system that has improved across-the-board. Levels of harm in acute settings have not reduced from 1:10 to 1:15, 1:20, or 1:40. At the systems level, over 30 years, there have been changes, ranging from clinicians' recognition of the importance of quality and safety, to widespread use of adverse event reporting systems and electronic charts. For every clinical condition there are now evidence- or consensus-based protocols by which to deliver care. Increasingly better information and communication technologies are in use, and a wider range of methods and theories for addressing safety and quality have emerged.

However, despite these *changes*, we have not been able to demonstrate systematic, widespread or ubiquitous *improvements*. And the resilient health care approach suggests we have focused on the relatively few things going wrong rather than the relatively many things going right, and we have not leveraged the underlying characteristics of the health care CAS—opinion leaders, champions, and naturally-occurring clinical networks, collaborations, and communities of practice, for example—as well as we might.

The Challenge Remaining

There have been many attempts to implement small- and large-scale, localized and systems-wide initiatives designed to address safety and quality. When large-scale interventions have been designed as a way of tackling these issues, challenges to progress have emerged. A major initiative in the English NHS delivered few measurable additional gains in improved care in intervention versus control hospitals (Benning et al., 2011a) and significant efforts in North Carolina, USA over a six-year period showed little evidence that rates of harm have changed on safety and quality indicators in 10 hospitals despite concerted effort and considerable expenditure (Landrigan et al., 2010). Another study, an action research interventional project encouraging greater levels of inter-professional care over a four-year period, 2007–2010, showed no improvement in systems-wide attitudes towards inter-professionalism despite active encouragement of staff including 272 initiatives and 2,407 encounters with health systems staff and strong expenditure support for the project (Braithwaite et al., 2012a, 2012b). This has led some commentators to go so far as to suggest that an entrenched characteristic of health systems is inertia (Coiera, 2011; Dunn et al., 2012; Ellingsen, Monteiro, and Røed, 2013).

The paradox, then, is that we are now able to demonstrate the magnitude of the safety and quality problem, and to appreciate better than ever before its dimensions, characteristics, scale, and scope, but we have not yet been able to diffuse what we know widely, to improve uptake beyond localized successes, to harness the leverage of the various stakeholders, or to scale up our efforts (Benning et al., 2011b; Wachter, 2004; Pittet and Donaldson, 2006). We need to do better, whether this takes the form of new models, better leadership, greater levels of teamwork, or more implementation ingenuity. A more recent proposition is to include a Safety-II perspective, supporting clinicians' everyday capacity to succeed under varying conditions, and facilitating much more a focus on ensuring that as many things as possible go right. These types of thinking and activities loom as the next set of considerations for stakeholders—and there are many of them, worldwide—working on the enterprise we know as safety and quality. It is very important that we make more progress than we have to date. Patients, worldwide, deserve nothing less.

CONCLUSION

The largely uncharted waters in patient safety and quality have hidden a key factor. Those working in the field have been slow to harness the role of patients and families in shaping and improving the processes of care, clinical decisions, organizational governance, and health care policies. At the end of the day, it is not the Minister's, or policy makers', or managers', or clinicians', health system. It belongs to society, to the community, to patients, and their families and carers. The potential for improving the system, and making it safer, providing higher quality of care, does not rest on the shoulders of patients, but they are its arbiter and yardstick. If every provider of care delivered services at a level that they themselves would like to receive, and care took into account patients' specific, informed preferences, and their aspirations, hopes, and concerns, to the extent possible, every time, we suspect safety and quality would improve markedly. Now there's a test for providers in every system, and a challenge which everyone ought to take on, every time care is offered. Involving patients and carers in improvement is a key building block, and where a more successful future lies.

ACKNOWLEDGMENT

Thanks go to Emily Hogden, who did background research, formatting, and word processing to help produce this chapter, and Danielle Marks and Kristiana Ludlow, for their assistance.

REFERENCES

Bastian, H., Glasziou, P., and Chalmers, I. (2010). Seventy-five trials and eleven systematic reviews a day: How will we ever keep up? *PLoS Medicine*, 7(9): e1000326, doi: 10.1371/journal.pmed.1000326.

Benning, A., Dixon-Woods, M., Nwulu, U., Ghaleb, M., Dawson, J., Barber, N., Franklin, B. D., Girling, A., Hemming, K., Carmalt, M., Rudge, G., Naicker, T., Kotecha, A., Derrington, M. C., and Lilford, R. (2011a). Multiple component patient safety intervention in English hospitals: Controlled evaluation of second phase. *BMJ*, 342, doi: 10.1136/bmj.d199.

Benning, A., Ghaleb, M., Suokas, A., Dixon-Woods, M., Dawson, J., Barber, N., Franklin, B. D., Girling, A., Hemming, K., Carmalt, M., Rudge, G., Naicker, T., Nwulu, U., Choudhury, S., and Lilford, R. (2011b). Large scale organisational intervention to improve patient safety in four UK hospitals: Mixed method evaluation. *BMJ*, 342: d195, doi: 10.1136/bmj.d195.

Berwick, D. (2013). *Berwick review into patient safety*. London: Department of Health.

Birken, S., Lee, S.-Y., and Weiner, B. (2012). Uncovering middle managers' role in healthcare innovation implementation. *Implementation Science*, 7(1): 28, doi: 10.1186/1748-5908-7-28.

Boan, D. and Funderburk, F. (2003). *Healthcare quality improvement and organizational culture: Insights*. Easton, MD: Delmarva Foundation.

Braithwaite, J. (2005). Invest in people, not restructuring. *BMJ*, 331(7527): 1272, doi: 10.1136/bmj.331.7527.1272-a.

Braithwaite, J. (2006). Analysing structural and cultural change in acute settings using a giddens–weick paradigmatic approach. *Health Care Analysis*, 14(2): 91–102, doi: 10.1007/s10728-006-0014-8.

Braithwaite, J. (2007). How to restructure-proof your health service. *BMJ*, 335(7610): 99–99, doi: 10.1136/bmj.39272.443137.59.

Braithwaite, J., Clay-Williams, R., Nugus, P., and Plumb, J. (2013). Health care as a complex adaptive system. In *Resilient Health Care*, ed. Hollnagel, E., Braithwaite, J., and Wears, R. L., pp. 57–73. Farnham: Ashgate Publishing Ltd.

Braithwaite, J. and Coiera, E. (2010). Beyond Patient Safety Flatland. *Journal of the Royal Society of Medicine*, 103(6): 219–225, doi: 10.1258/jrsm.2010.100032.

Braithwaite, J., Hyde, P., and Pope, C., (eds) (2010). *Culture and Climate in Health Care Organisations*. London: Palgrave Macmillan.

Braithwaite, J. and Mannion, R. (2011). Managing change. In *Healthcare Management*, ed. Walshe, K. and Smith, J., pp. 429–451. Maidenhead: McGraw-Hill.

Braithwaite, J., Marks, D., and Taylor, N. (2014). Harnessing implementation science to improve care quality and patient safety: A systematic review of targeted literature. *International Journal for Quality in Health Care*, 26(3): 321–329, doi: 10.1093/intqhc/mzu047.

Braithwaite, J., Runciman, W. B., and Merry, A. F. (2009). Towards safer, better healthcare: Harnessing the natural properties of complex sociotechnical systems. *Quality and Safety in Health Care*, 18(1): 37–41, doi: 10.1136/qshc.2007.023317.

Braithwaite, J., Westbrook, J., and Iedema, R. (2005). Restructuring as gratification. *Journal of the Royal Society of Medicine*, 98(12): 542–544, doi: 10.1258/jrsm.98.12.542.

Braithwaite, J., Westbrook, M., Nugus, P., Greenfield, D., Travaglia, J., Runciman, W., Foxwell, A. R., Boyce, R. A., Devinney, T., and Westbrook, J. (2012a). Continuing differences between health professions' attitudes: The saga of accomplishing systems-wide interprofessionalism. *International Journal for Quality in Health Care*, 25(1): 8–15, doi: 10.1093/intqhc/mzs071.

Braithwaite, J., Westbrook, M., Nugus, P., Greenfield, D., Travaglia, J., Runciman, W., Foxwell, A. R., Boyce, R. A., Devinney, T., and Westbrook, J. (2012b). A four-year, systems-wide intervention promoting interprofessional collaboration. *BMC Health Services Research*, 12(1): 99, doi: 10.1186/1472-6963-12-99.

Braithwaite, J., Westbrook, M. T., Hindle, D., Iedema, R. A., and Black, D. A. (2006). Does restructuring hospitals result in greater efficiency? An empirical test using diachronic data. *Health Services Management Research*, 19(1): 1–12, doi: 10.1258/095148406775322016.

Brennan, T. A., Leape, L. L., Laird, N. M., Hebert, L., Localio, A. R., Lawthers, A. G., Newhouse, J. P., Weiler, P. C., and Hiatt, H. H. (1991). Incidence of adverse events and negligence in hospitalized patients. *New England Journal of Medicine*, 324(6): 370–376, doi: 10.1056/NEJM199102073240604.

Carayon, P., Hundt, A. S., Karsh, B.-T., Gurses, A. P., Alvarado, C. J., Smith, M., and Brennan, P. F. (2006). Work system design for patient safety: The Seips model. *Quality and Safety in Health Care*, 15(Suppl 1): i50–i58, doi: 10.1136/qshc.2005.015842.

Catchpole, K. R., De Leval, M. R., McEwan, A., Pigott, N., Elliott, M. J., McQuillan, A., Macdonald, C., and Goldman, A. J. (2007). Patient handover from surgery to intensive care: Using formula 1 pit-stop and aviation models to improve safety and quality. *Pediatric Anesthesia*, 17(5): 470–478, doi: 10.1111/j.1460-9592.2006.02239.x.

Chassin, M. R., Galvin, R. W., and the National Roundtable on Health Care Quality. (1998). The urgent need to improve health care quality: Institute of Medicine national roundtable on health care quality. *JAMA*, 280(11): 1000–1005, doi: 10.1001/jama.280.11.1000.

Cheater, F. M., Hearnshaw, H., Baker, R., and Keane, M. (2005). Can a facilitated programme promote effective multidisciplinary audit in secondary care teams? An exploratory trial. *International Journal of Nursing Studies*, 42(7): 779–791, doi: 10.1016/j.ijnurstu.2004.11.002.

Choi, T. Y., Dooley, K. J., and Rungtusanatham, M. (2001). Supply networks and complex adaptive systems: Control versus emergence. *Journal of Operations Management*, 19(3): 351–366, doi: 10.1016/S0272-6963(00)00068-1.

Clark, J. (2012). Medical leadership and engagement: No longer an optional extra." *Journal of Health Organization and Management*, 26(4): 437–443, doi: 10.1108/14777261211251517.

Coiera, E. (2011). Why system inertia makes health reform so difficult. *BMJ*, 342: d3693–d3693, doi: 10.1136/bmj.d3693.

Cook, R. and Rasmussen, J. (2005). "Going solid": A model of system dynamics and consequences for patient safety. *Quality and Safety in Health Care*, 14(2): 130–134, doi: 10.1136/qshc.2003.009530.

Corallo, A. N., Croxford, R., Goodman, D. C., Bryan, E. L., Srivastava, D., and Stukel, T. A. (2014). A systematic review of medical practice variation in OECD countries. *Health Policy*, 114(1): 5–14, doi: 10.1016/j.healthpol.2013.08.002.

Corbett, A., Travaglia, J., and Braithwaite, J. (2011). The role of individual diligence in improving safety. *Journal of Health Organization and Management*, 25(3): 247–260, doi: 10.1108/14777261111143518.

Cunningham, F. C., Ranmuthugala, G., Westbrook, J. L., and Braithwaite, J. (2012). Net benefits: Assessing the effectiveness of clinical networks in Australia through qualitative methods. *Implementation Science*, 7: 108, doi: 10.1186/1748-5908-7-108.

Curley, C., McEachern, J. E., and Speroff, T. (1998). A firm trial of interdisciplinary rounds on the inpatient medical wards: An intervention designed using continuous quality improvement. *Medical Care* 36(8): AS4–AS12, doi: 10.2307/3767037.

DelliFraine, J. L., Langabeer, J. R. II, and Nembhard, I. M. (2010). Assessing the evidence of six sigma and lean in the health care industry. *Quality Management in Health Care*, 19(3): 211–225, doi: 10.1097/QMH.0b013e3181eb140e.

DeVita, M. A., Hillman, K., and Bellomo, R. (eds) (2006). *Medical emergency teams: Implementation and outcome measurement.* 1st edition. New York: Springer.

DeVita, M. A., Hillman, K., and Bellomo, R. (eds) (2011). *Textbook of rapid response systems.* 1st edition. New York: Springer.

Dixon-Woods, M., McNicol, S., and Martin, G. (2012). Ten challenges in improving quality in healthcare: Lessons from the health foundation's programme evaluations and relevant literature. *BMJ Quality & Safety*, 21(10): 876–884, doi: 10.1136/bmjqs-2011-000760.

Donabedian, A. (1966). Valuating the quality of medical care. *The Milbank Memorial Fund Quarterly*, 44(3): 166–206, doi: 10.2307/3348969.

Donaldson, L. (2000). *An organisation with a memory: Report of an expert group on learning from adverse events in the NHS.* London: HMSO.

Donaldson, L. (2001). Safe high quality health care: Investing in tomorrow's leaders. *Quality in Health Care*, 10 (Suppl 2): ii8–ii12, doi: 10.1136/qhc.0100008.

Donaldson, L. (2002). An organisation with a memory. *Clinical Medicine*, 2(5): 452–457, doi: 10.7861/clinmedicine.2-5-452.

Dowton, S. B. (2004). Leadership in medicine: Where are the leaders? *Medical Journal of Australia*, 181(11/12): 652–654. Available at: <http://europepmc.org/abstract/MED/15588200> (accessed September 28, 2015).

Dunn, A., Braithwaite, J., Gallego, B., Day, R., Runciman, W., and Coiera, E. (2012). Nation-scale adoption of new medicines by doctors: An application of the bass diffusion model. *BMC Health Services Research*, 12(1): 248, doi: 10.1186/1472-6963-12-248.

Eljiz, K., Fitzgerald, A., and Sloan, T. (2010). Interpersonal relationships and decision-making about patient flow: What and who really matters?" In *Culture and climate in health care organizations*, ed. Braithwaite, J., Hyde, P., and Pope, C., pp. 70–81. Basingstoke: Palgrave Macmillan.

Elkhuizen, S. G., Limburg, M., Bakker, P. J. M., and Klazinga, N. S. (2006). Evidence-based re-engineering: Re-engineering the evidence. *International Journal of Health Care Quality Assurance*, 19(6): 477–499, doi: 10.1108/09526860610686980.

Ellingsen, G., Monteiro, E., and Røed, K. (2013). Integration as interdependent workaround. *International Journal of Medical Informatics*, 82(5): e161–e169, doi: 10.1016/j.ijmedinf.2012.09.004.

Ellis, B. and Herbert, S. I. (2011). Complex adaptive systems (CAS): An overview of key elements, characteristics and application to management theory. *Informatics in Primary Care*, 19(1): 33–37. Available at: <http://www.ingentaconnect.com/content/bcs/ipc/2011/00000019/00000001/art00006> (accessed September 28, 2015).

Elshaug, A. G., Watt, A. M., Mundy, L., and Willis, C. D. (2012). Over 150 potentially low-value health care practices: An Australian study. *Medical Journal of Australia*, 197(10): 556–560, doi: 10.5694/mja12.11083.

Ezziane, Z., Maruthappu, M., Gawn, L., Thompson, E. A., Athanasiou, T., and Warren, O. J. (2012). Building effective clinical teams in healthcare. *Journal of Health Organization and Management*, 26(4): 248–436, doi: 10.1108/14777261211251508.

Fitzgerald, L., Ferlie, E., McGivern, G., and Buchanan, D. (2013). Distributed leadership patterns and service improvement: Evidence and argument from English healthcare. *The Leadership Quarterly*, 24(1): 227–239, doi: 10.1016/j.leaqua.2012.10.012.

Flodgren, G., Parmelli, E., Doumit, G., Gattellari, M., O'Brien, M. A., Grimshaw, J., and Eccles, M. P. (2011). Local opinion leaders: Effects on professional practice and health care outcomes. *Cochrane Database of Systematic Reviews*, 10(8), doi: 10.1002/14651858.CD000125.pub4.

Francis, R. (2013). *Report of the Mid Staffordshire NHS Foundation Trust Public Inquiry: Executive Summary*. London: HMSO.

Frankel, A., Graydon-Baker, E., Neppl, C., Simmonds, T., Gustafson, M., and Gandhi, T. K. (2003). Patient safety leadership walkrounds. *Joint Commission Journal on Quality and Patient Safety*, 29(1): 16–26. Available at: <http://www.ingentaconnect.com/content/jcaho/jcjqs/2003/00000029/00000001/art00003> (accessed September 28, 2015).

Fulop, N., Protopsaltis, G., King, A., Allen, P., Hutchings, A., and Normand, C. (2005). Changing organisations: A study of the context and processes of mergers of health care providers in England. *Social Science & Medicine*, 60(1): 119–130, doi: 10.1016/j.socscimed.2004.04.017.

Glynn, L. G. and Scully, R. (2010). The edge of chaos: Reductionism in healthcare and health professional training. *International Journal of Clinical Practice*, 64(6): 669–672, doi: 10.1111/j.1742-1241.2010.02385.x.

Greenfield, D., Braithwaite, J., Pawsey, M., Johnson, B., and Robinson, M. (2009). Distributed leadership to mobilise capacity for accreditation research. *Journal of Health Organization and Management*, 23(2): 255–267, doi: 10.1108/14777260910960975.

Haynes, A. B.,. Weiser, T. G., Berry, W. R., Lipsitz, S. R., Breizat, A.-H. S., Dellinger, E. P., Herbosa, T., Joseph, S., Kibatala, P. L., Lapitan, M. C. M., Merry, A. F., Moorthy, K., Reznick, R. K., Taylor, B., and Gawande, A. A. (2009). A surgical safety checklist to reduce morbidity and mortality in a global population. *New England Journal of Medicine*, 360(5): 491–499, doi: 10.1056/NEJMsa0810119.

Hendy, J. and Barlow, J. (2012). The role of the organizational champion in achieving health system change. *Social Science & Medicine*, 74(3): 348–355, doi: 10.1016/j.socscimed.2011.02.009.

Hillman, K., Chen, J., Cretikos, M., Bellomo, R., Brown, D., Doig, G., Finfer, S., and Flabouris, A. (2005). Introduction of the Medical Emergency Team (MET) system: A cluster-randomised controlled trial. *The Lancet*, 365(9477): 2091–2097, doi: 10.1016/S0140-6736(05)66733-5.

Hindle, D., Braithwaite, J., Travaglia, J., and Iedema, R. (2006). *Patient safety: A comparative analysis of eight inquiries in six countries*. Sydney: Centre for Clinical Governance Research in Health, University of NSW and Clinical Excellence Commission.

Hollnagel, E. (2009). *The etto principle efficiency-thoroughness trade-off: Why things that go right sometimes go wrong*. Farnham: Ashgate Publishing Ltd.

Hollnagel, E. (2014). *Safety-I and Safety-II: The past and future of safety management*. Farnham: Ashgate Publishing Ltd.

Hollnagel, E., Braithwaite, J., and Wears, R. L. (eds) (2013). *Resilient health care*. Farnham: Ashgate Publishing Ltd.

Hughes, R. (2008). Tools and strategies for quality improvement and patient safety. In *Patient safety and quality: An evidence-based handbook for nurses*, ed. Hughes, R., pp.1–39. Rockville, MD: Agency for Healthcare Research and Quality (US).

Jha, A. (2008). *World alliance for patient safety-summary of the evidence on patient safety: Implications for research*. Spain: World Health Organization.

Kauffman, S. (1995). *At home in the universe: The search for the laws of self-organization and complexity*. New York: Oxford University Press.

Kirchner, J. E., Parker, L. E., Bonner, L. M., Fickel, J. J., Yano, E. M., and Ritchie, M. J. (2012). Roles of managers, frontline staff and local champions, in implementing quality improvement: Stakeholders' perspectives. *Journal of Evaluation in Clinical Practice*, 18(1): 63–69, doi: 10.1111/j.1365-2753.2010.01518.x.

Kitson, A., Rycroft-Malone, J., Harvey, G., McCormack, B., Seers, K., and Titchen, A. (2008). Evaluating the successful implementation of evidence into practice using the parihs framework: Theoretical and practical challenges. *Implementation Science*, 3(1): 1, doi: 10.1186/1748-5908-3-1.

Kohn, L. T., Corrigan, J. M., and Donaldson, M. S. (2000). *To err is human: Building a safer health system*. Washington, D.C.: National Academies Press.

Kumar, R. D. C. (2013). Leadership in healthcare. *Anaesthesia & Intensive Care Medicine*, 14(1): 39–41, doi: 10.1016/j.mpaic.2012.11.006.

Kushniruk, A. W., Bates, D. W., Bainbridge, M., Househ, M. S., and Borycki, E. M. (2013). National efforts to improve health information system safety in Canada, the United States of America and England. *International Journal of Medical Informatics*, 82(5): e149–e160, doi: 10.1016/j.ijmedinf.2012.12.006.

Landrigan, C. P., Parry, G. J., Bones, C. B., Hackbarth, A. D., Goldmann, D. A., and Sharek, P. J. (2010). Temporal trends in rates of patient harm resulting from medical care. *New England Journal of Medicine*, 363(22): 2124–2134, doi: 10.1056/NEJMsa1004404.

Lawton, R. and Armitage, G. (2012). The role of the patient in clinical safety. In *The Health Foundation thought paper*, pp. 1–12. London: The Health Foundation.

Lawton, R., Taylor, N., Clay-Williams, R., and Braithwaite, J. (2014). Positive deviance: A different approach to achieving patient safety. *BMJ Quality & Safety*, 23(11): 880–883, doi: 10.1136/bmjqs-2014-003115.

Leape, L. L., Brennan, T. A., Laird, N., Lawthers, A. G., Localio, A. R., Barnes, B. A., Hebert, L., Newhouse, J. P., Weiler, P. C., and Hiatt, H. (1991). The nature of adverse events in hospitalized patients. *New England Journal of Medicine*, 324(6): 377–384, doi: 10.1056/ NEJM199102073240605.

McCannon, C. J., Hackbarth, A. D., and Griffin, F. A. (2007). Miles to go: An introduction to the 5 million lives campaign. *Joint Commission Journal on Quality and Patient Safety*, 33(8): 477–484. Available at: <http://www.ingentaconnect.com/content/jcaho/jcjqs/2007/00000033/00000008/art00002> (accessed September 28, 2015).

McGlynn, E. A., Asch, S. M., Adams, J., Keesey, J., Hicks, J., DeCristofaro, A., and Kerr, E. A. (2003). The quality of health care delivered to adults in the United States. *New England Journal of Medicine*, 348(26): 2635–2645, doi: 10.1056/NEJMsa022615.

McKee, L., Charles, K., Dixon-Woods, M., Willars, J., and Martin, G. (2013). "New" and distributed leadership in quality and safety in health care, or "old" and hierarchical? An interview study with strategic stakeholders. *Journal of Health Services Research & Policy*, 18(Suppl 2): 11–19, doi: 10.1177/1355819613484460.

MacMahon, J., MacCurtain, S., and O'Sullivan, M. (2010). Bullying, culture, and climate in healthcare organizations: A theoretical framework. In *Culture and climate in health care organizations*, ed. Braithwaite, J., Hyde, P., and Pope, C., pp. 82–96. Basingstoke: Palgrave Macmillan.

Mangione-Smith, R., DeCristofaro, A. H., Setodji, C. M., Keesey, J., Klein, D. J., Adams, J. L., Schuster, M. A., and McGlynn, E. A. (2007). The quality of ambulatory care delivered to children in the United States. *New England Journal of Medicine*, 357(15): 1515–1523, doi: 10.1056/NEJMsa064637.

Martin, J. (2002). *Organizational culture: Mapping the terrain*. Thousand Oaks, CA: Sage Publications.

Mennin, S. (2010). Self-organisation, integration and curriculum in the complex world of medical education. *Medical Education*, 44(1): 20–30, doi: 10.1111/j.1365-2923.2009.03548.x.

Mohr, J. J. and Batalden, P. B. (2002). Improving safety on the front lines: The role of clinical microsystems. *Quality and Safety in Health Care*, 11(1): 45–50, doi: 10.1136/qhc.11.1.45.

Øvretveit, J. (2009). *Leading improvement effectively: Review of research*. London: The Health Foundation.

Øvretveit, J. (2011). Understanding the conditions for improvement: Research to discover which context influences affect improvement success. *BMJ Quality & Safety*, 20(Suppl 1): i18–i23, doi: 10.1136/bmjqs.2010.045955.

Percarpio, K. B., Watts, B. V., and Weeks, W. B. (2008). The effectiveness of root cause analysis: What does the literature tell us?" *Joint Commission Journal on Quality and Patient Safety*, 34(7): 391–398. Available at : <http://www.ingentaconnect.com/content/jcaho/jcjqs/2008/00000034/00000007/art00003> (accessed September 28, 2015).

Pittet, D. and Donaldson, L. (2006). Challenging the world: Patient safety and health care-associated infection. *International Journal for Quality in Health Care*, 18(1): 4–8, doi: 10.1093/intqhc/mzi093.

Pittet, D., Hugonnet, S., Harbarth, S., Mourouga, P., Sauvan, V., Touveneau, S., and Perneger, T. V. (2000). Effectiveness of a hospital-wide programme to improve compliance with hand hygiene. *The Lancet*, 356(9238): 1307–1312, doi: 10.1016/S0140-6736(00)02814-2.

Pronovost, P., Needham, D., Berenholtz, S., Sinopoli, D., Chu, H., Cosgrove, S., Sexton, B., Hyzy, R., Welsh, R., Roth, G., Bander, J., Kepros, J., and Goeschel, C. (2006). An intervention to decrease catheter-related bloodstream infections in the ICU. *New England Journal of Medicine*, 355(26): 2725–2732, doi: 10.1056/NEJMoa061115.

Ranmuthugala, G., Plumb, J. J., Cunningham, F. C., Georgiou, A., Westbrook, J. I., and Braithwaite, J. (2011). How and why are communities of practice established in the health-care sector? A systematic review of the literature. *BMC Health Services Research*, 11(273), doi: 10.1186/1472-6963-11-273.

Rosenstein, A. H. and O'Daniel, M. (2008). A survey of the impact of disruptive behaviors and communication defects on patient safety. *Joint Commission Journal on Quality and Patient Safety*, 34(8): 464–471. Available at: <http://www.ingentaconnect.com/content/jcaho/jcjqs/2008/00000034/00000008/art00005> (accessed September 28, 2015).

Runciman, W. B., Hunt, T. D., Hannaford, N. A., Hibbert, P. D., Westbrook, J. I., Coiera, E. W., Day, R. O., Hindmarsh, D. M., McGlynn, E. A., and Braithwaite, J. (2012). Caretrack: Assessing the appropriateness of health care delivery in Australia. *Medical Journal of Australia*, 197(2): 100–105, doi: 10.5694/mja12.10510.

Runciman, W. B. and Moller, J. (2001). *Iatrogenic injury in Australia*. Adelaide: Australian Patient Safety Foundation.

Salas, E., DiazGranados, D., Weaver, S. J., and King, H. (2008). Does team training work? Principles for health care. *Academic Emergency Medicine*, 15(11): 1002–1009, doi: 10.1111/j.1553-2712.2008.00254.x.

Schmidt, I., Claesson, C. B., Westerholm, B., Nilsson, L. G., and Svarstad, B. L. (1998). The impact of regular multidisciplinary team interventions on psychotropic prescribing in Swedish nursing homes. *Journal of the American Geriatrics Society*, 46(1): 77–82. Available at: <http://europepmc.org/abstract/MED/9434669> (accessed September 28, 2015).

Scott, I. (2009). What are the most effective strategies for improving quality and safety of health care? *Internal Medicine Journal*, 39(6): 389–400, doi: 10.1111/j.1445-5994.2008.01798.x.

Shekelle, P. G., Pronovost, P. J., Wachter, R. M., Taylor, S. L., Dy, S. M., Foy, R., Hempel, S., McDonald, K. M., Ovretveit, J., Rubenstein, L. V., Adams, A. S., Angood, P. B., Bates, D. B., Bickman, L., Carayon, P., Donaldson, L., Duan, N., Farley, D. O., Greenhalgh, T., Haughom, J., Lake, E. T., Lilford, R., Lohr, K. N., Meyer, G. S., Miller, M. R., Neuhauser, D. V., Ryan, G., Saint, S., Shojania, K. G., Shortell, S. M., Stevens, D. P., and Walshe, K. (2011). Advancing the science of patient safety. *Annals of Internal Medicine*, 154(10): 693–696, doi: 10.7326/0003-4819-154-10-201105170-00011.

Sorbero, M. E., Farley, D. O., Mattke, S., and Lovejoy, S. L. (2008). *Outcome measures for effective teamwork in inpatient care: Final report*. Arlington, VA: RAND Corporation.

Stark, David. (2011). *The sense of dissonance: Accounts of worth in economic life*. Princeton, NJ: Princeton University Press.

Svyantek, D. J. and Bott, J. P. (2004). Organizational culture and organizational climate measures: An integrative review. In *Comprehensive handbook of psychological assessment: Industrial and organizational assessment*, ed. Thomas, J. C. and Hersen, M., pp. 507–524. Hoboken, NJ: John Wiley & Sons.

The Dartmouth Institute for Health Policy and Clinical Practice. 2014. *The Dartmouth Atlas of health care: Understanding of the efficiency and effectiveness of the health care system*. Available at: <http://www.dartmouthatlas.org/> (accessed September 26, 2014).

Vincent, C. (2003). Understanding and responding to adverse events. *New England Journal of Medicine*, 348(11): 1051–1056, doi: 10.1056/NEJMhpr020760.

Vincent, C., Neale, G., and Woloshynowych, M. (2001). Adverse events in British hospitals: Preliminary retrospective record review. *BMJ*, 322(7285): 517–519, doi: 10.1136/bmj.322.7285.517.

Wachter, R. M. (2004). The end of the beginning: Patient safety five years after "to err is human". *Health Affairs*, July–December (Suppl Web Exclusives): W4-534–W4-545, doi: 10.1377/hlthaff.w4.534.

Walshe, K. and Rundall, T. G. (2001). Evidence-based management: From theory to practice in health care. *Milbank Quarterly*, 79(3): 429–457, doi: 10.1111/1468-0009.00214.

Wears, R. L., Hollnagel, E., and Braithwaite, J. (eds) (2015). *Resileint health care, Volume 2: The resilience of everyday clinical work*. Farnham: Ashgate Publishing Ltd.

Wennberg, J. and Gittelsohn, A. (1973). Small area variations in health care delivery: A population-based health information system can guide planning and regulatory decision-making. *Science*, 182(4117): 1102–1108, doi: 10.1126/science.182.4117.1102.

Wilson, R. M., Runciman, W. B., Gibberd, R. W., Harrison, B. T., Newby, L., and Hamilton, J. D. (1995). The quality in Australian health care study. *Medical Journal of Australia*, 163 (9): 458–471. Available at: <http://www.ncbi.nlm.nih.gov/pubmed/7476634> (accessed September 28, 2015).

World Health Organization. (2010). *Patient safety workshop: Learning from error*. Geneva: World Health Organization.

Zhao, L., Yang, G., Wang, W., Chen, Y., Huang, J. P., Ohashi, H., and Stanley, H. E. (2011). Herd behavior in a complex adaptive system. *Proceedings of the National Academy of Sciences of the United States of America*, 108(37): 15058–15063, doi: 10.2307/41352044.

CHAPTER 15

....

IMPLEMENTING E-HEALTH

....

BILL DOOLIN

INTRODUCTION

....

As Bath (2008) observes, health care is an information-intensive process. Such information includes patient information for clinical care and management, secondary data for health service planning and delivery, and up-to-date information on the diagnosis and treatment of specific health problems. Unsurprisingly, a range of information technologies and systems have been developed to address the information needs of health care professionals, health service managers and planners, patients, and the public. The application of information and communication technology (ICT) in health care has become increasingly associated with the term "e-health". However, there is a degree of definitional ambiguity associated with this term. Some definitions emphasize specific technologies or contexts, such as the use of the Internet and other interactive technologies (Ahern, Kreslake, and Phalen, 2006), the networked exchange of health care information across organizations (Hill and Powell, 2009), or consumer-oriented health informatics (Ricciardi et al., 2013). Other definitions of e-health are more generic, simply encompassing ICT use in health care contexts and, in many ways, superseding previous usage of terms such as health information technology (IT) (Car et al., 2008; Oh et al., 2005; Ricciardi et al., 2013). In this chapter, e-health is defined broadly as *the application of ICT to support the organization, management, and delivery of health care*. Within this broad definition, e-health can refer to a range of information-based applications that (a) store, manage, and share patient health information; (b) inform and support clinical and patient decision-making; (c) enhance patient–provider interaction and service delivery (including remotely); (d) support evidence-based practice and epidemiological research; and (e) support health service planning and management (Ammenwerth, Schreier, and Hayn, 2010; Black et al., 2011; Car et al., 2008; Pagliari et al., 2005).

Definitions and descriptions of e-health tend to be overwhelmingly optimistic in terms of the benefits that ICT offers health care (Oh et al., 2005; Pagliari et al., 2005). The introduction of e-health is predicted to drive widespread changes to health care practice and improvements in the quality and efficiency of health care delivery (Alkhaldi et al., 2014; Blumenthal and Glaser, 2007). Belief in the capacity of e-health to achieve these changes has seen large-scale investment in ICT in health care internationally, and the development and implementation of large-scale e-health initiatives (in the order of billions of pounds or dollars) in various national health care systems (Adler-Milstein et al., 2014; Black et al., 2011).

Despite the optimism expressed about e-health and the investment being made in its development, an increasing number of commentators are pointing out that in many cases the benefits of e-health are more anticipated than realized in practice, and that empirical evidence for their achievement is lacking, inconclusive, modest, or mixed (Black et al., 2011; Goldzweig et al., 2009; Lau et al., 2010; Moxham et al., 2012). In a major review of primary studies and prior systematic reviews, Car et al. (2008) found that while e-health clearly has the potential to improve the quality and safety of health care, rigorous evidence demonstrating this impact was limited. In their review of over 150 international studies evaluating the outcomes of health IT adoption and use, Buntin et al. (2011) found that a large majority reported some form of positive outcome in terms of improvements in patient care. However, the authors also suggested that negative findings may be under-reported in the literature and that their examination of the studies reporting negative outcomes emphasized the criticality of what they call the "human element" (470) in implementing health IT. Similarly, a number of authors have directed attention towards the consideration of contextual and process issues in e-health implementation and integration in complex health care settings (Agarwal et al., 2010; Bath, 2008; Boddy et al., 2009; Car et al., 2008; Newell, 2011; Payton et al., 2011; Wears and Berg, 2005). Implementing e-health in a meaningful way requires more than the digitization and computerized management of patient information or the introduction of new technologies. It entails concomitant changes in work processes, interactions, and behavior by both clinicians and patients (Agarwal et al., 2010; Blumenthal and Glaser, 2007; DesRoches et al., 2010; Pope et al., 2013).

This chapter discusses e-health and its implementation. As Agarwal et al. (2010) argue, "Determining how best to manage the [health] IT implementation process ... is possibly one of the most pressing health policy issues" (801). The chapter briefly reviews the factors driving the development of e-health before introducing the main forms of e-health application in health care delivery, together with their benefits and risks. The focus is primarily on the management and use of health care information using ICT. The chapter then explores a range of issues that render e-health implementation and the realization of its anticipated benefits problematic. In doing so, it focuses on approaches that theorize the complex structures and processes involved in e-health implementation and attempt to identify the underlying mechanisms at work (Mair et al., 2012).

DRIVERS OF E-HEALTH

Health care systems in economically developed countries are facing a series of challenges, including an aging population, increased life expectancy but also increased incidence of long-term conditions, a wider range and increasing complexity of available treatments, increasing public expectations about access to and quality of health care, and increasing workloads and a shortage of qualified health care professionals. These challenges are increasing demand for and burden on health services, contributing to rising health care costs, and leading to variability in patient safety and quality of care (Car et al., 2008; Hill and Powell, 2009; Hovenga, 2010; Moxham et al., 2012). This is occurring at a time of increased fiscal constraint in most countries, where governments are attempting to curb or reduce public spending (Newell, 2011).

The application of ICT to health care delivery, in the form of the development of e-health applications, is increasingly seen as the means for solving three interrelated health care problems: accessibility, quality, and cost (Hill and Powell, 2009). At least in part, this reflects advances in ICT and its increasing pervasiveness in all parts of contemporary society (Car et al., 2008; Hovenga, 2010). Thus, e-health is expected to improve equitable access to health care by reaching less well-served populations, customizing care for individual patients, promoting changes in health behavior and disease management, and empowering patients as active participants in monitoring and maintaining their health (Agarwal et al., 2010; Ahern, Kreslake, and Phalen, 2006; Alkhaldi et al., 2014; Ammenwerth, Schreier, and Hayn, 2010; Blumenthal and Glaser, 2007; Stanimirović and Vintar, 2014).

E-health is further expected to improve the quality of care and enhance patient safety. In particular, the provision of critical and comprehensive information for clinical decision-making at the point of care, combined with computerized decision support, evidence-based prescribing, and electronic clinical communications, is anticipated to reduce the incidence of missed diagnoses, inappropriate clinical decisions, medical errors, and unnecessary tests and procedures. Such changes in information access and management are also expected to improve efficiency, enhance productivity, and reduce costs in health care (Agarwal et al., 2010; Alkhaldi et al., 2014; Ammenwerth, Schreier, and Hayn, 2010; Blumenthal and Glaser, 2007; Car et al., 2008; Stanimirović and Vintar, 2014).

While e-health implementation has predominantly occurred in the economically developed countries of North America, Europe, and the Western Pacific (Black et al., 2011; Moxham et al., 2012), increasing attention is being focused on the use of ICT to improve health care coverage and outcomes in developing countries (Blaya, Fraser, and Holt, 2010; Gerber et al., 2010). E-health implementation in such contexts can be challenging due to resource poverty, a shortage of skilled health care workers, lack of infrastructure, and distributed and rapidly growing populations, but can also have a larger impact than in more developed economies (Blaya, Fraser, and Holt, 2010; Fraser and Blaya, 2010).

E-Health Applications
for Information Management and Use

The electronic collection, storage, and retrieval of digitized patient information is central to ICT use by health care providers. Improving health care professionals' access to relevant patient information at the point of care should translate into improved quality of care, patient safety, and service efficiency (Car et al., 2008). Health information systems capture patient information at the point of care, integrate information from ancillary department such as laboratory, pharmacy, and radiology, and provide support to clinical decision-making and workflow (Black et al., 2011; Hill and Powell, 2009; Moxham et al., 2012). Increasingly, the emphasis on applying ICT in health care is shifting from the development of individual functional information systems to the exchange of health information across increasingly wider parts of the care continuum and involving a wider range of stakeholders, both within and between health care organizations and including patients and health consumers (Abraham, Nishihara, and Akiyama, 2011; Bath, 2008; Pagliari et al., 2005).

Figure 15.1 shows a conceptualization of e-health as the application of ICT to health care over three levels increasing of functionality and extent of the care continuum (Abraham, Nishihara, and Akiyama, 2011). Each level is associated with a particular type of electronic record: (1) an *electronic medical record* within a health care provider organization that combines clinical documentation with information from key ancillary departments; (2) an integrated *electronic health record* that allows the exchange of patient information between health care organizations; and (3) a *personal health record* that collects and stores information across the lifetime of a patient and extends access to

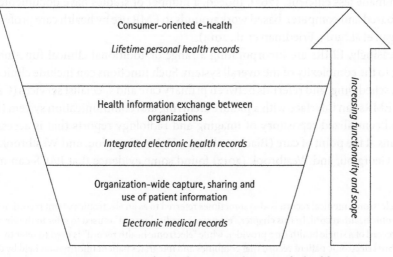

FIGURE 15.1 A multi-level conceptualization of e-health

that information to the patient, allowing patients to take a more active role in managing their own health. These three types of electronic record correspond roughly to the three main types of health IT outlined by Blumenthal and Glaser (2007, 2527).[1]

Information Management and Decision Support at the Point of Care

An electronic medical record (EMR) facilitates the digital collection, storage, and retrieval of patient information and has become regarded as a central part of the ICT infrastructure for health care providers (Dansky, Thompson, and Sanner, 2006). Such records assist clinicians at the point of care by making available more complete, current, and integrated information, including the patient's medical history and recent care details, laboratory test results, imaging reports, and prescriptions issued, across multiple encounters in a health care provider setting (Hill and Powell, 2009; Moxham et al., 2012). The expected benefits associated with EMRs derive from more efficient information management functions, improved accuracy and more complete capture of clinical information, immediate access by multiple users, savings in time and cost, improved clinician performance and productivity, and higher level analysis of data for audit and performance management (Black et al., 2011; Car et al., 2008; DesRoches et al., 2010).

However, there are potential risks or concerns associated with EMRs, including data security and unauthorized access, the impact on patient–provider interaction, and the implications for patient safety if paper-based records continue to be used in parallel. In some cases, data entry and retrieval by clinicians is persistently slower than the paper-based record systems EMRs replace (Black et al., 2011; Car et al., 2008). For example, in their review of EMR research, Greenhalgh et al. (2009) concluded that "while secondary work (audit, research, billing) may be made more efficient ... primary clinical work is often made less efficient" (767). Indeed, a number of studies have documented both paper-based and computer-based workarounds to EMR use by health care professionals (Flanagan et al., 2013; Friedman et al., 2014).

Increasingly, EMRs are incorporating a range of additional clinical functionalities, adding to the complexity of the overall system. Such functions can include clinical messaging, scheduling, and referrals between primary care and specialist services (Car et al., 2008). EMRs can interface with a picture archiving and communication system (PACS), a digital centralized repository of imaging and radiology reports that is accessible to clinicians at the point of care (Black et al., 2011; Hains, Georgiou, and Westbrook, 2012). Hains, Georgiou, and Westbrook (2012) found some evidence that PACS can improve

---

[1] An electronic medical record is also sometimes referred to as an electronic patient record or even an electronic health record. In this chapter, "electronic medical record" is used to refer to the electronic patient record of a single health care provider, while "electronic health record" is used to refer to a longitudinal electronic patient record that combines and integrates patient information held by different health care providers.

the efficiency of clinical work practices, and inconsistent evidence for their impact on clinical decision-making and communication between clinicians and radiologists. In fact, use of PACS could result in a decrease in communication and opportunistic interactions between clinicians and radiologists (Black et al., 2011).

EMRs are increasingly incorporating the ability to enter orders for medications, laboratory tests, and radiology tests electronically using computerized provider order entry (CPOE) systems. CPOE also include the electronic transfer of orders and return of results (Black et al., 2011). In their review, Black et al. (2011) found some evidence for an impact of CPOE use on efficiency, clinician performance, and appropriate ordering. Niazkhani et al. (2009) found that CPOE systems can improve order legibility and completeness, and reduce order turnaround times. However, in some cases, use of CPOE can negatively affect clinician workflow and workloads, such as increased time for order entry and interaction with the system, incompatibility between existing work practices and those required by the CPOE, or reduced opportunities for collaborative discussion (Black et al., 2011; Niazkhani et al., 2009).

E-prescribing refers to the ability to electronically prescribe and transfer prescriptions between the prescriber and the pharmacy. E-prescribing systems may include features that suggest generic alternatives, provide pre-populated order sets, allow clinicians to customize lists of frequently used orders, or trigger alerts for inappropriate or incorrect prescriptions (Abramson et al., 2012). Black et al. (2011) found moderate evidence for increased efficiency in time savings and more accurate communication as a result of e-prescribing, and some evidence of fewer medication errors and more optimal prescribing. Risks associated with e-prescribing, and CPOE more generally, include the introduction of new errors, user frustration with system interfaces and repetitive tasks, and "alert fatigue" (Aarts and Koppel 2009; Abramson et al., 2012).

EMRs, and indeed CPOE and e-prescribing systems, can incorporate a computerized clinical decision support system (CDSS). CDSS use a clinical knowledge-base, inputted patient information and inference mechanisms to generate case-specific advice. They have the potential to improve clinical decision-making by providing evidence-based and customized support (Car et al., 2008). In their review, Black et al. (2011) found mixed evidence for CDSS impact on clinician performance, which did not always result in higher quality care. This is consistent with Jaspers et al. (2011), who found that while CDSS can improve clinician performance, particularly with respect to medication ordering and preventive care reminders, the impact on patient outcomes is inconsistent.

Exchanging Health Information

An electronic health record (EHR) is "a longitudinal collection of patient-centric health-care information available across providers, care settings, and time" (Rosenthal, 2006). Just as the EMR is a central part of a health care provider's ICT infrastructure, the EHR is a central component of an integrated health information system in a given geographic area, whether at a community, regional, or national level. An EHR connects the EMRs of various health care providers and allows for the interoperable electronic exchange of information about an individual patient by multiple users across organizational and geographic boundaries (Abraham, Nishihara, and Akiyama, 2011; Blumenthal and Glaser, 2007; Car et al., 2008).

Health information exchange using an EHR typically involves a shared platform and standard syntax to ensure interoperability and the exchange of information between different types of systems. It also requires secure (and audited) access to the EHR to reduce the risk of threats to data integrity or breaches of patient confidentiality that are a concomitant consequence of increasing levels of information sharing (Car et al., 2008). However, there are major potential benefits in terms of improved clinician performance, enhanced cooperation across multiple care settings, personalization of patient care across the care continuum, and improved overall efficiency of health care delivery (Abraham, Nishihara, and Akiyama, 2011; Car et al., 2008).

EHRs are the focus of a number of countries' e-health efforts, not least because of potential cost savings in improved efficiency of health care delivery. However, successful implementations have been elusive and most countries have experienced difficulties in developing a sustainable approach for exchanging patient information at a national level (Bowden and Coiera, 2013; Deutsch, Duftschmid, and Dorda, 2010; Garrety et al., 2014; Greenhalgh et al., 2013). Reported challenges for EHR implementation and health information exchange include security and privacy concerns, responsibility for and governance of shared patient information, management of patient consent, clinician or provider distrust of information from other sources, achieving data integration and preserving data integrity, and defining standards for interoperability (Garrety et al., 2014; Pirnejad, Bal, and Berg, 2008; Zwaanswijk et al., 2011). Given the problematic and ongoing development of many EHR initiatives, it perhaps not surprising that there is limited empirical evidence for the attainment of their anticipated benefits (Car et al., 2008; Sheikh et al., 2011).

Extending Health Information Management to Consumers[2]

Dansky, Thompson, and Sanner (2006) suggest that "Health care is in the midst of a consumer-oriented technology explosion" (397), driven by the move towards more patient-centered models of health care delivery and consumer demands for Internet-based solutions to health care problems. A wide range of emerging consumer-oriented electronic tools and services offer the potential for individual health care consumers to more actively control their personal health information, manage their own health and well-being, self-manage their long-term conditions, and coordinate their care across

[2] "The term consumers encompasses patients, families, and caregivers, regardless of health status, whether or not they are actively receiving health care services" (Ricciardi et al., 2013, 376).

multiple providers. These include health information websites, provider-generated health care information and education resources, online health communities, and health-oriented social media networks related to a particular medical condition. In addition, ICT can be used to deliver health care to patients at a distance, facilitating new models of integrated care. Mobile devices are being used to deliver a wide range of online, interactive, and personally customizable applications for health behavior change, and personal monitoring devices are being developed to help patients monitor and manage their medical conditions, and to transmit relevant information to their health care providers (Agarwal et al., 2010; Blumenthal and Glaser, 2007; Forkner-Dunn, 2003; Hardiker and Grant, 2011; Hordern et al., 2011; Lluch and Abadie, 2013; Moxham et al., 2012; Ricciardi et al., 2013). While there is some evidence to support the benefits and efficacy of such consumer-oriented e-health applications and devices, more systematic evidence of their impact on health outcomes is needed (Åkesson, Saveman, and Nilssonet, 2007; Free et al., 2013; Hordern et al., 2011).

In particular, there is increasing interest in the concept and implementation of a personal health record (PHR) as a way of improving the quality of care and empowering consumers to manage their own health care. PHRs vary in the extent to which they are integrated with other health records and who controls the information they contain. A range of commercial providers offer stand-alone PHRs based on computers, mobile devices, or Internet applications. These allow consumers to enter and maintain personal health data. Some stand-alone PHRs enable a degree of information sharing with health care providers, but control of the information rests with the consumer (Archer et al., 2011; Detmer et al., 2008). Tethered PHRs allow patients to access and view certain parts of their EMR held by a health care provider, usually through a secure Internet portal. Control of the information remains with the provider, although some allow patients a limited ability to annotate their information (Ammenwerth, Schnell-Inderst, and Hoerbst, 2012; Archer et al., 2011; Blumenthal and Glaser, 2007; Detmer et al., 2008). The extent and type of information made available to patients varies considerably between health care providers (Collins et al., 2011). Some PHR portals offer additional functionality such as secure communication with the provider, appointments booking, and general health care information (Ammenwerth, Schnell-Inderst, and Hoerbst, 2012; Blumenthal and Glaser, 2007).

The "ideal" PHR is considered to be one that is integrated into the health care system and draws on comprehensive patient information from multiple sources, including the patient and all their health care providers (Archer et al., 2011; Kahn, Aulakh, and Bosworth, 2009). Implementing such a vision for PHRs faces a range of barriers, including the need for interoperability standards, the investment in infrastructure to integrate and securely maintain a lifetime of individual health information, concerns about protecting the privacy and confidentiality of patients and providers, consumer acceptance and trust, levels of consumer health literacy and comprehension of clinical information, balancing clinician and patient autonomy, and issues of custodianship of and liability for patient information (Archer et al., 2011; Beard et al., 2012; Detmer et al., 2008; Greenhalgh et al., 2008b; Kahn, Aulakh, and Bosworth, 2009). Given the nascent

stage of PHR implementation and use, there is only very limited evidence of their benefits (Ammenwerth, Schnell-Inderst, and Hoerbst, 2012).

PROBLEMATIZING E-HEALTH
IMPLEMENTATION

Van Gemert-Pijnen et al. (2012) argue that the complexity of health care innovation
has meant that e-health has not delivered on its potential, with many implementations resulting in abandoned projects, financial losses, under-used systems, or stakeholder dissatisfaction. Attempts to understand and remedy such results have produced
a stream of research studies that attempt to identify factors that enable and constrain
e-health implementation (Mair et al., 2012). Many such barriers and facilitators match
those in the IT project management literature more generally (e.g., adequate resources,
user attitudes and involvement, risk management, scope creep, legacy systems, data
quality, technical standards, system performance, training and support), but some seem
to have more salience for the health care context. These include concerns regarding data
security and patient privacy, problems with interoperability and integrating information from multiple sources, resistance from health care professionals with a high degree
of autonomy, and disruption to clinical workflow (e.g., Boonstra and Broekhuis, 2010;
Hill and Powell, 2009; McGinn et al., 2011).

   While such factor studies contribute to our knowledge of e-health implementation
outcomes, they do not necessarily address the processes involved in e-health implementation or the mechanisms that underlie it (Mair et al., 2012). There is a need for greater
use of theory to research e-health implementation processes (McEvoy et al., 2014). One
approach is the interplay of social theory with empirical data to develop phenomenon-
specific explanations that trace the mechanisms causing observed implementation
outcomes (Avgerou, 2013). Examining the body of research that takes this or a similar
approach in applying social theory to e-health suggests a number of insights into the
problematic nature of e-health implementation, which are discussed in the remainder
of the chapter.

E-Health Implementation ss a Complex and Emergent Process

A number of authors have argued that clinical environments are essentially complex
adaptive systems, sensitive to initial conditions and with properties that emerge as the
system responds to changes in circumstances (Bullas and Bryant, 2007). Such a system
is "replete with convoluted and highly inter-dependent relationships. Variation is the
norm, and nonlinear and novel responses are commonplace" (Abbott et al., 2014, e13).

This implies that introducing an e-health intervention will cause the system to adjust and adapt in unpredictable and non-linear ways, and that a particular approach to e-health implementation is unlikely to produce the same outcome in different clinical environments (Abbott et al., 2014).

In their case study of a discontinued EMR in a Finnish surgical clinic, Forsell, Karsten, and Vuokko (2010) analyzed escalating levels of complexity in issues with the EMR implementation. They were able to show how readily apparent first-order issues to do with the slow technical performance of the EMR combined and interacted to create second-order issues, such as dramatically increased workloads in dealing with patients and mistrust of the EMR system. These issues were reflected in the emergence of workaround practices and maintenance of parallel electronic and paper records. The clinicians' attitudes to the system and the disruptions to their everyday clinical work raised questions about insufficient information for patient treatment, the possibility of malpractice, and responsibility for mistakes or errors that might result from use of the EMR system. These third-order issues were more social and political, and had potential implications for other parts of the hospital, such as its reputation or financial position, undermining the organization's commitment to the EMR implementation. As the implementation issues interacted and escalated, they became more complex and harder to solve (Forsell, Karsten, and Vuokko, 2010).

As Mair et al. (2012) point out, "implementing and embedding new technologies of any kind involves complex processes of change at the micro level for professionals and patients and at the meso level for health-care organizations themselves" (357). Given the attempts by many countries to implement large-scale e-health programs, we can add the influence of macro level change for governments and health care systems (Greenhalgh et al., 2010). In their study of the (non-)use of an electronic outpatient booking system in England, Greenhalgh, Stones, and Swinglehurst (2014) draw on a version of structuration theory to conduct an analysis involving all three levels. They demonstrate how resistance to the nationally mandated e-health initiative was the result of the recursive relationship between and co-evolution of social structures, human agency, and technology that played out in a complex and emergent way at macro, meso, and micro levels (Greenhalgh and Stones, 2010). In doing so, they use the social theory to inform their empirical analysis of a particular e-health implementation. The authors suggest that their analysis reveals a mismatch between the model of clinical work and patient behavior assumed in government policy and inscribed in the online referral system and "the more complex, granular and exception-filled nature of real-world clinical practice" (Greenhalgh, Stones, and Swinglehurst, 2014, 218).

Greenhalgh, Stones, and Swinglehurst (2014) describe how the government's neoliberal policy of citizen choice and vision of an ICT-enabled health care system was mediated by the organizations charged with local implementation of the system, and enacted in relation to the internal structures of patients and doctors at the micro level of the technology in use. For example, the assumptions of rational choice based on abstracted performance information inscribed in the new system were inconsistent with patients' understanding of their role in the process and their patients' preference for referrals to their local hospital. Similarly, these assumptions conflicted with doctors' traditional selection of referrals based on their personal knowledge and professional contacts, and was perceived as interference with their contextual judgment. The conflict was also played out at the level of the locality, between the managers responsible for implementing the system, who interpreted doctors' resistance to using the system as threatening the quality of care, and doctors, who argued that their reluctance to use the system was because it threatened their professional standard of patient care (Greenhalgh, Stones, and Swinglehurst, 2014).

E-Health Implementations Often Lead to Unintended Consequences

Even where an e-health implementation is considered successful by (at least some of) its stakeholders, the complex and emergent nature of the implementation process may produce unintended, often adverse, consequences (Campbell et al., 2006). Systems intended to save time often add time to work processes, those expected to save money often create unexpected associated costs, while those designed to improve quality and patient safety often introduce new kinds of errors.

For example, Ash, Berg, and Coiera (2004) focused on the mismatch between how EMR and CPOE systems in a number of countries functioned and the reality of clinical work, and how this led to the emergence of unintended consequences when the systems were used in practice. For example, they found that, in many cases, the interface of the CPOE system was not conducive to work in a clinical use context characterized by multiple simultaneous activities and frequent interruptions. This sometimes led to confusion and juxtaposition errors resulting in incorrect medical orders for a given patient. The authors also found that many EMRs overemphasized structured and complete information entry, requiring the use of multiple fields and screens. This increased the time taken to record patient information and led to cognitive overload or loss of focus by the clinician. They make the interesting point that, in contrast to the "writing-as-thinking" cognitive process involved in the free text recording of data in prior paper-based systems, the excess of structure and detail entailed in an EMR hindered rather than helped the development of a cognitive pattern needed to understand a complex patient case.

Ash, Berg, and Coiera (2004) further analyzed how CPOE systems misrepresented the flexible and contingent nature of actual clinical work as a linear and predictable workflow. The relative inflexibility of the CPOE systems caused problems for their users, for example at times when urgency was needed, leading to workarounds that could potentially subvert patient safety. Similarly, computerizing the order process sometimes meant that the communication, cooperative problem-solving, and informal checking characteristic of the traditional medication ordering process was circumvented, removing a degree of redundancy and resilience that had previously caught errors made in medication management.

Unintended consequences of e-health implementations, such as those described above, arise more through interactions of the new technology with the organization's existing social structures and work arrangements than because of any technical flaws with an e-health application (Harrison, Koppel, and Bar-Lev, 2007). The emergent nature of unintended consequences means that they cannot necessarily be anticipated prior to implementation. As a result, e-health implementation needs to be less linear and more iterative as both the application and the implementation process are fine-tuned to address emerging consequences. Such an approach emphasizes adaptation to local experiences and practices (Harrison, Koppel, and Bar-Lev, 2007).

Making e-Health Implementations Work Involves Work

The complex and emergent nature of e-health implementation suggests that how e-health applications will function in the complex environments that characterize health care "can only be understood in the context of their use in particular practices" (Pols and Willems, 2011, 485). Pols and Willems (2011) argue that technology needs to be "tamed", but emphasize that the technology "is unleashed as well, affecting care practices in unforeseen ways" (484). Thus, while the "taming" of e-health technologies involves their integration into health care workflows, its "unleashing" may lead to the reconfiguration of the existing workflows. In either case, e-health implementation requires work (Nicolini, 2006; Pope et al., 2013).

A number of studies have examined the work needed to successfully integrate a new e-health technology into health care workflows. Goh, Gao, and Agarwal (2011) conducted a detailed case study of the replacement of a paper-based system of clinical documentation with the implementation of a computerized documentation system (CDS) in a large US hospital. Despite the disruption to the existing clinical workflows, the CDS was successfully integrated into the hospital's operations. The authors framed their analysis using concepts drawn from theory on organizational routines and adaptive structuration, and developed a model of the "adaptive routinization of health IT". The model proposes two mechanisms by which clinical work routines interact with the new technology, functional affordances, and symbolic expressions, and emphasizes the need to agentically manage these mechanisms to achieve a successful implementation.

In their analysis, Goh, Gao, and Agarwal (2011) suggest that the proposed users formed initial symbolic expressions about the CDS based on positive messages that emphasized efficiency and quality of care. These influenced how they anticipated and planned for changes their existing work routines. Once the CDS went live, however, the clinicians' impressions of the system became more negative as they experienced a loss of performance in using it and discovered that several previously available functional affordances were now absent. The authors found that the actions of certain key actors were influential in requesting changes to the CDS and developing workarounds that rapidly restored the functions its introduction had disrupted. Their leadership was a positive influence that helped to shape symbolic cues for other users, preventing the implementation from degenerating and possibly leading to abandonment of the system. Once this restoration phase was completed, clinicians began to explore and use new or previously unused functional affordances offered by the CDS. Personal innovativeness led to refinements in clinical work routines that used these more advanced features of the system.

Pope et al. (2013) analyzed the implementation of a CDSS designed to handle calls to emergency and urgent care services in three different UK settings. The CDSS is an expert system that uses a clinical evidence base to enable call-handlers to assess calls and assign appropriate care provision. The single e-health technology was implemented and used in the three settings in ways that reflected the different nature of the service provided and situated work practices in each context. The authors used Normalization Process Theory (NPT) to frame their analysis. NPT is a middle-range theory developed within the e-health field that attempts to explain how health care practices and innovations are implemented, embedded in everyday work, and sustained (integrated) in complex and emergent contexts through the actions of individuals and groups. The theory proposes four mechanisms that underlie this process of normalization: coherence (the work that people do to make sense of a practice), cognitive participation (the work done to enroll and engage individuals in relation to the practice), collective action (the work done in enacting the new practice), and reflexive monitoring (the work involved in assessing and adjusting a practice in use) (May and Finch, 2009; McEvoy et al., 2014).

Despite the variation in local contexts, in all three settings examined by Pope et al. (2013) coherence was achieved around the CDSS as suitable for call-handling work and a necessary development for dealing with increased demand for services and the need for evidence-based medicine. Again, in all three settings, staff were successfully enrolled in use of the CDSS, although more work and effort was involved obtaining their necessary active buy-in (cognitive participation) in settings where existing practices to be adjusted or accommodated, or where use of the CDSS involved a change in outcome for particular staff–patient interactions. Deployment of the CDSS changed the work of call-handlers in each setting; for example, by intensifying or extending it, changing the nature of expertise required, or offering a new "health worker" identity for the staff. Despite these changes, or perhaps because of them, the collective action necessary to bring the CDSS into use was achieved in all three cases. Finally, similar processes were used to monitor, appraise, and maintain the CDSS in each setting, although these process were not necessarily operationalized in the same ways and the adaptation of the system needed to keep it in place in each setting was different. As the authors conclude, "Implementation is more than simply putting technologies in place—it requires new resources and considerable effort, perhaps on an on-going basis" (Pope et al., 2013, 1).

E-Health Implementations Are Socio-Technical Problems

Commentaries on the problematic nature of e-health implementation have highlighted a perceived "technocentric" focus of many e-health policies and implementation approaches, in which the introduction of e-health is treated as predominantly a technological implementation and its social, organizational, and cultural aspects are overlooked or neglected (Greenhalgh et al., 2013; Wilson, Baines, and McLoughlin, 2014). This has led to calls for a socio-technical approach to e-health implementation and evaluation. There is a substantial body of research that views health care and ICT as constituting a socio-technical system in which people, technologies, and their social and organizational contexts interact in complex, interdependent, and mutually shaping ways. From this perspective, e-health implementation is not a technical problem, but rather a problem of socio-technical design (Aarts, Doorewaard, and Berg, 2004; Coiera, 2004; Wears and Berg, 2005). For example, Aarts, Doorewaard, and Berg (2004) analyzed the ultimately abandoned implementation of a CPOE system in a Dutch university hospital. Their analysis focused on the intertwining of technology and organizational arrangements in a process that mutually shaped both the CPOE system and the organizational practices that it supported.

Socio-technical perspectives on health IT have their roots in a number of research traditions (Berg, Aarts, and van der Lei, 2003). One stream of research utilizes actor-network theory (ANT) to understand the role that technologies play in stabilizing social arrangements—viewed as networks of materially heterogeneous elements. ANT emphasizes the inseparability and mutuality of technology and organization, and the importance of accounting for both human and non-human actants in understanding the outcomes of e-health implementations (Doolin, 1999). For example, Cho, Mathiassen, and Nilsson (2008) combined ANT with a process approach to analyze the implementation of a radiology information system and PACS in a Swedish hospital. They analyzed the implementation process as a sequence of episodes punctuated by critical events that shaped its trajectory by destabilizing the precarious actor-network (itself comprised of different and shifting configurations of actor-networks) that was forming around the emerging system. The authors' analysis revealed the complex socio-technical dynamics need to re-stabilize the incipient actor-network. These included ongoing negotiations around how the ICT would impact existing and new work practices and responsibilities between different groups of health care professionals with institutionalized power structures, and the important role played by the system's initial technical instability and poor technical performance in aligning the interests of various stakeholders.

A socio-technical approach to e-health implementation has a number of implications, including that implementation is an iterative and incremental process of organizational change in which the users of an e-health technology need to be centrally involved, and that e-health technologies should support rather than overly condition or structure clinical work (Berg, 1999; Berg, Aarts, and van der Lei, 2003). This latter implication suggests that e-health technologies should not be seen as ends in themselves, but as the means to achieve other, locally relevant health care ends (Greenhalgh et al., 2008a). A socio-technical approach to e-health implementation also allows those initiating and directing the implementation "to balance a concern with technology's potential and functionality *per se*, with the ways such functionality might be introduced to the organization, be adopted by groups of users and work teams, and the cumulative and integrated consequences that emerge as new sociotechnical systems of work are initiated, established and stabilised" (Cresswell et al., 2011, 60).

Large-Scale Versus Local E-Health Implementation

Studies and evaluations of e-health initiatives, such as the National Programme for IT (NPfIT) in England, suggest that large-scale, "top-down" e-health implementations are considerably more problematic than small or medium scale, "bottom-up" projects (Cresswell, Worth, and Sheikh, 2012b; Greenhalgh et al., 2010). Wilson, Baines, and McLoughlin (2014) go as far to suggest that there "is an emerging sense that technology implementations in complex policy areas at significant national scales are bound to fail" (564). A number of themes emerge from the literature addressing this issue. First, "multiple competing perspectives, complex interdependencies, inherent tensions, and high implementation workload" (Greenhalgh et al., 2010, 10) are exacerbated as the scale of the e-health implementation increases. Second, managing the tension between standardization, integration, or interoperability and responding to local requirements and priorities becomes increasingly problematic as the proposed implementation gets larger and more widespread. In particular, large centralized e-health implementations tend to limit the ability to customize a system to local needs, address the consequences of implementation at a local level, or use information in a locally meaningful way (Cresswell, Worth, and Sheikh, 2012b; Greenhalgh et al., 2009).

Third, the "success" of systems designed and developed locally and in-house appears to be difficult to replicate by commercial systems on a larger scale. Studies of e-health implementations that serve as exemplars and demonstrate significant benefits are often developed and refined locally in centers of clinical excellence, with high levels of involvement and ownership by their clinical users. Such local e-health solutions may not be readily transferable to different contexts of use (Black et al., 2011; Goldzweig et al., 2009). Similarly, aligning the various socio-technical dimensions in an e-health implementation is likely to be more achievable in smaller-scale projects where development occurs in an organic, incremental, and responsive fashion (Cresswell and Sheikh, 2013). For example, Abramson et al. (2012) examined the replacement of a well-established, locally-developed EMR with e-prescribing to a new, commercial EMR with clinical decision support for e-prescribing in a US hospital. Clinicians struggled with the transition to the new system, perceiving the new system to be over-engineered and rigid, and significantly reducing their efficiency without improving prescribing safety. Although some features of the commercial system were viewed as advantageous, most clinicians preferred prescribing with the simpler, locally-developed system that over time had become customized to their workflow and practice.

Resolving the tension between local needs or contingencies and system-wide requirements for interoperability and standardization may not be possible, but it does require managing (Greenhalgh et al., 2009). Allowing e-health implementation to occur at the local level before attempting larger-scale interoperability or integration may enable adjustment to change and increased complexity to be achieved in a more effective way (Cresswell, Worth, and Sheikh, 2012a). Alternatively, a "middle-out" approach, where shared goals and common standards are developed to form a high-level framework within which local e-health implementation can proceed in a more flexible way, may be feasible (Coiera, 2009). Similarly, Eason (2007) has suggested that large, centrally-directed e-health initiatives could be designed in ways that provide opportunities for local socio-technical development and implementation of systems that support a range of working practices. This would require not just technical features that allow flexibility for local customization but, perhaps more importantly, consideration of the structural implications of national policy imperatives. As Eason (2007) concludes, "Perhaps the main lesson is that the diversity of local sociotechnical systems cannot be denied and the needs of diverse settings will have to be recognized somewhere" (263).

CONCLUSION

There is little doubt that e-health in its various forms has the potential to offer significant benefits in health care delivery and accessibility, operational efficiency, and patient care and safety. ICT has become a pervasive and (mostly) useful part of modern society and there is no reason to believe that health care should be an exception. Nevertheless, the history of ICT implementation in this domain has often been troubled and many attempts to implement e-health have been equally problematic with their anticipated benefits remaining elusive. There is an important need for governments, policy makers, health care organizations, and individuals to learn from prior implementation attempts, regardless of how successful they may be perceived. There is no shortage of evaluations, case studies, and systematic reviews that endeavor to do this. However, this chapter has suggested that research that seeks to interweave concepts from social theory with empirical data is likely to be most able to address the complex structures and processes that characterize health care and attempt to identify the causal mechanisms underlying e-health implementation.

Reviewing examples of research that takes this approach has suggested a number of insights into (although not necessarily solutions to) the problematic nature of e-health implementation. Health care is a complex system characterized by many highly inter-dependent relationships. This makes e-health implementation a complex and emergent process, with unpredictable and non-linear effects across multiple levels that escalate as they interact. The implication is that attempts to impose standardized e-health implementations are unlikely to produce similar outcomes in different health care environments. This complexity and unpredictability often leads to unintended consequences, many adverse but some, potentially at least, resulting in improvements to clinical workflows or practice. This, in turn, suggests that making e-health implementations work requires ongoing efforts at the local level, involving iterative fine-tuning of e-health applications and systems in order to adapt them to the contingencies of such technologies in use.

Attempts to implement e-health need to avoid adopting a "technocentric" approach to implementation and instead actively take into account the consequences of the new technology for both the socio-technical arrangements that currently exist in specific implementation contexts and those that which may emerge and stabilize as users appropriate the technology and attempt to adapt it to their workflows and practices. Despite the tendency for governments and health services to initiate large-scale and ambitious centrally-directed e-health implementation programs, more successful results appear to have been achieved in implementations of local developed and customized e-health applications. There is no easy solution to managing the inevitable tension between locally relevant and useful e-health systems and the need for interoperability or integration on a larger scale, but the way forward may lie in approaches that take a middle position between top-down and bottom-up extremes, and that allow for local flexibility within commonly agreed standards and guidelines.

References

Aarts, J., Doorewaard, H., and Berg, M. (2004). Understanding implementation: The case of a computerized physician order entry system in a large Dutch University medical center. *Journal of the American Medical Informatics Association*, 11(3): 202–216, doi: 10.1197/jamia. M1372.

Aarts, J. and Koppel, R. (2009). Implementation of computerized physician order entry in seven countries. *Health Affairs*, 28(2): 404–414, doi:10.1377/hlthaff.28.2.404.

Abbott, P. A., Foster, J., Marin H. de F., and Dykes, P. (2014). Complexity and the science of implementation in health IT: Knowledge gaps and future visions. *International Journal of Medical Informatics*, 83(7): e12–e22, doi: 10.1016/j.ijmedinf.2013.10.009.

Abraham, C., Nishihara, E., and Akiyama, M. (2011). Transforming healthcare with information technology in Japan: A review of policy, people, and progress. *International Journal of Medical Informatics*, 80(3): 157–170, doi: 10.1016/j.ijmedinf.2011.01.002.

Abramson, E. L., Patel, V., Malhotra, S., Pfoh, E. R., Osorio, S. N., Cheriff, A., Cole, C. L., Bunce, A., Ash, J., and Kaushal, R. (2012). Physician experiences transitioning between an older versus newer electronic health record for electronic prescribing. *International Journal of Medical Informatics*, 81(8): 539–548, doi: 10.1016/j.ijmedinf.2012.02.010.

Adler-Milstein, J., DesRoches, C. M., Furukawa, M. F., Worzala, C., Charles, D., Kralovec, P., Stalley, S., and Jha, A. K. (2014). More than half of US hospitals have at least a basic EHR, but stage 2 criteria remain challenging for most. *Health Affairs*, 33(9): 1664–1671, doi: 10.1377/hlthaff.2014.0453.

Agarwal, R., Gao, G., DesRoches, C., and Jha, A. K. (2010). The digital transformation of healthcare: Current status and the road ahead. *Information Systems Research*, 21(4): 796–809, doi: 10.1287/isre.1100.0327.

Ahern, D. K., Kreslake, J. M., and Phalen, J. M. (2006). What is eHealth (6): Perspectives on the evolution of eHealth research. *Journal of Medical Internet Research*, 8(1): e4, doi: 10.2196/jmir.8.1.e4.

Åkesson, K. M., Saveman, B.-I., and Nilssonet, G. (2007). Health care consumers' experiences of information communication technology: A summary of literature. *International Journal of Medical Informatics*, 76(9): 633–645, doi: 10.1016/j.ijmedinf.2006.07.001.

Alkhaldi, B., Sahama, T., Huxley, C., and Gajanayake, R. (2014). Barriers to implementing eHealth: A multi-dimensional perspective. In *e-Health—for continuity of care*, ed. Lovis, C., Séroussi, B., Hasman, A., Pape-Haugaard, L., Saka, O., and Andersen, S. K., pp. 875–879. Istanbul: IOS Press, doi: 10.3233/978-1-61499-432-9-875.

Ammenwerth, E., Schnell-Inderst, P., and Hoerbst, A. (2012). The impact of electronic patient portals on patient care: A systematic review of controlled trials. *Journal of Medical Internet Research*, 14(6): e162, doi: 10.2196/jmir.2238.

Ammenwerth, E., Schreier, G., and D. Hayn, D. (2010). Health informatics meets eHealth. *Methods of Information in Medicine*, 49(3): 269–270.

Archer, N., Fevrier-Thomas, U., Lokker, C., McKibbon, K. A., and Straus, S. E. (2011). Personal health records: A scoping review. *Journal of the American Medical Informatics Association*, 18(4): 515–522, doi: 10.1136/amiajnl-2011-000105.

Ash, J. S., Berg, M., and Coiera, E. (2004). Some unintended consequences of information technology in health care: The nature of patient care information system-related errors. *Journal of the American Medical Informatics Association*, 11(2): 104–112, doi: 10.1197/jamia.M1471.

Avgerou, C. (2013). Social mechanisms for causal explanation in social theory based IS research. *Journal of the Association for Information Systems*, 14(8): 399–419.

Bath, P. A. (2008). Health informatics: Current issues and challenges. *Journal of Information Science*, 34(4): 501–518, doi: 10.1177/0165551508092267.

Beard, L., Schein, R., Morra, D., Wilson, K., and Keelan J. (2012). The challenges in making electronic health records accessible to patients. *Journal of the American Medical Informatics Association*, 19(1): 116–120, doi: 10.1136/amiajnl-2011-000261.

Berg, M. (1999). Patient care information systems and health care work: A sociotechnical approach. *International Journal of Medical Informatics*, 55(2): 87–101, doi: 10.1016/s1386-5056(99)00011-8.

Berg, M., Aarts, J., and van der Lei, J. (2003). ICT in health care: Sociotechnical approaches. *Methods of Information in Medicine*, 42(4): 297–301, doi: 10.1267/METH03040297.

Black, A. D., Car, J., Pagliari, C., Anandan, C., Cresswell, K., Bokun, T., McKinstry, B., Procter, R., Majeed, A., and Sheikh, A. (2011). The impact of eHealth on the quality and safety of health care: A systematic overview. *PLoS Medicine*, 8(1): e1000387, doi: 10.1371/journal.pmed.1000387.

Blaya, J. A., Fraser, H. S., and Holt, B. (2010). E-health technologies show promise in developing countries. *Health Affairs*, 29(2): 244–251, doi: 10.1377/hlthaff.2009.0894.

Blumenthal D. and Glaser, J. P. (2007). Information technology comes to medicine. *New England Journal of Medicine*, 356(24): 2527–2534, doi: 10.1056/NEJMhpr066212.

Boddy, D., King, G., Clark, J. S., Heaney, D., and Mair, F. (2009). The influence of context and process when implementing e-health. *BMC Medical Informatics and Decision Making*, 9: 9, doi: 10.1186/1472-6947-9-9.

Boonstra, A. and Broekhuis, M. (2010). Barriers to the acceptance of electronic medical records by physicians from systematic review to taxonomy and interventions. *BMC Health Services Research*, 10: 231, doi: 10.1186/1472-6963-10-231.

Bowden, T. and Coiera, E. (2013). Comparing New Zealand's "middle out" health information technology strategy with other OECD nations. *International Journal of Medical Informatics*, 82(5): e87–e95, doi: 10.1016/j.ijmedinf.2012.12.002.

Bullas, S. and Bryant, J. (2007). Complexity and its implications for health systems implementation. In *Information technology in health care 2007*, ed. Westbrook, J. I., Coiera, E., Callen, J. L., and Aarts, J., pp. 37–44. Amsterdam: IOS Press.

Buntin, M. B., Burke, M. F., Hoaglin, M. C., and Blumenthal, D. (2011). The benefits of health information technology: A review of the recent literature shows predominantly positive results. *Health Affairs*, 30(3): 464–471, doi: 10.1377/hlthaff.2011.0178.

Campbell, E. M., Sittig, D. F., Ash, J. S., Guappone, K. P., and Dykstra, R. H. (2006). Types of unintended consequences related to computerized provider order entry. *Journal of the American Medical Informatics Association*, 13(5): 547–556, doi: 10.1197/jamia.M2042.

Car, J., Black, A. D., Anandan, C., Cresswell, K., Pagliari, C., McKinstry, B., Procter, R., Majeed, A., and Sheikh, A. (2008). The impact of eHealth on the quality & safety of healthcare: A systemic overview & synthesis of the literature. Report for the NHS Connecting for Health Evaluation Programme, University of Edinburgh and Imperial College London.

Cho, S., Mathiassen, L., and Nilsson, A. (2008). Contextual dynamics during health information systems implementation: An event-based actor-network approach. *European Journal of Information Systems*, 17(6): 614–630, doi: 10.1057/ejis200849.

Coiera, E. (2004). Four rules for the reinvention of health care. *BMJ*, 328(7449): 1197–1199, doi: 10.1136/bmj.328.7449.1197.

Coiera, E. (2009). Building a national health IT system from the middle out. *Journal of the American Medical Informatics Association*, 16(3): 271–273, doi: 10.1197/jamia.M3183.

Collins, S. A., Vawdrey, D. K., Kukafka, R., and Kuperman, G. J. (2011). Policies for patient access to clinical data via PHRS: Current state and recommendations. *Journal of the American Medical Informatics Association*, 18(Suppl 1): i2–i7, doi: 10.1136/amiajnl-2011-000400.

Cresswell, K., Ali, M., Avery, A., Barber, N., Cornford, T., Crowe, S., Fernando, B., Jacklin, A., Jani, Y., Klecun, E., Lichtner, V., Marsden, K., Morrison, Z., Paton, J., Petrakaki, D., Prescott, R., Quinn, C., Robertson, A., Takian, A., Voutsina, K., Waring, J., and Sheikh, A. (2011). The long and winding road: An independent evaluation of the implementation and adoption of the National Health Service Care Records Service (NHS CRS) in secondary care in England. Report for NHS Connecting for Health Evaluation Programme, University of Birmingham.

Cresswell, K. and Sheikh, A. (2013). Organizational issues in the implementation and adoption of health information technology innovations: An interpretative review. *International Journal of Medical Informatics*, 82(5): e73–e86, doi: 10.1016/j.ijmedinf.2012.10.007.

Cresswell, K. M., Worth, A., and Sheikh, A. (2012a). Comparative case study investigating sociotechnical processes of change in the context of a national electronic health record implementation. *Health Informatics Journal*, 18(4): 251–270, doi: 10.1177/1460458212445399.

Cresswell, K. M., Worth, A., and Sheikh, A. (2012b). Integration of a nationally procured electronic health record system into user work practices. *BMC Medical Informatics and Decision Making*, 12: 15, doi: 10.1186/1472-6947-12-15.

Dansky, K. H., Thompson, D., and Sanner, T. (2006). A framework for evaluating eHealth research. *Evaluation and Program Planning*, 29(4): 397–404, doi: 10.1016/j.evalprogplan.2006.08.009.

DesRoches, C. M., Campbell, E. G., Vogeli, C., Zheng, J., Rao, S.R., Shields, A. E., Donelan, K., Rosenbaum, S., Bristol, S. J., and Jha, A. K. (2010). Electronic health records' limited successes suggest more targeted uses. *Health Affairs*, 29(4): 639–646, doi: 10.1377/hlthaff.2009.1086.

Detmer, D., Bloomrosen, M., Raymond, B., and Tang, P. (2008). Integrated personal health records: Transformative tools for consumer-centric care. *BMC Medical Informatics and Decision Making*, 8: 45, doi: 10.1186/1472-6947-8-45.

Deutsch, E., Duftschmid, G., and Dorda, W. (2010). Critical areas of national electronic health record programs—is our focus correct? *International Journal of Medical Informatics*, 79(3): 211–222, doi: 10.1016/j.ijmedinf.2009.12.002.

Doolin, B. (1999). Sociotechnical networks and information management in health care. *Accounting, Management and Information Technologies*, 9(2): 95–114, doi: 10.1016/S0959-8022(99)00005-3.

Eason, K. (2007). Local sociotechnical system development in the NHS national programme for information technology. *Journal of Information Technology*, 22(3): 257–264, doi: 10.1057/palgrave.jit.2000101.

Flanagan, M. E., Saleem, J. J., Millitello, L. G., Russ, A. L., and Doebbeling, B. N. (2013). Paper- and computer-based workarounds to electronic health record use at three benchmark institutions. *Journal of the American Medical Informatics Association*, 20(e1): e59–e66, doi: 10.1136/amiajnl-2012-000982.

Forkner-Dunn, J. (2003). Internet-based patient self-care: The next generation of health care delivery. *Journal of Medical Internet Research*, 5(2): e8, doi: 10.2196/jmir.5.2.e8.

Forsell, A., Karsten, H., and Vuokko, R. (2010). Issue orders and discontinued EPR. In *Information technology in health care: Socio-technical approaches 2010*, ed. Aarts, J. and Nøhr, C., pp. 118–126. Amsterdam: IOS Press, doi: 10.3233/978-1-60750-569-3-118.

Fraser, H. S. F. and Blaya, J. (2010). Implementing medical information systems in developing countries, what works and what doesn't. In *AMIA Annual Symposium Proceedings 2010*, pp. 232–236.

Free, C., Phillips, G., Galli, L., Watson, L., Felix, L., Edwards, P., Patel, V., and Haines, A. (2013). The effectiveness of mobile-health technology-based health behaviour change or disease management interventions for health care consumers: A systematic review. *PLoS Medicine* 10(1): e1001362, doi: 10.1371/journal.pmed.1001362.

Friedman, A., Crosson, J. C., Howard, J., Clark, E.C., Pellerano, M., Karsh, B.-T., Crabtree, B., Jaén, C. R., and Cohen, D. J. (2014). A typology of electronic health record workarounds in small-to-medium size primary care practices. *Journal of the American Medical Informatics Association*, 21(e1): e78–e83, doi: 10.1136/amiajnl-2013-001686.

Garrety, K., McLoughlin, I., Wilson, R., Zelle, G., and Martin M. (2014). National electronic health records and the digital disruption of moral orders. *Social Science and Medicine*, 101: 70–77, doi: 10.1016/j.socscimed.2013.11.029.

Gerber, T., Olazabal, V., Brown, K., and Pablos-Mendez, A. (2010). An agenda for action on global e-health. *Health Affairs*, 29(2): 233–236, doi: 10.1377/hlthaff.2009.0934.

Goh, J. M., Gao, G., and Agarwal, R. (2011). Evolving work routines: Adaptive routinization of information technology in healthcare. *Information Systems Research*, 22(3): 565–585, doi: 10.1287/isre.1110.0365.

Goldzweig, C. L., Towfigh, A., Maglione, M., and Shekelle, P. G. (2009). Costs and benefits of health information technology: New trends from the literature. *Health Affairs*, 28(2): w282–w293, doi: 10.1377/hlthaff.28.2.w282.

Greenhalgh, T., Morris, L., Jeremy C., Wyatt, J. C., Thomas, G., and Gunning, K. (2013). Introducing a nationally shared electronic patient record: Case study comparison of Scotland, England, Wales and Northern Ireland. *International Journal of Medical Informatics*, 82(5): e125–e138, doi: 10.1016/j.ijmedinf.2013.01.002.

Greenhalgh, T., Potts, H. W., Wong, G., Bark, P., and Swinglehurst, D. (2009). Tensions and paradoxes in electronic patient record research: A systematic literature review using the meta-narrative method. *Milbank Quarterly*, 87(4): 729–788, doi: 10.1111/j.1468-0009.2009.00578.x.

Greenhalgh, T. and Stones, R. (2010). Theorising big IT programmes in healthcare: Strong structuration theory meets actor-network theory. *Social Science and Medicine*, 70(9): 1285–1294, doi: 10.1016/j.socscimed.2009.12.034.

Greenhalgh, T., Stones, R., and Swinglehurst, D. (2014). Choose and book: A sociological analysis of 'resistance' to an expert system. *Social Science and Medicine*, 104: 210–219. doi: 10.1016/j.socscimed.2013.12.014.

Greenhalgh, T., Stramer, K., Bratan, T., Byrne, E., Mohammad, Y., and Russell, J. (2008a). Introduction of shared electronic records: Multi-site case study using diffusion of innovation theory. *BMJ*, 337: a1786, doi: 10.1136/bmj.a1786.

Greenhalgh, T., Stramer, K., Bratan, T., Byrne, E., Russell, J., and Potts, H. W. (2010). Adoption and non-adoption of a shared electronic summary record in England: A mixed-method case study. *BMJ*, 340: c3111, doi: 10.1136/bmj.c3111.

Greenhalgh, T., Wood, G. W., Bratan, T., Stramer, K., and Hinder, S. (2008b). Patients' attitudes to the summary care record and healthspace: Qualitative study. *BMJ*, 336: 1290, doi: 10.1136/bmj.a114.

Hains, I. M., Georgiou, A., and Westbrook, J. I. (2012). The impact of PACS on clinician work practices in the intensive care unit: A systematic review of the literature. *Journal of the American Medical Informatics Association*, 19(4): 506–513, doi: 10.1136/amiajnl-2011-000422.

Hardiker, N. R. and Grant, M. J. (2011). Factors that influence public engagement with eHealth: A literature review. *International Journal of Medical Informatics*, 80(1): 1–12, doi: 10.1016/j.ijmedinf.2010.10.017.

Harrison, M. I., Koppel, R., and Bar-Lev, S. (2007). Unintended consequences of information technologies in health care: An interactive sociotechnical analysis. *Journal of the American Medical Informatics Association*, 14(5): 542–549, doi: 10.1197/jamia.M2384.

Hill, J. W. and Powell, P. (2009). The national healthcare crisis: Is eHealth a key solution? *Business Horizons*, 52(3): 265–277, doi: 10.1016/j.bushor.2009.01.006.

Hordern, A., Georgiou, A., Whetton, S., and Prgomet, M. (2011). Consumer e-health: An overview of research evidence and implications for future policy. *Health Information Management Journal*, 40(2): 6–14.

Hovenga, E. J. S. (2010). Health care services, information systems & sustainability. In *Health informatics: An overview*, ed. Hovenga, E. J. S., Kidd, M. R., Garde, S., and Cossio, C. H. L., pp. 16–29. Netherlands: IOS Press, doi: 10.3233/978-1-60750-476-4-1.

Jaspers, M. W., Smeulers, M., Vermeulen, H., and Peute, L. W. (2011). Effects of clinical decision-support systems on practitioner performance and patient outcomes: A synthesis of high-quality systematic review findings. *Journal of the American Medical Informatics Association*, 18(3): 327–334, doi: 10.1136/amiajnl-2011-000094.

Kahn, J. S., Aulakh, V., and Bosworth, A. (2009). What it takes: Characteristics of the ideal personal health record. *Health Affairs*, 28(2): 369–376, doi: 10.1377/hlthaff.28.2.369.

Lau, F., Kuziemsky, C., Price, M., and Gardner, J. (2010). A review on systematic reviews of health information system studies. *Journal of the American Medical Informatics Association*, 17(6): 637–645, doi: 10.1136/jamia.2010.004838.

Lluch, M. and Abadie, F. (2013). Exploring the role of ICT in the provision of integrated care: Evidence from eight countries. *Health Policy*, 111(1): 1–13, doi: 10.1016/j.healthpol.2013.03.005.

McEvoy, R., Ballini, L., Maltoni, S, O'Donnell, C. A., Mair, F. S., and Macfarlane, A. (2014). A qualitative systematic review of studies using the normalization process theory to research implementation processes. *Implementation Science*, 9: 2, doi: 10.1186/1748-5908-9-2.

McGinn, C. A., Grenier, S., Duplantie, J., Shaw, N., Sicotte, C., Mathieu, L., Leduc, Y., Légaré, F., and Gagnon, M.-P. (2011). Comparison of user groups' perspectives of barriers and facilitators to implementing electronic health records: A systematic review. *BMC Medicine*, 9: 46, doi: 10.1186/1741-7015-9-46.

Mair, F. S., May, C., O'Donnell, C., Finch, T., Sullivan, F., and Murray, E. (2012). Factors that promote or inhibit the implementation of e-health systems: An explanatory systematic review. *Bulletin of the World Health Organisation*, 90(5): 357–364, doi: 10.2471/BLT.11.099424.

May, C. and Finch, T. (2009). Implementing, embedding, and integrating practices: An outline of normalization process theory. *Sociology*, 43(3): 535–554, doi: 10.1177/0038038509103208.

Moxham, C., Chambers, N., Girling, J., Garg, S., Jelfs, E., and Bremner, J. (2012). Perspectives on the enablers of e-health adoption: An international interview study of leading practitioners. *Health Services Management Research*, 25(3): 129–137, doi: 10.1258/hsmr.2012.012018.

Newell, S. (2011). Special section on healthcare information systems. *Journal of Strategic Information Systems*, 20(2): 158–160, doi: 10.1016/j.jsis.2011.05.002.

Niazkhani, Z., Pirnejad, H., Berg, M., and Aarts, J. (2009). The impact of computerized provider order entry systems on inpatient clinical workflow: A literature review. *Journal of the American Medical Informatics Association*, 16(4): 539–549, doi: 10.1197/jamia.M2419.

Nicolini, D. (2006). The work to make telemedicine work: A social and articulative view. *Social Science and Medicine*, 62(11): 2754–2767, doi: 10.1016/j.socscimed.2005.11.001.

Oh, H., Rizo, C., Enkin, M., and Jadad, A. (2005). What is eHealth (3): A systematic review of published definitions. *Journal of Medical Internet Research*, 7(1): e1, doi: 10.2196/jmir.7.1.e1.

Pagliari, C., Sloan, D., Gregor, P., Sullivan, F., Detmer, D., Kahan, J. P., Oortwijn, W., and MacGillivray, S. (2005). What is eHealth (4): A scoping exercise to map the field. *Journal of Medical Internet Research*, 7(1): e9, doi: 10.2196/jmir.7.1.e9.

Payton, F.C., Paré, G., LeRouge, C., and Reddy, M. (2011). Health care IT: Process, people, patients and interdisciplinary considerations. *Journal of the Association for Information Systems*, 12(2): i–xiii.

Pirnejad, H., Bal, R., and Berg, M. (2008). Building an inter-organizational communication network and challenges for preserving interoperability. *International Journal of Medical Informatics*, 77(12): 818–827, doi: 10.1016/j.ijmedinf.2008.05.001.

Pols, J. and Willems, D. (2011). Innovation and evaluation: Taming and unleashing telecare technology. *Sociology of Health & Illness*, 33(3): 484–498, doi: 10.1111/j.1467-9566.20130.01293.x.

Pope, C., Halford, S., Turnbull, J., Prichard, J., Calestani, M., and May, C. (2013). Using computer decision support systems in NHS emergency and urgent care: Ethnographic study using normalisation process theory. *BMC Health Services Research*, 13: 111, doi: 10.1186/1472-6963-13-111.

Ricciardi, L., Mostashari, F., Murphy, J., Daniel, J. G., and Siminerio, E. P. (2013). A national action plan to support consumer engagement via e-health. *Health Affairs*, 32(2): 376–384, doi: 10.1377/hlthaff.2012.1216.

Rosenthal, L. (2006). *Electronic Health Record*. US National Institute of Standards and Technology. Available at: <http://www.itl.nist.gov/div897/docs/EHR.html> (accessed October 9, 2015).

Sheikh, A., Cornford, T., Barber, N., Avery, A., Takian, A., Lichtner, V., Petrakaki, D., Crowe, S., Marsden, K., Robertson, A., Morrison, Z., Klecun, E., Prescott, R., Quinn, C., Jani, Y.,

Ficociello, M., Voutsina, K., Paton, J., Fernando, B., Jacklin, A., and Cresswell, K. (2011). Implementation and adoption of nationwide electronic health records in secondary care in England: Final qualitative results from prospective national evaluation in "early adopter" hospitals. *BMJ*, 343: d6054, doi: 10.1136/bmj.d6054.

Stanimirović, D. and Vintar, M. (2014). Development of eHealth at a national level: Comparative aspects and mapping of general success factors. *Informatics for Health and Social Care*, 39(2): 140–160, doi: 10.3109/17538157.2013.872108.

van Gemert-Pijnen, J. E., Wynchank, S., Covvey, H. D., and Ossebaard, H. C. (2012). Improving the credibility of electronic health technologies. *Bulletin of the World Health Organisation*, 90(5): 323–323A, doi: 10.2471/BLT.11.099804.

Wears, R. L. and Berg, M. (2005). Computer technology and clinical work: Still waiting for Godot. *Journal of the American Medical Association*, 293(10): 1261–1263.

Wilson, R., Baines, S., and McLoughlin, I. (2014). Introduction: Hiding in plain sight or disappearing in the rear view mirror? Whatever happened to the revolution in information for health and social care—learning from England and Australia. *Social Policy and Society*, 13(4): 563–568, doi: 10.1017/S1474746414000293.

Zwaanswijk, M., Verheij, R. A., Wiesman, F. J., and Friele, R. D. (2011). Benefits and problems of electronic information exchange as perceived by health care professionals: An interview study. *BMC Health Services Research*, 11: 256, doi: 10.1186/1472-6963-11-256.

CHAPTER 16

....

THE PARADOX OF HEALTH CARE PERFORMANCE MEASUREMENT AND MANAGEMENT

....

JENNY M. LEWIS

As a slightly rephrased version of a well-known aphorism has it, if it is not measured, it cannot be managed. At first blush, this reveals a belief that measurement and management are, or at least should be, tightly coupled. In other words, the measurement of performance is undertaken at the behest of management, and it is linked to some management purpose. A further step suggests an assumption that, armed with performance measures, management will take some action on that basis, towards achieving some desired goal. The following definition of performance management supports this, claiming that performance management is: "the use of performance indicators and management prescriptions, designed to improve such measured performance, to achieve public service performance objectives" (Cutler, 2011, 129).

This chapter examines the link between performance measurement and performance management in health care. In order to do so, it explores a paradox of performance measurement. A number of authors have described how performance measurement's introduction leads to various unintended and undesirable effects (for example: van Thiel and Leeuw, 2002; Hood, Margetts, and 6, 2010). Studies that report on the problems with performance measurement tend to treat these as technical obstacles of either measurement or management that can be overcome. There is generally little thought given to the idea that these problems cannot be solved because they are intrinsic to performance measurement itself (Lowe, 2013). Lowe argues that it distorts the priorities and practices of those who are delivering interventions and (paradoxically) produces worse outcomes for those who are meant to benefit from these interventions.

A different paradox of performance measurement and management in health care is the starting point here: In health care it often seems that there is both *too much* and *too little* performance measurement and management. How can this paradox be explained? And how can governments, responsible for delivering public services with standards of accountability, move beyond it?

Beginning with the too much (overload) side, it is apparent that performance measurement and management has moved up the agenda of those who have to find ways to account for their (individual and organizational) performance, whatever that might mean. Whether the discussion is framed as the rise of the performance movement (Radin, 2006), the audit society (Power, 1997), or the growth of administrative accountability (Flinders, 2001), there are some clear signs that performance measurement and management in the public sector is now a major industry.

National governments have created frameworks for performance measurement, as have individual departments within nations. There is no shortage of agencies, associations, departments, reports, rankings, and sets of indicators within wealthy nations, tasked with measuring performance. The following quote from an Organisation for Economic Co-operation and Development (OECD) report, highlights the international significance and scope of performance measurement:

> The trends to ex post controls and managerial flexibility do not mean there is less control—in fact there are more and more varied controls. Up to 50% of the work of external auditors is now performance audits (OECD, 2005, 84).

This quote also hints at the expected, but largely unrealized assumption that managerialism would reduce the level of central control—a point that is pertinent and will be returned to.

Not surprisingly, health care is one area where there has been a substantial focus on performance measurement. The relative size of expenditure on health care in many developed nations, combined with an ever-growing concern with demonstrating that health care costs are being contained, and that public funds are being used in an efficient and effective manner, ensures that the sector's financial performance is scrutinized carefully. In addition, the other important characteristics of health as a policy sector—matters of life and death are at stake, large and powerful professions are involved (and can perceive measurement as a threat), ensure that the quality of health care is also a major concern.

These two strands (finance and quality) are apparent in many national health system frameworks. For example, the NHS performance framework is self-described as "a performance management tool ... designed to strengthen existing performance management arrangements ... it improves the transparency and consistency of the process of identifying and addressing underperformance across the country" (Department of Health, 2012, 11). Performance is assessed in regard to finance and quality of service, with quality comprised of safety, patient experience, and effectiveness of care. This and other similar frameworks begin with a simple outline and a small number of components. But these then quickly expand into a raft of performance indicators, especially in regard to effectiveness.

As a general performance framework such as this unfolds into key components, the list of organizations with a stake in the measurement of health care quality expands. In England at the time of writing this chapter, this list includes the Department of Health, NHS England, the National Institute for Health and Care Excellence (NICE—which suggests quality indicators/measures), National Clinical Audits (NCA—which decides on which clinical indicators will be used), and Health Quality Improvement Partnership (HQIP—commissions, manages, supports and promotes national and local programmes of quality improvement), the Care Quality Commission (CQC—measures quality in the NHS and social care), and the Professional Standards Authority for Health and Social Care (oversees statutory bodies that regulate health and social care professionals in the UK and assesses their performance) as well as Clinical Commissioning Groups and Primary Care Trusts. This is a list of just the most obvious bodies with a stake in measuring health care quality. Financial regulation and performance assessment is undertaken by another agency, called Monitor. As might be expected, there is a concomitant list of performance indicators and league tables that seems to be forever increasing, producing contradictions and causing more than a little confusion for the public (Harford, 2014).

The deficit side of the paradox of performance measurement, again using an English example, was unhappily revealed in the case of the appalling care that was being given to patients in the main hospital serving Stafford, even as it was (on paper) apparently meeting the set standards. The letter to the Secretary of State that prefaces the Francis Inquiry into this case expresses bewilderment at how such a situation can arise:

> The NHS system includes many checks and balances which should have prevented serious systemic failure of this sort. There were and are a plethora of agencies, scrutiny groups, commissioners, regulators and professional bodies, all of whom might have been expected by patients and the public to detect and do something effective to remedy non-compliance with acceptable standards of care (The Mid Staffordshire NHS Foundation Trust Public Inquiry, 2013, 3).

How can this paradox of simultaneous overload and deficit be explained? How is it possible that the high level of oversight provided by so many agencies with an interest in performance can miss such catastrophic failure, even while measurement is being undertaken "by the book"? To understand this, it makes sense to first take a conceptual step back to the notion of accountability and the meaning of performance.

ACCOUNTABILITY AND PERFORMANCE

Accountability is an obligation to present an account of and answer for the execution of a set of responsibilities (OECD, 2005). It is often described as having three components: political or democratic accountability; judicial or legislative accountability; and bureaucratic or administrative accountability (e.g., Aucoin and Heintzman, 2000; Bovens, Schillemans, and Hart, 2008). While the first implies holding policy makers accountable to the people that have elected them, the judicial perspective is concerned with preventing and uncovering abuse, and the administrative perspective is centered on ensuring the effectiveness and quality of public services. To these three, another two types can be added—professional accountability, related to expertise and peer review, and social accountability, which refers to the need to provide accounts to the public at large (Bovens, 2007). These types might complement each other or compete. For example, in relation to health care, professional accountability can be expected to be both important and at odds with other forms of accountability—as Byrkjeflot, Christensen, and Lægreid (2013) found in a study of accountability in hospitals in Norway.

A useful description of accountability is that it is record keeping that gives rise to: "story-telling in a context of social (power) relations within which enforcement of standards and the fulfilment of obligations is a reasonable expectation" (Bovens, Schillemans, and Goodin, 2014, 3). This highlights the relational core of accountability, and also points to the fact that it is an enforcement mechanism that can be used as a management tool. Finally, accountability can be seen as a virtue (a desirable quality of some entity) and hence, as the outcome of an evaluation of performance in relation to a set of standards. It can also be seen as the mechanism (social, political, administrative) for assessing how agents are held to account (Bovens, Schillemans, and Goodin, 2014). Performance measurement and performance management, which are inherently relational and utilized as processes to achieve desired outcomes, are likewise both mechanisms and virtues.

Accountability is not a new concept, but it is often regarded as having become more prominent with the restructuring of relationships under new public management (NPM) as the earlier quote from the OECD alluded to in contrasting increased managerial flexibility along with increased controls. Beginning in the 1970s, NPM came to be seen as the solution to the budgetary challenges facing all sectors in many different countries (developed and developing), at all levels of government. With its basis in both scientific management ideas and transaction cost economics, NPM changed public sector accountability, tending to focus accountability towards administrative (rather than political or judicial) concerns. Administrative accountability was transformed into managerial accountability through a focus on results and targets (Day and Klein, 1987). Managerial accountability requires explicit standards of performance, so the need for performance information and performance management systems increased. Accounting systems were joined by a set of non-financial reporting systems as performance became a key organizational value. As a result, accountability came to be defined as demonstrating one's performance (van de Walle and Cornelissen, 2014).

Reflecting the dominant mood of the time, NPM with its focus on planning, targets, outputs, and a tighter oversight and control of the achievements of public sector organizations, came into play alongside a focus on saving money, reducing the time and effort expended, and cutting waste. In Hood's (1991) famous description of NPM, he argues that it was frugality and the reduction of waste that became its single minded focus. Performance measurement was (and is) a central plank of NPM reforms, with the link from inputs to outputs a major concern. A new-found belief that previous problems could be avoided if there was more measurement and more management grew. It was assumed that if the right systems could be put into place, then it would be a relatively easy task to identify efficiency savings while also continuing to deliver the desired outcomes.

Some argue that performance management in public services pre-dated NPM, for example, Cutler's (2011) historical study of the use of performance-related pay, management accounting, and performance indicators in NHS hospitals "before NPM." But most would agree that the particular aspect of accountability emphasized (administrative), the trend towards managerial accountability within this, and the values that were regarded as the most important (economy and efficiency), changed along with the rise of NPM. Cutler himself concludes that performance management became more sophisticated with NPM, at least in terms of discussion, even though it is not easy to demonstrate any increased effectiveness as a direct result of it.

As action became more oriented towards defined goals, increasingly demanding performance management systems, with expanding lists of performance measures and targets were required. An emphasis on demonstrating that taxpayers' money is being used effectively and that the specific goals set by politicians are met (Pollitt and Bouckaert, 2011) has led to an explosion of performance measures allegedly gauging the outcome or at least the output (as compared with input) of public services (Power, 1997). It is not difficult to see why the notion of performance measurement overload has arisen.

There is also a literature on the idea of an accountability deficit (Bovens, Schillemans, and Hart, 2008). The uncertainty of new forms of governing—networked governance in particular, with its dispersed and horizontal accountabilities across multiple levels—follows along this line of inquiry. Government departments have also become too large and too complex for ministers to accept personal responsibility for what is done by the civil servants who work within them (Day and Klein, 1987). But the arguments about deficit relate most directly to the democratic and legislative aspects of accountability, rather than administrative accountability. The efforts of governments to address increasing demands for results, and to demonstrate performance with respect to results, have led to increasing pressures to manage and report on outputs and outcomes. This, in turn, has led to greater efforts to specify goals and objectives, standards and performance targets (Aucoin and Heintzman, 2000).

In summary, the rise of performance measurement and management alongside NPM has changed the notion of accountability, focusing attention on the managerial aspects of public service delivery. This has produced a perceived need for more organizations, reports, and indicators to monitor performance, at the expense of a broader notion of accountability. Performance measurement increased markedly with the emphasis on public management reform in many countries, and it is now more extensive, more intensive, and more external in its focus (Pollitt and Bouckaert, 2011). And this has led to the idea that there is an overload of performance measurement. Moving on from accountability and public sector reform, the next section examines the purpose of all this measurement.

WHY MEASURE PERFORMANCE?

Performance measurement is seen to be important for numerous reasons. Colin Talbot (2005) lists the following: for accountability and transparency; for generating information to inform user choice; for reporting on success against stated aims; for improving efficiency; for increasing the focus on outcomes and effectiveness; for assisting decision making about resource allocation; and for adding value through issues like equity, probity, and building social capital. This list points to some of the different audiences for performance information (governments, managers, or service users). It also indicates some different purposes for it (meeting targets, making the best use of resources, or improving outcomes), and some possible values that might underlie it other than economy (equity, justice, inclusion).

Performance might be measured for the purposes of evaluation, to discover if a program is doing what it is supposed to do. It might be used in order to control the performance of those working in a program or service of interest. It might also be simply a means of controlling the budget for a particular area, or determining how much money is being spent to achieve some desired output. Sometimes performance measurement is undertaken in order to eliminate a program, sometimes it is used to support a new direction, and sometimes it is about maximizing returns on taxes and accountability to the public (Radin, 2006). Amongst the many different reasons why public managers measure performance, Behn (2003) has listed eight—to evaluate, control, budget, motivate, promote, celebrate, learn, and improve. Regardless of which of these is seen to be the central purpose, the issue of control (political and managerial) of public sector organizations is lurking in the background.

Since performance measurement is linked to notions of control, management, and consequences, it provides the potential for some actors to enhance their power. A crucial question then is: Who decides that performance should be measured? Performance indicators can be used to monitor the strategic or operational performance of an organization, to control the lower levels of an organization, to manage street-level bureaucrats, or to appraise performance (Carter, Klein, and Day, 1992). Carter and his colleagues posed the question: Are performance indicators tools of hierarchy, instruments of managerial self-examination, or devices for preserving accountability while decentralizing responsibility? The answer of course is that they can be any of these things. Their analysis of how government departments and public services implemented performance indicators during the Thatcher years indicated that performance indicators were an important tool to preserve hands-off (managerial) control in a system that was being devolved.

Performance reporting shifts power to the standard-setters, be they central government, professional bodies, consumer organizations or the news media (van de Walle and Cornelissen, 2014). Performance measurement has tended to be linked closely to locating and investigating failures, corruption and the abuse of power, so that those who are responsible can be sanctioned in some way. Once something is measured, it needs to be compared against something (a target or goal, or the same programme being delivered in another location). If it is found wanting, it is hard to avoid the implication that remedial action is needed. As many have reported in the UK, the development of performance measurement there has been primarily concerned with enhancing control and upwards accountability (Carter, Klein, and Day, 1992; Hood et al., 1999; Collier, 2008). This form of control can be expected to clash with professional forms that support the notion of local autonomy and discretion rather than external control and greater standardization.

Clearly, performance measurement has multiple concerns. As noted in the introductory section of this chapter, it might be what is done and how (processes as the key concern), or it might be the results of what is done (outputs or outcomes as the key concern). In addition, it might be merely a presentational device to assure the intended audience that all is well (ceremonial) (Collier, 2008). Ritual and ceremony are powerful in organizations (Meyer and Rowan, 1977). The symbolic use of performance information by organizations can allow them to avoid evaluation and inspection as long as they appear to comply. Some go so far as to claim that performance measurement has become an end in itself, its main purpose being to generate measures (Schick, 2001). But the mere existence of performance measures has an impact on the functioning of individuals and organizations. As one plain-language version stated, there are three ways to improve your score on any performance metric: first, actually improve performance; second, focus on ways to look good on the metric in question; and third, cheat (Harford, 2014).

Performance measurement is important as a means to discover what needs to be improved, which individuals and organization are meeting the set goals, and which are failing to do so and need either help or penalties. In short, there are many good reasons why governments, organizations and senior managers are in favo of measuring performance. The act of establishing performance measures and the multiplication of these feeds into the notion of overload, regardless of whether they are used to manage organizations. The sense of overload increases when the driver for measurement and reporting is external to the organization or the profession.

MEASURING WHAT?

A question that logically follows the decision to measure performance is the question of what should be measured. A good place to begin in answering this question is to distinguish between policy performance, organizational performance, and individual performance (see Talbot, 2005). A policy focus is the most complete, because it is not confined to a single organization or tier of government. But it is diffuse and difficult to pin down, and attributing performance to a particular policy is problematic. Focusing on organizations is easier because it allows performance to be related to resourcing and accountability and for models from the private sector to be imported and used. Individual performance is more closely related to human resource management. So health care performance measurement might occur at the policy or system level (regions or states), or at the organizational level (hospitals), or at the individual level (doctors).

The meaning of performance is not always obvious. Public executives are accountable for finances, fairness, and performance, claims Robert Behn (2014), arguing that the rules for the first two of these are very explicit, but the rules for the third are not. He goes on to claim that this vagueness of performance means that whoever wants to measure it must decide on the purpose of the organization, what specific aspects of performance should be measured, and what standard of comparison (targets) will be used. This gives that actor a substantial deal of power. He clearly envisages a good deal of organizational autonomy in this discussion and is firmly focused on performance in organizations rather than at a policy or system level.

The influential literatures behind performance measurement—principal/agent separation, and the public choice school—have buttressed the rise of measurement as a necessary means for ensuring that technical and allocative inefficiencies are minimized (Jackson, 2011). Some purposes of performance measurement have received much more political and organizational support than others—most notably, those which emphasize economy and efficiency (Pollitt, 1987). This can be at the expense of achieving other objectives such as effectiveness, professional development, and collegiality. As others have also noted, performance indicators are generally constructed around the "three Es" of economy, efficiency, and effectiveness. Other important objectives such as equity are more difficult, and so they often play a supplementary role (Carter, Klein, and Day, 1992).

Quality is even more difficult, for how can it be measured? In health care it is generally linked to safety, consumer experiences, and effectiveness. Abstract concepts such as access and equity must be turned into something that has meaning for evaluating good or bad performance. This is generally done through comparisons with other similar entities, and so measures become targets (achievement comparisons), time series (historical comparisons), and league tables (organizational comparisons) (Carter, Klein, and Day, 1992). Each of these suffer from a range of problems, which have been discussed at length in the literature on the problems of performance measurement (for example, Grizzle, 2002; Smith, 1995).

An illuminating example of the translation of objectives into components and indicators can be found in the Report on Government Services produced by the Australian Productivity Commission. This examines a number of broad service areas (including health care) and compares all of the Australian states and territories. Its general performance framework consists of equity, effectiveness, and efficiency as the three key components—all of which are said to be given equal prominence. These are then related to outputs (access, appropriateness and quality, and inputs per output unit) and outcomes (Steering Committee for the Review of Government Service Provision (SCRGSP), 2013). When this general performance framework is applied to public hospitals, examples of the specific performance indicators against the three components include:

1. equity of access by special needs groups (equity);
2. access, appropriateness, and quality (effectiveness); and
3. efficiency.

The relative difficulties of measurement noted above are made clear in this report: Some indicators are flagged as "comparable," including cost per casemix-adjusted separation (efficiency) and accreditation (safety). Others are denoted as "incomplete and/or not directly comparable," including waiting times (access). Another group of indicators is designated "yet to be developed," including equity of access by special needs groups (equity), and continuity of care (quality) (SCRGSP, 2013).

Having decided on objectives and possible indicators, a further choice to be made is between prescriptive measures (linked to objectives or targets), descriptive (which simply measure change) and proscriptive (which specify things that should not happen). Carter, Klein, and Day (1992) refer to these respectively as dials, tin-openers, and alarm-bells. Indicators as dials presume that standards of performance are unambiguous and can be simply read off. Indicators as tin-openers assume that performance is contestable and that measurement is therefore the beginning of the conversation, rather than the end of it.

Multiple assumptions sit behind whatever range of performance measures are chosen. More specifically, there are three assumptions made by the central target model of performance measurement. One of these is that it is possible to actually measure the outputs or outcomes of interest. A performance indicator is an estimate of something which cannot be measured directly, so good indicators are unbiased (or not very biased) estimates (Bevan and Hood, 2006). Another assumption is that failures of performance that are not reflected in the scoring system are not important (Bevan, 2006). And a further assumption is that gaming (reactive subversion) of any measurement system will occur, but it will be relatively small. Measurement is assumed to change behavior, and there will be some gaming in any system, but this is considered to be a relatively minor component of the behavior change that the system will set in train (Bevan and Hood, 2006). These are all rather large assumptions in practice.

In essence, performance measures are directed at different entities (policy, organizations, individuals), as well as different goals, and different values. The measures that are constructed are always imperfect and most of them are contestable. Not surprisingly then, a focus of much of the critical literature on performance measurement and management is either about the technical issues of what is measured and how this can be improved, or the unintended consequences of measurement. As an example, one article outlines 20 unintended consequences of measurement in health care (Mannion and Braithwaite, 2012). All of these factors add to the sense of overload because no matter how many new measures are created, it is never certain that the measures are the right ones, or that they will not generate more undesirable effects.

MEASUREMENT AND MANAGEMENT

Returning to where this chapter began, an important reason for measuring performance is that work that is not measured cannot be managed. Only when someone applies measures somehow do they accomplish something (Behn, 2003). If there are no criteria for measuring the value of what is being produced, then there is no way of arguing for why the something that is currently being done, is better than something else that could be done instead. There are many motivational issues at stake, because performance measures aim to discover what is working and what is not—or more personally, who is and is not doing what they should be. But just how closely linked are performance measurement and performance management in practice?

In their discussion of performance indicators as prescriptive dials or descriptive tin openers, Carter, Klein, and Day (1992) directly link the type of measure with the style of management: "The prescriptive PI will generally be a top-down management tool that lends itself to a command style of management ... the descriptive PI, which can be produced at any level of the organization, suggests the need for a more persuasive style of management ... performance—often bereft of normative standards, invariably full of ambiguity—is, in theory and practice, both contestable and complex" (50).

A comparative example that also shows indicators working with management strategies is provided by Bevan and Wilson (2013) in their comparison of England and Wales in a natural experiment of policy shifts after the devolution of government in the UK. They evaluated four models of reform that rely on some form of summary measurement of public services. In "trust and altruism," noble doctors always do their best, and indicators help them do their jobs. In "targets and terror," public servants are assumed to be selfish, whipped into shape by a central government with a dashboard of performance data. In the "quasi-market" system, the indicators are provided to the public, who act as consumers and make informed choices. Finally, "name and shame" uses league tables to humiliate losers and lionize winners.

In their comparison of schools and hospitals in England and Wales, Bevan and Wilson (2013) conclude that "name and shame" indicators work best, and that this is not because they provide information on performance to the bureaucracy (although they do that), nor because they help consumers make choices (which often consumers do not have), but simply because nobody wants to be at the bottom of a league table. This approach combined with targets and terror (a form of command and control) resulted in better performance in English hospitals in reducing waiting time (Bevan and Wilson, 2013).

Beyond economic treatments of how the use of different approaches changes behavior, there is a sizeable management literature on whether and how performance measurement is used. For example, Hammerschmid, van de Walle, and Stimac (2013) studied how public managers in different nations use performance information, finding considerable variation by country and by policy field, and that central governments used them less than local and regional governments. They argue that performance information use is better encouraged through organizational routines rather than through the personal education, training, and experience of managers. Jeanette Taylor (2009) found that agencies use performance information more for meeting external reporting requirements than for achieving internal improvements. She argued that technical problems, but also political and organizational issues were constraining the use of performance information. A comparative study of several European countries, found that Finland, the Netherlands, Sweden, and the UK were all doing more performance measurement (Pollitt, 2006), and that these measures were most often used by managers, not by politicians, and not by people further down the hierarchy.

Some claim that the mere establishment of indicators can be a good thing if it leads organizations to even think about performance (e.g., Moynihan, 2008). In contrast, Behn (2014) claims that it is pointless choosing a purpose, measures, and targets, without having leadership strategies to achieve those targets. In Behn's view, the organization is not the proper unit of analysis, the leadership team is. In other words, it is not the mechanisms but the executive and their practices that can make a difference to performance. This tackles the measurement-management gap head on, but notably, is referring to organizations and not whole policy systems with centrally determined indicators.

As Moynihan (2008) notes, the link between performance measurement and its actual use by managers is much more assumed than demonstrated. He defines performance management as a system that generates performance information through strategic planning and performance measurement routines, and connects this information to decision-making. His examination of how people interpret and use performance information in the US under a common performance framework (the Government Performance and Results Act) rests on a model of performance measurement that is socially constructed, taking the conversation back to the definition of accountability as fundamentally relational.

What he calls performance management doctrine is based on the logic that creation, diffusion and use of performance information will foster better decision-making, that liberating managers from traditional controls complements the creation of performance information, and that performance management will change the nature of accountability for the better (Moynihan, 2008). The more critical literature on performance management suggests it is destined to fail, because it is so flawed, because of measurement overload, because of ambiguity about which measures are accurate, and because of its numerous unintended and undesirable consequences, as has been described earlier.

However, Moynihan argues performance measurement is useful because it can change managerial behavior. He argues that the problem is that governments have adopted performance reporting requirements for agencies, without reducing traditional managerial controls (Moynihan, 2008). Others have likewise noted that schemes commonly go wrong because of their centralized and standardized approaches which ignore practical, tacit, locally specific knowledge (Hood, Margetts, and 6, 2010). Collier (2008) makes a related distinction between performance measurement and intelligence-led approaches to performance. The first addresses the need for legitimation through the collection and reporting of statistics. The second is aimed at using local and current knowledge and skills to address emerging challenges. Tensions between being either performance driven or intelligence-led reflect a clash of management and professional cultures. Many examples of what happens in practice point to an approach that is centralized, hierarchical, and tightly controlled, being widely applied.

Moynihan (2008) also notes that, based on his work, some leaders saw performance management reforms as an opportunity to improve their organizations. In line with a view of accountability and performance measurement as relational, and with Behn's (2014) comments on leadership, Moynihan claims that it is the dialogue that is important: Information needs to be presented and considered in written and oral form if it is to be used. Performance information does not indicate what should be done next (if it is a tin opener, in Carter, Klein and Day's terms). This can only be resolved by an interactive dialogue where actors discuss and try to persuade others by using the information to support their own arguments about what should be done. The question that arises then is whether performance management is aimed at following the directives and targets set by central government, or engaging in learning and improvement at the organizational level.

Related to this is a clash of performance cultures that is often obvious in the health sector. The individuals delivering the services that are measured are highly educated, very skeptical of performance measures that others have imposed on them as professionals, and well able to articulate their concerns. Over the last three decades, governments have in various ways circumscribed and changed professional autonomy and authority (Harrison, 1999; Lewis and Marjoribanks, 2003; Lewis, 2005) so that managers can have greater control in regard to their desired objectives of controlling expenditure on health care (Alford, 1975), and improving the quality of care. While management is concerned with driving efficiency from above, emphasizing the importance of hierarchy, competitiveness and the right to manage those lower down, professionals see efficiency as best achieved by the self-driven actions of those who have the expertise (Carter, Klein, and Day, 1992).

Medicine is governed through mutually reinforcing formal institutions, occupational practices, and the biomedical model, with its assumption that illness is related to specific (internal) causes and not social and psychological contexts. Harrison (2009) argues that the biomedical model has allowed cases to be standardized, categorized, and allocated to specific protocols—such as casemix measures which predefine the content of care for particular categories of patients. In addition, population-based approaches to researching clinical effectiveness have generated categories (assumed to be homogeneous), which allow for cases to be controlled bureaucratically. As a consequence, managers are now more easily able to control medical work. This leads Harrison to conclude that the amount of external control of the medical profession is increasing. The performance movement is obviously linked to this.

The professional perspective on performance measurement tends to be that it is too fraught with measurement problems to be of much use, too costly, and necessitates a focus on the easiest aspects to measure which are often the least important to quality care (Loeb, 2004). He goes on to describe the "public policy" perspective (central government) as one that sees measurement as integral to health care, and is unconcerned about imperfect measures being utilized, because evidence of some kind is needed to demonstrate that quality care is being provided. Again the clash of cultures is apparent in the distinction between local, accurate and tacit knowledge, and central, "good enough" and explicit standards.

Bovens and Schillemans (2014) advocate for accountability systems that are designed without the problems caused by centralization, standardization, and generic approaches. "Default" accountability—based on repetitive, predictable, and data-intensive mechanisms, rests on standardized and routine procedures (annual reports, standard forms). This is an outcome of a centrally constructed and controlled measurement system. A better approach is to design accountability systems that relate to specific contexts and conditions. The same argument can be made in relation to performance, as an aspect of accountability: what is needed is an approach that is more contextually driven.

Performance measurement, despite its breadth and complexity, can paradoxically still miss crucial information about performance. A focus on performance *management* rather than measurement indicates that there might be plenty of vertical management in the form of control and central direction, but less horizontal management as dialogue and local priorities. In health care this is particularly important because of the role of the professions and their expert knowledge. There are certainly aspects of practice that can be codified and counted, providing useful information about performance on things such as specific surgical procedures, and an ever growing sophistication in making this comparable on the basis of weightings. But the kind of intensive local feedback that is needed to improve organizational performance, as suggested by this overview, relies on context-specific approaches, management freedom to set priorities locally, and management activity that uses measurement through an ongoing dialogue.

CONCLUSION

Returning to the Mid Staffordshire case, the inquiry report contains 290 recommendations, all directed at changing the situation towards one where patients rather than numbers count:

> a high priority was placed on the achievement of targets; ... Management thinking during the period under review was dominated by financial pressures and achieving FT [Foundation Trust] status, to the detriment of quality of care; ... Statistics and reports were preferred to patient experience data, with a focus on systems, not outcomes. (The Mid Staffordshire NHS Foundation Trust Public Inquiry, 2013, 13)

Released shortly after this report was one exploring whether there should be ratings of health and social care providers (Nuffield Trust, 2013). This report recognized the multiple purposes of ratings—to increase accountability to the public, users, commissioners of care, and to Parliament (for publicly funded care); to aid choice by users and commissioners of care; to help improve the performance of providers; to identify and prevent failures in the quality of care; and to provide public reassurance as to the quality of care.

The recommendations include that measures of safety, effectiveness, and user experience be included in any rating. It also suggested that some measure of the quality of governance of providers may be important too, but noted that including direct measures of financial performance into a rating for quality might lead to providers making inappropriate trade-offs between financial issues and the quality of care. Instead, a once per year bringing together of quality ratings with financial health and overall governance was preferred (Nuffield Trust, 2013). The report also emphasized that inspections were needed in addition to data. The effects of the Francis Inquiry on this report are clear, and it is directly invoked in a number of places.

Again supporting the theme of overload, a bewildering array of levels and components of quality are listed in this report, illustrating how complicated measuring the performance of a national health system is. It lists the various quality initiatives by the Government and the Department of Health, the commissioning system, the regulatory system, other national level organizations, and professionally-led initiatives. The conclusion is that: "there are numerous initiatives and organizations involved in defining and assessing quality in health" (Nuffield Trust, 2013, 51), and that there ought to be some consideration of making the landscape more streamlined with less duplication of roles and data requirements, greater clarity, and less overlap with respect to who is measuring what. On the deficit side, the authors of this report note that data that is too aggregated "may prompt management to better performance, but quality of care for patients is delivered at a service level, say in departments or specialties or wards" (Nuffield Trust, 2013, 7). Providing information at this level was also seen as a means for better engaging with clinical staff.

Dealing with the performance measurement and management deficit through more dialogue and specificity is likely to improve performance but it might also exacerbate the overload problem. Performance measurement with a narrow focus on outputs, and overly centralized and routinized implementation without managers having the space or the time to exercise discretion in leadership, leads to an overload induced by default measurement systems. However, including more specificity and dialogue might increase the resources needed even further. Demands for more sophisticated measurement and interpretation, and a tighter connection to management practices are eminently sensible, but they are unlikely to come without costs (Lewis and Triantafillou, 2012). Even if performance measurement and management is designed in line with all this wise advice, there is no guarantee that the problem of both too much and too little will be resolved. Indeed, the only thing that is certain is that we will not be able to accurately predict what the unintended consequences of such changes might be.

A way to move beyond this paradox is first to accept that it is inherent to performance measurement and management in health care. All this measurement does not guarantee good performance, whatever that might be defined as, and neither does it guarantee that either central government or local managers will be able to use the information to improve performance. But what alternative is there? The risks of not collecting and analyzing comprehensive information on the quality of care are too high because the public rely on the health system to treat them (properly) when they fall ill. The risks of not tightly monitoring and controlling expenditure on health care are too large for governments overseeing national health systems to contemplate. An imperfect system is better than no system, so the focus should be on doing the best that is possible within these limitations.

For example, one suggested way forward is to use a mixed model of national and local targets instead (Bevan, 2006). A small number of national targets of easily measured priorities, plus a small number of local targets, supplemented by indicators and surveillance to cover other priority targets has been suggested as a way of overcoming the worst problems of the central target model. A more decentralized system of target setting could work with more contextual specificity and flexibility and dialogue with professionals at the local level. Although there is no specific mention of leadership and management in this, there is a point of convergence between this strategy and the recommendations focused on organizational performance that were described in the previous section. There is some agreement between those who come at this problem from behavioral economics, management and leadership, and professions and learning.

The performance of public services must be managed, and performance measurement is now firmly established as a tool for doing this. In health care, at least in centralized national systems, the need to maintain control through indicators is at cross-purposes with the need for greater local flexibility for managers and ongoing dialogue about the indicators, which appears more likely to actually improve performance. Moving towards a mixture of central and local measurement might work, but it will only work if local managers and professionals are given greater freedom to contribute to the discussion and to make changes. This is a difficult balancing act for governments, as relinquishing central control comes with social, economic, and political risks. And, just as for any other change in regard to health care, being seen as having done too little will be much worse than being seen to have done too much.

ACKNOWLEDGMENTS

This work was supported by an Australian Research Council Future Fellowship. Thanks to Nick Mays and Nick Black at the London School of Hygiene and Tropical Medicine, and Gwyn Bevan at the London School of Economics and Political Science for their useful insights and leads on the new English NHS.

References

Alford, R. (1975). *Health care politics: Ideological and interest group barriers to reform.* Chicago: University of Chicago Press.

Aucoin P. and Heintzman R. (2000). The dialectics of accountability for performance in public management reform. In *Governance in the twenty-first century: Revitalizing the public service*, ed. Peters, B.G., pp. 244–280. Montreal: McGill Press.

Behn, R. D. (2003). Why measure performance? Different purposes require different measures. *Public Administration Review*, 63(5): 586–606.

Behn, R. D. (2014). PerformanceStat. In *The Oxford handbook of public accountability*, ed. Bovens, M., Goodin, R. E., and Schillemans, T., pp. 456–471. Oxford: Oxford University Press.

Bevan, G. (2006). Setting targets for health care performance: Lessons from a case study of the English NHS. *National Institute Economic Review*, 197: 1–13.

Bevan, G. and Hood, C. (2006). What's measured is what matters: Targets and gaming in the English public health care system. *Public Administration*, 84(3): 517–538.

Bevan, G. and Wilson, D. (2013). Does "naming and shaming" work for schools and hospitals? Lessons from natural experiments following devolution in England and Wales. *Public Money and Management*, 33(4): 245–252.

Bovens, M. (2007). Analyzing and assessing public accountability: A conceptual framework. *European Law Journal*, 13(4): 837–868.

Bovens, M. and Schillemans, T. (2014). Meaningful accountability. In *The Oxford handbook of public accountability*, ed. Bovens, M., Goodin, R. E., and Schillemans, T., pp. 673–682. Oxford: Oxford University Press.

Bovens, M., Schillemans, T., and Goodin, R. E. (2014). Public accountability. In *The Oxford handbook of public accountability*, ed. Bovens, M., Goodin, R. E., and Schillemans, T., pp. 1–20. Oxford: Oxford University Press.

Bovens M., Schillemans, T., and Hart, P. 'T. (2008). Does public accountability work? An assessment tool. *Public Administration*, 86(1): 225–242.

Byrkjeflot, H., Christensen, T., and Lægreid, P. (2013). The many faces of accountability: Comparing reforms in welfare, hospitals and migration. *Scandinavian Political Studies*, 37(2): 171–195.

Carter N., Klein R., and Day P. (1992). *How organizations measure success: The use of performance indicators in government.* London and New York: Routledge.

Collier, P. M. (2008). Performativity, management and governance. In *Managing to improve public services*, ed. Hartley, J., Donaldson, C., Skelcher, C., and Wallace, M., pp. 46–64. Cambridge: Cambridge University Press.

Cutler, T. (2011). Performance management in public services "before" new public management: The case of NHS acute hospitals 1948–1962. *Public Policy and Administration*, 26(1): 129–147.

Day, P. and Klein R. (1987). *Accountabilities: Five public services.* London: Tavistock.

Department of Health (2012). *The NHS performance framework: Implementation guidance.* Available at: <https://www.gov.uk/government/publications/the-nhs-performance-framework-2012-13> (accessed September 23, 2015).

Flinders, M. (2001). *The politics of accountability in the modern state.* Aldershot: Ashgate.

Grizzle, G. A. (2002). Performance measurement and dysfunction: The dark side of quantifying work. *Public Performance & Management Review*, 25(4): 363–369.

Hammerschmid, G., van de Walle, S., and Stimac, V. (2013). Internal and external use of performance information in public organizations: Results from an international survey. *Public Money and Management*, 33(4): 261–268.

Harford, T. (2014). Underperforming on performance. *Financial Times*, 11 July 2014. Available at: <http://www.ft.com/cms/s/2/bf238740-07bd-11e4-8e62-00144feab7de.html#ixzz3PUpazKgY> (accessed January 22, 2015).

Harrison, S. (1999). Clinical autonomy and UK health policy: Past and futures. In *Professionals and the new managerialism in the public sector*, ed. Exworthy, M. and Halford, S., pp. 50–64. Buckingham: Open University Press.

Harrison, S. (2009). Co-optation, commodification and the medical model: Governing UK medicine since 1991. *Public Administration*, 87(2): 184–197.

Hood, C. (1991). A public management for all seasons? *Public Administration*, 69: 3–19.

Hood, C., Scott, C., James, O., Jones, G. W., and Travers, A. (1999). *Regulation inside government*. Oxford: Oxford University Press.

Hood, C., Margetts, H., and 6, P. (2010). The drive to modernize. A world of surprises? In *Paradoxes of modernization: Unintended consequences of public policy reform*, ed. Margetts, H., 6, P., and Hood, C., pp. 3–16. Oxford: Oxford University Press.

Jackson, P. M. (1988). The management of performance in the public sector. *Public Money and Management.*, Winter: 11–16.

Jackson, P. M. (2011). Governance by numbers: What have we learned over the past 30 years? *Public Money & Management*, 31(1): 13–26.

Lewis, J. M. (2005). *Health policy and politics: Networks, ideas and power*. Melbourne: IP Communications.

Lewis, J. M. and Marjoribanks, T. (2003). Challenging autonomy through financial constraints and incentives: Reforming general practice in Australia. *International Journal of Health Planning and Management*, 18: 49–61.

Lewis, J. M. and Triantafillou, P. (2012). Accountability as learning: A new source of government overload? *International Review of Administrative Sciences*, 78(4): 597–614.

Loeb, J. M. (2004). The current state of performance measurement in health care. *International Journal for Quality in Health Care*, 16(1): i5–i9.

Lowe, T. (2013). New development: The paradox of outcomes—the more we measure, the less we understand. *Public Money and Management*, 33(3): 213–216.

Mannion, R. and Braithwaite, J. (2012). Unintended consequences of performance measurement in healthcare: 20 salutary lessons from the English National Health Service. *Internal Medicine Journal*, 2012: 569–574.

Meyer, J. W. and Rowan, B. (1977). Institutionalized organizations: Formal structures as myth and ceremony. *The American Journal of Sociology*, 83(2): 340–363.

Mid Staffordshire NHS Foundation Trust Public Inquiry (The Francis Inquiry) (2013). *Report of the Mid Staffordshire NHS Foundation Trust Public Inquiry. Executive Summary*. London: HMSO.

Moynihan, D. P. (2008). *The dynamics of performance management: Constructing information and reform*. Washington D.C.: Georgetown University Press.

Nuffield Trust (2013). *Rating providers for quality: A policy worth pursuing? A report for the Secretary of State for Health*. London: Nuffield Trust.

OECD (Organisation for Economic Co-operation and Development) (2005). *Modernising government: The way forward*. Paris: OECD.

Pollitt, C. (1987). The politics of performance assessment: Lessons for higher education? *Studies in Higher Education*, 12(1): 87–98.

Pollitt, C. (2006). Performance management in practice: A comparative study of executive agencies. *Journal of Public Administration Research and Theory* 16(1): 25–44.

Pollitt, C. and Bouckaert, G. (2011). *Public management reform: A comparative analysis*, 3rd edition. Oxford: Oxford University Press.

Power M. (1997). *The audit society. Rituals of verification*. Oxford: Oxford University Press.

Radin, B. A. (2006). *Challenging the performance movement: Accountability, complexity and democratic values*. Washington, D.C.: Georgetown University Press.

Schick, A. (2001). Getting performance measures to measure up. In *Quicker, better, cheaper: Managing performance in American Government*, ed. Forsythe, D. W., pp. 39–60. Albany, NY: Rockefeller Institute Press.

SCRGSP (2013). *Report on government services 2013*. Canberra: Productivity Commission.

Smith, P. (1995). On the unintended consequences of publishing performance data in the public sector. *International Journal of Public Administration*, 18(2/3): 277–310.

Talbot, C. (2005). Performance management. In *The Oxford handbook of public management*, ed. Ferlie, E., Lynn, L., and Pollitt, C., pp. 491–517. Oxford: Oxford University Press.

Taylor, J. (2009). Strengthening the link between performance measurement and decision making. *Public Administration*, 87(4): 853–871.

Van de Walle, S. and Cornelissen, F. (2014). Performance reporting. In *The Oxford handbook of public accountability*, ed. Bovens, M., Goodin, R. E. and Schillemans, T., pp. 441–455. Oxford: Oxford University Press.

Van Thiel, S. and Leeuw, F. L. (2002). The performance paradox in the public sector. *Public Performance and Management Review*, 25(3): 267–281.

CHAPTER 17

HEALTH CARE TRANSPARENCY IN ORGANIZATIONAL PERSPECTIVE

CHARLOTTA LEVAY

INTRODUCTION

HEALTH care organizations are under considerable pressure to account for their operations and performance to outside audiences. There is an increasing demand for external reviews that shed light on vital health care processes and outcomes. Efforts abound to provide insight into otherwise obscure aspects of health services, especially as concerns the quality of care. This pursuit of transparency is expressed in the multiplication of quality assurance programs, performance indicators, medical audits, accreditation schemes, public report cards, and league tables. Taking an organizational perspective on these developments means looking at how they play out in health service organizations, but also at the underlying rationales and the governing tools employed.

This chapter analyzes organized efforts to enhance transparency in health care, with an emphasis on public quality reporting as a particularly influential ideal and practice. The chapter starts with a review of the concept of transparency and the driving forces behind current transparency reforms. It then treats the specific tools employed to render health care processes visible. Next, it explores the challenges involved in measuring and representing health care quality as well as the efficacy and consequences of public quality reporting. The chapter goes on to discuss how health professions respond to and participate in having their work increasingly scrutinized by outside observers. Finally it considers directions for future research.

MEANINGS OF TRANSPARENCY

Transparency is a prominent ideal in several policy areas, not just in health care. It is widely believed to promote accountability and efficiency in diverse contexts such as public administration, corporate governance, and international affairs (Ball, 2009; Fenster, 2006; Florini, 2000; Grigorescu, 2003). The transparency term appears frequently in policy documents since the 1980s (Hood, 2006a). In the social science literature, the use of "transparency" and its twin term "accountability" rose markedly in the mid 1990s (Drori, 2006). This transparency trend is multifaceted, and the different strains of thought do not clearly amount to a single, unified idea; they all affirm the value of openness about rules and behavior, but it varies to whom it applies—governments, organizations, or citizens—and what the underlying governance principles are (Hood, 2006a; Meijer, 2014). For instance, there is a grass roots democracy vision of transparency that suggests face-to-face contact between citizens and public officials, which is quite different from the notion that organizations should be obliged to disclose complex information about themselves to markets and regulators (Hood, 2006a). Transparency in the sense of citizens' knowledge of public affairs is often highlighted as a key value for the open, democratic society, but even then it can be construed differently—either as a value in itself, a human right (Birkinshaw, 2006), or as an instrumental value supporting central democratic institutions, such as the ability to hold governments accountable (Heald, 2006a).

So, transparency can denote many desired things, and the exact meaning is often left undefined. In fact, this mix of ambiguity and positive associations may explain some of the popularity of the term—while it is difficult to oppose transparency without appearing to protect a secret or a special interest, the term can be filled with meaning in strategic ways (Hood, 2001; Meijer, 2014). This is important to keep in mind in order to understand how transparency is invoked and pursued in health care. Still, it is possible to make some conceptual distinctions that are helpful when evaluating such initiatives and when relating them to similar initiatives that may be couched in a different terminology.

First, following Heald (2006b), we can distinguish between *nominal* transparency, when information is divulged, and *effective* transparency, when the information is actually accessible and intelligible to relevant audiences. For instance, an organization can be open about its documents and procedures and yet not be transparent if the information is perceived as incoherent by those meant to use it. "For transparency to be effective, there must be receptors capable of processing, digesting, and using the information," whether these receptors are the intended users directly or intermediate users interpreting the material for a wider audience (Heald, 2006b, 35). Many transparency reforms, not least in health care, can be criticized for relying on an overly linear conception of communication and so underestimating the need for knowledge and context to make sense of information (Fenster, 2006; Tsoukas, 1997). If transparency appears to be increasing according to some formal index, but the reality behind is quite different, there will be a gap between nominal and effective transparency that may described as a "transparency illusion" (Heald, 2006b).

Second, we can distinguish between different directions of transparency, especially in the vertical dimension. Transparency downwards occurs when the "ruled" can observe the conduct and results of their "rulers," as emphasized in theories of democracy and accountability. Transparency upwards occurs when hierarchical superiors can observe the conduct and results of subordinates, which amounts to and is often labeled as surveillance (Heald, 2006b). Since health services are regulated and frequently provided by public agencies, it is easy to conceive of transparency in health care as directed downwards, allowing citizens to hold government and public service accountable (Meijer, 2007). In practice, however, the implication is often that health care organizations are made to account for their conduct and results upwards, as part of governmental reporting requirements and public sector management (e.g., Gabe et al., 2012; Kousgaard, 2012; McGivern and Fischer, 2010). In this regard, transparency can be seen as a disciplinary technology and part of the general expansion of inspection and governmental "action at a distance" (Miller and Rose, 1990) that make up contemporary "audit society" (Power, 1997).

TRANSPARENCY PURSUITS AND THEIR DRIVERS

Efforts to make health care transparent through public reporting and external quality assessment follow naturally from new public management (NPM), that is reforms intended to make public services more efficient and accountable by applying business and market-like forms of control (Hood, 1995). Such reforms have been influential in the UK and other countries with publicly provided health care since the 1980s and onwards, supplanting previous "custodial" (Ackroyd, Hughes, and Soothill, 1989) forms of public management that left wide discretion to professional practitioners.

The use of performance indicators to control organizations and reward managers is a defining feature of NPM (Hood, 1995). Initially most indicators concerned aspects of finance and organization, but clinical indicators have become increasingly important (Exworthy et al., 2003). Another core element of NPM is the introduction of competition and consumer choice through internal markets and private alternatives (Hood, 1995), which also creates a demand for transparency. When purchaser-provider splits and market relations replace hierarchical organizational control, there is a need for independent audits, and when patients are meant to act like consumers making informed choices, there is a need for generally accessible and comparable quality information (Blomgren, 2007). Consequently, in many countries, external quality assessment and publicly available performance indicators for provider organizations have been part and parcel of public sector transformations inspired by NPM (e.g., Pollitt et al., 2010; Walshe et al., 2001; Torjesen and Gammelsæter, 2004; Van de Bovenkamp et al., 2014).

In the US, there have been similar developments driving demands for public reporting. In the 1980s, the field of American health became increasingly governed by market forces, price competition, and deregulation (Scott et al., 2000), and broad business models of utilization review, total quality management, and standardized treatment protocols were imported into the field (Caronna, 2004; Dranove, 2000). The US has been leading in the public disclosure movement, mainly propelled by the "business case for quality," arguing that high quality care will lower employers' health insurance costs, and by health plan pricing models directing patients to preferred providers (Marshall et al., 2003). An early federal release of largely unadjusted hospital mortality rates in 1986 was discontinued after a few years following criticism of the validity of rankings (Hannan et al., 2012), but it has been followed by a plethora of initiatives by a range of private and public actors to provide information about the comparative performance of health insurance plans, hospitals, and individual providers (Marshall et al., 2003).

Still, the pursuit of transparency in health care is not just the logical outgrowth of NPM and market forces. It has a different focus and underlying rationale centered on patient rights and democracy (Blomgren and Sahlin, 2007). It is also motivated by heightened concerns for quality of care among patients, purchasers, policy makers, and medical professionals (Makary, 2012; Marshall et al., 2003). Quality of care has risen on the policy agenda after repeated studies showing that quality is often highly variable around a mediocre mean, prompting intensified external scrutiny and an ever greater array of comparative performance measures (Davies, 2001). Influential ideas about "value-based" health care, focusing on maximizing health outcomes per money spent, rather than just keeping costs down, give a central role to public quality measures of health outcomes that matter to patients (Porter and Lee, 2013; Porter and Teisberg, 2006). Calls for greater transparency to confront appalling quality deficiencies, even among highly reputed provider institutions, resonate wider transparency policy discussions. People have a right to know about the quality of different provider organizations, it is argued, and transparency is necessary to make increasingly corporatized hospitals accountable (e.g., Makary, 2012).

The New Transparency Logic
and Its Technologies

The quest for transparency in health care is so widespread and consequential that it can be considered a new governing logic, as suggested by Blomgren and Sahlin (2007). Just as the field of health care underwent a comprehensive transformation when the logic of markets and managerialism became dominant in the 1980s (Scott, 2000), we can now see the contours of a new intuitional era of transparency. It is marked by new and redefined types of major actors and new types of governing mechanisms, such as news media relaying quality comparisons and transnational organizations setting authoritative standards of evaluation (Blomgren and Sahlin, 2007).

The transparency sought for cannot be achieved by simply making already existing data public; it is pursued through a range of interrelated technologies of transparency (Strathern, 2000), intended to create more clarity about processes and outcomes. According to Blomgren and Sahlin (2007), the main technologies involved can be categorized as *scrutiny, accountancy,* and *regulation* (see Figure 17.1), all of which have undergone an explosive growth in recent years. Scrutiny occurs when more or less independent parties review health services and single out good, bad, and acceptable performers, such as in the case of hospital rankings, medical audits, and special commission reports. Accountancy involves not just financial accounting but also other forms of continuous documentation and record keeping that make past activities visible and future activities amenable to control, for example medical records and quality accounting. Regulation in today's health care typically takes the form of "soft regulation," that is voluntary standards, guidelines, recommendations, and agreements designed to establish clarity and comparability, for example clinical guidelines derived from evidence-based medicine. These different technologies can replace one another, such as when public

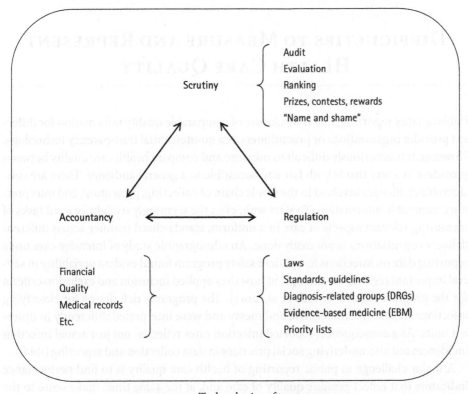

FIGURE 17.1 Technologies of transparency

Adapted from Blomgren and Sahlin (2007, 173).

reports of outcomes replace formal rules, which is a form of "regulation by revelation" (Florini, 2000). More importantly, they support and fuel one another, such as when intensified scrutiny requires more accountancy by organizations under inspection or leads to demands for new regulation (Blomgren and Sahlin, 2007).

As is clear from the examples given, transparency technologies demand an extensive labor of documentation, classification, and presentation (Quartz, Wallenburg, and Bal, 2013). What is more, they have a performative dimension, constituting the objects of scrutiny and transforming existing institutions and relations (Blomgren and Sahlin, 2007; cf. Miller and Rose, 1990; Power, 1997). For example, the administration of patient surveys is not a neutral device to take in the patient perspective; it is a governing technology which makes it possible to reconstruct disconcertingly placid patients into active consumers, by imbuing them with the appropriate attributes of sovereignty and rationality (Hasselbladh and Bejerot, 2007). Patient questionnaires are framed by a recently established body of formal knowledge of patient satisfaction, operated by organizations within the industry of performance measurement, and utilized for all kinds of improvement projects and monitoring systems (ibid.). It is this emergent landscape of new actors, technologies, and circuits of communication reshaping health care practices that warrants the characteristic of transparency as a new governing logic in health care (Blomgren and Sahlin, 2007).

DIFFICULTIES TO MEASURE AND REPRESENT HEALTH CARE QUALITY

Public quality reporting, that is disclosure of comparable quality information for different provider organizations or practitioners, is a quintessential transparency technology. However, it is notoriously difficult to measure and compare health care quality between providers in a way that is both fair and accessible to a general audience. There are considerable challenges involved in the whole chain of collecting, presenting, and interpreting comparable information. To start with, even the seemingly straightforward tasks of measuring relevant aspects of care in a uniform, standardized manner across different delivery organizations is not easily done. An ethnographic study of intensive care units reporting data on infections to a patient safety program found evident variability in several important regards, for example in how they applied inclusion and exclusion criteria for the program (Dixon-Woods et al., 2012). The program's definitions for classifying infections were seen as subjective and messy and were interpreted differently in different units. As a consequence, reported infection rates reflected not just actual infection incidences but also underlying social practices in data collection and reporting (ibid.).

A major challenge to public reporting of health care quality is to find performance indicators that reflect genuine quality of care and, at the same time, make sense to the general public. A classic typology for health care quality assessment distinguishes between measures of *structure* (e.g., qualifications of medical staff), *process* (e.g., adherence to clinical guidelines), and *outcomes* (e.g., recovery, survival, and patient satisfaction) (Donabedian, 1966/2005; Donabedian, 1980). Outcome measures are generally seen as more important and revealing since they go straight to what matters to patients (e.g., Donabedian, 1966/2005; Porter and Teisberg, 2006; Swensen et al., 2010). However, health outcomes depend on other things than the care provided, most notably the "case mix," that is the type of patients treated. Crude comparisons of outcomes can hence be highly misleading (Davies and Crombie, 1997; Mant, 2001). For instance, the most experienced and reputable surgeons and surgical units can have the worst outcomes since they receive the most difficult cases. In principle, this can be compensated by categorizing cases and adjusting outcomes accordingly. In practice, such case mix adjustment, or risk adjustment, is complicated (Davies and Crombie, 1997; Powell, Davies, and Thomson, 2003), and it is difficult for patients to understand the concept of risk-standardized outcomes (Lagu and Lindenauer, 2010). What is more, some relevant outcomes manifest themselves only after many years and are not available when they are needed (Donabedian, 1966/2005). For instance, survival after 5 or 10 years is an important indicator of cancer care quality, but it does not provide information about the current quality of provider organizations.

Process measures are more useful for quality comparison than they may first seem. In fact, if there is an established causal link between treatment and outcome, process measures are just as good indicators of quality of care as outcome measures, and if that link is lacking, outcome and process measures are equally useless (Donabedian, 1980, 103). Process measures are also more sensitive to differences in quality among provider organizations (Mant, 2001). For patients, however, it is difficult to make sense of most hospital process measures (Lagu and Lindenauer, 2010).

Another major challenge is to present comparative quality information so that it can be understood and used by the general audience. As we have seen, both risk-adjusted outcomes and process measures are hard to decipher without specialized knowledge. Numerous studies have shown that patients have difficulties in understanding publicly provided quality information (Faber et al., 2009). Public reports can be designed to be more accessible, for example by providing summary measures, using symbols instead of numbers, and rank-ordering providers according to quality performance (Hibbard, 2008). However, such aggregation can make the information less relevant and useful. For example, a hospital can have excellent quality for cardiovascular surgery but be poor at performing hip replacements, which would be masked by a summary score (Ginsburg, 2010).

In the practitioner-oriented literature, these challenges are usually approached pragmatically, with calls for balanced judgments, better-designed reports, and more use of measures that are relevant to patients (e.g., Hibbard, 2008; Lagu and Lindenauer, 2010; Swensen et al., 2010). But taken together, the challenges appear to create a double bind of nominal transparency—either public quality information gives a reasonably fair indication of quality but is difficult to understand, or it is relatively easy to understand but does not provide crucial information on quality.

EFFICACY OF PUBLIC QUALITY REPORTING

Notwithstanding the challenges of finding accurate and meaningful measures, public quality reporting is often promoted as a key policy tool to support and stimulate quality improvement (e.g., Makary, 2012; Marshall et al., 2003; Porter and Teisberg, 2006). Still, there is scant evidence that public reporting actually leads to better quality of care. There are individual studies and experiences of reporting systems supporting the claim (e.g., Hibbard, Stockard, and Tusler, 2003; Larsson et al., 2012), especially for process measures (Werner and Bradlow, 2010). But when the research is reviewed systematically, it is not possible to establish any positive effects overall (Chatterjee and Joynt, 2014; Fung et al., 2008; Ketelaar et al., 2011; Marshall et al., 2000). For instance, two particularly well-evaluated programs, the New York State's release of mortality data for individual cardiac surgeons and the regional Cleveland Health Quality Choice's quality comparisons of hospitals, both appeared to yield improved clinical outcomes, but other states and other hospitals without public reporting showed similar improvements in the same periods (Fung et al., 2008). Possible explanations for the lack of unambiguously positive results seem to be rooted in fundamental aspects of health care systems and organizational behavior.

There are two main pathways though which publicly reported quality data could lead to improved performance: the selection pathway, meaning that patients and their intermediaries compare data and reward better performing providers by selecting them, and the change pathway, meaning that performance data help providers identifying areas where they underperform (Berwick, James, and Coye, 2003; Fung et al., 2008). Public reports can also incite provider organizations to improve in order to uphold their reputation, which could either be seen as part of the selection effect (Berwick, James, and Coye, 2003) or as a separate, third pathway (Hibbard, 2008).

Each of these pathways has its weak links. First, even if citizens are highly interested in quality-of-care information, most data suggest that patients and other stakeholders do not make much use of comparative performance data when selecting provider or health plan (Davies, 2001; Faber et al., 2009; Marshall et al., 2000). There are several reasons for this, including lack of time for acutely ill patients to compare potential sources of care, lack of awareness of quality variations, lack of knowledge to make sense of the information available, and importance given to other factors, such as costs or recommendations from trusted family members or physicians (Faber et al., 2009; Lagu and Lindenauer, 2010). Second, even if evidence suggests that public release of performance data stimulates quality improvement activity at the hospital level, this does not automatically translate to actual improvements (Fung et al., 2008; Tu et al., 2009). Third, the actions taken by providers and institutions to protect their reputation are not only beneficial for quality of care.

While the positive effects of public quality reporting remain to be demonstrated, there are several well-established unintended negative consequences related to responses from health care organizations and individual providers striving to safe-guard their standing. Hospitals and individual surgeons tend to avoid treating more difficult, seriously ill patients so as to improve their quality ranking, which is what hap-pened in New York State following public report cards on cardiac surgery (Dranove et al., 2002; Werner and Asch, 2005). As a consequence, patients who need treatment the most get worse access (ibid.). So do racial and ethnic minorities, since they may be perceived to be at higher risk of poor outcomes (Chatterjee and Joynt, 2014). Even if publicly reported outcomes are well adjusted to take the risk of different types of patients into account, this may not compensate risk-averse providers sufficiently for the downside of treating sicker patients (Dranove et al., 2002). There are other prob-lematic ways in which actors may try to "game the system" in an attempt to do well in comparisons, such as when hospitals reclassify patients into or out of publicly reported diagnoses, or when they code a higher number of diagnoses to make patients seem sicker (Chatterjee and Joynt, 2014). Furthermore, public quality comparisons often stir anger, resentment, and disillusion among practitioners and managers in the organiza-tions concerned, especially if these people doubt the validity of measures employed and are worried that attention to what gets measured will crowd out other, more important quality issues (Davies, 2001; Hibbard, Stockard, and Tusler, 2003; Hoque, Davis, and Humphreys, 2004). Since public quality reports can actually be misleading (e.g., Bevan and Hood, 2006; Hood, 2006b; Paddock, Adams, and Hoces de la Guardia, 2015), such reactions cannot simply be discarded as self-serving. Finally, public rankings gener-ate substantial amounts of administrative work in health delivery organizations being ranked (Quartz, Wallenburg, and Bal, 2013), and potential benefits should be weighed against alternative use of resources.

GAMING AND WILLFUL BLINDNESS

The risk of gaming and low morale among organizations being monitored appears particularly high when public release of performance data is combined with financial rewards. One example is the NHS system of annual "star rating" of public hospitals and other public sector health-delivery organizations, which ran in England from 2000 to 2005 (Bevan and Hood, 2006; Hood, 2006b). Each organization was publicly rated with a summary score for different kinds of targets, a small set of key targets, and a wider set of indicators in a balanced scorecard. In addition to reputational effects of "naming and shaming," the indicators were linked to managers' bonuses and decisions to keep or fire them, "best to best" budgetary allocation, and "earned autonomy" for organizations performing high on measured metrics. Reported performance data indi-cated massive improvements, for example drastically reduced time spent by patients in the A&E. However, as analyzed by Hood (2006b) and Bevan and Hood (2006), there were several types of documented gaming, including instances of "hitting the target but missing the point" and in some cases putting patient safety at risk. One tactic to reach the waiting time target was to have patients wait in queues of ambulances outside the A&E Department before receiving them, which may have stalled ambulance responses to calls from seriously ill individuals. A related example is the recent scandal of the US Veterans Health Administration—another system featuring measurement and public reporting of performance results tied to managerial bonus incentives (Kizer and Kirsh, 2012)—with news reports revealing that long waiting times for veterans were cloaked in official waiting lists to generate favorable performance reviews (e.g., Oppel and Shear, 2014).

On paper, designers and administrators of transparency regimes can design a system to tackle the problem of gaming from the outset, for example by establishing independent third parties as regulators or evaluators. In reality, they operate in their own context of action and may have their own reasons to favor systems that produce only nominal transparency. The central managers of the NHS star rating did not put substantial resources into checking performance data and had no coherent antigaming strategy—a kind of gaming in itself, much like when Admiral Nelson put a telescope to his blind eye to avoid seeing a signal he did not want to obey (Hood, 2006b). According to Chang (2009), the star rating system was designed to advance political interests rather than rational performance improvement; the government's political objectives were infused into the formulation of measurements so that the information produced could be used to build a favorable image. Similarly, central administrators at the Veterans Health Administration had been aware but passive about waiting times dysfunctions well before the public scandal erupted in 2014. The oversight body of the Department of Veterans Affairs had issued reports identifying the problem since at least 2002, and the administration repeatedly agreed to recommendations but took no or inadequate action (Robbins, 2012).

There is no reason to believe that willful self-blinding by those responsible for systems to increase transparency is uncommon. Rather than singular cases of mismanagement, the examples just described may be instances of a wider phenomenon of "functional stupidity," that is an organizationally-supported lack of reflexivity, a refusal to use intellectual capacities in other than myopic ways to provide a sense of certainty that allows organizations to function smoothly (Alvesson and Spicer, 2012). A study of the construction of a Danish national quality program to render health care quality transparent and controllable shows that potentially disruptive information was actively kept out of sight in decision processes (Knudsen, 2011). Several critical systems design issues were well known to key actors and yet not discussed, for example that extensive external reviews can cause inspection overload and divert attention from important local concerns. The analysis suggests that blindness was actively self-imposed through forms of inattentiveness, for example by substituting actual knowledge of quality indicators by references to authoritative institutions. Information that could question the model being worked out was shut out, which made it easier for various stakeholders to communicate and reach decisions (ibid.).

Dynamic Effects of Transparency Efforts

Given the complexity of responses to efforts to make health care more transparent, their effects cannot be evaluated solely in the short run, on the basis of measurable scores in the organizations immediately concerned. Unexpected chains of events and more intangible consequences may transpire when various actors learn about new realities and start to act strategically upon them, and when perceptions of legitimate modes of control alter. Such dynamic effects can of course be constructive. For instance, as already mentioned, the US federal state's release of crude mortality data for identified hospitals in the mid-1980s was heavily criticized for poor validity, but it also spawned initiatives to provide more reliable quality assessments, using carefully risk-adjusted clinical data instead of administrative claims data (Asher et al., 2014). These include the Society of Thoracic Surgeons National Database, which provides performance assessment to participants, quality improvement initiatives, and, since 2010, voluntary public reporting of outcomes (Shahian et al., 2013). Even "strategic accounting" by health professionals can be a way to cope with unintended consequences of performance measurement, such as when doctors in Dutch hospital care found creative ways to sidestep pre-set combinations of diagnosis and treatment in order to provide innovative treatments unforeseen by the performance measurement system (Kerpershoek, 2010). However, there are also more problematic dynamic effects.

Reactivity, that is the change of behavior in reaction to being observed and evaluated, is a broader phenomenon than just gaming. Espeland and Sauder (2007) distinguish two principal mechanisms of reactivity: *self-fulfilling prophecy*, meaning changed behavior to conform with expectations embedded in measures, and *commensuration*, meaning changes in attention when qualities are transformed into quantities that share a simplified, de-contextualized metric. Both mechanisms were identified in a study of health professionals' reactions to performance measures and transparency regulation meant to curb malpractice (McGivern and Fischer, 2012). Doctors responded defensively to perceived threats of scapegoating by focusing less on actual practice and patient needs and more on representing their practice in standardized terms, hiding or avoiding practices that could draw negative attention. Therapists were anxious that poor patient ratings might put their job in jeopardy and made efforts to "be nice" and "patch up" instead of tackling more painful, underlying problems (ibid.).

A close study of Dutch hospitals' response to league tables found a host of reactive processes (Quartz, Wallenburg, and Bal, 2013). In the front stage, managers and professionals criticized the design and relevance of rankings and claimed they were of little consequence to hospital policies and external relations. In the backstage, clinical and administrative practices were thoroughly modified to comply with ranking criteria and to protect organizational reputation. This pragmatic compliance took many forms, ranging from a laboratory manager fulfilling accreditation requirements he considered meaningless for quality and safety, to hospitals developing IT systems and administrative structures to ensure data collection according to external demands (ibid.).

The performativity of transparency technologies extends to the evolution of transparency systems as such. Pollitt et al. (2010) detected a "logic of escalation" in the development of health care performance regimes in England and the Netherlands—once a system of quantitative performance indicators is in place, there is an endogenous dynamic or logic to the way it is likely to develop. Measures tend to multiply, and the use of performance indicators tends to move from formative approaches where measures are meant to indicate areas for improvement to summative approaches where targets and league tables are taken to define quality. Next, the summative approach is linked with incentives and sanctions, with associated pressures for gaming. Ownership of the performance regime becomes increasingly diffuse, with a whole industry of regulators and analysts using the regime partly to pursue their own ends. Finally, all of these tendencies combine to produce confusion and distrust among the lay public (ibid.). This logic of escalation cannot be immediately generalized to other contexts, but it is easily recognizable in the case of the US Veterans Health Administration, where measures multiplied and became more composite over the years and were increasingly used for compliance rather than data-driven development (Kizer and Kirsh, 2012).

Transparency and the Health Professions

Most of the complications of the pursuit of transparency in health care discussed in this chapter relate to the fact that health care is a complex activity performed by specialized experts. They operate not through a mass of information that can be relayed in bits and pieces, but through integrated bodies of knowledge that require years of formal training and immersed practice to master and wholly understand. There are limits to how far such expert work can become effectively transparent.

In his exposé of the paradoxes of the information society, Tsoukas (1997) emphasizes that expert systems develop their particular languages, values, and practices that cannot be completely articulated or understood by non-practitioners. There is an inevitable gap of knowledge separating participants in an expert system from those observing it, and there is no detached highground from which the system can be inspected. In order to be used effectively, expert systems depend on the trust of those who benefit from them (Giddens, 1990). Therefore, according to Tsoukas, attempts to make an expert system transparent to non-experts can only result in an illusory transparency and undermine the trust necessary for its functioning. "[T]he paradox is that the more information on the inner workings of an expert system observers seek to have, the less they will be inclined to trust its practitioners; the less practitioners are trusted, the less likely it is for the benefits of specialized expertise to be realized" (Tsoukas, 1997, 835). To illustrate the paradox, Tsoukas takes a proposal to install short-circuit cameras in operating theatres to record surgeons' likely mistakes. The laughter, joking, swearing, and music listening which are common and rather helpful practices from the perspective of those performing surgery may seem careless from the perspective of the patient, and the camera monitoring of surgeons undermines the mutual trust that could reconcile the two perspectives.

Given this problematic, it is hardly surprising that health professionals do not immediately embrace transparency technologies. They often respond with distrust in the validity of measures, concerns that vital aspects of quality will be ignored or harmed, fears of being evaluated on unjust grounds, frustration over blunt instruments of assessment, and general disillusionment about the whole process. Such reactions have been recorded in connection with public release of performance data (Davies, 2001; Hibbard, Stockard, and Tusler, 2003; Hoque, Davis, and Humphreys, 2004; Kerpershoek, 2010; Kousgaard, 2012; Levay and Waks, 2009; Quartz, Wallenburg, and Bal, 2013), consultant appraisal (McGivern and Ferlie, 2007), patient safety monitoring (Dixon-Woods et al., 2012), transparency regulation to prevent malpractice (McGivern and Fischer, 2012), evidence-based clinical guidelines (Timmermans and Oh, 2010), and audits using electronic patient records (Winthereik, van der Ploeg, and Berg, 2007).

These responses are consistent with classic theory of the professions. External evaluation and routinization go against the whole idea of autonomous professionalism. Professions can be defined as knowledge-based occupations that control their own work. They have the special privilege of freedom of control from outsiders, justified by their presumed ethics, self-regulation, and special knowledge that lay persons are not equipped to evaluate or regulate (Freidson, 1970, 2001). At the core of professional work lies inference, that is the ability of practitioners to connect information of diagnosis with a range of treatments (Abbott, 1988). If that connection can be made too easily, work gets routinized, and the professional domain may be taken over by competing professional groups. Likewise, if results are too easy to measure, the professional group is too easily evaluated by outsiders and may lose legitimate control of its work (ibid., 46, 51).

Yet, this is not the entire picture. Professional groups also have a strategic interest in displaying the efficacy of their particular competence. If the connection between diagnosis and treatment can only be performed on a case-to-case basis, and if results are too hard to measure, the profession's legitimacy will be weakened and it will lose ground to professional groups offering more demonstrable solutions (Abbott, 1988, 46, 51–53).

In fact, medical professionals take an active and pivotal part in developing technologies that make their practice more predictable, standardized, measurable, and hence amenable to external inspection. Medical professional organizations collaborate with regulatory entities to establish evidence-based practice guidelines, assessment tools, and standardized outcome measures (Timmermans and Oh, 2010). Such developments are sometimes seen as a partial loss of professional autonomy, since the profession is stratified between elite professionals setting standards of performance and rank-and-file practitioners performing increasingly routinized work (Freidson, 2001). But again, this is not the whole picture. Clinical guidelines can actually mean greater autonomy for ordinary professionals, since they make it easier for them to conduct and improve patient care without turning to university consultants or colleagues (Castel and Merle, 2002). Accreditation can also be perceived as useful by ordinary professionals, since it can help them to improve and legitimize services in the face of external demands (Levay and Waks, 2009) or to reposition a marginalized subspecialty in a competitive environment (Robelet, 2001). Even bad performance in public league tables can be used by professionals to argue for a larger share of resources for their organizational unit (Levay and Waks, 2009).

So, professional groups are affected by transparency technologies and respond to them in quite different manners. To some extent, the variation stems from differences in situation and outlook (cf. Bezes et al., 2012). For instance, medical professionals have generally been skeptical of evidence-based medicine, but some professional groups appear attracted by its signal for scientific expertise, such as marginalized doctors in Russia and nurses aiming for greater professionalization (Timmermans and Oh, 2010). To some extent, professional strategies evolve over time. For instance, Swedish doctors accepted to release comparable performance data from professionally controlled quality improvement registries only after pressures from investigative reporters and opinion-makers (Levay and Waks, 2009). However, doctors, especially those responsible for registries, then discovered advantages with public reporting, such as stronger motivation for improvement efforts among organizations reporting to registries (ibid.). To some extent, finally, consequences to professionals depend on how we understand professional autonomy. In the case of the Swedish quality registries, Bejerot and Hasselbladh (2011) conclude that doctors gradually lost control over registries to the government and were active participants in dismantling their own professional autonomy. In a different assessment, Levay and Waks (2009) conclude that doctors retained considerable control over the premises and criteria of external evaluation and so enjoyed a "soft autonomy."

FUTURE RESEARCH

This chapter has explored the nature and consequences of organized attempts to make health care processes and outcomes transparent. It has analyzed the challenges, unintended consequences, and wider implications of applying transparency technologies to complex professional activities that are not easily understood by a general audience. It has shown the uncertain foundation of claims that public quality reporting leads to quality improvement, described the perils of combining public performance indicators with financial reward systems, and pointed at the tendency of decision-makers to blind themselves to problematic aspects of transparency systems. It has discussed the performative potentials of transparency technologies to reshape health care practices and to both undermine and strengthen professional autonomy.

Studies referred to in this chapter have been conducted with varying approaches and theoretical perspectives, pertaining to quite different levels of health care and society. Two main strands of research are discernible: practitioner and policy-oriented research from a medical and quality of care perspective optimistically aiming to provide guidance for transparency initiatives, and theory-oriented social science research pessimistically expounding inexorable problems of transparency initiatives as social phenomena. Both strands can probably take cues from one another. And we can all take cues from classic quality of care scholar Avedis Donabedian's words on the frame of mind with which studies of health care quality are approached, given the social imperatives that give rise to quality assessment. His advice is equally valid for studies of health care transparency:

> Often associated with these [social imperatives] are the zeal and values of the social reformer. Greater neutrality and detachment are needed in studies of quality. More often one needs to ask, "What goes on here?" rather than, "What is wrong; and how can it be made better?" (Donabedian, 1966/2005, 721).

Finally, Gabe et al. (2012) propose an analytic framework to explore the consequences of public disclosure of health care performance data and develop a "sociology of disclosure." They identify three interconnected aspects of the drive for transparency that deserve particular attention: the capacity of different individuals to engage in *choice and calculativeness* when they take part of public information; the *strategies and tactics* employed by patients, health professionals, managers, and organizations in creating and receiving information; and the impact on *trust* between doctors and patients. Each aspect can be considered at three interacting levels: the micro level of professional-patient and inter-professional relationships; the meso level of the organization; and the macro level of the external regulatory environment (ibid.). Future social science research on health care transparency would gain from such a shared framework that makes it possible to build more systematically from one study to another.

REFERENCES

Abbott, A. D. (1988). *The system of professions: An essay on the division of expert labor.* Chicago: University of Chicago Press.

Ackroyd, S., Hughes, J., and Soothill, K. (1989). Public sector services and their management. *Journal of Management Studies*, 26(6): 603–619.

Alvesson, M. and Spicer, A. (2012). A stupidity-based theory of organizations. *Journal of Management Studies*, 49(7): 1194–1220.

Asher, A. L., Gliklich, R. E., Hernandez, A. F., Leavy, M. B., Mandel, K., Schwamm, L. H., and Shahian D. M. (2014). Quality improvement registries. In *Registries for evaluating patient outcomes: A user's guide*, 3rd edition, ed. Gliklich, R. E., Dreyer, N. A., and Leavy, M. B., pp. 171–197. Rockville, MD: Agency for Healthcare Research and Quality.

Ball, C. (2009). What is transparency? *Public Integrity*, 11(4): 293–307.

Bejerot, E. and Hasselbladh, H. (2011). Professional autonomy and pastoral power: The transformation of quality registers in Swedish health care. *Public Administration*, 89(4): 1604–1621.

Berwick, D. M., James, B., and Coye, M. J. (2003). Connections between Quality Measurement and Improvement. *Medical Care*, 41(Suppl 1): 130–138.

Bevan, G. and Hood, C. (2006). What's measured is what matters: Targets and gaming in the English public health care system. *Public Administration*, 84(3): 517–538.

Bezes, P., Demazière, D., Le Bianic, T., Paradeise, C., Normand, R., Benamouzig, D., Pierru, F., and Evetts, J. (2012). New public management and professionals in the public sector: What new patterns beyond opposition? *Sociologie du Travail*, 54(Suppl 1): e1–e52.

Birkinshaw, P. (2006). Transparency as a human right. In *Transparency: The key to better governance?*, ed. Hood, C. and Heald, D., pp. 47–57. Oxford: Oxford University Press.

Blomgren, M. (2007). The drive for transparency: Organizational field transformations in Swedish healthcare. *Public Administration*, 85(1): 67–82.

Blomgren, M. and Sahlin, K. (2007). Quests for transparency: Signs of a new institutional era in the health care field. In *Transcending new public management: The transformation of public sector reform*, ed. Christensen, T. and Lægreid, P., pp. 155–177. Aldershot: Ashgate.

Caronna, C. A. (2004). The misalignment of institutional "pillars": Consequences for the U.S. health care field. *Journal of Health and Social Behavior*, 45(Extra Issue): 45–58.

Castel, P. and Merle, I. (2002). Quand les normes de pratiques deviennent une ressource pour les médecins. *Sociologie du Travail*, 44(3): 337–355.

Chang, L.-C. (2009). The impact of political interests upon the formulation of performance measurements: The NHS star rating system. *Financial Accountability and Management*, 25(2): 145–165.

Chatterjee, P. and Joynt, K. E. (2014). Do cardiology quality measures actually improve patient outcomes? *Journal of the American Heart Association*. 3(1): e000404.

Davies, H. T. O. (2001). Public release of performance data and quality improvement: Internal responses to external data by US health care providers. *Quality in Health Care*, 10: 104–110.

Davies, H. T. O. and Crombie, I. K. (1997). Interpreting Health Outcomes. *Journal of Evaluation in Clinical Practice*, 3(3): 187–199.

Dixon-Woods, M., Leslie, M., Bion, J., and Tarrant, C. (2012). What counts? An ethnographic study of infection data reported to a patient safety program. *The Milbank Quarterly*, 90(3): 548–591.

Donabedian, A. (1980). *Explorations in quality assessment and monitoring*. Vol. 1: *The definition of quality and approaches to its assessment*. Ann Arbor, MI: Health Administration Press.

Donabedian, A. ([1966] 2005). Evaluating the quality of medical care. *The Milbank Quarterly*, 83(4): 691–729. Originally published 1966 in *The Milbank Memorial Fund Quarterly*, 44(3): 166–203.

Dranove, D. (2000). *The economic evolution of American health care: From Marcus Welby to managed care*. Princeton, NJ: Princeton University Press.

Dranove, D., Kessler, D., McClellan, M., and Satterthwaite, M. (2002). Is more information better? The effects of "report cards" on health care providers. Working Paper 8697. Cambridge, MA: National Bureau of Economic Research.

Drori, G. S. (2006). Governed by governance: The new prism for organizational change. In *Globalization and organization: World society and organizational change*, ed. Drori, G. S., Meyer, G.W., and Hwang, H., pp. 91–118. Oxford: Oxford University Press.

Espeland, W. N. and Sauder, M. (2007). Rankings and reactivity: How public measures recreate social worlds. *American Journal of Sociology*, 113(1): 1–40.

Exworthy, M., Wilkinson, E. K., McColl, A., Moore, M., Roderick, P., Smith, H., and Gabbay, J. (2003). The role of performance indicators in changing the autonomy of the general practice profession in the UK. *Social Science & Medicine*, 56(7): 1493–1504.

Faber, M., Bosch, M., Wollersheim, H., Leatherman, S., and Grol, R. (2009). Public reporting in health care: How do consumers use quality-of-care information? *Medical Care*, 47(1): 1–8.

Fenster, M. (2006). The opacity of transparency. *Iowa Law Review*, 91(3): 885–949.

Florini, A. (2000). The end of secrecy. *Foreign Policy*, 111(Summer): 50–63.

Freidson, E. (1970). *Profession of medicine: A study of the sociology of applied knowledge.* New York: Harper & Row.

Freidson, E. (2001). *Professionalism: The third logic.* Cambridge: Polity Press.

Fung, C. H., Lim, Y.-W., Mattke, S., Damberg, C., and Shekelle, P. G. (2008). Systematic review: The evidence that publishing patient care performance data improves quality of care. *Annals of Internal Medicine*, 148(2): 111–123.

Gabe, J., Exworthy, M., Jones, I. R, and Smith, G. (2012). Towards a sociology of disclosure: The case of surgical performance. *Sociology Compass*, 6(11): 908–922.

Giddens, A. (1990). *The consequences of modernity.* Cambridge: Polity Press.

Ginsburg, P. B. (2010). Provider price and quality transparency. In *The healthcare imperative: Lowering costs and improving outcomes: Workshop series summary*, ed. Yong, P. L., Saunders, R. S., and Olsen, L. A, Institute of Medicine (US) Roundtable on Evidence-Based Medicine, pp. 344–347. Washington, D.C.: National Academies Press.

Grigorescu, A. (2003). International organizations and government transparency: Linking the international and domestic realms. *International Studies Quarterly*, 47(4): 643–667.

Hannan, E. L., Cozzens, K., King, S. B. 3rd, Walford, G., and Shah, N. R. (2012). The New York state cardiac registries: History, contributions, limitations, and lessons for future efforts to assess and publicly report healthcare outcomes. *Journal of the American College of Cardiology*, 59(25): 2309–2316.

Hasselbladh, H. and Bejerot, E. (2007). Webs of knowledge and circuits of communication: Constructing rationalized agency in Swedish health care. *Organization*, 14(2): 175–200.

Heald, D. (2006a). Transparency as an instrumental value. In *Transparency: The key to better governance?*, ed. Hood, C. and Heald, D., pp. 59–73. Oxford: Oxford University Press.

Heald, D. (2006b). Varieties of transparency. In *Transparency: The key to better governance?*, ed. Hood, C. and Heald, D., pp. 25–43. Oxford: Oxford University Press.

Hibbard, J. H. (2008). What can we say about the impact of public reporting? Inconsistent execution yields variable result. *Annals of Internal Medicine*, 148(2): 160–161.

Hibbard, J. H., Stockard, J., and Tusler, M. (2003). Does publicizing hospital performance stimulate quality improvement efforts? *Health Affairs*, 22(2): 84–94.

Hood, C. (1995). The "new public management" in the 1980s: Variations on a theme. *Accounting, Organizations and Society*, 20(2/3): 93–109.

Hood, C. (2001). Transparency. In *Encyclopaedia of democratic thought*, ed. Clarke, P. B. and Foweraker, J., pp. 700–704. London: Routledge.

Hood, C. (2006a). Transparency in historical perspective. In *Transparency: The key to better governance?*, ed. Hood, C. and Heald, D., pp. 3–23. Oxford: Oxford University Press.

Hood, C. (2006b). Gaming in targetworld: The targets approach to managing British public services. *Public Administration Review*, 66(4): 515–520.

Hood, C. and Heald, D. (eds) (2006). *Transparency: The key to better governance?* Oxford: Oxford University Press.

Hoque, K., Davis, S., and Humphreys, M. (2004). Freedom to do what you are told: Senior management team autonomy in an NHS acute trust. *Public Administration*, 82(2): 355–375.

Kerpershoek, E. (2010). Performance measurement and strategic behavior in Dutch hospital care. Paper presented at the Third Biennial Conference of the European Consortium on Political Research Standing Group on Regulatory Governance on "Regulation in an Age of Crisis," University College Dublin, 17–19 June 2010.

Ketelaar, N. A., Faber, M. J., Flottorp, S., Rygh, L. H., Deane, K. H., and Eccles, M. P. (2011). Public release of performance data in changing the behaviour of healthcare consumers, professionals or organisations. *Cochrane Database of Systematic Reviews*, doi: 10.1002/14651858. CD004538.pub2.

Kizer, K. W. and Kirsh, S. R. (2012). The double edged sword of performance measurement. *Journal of General Internal Medicine*, 27(4): 395–397.

Knudsen, M. (2011). Forms of inattentiveness: The production of blindness in the development of a technology for the observation of quality in health services. *Organization Studies*, 32(7): 963–989.

Kousgaard, M. B. (2012). Translating visions of transparency and quality development: The transformation of clinical databases in the Danish hospital field. *International Journal of Health Planning and Management*, 27(1): e1–e17.

Lagu, T. and Lindenauer, P. K. (2010). Putting the public back in public reporting of health care quality. *Journal of the American Medical Association*, 304(15): 1711–1712.

Larsson, S., Lawyer, P., Garellick, G., Lindahl, B., and Lundström, M. (2012). Use of 13 disease registries in 5 countries demonstrates the potential to use outcome data to improve health care's value. *Health Affairs*, 31(1): 220–227.

Levay, C. and Waks, C. (2009). Professions and the pursuit of transparency in healthcare: Two cases of soft autonomy. *Organization Studies*, 30(5): 509–527.

McGivern, G. and Ferlie, E. (2007). Playing tick-box games: Interrelating defences in professional appraisal. *Human Relations*, 60(9): 1361–1385.

McGivern, G. and Fischer, M. (2010). Medical regulation, spectacular transparency and the blame business. *Journal of Health Organization and Management*, 24(6): 597–610.

McGivern, G. and Fischer, M. (2012). Reactivity and reactions to regulatory transparency in medicine, psychotherapy and counselling. *Social Science and Medicine*, 74(3): 289–296.

Makary, M. (2012). *Unaccountable: What hospitals won't tell you and how transparency can revolutionize health care*. New York: Bloomsbury Press.

Mant, J. (2001). Process versus outcome indicators in the assessment of quality of health care. *International Journal for Quality in Health Care*, 13(6): 475–480.

Marshall, M. N., Shekelle, P. G., Davies, H. T., and Smith, P. C. (2003). Public reporting on quality in the United States and the United Kingdom. *Health Affairs*, 22(3): 134–148.

Marshall, M. N., Shekelle, P. G., Leatherman, S., and Brook, R. H. (2000). The public release of performance data: What do we expect to gain? A review of the evidence. *Journal of the American Medical Association*, 283(14): 1866–1874.

Meijer, A. (2014). Transparency. In *The Oxford handbook of public accountability*, ed. Bovens, M., Goodin, R. E., and Schillemans, T. Oxford: Oxford University Press, doi: 10.1093/oxfordhb/9780199641253.013.0043.

Meijer, A. J. (2007). Publishing public performance results on the Internet: Do stakeholders use the Internet to hold Dutch public service organizations to account? *Government Information Quarterly*, 24(1): 165–185.

Miller, P. and Rose N. (1990). Governing economic life. *Economy and Society*, 19(1): 1–31.

Oppel, R. A. and Shear, M. D. (2014). Severe report finds V.A. hid waiting lists at hospitals. *New York Times*, 28 May.

Paddock, S. M., Adams, J. L., and Hoces de la Guardia, F. (2015). Better-than-average and worse-than-average hospitals may not significantly differ from average hospitals: An analysis of Medicare Hospital Compare ratings. *BMJ Quality & Safety*, 24(2): 128–134.

Pollitt, C., Harrison, S., Dowswell, G., Jerak-Zuiderent, S., and Bal, R. (2010). Performance regimes in health care: Institutions, critical junctures and the logic of escalation in England and the Netherlands. *Evaluation* 16(1): 13–29.

Porter, M. E. and Lee, T. H. (2013). The strategy that will fix health care. *Harvard Business Review*, 91(10): 50–70.

Porter, M. E. and Teisberg, E. O. (2006). *Redefining health care: Creating value-based competition on results*. Boston, MA: Harvard Business School Press.

Powell, A. E., Davies, H. T. O., and Thomson, R. G. (2003). Using routine comparative data to assess the quality of health care: Understanding and avoiding common pitfalls. *Quality and Safety in Health Care*, 12(2): 122–128.

Power, M. (1997). *The audit society: Rituals of verification*. Oxford: Oxford University Press.

Quartz, J., Wallenburg, I., and Bal, R. (2013). The performativity of rankings: On the organizational effects of hospital league tables. iBMG Working Paper W2013.02. Rotterdam: Institute of Health Policy and Management, Erasmus University Rotterdam.

Robbins, R. A. (2012). Editorial: VA administrators gaming the system. *Southwest Journal of Pulmonary and Critical Care*, 4: 149–154.

Robelet, M. (2001). La profession médicale face au défi de la qualité: Une comparaison de quatre manuels qualité. *Sciences Sociales et Santé*, 19(2): 73–98.

Scott, W. R., Ruef, M., Mendel, P. J., and Caronna, C. A. (2000). *Institutional change and healthcare organizations: From professional dominance to managed care*. Chicago: University of Chicago Press.

Shahian, D. M., Jacobs, J. P., Edwards, F. H., Brennan, J. M., Dokholyan, R. S., Prager, R. L., Wright, C. D., Peterson, E. D., McDonald, D. E., and Grover, F. L. (2013). The Society of Thoracic Surgeons National Database. *Heart*, 99(20): 1494–1501.

Strathern, M. (2000). The tyranny of transparency. *British Educational Research Journal*, 26(3): 309–321.

Swensen, S. J., Meyer, G. S., Nelson, E. C., Hunt, G. C. Jr., Pryor, D. B., Weissberg, J. I., Kaplan, G. S., Daley, J., Yates, G. R., Chassin, M. R., James, B. C., and Berwick, D. M. (2010). Cottage industry to postindustrial care: The revolution in health care delivery. *The New England Journal of Medicine*, 362(5): e12.

Timmermans, S. and Oh, H. (2010). The continued social transformation of the medical profession. *Journal of Health and Social Behavior*, 51(S): S94–S106.

Torjesen, D. A. and Gammelsæter, H. (2004). Management between autonomy and transparency in the enterprise hospital. Working Paper 1-2004. Bergen: Stein Rokkan Centre for Social Studies.

Tsoukas, H. (1997). The tyranny of light: The temptations and the paradoxes of the information society. *Futures*, 29(9): 827–843.

Tu, J. V., Donovan, L. R., Lee, D. S., Wang, J. T, Austin, P. C., Alter, D. A., and Ko, D. T. (2009). Effectiveness of public report cards for improving the quality of cardiac care: The EFFECT study: A randomized trial. *Journal of the American Medical Association*, 302(21): 2330–2337.

Van de Bovenkamp, H., De Mul, M., Quartz, J., Weggelaar, A.M., and Bal, R. (2014). Institutional layering in governing health care quality. *Public Administration*, 92(1): 208–223.

Walshe K., Wallace, L., Freeman T., Latham, L., and Spurgeon, P. (2001). The external review of quality improvement in health care organizations: A qualitative study. *International Journal for Quality in Health Care,* 13(5): 367–374.

Werner, R. M. and Asch, D. A. (2005). The unintended consequences of publicly reporting quality information. *Journal of the American Medical Association,* 293(10): 1239–1244.

Werner, R. M. and Bradlow, E. T. (2010). Public reporting on hospital process improvements is linked to better patient outcomes. *Health Affairs,* 29(7): 1319–1324.

Winthereik, B. R., van der Ploeg, I., and Berg, M. (2007). The electronic patient record as a meaningful audit tool: Accountability and autonomy in general practitioner work. *Science, Technology, and Human Values,* 32(1): 6–25.

PART IV

ISSUES IN THE
HEALTH CARE
ORGANIZATIONAL
FIELD

CHAPTER 18

RE-PLACING CARE

Governing HealthCare through Spatial Arrangements

LIEKE OLDENHOF, JEROEN POSTMA,
AND ROLAND BAL

A SPACE FOR PLACE

IN this chapter, we want to create a "space for place" (Gieryn, 2000) in health care management by analyzing the role that spatial arrangements, and especially re-placements, play in the governance of care. In projects we have been engaged in over the five years, we noticed that place increasingly became a focal point for policy makers, managers, professionals, and patients. Questions about governance of quality, efficiency, equity, and financial sustainability seemed to be increasingly linked to questions of place. In some projects the place–governance relation was clear: concentration of medical care for example deals with the explicit questions in which places care is and should be delivered, and the emphasis on home care clearly is an instantiation of a new (or renewed) spatial arrangement in health care. In others we had to dig deeper to understand the relation between place and governance, say in projects on self-management and telecare. Nevertheless, place was always there. This chapter emphasizes the importance of place in care by analyzing how re-placements are (and can be) used to govern health care and to what consequences.

Placing Place in Health Care and Governance Literature

Unfortunately, when studying place and re-placement, we are not much helped by the literature on health care management and policy, where place is an under-researched and under-theorized concept (Milligan, 2001). Surely, there is a wealth of studies that deals for example with the geographical spread of diseases, the planning and accessibility of health care services, the presence of (un)healthy food outlets in a certain area, and the design and construction of facilities such as hospitals. In these studies, place is usually conceptualized one-dimensionally as a geographical location, a dot on the map, where diseases or health facilities can be pinpointed. This conceptualization of place-as-location is also evident in studies on "place effects" that analyze health inequalities between places, such as neighborhoods, cities, or regions. To be able to measure these place-effects or determine the accessibility of care providers and (un)healthy food outlets, place itself needs to be geographically fixated on a map and materially stabilized in buildings such as hospitals, grocery stores, and junk food restaurants. However, by doing so, important relational, symbolic, and political dimensions of place are marginalized or completely stay out of view (Mcintyre, Ellaway, and Cummins, 2002; Kearns and Gesler, 1998).

An insightful example is research on "food deserts" that traditionally focuses on the physical distance of certain groups to food outlets. These studies ignore the symbolic meaning of food or perceived distances in cultural and class background. Even if the physical distance to food facilities were to be greatly reduced, it remains to be seen whether this would lead to a radical altering of eating habits and perceived health (Cummins, Flint, and Matthews, 2014), since both eating habits and health are intimately linked to socio-economic status and culture (Walker, Keane, and Burke, 2010). This example illustrates how relational, political, and symbolic dimensions matter a great deal for the distribution of health and therefore also for the operationalization of good health care governance in practice. To better understand the relation between place and health care governance, we need to go beyond place as self-evident and a neutral geographical location.

Unfortunately, also in governance literature, place is an under-theorized concept. Pollitt (2011) even calls place an "endangered species" as it is virtually absent in key handbooks on governance, sociology, and public administration (Pollitt, 2011, 2012; Gieryn, 2000). The absence of place can partly be explained by societal developments that seemingly render place irrelevant in governance issues, such as digitalization and globalization. Work on network governance (Kickert, Klijn, and Koppenjan, 1997), currently a popular concept in governance literature, is a case in point. On the one hand, network governance takes geography seriously in the sense that the position of an actor in a network is consequential for policymaking. On the other hand, however, *where* the action takes place stays completely out of the picture: networks can be anywhere, anyplace, and this does in no way affect their functioning. Networks are "without" or "beyond" place: they are "placeless."

The near absence of place in governance literature can also be explained by the ambition of scholars to make universal claims about society without having to worry about differences between places and unique particularities of places. As Gieryn (2000, 464) wryly remarks, many sociologists fear that attention for place may "rob social and cultural variables of their explanatory oomph." This however goes against "an enormous amount of empirical evidence to shows that [. . .] place still matter[s] in public administration and management" (Pollitt, 2011, 39). This evidence includes for example the notion that countries differ in the speed and shape of their uptake of "generic" policy programs or technologies, such as new public management (NPM) and information technologies; that the functioning and location of public services is highly dependent on place (e.g., the postal service is different in a city than in a rural area; waste incinerators tend to be located in lowly populated areas, or in places where the not-so-well-off tend to live, etc.); that buildings (their materiality as well as their symbolism) matter for the things that can be done in them (Yanow, 1996).

However, taking place seriously is not enough. Even though attention for place in governance literature is increasing, it is often not conceptualized as an analytical construct and thereby remains implicit. It then stays outside the realm of theory and is automatically equated with geographical locations or scales of policy making, such as neighborhoods, regions, or cities. Research on big societies, local governments, and neighborhood governance are a case in point. For example, the place of the neighborhood tends to become a fixed reality, that is usually also seen as something "good." This work tends to ignore that neighborhoods are not "one thing" but can be very different from the perspective of different actors (Latour and Hermant, 1998); that they are in a constant flux (Cresswell, 2004); that their boundaries are often not clear, and that they might have goods and bads in them. Place, although figuring prominently in this type of work, remains under-theorized, with the effect that many assumptions underlying the concept of the neighborhood are taken for granted.

In sum, place is either absent from the majority of governance and health care management and policy literatures, taken for granted, or used as a stand-in for other concepts such as scale. To get a better grip on place, we need to reconceptualize place and spatial relations, thereby "putting health into place" (Kearns and Gesler, 1998).

RE-PLACING PLACE: TOWARDS A CONCEPTUALIZATION

To get a better understanding of place, we use insights from scholars in human geography, sociology, and philosophy who have come to take place seriously as an analytical category in its own term (Harvey, 1996; Massey, 1997; Gieryn, 2000; Cresswell, 2004; Pollitt, 2012). Precisely because place is a "word wrapped in common sense" (Cresswell, 2004, 1), its underlying assumptions and conceptual boundaries need to be made explicit. Several scholars have already come to conceptual grips with place and in this chapter we build on their work.

The sociologist Thomas Gieryn defines place with three characteristics (Gieryn, 2000). First, place refers to a geographic location, a distinct spot. This could be any particular spot, from your favorite armchair to a whole continent or even the earth or beyond. Social action is always located at a particular geographically defined place. Second, place has materiality, it is "stuff." Places are "assemblages of things" worked upon by people, and any social process "happen[s] *through* the material forms that we design, build, use, and protest" (465, emphasis in original). Third, place is invested with meaning and value, it is symbolic. In Gieryn's definition, as in others' (Cresswell, 2004), places are "doubly constructed" in the sense that they are built by people, and also named, interpreted, and imagined. Place-shaping thus requires a continuous re-imagining of places in new ways as well as the political question to what purposes and what users places are being re-imagined for. Given a multitude of actors, different conceptualizations of places and different purposes exist that may well clash in mundane governance practices. The politics of place is thus always there, albeit sometimes simmering in the background.

Defining a term is also carving out its boundaries, so as important as arguing what it is, is arguing what it is not. Importantly, place is not the same as "space" which refers to abstract geometries, (e.g., economic, political, and commercial spaces (Lefebvre, 1991)), detached from human experience. Agnew (2002, 15–16, in Guenther, 2006) defines space and place as follows:

> Space represents a field of practice or an area in which an organization or set of organizations (such as states) operates, held together in popular consciousness by a map image or narrative story that makes the space whole and meaningful. Place represents the encounter of people with space. It refers to how everyday life is inscribed in space and takes on meaning for specified groups of people and organizations. Space can be considered as 'top down,' defined by popular actors imposing their control and stories on others. Place can be considered as bottom up, representing the outlooks and actions of ordinary people.

This definition of place beautifully shows how place is interrelated to space, yet as an analytical concept stands in its own right.

Moreover, place is also not (just) a geographical backdrop for a sociological or policy analysis; country comparisons for example do often not take into account the agentic, performative effects of the places that are studied. Although all our studies are situated, this does not mean that we always take place into account as an analytical category. Rather, place is often used as a boundary for statistical or other variables (as we argued earlier). Such work is not about place, but about those abstract categories that sociologist and epidemiologists are so good at defining (e.g., socio-economic groups, race, gender, and the like); they only become placed when for example they take into account the specific material arrangements of streets and shops and the ways these affect (health) behavior (Etman et al., 2014).

Finally, place is also not the same thing as landscape. Although social geographers have developed the insightful notion of "therapeutic landscape" to analyze and situate healing processes (Kearns and Gesler, 1998), in most notions of landscape the viewer remains outside of it. As Cresswell notes, "we do not live in landscapes, we look at them" (2004, 11). In contrast, places are "things to be inside of" (Creswell, 2004, 10).

To synthesize, place is a meaningful geographical location invested with material and symbolic value and based on lived experience. This conceptualization opens up new forms of analysis. We build on this to get a better understanding of the place-governance relation, but take it one step further by focusing on the action *in* and *through* place, that is re-placing. We thereby add a perspective of health care governance to the literature that is both spatial and dynamic.

A SPATIAL AND DYNAMIC GOVERNANCE APPROACH: GOVERNING BY RE-PLACING CARE

By studying the dynamics of place, the processes of re-placing of care come to the fore. Re-placements, here viewed as instantiations of steering by moving care practices from one place to another, then become an important aspect of governance. They are not only part and outcome of governance arrangements, but also allow certain types of governance to come into being. For example, medical tourism in the European Union (patients from the one country who go to another country to receive care) is a result of EU-legislation, but at the same time influences future health care governance. This more dynamic governance approach closely aligns with the notion of *place-shaping*. As Pollitt argues (2011, 45):

> if places are dynamic and constantly changing (as the practices and relations that temporarily 'fix' them changes), then government becomes—intentionally or otherwise—a major actor in defining what places are. By a myriad of actions, governments shape places—not simply through planning regulations but also by transport and communication investments, by the location of its own agency and staff, by negotiating with other place-makers such as firms and by manipulating place-related symbols such as local monuments or sites or festivals or supposedly unique cultural characteristics.

Importantly, the relationship between place-maker and place is not uni-directional in nature (i.e., the powerful place-maker shaping places to an ideal image), but reciprocal. Places also have performative effects on their own and determine the scope of what place-makers can do. Given their materiality and specific genealogy, places are only malleable to a certain extent. In addition, not only governments shape places, but a myriad of actors do through their conscious and unconscious actions. Places can thus be viewed as the collective product of permanent flows of mundane interactions (Massey, 1997; Cresswell, 2004). In this dynamic view, places are not so much roots but routes that embody interaction and movement.

When we apply this dynamic approach of governance to health care, not just the place where health care is provided is of special interest to us, but also the activity of re-placing services. Just like place, re-placements have multiple dimensions. To be able to re-place, and thereby govern health care, it is necessary to establish (1) new materialities, (2) (symbolic) meanings, and (3) geographical locations (cf. Gieryn, 2000). Filling in these dimensions in new ways, allows place-makers to steer care in new ways. Of course, the act of re-placing itself is only part of the story. Once care is re-placed, all kinds of intended and unintended effects occur. For example, re-placements of disease management from hospitals to the domain of the home may be aimed at decreasing costs and empowering patients, but may turn out a costly affair if patients are not sufficiently supported by relatives or unable to develop self-management skills (Pols, 2012). Re-placements of care thus require certain social fabrics (e.g., informal care), infrastructures (e.g., telemonitoring devices), as well as skills to make them work and sustainable in the long run.

We distinguish three types of arrangements that matter for the creation and maintenance of re-placements: (1) social arrangements that tie together actors and public services in new ways; (2) legal arrangements that attribute and delegate responsibilities for care ("governance proper"); (3) arrangements of skills and expertise that enable professionals, managers, and patients to cope with new responsibilities. An illustration of this is the transition from professional-led service provision towards empowerment of patients and informal care givers. In this case, care is often re-placed from health care facilities to patients' homes. The re-placement requires new social arrangements such as partnerships and task divisions between formal and informal care-givers. These partnerships can be promoted by decentralization laws as new legal arrangements that foster a bigger role for community participation (in the UK known as the "big society") and that extend and change the responsibilities and accountabilities of involved actors. With regards to skills and expertise, professionals may need to learn new negotiating and empowering skills, whereas citizens are expected to adopt organizing and self-management skills. As such, these social, legal, and skill arrangements also encompass new power distribution between actors. Therefore, the act of re-placing care is not a neutral decision but is a political choice that always produces certain consequences and effects.

EMPIRICAL CASES OF CARE RE-PLACEMENTS

To empirically flesh out re-placements of care and make visible the (un)intended consequences in social, legal, and skills arrangements, in this section we describe three cases:

- E-health and the notion of placeless care,
- Concentration of hospital care,
- Neighborhood-based care.

Although these empirical cases each zoom in on a different health care practice, they are all instantiations of steering by re-placement of care. Note also that these are just examples, and in no way are meant to give an overview of place-making activities in health care settings. They have been selected because of their illustrative power, but as argued before, other cases, such as medical tourism, could also have been described.

Placing Utopia

New technologies come with great expectations. This is especially so for the emerging field of e-health,[1] that has been hailed by many governments as a solution to many of the problems of access to, quality of and costs reductions in health care. E-health is, both literally and metaphorically a *utopian* technology. Metaphorically, e-health has come to stand for a plethora of information and communication technology (ICT) applications that will do many goods. The European Commission, in its green paper on mHealth, for example, expects mobile ICT applications to increase prevention and quality of life, lead to more efficient and sustainable health care systems, and empower patients, while also creating a new market where European businesses can prosper (European Commission, 2014). In its literal *utopian* sense, e-health is seen as "placeless"—Utopia is a combination of the Greek οὐ ("not") and τόπος ("place")—as both the provision of care and access to medical information become detached from their spatial embeddedness. Robotics, for example, would make it possible to operate on a patient from anywhere. And e-health "could serve as a basis for evidence-driven care practice and research activities, while facilitating patients' access to their health information anywhere and at any time" (European Commission, 2014, 3). In both its literal and metaphorical sense, e-health much resembles wider discussions on ICT applications; for example in the field of e-democracy (Pollitt, 2011).

Within social science literatures, especially from the field of Science & Technology Studies, this *Utopian* character of e-health has been challenged. Not only have scholars focused on the often exaggerated claims made on the possible effects of e-health, showing that many e-health applications do not live up to their promises, or how idealistic visions of e-health can actually become dystopias; what is more important here, they have shown the socio-material assemblages that are in fact needed to make e-health happen in the first place and in this sense have re-placed e-health as a technology that happens somewhere, in some place, with many actors involved, both social and material, in specific settings and contexts. Moreover, they have shown that the specificities of those assemblages matter, in the sense that they produce specific (types of) effects.

In her study of telemedicine applications, Jeannette Pols, for example, has shown that technologies that focus on self-monitoring, for example cardiovascular functions

---

[1] In this section, we will take e-health to stand for the broad development of using ICTs in the provision of health care. This includes fields otherwise known as telemedicine and mHealth (the use of mobile computer technologies such as smartphones).

do less in enhancing patients' social networks and interactions between patients and caregivers than do for example video-conferencing technologies used in homecare settings (Pols, 2012). The specific "affordances" (Abrishami, Boer, and Horstman, 2014) of e-health technologies, Pols claims, are often ignored in standard evaluations of such technologies, thus ignoring the socio-material settings that are needed to make these technologies work in the first place, leading to false expectations. For example, her study shows that the application of e-health often leads to more, rather than less time spent on patients, due for example to the many glitches of the technology, the possibility to have endless contact with caregivers and the expectation of patients that they can be "checked upon" at any time.

Similarly, Nelly Oudshoorn, in her study on telecare technologies in cardiovascular care shows the complex interactions and interdependencies between patients, carers, and technologies (Oudshoorn, 2011). She for example documents the coming into being of a new type of professional, telecare workers, who mediate between technologies, patients, and traditional health care professionals, "managing the consequences of the distributed nature of the work involved in diagnosing and monitoring the bodies of actors who are geographically separated" (Oudshoorn, 2011, 191–192). Such assemblages then also change the nature and distribution of diagnostic work (Buscher, Goodwin, and Mesman, 2010), as well as the distribution of responsibilities of who cares where (Milligan, Roberts, and Mort, 2011). Telecare relates to a transformation in which the clinical gaze is extended (Patton, 2010), thus also raising questions of the extension of public domains into the private lives of patients (Milligan, 2003). Although e-health to some extent empowers patients, giving them some form of control and knowledge over their own bodies, this is generally done within a predefined set of guidelines and regulations that actually re-centre the medical gaze (Oudshoorn, 2011). Oudshoorn therefore concludes that "[a]lthough telecare technologies have the potential, and were meant to bypass and partly re-place traditional health care professionals and institutions, [they] adapt to rather than transform the established hierarchy in the order of who cares" (2011, 296).

E-health is also a place-changing technology in the sense that clinics, but also the homes of patients, need to be attuned towards the demands of, and become part of, the new socio-technical assemblages generated through the use of telecare technologies (Langstrup, 2013). New technologies are brought into the home and sometimes connected to already existing infrastructures of telephone lines, computers, and TV-sets. Whereas in policy discourse, "the home" as a safe place where patients want to be is often evoked as one of the elements of e-health Utopia, what the home is actually changes through its application, making it part of wider and different networks. Whereas feminists have long-time argued that the home is not always the safe place where caring relations can thrive, e-health technologies also bring other types of insecurities, vulnerabilities, and responsibilities into the home environment. For example, when the Health care Inspectorate of the Netherlands studied home care, it found many unsafe practices, for example related to the use of infusion pumps (Inspectie voor de Gezondheidszorg,

2009). This also points at the need for transfer of skills to patients and informal carers in using homecare technologies, including e-health applications.

Realizing the *Utopia* of e-health thus comes with many new responsibilities, vulnerabilities, and changing social and material arrangements, expertise, and skills. The lack of attention to such changes leads to false expectations about the wonderful effects of e-health. By re-placing e-health in its socio-material setting, social scientists have been able to point at the many interdependencies that arise with the building of new care infrastructures, and the types of effects created by specific versions of e-health.

Concentration and Re-Placement of Hospital Care

Throughout Europe and the US, hospital care is being re-placed as a result of a trend of *concentration* (also called "centralization"). Concentration, predominantly achieved through mergers between hospitals and trusts, entails the re-placement of medical care from multiple hospital facilities to fewer, more specialized ones. Concentration is an often-used governance instrument for the re-placement of care because it is said to have two advantages: more efficiency due to economies of scale, and a better quality of care as a result of specialization (Sauerzapf et al., 2008). Economies of scale are supposed to result from the reduction of management costs and the elimination of excess capacity and duplication (Posnett, 1999). The quality of care argument follows the logic that physicians become more skilled by increasing the volume of treatments they perform, resulting in better care.

Concentration stands in a long tradition of planning of medical care that is focused on the geographic characteristic of place (Gieryn, 2000). Measures like distance and travel time are used as proxies for the geographic distribution of care, the accessibility of care for patients, and to demarcate the relevant market of hospitals (Schooling et al., 2011; Bosanac, Parkinson, and Hall, 1976; Morrisey, Sloan, and Valvona, 1988). However, this rational planning perspective fails to address changes in the "assemblage of things" and the processes of meaning-making that occur when care is being re-placed. The hospital is "an operational 'living' construct which 'matters' as opposed to being a passive 'container' in which things are simply recorded" (Kearns and Moon, 2002); something that is not only geographical, but also material, moral, psychological, social, and cultural (Martin et al., 2005; Kearns and Barnett, 2000). For example, in their analysis of resistance to the possible closing of St Bartholomew's Hospital in London, Moon and Brown (2001) distinguish four representations of the hospital: as community resource, as a site of expertise, as a heritage symbol, and as a site pertinent to the identity of Londoners. In addition, Hanlon (2001) shows that hospital restructuring not only involves changes in geographical location, but also in the relation between hospital executives, managers, professionals, and the citizens who support and rely on the hospital. Re-placing care thereby not only entails geographic changes, but impacts sense-making of the people that are affected.

Considering the multifaceted nature of place, it is no wonder that the results of concentration are mixed. On the one hand, authors have shown that concentration of care results in better outcomes for a number of (mostly complex) treatments, including breast cancer care, heart surgery for children, abdominal aortic aneurism surgery, and HIV/AIDS (Selby, Gillis, and Haward, 1996; Halm, Lee, and Chassin, 2002; Wittenberg et al., 2005; Glanville et al., 2010, Zuiderent-Jerak, Kool, and Rademakers, 2012). Also, research shows that concentration can improve efficiency of care, especially for small hospitals (Posnett, 1999). On the other hand, studies suggest that the positive correlation between volume and quality may work the other way around due to 'selective referral' (Luft, Hunt, and Maerki, 1987): patients are referred to facilities that are already performing better, which would mean that quality leads to more volume. Also, research shows that economies of scale are negligible, or even turn into diseconomies of scale, when facilities have reached a certain scale (Blank and Eggink, 2001; Blank et al., 2008).

Not only does concentration of medical care often fail to meet its goals, it results in all kinds of unforeseen problems and resistance from communities and professionals. First, there is a coordination problem. As care becomes more specialized, coordination between hospitals, primary care, long-term care, and "intermediary care" providers (e.g., for rehabilitation) becomes more important. Martin et al. (2005) show how hospitals, rehabilitation centres, and the home have different therapeutic qualities, requiring interaction and collaboration between professionals that work in different places. As concentration changes these professional networks, and leads to larger distances between care places, coordination becomes more complex. Second, different types of care in hospitals are intertwined in organizational and material arrangements and cannot easily be "carved out." Although concentration might yield benefits for a small number of complex treatments, the consequences for other types of care are unknown (Zuiderent-Jerak, Kool, and Rademakers, 2012). For example, Yudkin (2014) argues that the plea for concentrating stroke services in the NHS (comprising 0.5% of emergency department attendances) lacks an assessment on the impact of the other 99.5% of care that is being delivered in these facilities. The policy of concentration of stroke might go well against other types of care; the point is however that we don't know as no research is done on "that which is left behind." Third, concentration of care not only is said to serve public goals, but is also used strategically by health care organizations and professionals. On the basis of a study of five cases of concentration of care in the Netherlands, Zuiderent-Jerak, Kool, and Rademakers (2012) conclude that health care providers choose to concentrate care to improve their market position vis-à-vis competitors and to achieve operational efficiency. The quality of care argument is used to justify concentration, but it is unclear whether it holds ground in practice as monitoring is lacking.

Despite these difficulties, re-placing care through concentration can be a useful instrument to improve quality and efficiency of care. But, for concentration of medical care to be successful, additional, often invisible work (Suchman, 1995) is needed. In addition to the actual physical re-placement of care, this work needs to address the three types of arrangements that we discussed before: social arrangements, legal arrangements, and arrangements of skills and expertise. New social arrangements between professionals (e.g., protocols and formal and informal knowledge sharing) are necessary to establish coordination of care over larger distances and between different types of care. New legal arrangements (e.g., competition law) should guarantee that concentration not only serves the private interests of hospitals and professionals, but contributes to quality of care. New arrangements of professional skills and expertise (e.g., education and guidelines) are needed to equip professionals to deal with care that is increasingly specialized and standardized, while still being able to deal with problems of complexity (e.g., multi-morbidity). Only then can concentration of medical care become successful.

Replacing Care by Re-Imagining Neighbourhoods

> Neighborhood is a word that has come to sound like a Valentine. As a sentimental concept, 'neighborhood' is harmful to city planning. It leads to attempts at warping city life into imitations of town or suburban life. Sentimentality plays with sweet intentions in place of good sense (Jacobs 1992, 112).

Despite earlier criticism of sentimentality by the urban activist and scholar Jane Jacobs (1992), "the neighborhood" has re-emerged as an important locus in health policies that aim to re-locate care provision. In these policies, the neighborhood is "doubly constructed" (Cresswell, 2004) in the sense that neighborhoods are built physical places where care is provided and organized in concrete locations (e.g., elderly homes or private homes), while at the same the neighborhood is constructed and mobilized as a political symbol to advocate self-reliance of communities, decentralization of care to local governments, and the substitution of professional care for informal care. As various studies reveal, governments and care providers increasingly evoke the image of the neighborhood to promote community development (Lowndes and Sullivan, 2008; Wallace, 2010; Featherstone et al., 2012), informal care (Van Dijk, Cramm, and Nieboer, 2013; Milligan, 2001), aging in place (Gardner, 2011; Michael, Green, and Farquhar, 2006) and "tailor-made" service provision on a local level.

As sociologist Gieryn poignantly points out, neighborhoods are not given entities: "The very idea of the neighborhood is not inherent in any arrangements of streets and houses, but is rather an ongoing and discursive imagining of people" (Gieryn, 2000, 472). Hence, the neighborhood is a discursively imagined place and as such it can be clearly contrasted to large-scale "total" institutions on secluded terrains (Goffman, 1991) and the classical welfare state. When imagining neighborhoods as ideal places, they not only enable the integration of people with mental and physical disabilities into society (Oldenhof, Postma, and Putters, 2014), but also allow for the integration and joining-up of fragmented public services on a small-scale (Lowndes and Sullivan, 2008; Griggs and Roberts, 2012). Moreover, as ideal places, neighborhoods provide people the opportunity to grow old in one's own private home. Precisely because the neighborhood defies clear definition, the notion of the neighborhood can be strategically used by policy makers and politicians to achieve a variety of goals.

Nevertheless, the neighborhood is not merely an abstract symbol: it is connected to concrete re-location questions and therefore has actual consequences for people's lives. The inclusion and exclusion of citizens, for example, is to a large extent determined by place and the material placement of citizens in certain locations and not others. As Ootes remarks in her study of citizenship in long term-care: "Becoming a citizen depends on changing xyz coordinates. If we were to use a map to point out where mental health clients ought to be to become citizens, we would not point out large institutions, or geographically isolated areas. Instead we would advocate community living and point out community neighbourhoods in towns and cities" (Ootes, 2012, 94).

Consequently, contemporary re-placements of care—community-based care, substitution of formal by informal care, and decentralizations of welfare and care to local governments—only become possible when neighborhoods are given new symbolic meaning and are materially and geographically reshaped. This may imply the redrawing of neighborhood boundaries when services need to be re-integrated in new ways or the "relabeling" of neighborhoods from "deprived problem areas" to "sites for community development" (or the other way around when resources need to be attracted). It thus matters which specific versions of the neighborhood are being imagined and shaped into being. As a site for community development, the neighborhood foregrounds responsibilities of citizens while back-grounding the role of the state. Conversely, neighborhoods labeled as deprived areas that cluster health inequalities may invoke responsibilities of state actors to develop area-based health programs and neighborhood interventions. Each version of the neighborhood thus deals with specific responsibilities and leading actors.

In order to avoid the risk that re-placements become isolated policy acts that stay disconnected from existing social and institutional contexts, it is crucial that they are actively incorporated into the social and legal fabric of life. With the rise of neighborhood policies, new social arrangements are being adopted by local governments, such as co-production between citizens and professionals and private–public partnerships that address wicked problems on a neighborhood scale (Newman and Clarke, 2009). Although these social arrangements may not deliver what they promise (Lowndes and Sullivan, 2008), they do set into motion new relations between state and non-state actors and fundamentally redistribute responsibilities and power. These new social arrangements are often accompanied by new legal arrangements, or "governance proper" so to speak. Jurisdictional decentralizations of care responsibilities to local governments are a case in point as well as more specific "community rights to challenge," as can be witnessed in present-day discussions in England. These rights give citizens the power to challenge local governments in the provision of services, while simultaneously responsibilizing them as active citizens.

In addition to legal arrangements, the developments of alternative skill sets of professionals, citizens, and managers greatly matter for the day-to-day realization of care re-placements: even though they may often come as a casual afterthought of legal measures. For instance, the substitution of professional services by informal care work is partially enabled by the professionalization of lay people as caregivers and the re-training of professionals and managers as supportive coaches that promote empowerment and encourage self-organization of citizens (Postma, Oldenhof, and Putters, 2015). Local governments and service providers also discursively frame the neighborhood as a "small-scale" work territory for professionals that are employed by "large-scale" organizations (Lowndes and Sullivan, 2008; Postma, Oldenhof, and Putters, 2015). By doing so, new work forms, such as neighborhood-based teams, offer the possibility of shorter communication channels, improved coordination, and greater autonomy of professionals. The implementation of territory-based work formats is not just a way to coordinate actions of professionals, but also reconfigures the core meaning of professionalism. Current government reforms in the Netherlands that aim to transform "specialized professionals" into "holistically working generalists" that coordinate specialized expertise and develop an integrated overview of multi-problem cases, lead to new forms of organized professionalism (Noordegraaf, 2011; Postma, Oldenhof, and Putters, 2015). As neighborhood generalists, professionals are expected to deal with interrelated problems of health, well-being, housing, work, and education on a neighborhood scale, thereby transcending professional and organizational boundaries. As such, local governments steer professionals by using the "old" neighborhood as template for "new" professional work.

As becomes evident from many policy documents, the neighborhood is primarily viewed in a positive light. Jane Jacobs, however, warned us that the meaning of the neighborhood is not a-priori "good" in itself. The concept of neighborhood may actually do more harm than good when used in sentimental and nostalgic ways. When neighborhoods are projected as imitations of small-scale work territories of the old days or traditional village community life, the meaning of neighborhood becomes fixed and has little relevance for current day governance arrangements and settings such as big cities or dispersed rural areas. Critical voices moreover claim the neighborhood may become the new silo of today's society contributing to more rather than less fragmentation due to a proliferation of neighborhood-based work formats (Raad Maatschappelijke Ontwikkeling (RMO), 2009). Moreover, neighborhoods may not necessarily be healing places or therapeutic landscapes. They can be dangerous places that pose risks for one's health or well-being: a good illustration are "food deserts" which pose considerable health risks for inhabitants. Public health studies have therefore argued for a more balanced view: neighborhoods can both inhibit and promote health, depending on their physical characteristics and the availability of food and sport facilities (Macintyre and Ellaway, 2003; Etman et al., 2014). Such work has also sparked new neighborhood and landscape design that for example stresses green open spaces, friendly child routes to schools, a mix of work and living functions. New movements such as FunTheory make use of spatial interventions in neighborhoods to enhance healthy behavior (see, e.g., the much acclaimed Stockholm "piano stairs" or the dancing traffic light).[2] Evidence of

---

[2] See <http://www.youtube.com/watch?v=2lXh2noaPyw> and <http:// www.youtube.com/ watch?v=SB_ovRnkeOk> (accessed October 15, 2015).

the health effects of such architectural and planning interventions in neighborhoods is sparse though and not very convincing yet.

Importantly, the above shows that neighborhoods are not good or bad in themselves, but can and should be continuously re-imagined and re-structured, thereby enabling new re-placements of care in health care governance. By embedding care re-placements in legal, social, and skill-based infrastructures, they are made durable and become an inherent part of governance itself. It is therefore time to stop viewing neighborhoods merely as a neutral setting or as a fixed variable that determines health outcomes. Instead, the construction of neighborhoods should be taken seriously as an ongoing political and symbolic project that shapes our health care.

CONCLUSIONS

In this chapter, we have tried to unpack the notion of place in order to show its importance for governing health care. Rather than viewing place as just a context or backdrop for policymaking, we have argued that it is in fact at the heart of governing. The act of placing and re-placing care is crucial for the establishment of new governance arrangements in health care, as the empirical cases of e-health, concentration of hospital care, and neighborhood-based care have revealed. Although these re-placements of care are often discussed in non-place-related terms, they are deeply tied up to the symbolic and material construction of place and place-shaping efforts of various actors, such as professionals, citizens, managers, governments, and policy makers. Hence, places are not simply there, but are imagined and shaped into being by people. Moreover, they are continuously reshaped to achieve better health outcomes and new relations between patients, patients' relatives, professionals, and governmental actors. Based on our cases, we reflect on three aspects of re-placements that deserve more attention: unintended consequences of re-placements, the invisible work that comes with re-placing care, and their political-symbolic use.

Given the fact that not one agentic state actor is governing place, but a myriad of actors all engage in place-shaping efforts, it is no wonder that unintended consequences of re-placements arise. As for example the e-health case shows, re-placements of care do not always save costs and reduce the use of professional help, but actually may increase investments. Contrary to expectations, the presence of technologies unexpectedly raises the need of patients to be reassured by professionals that they use the technology "in the right way." Dealing with these new expectations and attuning the place of the home to newly brought-in technologies involves all kinds of material and social adjustments. This also is the case for concentrating hospital care. Carving out new places for specialized care in the existing care landscape may seem the obvious choice from a rational-planning perspective that favors economies of scale, but these economies of scale rapidly disappear (if they ever existed) when new coordination challenges arise between specialized hospitals. Moreover, they may give rise to new and unexpected vulnerabilities, as for example bacteria travel in-between places due to increased traveling of patients with multiple problems.

These unintended consequences of re-placements usually stay out of sight, as well as the amount of work that needs to be performed to make re-placements work and weave them into the changing fabric of social life. The neighborhood case showed that this invisible work goes beyond the visible legal and organizational arrangements that are implemented to re-place care to local communities and neighborhoods. A good illustration of this invisible work is the reframing of citizens as informal care-givers, long-term care patients as members of the community, and professionals as holistically working generalists that operate in the neighborhood as their work territory. This reframing is a subtle and incremental process that changes notions of health, professionalism, and citizenship by developing new skills and bodies of expertise that enable the enactments of care responsibilities at a local level. Similarly, "breaches" such as the finding of the Healthcare Inspectorate that homecare introduces new vulnerabilities point at the invisible but crucial work that is needed by patients and informal caregivers in making re-placements possible and safe. When this type of work is neglected, re-placements of care lead to higher costs for patients and the health system.

By making visible the work that goes behind re-placements, it also becomes possible to reflect on the symbolic and political use of place in health care governance. We argue the re-placing of care is always a symbolic and political affair since it encompasses a symbolic re-imagining of places and alternative conceptualizations of care practices as well as the political issue of power distribution. Re-placements of care shift the burden of responsibilities of care and coordination from one actor to the other, thereby raising the question whether care re-placements contribute to the fair distribution of responsibilities and resources. When patients are left alone at home without sufficient support to "age in place," the burden of care may become too great to bear. Likewise, patients with multi-problems who increasingly need to travel in-between hospitals because of specialization and concentration, have to become the coordinators of their own care journey, even when they are too vulnerable to continuously re-place and uproot themselves. It is therefore necessary to explicitly address the normative boundaries of re-placements. This is not an easy thing to do. From a policy point of view, there may even be an incentive to masquerade the amount of work that needs to be done to actually perform and keep on performing re-placements in practice. It is questionable whether decisions to re-place care would be undertaken with the same optimistic fervor when invisible work would have been taken into account. This is not to make a traditional argument for maintaining the status quo. Instead we believe that it is more fruitful to imagine different modes of doing re-placements, thereby allowing for a greater variety of choice and varieties of goodness.

This would also need a different type of research, in which place is taken seriously as an actor in its own right, focusing on the affordances and performativities of specific places, and reflexively monitoring what happens when care is re-placed. In this chapter we have already pointed at some of the work that is being done in this direction, but with the centrality of place in current health reforms, one would think that much more work needs to be done; if only to prevent all-too costly consequences of current and future re-placements.

References

Abrishami, P., Boer, A., and Horstman, K. (2014). Understanding the adoption dynamics of medical innovations: Affordances of the Da Vinci robot in the Netherlands. *Social Science & Medicine*, 117: 125–133.

Blank, J. L. and Eggink, E. (2001). A quality-adjusted cost function in a regulated industry: The case of Dutch nursing homes. *Health Care Management Science*, 4(3): 201–211.

Blank, J., Haelermans, C., Koot, P., and Van Putten-Rademaker, O. (2008). *Een Inventariserend Onderzoek naar de Relatie tussen Schaal, Bereikbaarheid, Kwaliteit en Doelmatigheid in de Zorg*. Achtergrondstudie bij: Schaal en Zorg. The Hague: Raad voor de Volksgezondheid en Zorg.

Bosanac, E. M., Parkinson, R. C., and Hall, D. S. (1976). Geographic access to hospital care: A 30-minute travel time standard. *Medical Care*, 14(7): 616–623.

Buscher, M., Goodwin, D., and Mesman, J. (eds) (2010). *Ethnographies of diagnostic work. Dimensions of transformative practice*. Basingstoke: Palgrave Macmillan.

Cresswell, T. (2004). *Place: A short introduction*. Malden, MA, Oxford, and Carlton: Blackwell Publishers.

Cummins, S., Flint, E., and Matthews, S. A. (2014). New neighbourhood grocery store increased awareness of food access but did not alter dietary habits or obesity. *Health Affairs*, 33(2): 283–291.

Etman, A., Kamphuis, C., Burdorf, A., Pierik, F. H., and Van Lenthe, J. (2014). Characteristics of residential areas and transportational walking among frail and non-frail elderly: Does the size of the area matter? *International Journal of Health Geographies*, 13(7): 1–7.

European Commission (2014). *Green paper on mobile health (mhealth)*. Brussels: European Commission.

Featherstone, D., Ince, A., Mackinnon, D., Strauss, K., and Cumbers, A. (2012). Progressive localism and the construction of political alternatives. *Transactions of the Institute of British Geographers*, 37: 177–182.

Gardner, P. J. (2011). Natural neighborhood networks. Important social networks in the lives of older adults aging in place. *Journal of Aging Studies*, 25(3): 263–271.

Gieryn, T. F. (2000). A space for place in sociology. *Annual Review of Sociology*, 26: 463–496.

Glanville, J., Duffy, S., Mahon, J., Cardow, T., Brazier, H., and Album, V. (2010). *Impact of hospital treatment volumes on patient outcomes*. York: York Health Economics Consortium, University of York.

Goffman, E. ([1961]1991). *Asylums: Essays on the Social Situation of Mental Patients and Other Inmates*. London: Penguin Books.

Griggs, S. and Roberts, M. (2012). From neighbourhood governance to neighbourhood management: A "roll-out" neo-liberal design for devolved governance in the United Kingdom? *Local Government Studies*, 38(2): 183–210.

Halm, E. A., Lee, C., and Chassin, M. R. (2002). Is volume related to outcome in health care? A systematic review and methodologic critique of the literature. *Annals of Internal Medicine*, 137(6): 511–520.

Hanlon, N. T. (2001). Hospital restructuring in smaller urban ontario settings: Unwritten rules and uncertain relations. *The Canadian Geographer/Le Géographe Canadien*, 45(2): 252–267.

Harvey, D. (1996). *Justice, nature and geography of difference.* Cambridge, MA: Blackwell Publishers.

Inspectie voor de Gezondheidszorg (2009). *Infuuspompen in de Thuissituatie: een Goede Ontwikkeling maar Toepassing moet Veiliger.* Utrecht: IGZ.

Jacobs, J. ([1961]1992). *The death and life of great American cities.* New York and Toronto: Vintage Books, original edition.

Kearns, R. A. and Barnett, J. R.(2000). "Happy Meals" in the starship enterprise: Interpreting a moral geography of health care consumption. *Health & Place*, 6 (2): 81–93.

Kearns, R. A. and Gesler, W. B. (1998). *Putting health into place: Landscape, identity and well-being.* Syracuse, NY: Syracuse University Press.

Kearns, R. A. and Moon, G. (2002). From medical to health geography: Novelty, place and theory after a decade of change. *Progress in Human Geography*, 26(5): 605–625.

Kickert, W., Klijn, E. H., and Koppenjan., J. (1997). *Managing complex networks: Strategies for the public sector.* London: Sage.

Langstrup, H. (2013). Chronic care infrastructures and the home. *Sociology of Health & Illness*, 35(7):1008–1022.

Latour, B. and Hermant, E. (1998). *Paris: Ville invisible.* Paris: La Decouverte.

Lefebvre, H. (1991). *The production of space.* Oxford, Malden, MA: Blackwell Publishing.

Lowndes, V. and Sullivan, H. (2008). How low can you go? Rationales and challenges for neighbourhood governance. *Public Administration*, 86(1): 53–74.

Luft, H. S., Hunt, S. S., and Maerki, S. C. (1987). The volume-outcome relationship: Practice-makes-perfect or selective-referral patterns? *Health Services Research*, 22(2): 157.

Macintyre, S. and Ellaway, A. (2003). Neighbourhoods and health: An overview. In *Neighbourhoods and health*, ed. Kawachi, I. and Berkman, L. F., pp. 20–44. New York: Oxford University Press.

Macintyre, S., Ellaway, A., and Cummins, S. (2002). Place effects on health: How can we conceptualise, operationalise and measure them? *Social Science & Medicine*, 55: 125–139.

Martin, G. P., Nancarrow, S. A., Parker, H., Phelps, K., and Regen, E. L. (2005). Place, policy and practitioners: On rehabilitation, independence and the therapeutic landscape in the changing geography of care provision to older people in the UK. *Social Science & Medicine*, 61(9): 1893–1904.

Massey, D. (1997). A global sense of place. In *Reading human geography*, ed. Barnes, T. and Gregory, D., pp. 315–323. London: Arnold.

Michael, Y. L., Green, M. K., and Farquhar, S. A. (2006). Neighbourhood design and active aging. *Health & Place*, 12: 734–740.

Milligan, C. (2001). *Geographies of care: Space and the voluntary sector.* Aldershot: Ashgate.

Milligan, C. (2003). Location or dis-location? Towards a conceptualization of people and place in the care-giving experience. *Social & Cultural Geography*, 4(4): 455–470.

Milligan, C., Roberts, C., and Mort, M. (2011). Telecare and older people: Who cares where? *Social Science & Medicine*, 72: 347–354.

Moon, G. and T. Brown (2001). Closing barts: Community and resistance in contemporary UK hospital policy. *Environment and Planning*, 19(1): 43–60.

Morrisey, M. A., Sloan, F. A., and Valvona, J. (1988). Defining geographic markets for hospital care. *Law and Contemporary Problems*, 51(2): 165–194.

Newman, J. and Clarke, J. (2009). *Publics, politics and power: Remaking the public in public services*. London: SAGE.

Noordegraaf, M. (2011). Risky business: How professionals and professional fields (must) deal with organizational issues. *Organization Studies*, 32: 1349–1371.

Oldenhof, L., Postma, J., and Putters, K. (2014). On justification work: How compromising enables public managers to deal with conflicting values. *Public Administration Review*, 74(1): 52–63.

Ootes, S. T. C. (2012). *Being in place: Citizenship in long-term mental healthcare*. Dissertation. Amsterdam: UvA.

Oudshoorn, N. (2011). *Telecare technologies and the transformation of healthcare*. Basingstoke: Palgrave Macmillan.

Patton, C. (2010). *Rebirth of the clinic: Places and agents in contemporary health care* Minneapolis, MN: University of Minnesota Press.

Pollitt, C. (2011). Time and place in public administration: Two endangered species? *Acta Wasaensia*, 238: 33–53.

Pollitt, C. (2012). *New perspectives on public services*. Oxford and New York: Oxford University Press.

Pols, J. (2012). *Care at a distance: On the closeness of technology*. Amsterdam: Amsterdam University Press.

Posnett, J. (1999). The hospital of the future: Is bigger better? Concentration in the provision of secondary care. *British Medical Journal*, 319(7216): 1063–1065.

Postma, J., Oldenhof, L., and Putters, K. (2015). Organized professionalism in healthcare: Articulation work by neighbourhood nurses. *Journal of Professions and Organization*, 2(1): 61–77.

Raad Maatschappelijke Ontwikkeling (2009). *De Wijk Nemen*. Amsterdam: Uitgeverij SWP.

Sauerzapf, V. A., Jones, A. P., Haynes, R., Crawford, S. M., and Forman, D. (2008). Travel time to radiotherapy and uptake of breast-conserving surgery for early stage cancer in Northern England. *Health & Place*, 14(3): 424–433.

Schooling, C. M., Kwok, M. K., Yau, C., Cowling, B. J., Lam, T. H., and Leung, G. M. (2011). Spatial proximity and childhood hospital admissions in a densely populated conurbation: Evidence from Hong Kong's "Children of 1997" Birth Cohort. *Health & Place*, 17(5): 1038–1043.

Selby, P., Gillis, C., and Haward, R. (1996). Benefits from specialised cancer care. *The Lancet*, 348(9023): 313–318.

Suchman, L. (1995). Making work visible. *Communications of the ACM*, 38(9): 56–64.

Van Dijk, H. M., Cramm, J. M., and Nieboer, A. P. (2013). The experiences of neighbour, volunteer and professional support-givers in supporting community dwelling older people. *Health and Social Care in the Community*, 21(2): 150–158.

Walker, R. E., Keane, C. R., and Burke, J. G. (2010). Disparities and access to healthy food in the United States: A review of food deserts literature. *Health & Place*, 16(5): 876–884.

Wallace, A. (2010). New neighbourhoods, new citizens? Challenging "Community" as a framework for social and moral regeneration under New Labour in the UK. *International Journal of Urban and Regional Research*, 34(4): 805–819.

Wittenberg J., Burgers, J. S., Van Croonenborg, J. J., Van Barneveld, T. A., Van Everdingen, J. J. E. (2005). *Goede Zorg, een Kwestie van Ervaring? Evidence-Rapport over de Relatie tussen Volume en Kwaliteit van Zorg.* Utrecht: Kwaliteitsinstituut voor de Gezondheidszorg CBO.

Yanow, D. (1996). *How does a policy mean? Interpreting policy and orgnanizational actions.* Washington, D.C.: Georgetown University Press.

Yudkin, J. S. (2014). Rigorous science is needed to justify the centralisation of services. *BMJ,* 349: g4324.

Zuiderent-Jerak, T., Kool, T., and Rademakers, J. (2012). *De Relatie tussen Volume en Kwaliteit van Zorg.* Utrecht and Rotterdam: Consortium Onderzoek Kwaliteit van Zorg.

CHAPTER 19

INTER-ORGANIZATIONAL NETWORKS IN HEALTH CARE

Program Networks, Care Networks, and Integrated Care

ROD SHEAFF AND JILL SCHOFIELD

SINCE the mid-1990s inter-organizational networks have become more common in health systems, having developed for dealing with problems which are complex, long-term, indivisible (Gray, 1985), linked to other problems (Williams, 2002), and have no single, well-defined, or even uncontested solution (van Bueren, Klijn, and Koppenjan, 2003); in short, "wicked"(van Bueren, Klijn, and Koppenjan, 2003). No single organization can solve them alone. Certain wicked problems have especially stimulated the spread of inter-organizational networks in health care (for short, henceforth referred to as "health care networks").

One is care coordination for patients with multiple chronic health problems, who often require primary medical care, community health services (e.g., nursing care at home), rehabilitative therapies, social care, and perhaps mental health care too, over long periods. This diversity of needs creates complex, persistent problems of service coordination whose occurrence in many health systems is well attested. An obvious solution is to set up a network of regular coordinating links for coordinated care planning, referrals, and information exchange about patients across the providers involved, with a view to easing patients' transitions between providers (e.g., the "revolving door" between acute hospital and primary care, or between physical and mental health care).

In liberal democracies, health policy has commonly been formed by networks ("policy communities") of organizations, such as groups of professional bodies or federations of health care organizations, whom governments choose, or are compelled, to consult about health policy (Rhodes, 1997; Trappenburg, 2005), and who collaborate in implementing it. In Germany, for example, three main networks (of sick-funds, of hospitals, and of doctors) collaboratively contribute to, interpret, and implement Federal health policy. Health care networks have also been used as implementation structures to implement particular programs or models of care. For instance, after 1990 the English NHS created networks of clinicians and managers responsible for specific care groups (e.g., cancer, mental health) to implement new service standards and coordinate service provision across primary, secondary and tertiary care, and between commissioners (payers) and service providers. Inter-organizational networks have undertaken social-marketing, even political campaigns, for health promotion, for instance to promote smoking control, healthier diet or (in Germany) workplace health promotion. By their nature these campaigns have to be pursued collectively with one organization (e.g., Smoke-Free Europe) coordinating a network of organizations and individuals.

Evidence-based medicine, and other clinical disciplines, into clinical practice is at a number of levels an inter-organizational activity. Inter-organizational networks have developed for the production of evidence about practice, whether for individual studies or more complete research programs, including world-wide collaborations of like-minded research centers (e.g., Cochrane Collaborations), and for "translating" evidence into practice. Clinical audit is often conducted by local networks of practitioners, especially in primary health care (e.g., in the USA, UK, Australia).

These patterns have developed across contrasting health systems and policy contexts. In many countries, including much of Europe, health system "reform" since 1990 has largely meant attempts to revert state-dominated health systems towards more market-like, or at least quasi-market, structures, transferring service providers from public to corporate or third-sector owners whose interests are increasingly discrepant from each other and which do not necessarily align with health policies other than that of health system "reform". By contrast, in the USA a fragmented health system with diverse ownership of organizations and multiple payment systems was the starting point. Inter-organizational networks among primary care providers, "vertical" networks between primary and secondary care, and between payers and providers (e.g., some Health Maintenance Organizations—HMOs) were intended to support an opposite reform trajectory, towards a more integrated and coherent whole. Because the idea and practice of inter-organizational networks appears applicable to addressing a wide variety of "wicked problems" in a wide variety of health systems, inter-organizational networks are of increasing interest and relevance for health care management. There is now a rich set of "proofs-of-concept" of the uses that inter-organizational networks can have in mitigating, even solving, the consequences of an increasingly complex inter-organizational division of labor in most health systems. Health networks also provide a way of harnessing diverse kinds of organizations (public, corporate, voluntary, etc.) and individuals (patients, carers, experts, etc.) towards common health policy goals.

Consequently, a large, complex body of research about the characteristics, kinds, and effects of health networks has appeared, although empirical studies of the actual effects produced by health care networks remains rather sparse (which has not inhibited an extensive normative literature from proposing how to manage inter-organizational networks and gain their supposed benefits). There is no lack of descriptions and taxonomies of health care networks, but one price paid for this abundance is conceptual confusion. Often the term "network" is conflated with the related concepts "communities of practice" (Wenger, 2000) "partnership," "collaborative," "consortia," and "integrated care." Another is a lack of coherent explanations linking the varieties of network with their structures, activities, and (so far as known) outcomes. This chapter proposes a conceptualization of health care networks in terms of what they produce, through what structures and under what management. On that basis it contrasts care networks with program networks, and how health care networks function (or not) as governance structures. It then compares these concepts with findings from some primary research on National Health Service (NHS) professional and clinical networks during 2005–10, and with published accounts of health networks in other health system settings. It draws out some implications for a new kind of inter-organizational network emerging in many health systems: "integrated care."

HEALTH NETWORKS: STRUCTURES, PROCESS, OUTCOMES

Inter-organizational networks can be narrowly defined as:

> groups of three or more legally autonomous organisations that work together to achieve not only their own goals but also a collective goal (Provan and Kenis, 2008, 231).

This concise definition has rich implications.

In practice network formation has many kinds of motive (Vincent, 2008), often including ideology (Vangen and Huxham, 2003) and interpersonal motives, and implies a "domain consensus" about what the network will and will not do (Tsasis, 2009). Nevertheless, the point of a network is to realize through collaboration joint goals (Uusikylä and Valovirta, 2007), which the member organization cannot achieve separately (Provan and Kenis, 2008), for instance achieving economies of scale in the management of (say) a health center (Wells and Weiner, 2007).

Pursuit of a common goal implies a "logic model" (Touati et al., 2009) of joint activities which, the network members think, will produce the collectively-intended outcomes. For short we call these "joint production" (Goodwin et al., 2004) activities the network's "core process." It occurs through member organizations transmitting resources between each other (Balkundi and Harrison, 2006) (e.g., work-in-progress; clients; money; information; expectations (Ebers, 1997), advice; social, emotional and psychological support (Wong, 2008)). A network's structure is the totality of such links. A rich literature conceptualizes these dyadic (one-to-one) direct links between pairs of member organizations in terms of strength, frequency, direction (A may send B information, but not vice versa), and contents. Further properties are visible only at whole-network level, properties such as "brokerage" (some network members act as intermediaries between others), hierarchies, power (Zolkiewski, 2001), and cliques (areas with denser links than elsewhere in the network).

One can define the effectiveness of a network's structure in either of two ways. One is as the extent to which the network, through that structure, collectively achieves its goals (Turrini et al., 2010). Then the substantive criterion of effectiveness (e.g., as the network's effects on clients (Provan and Milward, 1995; Turrini et al., 2010) or on hospital bed use) will vary between networks. Alternatively one might apply an arbitrary external criterion of effectiveness; perhaps an ideological one such as Pareto efficiency or generic criteria such as network innovation, change, and sustainability (Turrini et al., 2010). The efficiency of a network structure can then be defined in terms of whether the network had just the member organizations and links sufficient to achieve the relevant goal.

Substance and Structure

All inter-organizational networks thus have both a substantive aspect (goals, core process and its technology, resource requirements and work procedures) and a corresponding structure (membership, dyads, network-level properties) (Snehota and Håkansson 1995; Håkansson and Johanson, 1992). Social network analysis (SNA) allows powerful formal analysis of the latter. Transaction cost economics explains network structures in terms of minimizing transaction costs, although there was little evidence of this motivation for establishing a number of Netherlands (Van Raak, Paulus, and Mur-Veeman, 2005) or NHS care networks. Conversely, institutionalist and governance theories (Oliver and Ebers, 1998; Vincent, 2008) focus on the substantive relationships between network members, the network's overall activity and institutional setting (Williams, 2002).

Explanations of network effectiveness (Provan and Milward, 1995; Vollenberg, Kenis, and Raab, 2007) therefore need to consider both the structural and the substantive aspects (Vincent, 2008). Various theories relate an organization's substantive character (work-processes and their outcomes) to its structure. One which appears adaptable to network contexts is that of Donabedian (1980), provided that one adds:

1. an "environment" category of causal factors to accommodate (among other things) the effect of external mandates upon some networks;
2. a stronger contrast between a network's goals and the outcomes it actually produces, in recognition that networks (like organizations) sometimes fail to achieve their goals (e.g., the learning outcomes that did not materialize in some Netherlands health networks (Van Raak, Paulus, and Mur-Veeman, 2005)).

The environment from which a network emerges from supplies:

1. Its member organizations, hence the pre-existing goals, ideology, resources, and other characteristics which each brings to a prospective health care network; and

how much power each prospective member therefore wields when the network's collective goals are negotiated.

2. Physical, hence technical, constraints on the core processes required to achieve the network's collective goals and the several goals of its member organizations.

3. A set of policy mandates (for mandated networks) or market contexts (for business alliances), and regulatory and external social constraints (all networks).

In combination, the character of the member organizations, their goals, technologies required for the core process, and any external mandate together constrain the network's structure. Often the network members assume that in order to achieve their common goal it is sufficient just to complete certain proximate tasks (e.g., service change, evidence-based practice) which they assume will eventually produce the desired outcomes in turn (Van Raak et al., 2005). In any event, a joint project requires an agreed division of labor (Tsasis, 2009) among the network members. That imposes practical requirements as to which member organization is linked to which, and what they pass from one to another (resources (information, raw materials, knowledge); legitimation; money; clients, etc.). A care network, in which patients pass from provider to provider, as do referrals, clinical information, payments, equipment, and so on, is a familiar example. Network links develop out of resource-dependency ties and flows (Van Raak et al., 2005). A structure of links develops thus emerges from the operation of its core process. Commonly a network's core process also involves artifact production, whether of physical (products, services) or symbolic (e.g., new knowledge, new guidance). Managerial artifacts are typically symbolic (e.g., logos, publications), promoting the network's goals, shared identity, or culture (Schein, 1996), and participation in it.

A network's core process literally produces whatever outcomes the network achieves. How far they approximate to the network's goals depends (at least) on whether the network:

1. bases its core process on an empirically valid logic model;
2. pursues mutually consistent logic models and/or goals;
3. puts its logic model into practice;
4. meets facing little no external opposition to its activities.

As its outputs and environment change network members may in the light of experience revise their assumptions about what joint activity will enable them to realize their joint goals, and indeed the goals themselves (Shortell, Zukoski, and Alexander, 2002).

Figure 19.1 summarizes the resulting modified Donabedian model, simplified by ignoring multiple feed-back loops (e.g., network revising its core processes or objectives; community health partnerships recruiting additional members to enhance their external legitimacy (Zukoski and Shortell, 2001)) and ways in which (other) environmental factors (e.g., external community support (Hasnain-Wynia, Sofaer, and Bazzoli, 2003), external normative pressures (Van Raak, Paulus, and Mur-Veeman, 2005)) may moderate the relationships between structure, process and outcomes (Tolson et al., 2007).

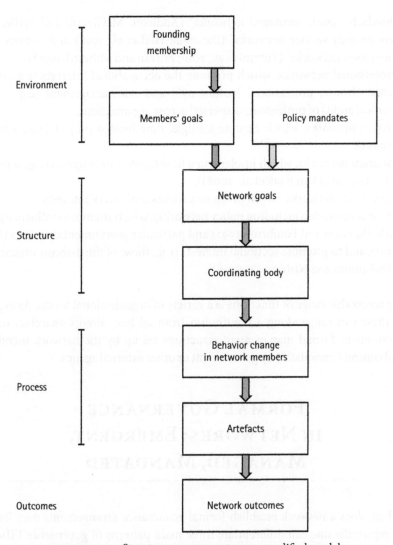

FIGURE 19.1 Structure, process, putcome: modified model

Health Network Types

This revised Donabedian model implies—and to that extent has some empirical support (Abrahamson and Fombrun, 1992; Goodwin et al., 2004)—that networks' structures vary according to their environments, membership, and goals. It implies that a taxonomy of health care networks should distinguish them by goals (intended outcomes), core processes and structures. Southon, Perkins, and Galler (2005) distinguish:

1. Care networks, which coordinate a care pathway and its component clinical interventions across multiple providers (also described as "providing networks"

(Bardach, 1994), "managed networks" (Addicott, McGivern, and Ferlie, 2007), "community service networks" (Banaszak-Holl et al., 1998) and "service implementation networks" (Turrini et al., 2010; Provan and Milward, 1995)).

2. Professional networks, which promote the occupational interests (e.g., occupational closure, professional "autonomy") and self-management (e.g., through medical audit) of professions dispersed across organizations.
3. Project networks, which execute a single, time-limited project (e.g., a building project).
4. Program networks, which implement a health policy or program (e.g., a model of palliative care (Van Raak et al., 2008)).
5. Experience networks, which promote patients' and carers' interests.
6. Interest networks (including policy networks), which attempt to influence policies (Abrahamson and Fombrun, 1992) and particular government decisions (Useem, 1983), and to promote sectional interests (e.g., those of third-sector organizations (Tsukamoto and Nishimura, 2006)).

Cutting across this range of functions is a variety of organizational forms. As explained below, these can range along a continuum from ad hoc, almost anarchic, informal organizations to formal management structures set up by the network members to external control ("mandate") by government or other external agency.

Formal Governance in Networks: Emergent, Managed, Mandated

How, then, does a network establish formal governance arrangements over its members? Empirically one can differentiate three main patterns of governance (Thomson, Perry, and Miller, 2009):

1. Emergent networks, whose goals stem from the network members and are not necessarily explicit at whole-network level.
2. Managed networks, whose member organizations establish formal network management structures (Gray, 1985) to aid collaboration (Tsasis, 2009; Tsukamoto and Nishimura, 2006) in pursuit of goals which they formulate collectively.
3. Mandated networks, a special case of managed network, whose goals are mandated by government or another external power.

These three variants have been regarded as phases of a "punctuated transformation" (Abrahamson and Fombrun, 1992) within a network's life-cycle (D'Aunno and Zuckerman, 1987).

Non-Governance of Emergent Networks

As noted, inter-organizational networks frequently emerge as repeated ad hoc interactions between organizations become routine and normalized, and usually without any overall management. The network's goals may remain tacit, even concealed (Child and Faulkner, 1998).

Since participation in the network is voluntary the member organizations have to assume that they are "symbionts" (mutually beneficial to each other) (Abrahamson and Fombrun, 1994), especially when they are few. Through repeated interactions (Tsasis 2009), network members come to trust each other (Huxham and Vangen, 2005; van Wijk, Jansen, and Lyles, 2008). Emergent collaboration thus requires cognitive, discursive, and normative convergence (Mowery, Oxley, and Silverman, 1996; Roussos and Fawcett, 2000; Tolson et al., 2007; Thomson, Perry, and Miller, 2009; van Bueren, Klijn, and Koppenjan, 2003) convergence; a low cultural distance (van Wijk, Jansen, and Lyles, 2008) between network members, or an ideological convergence of the kind that assisted AIDS network formation in Canada (Tsasis, 2009).

Coordination between the network members thus occurs through a combination of trust (Uzzi, 1997), persuasion, and reciprocity in dealings between them (Powell, 1990). These relationships have been compared to "*socially—not legally—binding*" (Jones, Hesterly, and Borgatti, 1997) contracts, although an inter-organizational coordination and relationships within most health networks is distinctively non-contractual. In the absence of collective self-governance, inter-organizational coordination emerges as a post facto pattern; perhaps like the "hidden hand" which Adam Smith perceived in markets, and equally in need of management.

Managed Networks

"*Conscious coordinative efforts*" (Thorelli, 1986) and a coordinating body to execute them (Thomson, Perry, and Miller, 2009; Tsukamoto and Nishimura, 2006) are often added to an emergent network's core process, especially as a network grows. The network coordinating body ("lead organization") may be an existing network member, often a dominant one (Provan and Kenis, 2008; Banaszak-Holl et al., 1998), through which network coordination is then centralized and brokered. Its central "broker" position gives it the strong relational ties and trust that facilitate inter-organizational knowledge transfer (van Wijk, Jansen, and Lyles, 2008). Evidence-basing quality standards, safety standards and working practices is nowadays de rigeur in most health systems. A coordinating body's ties with organizations outside the network help such knowledge to enter the network (Burt, 2004; Uzzi, 1996). Specialized tasks are often undertaken by project sub-groups (Touati et al., 2006; Van Raak, Paulus, and Mur-Veeman, 2005; Huxham and Vangen, 2005), sub-sets of network members (Provan and Sebastian, 1998) or by giving different member organizations the lead role for particular tasks or issues (Zukoski and Shortell, 2001).

The revised Donabedian model implies that the network coordinating body's function is, firstly, to formulate the network's collective task (Wells and Weiner, 2007) and objectives (Zukoski and Shortell, 2001), focusing on some issues and actions and ignoring others so as to accentuate the presumed convergence of member organizations' interests; then to establish the joint productive process (maybe from scratch) (Provan and Kenis, 2008) and any concomitant artifact-production. Finally action planning is required to get it all implemented (Zahner, 2005).

To say that these things are required is not to say that they always occur (e.g., action planning was reported in only 60% of Wisconsin public health partnerships) (Zahner, 2005). Management and leadership techniques applied within hierarchies are not always relevant to networks (Huxham and Vangen, 2005), whose management relies heavily on, say, informal discussion and problem-solving besides formal activities such as meetings, and so on (Williams, 2002). Decisions have to be implemented participatively and by persuasion not command or coercive "performance management" (Vangen and Huxham, 2003). "Reticulist" skills of boundary-spanning, relationship-building, resolving conflicts and non-compliance (Van Raak et al., 2008) with network decisions, influencing (Williams, 2002), pressurizing (even "thuggery" (Huxham and Vangen, 2005)), brokering disputes to align network-members interests (Kickert and Koppenjan, 1997) and of promoting transparency and network members' accountability to the rest of the network (Fawcett et al., 2000). The reticulist also has to deal with conflicts, encourage involvement, and build trust on basis of experience of relationality, including fairness, consistency, and reciprocity (O'Toole, 1997; Agranoff and McGuire, 2001) of the network managers' own behaviors. All this requires resources: specially employed managers (Turrini et al., 2010) and a budget (Zahner, 2005).

Mandated Networks

In a mandated network the management activities are undertaken on behalf of an external power (for health networks, usually government) and its policies (the "mandate") rather than the network members' goals. The lead network body may become a network administrative organization (NAO), as Provan and Kenis (2008) name it, whose sole role is to manage the network. It *"is not another member organization providing its own services"* (Provan and Kenis, 2008).

A mandated network is thus one specific form of implementation structure (Porter and Hjern, 1981)). Policy implementation deficits in mandated networks often arise because of characteristics which also found in other implementation structures:

1. Communication links between organizations do not always arise spontaneously and have to be artificially constructed.
2. The relevant organizations may have discrepant interests (e.g., in many Mediterranean health systems, general practioners (GPs) work as private practitioners besides being public servants).

3. The relevant organizations may not contribute, or even have, the resources which the policy requires (often the case for primary and community care in Eastern Europe during the 1990s).

4. Some of these organizations, especially organizations and professionals who fear loss of power, autonomy, resources, or clientele, may passively resist the mandate (Touati et al., 2006).

Unlike other implementation structures, managed mandated networks have a network coordinating body. Bodies that oppose the policy are typically excluded (e.g., there were no tobacco firms in the World Health Organization (WHO) Tobacco Free Europe campaign).

One way to explore how these differences in management might relate to a health network's structure and core process is to use the revised Donabedian framework to compare systematically program networks (usually mandated) and care network (usually not).

Program Networks

Program networks are very relevant to the work of the managers responsible for implementing health programs or models of care, and to clinicians specializing in such a disease or program. Examples of such programs include those advocated by WHO for the management of particular diseases (e.g., diabetes) across primary, secondary, and tertiary care; evidence-based, inter-organizational models of care promoted by national bodies such as IQWIG (Germany) or NICE (UK); or programs advocated "from below" such as Psichiatrica Democratica in Italy (Ramon, 1983).

Mandated health networks are either artificially constructed de novo (Lewis, Baeza, and Alexander, 2008; Billett, Clemans, and Seddon, 2005) or captured from emergent or existing managed network(s). Because a policy mandate substitutes external goals and governance for the network's own, some writers regard use of inter-organizational networks for implementing external policies or models of care as "the distortion of a technique" (Addicott, McGivern, and Ferlie, 2007). The first mandated NHS networks were mandated to implement new models of cancer care, in particular faster referral systems (The Expert Advisory Group on Cancer to the Chief Medical Officers of England and Wales, 1995). Another was mandated by the secretary of state for health to break a logjam, in a major city, over the rationalization of hospital services for children (Sheaff et al., 2011). Certain existing inter-organizational networks (e.g., for cardiac heart disease (CHD)) also became subject to health policy mandates in the early 2000s. Their "capture" was either effected by making their existing "lead" coordinating body externally accountable or by introducing a new network "host" organization which was not previously a network member (e.g., a Strategic Health Authority, not a service provider). Often, too, "capture" involved merging networks.

NHS networks' existing goals were supplemented or replaced with policy targets (e.g., to reduce hospital waiting times), a "reform" (e.g., to introduce clinical audit, NICE guidance) or models of care (e.g., the National Service Frameworks (NSF) (Department of Health, 1999, 2001, 2002) combining evidence-based clinical standards (Currie and Harvey, 2000) with organizational requirements such as workforce reviews). The mandates themselves grew over time, for instance by adding requirements for greater lay participation in the networks. Networks were also sometimes used ad hoc to help implement new policies having little specific or direct connection with their original mandate, for example the EU working time directive (limiting doctors' hours of work). Unstable mandates were problematic for the network coordinators:

> [NHS regional body] is sending, different information [about CHD services] depending on how at a higher level things are changing all the time, people are just getting fed up with it and just saying well you said something different last week, or you said something different the month before (CHD network coordinator).

The widest mandates were however in primary care, where inter-organizational networks were used to coordinate and supervise general practices (which are independent organizations) at "arm's length"; a role which NHS Clinical Commissioning Groups have inherited and expanded (Department of Health, 2010).

The networks' coordinating ("lead") bodies became an officially-recognized mediators between the networks' other member organizations and higher NHS management, an external brokerage role. Being reinforced with sanctions, these external links were in some ways stronger than the coordinating bodies' internal links to the (other) member organizations, leading the former to develop a strong institutional isomorphism with regional and national level NHS management. (A similar pattern is reported of social care providers in Japan (Tsukamoto and Nishimura, 2006)). The mix of individuals participating shifted somewhat from clinicians towards managers (Ross et al., 2009).

The mandates often stipulated which organizations should be network members, resulting in the possible inclusion of involuntary members (Huxham and Vangen, 2005) and members with conflicting interests. Contemporary voluntary networks in the NHS dealt with conflicts by negotiation, voice, or peaceful co-existence. But dissident organizations, or those which considered the network ineffective or just irrelevant to their organization-level goals could not withdraw. Their representatives would then participate either in passive, tokenistic ways ("symbolic participation") or mainly with an eye to appropriating network resources (Tsasis, 2009; Huxham and Vangen, 2005). The need for compromises between conflicting member organizations was liable to make the definition of network objectives and its core process slow and ambiguous (Uusikylä and Valovirta, 2007). Since the member organizations were motivated extrinsically by the mandate rather than intrinsically as in a voluntary network, incentives or soft coercion were also required at times to make them comply with NAO decisions (Sheaff et al., 2003). A mandate did not guarantee practical collaboration (Gray, 1985).

Some networks were mandated to implement a policy or program within each member organization rather than jointly across them; for instance the promotion of evidence-based practice (Tolson et al., 2007) at individual clinician or inter-disciplinary team (Touati et al., 2006) level. A similar pattern is found in some American HMOs. Processes through which network member organizations mutually helped each other implement such program included:

1. Operationalizing a national mandate for local conditions, for example by defining a model or care or standards of clinical quality that applied across the network but not more widely.
2. Jointly learning about the program, including how to implement it severally, for example by sharing of practical and tacit information.
3. Recruiting other organizations (e.g., primary care doctors) whose help was necessary.
4. Devising ways of producing and presenting evidence of compliance and health impacts in each member organization.

The mandated program networks produced artifacts which included rules of working practice; policy and managerial guidance; evidence-basing of current treatments and translating relevant new evidence into practice; data-bases, IT systems, and research to monitor and evaluate compliance with program; evaluating existing working practice against program norms; local technical guidance and policy for new models of care or technologies; care pathway mapping and revision; consultations with local community representatives; framework contracts and other incentive systems. Voluntary networks also produced many similar artifacts however.

Whilst expansion of a network's mandate may bring a corresponding diversification of its activities and artifacts, one kind of artifact was distinctive, even essential, to the mandated networks. That was the production of artifacts—especially symbolic artifacts—designed to demonstrate that the network had fulfilled its mandate, beginning by demonstrating that the required network actually existed. Following (Foucault et al., 1991), production of such artifacts can be understood as a form of "dressage." Their practical purpose was to demonstrate obedience.

One would therefore predict that mandated program networks would have more and stronger links between the NAO and each member organization, than directly between (other) member organizations. Social network analysis would show the coordinating body either at the center of a "star" pattern of links to the other member organizations, or at the apex of an hierarchy of member organizations; or rather, a quasi-hierarchy (Exworthy, Powell, and Mohan, 1999), in which an hierarchical structure of links between the individuals participating was distributed across the network as a whole, irrespective of organizational boundaries (Figure 19.2).

In theory, and sometimes in practice (Provan and Milward, 1995; Vollenberg, Kenis, and Raab, 2007), mandated program networks are most effective when the mechanisms of external control upon member organizations are direct and unfragmented, and there

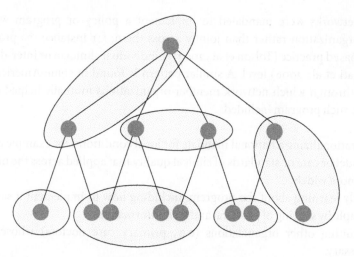

FIGURE 19.2 Quasi-hierarchy

are local monitoring and control mechanisms. In US mental health networks decentralized communication (etc.) links reduced network effectiveness in terms of clients' health status and well-being (Provan and Milward, 1995). The coordinating body's central position is associated with better transfer of knowledge (van Wijk, Jansen, and Lyles, 2008).

CARE NETWORKS

Of all health care networks, care networks are the type most immediately relevant to everyday clinical practice, hence to clinicians, for a wide range of chronic diseases (e.g., dementia care networks in Canada (Lemieux-Charles et al., 2005)) and for patients with multi-morbidity. They are also relevant to those organizations and managers, including case managers, who have to coordinate and/or finance such care across multiple organizational boundaries.

The practical function of a care network is jointly to manage service delivery, especially for prolonged, complex episodes of care (Tsukamoto and Nishimura, 2006) across numerous providers, possibly including non-health organizations (Blumenthal and Buntin, 1998) (e.g., social care, housing services). Often known nowadays as "integrated" care projects, these care networks often develop where care coordination is missing or inadequate. Their aims often include changing or extending an existing care pathway (de Rijk, Van Raak, and van der Made, 2007), which can in itself strongly motivate health workers and organizations members to cooperate (Van Raak et al., 2005).

Care networks' core productive process is an implicit or explicit inter-organizational care pathway (or several), perhaps formalized as a multi-agency, multi-disciplinary care protocol (Van Raak, Paulus, and Mur-Veeman, 2005) with a shared understanding and norms as to its division of labor (Thorelli, 1986). The member organizations apply agreed criteria (again, maybe tacit) when referring patients between organizations, harmonizing its member organizations' work routines (de Rijk, Van Raak, and van der Made, 2007), and making professions' or providers' roles more complementary within the wider care pathway. Correspondingly, NHS care networks' typical artifacts included intangibles (general guidance, policies, etc. as in program networks) but also "tools of the work" such as new referral routes; patient information exchange through shared (e.g., patient-held) clinical records and tools (e.g., a Common Assessment Framework, pain assessment tools, medicines charts, district nursing records (Tolson et al., 2007), clinical audits); physical inputs to care (shared equipment, co-location of services), technical training; knowledge-sharing about clinical and social care; funding for services; support groups (for clinicians and/or patients) for specific diseases or services; and guidance about when and how, to access and use existing models of care or technologies.

Care network members are often single professionals, groups of professionals, or departments with a larger organization, not only entire provider-organizations. Typically, therefore, different organizational levels are represented in the network's membership. Consequently the individuals who participate often have to refer back to higher management within their respective member organizations before they can commit themselves to the network's collective decisions and actions, with a corresponding risk of inertia at the collective, network level (Thomson, Perry, and Miller, 2009). An apparent solution is for member organizations to be represented in the care network by one or more of their senior clinicians.

Patient care involves the direct referral of patients from member organization to member organization, the providers dealing directly with each other and transferring such resources as referral requests, clinical information, equipment, and pharmaceuticals, and money along the care pathway. These activities do not inherently require a coordinating body at all. Nevertheless, one might still exist for the reasons noted above. In NHS care networks, such bodies distributed budgetary or real inputs (e.g., case managers, psychologists) (Touati et al., 2009) to patient care, facilitated patient transfers, and matched supply and demand for services across providers (Van Raak et al., 2008). Many NHS clinical commissioning groups now operate referral "hubs" to screen, and where feasible divert, hospital referrals. With or without external ties or a central coordinating body, the practically indispensable structure of a care network is the "horizontal" links making up the care pathway.

PROGRAM NETWORKS, CARE NETWORKS, AND NETWORK THEORY

In summary, one would therefore predict care networks to have denser and stronger links (i.e., more frequent and diverse interactions) directly between providers than between the providers and any non-provider coordinating body outside the care pathway. That is, a predominantly "flat" structure. In US mental health networks, for example, strong integration of the "clique" of main service-providing organizations increased network effectiveness in terms of clients' health status and well-being as perceived by families and therapists (Provan and Milward, 1995). In contrast program networks would have a more centralized, even hierarchical, structure.

Framed in terms of our revision of Donabedian's theory, Table 19.1 systematically compares typical program and care networks.

The cell contents in Table 19.1 are of course generalizations for which counter-examples might probably be found, but the secondary evidence referred to above suggests that they have some face validity. The "Outcomes" are those which ensue if the network processes do operate as the network members intended. That leaves open whether these outcomes could have been more fully achieved if a particular network were differently ("better") managed, and whether a non-network structure might not have achieved them equally well. "Standardization" here refers both to more uniform care provision (for each care group) and, nowadays, to greater use of evidence-based practice. However, the main point is that the differences in network membership and goals of the two kinds of networks then produce correspondingly different network structures (and governance), distinct kinds of core working processes, and correspondingly different kinds of outcomes.

Table 19.1 Program and Care Networks: typical characteristics

	Program Networks	Care Networks
Environment: Goals, members.	Mandated by government or expert body external to network.	Local provider organizations and individual practitioners seek shared model(s) and standards of care.
Structure: Links, governance	Quasi-hierarchy, formally managed by a network coordinating body at its apex/center. Strong external linkages.	Mainly "horizontal" links between care providers (individuals and/or organizations). Formal coordinating body optional.
Process: Core joint work	Disseminate policy/program and operationalize general norms for local conditions. Legitimate and monitor compliance.	Refer and treat patients, and coordinate their care, according to jointly designed care pathways, care plans, and case management systems.
Outcomes:	Compliance with policy program and/or normative model(s) of care.	Increased continuity of care; care coordination; standardization of care.

HYBRID NETWORKS

Nevertheless, a comparison of three mandated and two voluntary NHS networks during 2006–10 (Sheaff et al., 2011) suggested that NHS networks had neither the unambiguously quasi-hierarchical structure predicted above for a program network, nor the predominantly horizontal structure predicted for a care network. None completely matched either ideal type described in Table 19.1.

The mandated networks had a markedly non-hierarchical structure. They were dense; their member organizations had lots of direct links with each other (densities of 51% or above at whole network level). These were high scores compared to those reported for some other networks (Provan and Milward, 1995; Dunn and Westbrook, 2011)), substantially higher than for a pure hierarchy of equivalent size. No one member organization monopolized the links to other network members. Because of their usually direct links to each other, member organizations had little scope to become, and little need to use, intermediaries ("brokers"). Although the three mandated networks were somewhat more centralized than two non-mandated NHS networks, all five networks had low centralization. All the networks, even the mandated ones, also all had low "efficiency" scores, meaning that most members had links to many other member organizations besides the coordinating body. It is often assumed that predominantly centralized networks will be more effective than networks with decentralized, cohesive links between network members (Provan and Milward, 1995; Vollenberg, Kenis, and Raab, 2007). Provan and Kenis (2008) argue that dense direct links between member organizations, in addition to links with the coordinating body, are redundant and therefore reduce network efficiency.

These patterns apparently contradict the above predictions that mandated networks would be more hierarchical, more centralized, and less dense than voluntary networks. How can this be explained? The empirical comparison assumed that care networks and mandated program networks are separate, distinct entities. But what if a program network's mandate were to implement a prescribed care pathway, or if a care network was "captured" and became a mandated program care network? Either way the consequence would be to create a hybrid care-and-program network. Indeed the NHS clinical and professional networks we studied were mandated to implement National Service Frameworks which, to varying extents, stipulated what care pathways the networks had to construct for specific patient groups.

It follows from the above predictions that the structure of a hybrid, mandated care-and-program network would be the superset of the mainly horizontal, direct inter-provider links that would exist in care network and the more centralized pattern of links in a mandated program network. This superimposition of structures would produce the combination of high density and low centralization observed in the NHS networks. In that case these network characteristics reflect not inefficiency but the networks' dual function, hence dual core processes. Indeed the two sets of links may be mutually reinforcing; the links which support, say, the clinical "integration" of a care pathway can promote its functional "integration" and vice versa (Touati et al., 2006).

INTEGRATED CARE

As a specific kind of hybrid program and care network, integrated care networks are of interest because they address important health policy and management issues that recur across many health systems. These are to reduce the pressures upon, and the costs of, inpatient care which in modern health systems takes the greater share of expenditure; and to reduce the waste and, especially for older people, distress and iatrogenesis caused by preventable hospital admissions. To achieve these ends requires inter-organizational coordination at both managerial and clinical levels, and often the financial level too, with non-health services (social care, housing, etc.) as well as among health care providers.

Like health policies in other countries (e.g., Belgium, Netherlands), recent NHS policy has increasingly mandated efforts to reduce hospital bed use by substituting complex packages of primary medical, community health and social services, especially for frail older people, both to prevent referrals and to expedite discharge. Where, as in many health systems, primary care is organizationally fragmented this mandate necessitates strengthening existing care networks, even establishing new ones. It implies the use, for each patient, of a single care plan and a care coordinator (Tracy et al., 2005). In many countries this increasingly salient "integrated care" agenda leads towards policy mandates to establish care networks for both the vertical and the horizontal "integration" of services provided by separate organizations.

The foregoing analysis suggests that mandated integrated care networks are likely to have an especially dense structure of links, and two core processes operating in parallel: implementation of a policy program and the operation of care networks spanning primary and secondary care, and services for physical and for mental health care. Three implications follow.

Analyses of how network structure affects network effectiveness have focused on mandated program networks. Few as these studies are, there are still fewer equivalent analyses of mandated care networks. Such studies face the methodological challenge of analytically separating the two or more groups of structures nested within the overall network structure. How to manage care networks across organizational boundaries is a second issue that health services will need stronger evidence about in future. Many studies report specific interventions and particular projects for care integration, but fewer analyze the mechanisms of inter-organizational coordination within such networks. An important aspect of this is the transfer of clinical and administrative information about individual patients across organizational boundaries; something which the NHS, at least, has not found easy. The term "integrated" care is, thirdly, often unintentionally ironic. The one thing which care networks inherently exclude is organizational integration of the relevant services under single ownership, management, information systems, and financing (e.g., with all services under one managerial hierarchy). At best they allow closer coordination of patient transfers between separate providers, harmonize working practices at the boundaries, promote common models of care, and standardize clinical practices and information-sharing between providers; better co-ordination certainly, and desirable, but not "integration." That it falls short of such integration, where desirable, is the fundamental weakness of a network-based mode of organization. Indeed the logical culmination of "integration" policy would be to minimize the inter-organizational barriers to patient transfer—barriers also to the coordination and continuity of care—by combining the separate providers into a single organization. Indeed primary care centers ("polyclinics") in parts of Scandinavia do exactly that (Øvretveit, Hansson, and Brommels, 2010). On that logic, mandated care networks might fore-shadow eventual organizational integration.

Conclusion: Health Networks as Productive Processes

In conclusion, what does a network perspective, in particular a theory of networks on the lines based on the revisions of Donabedian's theory suggested earlier, contribute to the management and understanding of health systems?

First, it highlights the inter-organizational character of much health care work. Care for people with multiple chronic conditions, implementing new models of care, translating evidence into practice and inter-sectoral health promotion (to name but some) are usually achieved through a process of production distributed across organizations. A network perspective thus draws attention to the main management tasks and skills involved. It suggests that for much of health care management, hierarchical "leadership" or the application of some managerial "panaceas" ("fads") are of less practical use than the tasks (and skills) of a negotiating agreed working practices across multiple, probably different, organizational cultures, of dealing with discrepant ideologies and unequal distributions of power, and of negotiating the ways in which formal health services are intercalated with the informal (co-)production of care by patients themselves and their informal carers. Similarly, the foregoing perspective on networks supplements and corrects the anyway empirically dubious neo-classical micro-economic approaches to analyzing, and making recommendations for inter-organization coordination through market mechanisms (competition, financial incentives). To these micro-economic accounts a network perspective on the above lines adds recognition of all the intrinsic motivations (e.g., alleviating health problems, promoting better health, caring for patients) and most of the extrinsic motivations (non-financial extrinsic motives such as reputation and professional recognition) which lead individuals and organizations—and networks—to provide health care.

Not least, a network perspective on the above lines suggests why health networks have proliferated. They have often been created as new process of health care provision which offer a practical, often ad hoc, workaround for the inadequacies of market and quasi-market structures when it comes to coordinating such activities as caring for people with multiple chronic conditions and implementing new models of care across organizational boundaries. They offer a practical way of surmounting problems that fragmentation of services, organizational barriers, privatization, paywalls, and competition create for these kinds of health care process. Such problems were likely to increase in any event as health care became more complex and often, at the clinical and professional levels, more specialized and compartmentalized. But pro-market health "reform" programs, especially in Europe since 1991, have often exacerbated them. Hence the development of networks.

The evidence outlined in this chapter appears on balance consistent with, and tends to confirm at least the face validity of, an explanation of a health networks as a complex productive processes. Networks' characteristics as productive processes (producing coordinated care, new models of care, evidence-based clinical practice, etc, as the case may be) go a long way towards explaining their structures and internal governance. It therefore suggests an objective basis for the constructive empirical evaluation of a network's structures and management, an evaluation in the network's terms, that is in terms of how they contribute to producing the network's own stated objectives. In that sense this chapter has extended labor process theory to inter-organizational health care, albeit a version of labor process theory stripped of some of the wrong empirical assumptions and predictions of earlier, organizational-level versions of that theory (Braverman 1974). However the evidence discussed above also suggests that if such a theory is to have empirical purchase on observed health care networks, hence practical value, it must be applied in a particular way. When applied to hybrid networks (as health networks often are), it must be used analytically, to understand observed, hybrid networks as sets of multiple overlapping productive processes. Thus a real health care network might predominantly function as, say, a care network but simultaneously also function secondarily as, say, a professional or a program network. Then the above theoretical framework can be applied to each component, an approach likely to reveal both the tensions within a given network (e.g., the tension between financial and care coordination mechanisms, in the case of certain German mental health networks (Sheaff et al., 2015)) and the scope for synergies between parallel processes of production (continuing the same example, the use of care pathways both to coordinate care and as a way of introducing new models of care).

Certain research implications follow. The above theory is far from complete, requiring elaboration further empirical testing and refinement regarding at least:

1. How, in care networks, clinical techniques (the "technology" of care) constrain—even determine—the structure of links necessary for the network to function.
2. Deeper understanding of which patterns of linkage, artifact production, and management which are specific characteristics of each type of network noted above (care network, program network, etc.).

3. How contextual factors, for example the juridical framework, wider social ideologies and national "culture" influence the goals that health networks set themselves and how their members use (or not) the links they set up between themselves.

From the above perspective on networks, it makes sound sense for researchers to compare networks of similar kinds in terms of governance and effectiveness in achieving their declared outcomes (i.e., to compare care network with care network, or program network with program network). It makes less sense to compare networks of different kinds in these terms or, therefore, to expect to find many universal recipes for successfully establishing and managing health networks. Rather, a contingency approach is required, one which (as the realists might say) differentiates what kinds of network structure and management work best for which purposes, for whom, and under which contextual conditions. The same reasoning similarly indicates both the uses and the limitations of social network analysis. It also indicates the need for mixed methods research, so that future studies not only describe health network structure (formally, even mathematically), but also explain how that structure functions as the medium through which a core network process is sustained, coordinated, and (sometimes) managed, and adapted (or not) to produce specific outcomes: which requires qualitative methods.

Returning finally to governance and mandated "integrated care" networks, the foregoing also suggests that the chief policy uses of mandated care networks therefore appear to lie not only, or even mainly, in care coordination, but elsewhere. They lie in moderating the effects of, whilst still preserving, the existing patterns of separate ownership, control, and even competition among those health care providers which already are, or which policy makers want to make, independent of the state.

ACKNOWLEDGMENTS

The NHS research described above was funded by the UK National Institute for Health Research Health Services and Delivery Research Programme (SDO project 08-1508-104). The researchers were Rod Sheaff, Jill Schofield, Nigel Charles, Lawrence Benson, Russell Mannion, and David Reeves. The views expressed above are those of the chapter authors alone and do not necessarily reflect those of the HS&DR Programme, NIHR, NHS, or the Department of Health.

REFERENCES

Abrahamson, E. and Fombrun, C. J. (1992). Forging the iron cage: Interorganisational networks and the production of macro-culture. *Journal of Management Studies*, 29(2): 175–94, doi: 10.1111/j.1467-6486.1992.tb00659.x.

Abrahamson, E. and Fombrun, C. J. (1994). Macrocultures: Determinants and consequences. *Academy of Management Review*, 19 (4): 728–55. doi: 10.5465/AMR.1994.9412190217.

Addicott, R., McGivern, G., and Ferlie, E. (2007). The distortion of a managerial technique? The case of clinical networks in UK health care. *British Journal of Management*, 18(1): 93–105.

Agranoff, R. and M. McGuire. (2001). Big questions in public network management research. *Journal of Public Administration Research and Theory*, 11(3): 295–326.

Balkundi, P. and D. A. Harrison. (2006). Ties, leaders, and time in teams: Strong inference about network structure's effects on team viability and performance. *Academy of Management Journal*, 49(1): 49–68.

Banaszak-Holl, J., Allen, S., Mor, V., and Schott, T. (1998). Organizational characteristics associated with agency position in community care networks. *Journal of Health and Social Behavior*, 39(4): 368–385.

Bardach, E. (1994). Can network theory illuminate interagency collaboration. Workshop on network analysis and innovations in public programs, LaFollette Institute of Public Affairs, University of Wisconsin-Madison.

Billett, S., Clemans, A., and Seddon, T. (2005). Forming, developing and sustaining social partnerships. Adelaide: National Centre for Vocational Education Research.

Blumenthal, D. and Buntin, M. B. (1998). Carve outs: Definition, experience, and choice among candidate conditions. *American Journal of Managed Care*, 4 (Suppl.): SP45–SP57.

Braverman, H. (1974). *Labour and monopoly capital*. New York: Monthly Review Press.

Burt, R. S. 2004. Structural holes and good ideas. *The American Journal of Sociology*, 110(2): 349–399, doi: 10.2307/3568221.

Child, J. and Faulkner, D. (1998). *Strategies of co-operation*. Oxford: Oxford University Press.

Currie, V. L. and Harvey, G. (2000). The use of care pathways as tools to support the implementation of evidence based practice. *Journal of Interprofessional Care*, 14(4): 311–24.

D'Aunno, T. A. and Zuckerman, H. S. (1987). A life-cycle model of organizational federations: The case of hospitals *Academy of Management Review*, 12(3): 534–545, doi: 10.5465/AMR.1987.4306568.

Department of Health. (1999). *A national service framework for mental health*. London: Department of Health.

Department of Health. (2001). *National service framework for older people*. London: Department of Health.

Department of Health. (2002). *A national service framework for coronary heart disease*. London: Department of Health.

Department of Health. (2010). *Equity and excellence: Liberating the NHS*. Cm 7881. London: Department of Health.

De Rijk, A., Van Raak, A., and van der Made, J. (2007). A new theoretical model for cooperation in public health settings: The RDIC model. *Qualitative Health Research*, 17(8): 1103–1116.

Donabedian, A. (1980). *The definition of quality and approaches to its assessment*. Ann Arbor, MI: Health Administration Press.

Dunn, A., and Westbrook, J. (2011). Interpreting social network metrics in healthcare organisations: A review and guide to validating small networks. *Social Science & Medicine*, 72(7): 1064–1068, doi: 10.1016/j.socscimed.2011.01.029.

Ebers, M. (1997). Explaining inter-organizational network formation. In *The formation of inter-organizational networks*, ed. Ebers, M., pp. 1-26. Oxford: Oxford University Press.

Exworthy, M., Powell, M., and Mohan, J. (1999). The NHS: Quasi-market, quasi-hierarchy and quasi-network? *Public Money and Management*, 19(4): 15–22.

Fawcett, S., Francisco, V., Paine-Andrews, A., and Schultz, J. (2000). A model memorandum of collaborations: A proposal. *Public Health Reports*, 15(May–June): 175–190.

Foucault, M., Burchell, G., Gordon, C., and Miller, P. (1991). *The Foucault effect: Studies in governmentality*. Chicago: University of Chicago Press.

Goodwin, N., 6, P., Peck, E., Freeman, T., and Posaner, R. (2004). *Managing across diverse networks of care: Lessons from other sectors*. Birmingham: University of Birmingham.

Gray, B. (1985). Conditions facilitating interorganizational collaboration. *Human Relations*, 38(10): 911.

Håkansson, H. and Johanson, J. (1989). A model of industrial networks. Uppsala: Department of Business Administration, University of Uppsala.

Hasnain-Wynia, R., Sofaer, S., and Bazzoli, G. (2003). Members' perceptions of community care network partnerships' effectiveness. *Medical Care Research & Review*, 60(4): 40–62.

Huxham, C. and Vangen, S. (2005). *Managing to collaborate: The theory and practices of collaborative advantage*. London: Routledge.

Jones, C., Hesterly, W. S., and Borgatti, S. P. (1997). A general theory of network governance: Exchange conditions and social mechanisms. *Academy of Management Review*, 22(4): 911–945.

Kickert, W. and Koppenjan, J. (1997). Public management and network management: An overview. In *Managing complex networks. Strategies for the public sector*, ed. Kickert, W., Klijn, E. H. and Koppenjan, J., pp. 35–61. London: Sage.

Lemieux-Charles, L., Chambers, L. W., Cockerill, R., Jaglal, S., Brazil, K., Cohen, C., LeClair, K., Dalziel, B., and Schulman, B. (2005). Evaluating the effectiveness of community-based dementia care networks: The dementia care networks' study. *The Gerontologist*, 45(4): 456–464.

Lewis, J., Baeza, J., and Alexander, D. (2008). Partnerships in primary care in Australia: Network structure, dynamics and sustainability. *Social Science & Medicine*, 67(2): 280–291.

Mowery, D., Oxley, J., and Silverman, D. (1996). Strategic alliances and interfirm knowledge transfer. *Strategic Management Journal*, 17: 77–91.

Oliver, A. L. and Ebers, M. (1998). Networking network studies: An analysis of conceptual configurations in the study of inter-organizational relationships. *Organization Studies*, 19(4): 549–583, doi: 10.1177/017084069801900402.

O'Toole, L. J. (1997). The implications for democracy in a networked bureaucratic world. *Journal of Public Administration Research and Theory*, 7(3): 443–459.

Øvretveit, J., Hansson, J., and Brommels, M. (2010). The creation of a comprehensive integrated health and social care organisation in Sweden. *Health Policy*, 97(2): 113–121.

Porter, B. and Hjern, D. (1981). Implementation structures: New unit of administrative analysis. *Organization Studies*, 2: 211–227.

Powell, W. W. (1990). Neither market nor hierarchy: Network forms of organization. *Research in Organizational Behavior*, 12: 295–336.

Provan, K. and Kenis, P. (2008). Modes of network governance: Structure, management, and effectiveness. *Journal of Public Administration Research and Theory*, 18(2): 229–252.

Provan, K. and Milward, H. (1995). A preliminary theory of interorganizational network effectiveness: A comparative study of four community mental health systems. *Administrative Science Quarterly*, 40: 1–33.

Provan, K. and Sebastian, J. (1998). Networks within networks: Service link overlap, organizational cliques, and network effectiveness. *Academy of Management Journal*, 41(4): 453.

Ramon, S. (1983). Psichiatria democratica: A case study of an Italian community mental health service. *International Journal of Health Services: Planning, Administration, Evaluation*, 13(2): 307–324.

Rhodes, R. (1997). *Understanding governance*. Buckingham: Open University Press.

Ross, J. W., Hooper, L., Stenhouse, E., and Sheaff, R. (2009). What are child-care social workers doing in relation to infant mental health? An exploration of professional ideologies and practice preferences within an inter-agency context. *British Journal of Social Work*, 39(6): 1008–1025, doi: 10.1093/bjsw/bcn029.

Roussos, S. T. and Fawcett, S. B. (2000). A review of collaborative partnerships as a strategy for improving community health. *Annual Review of Public Health*, 21(1): 369–402, doi: 10.1146/annurev.publhealth.21.1.369.

Schein, E. H. (1996). Culture: The missing concept in organization studies. *Administrative Science Quarterly*, 41(2): 229–240.

Sheaff, R., Charles, N., Mahon, A., Chambers, N., Morando, V., Exworthy, M., Abzug, R., Mannion, R., and Llewellyn, S. (2015). NHS commissioning practice and health system governance: A mixed-methods realistic evaluation. *Health Services and Delivery Research*, 3(10): 1–184, doi: 10.3310/hsdr03100.

Sheaff, R., Rogers, A., Pickard, S., Marshall, M. N., Campbell, S., and Roland, M. O. (2003). A subtle governance: "Soft" medical leadership in English primary care. *Sociology of Health and Illness*, 25(5): 408–428.

Sheaff, R., Schofield, J., Charles, N., Benson, L., Mannion, R., and Reeves, D. (2011). *The management and effectiveness of professional and clinical networks*. London: SDO.

Shortell, S., Zukoski, A., and Alexander, J. (2002). Evaluating partnership for community health improvement: Tracking the footprints. *Journal of Health Politics Policy and Law*, 27(1): 49–91.

Snehota, I. and Håkansson, H. (1995). *Developing relationships in business networks*. London: Routledge.

Southon, G., Perkins, R., and Galler, D. (2005). Networks: A key to the future of health services. *Australian Health Review*, 29(3): 317–326.

The Expert Advisory Group on Cancer to the Chief Medical Officers of England and Wales. (1995). *A policy framework for commissioning cancer services : A report by the expert advisory group on cancer to the chief medical officers of England and Wales*. London: Department of Health.

Thomson, A. M., Perry, J. L., and Miller, T. K. (2009). Conceptualizing and measuring collaboration. *Journal of Public Administration Research and Theory*, 19(1): 23–56, doi: 10.1093/jopart/mum036.

Thorelli, H. B. (1986). Networks: Between markets and hierarchies. *Strategic Management Journal*, 7(1): 37–51.

Tolson, D., McIntosh, J., Loftus, L., and Cormie, P. (2007). Developing a managed clinical network in palliative care: A realistic evaluation. *International Journal of Nursing Studies*, 44(2): 183–195.

Touati, N., Pineault, R., Champagne, F., Denis, J.-L., Brousselle, A., Contandriopoulos, A.-P., and Geneau, R. (2009). Evaluating service organization models: The relevance and methodological challenges of a configurational approach. *Evaluation*, 15(4): 375–401, doi: 10.1177/1356389009341729.

Touati, N., Roberge, D., Denis, J. L., Cazale, L., Pineault, R., and Tremblay, D. (2006). Clinical leaders at the forefront of change in health care systems: Advantages and issues. Lessons learned from the evaluation of an integrated oncological services network. *Health Services Management Research*, 19: 105–122.

Tracy, S., Hartz, D., Nicholl, M., McCann, Y., and Latta, D. (2005). An integrated service network in maternity: The implementation of a midwifery-led unit. *Australian Health Review*, 29(3): 332.

Trappenburg, M. (2005). Fighting sectional interests in health care. *Health Care Analysis*, 13(3): 223–237.

Tsasis, P. (2009). The social processes of interorganizational collaboration and conflict in nonprofit organizations. *Nonprofit Management and Leadership*, 20(1): 5–21, doi: 10.1002/nml.238.

Tsukamoto, I. and Nishimura, M. (2006). The emergence of local non-profit: Government partnerships and the role of intermediary organizations in Japan. *Public Management Review*, 8(4): 567–581, doi: 10.1080/14719030601022965.

Turrini, A., Cristofoli, D., Frosini, F., and Nasi, G. (2010). Networking literature about determinants of network effectiveness. *Public Administration*, 88(2): 528–550. doi: 10.1111/j.1467-9299.2009.01791.x.

Useem, M. (1983). Business and politics in the United States and United Kingdom: The origins of heightened political activity of large corporations during the 1970s and early 1980s. *Theory and Society*, 12(3): 281–308.

Uusikylä, P. and Valovirta, V. (2007). Three spheres of performance governance spanning the boundaries from single-organization focus towards a partnership network. *Evaluation*, 13(4): 399–419.

Uzzi, B. (1996). The sources and consequences of embeddedness for the economic performance of organizations: The network effect. *American Sociological Review*, 61(4): 674–698.

Uzzi, B. (1997). Social structure and competition in interfirm networks: The paradox of embeddedness. *Administrative Science Quarterly*, 42(1): 35.

Van Bueren, E. M., Klijn, E.-H., and Koppenjan, J. F. M. (2003). Dealing with wicked problems in networks: Analyzing an environmental debate from a network perspective. *Journal of Public Administration Research and Theory*, 13(2): 193–212, doi: 10.1093/jpart/mug017.

Vangen, S. and Huxham, C. (2003). Enacting leadership for collaborative advantage: Dilemmas of ideology and pragmatism in the activities of partnership managers. *British Journal of Management*, 14(December): S61–S76, doi: 10.1111/j.1467-8551.2003.00393.x.

Van Raak, A., Meijer, E., Meijer, A., and Paulus, A. (2005). Sustainable partnerships for integrated care: The role of decision making and its environment. *International Journal of Health Planning & Management*, 20: 159–180.

Van Raak, A., Paulus, A., Cuijpers, R., and Veldec, C. T. (2008). Problems of integrated palliative care: A Dutch case study of routines and cooperation in the region of Arnhem. *Health & Place*, 14(4): 768–778.

Van Raak, A., Paulus, A., and Mur-Veeman, I. (2005). Why do health and social care providers co-operate? *Health Policy*, 74(1): 13–23.

Van Wijk, R., Jansen, J. J. P., and Lyles, M. A. (2008). Inter- and intra-organizational knowledge transfer: A meta-analytic review and assessment of its antecedents and consequences. *Journal of Management Studies*, 45(4): 830–853, doi: 10.1111/j.1467-6486.2008.00771.x.

Vincent, S. (2008). A transmutation theory of inter-organizational exchange relations and networks: Applying critical realism to analysis of collective agency. *Human Relations*, 61(6): 875–899, doi: 10.1177/0018726708092408.

Vollenberg, M., Kenis, P., and Raab, J. (2007). Provan and Milward 1995 revisited: A case-study on network structure and network effectiveness of a Dutch mental health care network. Paper presented at the 9th Public Management Research Conference, 25–27 October.

Wells, R. and Weiner, B. J. (2007). Adapting a dynamic model of interorganizational cooperation to the health care sector. *Medical Care Research and Review*, 64(5): 518–543, doi: 10.1177/1077558707301166.

Wenger, E. (2000). Communities of practice: The organizational frontier. *Harvard Business Review*, January/February: 139–145.

Williams, P. (2002). The competent boundary spanner. *Public Administration*, 80(1): 103–124, doi: 10.1111/1467-9299.00296.

Wong, S.-S. (2008). Judgments about knowledge importance: The roles of social referents and network structure. *Human Relations*, 61(11): 1565–1591, doi: 10.1177/0018726708096638.

Zahner, S. (2005). Local public health system partnerships. *Public Health Reports*, 120(January/February): 76–83.

Zolkiewski, J. (2001). The complexity of power relationships within a network. In *Proceedings of the 17th IMP International Conference, Oslo, Norway*.

Zukoski, A. and Shortell, S. (2001). Keys to building effective community partnerships. *Health Forum Journal*, 44(5) (September/October): 23–25.

CHAPTER 20

....

PUBLIC–PRIVATE PARTNERSHIPS IN HEALTH CARE

....

SIMON BISHOP AND JUSTIN WARING

INTRODUCTION

....

SINCE the mid-1990s, public–private partnerships (PPPs) have become a prominent feature of public service reform. Internationally, PPPs can now be found across many areas of public service renewal and development, from major transport or energy infrastructure projects to provision of local libraries and community services. One of the most significant and contentious areas in which PPPs have become commonplace is in the organization and delivery of health care. Health care systems across the world are increasingly turning to PPPs as a means of securing new investment and funding, expanding service capacity, fostering competition and choice, bringing about efficiencies and cost savings, and for stimulating innovation and improvement. PPPs have come in many guises but generally involve public and private sector actors coming together to jointly engage in one or more of the activities that make up the delivery of health care services. This has included projects focused on infrastructure development with public–private agreements over the financing, design, construction, and/or operation of new health care facilities, as well as projects focused on cross-sector delivery of clinical services. As one prominent example, the private finance initiative (PFI), whereby the private sector is contracted to finance, construct, and maintain health care facilities, has been adopted around the world including in Mexico, Australia, Canada, and across Europe (Hodge, Greve, and Boardman, 2010). However, many other models of health care PPP have now been developed including for the provision community health programmes such as in South Africa and Botswana (Marek et al., 2005) as well as for the delivery of hospital services such as in Spain, Portugal, Sweden, and the UK (Acerete, Stafford, and Stapleton, 2011).

This chapter provides an introduction to PPPs and outlines key tensions in the management of PPPs in health care, given the influence of established sectoral and professional boundaries, cultures, and identities. The chapter draws upon both international literature and findings from the authors' own case studies of two PPPs, both Independent Sector Treatment Centres (ISTCs) operating in the English National Health Service (NHS) (Waring, Currie, and Bishop, 2013). The chapter first outlines the policy history and drivers of PPPs, and outlines central concerns and debates at the general level. The chapter then considers PPPs within the context of health care, highlighting particular challenges of governance, innovation, culture, and employment management. These sections include key areas of consideration for health care managers, and public managers more broadly, engaged in the organization and delivery of services through PPPs.

INTRODUCTION TO PPPS

Context of PPP Development

Over the past 20 years, public–private partnerships (PPPs) have become part of the mainstream policy approach to addressing myriad challenges of public service finance, governance, and delivery (Hodge, Greve, and Boardman, 2010; Grimsey and Lewis, 2007). Although PPPs are often thought of as a contemporary phenomenon, prior to the rise of centrally managed economies in the twentieth century, the boundaries between public and private were often blurred; economic, humanitarian, and military ventures have involved a mix of state power and private finance over many centuries (Wettenhall, 2005, 2010). Contemporary PPPs are, however, most frequently examined as a product of the neo-liberal economic and political trends that rose to prominence in the early 1980s; an era which saw the power and legitimacy of the State to act monopolistically compressed (Davies, 2014). Correspondingly, this period saw an elevated belief in the private sector, via the renewed freedoms of the marketplace, to deliver economic prosperity as well as social value (Palley, 2004). In a number of the world's largest economies this resulted in both the privatization of national assets and a move towards new public management (NPM) in the remaining public sector (Hood, 1991).

During the 1980s governmental and policy actors in the US began to proclaim efficacy for new forms of collaboration between the public and the private sector to deliver social goods, particularly in projects of urban renewal and for infrastructure development (Osborne, 2002; Yescombe, 2011). PPP began to be advocated at the international level by organizations such as the World Bank, the International Monetary Fund, and the Organisation for Economic Co-operation and Development to further the involvement of private capital in public services provision (Parker and Figueira, 2010). This was also supported by international trade agreements and regulatory reforms, which have increasingly opened up national public services to global private sector investment and competition (Price, Pollock, and Shaoul, 1999). A further key development came in the form of the private finance initiative (PFI), first introduced in the UK in 1992 as a means of stimulating service development through private investment while controlling short-term public borrowing or tax increases. Early PFI schemes typically involved private financing, design and construction of new buildings and facilities, to be leased back to the public sector in long-term agreements of up to 30 years (Broadbent, Gill, and Laughlin, 2003). During the latter half of the 1990s and the early 2000s, these schemes became a central part of both the expansion and "modernization" of public services, and used to fund transport, health, education, and prison developments (Edwards and Shaoul, 2003). By 2009, contracts for 641 PFI projects had been signed in the UK, valued at some £273.8 mllion (Hellowell, 2010).

Outside the US and UK, other Anglo-Saxon countries including Canada, Australia, and New Zealand also saw a rapid growth in the number of PPP projects over the 1990s and 2000s (Flinders, 2010), with long-term "PFI"-like contracts signed for infrastructure developments across a number of public service domains. For example, in Canada 30 PFI type projects were signed between 2000 and 2009, ranging in value from CAD$27 million for a water treatment plant to CAD$1.9 billion for a rapid transit line (Boardman and Vining, 2010). Over the same period, Australia has established 49 projects totalling AUS$32.2 billion in roads, airports, hospitals, and schools as well as other areas (Hodge and Duffield, 2010). Although the UK has been to date the dominant adopter of PPPs in Europe (accounting for 57.7% of European projects by value in 2007 (Blanc-Brude, Goldsmith, and Välilä, 2007)), over the past ten years there has been a general growth in the number of projects across the continent, with southern European and Scandinavian countries more heavily involved than countries in western and northern Europe (Hammerschmid and Ysa, 2010). PPPs have also now been widely adopted in developing and post-communist countries such as in Poland, often seen as an important source of investment and a key route to national development as well as public sector reform (Osborne, 2002).

MEANINGS OF PPP

A number of rationales have underpinned the promotion and adoption of PPPs. These include the need for new sources of public investment, increasing utilization of scarce resources, improving efficiency through market mechanisms, importing private-sector knowledge to the public sector, and sharing of public risk (Vining and Boardman, 2008). In defining PPPs, some have put forward a normative view of the "true-spirit" of partnership, including characteristics such as high-trust relationships between sectors, collaborative decision-making, joint management, and an equitable sharing of risk (Bovaird, 2006; Entwistle and Martin, 2005; Klijn and Teisman, 2005). Brinkerhoff and Brinkerhoff (2011) propose mutuality, shared responsibility, commitment to shared goals, a common organizational identity, and aligning of distinctive and valuable competences as essential elements for partnership working. Many commentators have seen PPPs as indicative of a new "hybrid" form of governance, sitting between purely market-based forms of control on one hand and fully integrated public bureaucracy on the other (Powell et al., 2005). This has led to suggestions that PPPs are one part of an ongoing shift towards more "network" forms of public service governance, characterized by cross-boundary and multi-agency working and the potential for reciprocity and cooperation between actors of all sectors to provide public goods (Rhodes, 1997; Diamond and Liddle, 2005).

In practice, the language of PPP has been applied very widely, used to describe many varieties of mixed public–private collaboration "no matter how short term or insignificant" (Field and Peck, 2003, 496) and regardless of whether "ideal" criteria for partnership have been met (Linder, 1999; Hodge and Greve, 2005). For example, the label of PPP has been applied to consortiums in which public and private sector organizations invest and work together on the regeneration of a geographic area (Kort and Klijn, 2011), but it has also been applied to contractual arrangements in which a private contractor provides services to predetermined financial and quality criteria (Hodge and Duffield, 2010). Further, the PPP label has also been applied to instances in which non-government organizations (NGOs) such as UNICEF are supported by private actors through philanthropic donations or resource sharing (Bull, 2010). The meaning of PPP is also confused by the fact that that different countries and industries have their own historical and institutional norms of collaboration between sectors (Hodge, Greve, and Boardman, 2010). In countries with relatively market-based welfare regimes, such as in the US, collaboration between public agencies and private business is relatively common; whereas more social democratic nations have traditional maintained a division between public and private sectors in the provision of welfare service (Esping-Anderson, 1990).

To clarify the understanding of PPPs, a number of typologies have been proposed which identify categories of PPP based on how roles, responsibilities and risks are shared between the public and private actors. Gidman et al. (1995) suggest a range of relationships between the public and private sector, from passive private sector investment in the state, through various levels of joint venture and contracting arrangements, to governmental support for private sector growth. Hodge and Greve (2007) distinguish PPPs by the degree to which they involve either "tight" or "loose" forms of collaboration between the public and private partners. For example, "issue networks" involve relatively loose forms of collaboration amongst actors with significant common interests. "PFI" or "contract-based" PPPs on the other hand involve tight financial contracts but looser inter-organizational operational relationships. Within this latter category, the nature of contractual relationships is further commonly distinguished by which activities are taken on by the private sector, with projects identified by an array of terms such as "Finance, Build, Operate" (FBO), or "Build, Operate, Own, Transfer" (BOOT). Waring, Currie, and Bishop (2013) develop the tight/loose distinction by identifying three linked dimensions in which PPP activities been seen to vary. The first relates to the relative level of public and private *financing and risk sharing*, the second relates to the level of each partners involvement in *strategic planning and design* and the third relates to additional *resource sharing* such as through joining management capabilities, human resources, IS, or governance arrangements. While such typologies provide the basis of comparison and analysis, it should also be noted that the nature of inter-organizational relations within any single PPP may be multifarious—as multiple partners from different institutional backgrounds come together—as well as open to contingent change over time (Lowndes and Skelcher, 1998).

DEBATES AND CONTROVERSIES

Although now widespread, PPPs have been a controversial policy development for a number of reasons. First, many have questioned the long-term value for public money of partnership agreements, particularly those which lock the public sector into long-term contracts, unable to take account of future changes to the market. Although such agreements spread the cost of new infrastructure over the lifetime of the project, this is usually at the expense of an increased cost of borrowing (Yescombe, 2011) and large questions remain about how the overall economic costs and benefits of PPP projects—including externalities—should be calculated (Boardman and Vining, 2010). Underlining this debate, a number of PFI projects have been found to involve inequitable sharing of risk, offering poor value for money and leaving public sector organizations with high levels of debt (Edwards and Shaoul, 2003; Toms, Beck, and Asenova, 2011). A second area of critique has been around the ability of public and private organizations to overcome institutional differences to engage in "true" partnership working. Embedded characteristics of the public sector, such as the need for political control of projects, contrast with those of the private sector, such as profit maximization and the avoidance of risk, meaning that there is always likely to be a separation of responsibilities and a reliance on explicit formal contract terms inhibiting open sharing of resources and risks (Klijn and Teisman, 2003). A third area of controversy has been around the values and ethos promoted by PPPs, with some case study evidence suggesting that the growth of PPP contracts have led to a reduction in the capacity of public servants to work in the public interest, limiting the scope for individual discretion and professional autonomy in the face of strict contractual and performance criteria (Smith, 2012). Alongside other NPM reforms, PPPs have been argued to undermine the moral purpose of public organizations by promoting economic rationality above other principles and values (Fevre, 2003; Davies, 2014). Fourth, questions have also been raised about the outcome quality in PPPs, particularly in circumstances in which they are seen to promote cost-reduction over maintaining or improving quality (Hebson, Grimshaw, and Marchington, 2003)

Given this controversy, PPPs have faced strong political and public resistance leading, in places, to the approach being reined in. At the same time, many of the long-term PPP projects signed during the 1990s and 2000s have several years left to run. Further, in times of fiscal constraint it appears likely that governments will continue to look to the private sector for both investment and to stimulate cost-saving reform, including through engaging in changing forms of partnership with the private sector. Turning now to the field of health care, we consider the basis and implications for the changing relationship between the public and private sector, and consider the challenges in managing health services within an environment of PPPs.

INTRODUCTION TO HEALTH CARE PPPs

In line with the trends identified above, PPPs have become a prominent and contentious feature of health care reform. Health care PPPs are often premised on the idea that neither public nor private sector can adequately meet the manifold challenges of ageing populations, an increase in chronic "lifestyle" diseases, assimilating new treatments technologies and the need to control public health care spending. Through new forms of collaboration, it is suggested that health care PPPs can expand access, coverage, and provision of health care, support investment for the future, engender innovation, and improve the experiences of patient and clinicians.

As with PPPs across public service sectors, forms of collaboration between the public and private sector in health care have been highly varied. Significant differences can be observed, for example, in the experience of the developing (low and middle income) and developed (high income) nations. In developing countries across Africa, the Indian sub-continent and the Caribbean, PPPs have been seen as addressing long-standing gaps in health care provision, including a lack of funding, uneven levels of coverage, limited access to specialist clinicians, medicines, or technologies, and outdated hospital infrastructure. Developing new forms of partnership between government actors and both for-profit and non-profit organizations has been seen as essential for addressing global health challenges, such as vaccines for infectious diseases and improving access to health services (Nishtar, 2004). In India, a range of significant developments in primary, community, specialist, and remote (tele-) care services have been established through PPPs (Raman and Björkman, 2008). These combine long-term public financing for public health care, with extended opportunities for private care providers to offer both public and private health care under contract, with some evidence to show improved access and care standards for poor communities (Ghanashyam, 2008). Similarly, Downs et al. (2013) argue that partnership working in Lesotho has enabled the country to develop new hospital infrastructure in a relatively short period of time that has enhanced the quality and standards of care for local populations.

In developed countries, PPPs are commonly advocated as a way of addressing the rising demand for health care services (Barrows et al., 2011), adding to the "mix" of available forms of funding and delivery. Here PPPs have commonly taken the form of investment in new acute-care infrastructure, as seen in Spain, New Zealand, and Australia (Acerete, Stafford, and Stapleton, 2011; Barrows et al., 2011), but can also involve novel collaborative approaches to developing, managing, and carrying out clinical services (Waring, Currie, and Bishop, 2013). Differences in the trajectory along which countries have moved to adopt new forms of PPP can in part be related to the established mix of public and private actors involved in the provision of the countries health care services. In countries such as the US or Canada, where health care services have historically been financed and provided through a combination of public and private channels, the premise of partnership working is less considered a divergent break from the past. Similarly, in European countries with public health insurance "Bismark" systems of health care, such as Germany, France, the Netherlands, and Belgium, there has traditionally been a wide range of actors, including private, for-profit, and charitable organization involved in commissioning, funding, and providing health care services over the long term. Although the mix between public and private provision in each of these countries has changed over time, for example with an increase in private provision in Germany since reunification (Maarse, 2006), a long-standing legitimate role for private providers has meant there has been less policy emphasis on PPP to bring new providers into these markets. There are however some exceptions to this with several PFI-type schemes for health care established in France and the Netherlands (Acerete, Stafford, and Stapleton, 2011; Hodge, Greve, and Boardman, 2010).

In countries where health services have traditionally been funded, owned, and provided directly by the state, such as the UK, Australia, New Zealand, and Scandinavia, there has been a greater pressure on governments to pluralize supply and bring new actors into the health economy. These countries have been particularly active in trialing PPPs and have introduced a range of new intersectoral arrangements. This has commonly included PFI-type contracts for new health care facilities but has also included a number of country-specific developments (Hodge, Greve, and Boardman, 2010; Maarse, 2006; McKee, Edwards, and Atun, 2006). For example in Sweden there has been an emphasis on hospital franchising whereby entire public hospitals have been taken over by private companies to manage both the estates and the clinical services as part of the publicly funded health provision (Sveman and Essinger, 2001). Similarly, southern European countries such as Portugal, Spain, and Italy have also been active in adopting PFI schemes for hospital building, partially as a response to severe restrictions in central government borrowing. Among these, Spain is notable for developing the "Alzira" model of PPP service provision, named after the area of Valencia in which it was first established. In this model, the private sector finances, builds, and operates hospital and/or primary care facilities as well as provides clinical services under contracts of commonly 15 to 20 years (Global Health Group, 2009). These are funded by capitation payment from the public health budget based on the size of the population served by the facilities. The first of these opened in 1999 led by further contracts in Valencia, Madrid, and Portugal as well as several developing countries, albeit with significant variation in the nature of contracts and services provided in each iteration (Acerete, Stafford, and Stapleton, 2011). The Alzira model has been seen to have played an important role in the development of health care-specific PPPs, including as part of the inspiration for the UK Independent Sector Treatment Centres (Acerete, Stafford, and Stapleton, 2012), which are discussed further below.

Although the adoption of PPPs in health care is widespread, the institutionalized boundaries between public and private sectors can pose particular challenges to policy-makers and service managers. These challenges of organizing and managing across sectoral boundaries are exemplified by the English NHS. Somewhat ironically, the UK is one of the world's leading exponents of health care PPPs, despite widespread public concern about the threat to core service principles and the possibilities of privatization (Pollock, 2006). The NHS was founded in 1948 and since that time has been predominately funded through central taxation, with universal care provided through a largely nationalized care system. For the first 40 years of operation public resources were allocated to public providers through forms of bureaucratic planning, but for the previous 20 years resources have flowed through contracts between commissioners and providers, with an increased emphasis on mixed-market provision. Looking back at the history of the NHS, it is important to also recognize the long-standing role of the private sector in care organization and delivery. This can be seen, for example, in the role of community pharmacies which provide a first point of contact for patients, providing medicines advice and dispensing prescriptions. Furthermore, general practitioners have provided primary care service to the NHS under an independent contract since the inception of the service, meaning that (in technical terms) the majority of patient contacts within the NHS have been provided by private contractor. In addition, specialist NHS doctors can maintain private practice and are able to use both private and public health care facilities to provide this care. As such, the linkages between the public and private sector in the English NHS are perhaps more complicated than often perceived.

That said, over the last 30 years the NHS has been at the forefront of using PPPs as vehicle for service modernization. During this time, the form and function of PPPs has evolved over what we describe as three distinctive time periods, each building on the former. The first period is found in the 1990s where partnership working was primarily concerned with securing new lines of investment in NHS infrastructure without requiring additional taxation or public borrowing. The PFI approach to funding support the construction of new hospital buildings, such as the Norfolk and Norwich University (see Example 1). Under long-term contract, the PFI programme allowed consortia of private contractors to fund, design, and construct new buildings (National Audit Office, 2005). This model has since been extended to include major infrastructure projects, such as University College Hospital, London.

The second period corresponds with the 2000s where the PFI model was extended to allow for new forms of partnership working in the management of infrastructure as well as the co-delivery of frontline services including pre-existing NHS care pathways and clinical teams. This was initially outlined in the *NHS Plan* (Department of Health (DH), 2001) which set out a long-term strategy to tackle the endemic problems of under-capacity, lack of choice and lack of competition within the NHS though allowing private providers to work within the NHS system. A prominent example is the introduction of Independent Sector Treatment Centres (ISTCs) for the delivery of high-demand, low-risk elective diagnostic and treatments services, such as day surgery. These could be wholly or partly owned and managed by a private provider, which were also under contract to provide clinical services in coordination with the wider public health care system. Approximately 50 such centres were set up in the 2000s during two distinct waves of contracting, with most contracts set to run for an initial period of five years.

The third stage of PPPs in the NHS follows reforms outlined in the 2010 White Paper *Equity and Excellence* (DH, 2010), which effectively creates a more open and competitive market of care provision within the NHS. Since this point, a large number of primary and community health care services have been made available for open tender to private and social enterprise providers. This has seen both a significant re-designation of services, especially community services as social enterprises, as well as a number of private contractors winning contracts to provide a range of specialist support services, such as Care UK and Virgin Healthcare. The central government emphasis is now less on collaborative working and more on competition between public and private organizations, with sections of the NHS workforce often being transferred to the management of private or social enterprises. At the same time, the nature of health care service delivery across complex pathways of care necessitates close ongoing relationships between organizations of all sectors.

The evolution of health care PPPs over time means that examples of PPP projects can be found across the range of partnership configurations, from relatively "loose" financial or funding arrangements providing acute and primary care infrastructure to more "tight" joint ventures where there is "full service" partnership working across service financing, planning, and delivery. The wide spectrum of arrangements now in operation provides an opportunity to examine a wide range of issues central to a critical analysis of PPPs at a more general level, including "upstream" governance issues, such as how contractual obligations are determined or risks allocated, as well as "downstream" management and organization issues, such as how care pathways are configured or clinical teams managed. Focusing particularly on the context of the English NHS, the remainder of the chapter considers these issues by outlining four organizational and management challenges brought about by the introduction of PPPs in health care; governance and accountability; management culture and identity; managing workforce and employment; and managing learning and innovation.

Example 1 Norfolk and Norwich University Hospital

Norfolk and Norwich University hospital was the first example of a large-scale PFI arrangement for the construction of new hospital facilities within the NHS. In 1996 approval was given for partnership between the NHS Trust and Octagon Consortium to construct a new 809 bed hospital, with a second stage approved in 2000. The consortium comprised a number of private sector design, construction and support service providers, including John Laing plc, Anshen and Allen, WSP Group, Hoare Lea and Serco. The new hospital was opened 2001 ahead of schedule and on budget, and has since attracted several awards for its design. Under the arrangement, Norfolk and Norwich University Hospital NHS Trust pays the private consortium an annual fee for the use of the facilities which include charges for estates management, maintenance and support services, such as catering, portering and cleaning. In 2004 the Association of Chartered Certified Accountants estimated that over the 35 life of contractual arrangement the cost of the partnership could reach over £1.1 billion, as compared to the £229 million required to build the hospital.

Example 2 University College Hospital, London

University College Hospital is one of several hospital sites managed by University College London Hospitals (UCLH) NHS Foundation Trust. The state-of-the-art 665-bed hospital was opened in 2005 providing an extensive range of acute and specialist services, such as emergency medicine, hyper-acute stroke, and cancer care. The new hospital facilities were developed through one of the biggest public–private partnership arrangements in the English NHS, initially comprising a Private Finance Initiative to fund, design, and build the hospital and now includes an ongoing contractual arrangement with a private partner for the provision of support and facilities management. The PPP was established in 2000 between UCLH and a newly formed partner organization Health Management (UCLH) plc. This partner organization involve a consortium of several leading private sector contractors including AMEC, Balfour Beatty, and Interserve, and invested over £4,200 million in developing the new hospital. This partnership arrangement ensured the provision of the necessary financial resources to fund the project together with specialist services design and construction, project management and facilities management. Interserve continues to provide a range of services to the NHS Foundation Trust as a part of its role in facilities management, including restaurant and café services, portering, domestic services, laundry, waste management, and security.

Example 3 Circle Partnership

Circle Partnership was formed in the late 2000s. It was established on the basis of mutual ownership, through an initial investment partnership of health care professionals, mostly doctors working in the NHS. As the partnership expanded additional private equity investment was secured and the partnership was rebranded as Circle. The partnership's early activities focused on the provision of low-risk, high-volume elective services within Independent Sector Treatment Centres. These centres were introduced in the mid-2000s with the aim of reducing waiting and expanding NHS provision for high demand services based upon contractual partnership with private providers. Circle Partnership acquired the contracts of existing private providers and assumed operational responsibility for three ISTCs. In most instances the facilities and resources involved are co-finance or subsidized through public health care agencies. In addition, many of these services involved the transfer or secondment of NHS employees to the management of Circle partnership. Since this time, the partnership has secured the contracts for several other NHS acute and diagnostic services and opened its own private health care facilities. In 2012, Circle Partnership made history within the NHS by winning the management franchise contract to operate an established NHS acute hospital. Under existing NHS management arrangements the hospital had been identified as poor performing and the decision was made to give Circle Partnership to assume management responsibilities, but where the estates, facilities, and workforce remain NHS.

Example 4 Care UK

Care UK are a well-established private sector provider of health care in the UK, being founded in 1982, especially in the development and management of primary care services. The scale and scope of their services have increased significantly since the early 2000s to become one of the largest private providers on health and social care, often working in partnership with local NHS commissioners and provider organizations. There areas of service provision include a range of NHS service under contract with commissioners, including GP and diagnostic service; health and social care for the elderly, such as care homes and day care centres; a range of learning disability services; and community mental health services, such as eating disorder clinics.

Example 5 Virgin Care

Virgin is a well-known global brand in the area of aviation, rail, telephony, and media and leisure services. In the mid-2000s, Virgin acquired a stake in Assura Medical services, a company that specialized in developing primary and community estates and facilities. By the late 2000s, Assura Medical Service brought within the Virgin Group and started managing walk-in centres to expand the provision of urgent care. In 2011, Assura Medical was rebranded as Virgin Care and since this time has grown to manage and provide over 200 community health and social care services across England under contractual arrangement with NHS commissioners. This includes, for example, an extensive range of community services, younger people's service, sexual health services, GP and urgent care services, and prison health services. Virgin Care illustrates a contractual partnership arrangement whereby it competes with or acquires existing NHS providers to secure contracts with local care commissioners.

MANAGEMENT CHALLENGES

Governance and Accountability

The challenge of governance has been a central concern in the adoption of PPPs. Involving private sector organizations in the provision of public services requires a degree of authority to be distributed outside the bounds of integrated public bureaucracies. Forms of governance are therefore required which on the one hand allow private actors sufficient autonomy to develop innovations and introduce change in line with public interests, but on the other hand provide adequate controls to protect each party from opportunistic behavior of others in the partnership (Skelcher, 2010). In a number of high-profile health care PPPs it has been seen that asymmetries of information have lead the public sector to over-pay for services provided by the private sector (Shaoul, Stafford, and Stapleton, 2008), or have even locked the state into paying large sums for services for which there is insufficient demand or are no longer required (Pollock and Godden, 2008). Equally, examples have been identified in which public managers engage in restrictive or controlling forms of contract management over private contractors (Grimshaw, Vincent, and Willmott, 2002). A key governance challenge therefore is the equitable balancing of risk and reward, with managers on both sides required to evaluate exposure to risk and remain cautious in evaluating partners (Grimsey and Lewis, 2007). This has required significant changes to the skills and knowledge of public managers, who are obliged to operate in an increasingly commercialized and contract-based environment and to scrutinize financial and contractual terms (English, 2005).

Skelcher (2010) identifies four distinct facets of governance important to consider. First, the legal basis for the partnership, with a number of potential forms available including limited company, public consortium, or memorandum of association. Choosing a suitable legal form requires consideration of the aims of the parties involved and sets the character collaborative working, whether open-ended or tightly proscribed. Second, the regulatory rules and systems which control the relationship between partners require consideration. These are commonly enshrined in the PPP contract which details the agreed obligations, systems of interaction and reporting, incentives, and penalties. Here there has been an advocacy of "relational" or partnership contracting which emphasizes mutual interests and allow greater scope for informal settlements and shared decision-making (Bovaird, 2006). Studies have though also shown how embedded institutional differences between NHS organizations and private health care providers lead to difficulties in establishing such open-ended, trusting relationships, with contract management frequently involving recourse to contractual terms (Hebson, Grimshaw, and Marchington, 2003). The third important facet of governance is the democratic aspect, which relates to the degree of accountability and transparency extended to private actors. In health care, there has been a strong critique that external providers are not open to the same level of scrutiny as public bodies, with commercial confidentiality limiting public access to information on organizational processes and decision-making (Pollock, 2006). Fourth, PPPs are also affected by the distinct corporate governance of the partners involved. A number of private health care companies working with the NHS, such as Circle Health care Partnerships, have sought to emphasize forms of socially orientated corporate governance and codes of ethics which align them with the interests of patients and staff. However, there has so far been little research in this area.

In the authors' own studies of ISTCs, we have also seen how the divisions of accountability and control can emerge informally in the development and operation of partnership arrangements (Waring, Currie, and Bishop, 2013). While elements of contract governance were established in the planning phase of the ISTCs, there remained considerable scope for norms of interaction and reporting, as well as divisions of accountability and control, to be shaped over the course of the agreement. For example, the extent to which legal or punitive aspects of contracts needed to be enforced was dependent on the nature of relationships between contract managers in the NHS and counterparts within the private providers. These relationships in turn were dependent on a number of locally contingent factors, including the opportunities for interpersonal communication, the changing local political attitudes to private sector involvement, as well as the market positioning of the ISTC companies. As new service providers, the private companies involved in our study sites were each keen to demonstrate compliance with central government audit and local contractual requirements in order to establish legitimacy as NHS partners. However, we also saw how the approach to achieving this compliance varied between ISTC sites and over time. Moreover, in other circumstances private partners' aims and interests may be served by following other approaches to contract engagement (Edwards and Shaoul, 2003) and engaging in PPPs requires public managers to consider appropriate forms of governance to promote the equitable sharing of risk (Skelcher, 2010).

Managing Innovation

In various ways, PPPs are advocated as bringing about innovation and improvement in the organization and delivery of public services. As well as being presented as an innovation in themselves, PPPs are also described in policy documents as engendering innovation through the opportunities afforded for public and private organizations to share previously siloed resources and capabilities. Public sector partners can contribute specialist professional or technical expertise or greater appreciation of public need, and private partners can offer the business acumen and experiences in commercial sectors. From this view, PPPs are indicative of a form of innovation through hybridity; that is the recombination of character traits into a new mode of service organization (Billis, 2010; Waring and Bishop, 2014).

Further, PPPs are described as fostering ongoing innovation and improvement in the day-to-day organization of public service, in part because private businesses are assumed to be dynamic and responsive to external change, and also because PPPs are expected to create new opportunities for knowledge sharing between public service professionals and providers. A significant body of research shows how sectoral, organizational, and professional boundaries within "traditional" health care organizations can stymie innovation and implementation of new technologies or evidence (Cooksey 2007; Ferlie et al., 2005). PPPs are seen as a means of stimulating the formation of new clinical communities through which more productive, integrated and patient-centered services can be developed. For example, the Confederation of British Industry (CBI, 2008) describe a number of innovations brought about by partnership working between the NHS and private industry including reduced "backroom" administration in areas such as patient booking, realigned human resources to develop more productive clinical processes, and utilized quality assurance methodologies to reduce waste and enhance productivity.

Despite these claims, whether health care PPPs do indeed represent a radical innovation and improvement in health care organization requires critical examination. In their study of Independent Sector Treatment Centres, for example, Gabbay et al. (2011) suggest radical building designs, stark aesthetic improvements, and the abundance of the new technologies are not necessarily reflected in new ways of working. In other words, innovation might be more "style over substance" aimed at giving the impression of being distinct from traditional NHS services and like other retail sectors, but without necessarily changing the core business of care. Similarly, case studies by the authors suggest innovation in health care PPPs can be limited to establishing more efficient, standardized, and low risk services; where care service become less specialized or differentiated but align instead with highly standardized service models and templates (Waring, Currie, and Bishop, 2013). In these cases, radical innovation was not necessarily welcomed by PPP leaders because of its potentially de-stabilizing effect on relatively standardized services, and opportunities for change were only welcomed when directed towards increased management control.

Looking further at the nature of innovation within PPPs, the author's studies also describe a difference between those based upon the "top-down" transfer of business and management practices, and those based upon "bottom-up" learning amongst clinical teams (Waring, Currie, and Bishop, 2013). Our research found a greater proclivity for PPP leaders to introduce strategies or approaches that had been tried and tested in other settings and, as suggested above, aligned primarily to the goal of enhanced productivity rather than creating space for bottom-up learning and innovation. By promoting more standardized approaches to care, PPPs can have the effect of potentially de-skilling staff in more narrow roles rather than encouraging broader development and advanced learning. Where this has been specifically studied, health care PPPs have been found not to engender the type of learning environment anticipated by policy makers (Turner et al., 2011). Somewhat paradoxically, Turner et al.'s (2011) comparative study found PPPs did produce innovation, but not within the new organizations; rather it was the existing NHS hospitals who sought to innovate existing service models and care in the face of new competition.

Managing Culture and Values

A significant challenge faced by PPPs relates to the underlying cultural and ideological characteristics that have distinguished public and private sectors and potentially inhibit collaboration. Public and private sectors are typically associated with having distinct funding arrangements, accountability systems, client relations, and modes of working. These are reflected in, and reinforced by, the idea that each sector is characterized by a particular culture, manifest in systems of meanings, beliefs, values, norms, and routines. Although public service reforms over the last three decades have arguably blurred these distinctions (Boyne, 2002), it remains the case that PPPs face intractable differences in managing cultural difference and conflict. In the US, Perry and Wise (1990) suggest public service employees are motivated by an attraction to public governance, civic duty, compassion, and self-sacrifice. In the UK context, Pratchett and Wingfield (1996) describe public sector organization as characterized by an ethos of political accountability, bureaucratic behavior, public interest, and loyalty. These cultural attributes potentially conflict with the beliefs, motives, and values that inform private sector work, such as competitive behavior, enterprise and entrepreneurship, accountability to share-holders, and private value.

A key challenge faced by PPPs is therefore how to recognize, cope with, and manage cultural differences. For example, inherent differences between sectors mean that build-ing sufficient trust for meaningful cooperation can take significant time and effort (Klijn and Teisman, 2005); a number of case studies in health care organizations have shown productive relationships have failed to develop resulting in significant frustration and waste on both sides (Grimshaw, Vincent, and Willmott, 2002). Public sector managers have been found to act defensively in light of perceived profit-motivated behavior of pri-vate sector counterparts and private sector managers may be faced with the need to fos-ter behavioral and identity change amongst resistant public sector professional-grade employees (Waring, Currie, and Bishop 2013).

Looking at the experiences of public sector clinicians involved in health care PPPs, the authors' studies found four prominent points of cultural difference between NHS staff and their private sector partners (Waring and Bishop, 2010; Waring, Currie, and Bishop, 2013). The first related to the perceived goals or purpose of the service. Public sector clinicians advocated individual patient care as an end in itself, they perceived private partners as motivated to make a profit, with patient care a means to this end. Second, public sector clinicians often perceived the broader ethos or ideology of care as a pub-lic good, and contributing to societal well-being. In contrast, PPPs can be experienced as advancing private interest and value ahead of the public good. In other cases, PPPs have been seen as displacing or subverting the underlying goals and ideals of public sec-tor workers (Hebson, Grimshaw, and Marchington, 2003). Third, clinicians described a shift in the norms and customs of day-to-day work with a shift from more collegial and team based practices towards more standardized, machine-like modes of working. This shift towards standardization and rationalization was seen as reflecting the pursuit for efficiency at the expense of service quality and patient safety (Waring and Bishop, 2011). Finally, work in these PPPs was also felt to change patterns of accountability and responsibility, with emphasis given to contractual obligations and performance indica-tors ahead of patient experience of professional judgments (Bishop and Waring, 2011). Again, this was seen as stemming from the PPPs more consumerist and commercial approach. Together these cultural differences were seen as transforming the sense of public professionalism shared by many frontline clinicians (Waring and Bishop, 2010).

Managing Employment

The rise of PPPs has been seen to have a number of implications for both the manage-ment of work and the nature of employment in health care. Prior to market reforms of the 1990s and 2000s the NHS was traditionally seen as both a highly integrated and cen-trally governed employer. This picture has changed in recent years to one characterized by increasingly local flexibility for management to shape employment within national frameworks. For example, the New Labour government's program of "workforce modernization" included general guidelines for "best practice" employment while advocating the rationalization of work roles with increased emphasis on organizational level management actively aligning technical skills with tasks in ways which broke from traditional professional groupings. In bringing new private sector organizations into the health care economy, PPPs could be seen as furthering a move away from nationally standardized employment conditions and practices towards a system with increasing flexibility for the nature of employment to be determined within the organization. This potentially allows management greater control of employment and allows them to "fit" human resource management practices to the nature of activities being undertaken, local operating circumstances, available resources, ambitions for organizational culture, or strategic intent. However, while reforming public service employment has been stated as one of the policy aspirations for expanding the PPP programme (DH, 2006), research has also shown how a number of complexities and operating difficulties surface as relationships between the public and private sector are established.

A sizable body of work has shown managing employment across networks of close inter-organizational relationships can cause difficulties for both management and employees (Marchington et al., 2004; Rubery et al., 2004). PPP projects have been seen to introduce considerable complexity in the structure of public service delivery with lines of hierarchy and accountability fragmented into increasingly complex sets of inter-organizational arrangements (Forrer et al., 2010). Engaging in sub-contracting, outsourcing, and tight partnership arrangements can mean that the control of, and responsibility for, employment can become distorted, introducing a break in the link between control of employment, line management, and work practice. For example, in certain PPPs arrangements public sector staff see their work either fully or partially transferred to private partners, albeit with their terms and conditions of employment protected by the contractual terms of partnership (through detailing the specifications of staffing levels and skill mix required to maintain quality) and/or wider employment regulations. In these circumstances, managers within the private partner may find themselves unable to make explicit changes to the employment of the staff transferred to them from the public sector and constrained in terms of their ability to shape their human resource management (HRM) systems internally, having to negotiate any changes with "parent" public sector organization. This can also lead to confusion over day-to-day aspects of management, including managers' ability to check the quality of work or manage performance for those employed externally. Even where private partners are able to control employment within their own organizations, close inter-organizational working can still introduce complexity into lines of authority, as for example the staff of subcontractors work on behalf of public managers, but not directly answerable to them.

In addition, PPPs have been seen to introduce a number of forms of employment inconsistency across complex health care "supply chains." A common criticism of new PPP arrangements is that they can introduce a "two-tiered" workforce, whereby private sector and public sector employees are subject to substantively different forms of employment. This can be particularly problematic when staff under different forms of employment share the same workplace, with public and private staff working side-by-side. In early forms of PFI, it was particularly lower status occupational groups such as cleaning, catering, and site services staff who saw their work transferred to the private sector. In later forms of partnership, our own case studies have reported on instances in which private companies directly employ higher status health care professionals, including medical and nursing staff, to work alongside clinical staff who remain on NHS contracts (Bishop and Waring, 2011). These arrangements presented difficulties for management in terms of justifying variations in employment and maintaining the commitment of staff without the ability to harmonize employment terms and conditions. These problems were particularly acute where staff of the same clinical-professional grading worked within the same teams and on the same patients, but with differing systems of management and employment. It should however also be noted that the legitimacy and acceptance of such multi-employer systems could be dependent on wider industry and sectoral norms, and therefore subject to change as more diverse and heterogeneous systems of health care delivery become further established.

Conclusion

In conclusion, various claims for the benefits of PPPs have been made over the years, often centered on notions of efficiency, value for public money, expanding investment or bringing change, and innovation. These claims are particularly appealing for leaders in the health sector, facing serious challenges in light of restricted resources and increasing demand. However, after several years of study, the collected evidence for each of these claims is, at best, mixed. While there have been instances in which PPPs have appeared to deliver on promises, there have been many others which have not. Perhaps as importantly, the appropriate methods of measuring even the economic benefits of PPPs remain disputed (Boardman and Vining, 2010), let alone the wider organizational and cultural aspects of partnership. Moreover, there have been several consequences of PPPs that remain controversial regardless of the outcomes of individual projects, including long-term public indebtedness and fragmentation of public services. In our chapter above, we have described how PPPs present several organizational challenges for managers in both public and private sector organizations as they seek to maintain service continuity whilst introducing innovation and improvement. These are important areas of consideration for health care managers given that the penchant for partnerships continues to expand; in a number of countries around the world, partnerships between the public and private sector are now a core part of how health care services are financed, planned, and delivered.

Surveying the current field of research into health care PPPs, a number of important areas for future research can be proposed. At the macro level, current research has tended to focus on policy developments within individual countries, placing national developments within the international context. There is considerable scope for purposeful comparative work to examine how aspects of the political economy, the regulatory environment, and approaches to public financing interact with policy formulation around PPPs. At the meso level, studies of PPPs have considerable potential to contribute to debates on how new organizational forms are established, for example by considering how tensions between the institutional logics inherent in each sector play out at the inter-organizational level. At the micro level, work is needed to report on the evolving character of PPPs as both providers of essential services and as places of work for public service employees. Both advocacy of and resistance towards PPPs center on the capacity of new organizational arrangements to change behavior; detailed work is therefore needed to examine how and indeed whether this takes place. As PPPs are often years in the making and have been found to evolve over time, each of these areas would benefit from longitudinal work that is able to detail and explore the processes and outcomes of change.

References

Acerete, B., Stafford, A., and Stapleton, P. (2011). Spanish healthcare public private partnerships: The "Alzira model". *Critical Perspectives in Accounting*, 22(6): 533–549.

Acerete, B., Stafford, A., and Stapleton, P. (2012). New development: New global health care PPP developments—a critique of the success story. *Public Money & Management*, 32(4): 311–314.

Anderson, E. (1990). *The three worlds of welfare capitalism*. Cambridge: Polity Press

Barrows, D., MacDonald, I., Supapol, A., Dalton-Jez, O., and Harvey-Rioux, S. (2011). *Public private partnerships in Canadian healthcare: A case study of the Brampton Civic Hospital*. Geneva: OECD.

Billis, D. (ed.) (2010). *Hybrid organizations and the third sector: Challenges for practice, theory and policy*. Basingstoke: Palgrave Macmillan.

Bishop, S. and Waring, J. (2011). Inconsistency in health care professional work: Employment in independent sector treatment centres. *Journal of Health Organization and Management*, 25(3): 315–331.

Blanc-Brude F., Goldsmith H., and Välilä T. (2007). Public–Private Partnerships in Europe: An Update, Economic and Financial Report, EFR 2007-03, EIB.

Boardman, A. and Vining, A. (2010) Assessing the economic worth of public–private partnerships. In *International handbook on public–private partnership*, ed. Hodge, G. A., Greve, C., and Boardman, A. E., pp. 159–186. Cheltenham and Northampton, MA: Edward Elgar Publishing.

Bovaird, T. (2006). Developing new forms of partnership with the "market" in the procurement of public services. *Public Administration*, 84(1): 81–102.

Boyne, G. A. (2002). Public and private management: What's the difference? *Journal of Management Studies*, 39(1): 97–122.

Brinkerhoff, D. W. and Brinkerhoff, J. M. (2011). Public–private partnerships: Perspectives on purposes, publicness, and good governance. *Public Administration and Development*, 31(1): 2–14.

Broadbent, J., Gill, J., and Laughlin, R. (2003). Evaluating the private finance initiative in the National Health Service in the UK. *Accounting, Auditing & Accountability Journal*, 16(3): 422–445.

Bull, B., (2010). "Public–private partnerships: The United Nations experience. In *International handbook on public–private partnership*, Hodge, G. A., Greve, C., and Boardman, A. E., pp. 479–498. Cheltenham and Northampton, MA: Edward Elgar Publishing.

Confederation of British Industry (CBI). (2008). *ISTCs and the NHS*. London: CBI.

Cooksey, D. (2007). *The Cooksey Review*. London: TSO.

Davies, W. (2014). *The limits of neoliberalism, authority sovereignty and the logic of competition*. London: Sage.

Department of Health (DH) (2001). *The NHS plan*. London: TSO.

Department of Health (DH) (2010). *Equity and excellence: Liberating the NHS*. London: TSO.

Diamond, J. and Liddle, J. (2005). *Management of regeneration*. London: Routledge.

Downs, S., Montagu, D., Da Rita, P., Brashers, E., and Feachem, R. G. A. (2013). *Health system innovation in Lesotho: Design and early operations of the Maseru public–private integrated partnership*. Healthcare Public–Private Partnerships Series, No. 1. San Francisco, CA: The Global Health Group, Global Health Sciences, University of California, San Francisco, and PwC.

Edwards, P. and Shaoul, J. (2003). Partnerships: For better, for worse? *Accounting, Auditing & Accountability Journal*, 16(3): 397–421.

English, L. M. (2005). Using public–private partnerships to achieve value for money in the delivery of healthcare in Australia. *International Journal of Public Policy*, 1(1–2): 91–121.

Entwistle, T. and Martin, S. (2005). From competition to collaboration in public service delivery: A new agenda for research. *Public Administration*, 83(1): 233–242.

Esping-Andersen, G. (1990). The three political economies of the welfare state. *International Journal of Sociology*, 20(3): 92–123.

Ferlie, E., Fitzgerald, L., Wood, M., and Hawkins, C. (2005). The nonspread of innovations: The mediating role of professionals. *Academy of Management Journal*, 48(1): 117–134.

Fevre, R. (2003). *The new sociology of economic behaviour*. London: Sage.

Field, J. E. and Peck, E. (2003). Public–private partnerships in healthcare: The managers' perspective. *Health & Social Care in the Community*, 11(6): 494–501.

Flinders, M. (2010). Splintered logic and political debate. In *International handbook on public–private partnership*, ed. Hodge, G. A., Greve, C., and Boardman, A. E., pp. 115–131. Cheltenham and Northampton, MA: Edward Elgar Publishing.

Forrer, J., Kee, J. E., Newcomer, K. E., and Boyer, E. (2010). Public–private partnerships and the public accountability question. *Public Administration Review*, 70(3): 475–484.

Gabbay, J., Le May, A., Pope, C., Robert, G, Bate, P., and Elston, M. (2011). *Organisational innovation in health services*. Bristol: Policy Press

Ghanashyam, B. (2008). Can public–private partnerships improve health in India? *The Lancet*, 372(9642): 878–879.

Gidman, P., Blore, I., Lorentzen, J., and Schuttenbelt, P. (1995). *Public–private partnerships in urban infrastructure services*, UMP Working Paper Series, Vol. 4. Washington, D.C.: UNDP/UNCHS/World Bank-UMP.

Global Health Group (2009). *Public–private investment partnerships: An innovative approach for improving access, quality, and equity in healthcare in developing countries*. San Francisco, CA: Global Health Group, University of California.

Grimsey, D. and Lewis, M. (2007). *Public private partnerships: The worldwide revolution in infrastructure provision and project finance.* Cheltenham and Northampton, MA: Edward Elgar Publishing.

Grimshaw, D., Vincent, S., and Willmott, H. (2002). Going privately: Partnership and out-sourcing in UK public services. *Public Administration,* 80(3): 475–502.

Hammerschmid, G. and Ysa, T. (2010). Empirical PPP experiences in Europe: National varia-tions of a global concept. In *International handbook on public-private partnerships,* ed. Hodge, G. A., Greve, C., and Boardman, A. E., pp. 333–353. Camberley; Cheltenham; Northampton: Edward Elgar.

Hebson, G., Grimshaw, D., and Marchington, M. (2003). PPPs and the changing public sector ethos: Case study evidence from health and local authority sectors. *Work, Employment and Society,* 17(3): 481–501.

Hellowell, M. (2010). The UK's private finance initiative: History, evaluation, prospects. In *International handbook on public–private partnership,* ed. Hodge, G. A., Greve, C., and Boardman, A. E., pp. 307–332. Cheltenham and Northampton, MA: Edward Elgar Publishing.

Hodge, G. and Duffield, C. (2010). The Australian PPP experience: Observations and reflec-tions. In *International handbook on public–private partnership,* ed. Hodge, G. A., Greve, C., and Boardman, A. E., pp. 399–438. Cheltenham and Northampton, MA: Edward Elgar Publishing.

Hodge, G. A. and Greve, C. (2005). PPPs: A policy for all seasons? In *The challenge of public-private partnerships: Learning from international experience,* ed. Hodge, G. and Greve, C., pp. 330–349. Cheltenham: Edward Elgar.

Hodge, G. A. and Greve, C. (2007). Public–private partnerships: An international performance review. *Public Administration Review,* 67(3): 545–558.

Hodge, G. A. and Greve, C. (2009). PPPs: The passage of time permits sober reflection. *Economic Affairs,* 29(1): 33–39.

Hodge, G. A., Greve, C., and Boardman, A. E. (2010). *International handbook on public–private partnership.* Cheltenham and Northampton, MA: Edward Elgar Publishing.

Hood, C. (1991). A public management for all seasons? *Public Administration,* 69(1): 3–19.

Klijn, E. H. and Teisman, G. R. (2003). Institutional and strategic barriers to public–private partnership: An analysis of Dutch cases. *Public Money and Management,* 23(3): 137–146.

Klijn, E. H. and Teisman, G. (2005). Public–private partnerships as the management of co-production: Strategic and institutional obstacles in a difficult marriage. *The challenge of public–private partnerships: Learning from international experience,* ed. Hodge, G. and Greve, C., pp. 95–116. Cheltenham: Edward Elgar.

Kort, M. and Klijn, E. H. (2011). Public–private partnerships in urban regeneration pro-jects: Organizational form or managerial capacity? *Public Administration Review,* 71(4): 618–626.

Linder, S. H. (1999). Coming to terms with the public–private partnership a grammar of multi-ple meanings. *American Behavioral Scientist,* 43(1): 35–51.

Lowndes, V. and Skelcher, C. (1998). The dynamics of multi-organizational partnerships: An analysis of changing modes of governance. *Public Administration,* 76(2): 313–333.

McKee, M., Edwards, N., and Atun, R. (2006). Public–private partnerships for hospitals. *Bulletin of the World Health Organization,* 84(11): 890–896.

Maarse, H. (2006). The privatisation of health care in Europe: An eight-country analysis. *Journal of Health Politics, Policy and Law,* 31(5): 981–1011.

Marchington, M., Grimshaw, D., Rubery, J., and Willmott, H. (2004). *Fragmenting work: Blurring organizational boundaries and disordering hierarchies.* Oxford: Oxford University Press.

Marek, T., O'Farrell, C., Yamamoto, C., and Zable, I. (2005). *Trends and opportunities in public-private partnerships to improve health service delivery in Africa.* Washington, D.C.: The World Bank.

National Audit Office Report (2005). *The refinancing of the Norfolk and Norwich PFI Hospital.* London: NAO (HC 78, 2005-06).

Nishtar, S. (2004). Public-private "partnerships" in health: A global call to action. *Health Research Policy and Systems,* 2(1): 5.

Osborne, S. (2002). *Public-private partnerships: Theory and practice in international perspective.* London: Routledge.

Palley, T. I. (2004). From Keynesianism to neoliberalism: Shifting paradigms in economics. In *Neoliberalism: A critical reader,* ed. Saad-Filho, A. and Johnston, D., pp. 20–29. London: Pluto Press.

Parker, D. and Figueira, C. (2010). PPPs in developed and developing economies: What lessons can be learned. In *International handbook on public-private partnership,* ed. Hodge, G. A., Greve, C., and Boardman, A. E., pp. 526–547. Cheltenham and Northampton, MA: Edward Elgar Publishing.

Perry, J. (1997). The antecedents of public service motivation. *Journal of Public Administration Research and Theory,* 7(2): 181–187.

Perry, J. and Wise, L. (1990). The motivational base of public service. *Public Administration Review,* 50(3): 367–373.

Pollock, A. M. (2006). *NHS plc: The privatization of our health care.* London: Verso.

Pollock, A. M. and Godden, S. (2008). Independent sector treatment centres: Evidence so far. *BMJ,* 336(7641): 421.

Powell, W. W., White, D. R., Koput, K. W., and Owen-Smith, J. (2005). Network dynamics and field evolution: The growth of interorganizational collaboration in the life sciences. *American Journal of Sociology,* 110(4): 1132–1205.

Pratchett, L. and Wingfield, M. (1996). Petty bureaucracy and woollyminded liberalism? The changing ethos of local government officers. *Public Administration,* 74(4): 639–656.

Price, D., Pollock, A. M., and Shaoul, J. (1999). How the World Trade Organization is shaping domestic policies in health care. *The Lancet,* 354(9193): 1889–1892.

Raman, A. V. and Björkman, J. W. (2008). *Public-private partnerships in health care in India: Lessons for developing countries.* London: Routledge.

Rhodes, R. A. (1997). Understanding governance: Policy networks, governance, reflexivity and accountability. Maidenhead: Open University Press.

Rubery, J., Carroll, C., Cooke, F. L., Grugulis, I., and Earnshaw, J. (2004). Human resource management and the permeable organization: The case of the multi-client call centre. *Journal of Management Studies,* 41(7): 1199–1222.

Shaoul, J., Stafford, A., and Stapleton, P. (2008). The cost of using private finance to build, finance and operate hospitals. *Public Money and Management,* 28(2): 101–108.

Skelcher, C. (2010). Governing partnership. In *International handbook on public-private partnership,* ed. Hodge, G. A., Greve, C., and Boardman, A. E., pp. 292–306. Cheltenham and Northampton, MA: Edward Elgar Publishing.

Smith, A. (2012). "Monday will never be the same again": The transformation of employment and work in a public-private partnership. *Work, Employment & Society,* 26(1): 95–110.

Sveman, E. and Essinger, K. (2001). Procurement of health care services in Sweden in general, and the example of procurement of acute care in the Stockholm region. In *European integration and health care systems: A challenge for social policy*. Paper prepared for delivery at the conference on European Integration and Health Care Systems: A Challenge for Social Policy. A conference organized during the Belgian Presidency of the European Union, December 7–8, 2001. Stockholm: Swedish Federation of County Councils.

Teisman, G. R. and Klijn, E. H. (2002). Partnership arrangements: Governmental rhetoric or governance scheme? *Public Administration Review*, 62(2): 197–205.

Toms, S., Beck, M., and Asenova, D. (2011). Accounting, regulation and profitability: The case of PFI hospital refinancing. *Critical Perspectives on Accounting*, 22(7): 668–681.

Turner, S., Allen, P., Bartlett, W., and Perotin, V. (2011). Innovation and the English National Health Service: A qualitative study of the independent sector treatment centre programme. *Social Science and Medicine*, 73(4): 522–529.

UK Trade and Investment (2013). *Healthcare UK: Public private partnerships*. London: UKTI.

Vining, A. R., and Boardman, A. E. (2008). Public–private partnerships: Eight rules for governments. *Public Works Management & Policy*, 13(2): 149–161.

Waring, J. and Bishop, S. (2010). Lean healthcare: Rhetoric, ritual and resistance. *Social Science & Medicine*, 71(7): 1332–1340.

Waring, J. and Bishop, S. (2011). Healthcare identities at the crossroads of service modernization: The transfer of NHS clinicians to the independent sector? *Sociology of Health & Illness*, 33(5): 661–676.

Waring, J. and Bishop, S. (2013). McDonaldization or commerical re-stratification: Corporatization and the multimodal organisation of English doctors. *Social Science and Medicine*, 82: 147–155.

Waring, J., Currie, G., and Bishop, S. (2013). A contingent approach to the organization and management of public–private partnerships: An empirical study of English health care. *Public Administration Review*, 73(2): 313–326.

Wettenhall, R. (2005). The public–private interface: Surveying the history. In *The challenge of public–private partnerships: Learning from international experience*, ed. Hodge, G. and Greve, C., pp. 22–43. Cheltenham: Edward Elgar.

Wettenhall, R. (2010). Mixes and partnership through time. In *International handbook on public–private partnership*, ed. Hodge, G. A., Greve, C., and Boardman, A. E., pp. 17–42. Cheltenham and Northampton, MA: Edward Elgar Publishing.

Yescombe, E. R. (2011). *Public–private partnerships: Principles of policy and finance*. Oxford: Butterworth-Heinemann.

CHAPTER 21

....

ACCOUNTABILITY IN
HEALTH CARE

....

KARSTEN VRANGBÆK AND HALDOR BYRKJEFLOT

> The rhetoric of reform usually poses questions of accountability in terms of whether government employees are more accountable after the reform than they were before. While it is not impossible to discuss accountability in terms of more or less, doing so implies a uni-dimensional, linear concept that does not reflect the complexity of public management. (...) A more useful approach, (...) recognizes the various dimensions of accountability and the complex context of public accountability. (Romzek, 2000, 22)
>
> Accountability is a word that is loaded with meanings that strike fear in the heart and soul of our health care system (Harber and Ball, 2003).

INTRODUCTION

....

THE quotation by Romzek suggests that accountability is a core part of most reforms. Accountability is a multidimensional phenomenon, where health care institutions may be subject to several different types of accountability demands and logics at any given point in time. The concept of "accountability regime" is useful for capturing this. The second quote, by Harber and Ball (2003), refers to experiences of those working in the health care system or in the public sector. It illustrates that a careful balance must be struck between external, sanction-based accountability, and the intrinsic motivation and trust-based interactions in the highly professionalized system of health care.

Recent academic literature has outlined how the accountability discourse has expanded and how accountability has become a "magic word" (Pollitt and Hupe, 2013) associated with a multitude of reforms and organizational changes in the public as well as private sector. Accordingly there has been an inflation in the use of the term, but there is also "a minimal conceptual consensus" that provides us with a point of departure (Bovens, Goodin, and Schillemans, 2014). At the core of the concept of accountability are specific types of relationships between actors and levels within systems, where actors have obligations to account for their decisions and behavior. Actors in these systems must explain and justify their behavior in forums of different kinds, and such account giving may actually have consequences (Bovens, 2007). However, such relationships play out in different, interrelated spheres of modern societies and take a variety of forms. It is therefore important to consider the specific contexts for accountability structures (Romzek, 2014; Mansbridge, 2014). National, sector specific, organizational, and micro-level context determine how the balance can be struck between formal and informal accountability mechanisms (Romzek, 2014), and to which extent the systems can rely on a core of trust and selection-based social accountability (Mansbridge, 2014). The distinction between informal and formal is a classical one in organization theory and refers to the distinction between formalized structures and regulations on the one hand and shared norms and expectations on the other (Romzek, 2014). Selection and trust-based accountability refers to the traditional model of health care where formal education and subsequent licensing of medical professionals is the central mechanism for governance and knowledge development (Mansbridge, 2014).

We suggest that a comprehensive framework distinguishing between form, direction, and function of accountability is helpful for understanding the complex accountability structures within health care, in the context of NPM and post-NPM reforms introduced since the 1990s (Lægreid, 2014). We use the two Nordic countries of Denmark and Norway to illustrate selected aspects of this comprehensive framework, and we address the issue of whether the traditional trust-based (Mansbridge, 2014) and somewhat informal (Romzek, 2014) accountability logics within the public decentralized health systems in Denmark and Norway have changed in terms of form, direction, and function. We discuss whether recent reforms have implied a change towards more formalized (Romzek, 2014) and sanctions-based (Mansbridge, 2014) accountability forms and we discuss the possible consequences of such changes.

ACCOUNTABILITY CONCEPTS FOR HEALTH CARE

Accountability in health care remains a sparsely analyzed field although it is possible to find examples of literature at least back to the 1970s that refers to the concept (Etzioni, 1975; Day and Klein, 1987; Emanuel and Emanuel, 1996; Relman, 1988; Tuohy, 2003; Brinkerhoff, 2004; Rosen, Israeli, and Shortell, 2012; Denis, 2014). A starting point in this literature is the distinction between responsibility and accountability, and it is indicated that there has been a movement from the first to the latter. The physician profession has been the core of health care, but as the patient perspective has become more important there has also been a change from trusting to checking. Since the end of the 1980s it has been argued that health care had moved from the era of responsibility to accountability (Relman, 1988). Most states had relied on professional self-regulation in health care, where the state delegated decision-making authority to the professional bodies of medicine. This worked as long as the quality of the relationship between doctor and patient was in focus, but new ways of governance had to be developed as the states faced the challenges of expansion in funding needs and demands for cost and quality control (Tuohy, 2003). The role of indirect instruments and third parties for maintaining accountability was now brought into the limelight as many governments developed a policy for information gathering and performance management. One way of framing the issue was to see the new regime as part of an "audit society" where control was pushed further into organizational structures, inscribing in it systems that could be audited (Power, 1997, 42).

Although the narratives are similar and most seem to worry about the consequences for established trust relations (Rosen, Israeli, and Shortell, 2012), there were also differences among scholars in the way they framed the accountability problematic. Some were more preoccupied with context and how accountability was related to national and organizational cultures (Saltman, 2012) and politics (Mattei, 2009), whereas others were seeking to develop the ideal model of accountability across national systems, focusing more on the variations among the various domains of the health care systems in any country (Emanuel and Emanuel, 1996). It is clear from these contributions that accountability illustrates central dilemmas in the current governance of health care systems (Thomas, 2003). In the following we will depart from a framework for studying accountability developed by Mark Bovens, which may be used to identify and analyze such dilemmas.

Bovens' (2007) often-cited definition of accountability is based on the distinction between an actor and a forum, and includes the precondition that some form of instrumental authority is involved: The actor may face consequences on the basis of being held accountable by the forum, and the forum actually has the necessary authority to both demand accountability and impose sanctions.

The social expectations of when and how to give account, the content of account giving and the types of potential sanctions associated with account giving vary over time and across different social spheres. Formal rules for accountability relationships represent conscious attempt to establish such expectations and obligations. But accountability also has a more informal and dynamic side, since the formal rules are constantly interpreted and applied in practice. Indeed some types of accountability primarily rest on informal and normative basis (Romzek, 2014), where social sanctions are the main mechanism for ensuring trust-based relationships (Mansbridge, 2014). Such informal, trust and selection-based accountability (Mansbridge, 2014) has been particularly important within the field of health care, due to the high degree of information asymmetry between managerial/public principals and professional agents. This information asymmetry makes it difficult to monitor behavior and makes the cost of monitoring and sanctioning relatively high. At the same time a high degree of flexibility is necessary for health professionals in making decisions on treatment. Selection and trust-based accountability in health care rests on the formal education and subsequent licensing of medical professionals. Once you have been selected into the profession, you are formally entrusted with treating patients and being part of the medical community. Within the medical community a number of informal norms exist to reinforce a constant focus on applying the most up-to-date evidence in treatment practices. This informal, normative pressure operates through medical societies and peer group discussions at the general level, and within the specific organizational settings for delivering health care. Ideally this ensures a high level of professional ethics and best practice. However, one might argue that the degree of actual scrutiny of practices in peer-based systems can be relatively weak, and that there are few formal opportunities for sanctioning if things go wrong. Sanctions are often relatively subtle and relate to lack of promotion and gradual exclusion of the social community. The efficiency of this type of accountability scheme is thus based on the premise that there are a significant number of agents with trustworthy internal motivations for delivering high quality services within this field, and that these internal motivations are backed by widely accepted social norms within the profession to ensure a high level of quality. This premise has been questioned particularly in the past three decades for a number of reasons. First, the availability of information about performance is much greater today than in previous decades. This means that poor performance is much more likely to be discovered by the public. Several highly publicized scandals, for example in England, bear witness to this (Peckham, 2014), but discussions about comparative performance have also been important drivers of health policy in the Nordic countries. Second, although the medical profession may consist of many idealistic and intrinsically motivated individuals, their normative orientation tends to be focused on clinical issues for the individual patient and not the broader and sometimes conflicting societal goals within health systems. Health care professionals may thus work hard to optimize within their clinical performance, but at the same time the system may fail to live up to broader objectives of cost containment, equity, responsiveness, and promoting public health (Papanicolas and Smith, 2013). To ensure such broader objectives and to reinforce the internal normative structures within health professions there has been a pressure to introduce additional accountability structures over the past three decades.

In the words of Mansbridge (2014) the combined result of such changes is that the core of trust and selection based accountability in regards to the professional staff, has increasingly become circumscribed by political, administrative/managerial or market based mechanisms to scrutinize performance and issue sanctions, if particular health professionals or organizational units fail to live up to standards. Some of these new accountability structures are generated by developments within the health care sector itself, while others are a product of general trends in public administration, which has meant that many parts of modern societies have become characterized by a multitude of accountability forms. Such general reforms have introduced new governance forms, which have added to the complexity and ambiguity of the overall accountability structure (Lægreid, 2014). To disentangle the complexity of the new accountability structure we find it useful to introduce an analytical distinction between six different accountability forms (Mulgan, 2000; Willems and Van Dooren, 2012).

Political accountability denotes the relationship between political leadership and citizens, in the sense that politics and policies are displayed and performed in a variety of areas where citizens may act as a forum towards political leaders. We emphasize the formal "democratic chain of command" from voters to parliament and from parliament to executive powers (see column 2 in Table 21.1). Important accountability mechanisms in these relations are elections, where voters hold politicians to account, parliamentary scrutiny and questions and budgets and budget controls, transparency rules and administrative policy regulations for steering the bureaucracy (column 3 in Table 21.1).

By *administrative accountability* we emphasize accountability relationships inside the administration or by external audit institutions. Important relations are thus between higher- and lower-level administrators in hierarchical relations, and between internal and external auditors and public organizations. There has been a development where traditional "weberian" bureaucratic accountability has been supplemented or in some cases substituted by new public management (NPM)-style "managerial accountability" based on performance measurements, contracting, benchmarking, and so on. External audit is another administrative accountability form. Some types of external auditing have existed for a long periods of time (e.g., general accounting offices and ombudsmen), while others are more recent (e.g., accreditation of hospitals).

Professional accountability refers to accountability relationships that are oriented towards operational quality performance and professional standards. Much of this takes place internally within professional ranks, but there are also external and formal channels for professional scrutiny of conduct, for example through the complaint system, whistleblower arrangements, and audit agencies. Accountability relations are thus between peers and within medical hierarchies. Primary accountability mechanisms are peer reviews, whistleblowers and external examiners and health professionals, and increasingly also between administrators and professionals.

Public accountability refers to the external scrutiny of health care administration and organizations by more or less organized civic society groups and mass media. Both play an important role in health although in a rather ad hoc fashion and with clear bias in terms of which civic society groups (patients, industry, etc.) that have most resources to exercise this type of accountability.

Market accountability has traditionally played the most important role in market- and contract-based health care systems. However, in recent decades there has been an increase in the number of private actors and contractual relationships in most public health systems also. At the same time there has been an increased emphasis on patient choice as a policy tool in health care. A number of performance measurement systems have been developed to support choice including measurements of patient experiences, waiting times, and quality.

Judicial accountability concerns the use of formal legal interventions through civil and administrative courts. This type of accountability has traditionally played a less

Table 21.1 Accountability dimensions in health care

Accountability form	Accountability forum ↔ Account-giver	Account mechanism	Main function	Typical direction
Political	Voters ↔ parliament Parliament ↔ government Government ↔ administration	Elections Parliamentary scrutiny, questions, votes of no-confidence, etc. Budgets and budget control	Democratic Constitutional	Vertical
Administrative	Higher level ↔ lower level administrative staff/units (Administrative chain of command) Internal audit ↔ Public organizations/ hospital units External audit ↔ administration/ hospital units	Hierarchical scrutiny and intervention. Hard or soft contracts. Benchmarking and performance indicators Internal or external audit, accreditation, etc.	Democratic Constitutional Performance	Vertical Diagonal
Professional (individual)	Formal or informal profession groups ↔ Individual professional Profession based external committees for evaluation of complaints, malpractice, etc. ↔ Individual professionals Administrative bodies ↔ Individual professionals	Professional peer review Whistleblowers Profession based external scrutiny, for example through complaint procedures Administrative examination of professional conduct of individual professionals	Constitutional Performance	Horizontal Diagonal (Vertical)
Public	Mass media ↔ health administration*, organizations and professionals Organized civic society ↔ health administration*, organizations and professionals "Ad hoc" action groups or individuals (e.g., e-based) ↔ health administration*, organizations and professionals	Framing, agenda-setting, information channel, watchdog Monitoring, critical dialogue, petitions, protest campaigns, etc. Same.—But growing importance of e-based virtual communities and communication forms	Democratic	Horizontal

(Continued)

Table 21.1 (Continued)

Accountability form	Accountability forum ↔ Account- giver	Account mechanism	Main function	Typical direction
Market	Shareholders/owners ↔ health organizations Consumers ↔ health organizations, individual professionals Purchasers/contracting agencies/insurers ↔ Health organizations	General assemblies, boards. Sale and purchase of shares. Profit. Performance indicators Choice of health organizations and professionals. Consumer panels and surveys. Reputation. Performance indicators Monitoring adherence to contracts. De-selection for future contracts	Performance	Horizontal
Judicial	Judicial courts ↔ health administration*, organizations and professionals Administrative courts ↔ health administration*, organizations and professionals	Formal judicial trials and procedures	Constitutional	Diagonal

*Public or private insurers and public or private bodies responsible for organizing and delivering health services

prominent role in the Nordic, universalistic health systems than in insurance-based systems, as the legislation typically specifies general obligations for public health systems rather than specific rights. However, there has been a tendency to inscribe more rights into the health legislation in recent years (waiting time guarantees, choice of provider, information and informed consent, etc.).

FUNCTION AND DIRECTION OF ACCOUNTABILITY

Classical accounts of accountability distinguish between a constitutional, democratic, and performance function of accountability (Willems and Van Dooren, 2012). Public authorities are held accountable for a variety of well-established rules and procedures to prevent unfairness and abuse of power. Procedural rules regarding due process, equal treatment, openness, and impartiality belong to this category. "Constitutional" rules are meant to provide boundaries for the exercise of public power and to safeguard rights for the individual. Such concerns are also important within health care. The principle of equal rights is safeguarded in universalistic health systems, and all European health systems have a set of minimum requirements for health care insurers and providers. But the issue of "policing the boundaries" of professional conduct and safeguarding rights has a deeper meaning within health care. This is based on the high degree of information asymmetry between professionals and patients, and by the potentially severe consequences for the individual if professionals fail to live up to general standards. This accountability relationship deals with protection of personal integrity, dignity, and safety in all relationships between professionals, pharmaceutical and medical device producers, and patients.

The "democratic" function refers to the interest of citizens (or elected representatives) to be able to control the legislative and executive powers of the state. Citizens should be able to hold representatives accountable for decisions and to select other representatives if necessary. Within health care this means having the means to control and select the formal democratic decision-makers that set the regulatory boundaries for health care and determine principles for allocation of public resources in the sector. In public integrated health systems such as the Nordic systems and the UK this also extends to controlling the public health care delivery organizations and their employees.

The "performance" function deals with the output dimension of public activities (Scharpf, 1999). Citizens and patients should ideally be able to hold health care providers accountable for the results they achieve. Collectively we should be able to judge whether we get optimal societal value for the resources allocated to health care. The types of measurements to support performance accountability range from quality data reported into clinical databases to process data (e.g., waiting times and adherence to standards) and service quality data (e.g., measured as patient-perceived quality). Performance data is often made publicly available to allow comparisons and questioning (public accountability) and to support efforts to develop incentive schemes and sanctions by political, administrative, or private principals (political, administrative, and market accountability).

The performance function has become more important in recent decades for the public sector in general (Hood, 1991; Van Dooren, Bouckaert, and Halligan, 2010). This is expressed in a significant growth in monitoring and auditing mechanisms focusing on the three e's of efficiency, economy, and effectiveness. Within health care we have seen an explosion in performance measuring systems focusing on quality, service, and efficiency.

An additional theoretical distinction should be made about the *"direction" of accountability* relations.

Schillemans (2011) distinguishes between horizontal and vertical accountability relationships. Vertical accountability refers to situations where a superior demands an account from a subordinate. As with classical hierarchical accountability, a defining characteristic is that authority and distribution of roles are formalized or of a strong character; as is the case between a minister and a ministry. In horizontal accountability mechanisms, the situation is rather an absence of hierarchical relations. Instead there is an accountability relationship to a third party, a peer, or a non-hierarchical forum. The relationship may or may not be formalized; there is no subordination of one actor towards the other, as in the relationship between a semi-autonomous audit agency and an administrative institution or the relationship between interest groups and service producers. Bovens (2007) also suggests this distinction, but includes the possibility of a diagonal arrangement: In diagonal accountability relationships the forum is not hierarchically superior to the actor, but still has sanctioning powers and acts on behalf of another authority. Ombudsmen or independent complaint boards could be examples of such accountability arrangements; they are not superior to the actors they hold accountable, but act on behalf of "the system" or "the public interest." Sometimes horizontal accountability is reinforced by vertical accountability as political, administrative, or private superiors hold subordinate units jointly accountable.

We now have several dimensions to describe accountability within health systems. First, we can distinguish between different accountability *forms*, each with several different forums and account-givers and associated accountability mechanisms. Second, we distinguish between different *functions* of accountability. While democratic and constitutional functions have traditionally been closely linked to political, judicial, and administrative accountability forms, and performance more closely to market and professional accountability forms, it is important to realize that different forms may include concerns for several different functions. For example, professional accountability typically is concerned with a due process and equity as well as performance. Similarly it can be argued that the performance function of accountability has gained importance in public health systems over the past three decades with the introduction of NPM perspectives and tools and that this is combined with different forms of administrative accountability. Third, we distinguish between different *directions* of accountability. We suggest that horizontal accountability forms have gained importance over time, as more services are delivered in networked structures and as traditional forms of government are giving way to new types of "governance" relations.

In this sense there tends to be a dynamic interaction between the different dimensions as pointed out by Willems and Van Dooren (2012) and accountability regimes should be seen as snapshots of forms, functions, and direction of accountability in a particular context at a given point in time (Goodin, 2003; Tuohy, 2003; Mattei, 2009). Reforms can shift the relative importance of different forms, functions, and directions over time. This may happen through formal rules, or more implicitly by introducing new institutional structures and relationships. The result can be new configurations of the trust-based accountability core and the formal, sanction-based periphery (Mansbridge, 2014). Understanding the gradual development of accountability regimes provides important insights into the governance of modern health care systems.

EXAMPLES OF DEVELOPMENTS
IN ACCOUNTABILITY FOR HEALTH CARE

The Nordic countries as well as United Kingdom belong to the group of public integrated health systems with a strong public role in stewardship, financing, and delivery of services. Whereas the Nordic countries traditionally emphasize democratic governance at both the central and decentralized levels, the National Health Service (NHS) in the United Kingdom historically represented a more centralized system.

The dominant accountability forms in the Nordic countries have traditionally (until the early 1980s) been professional accountability at the clinical level nested within democratic/political and administrative accountability at national and decentralized levels for managing the system. Judicial accountability has been less prominent than in market-based systems, and market accountability has been of limited relevance due to the dominance of public financing and public provision. This is in stark contrast to, for example the US health care system. Prior to the 1980s the public had limited insight and limited options for comparing health services, and thus played a relatively indirect role in accountability terms, primarily as voters at local, regional, and national level.

However, a number of changes have been introduced from the 1980s and onwards in the Nordic countries, the UK, and most other European health care systems (Vrangbæk, 1999; Magnussen, Vrangbæk, and Hagen, 2009; Byrkjeflot, 2011; Olejaz et al., 2012; Ringard et al., 2013; Lægreid, 2014). The reforms and dominant change trends can be labeled under the following headlines: (a) NPM style reforms from the 1980s and onwards introducing choice, economic incentives, performance measurements, and transparency (activity, service, and clinical quality); (b) structural reforms changing the balance between central and decentralized governance; (c) changes in the public/private mix of health care by introducing more private providers and encouraging voluntary private insurance; (d) various reforms and changes to promote integration of care; and (e) digitalization and e-based solutions for communication, monitoring, and delivering services.

In terms of accountability this has resulted in the following changes:

1. Accountability relations have become more complex and layered over time (Bovens and Schillemans, 2011), with new combinations of form, function, and direction.
2. Administrative accountability has changed to increasingly incorporate "management" and "market" accountability dimensions. In some cases these NPM-related accountability types have replaced more traditional forms, but more often they have been added on top of existing forms sometimes creating tensions and lack of clarity for the involved account-givers (Lægreid, 2014; Byrkjeflot, 2011; Vrangbæk, 1999).

3. Professional accountability is increasingly challenged by attempts to superimpose external administrative or market based accountability forms. Professional accountability has become more formalized, standardized, and transparent (Timmermans, 2005).

4. Although judicial accountability in general is still expected to play a minor role, particularly in the NHS type of systems, there is a tendency to develop more specific rights within health care. This leads to more opportunities for taking judicial action (Hogg, 1999)

5. Market accountability has become more important due to increased use of choice, contracting and privatization within health care.

6. Social accountability plays a strong role, but various types of ad hoc e-based virtual interest groups and campaigns have supplemented mass media and locality-based movements.

7. Horizontal accountability has gained importance in post-NPM efforts to create less fragmented health care services and provide seamless service delivery across different health and social care levels. Intergovernmental relationships have become tighter with more formalized mandatory collaboration between regions (hospitals) and municipalities. Regions, municipalities, and delivery organizations engage in "dynamic accountability" relationships based on networks, recursivity, deliberation, innovation, inclusion, and publicity (Sabel and Zeitlin, 2008; Mansbridge, 2014). However, stronger accountability pressures from the state level in terms of monitoring and sanctioning mechanisms reinforce this type of horizontal dynamic accountability in case regions and municipalities fail to reach acceptable progress.

Based on these observations we can conclude that there are indications of circumscribing the traditional core of selection and trust-based accountability with a thicker, more complex and more penetrating layer of monitoring and sanctioning accountability (Mansbridge, 2014). This can be seen at the clinical level, where traditional reliance on selection and trust-based accountability forms is challenged by IT-based systems for monitoring performance, and by the widespread use of clinical guidelines, standards, and operation procedures. In terms of the criteria developed by Mansbridge this can partly be explained by a reduction in the price of monitoring due to the introduction of IT solutions and collection of "big data." Alternatively one can argue that some of the cost has been shifted to those being monitored, as they are responsible for taking the time to enter data and thus supply the basis for (self-) monitoring. A similar development has taken place in the accountability relations for hospitals and public authorities (regions and municipalities). Hospital managers are increasingly held to account for process and outcome quality in addition to traditional economic management. Rising expectations among patients and in the general population contribute to this development. The authority of health care professionals has been weakened and people are less inclined to accept quality differences or failures. A third impetus for the development is a growing need among state-level politicians and administrators for being able to manage increasing costs and medical technology advances. This has necessitated a tighter control regime and better monitoring of performance.

Accountability relations between state and regions are also changing. The state has implemented stronger governance of economic performance and tougher sanctions for budget overruns. Productivity increases are mandatory and failure to deliver such increases result in economic sanctions. In addition the two Nordic states also use softer means in the form of benchmarking and publication of comparative data in order to hold regions and their hospitals accountable and to enable citizens/patients to do the same.

LIMITATIONS AND CRITICAL ISSUES FOR STUDYING ACCOUNTABILITY IN HEALTH CARE IN THE FUTURE

In this chapter we have used some of the more recent perspectives in public administration research on accountability to analyze developments in health care. We have also briefly reviewed the literature in on health care accountability, but not in a comprehensive way. Our impression is that the health care literature on accountability has been centered on the relationship between the medical profession and a few of the other dimensions mentioned (e.g., state or market), but that there has been fewer attempts to give an overview of the multiple dimensions of accountability or discuss other dimensions like administrative or social accountability. Our framework can contribute to a more systematic discussion of such issues. The limits of our perspective are that we do not really seek to explain the development or make the systematic cross-national comparisons that may give us a better understanding of the context or the drivers for change. Our perspective is also limited to giving an overall view of the system rather than studying accountability relations from the perspective of the organizations and the actors that are affected by them.

The balancing act between responsibility and accountability will continue to be important in further studies. Responsibility is a more active process—it relates to delegated authority within a hierarchical system. Accountability is more about providing documentation for your competence, trustworthiness, and control ambitions in a system of checks and balances. The inflation of accountability forms is a challenge for most health care systems, but it may perhaps be an even greater challenge for the public systems where health care historically has to a greater extent been integrated into local and central systems for democratic governance. The challenges may be somewhat different in private market dominated systems like the United States, where the focus is on creating accountable care organizations rather than changing the system of health care regulation as such in order to maintain and rationalize a system for public provision of health care (Fisher and Shortell, 2010). There are few comparative studies of accountability regimes in health care (but see Tuohy, 2003; Byrkjeflot, Christensen, and Lægreid, 2014; Byrkjeflot, Neby, and Vrangbæk, 2012). Such studies and also historical case studies of single systems may be useful also in giving input to current reforms, cautioning ambitious reformers against making promises of developing "crystal clear" accountability relations, and so on as they usually tend to do when new reforms are introduced in health care. Unfortunately there is no all-encompassing accountability theory that can help us understand the complex linkages and predict how different regimes are really operating and how they will develop (Dubnick and Frederickson, 2011). It is, however, useful to map the set of accountability relationships in any given system, firstly in order to avoid seeing the trees only and not the forest and secondly to be prepared for surprises relating to accountability relations in health care.

The "top-down" approach to the analysis of accountability structures is valuable in itself but obviously does not make it possible to understand how accountability logics work "on the ground." We therefore suggest that the "top-down" mapping should be supplemented by a "bottom-up" analysis of accountability regimes as seen from the perspective of different actors within the health system.

The purpose would be to analyze the accountability pressures facing specific actors in health systems and the relative importance of different accountability logics and of how organizations and professionals prioritize and deal with the different types of accountability demands. This type of "bottom-up" analysis would provide a supplementary and perhaps more realistic picture of how the complexity of formal accountability systems appear on the ground. This accountability from below is similar to what for instance Sinclair (1995) has done. The public servants she has interviewed feel the pain of accountability as they speak of a "blowtorch applied to the belly." "Accountability is multiple and fragmented," she concludes "being accountable in one form often requires compromises of other sorts of accountability" (Sinclair, 1995, 226, 231). Similarly in the studies of accountability in the NAV reforms[1] in Norway (Fimreite and Lægreid, 2009), it was demonstrated how organizations must be accountable upwards to political sovereigns, horizontally to other network partners and agencies, and downwards to citizens and clients. Not surprisingly the study also concluded that it is a very difficult task to balance such multiple accountability relations and logics.

References

Bovens, M. (2007). Analysing and assessing accountability: A conceptual framework. *European Law Journal*, 13(4): 447–468.

Bovens, M., Goodin, R. E., and Schillemans, T. (eds) (2014). *The Oxford handbook of public accountability*. Oxford: Oxford University Press.

---

[1] "Ny Arbeids og Velferdsforvaltning" ("New work and welfare administration").

Bovens, M. and Schillemans, T. (2011). The challenge of multiple accountability: Does redundancy lead to overload? In *Accountable governance: Promises and problems*, ed. Dubnick, M. J. and Friederickson, H. G, pp. 3–21. London: M. E. Sharpe.

Brinkerhoff, D. W. (2004). Accountability and health systems: Toward conceptual clarity and policy relevance. *Health policy and planning*, 19(6): 371–379.

Byrkjeflot, H. (2011). Healthcare states and medical professions: The challenges from new public management. In *The Ashgate research companion to new public management*, ed. Christensen, T. and Lægreid, P., pp. 147–161. Aldershot: Ashgate.

Byrkjeflot, H., Christensen, T., and Lægreid, P. (2014). The many faces of accountability: Comparing reforms in welfare, hospitals and migration. *Scandinavian Political Studies*, 37(2): 171–195.

Byrkjeflot, H., Neby, S., and Vrangbæk, K. (2012). Changing accountability regimes in hospital governance: Denmark and Norway compared. *Scandinavian Journal of Public Administration*, 15(4): 3–23.

Day, P. and Klein, R. (1987). *Accountability: Five public services*. London: Tavistock.

Denis, J. L. (2014). Accountability in healthcare organizations and systems. *Healthcare policy/Politiques de sante*, 10(SP): 8–11.

Dubnick, M. J. and Frederickson, H. G. (2011). Introduction: The promises of accountability research. In *Accountable governance: Promises and problems*, ed. Dubnick, M. J. and Friederickson, H.G. London: M.E. Sharpe.

Emanuel, E. J. and Emanuel, L. L. (1996). What is accountability in health care? *Annals of Internal Medicine*, 124(2): 229–239.

Etzioni, A. (1975). Alternative conceptions of accountability: The example of health administration. *Public Administration Review*, 35(3): 279–286.

Fimreite, A. L. and Lægreid, P. (2009). Reorganizing the welfare state administration: Partnership, networks and accountability. *Public Management Review*, 11(3): 281–297.

Fimreite, A. L., Tranvik, T., Selle, P., and Flo, Y. (2007). Når sektorbåndene slites. Utfordringer for den norske velferdsmodellen. *Tidsskrift for Samfunnsforskning*, 2: 165–193.

Fisher, E. S. and Shortell, S. M. (2010). Accountable care organizations: Accountable for what, to whom, and how. *Jama*, 304(15): 1715–1716.

Goodin, R. E. (2003). Democratic accountability: The distinctiveness of the third sector. *European Journal of Sociology*, 44(3): 359–393.

Harber, B. and Ball, T. (2003). From the blame game to accountability in health care. *Policy*, 49: 49–54.

Hogg, C. (1999). *Patients, power and politics: From patients to citizens*. London: SAGE Publications Ltd.

Hood, C. (1991). A public management for all seasons? *Public Administration*, 69: 3–19.

Lægreid, P. (2014). New public management and accountability. In *The Oxford handbook of public accountability*, ed. Bovens, M., Goodin, R. E., and Schillemans, T., pp. 324–339. Oxford: Oxford University Press.

Magnussen, J., Vrangbæk, K., and Hagen, T. P. (2009). *Nordic healthcare systems. Recent reforms and current policy challenges*. Berkshire: World Health Organization/McGraw-Hill Open University Press.

Mansbridge, J. (2014). A contingency theory of accountability. In *The Oxford handbook of public accountability*, ed. Bovens, M., Goodin, R. E., and Schillemans, T., pp. 55–68. Oxford: Oxford University Press.

Mattei, P. (2009). *Restructuring welfare organizations in Europe*. Basingstoke: Palgrave Macmillan.

Mulgan, R. (2000). Accountability: An ever-expanding concept? *Public Administration*, 78(3): 555–573.

Olejaz, M., Nielsen, A. J., Rudkjøbing, A., Birk, H. O., Krasnik A., and Hernández-Quevedo, C. (2012). Denmark: Health system review. *Health Systems in Transition*, 14(2): 1–192. Available at: <http://www.euro.who.int/en/about-us/partners/observatory/publications/health-system-reviews-hits/full-list-of-country-hits/denmark-hit-2012> (accessed October 7, 2015).

Papanicolas, I. and Smith, P. (2013). *Health system performance comparison: An agenda for policy, information and research*. Milton Keynes: McGraw-Hill International.

Peckham, S. (2014). Accountability in the UK healthcare system: An overview. *Healthcare policy = Politiques de sante*, 10(SP): 154–162.

Pollitt, C. and Hupe, P. (2011). Talking about government: The role of magic concepts. *Public Management Review*, 13(5): 641–658.

Power, M. (1997). *The audit society: Rituals of verification*. Oxford: Oxford University Press.

Relman, A. S. (1988). Assessment and accountability: The third revolution in medical care. *New England Journal of Medicine*, 319: 1220–1222.

Ringard, Å., Sagan, A., Saunes, I. S., and Lindahl, A. K. (2013). Norway: Health system review. *Health Systems in Transition*, 15(8): 1–162.

Romzek, B. S. (2000). Dynamics of public sector accountability in an era of reform. *International Review of Administrative Sciences*, 66: 21–44.

Romzek, B. (2014). Accountable public services. In *The Oxford handbook of public accountability*, ed. Bovens, M., Goodin, R. E., and Schillemans, T. Oxford: Oxford University Press. DOI: 10.1093/oxfordhb/9780199641253.013.0030.

Rosen, B., Israeli, A., Shortell, S. (2012). Accountability in health care reconsidered. In *Accountability and responsibility in health care: Issues in addressing an emerging global challenge*, Vol. 1, ed. Rosen, B., Israeli, A., and Shortell, S., pp. 7–22. Singapore: World Scientific.

Sabel, C. F. and Zeitlin, J. (2008). Learning from difference: The new architecture of experimentalist governance in the EU. *European Law Journal*, 14(3): 271–327.

Saltman, R. B. (2012). Context, culture and the practical limits of health sector accountability. In *Accountability and responsibility in health care: Issues in addressing an emerging global challenge*, Vol. 1, ed. Rosen, B., Israeli, A., and Shortell, S., pp. 189–207. Singapore: World Scientific.

Schillemans, T. (2011). Does horizontal accountability work? Evaluating potential remedies for the accountability deficit of agencies. *Administration & Society*, 43(4): 387–416.

Sinclair, A. (1995). The chameleon of accountability: Forms and discourses. *Accounting, Organizations and Society*, 20(2): 219–237.

Timmermans, S. (2005). From autonomy to accountability: The role of clinical practice guidelines in professional power. *Perspectives in Biology and Medicine*, 48(4): 490–501.

Thomas, P. G. (2003). Accountability in modern government. In *Handbook of public administration*, ed. Peters, B. G. and Pierre, J., pp. 557–568. London, Thousand Oaks, CA, and New Delhi: Sage.

Tuohy, C. H. (2003). Agency, contract, and governance: Shifting shapes of accountability in the health care arena. *Journal of Health Politics, Policy and Law*, 28(2/3): 195–215.

Van Dooren, W., Bouckaert, G., and Halligan, J. (2010). *Performance management in the public sector*. London: Routledge.

Vrangbæk, K. (1999). New public management i sygehusfeltet—udformning og konsekvenser. In *Når styringsambitioner møder praksis—Den svære omstilling af sygehus- og sundhedsvæsenet i Danmark og Sverige*, ed. Bensten, E. Z., Borum, F., Erlingsdottir, G., and Sahlin-Andersson, K., pp. 33–56. København: Handelshøjskolens forlag.

Willems, T. and Van Dooren, W. (2012). Coming to terms with accountability. *Public Management Review*, 14(7): 1011–1036.

CHAPTER 22

....

PHARMACEUTICALS, MONEY, AND THE HEALTH CARE ORGANIZATIONAL FIELD

....

WENDY LIPWORTH

HEALTH CARE AS A SOCIAL INSTITUTION

....

THERE are many different ways of conceptualizing health care organizations and their roles in society. One view is that health care is first and foremost a "social institution"— that is, an institution that exists to fulfill "collective goods." These are goods that are intrinsically desirable (as opposed to simply being desired) and that are generated and maintained by institutional role occupants, who in turn have an institutionally derived "right" to the goods (Miller, 2009). In the case of health care, these collective goods consist of those that promote survival by extending lives that would otherwise be cut short; those that promote ontological security by restoring and maintaining basic physical and social functioning, and those that promote human flourishing by ensuring quality of life (Little et al., 2012; Montgomery and Lipworth, 2014).

Like all social institutions, the institution of health care is "normative" in the sense that it generates institutional rights and duties (deontic properties), and correspond-ing social norms. These, in turn, attach to specific institutional roles, and morally con-strain the activities of institutional role occupants (Miller, 2009). The rights, duties, and norms that characterize a social institution are expressed through, and exert their force through, the institution's "logic"—that is, the "taken-for-granted" belief and meaning systems that are evident in institutional patterns of activity, discourse and policy (Scott, 2014).

In its idealized form, the health care social institution is dominated by health care practitioners who adhere to a "professional" institutional logic. According to such a logic, clinical practitioners are given the resources they need to practice, either from governments or from private insurers, and they are allowed considerable autonomy over their education, credentialing, quality assurance, and pricing. In return, they are expected to behave as disinterested "others" and to prioritize the collective goods they produce over purely commercial considerations (Miller, 2009; Reay and Hinings, 2009; Goodrick and Reay, 2011; Scott, 2014).

There are also a number of other occupational groups within the health care organizational field, each of which adheres to its own characteristic institutional logic or set of logics. These groups include health researchers in academic institutions, with their "scientific" and "academic" logics (e.g. Owen-Smith, 2003; Miller, 2009; Swan et al., 2010; Arman, Liff, and Wikström, 2014), and health service administrators, and health policymakers, with their "managerial," "government/state," "bureaucratic," or "administrative" logics (e.g. Miller, 2009; Goodrick and Reay, 2011; Waldorff, 2013; Blomgren and Waks, 2015; Currie and Spyridonidis, 2015). While the rights, duties, and norms of these groups are not identical to those of professionals engaged in direct patient care, these occupational groups are also expected to prioritize the collective goods they produce over purely commercial considerations.

The Commercialization of the Health Care Organizational Field

While the institution of health care is often viewed idealistically as one in which commerce is a means to an end rather than an end in itself, the fact is that the logic of the health care organizational field is, and always has been, in part a "market logic"—that is a logic characterized by the promotion of free and unregulated competition and the use of financial criteria and consumer satisfaction to judge success (Glynn and Lounsbury, 2005; Scott, 2008; Goodrick and Reay, 2011; Pache and Santos, 2011).

Many believe that the health care institution is becoming increasingly tolerant of market structures, values, and norms. This has been attributed to, among other things, the privatization of health care services (Janssen and Vandermade, 1990; Collyer and White, 2011), and the increasing tendency for clinicians to emphasize their "technical expertise" as validated by the market and measured through metrics such as "cost effectiveness" and "consumer satisfaction" (Reay and Hinings, 2009; Scott, 2014). Similar trends have been observed in academic settings, where biomedical scientists race to commercialize their discoveries (with some of them leaving academia to become "entrepreneurs"), and with the increasing focus of government funding bodies and academic organizations on commercial measures of productivity (Shapin, 2008; Smith, 2012).

Alongside this "marketization" of clinical and academic organizations, there has been an enormous growth in the size and power of several "for-profit" industries within the health care organizational field. These include the pharmaceutical industry, the biotechnology industry, medical devices and diagnostics industries, as well as industries dedicated to the production of health foods and complementary and alternative medicines.

In the remainder of this chapter, I will map the contemporary health care organizational field, with a particular emphasis on the pharmaceutical industry and the organizational forms with which pharmaceutical companies interact. I will then describe the various ways in which stakeholders have responded the rise of the pharmaceutical industry within the health care organizational field. This will be followed by some suggestions as to how tensions between and within stakeholder groups might be conceptualized, and how actors within the health care organizational field might better accommodate the presence of the pharmaceutical industry without completely sacrificing their commitment to their professional, academic, or administrative values and norms.

MAPPING THE HEALTH CARE ORGANIZATIONAL FIELD

The Rise of the Pharmaceutical Industry

Many of the pharmaceutical companies we know today began their lives in the late nineteenth and early twentieth century when apothecaries began manufacturing drugs such as morphine, quinine, and strychnine, and dye and chemical companies began to discover medical applications for their products. Several pharmaceutical companies whose names persist to this day, such as Merck, Schering, Roche, Smith Kline, Parke-Davis, Bayer, Ciba, Geigy, and Sandoz first emerged at this time (Daemmrich and Bowden, 2005).

The "modern" pharmaceutical industry came into its own between 1930 and 1960, with the development of an array of revolutionary medicines including immunosuppressants, antibiotics, antimalarials, synthetic vitamins, hormones, antihistamines, and anesthetic agents. During the 1970s and 1980s, new techniques for targeting therapies against physiological processes enabled the development of (among others) antihypertensives, cholesterol reducing drugs, tranquilizers, antidepressants, anti-inflammatory drugs, contraceptives, and cancer therapies. Since the 1980s, developments in molecular biology, genomics, biotechnology, and information technology have contributed to further therapeutic breakthroughs (Le Fanu, 2000; Daemmrich and Bowden, 2005).

Today, the pharmaceutical industry is facing a number of challenges including decreasing productivity, increasing research and development costs, growing competition from manufacturers of generic medicines, threats to global intellectual property regimes, and increasing demands from those who pay for medicines that companies demonstrate not only the safety and efficacy of new medicines but also genuine "innovation" and value for money (Kaitin, 2010; Munos and Chin, 2011; Khanna, 2012).

Pharmaceutical companies have begun to respond to these challenges by outsourcing much of their research, development, and manufacture to countries such as Brazil, Russia, India, and China (George et al., 2013; Rafols et al., 2014); by relying less on discovering "blockbuster drugs" and more on developing "personalized medicines" (Paul et al., 2010, Zuckerman and Milne, 2012); by joining with other companies and with universities in various kinds of "open innovation" initiatives and research and development (R&D) "partnerships" (Hunter and Stephens, 2010; Bianchi et al., 2011); by leveraging the "big data" that can be generated and analyzed through new biological, information, and computational technologies (Allarakhia and Steven, 2011; Lesko, 2012; Menius and Rousculp, 2014); and by tailoring their R&D to the mandates of consumers, clinicians and funding bodies (Epstein, 2012; Basch, 2013).

Despite the challenges it faces, the pharmaceutical industry is enormously profitable and powerful, with global sales of over $1 trillion. The growing global burden of both infectious and chronic disease, together with international trade liberalization, bode well for the future of the industry, and it has been projected that the global pharmaceutical market could be worth more than $1.6 trillion by 2020 (PWC, 2012). The health care organizational field is therefore likely to remain highly commercialized, and the pharmaceutical industry is likely to remain a central force in this institutional trend.

ORGANIZATIONAL FORMS THAT INTERACT WITH PHARMACEUTICAL COMPANIES

This growth of the pharmaceutical industry has had far-reaching effects on other organizational forms within the health care organizational field. In some cases, these organizational forms owe their existence—or at least their prominence—to the pharmaceutical industries, while in other cases pre-existing organizational forms have been changed in profound ways by the existence of the pharmaceutical industry.

Organizations That Are Supported by the Pharmaceutical Industry

There are a number of organizational forms within the health care organizational field that rely heavily on the pharmaceutical industry to fund their core activities or to provide them with other kinds of support. These include academic researchers, clinicians, biomedical journals, and patient advocacy organizations.

Academic basic scientists are encouraged by both universities and funding organizations to commercialize their discoveries, and this often entails them joining with pharmaceutical companies in various kinds of "public-private" partnerships (Jakobsen, Wang, and Nwaka, 2011; Goldman, Compton, and Mittleman, 2013). Similarly, almost all clinical trials internationally are now funded by the pharmaceutical industry (Buchkowsky and Jewesson, 2004; DeMets and Califf, 2011).

Practicing clinicians rely heavily on the pharmaceutical industry not only to produce the medicines they prescribe, but also to "educate" them about these medicines. A significant proportion of formal continuing medical education programs are funded by the pharmaceutical industry, and many clinicians rely on pharmaceutical representatives ("drug reps") for information about new medicines (Holmer, 2001; Rodwin, 2010). Professional medical associations also often rely on industry funding for their conferences, journals, patient educational materials, advocacy activities, research grant programs, and clinical practice guidelines (Rothman et al., 2009; Dalsing, 2011).

Biomedical journals gain much of their prestige and their "impact factors" from publishing the results of "pivotal" clinical trials. They therefore rely on their relationships with the authors of pharmaceutical industry-funded clinical trials in order to attract these publications. Journals also derive much of their income from the pharmaceutical industry in the form of advertising, purchase of article reprints (which are precious marketing materials for pharmaceutical companies) and sponsorship of special issues and supplements (Hopkins, Galligher, and Levine, 1999; Fugh-Berman, Alladin, and Chow, 2006; Fugh-Berman, 2010).

Finally, most patient advocacy organizations derive their income from pharmaceutical companies, who then work closely with these groups to advocate for access to medicines that might otherwise not be registered for marketing or funded as part of public or private insurance schemes (Rothman et al., 2011; Rose, 2013).

Medicines Policymaking Organizations

Many medicines policymaking organizations owe their very existence—or at least their prominence—to the pharmaceutical industry. These include drug regulatory agencies, such as the US Food and Drugs Administration (FDA), and the European Medicines Agency (EMA) that assess the safety and efficacy of new and existing medicines (Annas and Elias, 1999; Daemmrich and Bowden, 2005). They also include public and private organizations devoted to conducting "health technology assessments" of new medicines, making resource allocation decisions, and producing clinical practice guidelines (Stevens, Milne, and Burls, 2003; Volmink et al., 2004; Steinbrook, 2008). In some cases, these regulatory and funding organizations are supported financially by industry, deriving their operating budgets from hefty "submission fees" from the companies who want to have their medicines registered or subsidized (Salkeld, 2011; Wolfe, 2014).

Related Commercial Organizations

A new commercial organizational form that has emerged as a direct result of the growth of the pharmaceutical industry is that of the "contract research organization" (CRO). These organizations have emerged as a result of the increasing cost and complexity of drug development, regulation, funding, and marketing, and pharmaceutical companies now have the option of outsourcing almost any of their functions to CROs (Mirowski and Van Horn, 2005; Kaitin, 2010). CROs now number in the thousands globally and, together with other similar organizations such as medical writing companies, have functions as specialized as generating pathology reports for toxicology analyses (Rovira, Foley, and Clemo, 2011), accessing crowd-sourced cohorts for clinical research studies (Swan, 2012), and writing clinical research articles and regulatory documents (Leventhal, 2013).

Another group of commercial organizations that interact frequently with the pharmaceutical industry are the venture capital organizations that provide start-up funds for small pharmaceutical or biotechnology companies (Guston, 1999; Samila and Sorenson, 2010; Ratcliffe, 2011; Sanberg et al., 2014). Pharmaceutical and biotechnology companies might also seek capital support at the later stages of drug development from new kinds of organizations such as "no research, development only" (NRDO) companies, which license compounds in or beyond the clinical development phase (Thiel, 2004; Herson, 2006).

There are, therefore, many different organizational forms within the health care organizational field that interact "frequently and fatefully" (Scott et al., 2000, 13) with the pharmaceutical industry, and that would not exist at all, or would not exist in a form that we would recognize today—if the pharmaceutical industry was not as influential as it is.

RESPONSES TO THE PHARMACEUTICAL INDUSTRY

The rise of the pharmaceutical industry within the health care organizational field has provoked passionate responses from many institutional actors, generating major controversies within academic, political, and public debates. As Santoro notes:

> Perhaps no business engages the worlds of science, medicine, economics, health, human rights, government, and social welfare as much as the pharmaceutical industry. As the twenty-first century begins, however, there is growing controversy and even hostility in the relationship between the pharmaceutical industry and the public (Santoro and Gorrie, 2006, 1).

These responses can be grouped into three broad categories: criticism of the pharmaceutical industry, support for the pharmaceutical industry, and uncertainty about the pharmaceutical industry.

Critics of the Pharmaceutical Industry

Many social and political scientists, economists, journalists, bioethicists, and other commentators are intensely critical of the pharmaceutical industry. These criticisms are broad ranging, focusing on (among other things) pharmaceutical companies' history of developing drugs for commercial gain rather than to address genuine unmet global health needs; creating new "diseases" or expanding disease definitions to enlarge their markets; exploiting research participants; distorting the design, analysis, and publication of research; abusing tax breaks and intellectual property laws; overstating their role in, and the cost of, drug development and therefore over-pricing medicines; providing incomplete or misleading information to regulatory and funding agencies; interfering with policymaking processes; failing to monitor the safety and effectiveness of their products once they are on the market; continuing to promote products that they know to be ineffective or harmful; and engaging in aggressive, misleading, manipulative, and sometimes illegal, marketing, advertising, and medical "education."

An entire genre of literature has emerged in which the industry is condemned for these and other misdeeds. This quotation from Marcia Angell, a strong critic of the industry who was once editor of the prestigious *New England Journal of Medicine*, is typical:

> contrary to its public relations, the industry discovers few genuinely innovative drugs, spends less than half as much on research and development (R&D) as on marketing and administration,…put(s) most of their efforts into turning out higher-priced versions of existing medicines and persuading us to take more of them… (and) uses its immense wealth and power to co-opt nearly every institution that might stand in its way (Angell, 2004, xvi).

At times, these behaviors are viewed as evidence of outright corruption on the part of the pharmaceutical industry. Angell, for example, highlights evidence of companies "rigging prices," "offering kickbacks," engaging in anticompetitive practices, and attempting to cover up these activities (Angell, 2004, 230).

Others view industry misbehavior less as outright corruption than as the expected, but nonetheless corrosive, effects of a commercial imperative playing itself out within the health care organizational field. In his book, evocatively entitled "Pharmageddon," David Healy captures this view in his claim that:

> Pharmaceutical companies … have no interest in what molecules might reveal about how humans work. Molecules are only interesting insofar as they can be used to capture market niches (Healy, 2012, x).

In the book "White Coat Black Hat," the bioethicist Carl Elliott argues similarly that:

> if more academics think like businesspeople now, it is partly because the world in which drugs are tested, developed and marketed is so completely ruled by business (Elliott, 2010, xii).

And in "Powerful Medicines," Jerry Avorn, a Harvard physician and pharmaco-epidemiologist claims that:

[t]he scent of economic incentive is everywhere in medicine, occasionally rising to the level of stench (Avorn, 2005, 401).

According to these critics, the pharmaceutical industry's attempts to justify its actions are unconvincing. Avorn, for example, takes issue with the industry's claim that high drug prices are a fair and necessary reward for investment in drug development. He describes this as a "Research Ultimatum" and argues that while industry's claims are:

pregnant with portent for the future of medicine … for many scientists, its logic just leaves stretch marks on our credulity, and fails to deliver on most of the policy implications it implies (Avorn, 2005, 199).

Similarly, critics of the pharmaceutical industry are skeptical about the industry's willingness to reform itself. As Angell argues:

Sadly, there is little sign that the pharmaceutical industry is responding to its current difficulties by changing its behavior. It continues to make me-too drugs as its major product, to use its massive marketing muscle to promote them relentlessly, to charge prices as high as it can get away with, and to act as if it puts short-term profits ahead of everything (Angell, 2004, xxi).

The pharmaceutical industry is seen to be not only immoral in its own right, but also to have a corrosive influence on the other institutional actors and organizations with which it interacts in the health care organizational field. Healy, for example, argues that doctors are:

Locked into the distribution channel for prescription-only drugs, hemmed in by their science, … (and thus) increasingly resemble the employees of the occupational health department of a factory that in the course of business exposes its workers to disability-inducing aerosols (Healy, 2014).

Hardly a week goes by without a report in a medical journal about a newly discovered "conflict of interest" involving health care practitioners, academic researchers, journal editor's or policy makers. The view is that these once independent endeavors are now "for sale" (Angell, 2000). Those who benefit financially or otherwise from interactions with industry are seen to be "easily fooled" (Elliott, 2010, xiv) and to lose their capacity and/or willingness to be objective in fulfilling their primary obligations to patients or the public. Discussing industry support of medical education, Avorn cautions that:

The more that medical schools and their teaching hospitals become dependent on support from industry to fund their research and educational activities, the easier it is for their faculties to become convinced that what's good for those companies is good for their institutions (Avorn 2005, 214).

The capacity for industry wrongdoing to taint the reputations of other organizational forms is also evident in the suspicion that arises when these organizations fail to detect or respond to industry wrongdoing. For example, when several pharmaceutical companies were found to have obscured evidence about the link between antidepressants and suicide in adolescents and children, this also revealed what was seen to be a "culture of denial" within regulatory bodies such as the US Food and Drug Administration (Avorn, 2005). The case of the anti-inflammatory drug "Vioxx" is also illustrative: when it emerged that the manufacturer (Merck) had known about, and hidden, information about an increased risk of heart attacks, the academic researchers who had been involved in Vioxx trials, and had authored journal articles, were taken to task for not disclosing all that they knew, and were forced to defend themselves publicly against these accusations (Curfman, Morrissey, and Drazen, 2005; Bombardier et al., 2006).

Supporters of the Pharmaceutical Industry

While the discourse about the pharmaceutical industry is dominated by the voices of critics, these voices are balanced to some degree by the those who focus on the ways in which the pharmaceutical industry has "revolutionized" health and medicine over the past century and on its promise for the future.

Not surprisingly, those who work within the pharmaceutical industry emphasize the many life-saving health technologies that exist only because of the industry, and the risks that pharmaceutical companies take to develop these medicines. This statement from the International Federation of Pharmaceutical Manufacturers and Associations (IFPMA) is typical:

> The research-based pharmaceutical industry plays a unique role in developing new medicines and vaccines to prevent and treat diseases, and improve the lives of patients. Its key contribution to medical progress is turning fundamental research into innovative treatments ... Despite challenging business conditions, the industry undertakes investments that are considerably more risky than those in other high-technology sectors. By investing billions of dollars and thousands of scientist-hours, it pushes the limits of science, improves global health and contributes to the prosperity of society (International Federation of Pharmaceutical Manufacturers & Associations (IFPMA), 2011, 11).

The industry also defends the roles it plays in policymaking, advocacy, and continuing medical education, seeing no conflict in the goals of industry and those of other stakeholders:

> Just as it leads in biomedical innovation, the pharmaceutical industry is proud to play a leading role in sponsoring continuing medical education (CME) for

physicians—an effort that serves the overriding mutual interest to ensure that patients receive the most up-to-date and appropriate care (Holmer, 2001, 2012).

Support for the pharmaceutical industry also comes from outside the industry from people who emphasize the important roles that industry plays in developing and manufacturing medicines and supporting biomedical research, policymaking, and medical education. These supporters of industry may attempt to defend the industry against what they see as unwarranted attacks. Barton and Stossel, for example, deride the "movement" that has emerged to address financial conflicts of interest as follows:

> The [financial conflict of interest] narrative has buried its opposition in an avalanche of one-sided rhetoric, forming what behavioral economists call an 'availability cascade' of industry vilification and unsubstantiated accusations (Barton, Stossel, and Stell, 2014, 666).

De George acknowledges that the pharmaceutical companies sometimes misbehave, but pleads for a more nuanced view of industry's failings, noting that:

> those who are a party to the dispute focus on the period of [patent] protection and often forget the long-term benefits to all that follow when the protection expires (De George, 2009, 170).

More generally, Santoro complains about the well-rehearsed platitudes and taken-for-granted axioms that characterize criticisms of the pharmaceutical industry, arguing that "among observers outside the industry, the greed and moral failings of the industry approach the state of a truism" (Santoro and Gorrie, 2006, 3).

Uncertainty about the Pharmaceutical Industry

While the literature on the pharmaceutical industry is dominated by strongly negative and, to a lesser extent, strongly positive claims, there is also evidence that some organizational field actors are uncertain about the moral status of the industry and those who interact with it.

In a qualitative interview study of Australian medical specialists, for example, Doran et al. found that while some doctors feel confident about engaging with industry as researchers and prescribers, and others avoid industry altogether, a significant proportion fit into a group they referred to as "ambivalent engagers." These doctors recognized, for example, that the profit motive simultaneously drives pharmaceutical innovation, which they support, and underpins industry misconduct, which worries them (Doran et al., 2006). Other studies have revealed similar ambivalence among clinicians, researchers, and policy makers about the industry and their interactions with it (Prosser, Almond, and Walley, 2003; Glaser and Bero, 2005; Morgan et al., 2006).

Uncertainty about the pharmaceutical industry is also evident at the organizational level in the tendency for universities, teaching hospitals, and governments to demand that biomedical researchers engage with industry and commercialize their discoveries, while at the same time expecting these interactions to be limited, disclosed, and defended (Zinner et al., 2010; Chapman et al., 2012). Similarly, policymaking committees, such as those making regulatory or funding decisions, or producing clinical practice guidelines, are expected to include people with high levels of expertise—many of whom are employees of industry or academic "key opinion leaders" who have close ties to industry—while at the same time ensuring that decision-making is free of industry influence (Rockey and Collins, 2010; Norris et al., 2012).

UNDERSTANDING AMBIVALENCE

The discourse about the pharmaceutical industry and those who interact is clearly shaped by a deep ambivalence about the industry. This ambivalence manifests itself at two levels: in debates between those who are wholeheartedly "for" industry and those who are "against" it, and in the inner conflicts of those who appreciate and rely on industry but distrust it at the same time.

The ambivalence towards the pharmaceutical industry has been explained in a variety of ways, which can be categorized broadly as socio-political, moral, intersubjective, and "logical." Taking a socio-political view, Santoro views ambivalence as: "the unraveling of a "grand bargain" between the pharmaceutical industry and society. This grand bargain, he argues:

> was a complex, implicit social contract that allowed the modern global pharmaceutical industry to emerge in the second half of the twentieth century" and that was beneficial to industry and society alike.

Today, however, "this grand bargain is in tatters and public mistrust and resentment of the industry run feverishly high" (Santoro and Gorrie, 2006, 1).

The creation and subsequent breakdown of this social contract has likely been hastened by the fact that the governments and courts worldwide have intervened in numerous ways over the years to "protect the pharmaceutical industry from the downsides of drug development work" (Avorn, 2005, 202) through tax breaks and intellectual property protections that are not offered to other kinds of companies. This has, in turn, created expectations of the pharmaceutical industry that might not be applied to other corporate entities, and that have been unfulfilled, leading to a sense of betrayal.

Taking a more morally oriented view, De George attributes the tension between the pharmaceutical industry and its critics to "an apparent conflict of two rights" in which:

> On the one hand (there) is the right of for-profit corporations to make a profit within the bounds set by law and ethics ... In this respect there are no special rules for

corporations in the health care industries. On the other hand (there) are the human rights of all people to life, and so to health care, which seems to impose obligations on those able to provide such care. These are obligations not placed on other corporations (De George, 2009, 171–172).

The ambivalence about the pharmaceutical industry therefore stems from the sense that the pharmaceutical industry has failed to fulfill its obligations to those with a right to health care.

De George goes on to note, however, that the positive right to health care in fact rests primarily with governments, and not with corporations. Insofar as pharmaceutical companies do have obligations, these are limited to producing the life-saving drugs they develop in sufficient quantities, and doing their "fair share," along with governments to rescue those in need. Matters are complicated further by the idea that the pharmaceutical industry as a whole might have obligations that are not held by individual companies (De George, 2009). Ambivalence towards the pharmaceutical industry is therefore exacerbated by different stakeholders having different ideas as to what obligations rest with government, the industry as a whole, and individual pharmaceutical companies.

Elliott interprets ambivalence towards the pharmaceutical industry intersubjectively in terms of trust. He likens commercialized medicine to the Internet, which has been "transformed by commerce" and which has, in turn, "opened a window for deception" (Elliott, 2010, xv). Yet, unlike the Internet, which "does not operate on trust anymore" medicine still "operates by the old rules":

> Medical journals still trust authors; patients still trust doctors; researchers trust subjects; and subjects trust researchers. Nobody wants to admit that the world has changed. Nobody is willing to concede that trust may no longer be warranted (Elliott, 2010, xv).

This ongoing need and desire to trust in an entity that is not fully trustworthy is therefore a compelling explanation for the ambivalence that people feel towards the pharmaceutical industry.

A fourth way of understanding the ambivalence towards the pharmaceutical industry is that it stems from the ways in which organizational field actors respond to instances in which there are conflicting or competing institutional logics. As explained previously, the rights, duties, and norms that characterize a social institution are expressed through, and exert their force through, the institution's "logic"—that is, the "taken-for-granted" belief and meaning systems that are evident in institutional patterns of activity, discourse and policy (Scott, 2014).

These logics are often multiple and may compete or conflict, and researchers have identified a number of strategies that institutional actors use to navigate competing logics. These include continued efforts to ensure that one logic prevails and another is extinguished. They also include a variety of methods of accommodating more than one logic, including: compartmentalization, in which actors selectively accept some parts of a new logic which rejecting others; ceremonial compliance, where actors reject all or some of an undesirable logic, but do so covertly while pretending to be accepting of the new logic; pragmatic collaboration, where actors "agree to disagree" in order to be able to work together on shared tasks and common goals; and balancing, where actors embrace two logics simultaneously and either try to find some kind of "middle ground" or embrace one logic at some times, and another logic at other times (Kitchener, 2002; Nelson, 2005; Meyer and Hammerschmid, 2006a, 2006b; Thornton and Ocasio, 2008; Reay and Hinings, 2009; Pache and Santos, 2011). This latter group of strategies might result in the formation of a "hybrid" logic (Montgomery and Oliver, 1996; Glynn and Lounsbury, 2005).

It is possible that some of those who are unequivocal in their criticism or defense of the pharmaceutical industry have "chosen" either to embrace or fully reject the existence of a market logic within the health care organizational field and are determined to either rid the organizational field of the industry altogether or allow the field to become one that is dominated by the industry and its market logic. This would be consistent with the first strategy described above: that of competition aimed at achieving complete dominance in a "zero sum game."

On closer inspection, however, it seems that even the strongest critics of the pharmaceutical industry accept the need for the industry in one form or another and are more concerned with addressing market *failure* than with ridding the organizational field of the market itself. In this regard it is noteworthy that some of the strongest critics of the pharmaceutical industry explicitly make the distinction between the evils of markets per se, and the problem of market failure. Angell, for example, argues that the "profitability of the pharmaceutical industry and the poor access to drugs in many parts of the world" has "thrived under conditions of characterized by enormous asymmetry of information between buyers and sellers" and is a "classic case of market failure" (Angell, 2004, x). Avorn places the blame for market failure firmly on the pharmaceutical industry, arguing that:

> Although the industry extols the virtues of unfettered markets, several companies have developed creative strategies to disable these very markets (Avorn, 2005, 225).

If we accept that most institutional actors—including those who are most critical of industry—have not rejected the pharmaceutical industry completely, then the question arises as to what strategies they are using to accommodate the market logic within the health care organizational field.

The main strategy used to accommodate the industry and its market logic seems to be that of compartmentalization (also referred to as loose coupling, bricolage, segmentation, or selection), in which actors explicitly embrace some parts of the market logic, while explicitly rejecting others. This approach is most clearly evident in calls to "distance" or "disentangle" science, medicine, publishing, policymaking, and consumer from the pharmaceutical industry so that the influence of industry is more limited.

The idea that it is both desirable and possible to compartmentalize the market logic is obvious in the almost endless debates about exactly what kinds of interactions with industry are, and are not acceptable, and which of these interactions need to be disclosed to other stakeholders. Rules for interactions with the pharmaceutical industry almost always allow some kinds of interactions, reject others, and insist that certain kinds of interactions are disclosed in the public domain. Importantly, every set of rules and guidelines is unique with respect to where it draws these lines.

A second strategy used by institutional actors to manage the tension between the market logic and other logics is that of "decoupling." This is evident in the approaches (described above) of many clinical, research, publishing, and policymaking organizations to conflicts of interest On the one hand, these organizations behave as if reliance on industry is a necessary and even desirable part of everyday business, and they expect and encourage their employees to engage with industry. But at the same time, they expect these same employees to declare and be able to defend all interactions with industry. It is likely that individual institutional actors also engage in a kind of decoupling process in order to cope with the cognitive dissonance that must arise when they are put in these ambiguous situations.

A third strategy that is evident is that of "balancing." Here institutional actors try to find a "middle ground" or "sweet spot" where the primary goals of industry and those of researchers, clinicians, policy makers, and journal editors can *all* be satisfied. This approach is evident when people argue that companies and patients both benefit from adequately rewarded pharmaceutical innovation, even if this means that the price of patented medicines places them out of some people's reach. The idea that there is a "middle ground" is also evident in claims that both the industry and other stakeholders can benefit from properly controlled industry involvement in research, policymaking, publishing, education, and consumer advocacy. This strategy might also entail "reframing" commercial values, norms, goals, and activities so that they sound more compatible with those of other stakeholders.

Another approach to balancing is not to attempt to find a middle ground, but rather to fully embrace the entirety of one logic in some circumstances, and fully embrace another, competing, logic at other times. This "dialectical" strategy is evident, for example, in the attitudes of those who want there to be no limits at all on the commercialization of biomedical research, but who simultaneously believe that no commercial influence should be allowed when it comes to policymaking or medical education.

There are, therefore, at least four different strategies that actors within the health care organizational field use to manage the ambivalence that arises from tensions between the market logic of the pharmaceutical industry, and the professional, scientific or administrative logics that have, at least in theory, traditionally dominated the field.

ADDRESSING AMBIVALENCE

It is highly unlikely that ambivalence towards the pharmaceutical will ever be overcome. As Santoro notes:

> Given the divergent ends of a for-profit industry and a product with immense public health implications, there will always be some tension in the relationship between the pharmaceutical industry and society (Santoro and Gorrie, 2006, 2).

Put another way, it seems highly unlikely that a "hybrid logic" will ever be created that will comfortably accommodate both market and professional logics and in which the pharmaceutical industry will sit comfortably within the health care organizational field.

This is not necessarily a bad thing—after all, ongoing ambivalence ensures that the necessary checks and balances will always be in place so that any one institutional logic does not come to completely overpower the organizational field. We would not want critics to stop pointing out industry wrongdoing. Nor would we want the industry to stop defending itself and reminding us of all the ways it contributes to our survival, security, and flourishing.

In a sense, the strong pro- and anti-pharma positions reflect opposite poles of a "dialectic." The existence of this dialectic reflects the fact that the health care organizational field, like all complex psycho-social realities, inevitably contains within it potentially polarized elements (Bhaskar et al., 1998). The best way to deal with these kinds of social realities is through dialectical forms of reasoning and debate, which involve explicit thinking in terms of contradictions (Flak, Nordheim, and Munkvold, 2008), and which challenge the idea that apparent contradictions about the nature of social reality are necessarily reflective of a poor grasp of what is "really" going on. If people have apparently opposing views about the nature of social reality, then dialectic provides a way of *making sense* of these apparently "oppositional, and nonreducible" aspects of psycho-social reality (Linehan, 1993, 33).

But while we do not want to (and could not in any case) do away with ambivalence about the pharmaceutical industry, we would be well served if people could be given a deeper understanding of *why* there is so much conflict between stakeholder groups, and why they may feel confused about their own stances. This would help to reduce the cognitive dissonance that is so evident in the current discourse about the pharmaceutical industry, and that likely impairs people's ability to think about problems in nuanced ways. As a start, people might be helped to understand that the pharmaceutical industry is part of a social institution that exists to promote survival, security, and human flourishing, but may not always be successful in doing so. In this way people might feel less pressure to adopt a strong pro- or anti-industry stance.

It would also be helpful if the ambivalence about the pharmaceutical industry could be rendered somewhat less "vitriolic" (Santoro and Gorrie, 2006, 4). This is not (only) because a declining public image is "a bitter pill" for those who work within or collaborate with the pharmaceutical industry, and do so with the best intentions (Santoro and Gorrie, 2006, 4), but rather because polemic of the kind illustrated above has the potential to over-simplify issues, prevent interchange and cooperation between industry and other stakeholders, and obscure potentially creative solutions to problems.

These creative solutions will almost always need to be multifaceted, consisting of a mixture of external regulation, internal regulation, incentives, punishment, transparency, and disengagement. The appropriate mix of strategies will depend on the nature of the problem. For some kinds of problems, it will be absolutely necessary to insist on strong external regulation, mandated transparency, and/or punishment of those who transgress. There should be no leeway, for example, when it comes to obvious abuses of clinical trial participants, burying of safety data, or bribing of policy makers or clinicians.

In other cases, a "softer" and more collaborative approach may be warranted. For example, there are differing views as to the harms and benefits of direct-to-consumer advertising, off-label promotion, and the expansion of "treatable" disease categories, and these debates would benefit from greater engagement between critics of the industry and those within it. Scholars have begun to call for such dialogue and cooperation (Fisher, 2007). Empirical research shows that those within the pharmaceutical industry apply moral principles that are very similar to those of clinicians and researchers. Like clinicians and researchers, industry employees (at least those in medical and regulatory departments) are concerned about doing good, not doing harm, and achieving justice, both for their companies and for the general public (Lipworth and Little, 2014). They also have a variety of sophisticated ways of working through competing commercial and medical or scientific goals (Lipworth, Montgomery, and Little, 2013). This suggests that there would be ways for those with concerns about the pharmaceutical industry to engage more with employees of pharmaceutical companies. However, this collaboration should not occur at the expense of a robust, external discourse in which serious and unquestionable wrongdoing can be detected and addressed.

None of these strategies will ever completely resolve the tensions between market and other logics within the health care organizational field, nor would we want them to for the reasons given above. But the approaches outlined here might help to overcome the "hostile interdependence" and cognitive dissonance that unsettle actors in the increasingly commercialized health care organizational field.

REFERENCES

Allarakhia, M. and Steven, W. (2011). Managing knowledge assets under conditions of radical change: The case of the pharmaceutical industry. *Technovation*, 31(2/3): 105–117.

Angell, M. (2000). Is academic medicine for sale? *New England Journal of Medicine* 342(20): 1516–1518.

Angell, M. (2004). *The truth about the drug companies: How they deceive us and what to do about it*. New York: Random House.

Annas, G. J. and Elias, S. (1999). Thalidomide and the *Titanic*: Reconstructing the technology tragedies of the twentieth century. *American Journal of Public Health*, 89(1): 98–101.

Arman, R., Liff, R., and Wikström, E. (2014). The hierarchization of competing logics in psychiatric care in Sweden. *Scandinavian Journal of Management*, 30(3): 282–291.

Avorn, J. (2005). *Powerful medicines: The benefits, risks and costs of prescription drugs*. New York: Vintage Books.

Barton, D., Stossel, T., and Stell, L. (2014). After 20 years, industry critics bury skeptics, despite empirical vacuum. *International Journal of Clinical Practice*, 68(6): 666–673.

Basch, E. (2013). Toward patient-centered drug development in oncology. *New England Journal of Medicine*, 369(5): 397–400.

Bhaskar, R., Archer, M., Collier, A., Lawson, T., and Norrie, A. (eds) (1998). *Critical realism: Essential readings*. Abingdon: Routledge.

Bianchi, M., Cavaliere, A., Chiaroni, D., Frattini, F., and Chiesa, V. (2011). Organisational modes for Open Innovation in the bio-pharmaceutical industry: An exploratory analysis. *Technovation*, 31(1): 22–33.

Blomgren, M. and Waks, C. (2015). Coping with contradictions: Hybrid professionals managing institutional complexity. *Journal of Professions and Organization*, 2(1): 78–102.

Bombardier, C., Laine, L., Burgos-Vargas, R., Davis, B., Day, R., Ferraz M. B., Hawkey, C. J., Hochberg, M. C., Kvien, T. K., Schnitzer, T. J., Weaver, A., Reicin, A., and Shapiro, D. (2006). Response to expression of concern regarding VIGOR study. *New England Journal of Medicine*, 354(11): 1196–1198.

Buchkowsky, S. S. and Jewesson, P. J. (2004). Industry sponsorship and authorship of clinical trials over 20 years. *Annals of Pharmacotherapy*, 38(4): 579–585.

Chapman, S., Morrell, B., Forsyth, R., Kerridge, I., and Stewart, C. (2012). Policies and practices on competing interests of academic staff in Australian universities. *Medical Journal of Australia*, 196(7): 452–456.

Collyer, F. and White, K. (2011). The privatisation of Medicare and the National Health Service, and the global marketisation of healthcare systems. *Health Sociology Review*, 20(3): 238–244.

Curfman, G. D., Morrissey, S., and Drazen, J. M. (2005). Expression of concern: Bombardier et al., "Comparison of upper gastrointestinal toxicity of rofecoxib and naproxen in patients with rheumatoid arthritis," N Engl J Med 2000; 343:1520–1528. *New England Journal of Medicine*, 353(26): 2813–2814.

Currie, G. and Spyridonidis, D. (2015). Interpretation of multiple institutional logics on the ground: Actors' position, their agency and situational constraints in professionalized contexts. *Organization Studies*, doi: 0170840615604503.

Daemmrich, A. and Bowden, M. (2005). A rising drug industry. *Chemical & Engineering News* 83(25). Available at: <http://pubs.acs.org/isubscribe/journals/cen/83/i25/html/8325intro.html> (accessed September 28, 2015).

Dalsing, M. C. (2011). Industry working with physicians through professional medical associations. *Journal of Vascular Surgery*, 54: 41S–46S.

De George, R. (2009). Two cheers for the pharmaceutical industry. In *Ethics and the Business of Biomedicine*, ed. Arnold, D., pp. 169–197. Cambridge: Cambridge University Press.

DeMets, D. L. and Califf, R. M. (2011). A historical perspective on clinical trials innovation and leadership: Where have the academics gone? *Jama-Journal of the American Medical Association*, 305(7): 713–714.

Doran, E., Kerridge, I., McNeill, P., and Henry, D. (2006). Empirical uncertainty and moral contest: A qualitative analysis of the relationship between medical specialists and the pharmaceutical industry. *Social Science & Medicine*, 62(6): 1510–1519.

Elliott, C. (2010). *White coat, black hat: Adventures on the dark side of medicine*. Boston, MA: Beacon Press.

Epstein, R. S. (2012). R&D transformation and value-based innovation. *Journal of Comparative Effectiveness Research*, 1: 1–2.

Fisher, M. A. (2007). Medicine and industry: A necessary but conflicted relationship. *Perspectives in Biology and Medicine*, 50(1): 1–6.

Flak, L., Nordheim, S., and Munkvold, B. (2008). Analyzing stakeholder diversity in G2G efforts: Combining descriptive stakeholder theory and dialectic process theory. *E-Service Journal*, 6(2): 3–23.

Fugh-Berman, A. J. (2010). The haunting of medical journals: How ghostwriting sold "HRT". *Plos Medicine*, 7(9).

Fugh-Berman, A., Alladin, K., and Chow, J. (2006). Advertising in medical journals: Should current practices change? *Plos Medicine*, 3(6): 762–768.

George, M., Selvarajan, S., Suresh-Kumar, S., Dkhar, S. A., and Chandrasekaran, A. (2013). Globalization of clinical trials: Where are we heading? *Current Clinical Pharmacology*, 8(2): 115–123.

Glaser, B. E. and Bero, L. A. (2005). Attitudes of academic and clinical researchers toward financial ties in research: A systematic review. *Science and Engineering Ethics*, 11(4): 553–573.

Glynn, M. A. and Lounsbury, M. (2005). From the critics' corner: Logic blending, discursive change and authenticity in a cultural production system. *Journal of Management Studies*, 42(5): 1031–1055.

Goldman, M., Compton, C., and Mittleman, B. B. (2013). Public–private partnerships as driving forces in the quest for innovative medicines. *Clinical and Translational Medicine*, 2(1): 2–2.

Goodrick, E. and Reay, T. (2011). Constellations of institutional logics: Changes in the professional work of pharmacists. *Work and Occupations*, 38(3): 372–416.

Guston, D. H. (1999). Stabilizing the boundary between US politics and science: The role of the Office of Technology Transfer as a boundary organization. *Social Studies of Science*, 29(1): 87–111.

Healy, D. (2012). *Pharmageddon*. Berkeley: University of California Press.

Healy, D. (2014). Dr David Healy (Blog). Available at: <http://davidhealy.org/professional-suicide/> (accessed September 28, 2015).

Herson, J. (2006). Innovation in pharmaceuticals: Speeding up the development of new cures. *Futurist*, 40(1): 25–29.

Holmer, A. F. (2001). Industry strongly supports continuing medical education. *Jama-Journal of the American Medical Association*, 285(15): 2012–2014.

Hopkins, F., Galligher, C. and Levine, A. (1999). Medical affairs and drug information practices within the pharmaceutical industry: Results of a benchmark survey. *Drug Information Journal*, 33: 69–85.

Hunter, J. and Stephens, S. (2010). Is open innovation the way forward for big pharma? *Nature Reviews Drug Discovery*, 9(2): 87–88.

International Federation of Pharmaceutical Manufacturers & Associations (IFPMA) (2011). The Pharmaceutical industry and global health: Facts and figures. Available at: <http://www.

ifpma.org/fileadmin/content/Publication/2011/2011_The_Pharmaceutical_Industry_and_Global_Health_low_ver2.pdf> (accessed September 28, 2015).

Jakobsen, P. H., Wang, M.-W., and Nwaka, S. (2011). Innovative partnerships for drug discovery against neglected diseases. *Plos Neglected Tropical Diseases* 5(9): e1221, doi:10.1371/journal.pntd.0001221.

Janssen, R. and Vandermade, J. (1990). Privatisation in health-care: Concepts, motives and policies. *Health Policy*, 14(3): 191–202.

Kaitin, K. (2010). Deconstructing the drug development process: The new face of innovation. *Clinical Pharmacology and Therapeutics*, 87(3): 356–361.

Khanna, I. (2012). Drug discovery in pharmaceutical industry: Productivity challenges and trends. *Drug Discovery Today*, 17(19/20): 1088–1102.

Kitchener, M. (2002). Mobilizing the logic of managerialism in professional fields: The case of academic health centre mergers. *Organization Studies*, 23(3): 391–420.

Le Fanu, J. (2000). *The rise and fall of modern medicine*. New York: Carroll & Graf.

Lesko, L. J. (2012). Drug research and translational bioinformatics. *Clinical Pharmacology & Therapeutics*, 91(6): 960–962.

Leventhal, P. (2013). Medical writing around the world. *Medical Writing*, 22(2): 79.

Linehan, M. (1993). *Cognitive-behavioral treatment of borderline personality disorder*. New York: Guildford Press.

Lipworth, W. and Little, M. (2014). Deriving and critiquing an empirically-based framework for pharmaceutical ethics. *American Journal of Bioethics (AJOB) Empirical Bioethics*, 5(1): 23–32.

Lipworth, W., Montgomery, K. and Little, M. (2013). How pharmaceutical industry employees manage competing moral commitments. *Journal of Bioethical Inquiry*, 10(3): 355–367.

Little, M., Lipworth, W., Gordon, J., Markham, P., and Kerridge, I. (2012). Values-based medicine and modest foundationalism. *Journal of Evaluation in Clinical Practice*, 18(5): 1020–1026.

Menius, J. A. Jr. and Rousculp, M. D. (2014). Growth in health care data causing an evolution in the pharmaceutical industry. *North Carolina Medical Journal*, 75(3): 188–190.

Meyer, R. and Hammerschmid, G. (2006a). Public management reform: An identity project. *Public Policy and Administration*, 21(1): 99–115.

Meyer, R. E. and Hammerschmid, G. (2006b). Changing institutional logics and executive identities: A managerial challenge to public administration in Austria. *The American Behavioral Scientist*, 49(7): 1000–1014.

Miller, S. (2009). *The moral foundations of social institutions: A philosophical study*. New York: Cambridge University Press.

Mirowski, P. and Van Horn, R. (2005). The contract research organization and the commercialization of scientific research. *Social Studies of Science*, 35(4): 503–548.

Montgomery, K. and Lipworth, W. (2014). Using the survival-security-flourishing model to explain the emergence and shape of the medical profession. In *Debates in values-based practice: arguments for and against*, ed. Loughlin, M., pp. 198–208. Cambridge: Cambridge University Press.

Montgomery, K. and Oliver, A. L. (1996). Responses by professional organizations to multiple and ambiguous institutional environments: The case of AIDS. *Organization Studies*, 17(4): 649–671.

Morgan, M. A., Dana, J., Loewenstein, G., Zinberg, S., and Schulkin, J. (2006). Interactions of doctors with the pharmaceutical industry. *Journal of Medical Ethics*, 32(10): 559–563.

Munos, B. H. and Chin, W. W. (2011). How to revive breakthrough innovation in the pharmaceutical industry. *Science Translational Medicine*, 3(89).

Nelson, A. J. (2005). Cacophany or harmony? Multivocal logics and technology licensing by the Stanford University Department of Music. *Industrial and Corporate Change*, 14(1): 93–118.

Norris, S. L., Holmer, H. K., Burda, B. U., Ogden, L. A., and Fu, R. (2012). Conflict of interest policies for organizations producing a large number of clinical practice guidelines. *Plos One*, 7(5).

Owen-Smith, J. (2003). From separate systems to a hybrid order: Accumulative advantage across public and private science at Research One universities. *Research Policy*, 32: 1081–1104.

Pache, A.-C. and Santos, F. (2011). Inside the hybrid organization: An organizational level view of responses to conflicting institutional demands, ESSEC Working Paper 11001, ESSEC Business School. Available at: <http://hal-essec.archives-ouvertes.fr/hal-00580128/fr/> (accessed September 28, 2015).

Paul, S. M., Mytelka, D. S., Dunwiddie, C. T., Persinger, C. C., Munos, B. H., Lindborg, S. R., and Schacht, A. L. (2010). How to improve R&D productivity: The pharmaceutical industry's grand challenge. *Nature Reviews Drug Discovery*, 9(3): 203–214.

Prosser, H., Almond, S., and Walley, T. (2003). Influences on GPs' decision to prescribe new drugs: The importance of who says what. *Family Practice*, 20(1): 61–68.

PWC (2012). Pharma 2020—From vision to decision. Pharma 2020. Available at: <https://www.pwc.com/gx/en/pharma-life-sciences/pharma2020/assets/pwc-pharma-success-strategies.pdf> (accessed September 28, 2015).

Rafols, I., Hopkins, M. M., Hoekman, J., Siepel, J., O'Hare, A., Perianes-Rodriguez, A., and Nightingale, P. (2014). Big Pharma, little science? A bibliometric perspective on Big Pharma's R&D decline. *Technological Forecasting and Social Change*, 81: 22–38.

Ratcliffe, L. T. (2011). A venture capital view of challenges, opportunities, and innovation in biomedical research. *Clinical Pharmacology & Therapeutics*, 89(2): 174–176.

Reay, T. and Hinings, C. B. (2009). Managing the rivalry of competing institutional logics. *Organization Studies*, 30(6): 629–652.

Rockey, S. J. and Collins, F. S. (2010). Managing financial conflict of interest in biomedical research. *Jama-Journal of the American Medical Association*, 303(23): 2400–2402.

Rodwin, M. A. (2010). Drug advertising, continuing medical education, and physician prescribing: A historical review and reform proposal. *Journal of Law Medicine & Ethics*, 38(4): 807–815.

Rose, S. L. (2013). Patient advocacy organizations: Institutional conflicts of interest, trust, and trustworthiness. *Journal of Law Medicine & Ethics*, 41(3): 680–687.

Rothman, D. J., McDonald, W. J., Berkowitz, C. D., Chimonas, S. C., DeAngelis, C. D., Hale, R. W., Nissen, S. E., Osborn, J. E., Scully, J. H. Jr., Thomson, G. E., and Wofsy, D. (2009). Professional medical associations and their relationships with industry: A proposal for controlling conflict of interest. *Jama-Journal of the American Medical Association*, 301(13): 1367–1372.

Rothman, S. M., Raveis, V. H., Friedman, A., and Rothman, D. J. (2011). Health advocacy organizations and the pharmaceutical industry: An analysis of disclosure practices. *American Journal of Public Health*, 101(4): 602–609.

Rovira, A. R. I., Foley, G. L., and Clemo, F. A. (2011). Sponsor-CRO practices that facilitate the creation of a high-quality pathology report: A pharmaceutical sponsor's perspective. *Toxicologic Pathology*, 39(6): 1013–1016.

Salkeld, G. (2011). Pharmaceutical benefits scheme cost recovery. *Australian Prescriber*, 34(3): 62–63.

Samila, S. and Sorenson, O. (2010). Venture capital as a catalyst to commercialization. *Research Policy*, 39(10): 1348–1360.

Sanberg, P. R., Gharib, M., Harker, P. T., Kaler, E. W., Marchase, R. B., Sands, T. D., Arshadi, N., and Sarkar, S. (2014). Changing the academic culture: Valuing patents and commercialization toward tenure and career advancement. *Proceedings of the National Academy of Sciences of the United States of America*, 111(18): 6542–6547.

Santoro, M. and Gorrie, T. (eds) (2006). *Ethics and the pharmaceutical industry.* Cambridge: Cambridge University Press.

Scott, W. (2008). Lords of the dance: Professionals as institutional agents. *Organization Studies*, 29: 219–238.

Scott, W. (2014). *Institutions and organizations.* Thousand Oaks, CA: Sage Publications.

Scott, W. R., Reuf, M., Mendel, P., and Caronna, C. A. (2000). *Institutional change and health care organization: From professional dominance to managed care.* Chicago: University of Chicago Press.

Shapin, S. (2008). *The scientific life: A moral history of a late modern vocation.* Chicago: University of Chicago Press.

Smith, K. (2012). Fools, facilitators and flexians: Academic identities in marketised environments. *Higher Education Quarterly*, 66(2): 155–173.

Steinbrook, R. (2008). Saying no isn't nice: The travails of Britain's national institute for health and clinical excellence. *New England Journal of Medicine*, 359(19): 1977–1981.

Stevens, A., Milne, R., and Burls, A. (2003). Health technology assessment: History and demand. *Journal of Public Health Medicine*, 25(2): 98–101.

Swan, J., Bresnen, M., Robertson, M., Newell, S., and Dopson, S. (2010). When policy meets practice: Colliding logics and the challenges of "Mode 2" initiatives in the translation of academic knowledge. *Organization Studies*, 31(9–10): 1311–1340.

Swan, M. (2012). Scaling crowdsourced health studies: The emergence of a new form of contract research organization. *Personalized Medicine*, 9(2): 223–234.

Thiel, K. A. (2004). Goodbye Columbus! New NRDOs forego discovery. *Nature Biotechnology*, 22(9): 1087–1092.

Thornton, P. H. and Ocasio, W. (2008). Institutional logics. In *The SAGE handbook of organizational institutionalism*, ed. Greenwood, R., Oliver, C., Suddaby, R., and Sahlin-Andersson, K., pp. 99–129. London: SAGE Publications Ltd.

Volmink, J., Siegfried, N., Robertson, K., and Gulmezoglu, A. M. (2004). Research synthesis and dissemination as a bridge to knowledge management: The Cochrane Collaboration. *Bulletin of the World Health Organization*, 82(10): 778–783.

Waldorff, S. B. (2013). Accounting for organizational innovations: Mobilizing institutional logics in translation. *Scandinavian Journal of Management*, 29(3): 219–234.

Wolfe, S. M. (2014). The Washington brief. Does $760m a year of industry funding affect the FDA's drug approval process? *BMJ*- 349.

Zinner, D. E., DesRoches, C. M., Bristol, S. J., Clarridge, B., and Campbell, E. G. (2010). Tightening conflict-of-interest policies: The impact of 2005 ethics rules at the NIH. *Academic Medicine*, 85(11): 1685–1691.

Zuckerman, R. and Milne, C.-P. (2012). Market watch: Industry perspectives on personalized medicine. *Nature Reviews Drug Discovery*, 11(3): 179.

CHAPTER 23

MANAGEMENT CONSULTING IN HEALTH

IAN KIRKPATRICK, CHRIS LONSDALE, AND INDRANETH NEOGY

INTRODUCTION

THERE can be few topics that have generated so much heated debate and controversy as the increasing role played by management consultants in public services, in particular, health care. In the US, health care has become one of the most profitable areas for management consulting, with annual growth of 18.4% reported in 2013 (Sager, 2013). The UK has seen a similar trend, with it being announced recently that National Health Service (NHS) annual expenditure on management consultants had returned to a previous high of £600 million (Oliver, 2014). In many countries this trend has been widely criticized, with sensational newspaper headlines talking about how health systems are being "hijacked" by consultants (Rose, 2012) and reports of large-scale (and costly) project failures. The perception sometimes given is that management consultants are at best shaping policy to suit their own interests and, in the worst case, "wining and dining" at the tax-payers' expense. But how correct are these assumptions? What do we know about management consulting in the health sector, why are governments and managers using them and with what conseqeunces?

In this chapter, our aim is to begin to address some of these questions. To do so, we provide a brief review of the literature from economics and organizational theory on the nature and role of management consultants in the wider economy. We then focus more specifically on the case of public services and health. Drawing on a variety of sources, we offer an overview of the role that management consultants are playing in the health sector, an account of the factors that have driven increased spending on consulting advice, and a discussion of the past and future consequences. We look in detail at what many have described as a "revolving door" relationship between government and leading global consulting firms. Lastly, we consider the changing practices of public sector clients in the procurement of consulting advice.

A key conclusion we will draw in this chapter is that management consultants have played (and are likely to continue to play) a significant role in the inception and implementation of new public management (NPM) reforms in health services. In the process consultants have been transformed from arms-length vendors of specialist services into what might best be described as "partners" in government, an almost permanent feature of the public sector organizational landscape.

However, before we begin it is important to note that while there is considerable research on the role of management consultants in the wider economy, research specifically within the health sector remains very much in its infancy. As a result, in this chapter we have been forced to supplement a limited range of academic sources with extensive material from practitioner publications, websites, and (where available) government publications. A further caveat is that much of the ongoing debate about the role and impact of management consultants in health (at least that which is available in English) has been heavily concentrated within one national case: the UK NHS. The reasons for this are hard to gauge, but may have much to do with the fact that the UK has been (and remains) at the forefront of public management reforms over past decades (Pollitt and Boukaert, 2011). Either way, the implication is that while it is possible to make general reference to the international experience (notably the US), the bulk of the discussion that follows will be focused on the UK.

Both of these caveats mean that the conclusions we are able to draw in this chapter are inevitably quite tentative. As we shall argue in the closing section, more sustained research is needed on the nature and impact of management consulting interventions in health care to strengthen the evidence base. This research should also be comparative to account for the impact that different national institutions might have. As such, our aim is essentially to perform a ground clearing exercise, to draw initial conclusions and also set out an agenda for future work on this topic.

MANAGEMENT CONSULTING: DEFINITIONS AND DEBATES

What Is Management Consulting?

A useful starting point for understanding management consulting is the industry definition. According to the Management Consultancies Association (MCA), the relevant employers' organization in the UK, management consulting is "the practice of creating value for organizations, through improved performance, achieved by providing objective advice and implementing business solutions" (Management Consultancies Association, 2015). This definition, however, glosses over a great deal of debate and controversy regarding what management consulting is, or how one might define it as a field or sector. This is apparent even within many core practitioner texts on the topic (O'Mahoney and Markham, 2013). Nikolova and Devinney (2012), for example, highlight differences between so-called "expert" models of consulting, where consultants are essentially sellers of expertise, responsible for objectively diagnosing and solving problems for the client, and "social learning models," which focus more on the role of consultants as helpers, enabling clients to solve their own problems.

Difficulties also arise when we seek to define the consulting industry or sector. In their annual survey, the European Federation of Management Consulting Associations (FEACO) segment the industry into four primary categories: general consulting, including "business consulting and IT consulting"; development and systems integration consulting; outsourcing and value added services; and other services (training, executive search, etc.). Reviews of the industry also highlight wide variations in "functional focus and structure, ranging from large global corporations to medium-sized domestic firms, small partnerships, solo practitioners, academic consultants and corporate 'internal' consultants" (Kitay and Wright, 2007, 1618).

This variety is partly accounted for by the relative lack of any significant state or even professional regulation of the sector. According to Kubr (2002, 130–131): "[E]ven in sophisticated business cultures, virtually anyone can call himself or herself a management or business consultant and offer services to business clients without any diploma, certificate, license credentials, recommendations, or registration." While professional bodies exist, such as the Institute of Consulting in the UK, they have no ability to control entry to the sector and membership is low relative to employment (Kirkpatrick, Muzio, and Ackroyd, 2012). This fact has made it hard to define, let alone police, the boundaries of the industry, with numerous overlaps existing between the work of management consultants and other professions involved in business services such as IT, accounting, project management, and finance (Kipping and Kirkpatrick, 2013).

This ambiguity over what constitutes "management consulting" also has much to do with the historical development of the sector. Following Kipping (2002), it can be seen how this development over the twentieth century was characterized by successive and overlapping waves of change. The dominant consultancies in the first wave provided services related to the "scientific" organization of individual work and the production process in factories and offices. By contrast, the most visible consultancies in the second wave (from the 1950s) concentrated on advice to top management in terms of corporate strategy and structure. Finally, those in the, still emerging, third wave focus on the use of information and communication technologies to control far-flung and extensively networked client organizations. Over this timeframe, changes to both the predominant types of client organization and the concerns of senior management have provided opportunities for consultancies to offer new types of services.

However management consulting is defined, as an activity there can be no denying its impressive scale and growth in recent times. Worldwide, total revenue was estimated to be $3 billion in 1980 but by 2013 had risen to $228 billion (Kennedy, 2013). Over 60% (around $138 billion of revenue) of this market is accounted for by the US management consulting industry (Statistica, 2015). According to the most recent figures from the MCA, the UK consulting industry was worth around £9 billion in 2013 (around 6% of global turnover) with headline growth for 2014 predicted at around 8% (O'Mahoney and Markham, 2013). In terms of the breakdown of expenditure, FEASCO estimate that "business consulting" accounts for over 52% of turnover (FEASCO, 2010).

The growing significance of the sector is also reflected in the numbers employed. Precise calculations of employment are hard to come by given different definitions of the sector (Fincham, 2006), although even conservative estimates show rapid growth. Kirkpatrick, Muzio, and Ackroyd (2012), for example, estimate that numbers employed in the sector rose from approximately 1,950 in 1964, to 42,000 in 2000, rising to almost 95,000 by 2008.

Lastly, in terms of industry structure, there are, as mentioned, a great many sources of consulting advice ranging from sole practitioners to large multi-functional consulting firms and the advisory services of the major audit firms. Similar to other kinds of business service, the sector is dominated in numerical terms by small and medium-sized enterprises. However, management consulting is also distinctive for the role played by the largest firms. While representing only 2% of the top 500 companies, the ten largest firms account for more than 50% of total fee income (O'Mahoney and Markham, 2013). The ranking of these global firms is constantly evolving. In 2009, for example, the top ten firms were made up of, in rank order: Deloitte, IBM, PWC, Accenture, E&Y, CSC, KPMG, Fujitsu, HP, and Capgemini. Interestingly, many of the firms that are traditionally thought of, in terms of brand reputation, as leading management consultancy firms, most notably McKinsey and Boston Consulting Group, are no longer at the top of the tree (Adams, 2011).

Explaining the Rise of Management Consulting

The facts and figures presented above testify not only to the scale and diversity of the sector, but also to its meteoric rise in recent decades. According to O'Mahoney and Markham (2013), in the period from 1980 to 2008, global management consulting revenues increased by approximately 10,000%. The significance of this rise is also captured by figures for the increase in the ratio of consultants to managers, which is calculated to have risen from 1:100 in 1965 to 1:13 in 1995 (McKenna, 2006). But how are we to explain this change, especially at a time when managers themselves (the clients of consultants) are significantly better qualified and arguably more knowledgeable (Stern, 2010)? In the wider consulting literature, this question has been debated extensively, with observers stressing either demand or (perhaps more crucially) supply-side explanations for consulting growth. In the context of this chapter, it is not possible to do justice to this increasingly sophisticated literature. However, given the significance of this question to our own concerns (the role of consulting in health) it is worth briefly summarizing the main contours of the debate.

A first perspective is that consulting growth arises naturally from the changing needs and consequent demands of clients for advice and services that add value to their business. Such a positive evaluation may even extend to the role that consultants sometimes play as "political agents" of change on behalf of the client, reinforcing or legitimating commitments to policies that have already been decided (Clark and Greatbatch, 2002). Demand-side factors are frequently captured in industry surveys. A 2006 study by the MCA, for example, reported that 66% of clients stated they recruited consultants because staff didn't possess the necessary skills, 45% said they provided original thinking, 34% objective perspective, 17% to provide interim cover, 17% to gain access to methodologies, and 10% to validate an internal decision (O'Mahoney and Markham, 2013).

These themes are also reflected in the academic literature on management consultancy, especially those accounts which emphasise structural explanations for consulting demand (Fincham, 1999). Typical of this view is the work of Canback (1998), who argues that the demand for consultants ("symbolic analysts") is linked to rising international transaction costs encountered by client organizations which stem from the need to "deploy considerable coordination resources in order to realise production scale and scope economies" (Canback, 1998, 4). To address this challenge, clients must either develop their own consulting operations or outsource the activity. In the longer term, according to Canback, outsourcing becomes more economical because management consultants have lower production costs of giving advice relative to insiders. They are also able to achieve substantial economies of knowledge, arising from their work across large numbers of clients or sectors (also see Czerniawska, 2002).

A related argument is to explain the rise of management consulting in terms of the changing nature and function of management itself. Hence David (2012) notes how major consulting firms "rode the coattails" of US corporations in expanding around the world in the post-war period. It is this wave of expansion that helped cast management consulting firms as bringers of "best practice" to the world, as the agents of globalization (Wood, 2002), or, in a less positive light, as agents of "Americanization" (Kipping and Wright, 2012, 168).

This demand-side explanation, however, contrasts sharply with more critical perspectives which, in recent years, have begun to stress the agency of consultants themselves as fashion setters, effectively creating demand for their own services (Sturdy et al., 2009). Here, the emphasis is on the "symbolic nature of consultant strategies and consultancy as a powerful system of persuasion" (Fincham, 1999, 335). In common with other agents such as gurus, business schools, and mass media organizations, consultants are seen as key players in the commodification and dissemination of management fashions (Jung and Kieser, 2012; Suddaby and Greenwood, 2001). While these fashions may promise quantum leaps in performance, it is suggested that more often than not they are based on hyperbole and un-substantiated advice (Sorge and van Witteloostuijn, 2004). Indeed, to a greater extent than with other business services professions, consultants are accused of actively generating "demand for their own services [. . .] by stirring up managers' fear and greed and by making managers dependent on them" (Kieser, 2002, 182). The result is an artificially inflated uptake of management fads, not to mention the costs associated with cynicism and disillusionment when change interventions fail to produce the promised results (Sturdy et al., 2009).

Therefore, significant concerns have been raised about the role of consultants in promoting the consumption of their services and the hidden costs associated with this. However, while this critical lens is useful, it is important not to get too carried away with the idea that consultants are entirely the arbiters of their own destiny or to overstate the naivety of clients. Much of the latest research on this topic has emphasized the knowledge and agency of clients in the process of negotiating consultancy projects (Czarniawska and Mazza, 2003). There is also a growing body of evidence that clients have started to become more systematic and demanding in their use of consulting firms, especially with regard to procurement practices (Werr and Perner, 2007; Jung, 2008). Indeed, it is argued by some that client procurement functions are going too far in their efforts to drive down margins and are driving a wedge between client end-users and consultants (O'Mahoney, Heusinkveld, and Wright, 2013).

MANAGEMENT CONSULTING IN HEALTH

In this section, we turn to the more specific concerns of the chapter—the nature, drivers, and impact of management consulting activity in the health sector. As noted earlier, the limitations of data mean that we will focus primarily on the UK experience, although, where possible, reference will be made to other national cases, the US in particular.

Historical Evolution

It seems that in Europe and North America management consulting firms have been involved with health care for some time, although precisely when this involvement began is hard to gauge (Kipping and Saint-Martin, 2005). Where the UK NHS is concerned, the story really begins with McKinsey in 1972. The contribution of McKinsey to what would come to be known as the Grey Book (Edwards, 1995) sits well with Kipping's (2002) categorization of McKinsey as the archetypal "strategy and structure" consulting firm. This report (in collaboration with Brunel University) concentrated on rearranging the management and structure of the NHS. True to the spirit of the age, McKinsey modified popular matrix management concepts to fit the NHS context, ushering in a regional structure and model of consensus management (Harrison and Pollitt, 1994).

It was to be some time before management consulting firms again acquired a similar strategic role in directing policy in the NHS. The introduction of general management after 1983 (effectively scrapping the organizational model set out in the Grey Book) followed not consultant advice but a report by Sir Roy Griffiths, of the large retailer JD Sainsbury. The next major reform program, set out in the 1989 white paper "Working for Patients," and ushering in the purchase-provider split in the NHS, had also not been the product of consultant advice. Instead, these proposals emerged from a small clique of politicians, who, in turn, had been influenced by a Stanford Professor Alan Enthoven.

These reforms did, however, provide great opportunities for consulting firms. Many of the requirements of the new quasi-market, created in 1991, called for better tracking of activity and systems for billing. All of this fell neatly into the domain of what Kipping (2002) called the wave of "information and communication" consulting. There was a need for the design and implementation of ICT systems to facilitate the development of internal markets. As we shall see, the major consulting firms have been heavily involved in this activity, including Fujitsu/ICL, KPMG, Deloitte, and Andersen Consulting (ancestor of Accenture).

Although the election of the "New Labour" administration in 1997 partially de-emphasized the role of the quasi-market, an ongoing commitment to "modernizing" government, including the NHS, ensured that even greater emphasis was placed on information systems to deliver improvements. This also chimed with wider moves towards "e-government," promoting IT as a tool to overcome organizational (spatial) boundaries and make services more "joined up" (Bohlen et al., 2005). The New Labour government's enthusiasm for outsourcing across the public sector also created opportunities for many firms to give advice as well as implementation support to the NHS. In particular, the consulting firms attached to large accounting firms (for example, KPMG, Deloitte, and PwC) found outsourcing and the Private Finance Initiative (PFI) to be useful cross-selling opportunities. Therefore, alongside the implementation of contracts by the accounting firms, management consultants got involved in projects relating to service redefinition and tendering strategies (Craig, 2006).

Most recently, the arrival of the Coalition government in 2010 raised consulting firms' involvement to a new level. McKinsey consultants were heavily involved (Rose, 2012) in drafting the new Health and Social Care Bill and within days of the 2010 general election had signed a £330,000 contract to advise Monitor. Crucially, in the new act Monitor had a responsibility to oversee a new level of marketization—enforcing competitive tendering on commissioning organizations. This tendering requirement and the complete reorganization of primary care governance has, as we shall see, opened many more opportunities for consulting firms.

Expenditure on Management Consulting in Health Systems

Reliable figures on the extent of management consulting in health systems and how this has changed over time are very hard to come by. In the UK NHS, following the 1974 reorganization, although consultant involvement almost certainly increased, only figures for total government spending on consultants are available. In 1979, this figure stood at around £6 million, but grew exponentially to £246 million by 1990 (Saint-Martin, 2012). This dramatic increase was noted in a report by the UK government's Efficiency Unit in

1994, which stated that "government spending on external consultancy increased 'nearly fourfold' between 1985 and 1990" (Efficiency Unit, 1994, 64).

From 1990 to 2005, UK government spending on consultants increased at an even faster pace. By 2001, billed amounts had reached £600 million and they rose further, to £1.58 billion, by 2005 (NAO, 2006). This latter rise is partly attributable to a number of large-scale initiatives aimed at implementing various forms of "e-government" (for example, tax returns and passport applications). However, the National Audit Office (2006) attributed part of a further jump in expenditure to £2.8 billion by 2005–2006 projects within the NHS. Specifically, they estimated that the proportion spent on health was around 20%, or £600 million.

To some extent, these estimates were confirmed after 2007 when, for a brief period, the UK government did publish annual NHS expenditure on external consultants. This data reveals NHS spending rising from £200 million in 2007 to over £400 million by 2010 (Macleod, 2014). The most recent estimates for 2014–15 suggest a continued upward trend with spending rising to £640 million, despite a stated government commitment to "reduce their management costs by 46% over the next four years" (Consultancy.uk, 2014). These figures mean that health care consulting now accounts for roughly 5% of the total turnover of the UK consulting industry.

All the indications are that this growth in consultant expenditure has been replicated in other countries. According to Consulting.uk (2015), in 2012 the global health care consulting market was worth approximately $6 billion, but is forecast to grow to $7 billion by the end of 2015. In this context, "the US market is with a distance the largest market for health care consulting, making up almost two thirds (62%) of the $6.33 billion."

The Focus of Management Consulting in Health

Although management consulting activity in health appears to be increasing in many countries, our knowledge of the specifics remains patchy. Where the UK NHS is concerned, the indications are that almost every major firm has been involved at some point, including the current top ten. Many other firms have also been major players in the health sector, most notably McKinsey, who have perhaps the longest relationship, and home grown UK firms such as PA Consulting. In addition to this, the regular presence of HR consulting firms, such as Hays and Mercer, should be noted. With the rise of "lean management" as a philosophy, firms such as GE Healthcare have also become prominent recently (Sloan et al., 2014).

In terms of the kinds of services these firms provide, the data on the NHS are limited. One of the best estimates comes from a Royal College of Nursing (RCN) report (2009) which, drawing on freedom of information requests, pieced together an overview of consulting activity undertaken in the years 2007–2008 and 2008–2009. In this period, the RCN found that 22% of expenditure on consulting was on the operation of "direct patient care." This included activities such as clinical service reviews, productive ward and related initiatives, specialist advice on clinical pathway design, and quality of care initiatives, such as benchmarking and audit. The remaining 78% was split across what might be seen as "the business side" of health care. Important categories included advice on PFI, commissioning services, support for Foundation Trust applications, and market testing and development initiatives. Other sources testify to the fact that management consulting firms have become involved in providing strategic "turnaround" services. A high profile example of this recently is the regulatory body, Monitor, which is reported to have spent 40% of its 2013 annual budget (approximately £9 million) on projects provided by four major consulting firms, KPMG, McKinsey, PwC, and Deloitte (*Yorkshire Post*, 2014). Individual trusts have also engaged consultants to conduct "strategic reviews" of services (typically over a five-year period), with evidence to suggest that McKinsey has become a leading "go-to" specialist in this area. Recent examples include West Dorset Clinical Commissioning Group, currently spending £2.7 million with McKinsey to conduct a "strategic review" (National Health Executive, 2015) and South Tees Hospitals NHS Foundation Trust, reported to have spent £500,000 for "advice on cost cutting" (Guillot, 2014).

A different area of activity relates to the provision of corporate services, increasingly outsourced following the Health and Social Care Act in 2012. This Act led, not only to the formation of Clinical Commissioning Groups (CCG), led by GPs, but also to the creation of separate organizations, Commissioning Support Units, to assist with commissioning activity. Early reports suggest that many of the providers of these support services are management consulting firms, offering a variety of services covering strategy, performance management, planning, change management, governance, procurement, and organizational design.

The activities mentioned so far point to how management consultants have become deeply involved in most aspects of the business of managing and organizing health care within the NHS. Even this, however, may not capture the full extent of their involvement. While firms, such as McKinsey, are providing high-level strategic reviews of services, there is also evidence that they are working as think-tanks, producing reports on the future of the system as a whole (Engwall, 2012). Recent examples of this include PwC's initiative to promote policy transfer related to the development of health care economies (PwC, 2015) and McKinsey's joint venture with the London School of Economics to develop international models for effective hospital management, including clinical leadership (Dorgan et al., 2010). Deloitte has also moved into think-tank activities, publishing a report on the cost saving potential of better resourced GP services (Campbell, 2014).

Various other new directions are also apparent in the NHS, including the implementation of lean systems (Sloan et al., 2014) and new technologies. The latter include systems for managing health records and supporting data analytics and data mining to improve clinical decision making. In this respect, consultancies such as Accenture Health and PA Consulting are now fully engaged with the latest fashion of "big data" and health analytics. By contrast, KPMG's signature project in the UK health sector is a partnership with the NHS Leadership Academy to "transform the culture of the NHS" through the development of various online and residential programmes to train the next generation of clinical leaders (NHS Leadership Academy, 2013). This kind of involvement in deep organizational change highlights how the internal consulting and change management capacity of the NHS no longer seems to be able to function without outside help.

In terms of the experience of other countries, in the US the evidence suggests while, as with the UK, the largest global firms are present in the health care market (for example, Deloitte, Accenture, and KPMG), a majority of top ten firms have, if anything, an even stronger health care specialization (Huron Consulting Group, 2014). This may in part be due to the greater geographic size of the US market and the greater number of health care firms. A further crucial contrast with the UK is the wider range of activities that health care firms seek advice and support for. Particular areas of difference include a greater emphasis on sales and marketing (e.g., Huron), billing and regulatory compliance (e.g., Navigant). This is unsurprising, of course, given that health care in the US is provided in a market-based system where greater attention is paid to sales and marketing and where there is a multiplicity of commercial transactions (Woolhandler, Campbell, and Himmelstein, 2003).

Accounting for the Growth of Management Consulting in Health Systems

Explanations for the growth of management consulting advice in the health care sector are arguably no different to those that apply to the wider economy. As we suggested above, this may be especially true in the US, where the marketization of health services, with multiple providers and buyers, generates a strong commercial demand for external advice. However, in health systems that are both state-funded and managed, including the UK NHS, a more complex set of dynamics are apparent.

From the earliest point, management consultants in the NHS have been viewed by their clients (mainly government ministers and senior civil servants) as critical agents in the process of re-structuring and modernization. Initially, in the 1970s, this emphasized the need for "rational planning" and advice on how to make the administration of welfare states more "scientific" and professional (Saint-Martin, 2012). Later on, however, this demand for outside advice was shaped by the rise of the NPM and a growing interest in making government activities more "corporate" and "business like" (Pollitt and Bouckaert, 2014).

The enthusiasm for outside advice also coincided with a declining trust in, and self-confidence of, the established professions and civil service (Aucoin, 2011). This was notably the case following the election of the first Thatcher administration in 1979. The new government felt that civil servants were neither naturally committed to their goal of creating a minimalist state (Bakvis, 1997), nor sufficiently competent to design and implement the large-scale changes they envisaged. Thus, a major subtext of public sector reform would be the injection of outside experts that the governing politicians felt could be trusted to further their aims.

However, while it is legitimate to emphasize the neo-liberal ideological preference of politicians to favor the use of management consultants, one should not over-state this point. While, in the first half of the 1990s, New Labour had been critical of rising expenditure on management consultants, it also began to make greater use of them soon after taking office, albeit with a different focus on modernization and e-government (Kipping and Saint-Martin, 2005). It is also important to note how more specific conditions facing public (including health) sectors around the world may have driven the demand for management consultants.

With regard to these conditions in the UK, two main points can be made. The first relates to the sheer scale and pace of management reforms over the previous three decades. Indeed, it is no exaggeration to say that history of the NHS since the 1980s is a story of one major reorganization after another. If anything, this process has intensified in recent years under the current coalition government, whose re-structuring of the NHS was described by one commentator as a "change so big it could be seen from space" (Kirkpatrick and McCabe, 2011). As a recent King's Fund report (Appelby et al., 2015) noted, the demands created by these complex changes have been immense and in the process this has generated increased demand for consulting advice (Oliver, 2014).

Second, and closely related, is the fact that management capacity within the NHS has, and continues to remain, extremely limited. Despite the political and media rhetoric concerning the rising number of "bureaucrats," "men in grey suits," and "pen pushers," the facts are that management numbers remain small by comparison to organizations in the rest of the economy (King's Fund, 2011). Recent estimates suggest that the proportion of dedicated management specialists in the NHS (including central functions) accounts for less than 3% of the workforce, compared with approximately 7% of the UK workforce as a whole. As such, it is easy to see why a small (and decreasing) number of over-worked NHS managers may call on the assistance of external management consultants.

While the above concern the demand side, supply-side factors have also played a role in the growth of consultant usage. The role that consultants themselves have played in shaping and creating demand for their services should not be under-estimated. According to Saint-Martin (2012), consultants have done this partly through their participation in cycles of fashion and management fads, many of which, such as "corporate culture" and "TQM," have been immensely influential in the public sector. A specific example of this demand creation strategy is PFI, which led to a step-change in the number of consultancies operating within the Department of Health (Leys and Player, 2011).

By all accounts the PFI program in the NHS has been extensive. HM Treasury figures from 2009 showed that the 106 PFI schemes created had a capital value of about £11 billion and were expected to raise over five times that sum in the coming 30 years (Leys and Player, 2011). The first wave of consultants involved in PFI came from the "Big Five" (Deloitte, PwC, E&Y, KPMG, and Andersen) (Craig, 2006), initially as auditors but then as suppliers of specialist advice on PFI contracts and their operation. According to Craig (2006), this led to a situation in which consultants actively sought to create demand for PFI by devising the protocols for assessing the value of using PFI for particular projects. "Unsurprisingly," he suggests, "time and again PFI emerged as the preferred method for building and running public infrastructure" (Craig, 2006, 143). An illustration is the case of West Middlesex hospital, where the financial analysis suggested the public sector comparator benchmark for the project was initially cheaper than the PFI proposal. In response, KPMG simply arranged for a further analysis where the cost estimates were revised in order to make PFI seem more attractive. Craig is not alone in having doubts over PFI evaluation practices (Price and Green, 2000).

A final way in which management consultants have arguably created demand for their services is through an active set of lobbying and agenda-setting activities. Kipping and Saint-Martin (2005) highlight the "revolving door" between governments and various management consultancies. This has most notably been the case in the US, where there is a strong tradition of using outsiders and political appointees, but is also apparent in the UK (Leys and Player, 2011). Increasingly, it is suggested, consultancies have been transformed almost into "partners in governance," deeply embedded, through networking and lobbying strategies, in the formation of public policies, as well as being important beneficiaries of them (Saint-Martin, 2012). In the next section, we explore this phenomenon in more detail, making specific reference to the NHS.

The Revolving Door: Consultants as Partners in Government

Relationships between management consulting firms and the UK government have become increasingly close in recent decades. In the 1980s, the MCA created a "Public Sector Working Party" to develop a more coordinated strategy for promoting management consulting in government, including a sub-group with direct links to the Cabinet Office (Saint-Martin, 2012). Individual consulting firms themselves also established "government services divisions" and many now have dedicated health services divisions (for example, Accenture Health). In many cases, these divisions have been made up of former civil servants or professionals with public sector expertise (Bakvis, 1997).

This strategy of close networking with government has, as noted earlier, frequently been termed a "revolving door." One manifestation of this has been a stream of senior politicians with close associations with consulting firms. Notable examples include Margaret Hodge (PWC) and Patricia Hewitt (Anderson Consulting). On the other side of the equation is the growing practice of management consulting firms seconding their own senior staff, sometimes with no fee, as advisors to public policy makers (Saint-Martin, 2012). In the NHS, we can see numerous examples of this kind of exchange, with one of the most significant being the regulatory body, Monitor, set up to oversee the practice of semi-autonomous Foundation Trusts. It is notable that out of nine members, the Monitor executive team contains six former management consultants (_Yorkshire Post_, 2014). Given this high representation of consulting firm alumni, it is perhaps not entirely surprising that, as we noted earlier, Monitor has become a significant user of outside consultants.

Perhaps the deepest partnership of all has been between the UK government and McKinsey (McDonald, 2014). As we saw, McKinsey's relationship with the NHS dates back to the publication of the _Grey Book_ report on NHS management in 1972. In part, the close relationship has been underpinned by an ideological alignment between the

Tory privatization agenda and the McKinsey belief that "almost any service could, and should, be commercialized" (Craig, 2006, 43). It has also been rooted in the brand image and reputation of McKinsey as the consulting firm of choice which every company (and government) wished to be associated with (McKenna, 2006). But equally important have been strong personal connections, including those of William Hague, an ex-McKinsey partner who would later go on to be leader of the Conservative Party.

McKinsey's close relationship with the UK government was a particular feature of the New Labour years. Prime Minister Tony Blair centralized policy and implementation around his own office and talked openly of his frustrations with the pace of civil service action (Craig, 2006). This provided an opportunity for consultancies, including McKinsey, which was particularly active within the NHS. It is reported that McKinsey designed the terms of the Foundation Trust regulatory regime for the Department of Health (Ham, 2009), established the "Cambridge Health Network," a forum for bringing together NHS leaders with private sector firms, including management consultancies (Leys and Player, 2011), reviewed the organization of the Department of Health (Ham, 2009), undertook scoping work for the Practice Based Commissioning program (controversially putting itself forward as one of the companies offering such support services) (Leys and Player, 2011) and advised on the "World Class Commissioning" framework (Cowper, 2008). McKinsey also offered its expertise in the area of IT, following the 2002 Wanless Report (Craig, 2006). It provided the initial feasibility study for what would become, first, the NHS National Programme for IT and then Connecting for Health, the largest of the New Labour transformation projects involving management consultants (Craig, 2006).

McKinsey's relationship with the UK government and NHS survived New Labour's election defeat in 2010, with former Senior Partner and Tony Blair advisor, David Bennett, appointed as the Chief Executive of the regulatory body, Monitor, in the early days of the Coalition government (Leys and Player, 2011, 84). Indeed, McKinsey has shown considerable political flexibility. While the firm was working closely with the last Labour Government on health, it was simultaneously investing consultant time in helping the Conservative Shadow minister for Health create proposals for a major reorganization of the NHS. It has been alleged (Rose, 2012) that many of the proposals in the subsequent parliamentary bill "were drawn up by McKinsey and included in the legislation wholesale." It was further alleged that "McKinsey's involvement in the Bill is so great that its executives attend the meetings of the 'Extraordinary NHS Management Board' convened to implement it." McDonald (2014) notes that extensive lobbying of the new administration was rewarded by further contracts in the first six weeks of the Coalition government.

Hence, from this case, it is possible to note how revolving door relationships have contributed to a deep partnership between one leading management consulting firm (McKinsey) and the UK government. In the context of the NHS, this has potentially impacted upon the demand for its consulting advice and on the very formulation and inception of policy itself. However, it would be a mistake to assume that politicians and managers (clients) have simply been hoodwinked into buying more consulting advice.

As Saint-Martin (2012, 458) suggests, while consultants can be viewed as clever manipulators, this could ignore the "opposite scenario" whereby "consultants allow policy makers to diffuse blame and provide a layer of protection from attack on proposed policies by political adversaries." A further paradox is that while these revolving door relationships mean that consultants have contributed to the privatization agenda for public services, their increasingly intimate relationship with government has also "transformed them into somewhat less 'private' and more 'public' actors" (ibid.).

Assessing the Outcomes of Management Consulting Involvement in Health

Much of the discussion so far in this chapter raises questions about the impact of management consulting advice in health care and how this advice should be evaluated. The available literature in the UK has been strongly critical, making reference to a succession of unsuccessful projects (Lapsley, 2009; Craig, 2006), the costs of which, in some cases, have been astronomical. Perhaps the most widely cited example is the NHS National Programme for IT, later Connecting for Health, which has become a byword for big project failure (Campion-Awwad et al., 2014). The original cost estimates for this project were around £2.6 billion, later dwarfed by a final bill of over £10 billion (Todd, 2013). Reviews of what went wrong emphasize many of the usual failings associated with poor planning, a lack of consultation, an over-centralized system design, and a lack of management capabilities to implement change (Campion-Awwad et al., 2014).

Making the situation worse for the NHS was the fact that, due to the legal complexities of terminating such a large contract, the government has been unable to reclaim much of the money lost. Accenture, for example, were theoretically liable for £1 billion when they walked away from their £2 billion contract, but in the end only around £63 million was collected (Campion-Awwad et al., 2014). Nor have the main consultancy firms involved suffered much in terms of reputational damage and loss of repeat business. Fujitsu were officially rated as "high-risk" after their failures, but appear to have overturned this with legal action (Jackson, 2014). Accenture are also back in the game, being recently shortlisted for a project to develop a new NHS email system (Flinders, 2014).

At face value, Connecting for Health (and other projects) may be viewed as a salutary warning of the dangers of relying on external management consultants. However, even this conclusion must be treated with caution. For every failed project other successful ones can be highlighted (Leaman, 2010). In practice, it is also hard to accurately assign blame for project failures between the civil servants, who created the tendering process, and the firms putting in bids. Where Connecting for Health is concerned, it is worth noting that there was significant political enthusiasm for a "big bang" project (Campion-Awwad et al., 2014, 11–12) prompted not by management consultancies, but rather a meeting between the PM and senior IT industry figures, including Bill Gates. Lastly, clear evaluations are hard simply because of the absence of any benchmark for comparison with in-house consulting services which, in the NHS and elsewhere, appear to have been significantly run down.

Putting aside these difficulties associated with a straightforward cost-benefit analysis of management consulting, one might pose a bigger question regarding their contribution to wider programmes of NPM reform. Here, it can be argued that many consulting firms have "over promised" and that not much has changed. As McDonald (2014, 180) suggests, while McKinsey have been camped out inside the NHS for years, they have "failed to move the stultified British bureaucracy an inch." However, on the other hand, as Aucoin (2011) suggests, management consultancies have been commissioned repeatedly by the UK Government to design and drive through reforms which they believed civil servants could not or would not do. As such, most of these management consulting projects have arguably delivered what the ultimate customer (ruling politicians) wanted—irrespective of the failure to provide success against the metrics of other stakeholders (for example, a working IT system, value for money in a turnaround project, etc.). In terms of the wider ideological project of reform, bringing in the management consultants has arguably been money well spent.

The Client Response: Changing Procurement in the NHS

In this final section, we turn to the question of how, and with what success, NHS organizations have responded to the expansion of management consulting by developing effective procurement policies and practices. According to Kipping and Saint-Martin (2005), the long-term trend in public sectors around the world has been for governments to become more knowledgeable consumers, although arriving at this point has been a slow and torturous process. Evidence on procurement practice needs be assessed in terms of the three broad stages of the procurement process: needs assessment, sourcing, and contract management.

There has been a great deal of criticism of the NHS with respect to the first stage, needs assessment. Some criticisms have focused on the types of projects being requested, with the aforementioned Royal College of Nursing report arguing that 78% of project expenditure was unrelated to patient care (Royal College of Nursing, 2009). Others relate to whether projects could be undertaken by internal staff. Responding to this criticism in 2009, the NHS Chief Executive explained that much of the consultant expenditure was required for implementation support because tight "talent markets" meant that "there simply were not the people out there for us to recruit" (House of Commons Health Committee, 2009, 4). A related issue is the quality of project scoping. Wye et al. (2014) commented on a failure of many consultancy projects in the NHS to be directed at "clearly identified and recognised problems."

In terms of the sourcing stage, a complex picture emerges. NHS organizations operate with a bewildering array of sourcing options, including: local procurement (by either provider or commissioning organizations), regional procurement hubs, NHS Supply Chain, NHS Shared Business Services (SBS) or contracts arranged by the Crown

Commercial Service (CCS), an agency of the Cabinet Office. Co-ordinating the practice of all of these purchasers is a difficult task. Accordingly, an option the UK government is now trying to promote is the national framework agreement, *Consultancy One* led by CCS and available to all UK public sector organizations, including the NHS. CCS (2015, 3) explains that Consultancy One aims to "reduce the time and costs associated with the procurement by offering a facility, which has already been competitively tendered ... It will promote strategic relationships with suppliers to drive value for money and leverage off the central government collective buying power." In terms of its details, the framework agreement is for three years, contains 65 suppliers, divided into 15 activity areas, and claims to offer market competitive prices (Crown Commercial Service, 2015).

Although the use of *Consultancy One* framework has been quite limited in the NHS (and public sector more widely) (National Audit Office/Audit Commission, 2010), it has led to some savings. Indeed, it has recently been criticized for being too cost-focused (O'Mahoney, Heusinkveld, and Wright, 2013; Radnor and O'Mahoney, 2013). It is interesting to note, for example, that the preferred supplier selection criteria used under the framwork placed a 70% weighting on "quality" and only a 30% weighting on price (Crown Commercial Service, 2015).

Given the complex nature and co-production of management consultancy services, significant emphasis needs to be placed upon contract management. Here, concerns regarding NHS practice have been expressed by Wye et al. (2014) who found that aspects of co-production were ineffective in some of the cases reviewed in their study, adversely affecting the value obtained. In particular, contracts provided insufficient mechanisms to ensure that local health care staff had enough time to learn new skills and understand how to apply suggested practices. Post-project evaluation has also been criticized as weak and at odds with the peer review evaluation system used for academic research contracts commissioned by the NHS (House of Commons Health Committee, 2009).

Many of the criticisms of management consultant use in the UK NHS have focused upon their cost and their effectiveness in effecting positive change. Both of these are affected by procurement practices. The evidence above suggests that some progress has been made in the area of sourcing, but that the capabilities of the NHS across all three stages of the process are still contain weaknesses.

CONCLUDING DISCUSSION

Drawing on a wide range of available sources, this chapter has sought to provide an initial road map of current research and debates on the role of management consulting, specifically in relation to health care. Focusing primarily on the UK NHS, it can be seen how the involvement of consultants has increased exponentially since the late 1970s and how this can be attributed both to a mix of demand and supply factors. We have also noted that this change is not captured by figures on rising expenditure alone. A key conclusion of the chapter is that management consultants have played (and are likely to continue to play) a significant role in the inception and implementation of NPM reforms in health services. In the process they have moved from being arms-length vendors of specialist services to embedded "partners" in government. However, this shift has not made government complacent about the costs or effectiveness of consulting advice. At the same time as health organizations have worked more closely with management consultants, they have also become somewhat more knowledgeable and discerning clients and purchasers of consulting advice, IT projects apart.

Notwithstanding these conclusions about the changing role of management consultants in the health sector, it is clear that much work still needs to be done to make sense of these developments. As we noted earlier, this chapter, at best, provides a ground-clearing exercise, setting out a possible framework for discussion. Significantly, it also highlights the need for a more sustained program of research in future. This need is especially pronounced with regard to the *nature* and role of management consultants in health, the *drivers* of their use, and wider *consequences*.

In terms of the nature and role of consultants in health, a first priority must be for more systematic tracking of data, relating to levels of expenditure and the kinds of projects that are being commissioned. While data on expenditure are available there is a general lack of transparency making it hard to discern clear trends and even harder to comment on the effectiveness or value for money of consulting interventions. Future research could help to develop a finer grained picture to explore patterns of consulting involvement within and between health systems over time.

With regard to drivers of consulting use, more attention could focus on how far the kind of demand- and supply-side explanations that feature in the wider literature apply in the context of public services. Useful here would be more case studies focusing on the interaction between clients and consultants over the life span of particular projects in health settings. While there is some evidence of revolving door relationships, we know little about the motivations of clients (including managers and clinicians) who have asked for consulting advice in particular areas.

Related to this is the need to gain a better understanding of the impact and wider consequences of consulting advice. An obvious line of enquiry here might be to conduct more formal evaluations of consulting projects, maybe adopting the same kind of methodology that is frequently used to assess the evidence base for clinical interventions. Wider questions might also be asked about the consequences of what seems to be an increasingly deep partnership between health organizations and consulting firms (as noted in the UK NHS). One concern here may be that in future there will be a shift towards a more oligopolistic relationship between the NHS and a smaller number of global firms. The latter are not only more deeply connected to relevant policy networks (the "revolving door") but have the resources to successfully tender for projects in the face of an increasingly demanding NHS procurement regime.

Lastly, there is clearly a need for more comparative research to understand how far the issues discussed in this chapter are being played out in other health systems. A starting point here might be to look at other European health systems which, like the NHS, rely on substantial public funding, and where there have been similar moves to commercialize services and strengthen management capabilities (Saltman, Durán, and Dubois, 2011; Kirkpatrick et al., 2013). While these conditions are similar to those that prevail in the UK NHS, it is not clear if they have led to the same level and type of involvement of management consultants. More work could also focus on insurance-based health systems where private sector business interests are already more established, notably the US. Our review suggests that the US is by far the largest health market for management consulting, although very little is known about the nature and consequences of this.

Lastly, there is scope to develop new theoretical insights from this line of research. As we saw, much of the critical research of consulting has emphasized the agency of consultants in promoting their services (through commodification) and the generation of client demand. This connects to wider debates about the emergence of management ideas or fashions (Abrahamson, 1996). It also links to the literature on the changing dynamics of organizational fields and the role of "institutional entrepreneurs" as agents actively transforming dominant logics that prevail in these fields (see Muzio, Brock, and Suddaby, 2013, for a summary). In this regard, the changing role of consultants in health services in helping to reshape wider policy agendas and organizational landscapes may represent a very salient case of entrepreneurship in action, one that highlights implications that go beyond those already identified in much of the literature.

References

Abrahamson, E. (1996). Management fashion. *Academy of Management Review*, 21(1): 254–285.

Adams, S. (2011). The most prestigious consulting firms. *Forbes*, August 25. Available at: <http://www.forbes.com> (accessed April 2015).

Appelby, J., Baird, B., Thompson, J., and Jabbal, J. (2015). *The NHS under the coalition government: Part II*. London: King's Fund.

Aucoin, P. (2011). The political-administrative design of NPM. In *New public management*, ed. Christensen, T. and Laegreid, P., pp. 33–46. Farnham: Ashgate.

Bakvis, H. (1997). Advising the executive: Think tanks, consultants, political staff and kitchen cabinet. In *The hollow crown: Countervailing trends in core executives*, ed. Weller, P., Bakvis, H. and Rhodes, R., pp. 84–125. London: Macmillan.

Bohlen, M. H., Gamper, J., Polasek, W., and Wimmer, M. A. (2005). *E government: Towards electronic democracy*. Berlin: Springer.

Cabinet Office (2015). Cabinet office controls guidance: Version 4.0. Available at: <http://www.gov.uk/government/publications> (accessed April 2015).

Campbell, D. (2014). NHS can save billions with a small rise in spending on GPs say researchers. *The Guardian*, 28 November. Available at: <http://www.theguardian.com/society/2014/nov/28/nhs-spending-gps-hospital-doctors-patient> (accessed March 2015).

Campion-Awwad, O., Hayton, A., Smith, L., and Vuaran, M. (2014). *The national programme for IT in the NHS: A case history*. Cambridge: University of Cambridge.

Canback, S. (1998). The logic of management consulting, part 1. *Journal of Management Consulting*, 10(2): 3–11.

Canback, S. (1999). The logic of management consulting, part 2. *Journal of Management Consulting*, 10(3): 3–12.

Clark, T. and Greatbatch, D. (2002). Whose idea is it anyway? Collaborative relationships in the creation of management guru ideas. In *Management consulting: Emergence and dynamics of a knowledge industry*, ed. Kipping, M., pp. 129–145. Oxford: Oxford University Press.

Consultancy.uk (2014). NHS spends £640 million on management consultants. *Consultancy. uk*, 23 December. Available at: <http://www.consultancy.uk/news/1240/nhs-spends-640-million-on-management-consultants> (accessed April 2015).

Cowper, A. (2008). World class commissioning: Quality assurance. *Health Services Journal*, June. Available at: <http://www.hsj.co.uk/resource-centre/world-class-commissioning-quality-assurance/1335452.article> (accessed April 2015).

Craig, D. (2006). *Plundering the public sector: How new labour are letting consultants run off with £70 billion of our money*. London: Constable.

Crown Commercial Service (2015). ConsultancyONE: Framework agreement. Available at: <http://ccs-agreements.cabinetoffice.gov.uk/contracts/rm1502> (accessed March 2015).

Czarniawska, B. and Mazza, C. (2003). Consulting as a liminal space. *Human Relations*, 56: 267–290.

Czerniawska, F. (2002). *Management consultancy: What next? Growth and future directions*. Basingstoke: Palgrave Macmillan.

David, R. (2012). Institutional change and the growth of strategy consulting in the United States. In *The Oxford handbook of management consulting*, ed. Kipping, M. and Clark, T., pp. 71–92. Oxford and New York: Oxford University Press.

Dorgan, S., Layton, D., Bloom, N., Homkes, R., Sadun, R., and Van Reenen, J. (2010). *Management in health care: Why good practice really matters*. London: McKinsey and Co and London School of Economics.

Edwards, B. (1995). *The national health service: A manager's tale: 1946–1994*. London: Nuffield.

Efficiency Unit. (1994). *The government's use of external consultants: An efficiency unit scrutiny*. London: HMSO.

Engwall, L. (2012). Business schools and consultancies: The blurring of boundaries. In *The Oxford handbook of management consulting*, ed. Kipping, M. and Clark, T, pp 365–388. Oxford and New York: Oxford University Press.

FEASCO (2010). *Survey of the European management consultancy 2009/10*. Brussels: FEASCO.

Fincham, R. (1999). The consultant–client relationship: Critical perspectives on the management of organizational change. *Journal of Management Studies*, 36(3): 335–351.

Fincham, R. (2006). Knowledge work as occupational strategy: Comparing IT and management consulting. *New Technology, Work and Employment*, 21(1): 16–28.

Flinders, K. (2014). Accenture and BT to battle for NHS email contract. *Computer Weekly*, 19 December. Available at: <http://www.techtarget.com/contributor/Karl-Flinders/2014> (accessed April 2015).

Guillot, T. (2014). Teesside health chiefs could pay consultancy firm over £500k for advice on cost cutting. *Gazette Live*, June 26. Available at: <http://www.gazettelive.co.uk/news/tees-side-news/south-tees-hospitals-nhs-foundation-7327196> (accessed April 2015).

Ham, C. (2009). *Health policy in Britain*. Basingstoke: Palgrave Macmillan.

Harrison, S. and Pollitt, C. (1994). *Controlling the health professionals: The future of work and organisation in the NHS*. Buckingham: Open University Press.

House of Commons Health Committee (2009). *The use of management consultants by the national health service, fifth report of session 2008/9*. London: HMSO.

Huron Consulting Group (2014). Largest health care management consulting firms. *Modern Healthcare*, August 25. Available at: <https://www.huronconsultinggroup.com/Insights/

Perspective/Healthcare/~/media/82C3BBCB6D7D4240BD2B7A80177D0C08.ashx>
(accessed April 2015).

Jackson, M. (2014). BDUK Blacklist No more: Government lose £900m IT case vs Fujitsu UK. *ISP Review*, July.

Jung, N. (2008). Do clients really become more professional? Analysing clients new ways of managing consultants. Paper presented at the Annual Meeting of the Academy of Management, Anaheim, 8–13 August.

Jung, N. and Kieser, A. (2012). Consultants in the management fashion arena. In *The Oxford handbook of management consulting*, ed. Kipping, M. and Clark, T. pp 327–346. Oxford and New York: Oxford University Press.

Kennedy Consulting Research and Advisory (2013). *Global consulting market index 2013*. New York: Kennedy Consulting Research & Advisory.

Kieser, A. (2002). Managers as marionettes? Using fashion theories to explain the success of consultancies. In *Management consulting*, ed. Kipping, M. and Engwall, L., pp. 167–183. Oxford: Oxford University Press.

King's Fund (2011). *The future of leadership and management in the NHS: No more heroes*. London: The King's Fund.

Kipping, M. (2002). Trapped in their wave: The evolution of management consultancies. In *Critical consulting: New perspectives on the management advice industry*, ed. Clark, T. and Fincham, R., pp. 28–49. Oxford: Blackwell.

Kipping, M. and Kirkpatrick, I. (2013). Alternative pathways of change in professional services firms: The case of management consulting. *Journal of Management Studies*, 50(5): 777–807.

Kipping, M. and Saint-Martin, D. (2005). Between regulation, promotion and consumption: Government and management consultancy in Britain. *Business History*, 47(3): 449–465.

Kipping, M. and Wright, C. (2012). Consultants in context: Global dominance, societal effect and the capitalist system. In *The Oxford handbook of management consulting*, ed. Clark, T. and Kipping, M., pp. 165–185 Oxford, Oxford University Press.

Kirkpatrick, I., Bullinger, B., Lega, F., and Dent, M. (2013). The translation of hospital management reforms in European health systems: A framework for comparison. *British Journal of Management*, 24: 48–61.

Kirkpatrick, I. and McCabe, C. (2011). A full blooded market system: At what cost to the NHS? *British Medical Journal*, 343, doi: 10.1136, 13 July.

Kirkpatrick, I., Muzio, D., and Ackroyd, S. (2012). The sociology of professions. In *The Oxford handbook of management consulting*, ed. Clark, T. and Kipping, M., pp. 187–206. Oxford: Oxford University Press.

Kitay, J. and Wright, C. (2007). From prophets to profits: The occupational rhetoric of management consultants. *Human Relations*, 60(11): 1613–1640.

Kubr M. (2002). *Management consulting: A guide to the profession*. Geneva: International Labour Office.

Lapsley, I. (2009). New public management: Cruelest invention of the human spirit? *Abacus*, 45(1): 1–21.

Leaman, A. (2010). NHS spending on management consultants is not wasteful. *The Guardian*, September 7. Available at: <http://www.theguardian.com/commentisfree/2010/sep/07/nhs-management-consultants-not-wasteful> (accessed April 2015).

Leys, C. and Player, S. (2011). *The plot against the NHS*. London: Merlin Press.

McDonald, D. (2014). *The firm: The inside story of McKinsey, the world's most controversial management consultancy*. London: Oneworld Publications.

McKenna, C. (2006). *The world's newest profession: Management consulting in the twentieth century*. New York: Cambridge University Press.

Macleod, N. (2014). Management consulting in the public sector, Unpublished dissertation, University of Leeds Business School.

Management Consultancies Association (2009). *Improving care, reducing cost*. London: Management Consultancies Association.

Muzio, D., Brock, D., and Suddaby, R. (2013). Professions and institutional change: Towards an institutionalist sociology of the professions. *Journal of Management Studies*, 50(5): 699–721.

National Audit Office (2006). *Central Government's use of consultants*. London: NAO.

National Audit Office/Audit Commission (2010). *A review of collaborative procurement across the public sector*. London: National Audit Office.

National Health Executive (2015). NHS bill for consultants more than doubles despite government promises to cut spending. Available at: <http://www.nationalhealthexecutive.com/Health-Care-News/nhs-bill-for-consultants-more-than-doubles-despite-government-promises-to-cut-spending> (accessed March 2015).

NHS Leadership Academy (2013). Available at: <http://www.leadershipacademy.nhs.uk/news/largest-ever-leadership-programme-to-transform-nhs-culture-announced/> (accessed April 2015).

Nikolova, N. and Devinney, T. (2012). The nature of client–consultant interaction: A critical review. In *The Oxford handbook of management consulting*, ed. Clark, T. and Kipping, M., pp. 285–302. Oxford: Oxford University Press.

Oliver, D. (2014). Stop wasting taxpayers' money on management consultancy for the NHS. *BMJ*, 349. Available at: <http://www.ncbi.nlm.nih.gov/pubmed/25491703>> (accessed April 2015).

O'Mahoney, J., Heusinkveld, S., and Wright, C. (2013). Commodifying the commodifiers: The impact of procurement on management knowledge. *Journal of Management Studies*, 50: 204–235.

O'Mahoney, J. and Markham, C. (2013). *Management consultancy*. Oxford: Oxford University Press.

Pollitt, C. and Bouckaert, G. (2011). *Public management reform: A comparative analysis— new public management, governance, and the neo-Weberian state*. Oxford: Oxford University Press.

Price, D. and J. Green. (2000). Capital planning and the private finance initiative: Cost minimisation or health care planning. *Critical Public Health*, 10(1): 71–80.

PwC (2015). Time for a health and social care reset. Available at: <http://pwc.blogs.com/publicsectormatters/2013/09/time-for-a-health-and-social-care-reset.html> (accessed April 2015).

Radnor, Z. and O'Mahoney, J. (2013). The role of management consultancy in implementing operations management in the public sector. *International Journal of Operations and Production Management*, 33(11): 1555–1578.

Rose, D. (2012). The firm that hijacked the NHS. *The Mail on Sunday*, February 12. Available at: <http://www.dailymail.co.uk/news/article-2099940/NHS-health-reforms-Extent-McKinsey—Companys-role-Andrew-Lansleys-proposals.html> (accessed April 2015).

Royal College of Nursing (2009). *NHS expenditure on management consultants*. London: Royal College of Nursing Policy Unit.

Sager, I. (2013). Where the growth is in management consulting. Available at: <http://www.bloomberg.com/bw/articles/2013-06-13/where-the-growth-is-in-management-consulting> (accessed April 2015).

Saint-Martin, D. (2005). Management consultancy. In *The Oxford handbook of public management*, ed. Ferlie, E., Lynn, L., and Pollitt, C., pp. 671–694. Oxford: Oxford University Press.

Saint-Martin, D. (2012). Governments and management consultants: Supply, demand and effectiveness. In *The Oxford handbook of management consulting*, ed. Clark, T. and Kipping, M., pp. 447–466. Oxford: Oxford University Press.

Saltman, R., Durán, A., and Dubois, H. (2011). *Governing public hospitals: Reform strategies and the movement towards institutional autonomy*. Copenhagen: European Observatory on Health Systems and Policies.

Sloan, T., Fitzgerald, A., Hayes, K., Radnor, Z., Robinson, S., and Sohal, A. (2014). Lean in health care: History and recent developments. *Journal of Health Organization and Management*, 28(2): 130–134.

Sorge, A. and van Witteloostuijn, A. (2004). The (non)sense of organizational change: An essay about universal management hypes, sick consultancy metaphors, and healthy organization theories. *Organization Studies*, 25: 1205–1231.

Statistica (2015). Revenue of management consulting in the United States 2009 to 2014. Available at: <http://www.statista.com/statistics/293754/revenue-of-management-consulting-in-the-us/> (accessed April 2015).

Stern, S. (2010). Consultants face need for survival strategy. *Financial Times*, June 7. Available at: <http://www.ft.com/cms/s/0/d982d768-7189-11df-8eec-00144feabdco. html#axzz3n3Kb8VHm> (accessed March 2015).

Sturdy, A., Handley, K., Clark, T., and Fincham, R. (2009). *Management consultancy: Boundaries and knowledge in action*. Oxford: Oxford University Press.

Suddaby, R. and Greenwood, R. (2001). Colonizing knowledge: Commodification as a dynamic of jurisdictional expansion in professional service firms. *Human Relations*, 54(7): 933–953.

Timmins, N. (2012). *Never again: The story of the health and social care act 2012*. London: King's Fund/Institute for Government.

Todd, R. (2013). NPfIT to cost £10 billion. Available at: <http://www.digitalhealth.net/news/28736/npfit-to-cost-%C2%A310-billion> (accessed March 2015).

Washburn, S. (1996). Challenge and renewal: A historic view of the profession. *Journal of Management Consulting*, 9(2): 47–53.

Werr, A. and Pemer, F. (2007). Purchasing management consulting services: From management autonomy to purchasing involvement. *Journal of Purchasing and Supply Management*, 13: 98–112.

Wood, P. (2002). European consultancy growth: Nature, causes and consequences. In *Consultancy and innovation: The business service revolution in Europe*, ed. Wood, P., pp. 35–71. London: Routledge.

Woolhandler, S., Campbell, T., and Himmelstein, D. (2003). Costs of health care administration in the United States and Canada. *New England Journal of Medicine*, 349: 768–775.

Wye, L., Brangan, E., Cameron, A., Gabbay, J., Klein, J., Anthwal, R., and Pope, C. (2014). What do external consultants from private and not-for-profit companies offer health care commissioners? A qualitative study of knowledge exchange. *BMJ Open*, 5. Available at: <http://www.bris.ac.uk/social-community-medicine/people/lesley-wye/pub/34822044> (accessed April 2015).

Yorkshire Post (2014). NHS regulator spends £40 million of budget on consultants. Available at: <http://www.reasonandreality.org/?p=2400> (accessed March 2015).

Index

Note: Tables and figures are indicated by an italic *t* and *f* following the page number.